Publications of The National Museum
Ethnographical Series, vol. 18

Fifty Years of Arctic Research

Anthropological Studies
From Greenland to Siberia

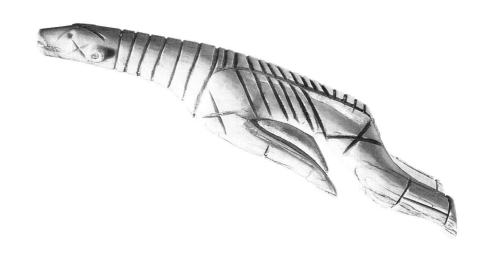

Editors: R. Gilberg & H. C. Gulløv

Department of Ethnography
The National Museum of Denmark
Copenhagen 1997

Copyright:	The National Museum of Denmark & authors 1997
Editors:	Rolf Gilberg & Hans Christian Gulløv
Translation:	Peter Crawford pp:15-18; Maja Gilberg Barker rest of the book
Layout:	Rolf Gilberg
Production:	Erik Gregersen, DK-4300 Holbæk
Composing:	Times
Paper:	130 gr Arctic Silkmat Acid-free paper (N 120 z 3948)
Impression:	1.000 issues printed
Printer:	Holbæk Center-Tryk/Erik Gregersen
ISBN:	87-89385-60-1

Published with support from:
Dronning Margrethe og Prins Henriks Fond
Augustinus Fonden
Landsdommer V. Gieses Legat
Konsul George Jorck og hustru Emma Jorck's Fond
Hielmstierne-Rosencroneske Stiftelse
Overretssagfører L. Zeuthens Mindelegat
Rockwool Fonden
Rock Foundation, Inc.

Abriviations

A.D.	= anno domini, that is time after year zero
B.C.	= before Christ, that is time before year zero
B.P.	= before present, that is time before year 1997
c.	= circa
°C	= celsius degree
cm	= centimeters (= 0.3937 inch)
etc	= and so on, and the like
km	= kilometer (= 0.62137 miles)
m	= meter (= 3.937 inches)
mm	= millimeter
p.	= pages
pp:	= from page to page
÷	= minus

Frontpage:

Polar bear carved in walrus ivory, 15.6 cm long, Dorset Culture, c. 500 A.D. - 1000 A.D.
Excavated 1954 by Jørgen Meldgaard at the Alarnerk Site, Igloolik, Arctic Canada. 208 house ruins distributed on raised beaches from 23 metres to 8 metres above present sea level represented the development of the Dorset Culture from c. 900 B.C. to 1200 A.D.

Back cover: See page 5 and 73

Content

Preface

The Department of Ethnography has a long tradition of Arctic research and a long history as one of the oldest ethnographical museums on the world. Some of the objects in the museum originate from the 17th-century Ole Worm Collection. After Worm's death in 1654 his collection became part of the Royal Kunstkammer, from which Christian Jürgensen Thomsen in the 1840s created an independent museum, the Royal Ethnographical Museum, which opened to the public in 1849. Then in 1892 the National Museum of Denmark was created and the Royal Ethnographical Museum became a part of it.

The Department of Ethnography has been particulary active in the Arctic over the last two centuries. A few of the activities we can mention are Gustav Holm's finds and collections from his East Greenland Expedition to Ammassalik 1883-1885, and Knud Rasmussen's finds and collections from his Fifth Thule Expedition across Arctic America 1921-1924.

When the Department of Ethnography again became an independent department of the National Museum of Denmark in 1920-1997, the staff engaged in Arctic research. For more than fifty years Jørgen Meldgaard has worked as an Arctic archeologist at the Department of Ethnography and since 1959 as a curator.

In 1997 Meldgaard retired from the museum but he still keeps an office there. The Department of Ethnography considers Meldgaard's retirement an appropriate occasion to review the past half a century of Arctic activities. It is our hope that this collection of papers focusing on Arctic science will inspire future researchers.

The editors

Jørgen Meldgaard

Introduction

Rolf Gilberg & Hans Christian Gulløv

In March 1997, an era in Danish Arctic research ended. This happened when Jørgen Meldgaard retired from his position at the National Museum of Denmark after almost 40 years as a curator and half a century in the service of eskimology. As the last in a line of unique Danish Arctic scholars Meldgaard has succeeded through his work in passing on a research tradition, which in this century has also included Therkel Mathiassen (1892-1967), Kaj Birket-Smith (1893-1977), Erik Holtved (1899-1981), Helge Larsen (1905-1984), and Eigil Knuth (1903-1996). Their pioneer work within arctic cultural history and Eskimo archaeology was carried out for the National Museum of Denmark.

The Beginning

Ever since Jørgen Meldgaard arrived in 1945 at the Department of Ethnography fresh from high school, his work has been closely tied to all the multifarious activities of the department. Helge Larsen, who had lived in the United States during the war, returned home to Denmark with new ideas from abroad; after five years of German occupation the museum was able to resume its research in the Arctic.

Eigil Knuth had conceived the plans for the Danish Peary Land Expedition, and the first team travelled north in 1947. Knuth was looking for employees for his archaeological investigations, and *"as a young archaeology student I was sitting in the reading room one day with some fellow students, when the then curator P. V. Glob came rushing in, shouting 'Who wants to go to Greenland? Raise your hand!' And I was the first to raise my hand. I literally jumped on board the old ship Godthåb, which for four weeks thumped across the Atlantic with sails and* *steam through storms, and struggled through the ice. I ended up in the northernmost part of North East Greenland - and was deeply fascinated. After this first expedition I was stuck with arctic archaeology".*

New horizons

1948 was in many ways a landmark year for Arctic archaeology. That summer, Louis Giddings was digging at Cape Denbigh, and when he returned to the University of Alaska he met Helge Larsen and Erik Holtved, who had worked in the Bristol Bay area. The enormous depth of Arctic prehistory and the Paleo-Eskimo Cultures were revealed in long conversations between the three. That same summer Eigil Knuth found tools in the very north of Greenland, and he could draw striking parallels to the Denbigh Flint complex. With these discoveries in 1948 a new chapter in arctic archaeology had begun, and today it is considered a turning point in the history of Arctic research (McGhee 1996:25-41).

This summer was also the arctic test for Meldgaard. Together with Hans-Georg Bandi several settlements were excavated, and the cultural ties north of Greenland to the Dorset and Thule Cultures in the Smith Sound region and to Arctic Canada were emphasized (Bandi this volume; Bandi & Meldgaard 1952).

Concurrent with his studies in prehistoric archaeology, Meldgaard had the opportunity in 1949 to participate in the National Museum's expedition to the Norse settlements in South West Greenland. On this expedition another topic of research was revealed to this young student, and this was later to turn into a major involvement. The investigations, which were a continuation of the Norse research in Greenland from the inter-war period, was lead by curator C. L. Vebæk, whose working skills are legendary (Vebæk 1992).

Helge Larsen had noticed Meldgaard's skills and invited him to join him as his assistant on an expedition to Alaska in the summer of 1950, where the excavations of the caves at Trail Creek were to be completed. Here, they uncovered traces from the late Pleistocene, when the Bering Land Bridge was still open. Also the Ipiutak mens' house at Deering was excavated this summer, and Meldgaard was among the participants (Larsen 1953, 1968).

In the storage spaces at the National Museum of Denmark was a collection of stone objects, 182 pieces, donated by horticultural consultant Hans Mosegaard, who had picked them up near the West Greenlandic settlement Saqqaq in Disko Bay. Meldgaard was given the task of describing this collection, and he came to the conclusion that the material represented a Pre-Thule West Greenland Paleo-Eskimo Culture which was closely related to the early Alaskan cultures Ipiutak, Near Ipiutak, and the Denbigh Flint Complex. He explained the Dorset types, in the collections described by the Norwegian Solberg (1907), as a result of later influences from the Canadian Dorset Culture. For the first time the burin was described as a tool in Eskimo archaeology, and the results of the examination of Mosegaard's collection were published in American Antiquity (Meldgaard 1952).

In the summer of 1952 Meldgaard travelled to Greenland again with Inge Kleivan, George Nelleman, and Claude Desgoffe in order to conduct excavations as well as ethnographic research in Godthåb (Nuuk) District (Meldgaard 1953). The collected antiquarian information was passed on to the Geodetic Institute in Copenhagen and comprises the basic material in the complete survey of Godthåb's settlement patterns (Gulløv 1983). In Godthåb Meldgaard presented the idea of converting one of the buildings of the former Moravian Mission into a National Museum. His ideas was realized 14 years later (Schultz-Lorentzen this volume).

After finishing his dissertation in 1953 on European prehistoric archaeology at Aarhus University, Meldgaard travelled with George Nellemann, professor P. V. Glob, and curator Helge Larsen to Disko Bay in West Greenland to dig the large midden at Sermermiut. The result was the establishment of the three phases of Greenland's prehistory: Saqqaq, Dorset, and Thule. The monograph is now a classic in Greenlandic archaeology (Larsen & Meldgaard 1958).

The Dorset Culture

Immediately after his return he travelled west again and spent one year at the McGill University in Canada as preparation for his archaeological investigations at Igloolik. With Richard Emmerick of Philadelphia, and Father Guy Mary-Rousselière of Churchill, he explored Arctic prehistory on the raised beach terraces at Fury and Hecla

Strait, and this place is now considered a classic location within Eskimo archaeology. It is the source of material for a large number of publications which have since come from Meldgaard's hand (for instance 1955, 1957, 1960, 1962, 1986, 1991).

His work at Igloolik can, thus, be seen as a continuation of the efforts of Knud Rasmussen's Fifth Thule Expedition in the same area three years earlier (Meldgaard 1971). But Meldgaard also had access to the exciting find from nearby Abverdjar, an important incentive for his future research on Paleo-Eskimo cultures. This is a topic which has occupied research of the entire Canadian Arctic and which has been taken on by following generations of researchers (Harp this volume; Maxwell this volume; Plumet this volume; Rowley & Rowley this volume). Meldgaard continued his investigations at Igloolik in 1957 and 1965, but the year 1954 remains a turning point in his Arctic life - it was the year he received a namesake among the local Inuit, George Quviq Qulaut.

Vinland

In the summer of 1956 he travelled the coasts of Holsteinsborg District (Sisimiut) looking for traces of Eskimos and Norse inhabitants. He continued the scenario descriptions of the sagas by hand along the coast of Labrador (Meldgaard 1961). At Lake Melville, the southern border of the Neo-Eskimo habitation, test digs were made, but the material found was entirely of Indian origin. This region has since then been the focus of significant research efforts (Fitzhugh 1972; Kaplan this volume).

However, at the northern tip of Newfoundland he found the area which convinced him in his search for the Lands of the Sagas: Here is the begining of Vinland.

"As a student of Brøndsted, and inspired by his encouragement, I left for the coast of Labrador and the northern part of New Foundland for a short period in the later summer of 1956. The Finnish geographer, V. Tanner, had in 1941 persuasively pointed out the localities along this coast. I returned home convinced that the long sand beaches of Markland, the Furdu beaches, and the striking foreland, Kjalarnes, could be identified in South East Labrador; Leifsboderne in the northernmost part of Newfoundland. But ruins and antiquities did not appear. Concrete and reliable evidence has been dug up over the last 30 years. Our break through came in 1962 when Helge Ingstad found the l'Anse aux Meadows site on the north tip of Newfoundland and began excavating ruins, which turned out to originate from the period around 1000 A.D. Most recently, Birgitta Wallace has followed up on Helge and Anna Stine Ingstad's many years of excavating. She has show that these are probably Leif's houses, a gateway, and the base for summer migrations in pursuit of Vinland's blessings in the south along the coasts of Gulf of the St. Lawrence." (Meldgaard 1992).

A Birthday Tribute

George Qulaut

Dear Dr. Jorgen (George) Meldgaard

It is with great pleasure I am writing this very special letter to you.

First of all on behalf of my family, especially my mother, and indeed all Iglulingmiut, we wish you a very happy 70th birthday.

I understand you will be retiring from your position as curator of the Eskimo Collections at the National Museum of Denmark, after a long and very successful career in Arctic anthropology. To me it seems that your work has just begun for it will inspire and inform future generations in your profession for years to come.

When I think back to the time when my grandfather, Itikutuk, told me stories of the various Qallunaat that my father had guided, he mentioned you in particular. He referred to you as Nagvaqsiuti - "one who gathers or finds things". This is what we Iglulingmiut call archaeologists. He had admired your ability to walk great distances in a very short time. For this ability you were also known among the Iglulingmiut elders as Pisukkaaluk - "a great walker". I have many fond memories of my grandfather's stories about your visit to the Iglulik area in the spring and summer of 1954.

As for my father, he mentioned he truly enjoyed your company, for he learned a great deal about our ancestors through your findings. One of the things he had talked about was making, with your help, a caribou antler harpoon head, an exact duplicate of one you had found in one of the old camp sites. He was amazed how well it performed when used on a walrus, noting that it worked just as well, if not better, than his own metal harpoon heads. One of the greatest memories he shared with me concerned my birth at Qangiq, in the vicinity of Alangniq, in July of 1954, when he named me after you.

Since Inuit can not pronounce the name "Jorgen" he asked Attamarik - Father Guy Mary-Rousseliere, who was your colleague at the time, if he would baptize me using an equivalent but pronounceable name. And so I became George and I am very proud to be named after you. If I remember correctly, my father also mentioned that you excavated the well-known "swimming polar bear" carving on the very day of my birth.

During my travels throughout Nunavut I find people telling me how much they envy the Iglulingmiut for cherishing their culture and keeping it strong. Your work and example among us has, I believe, contributed to these positive attitudes.

I will close on a personal note. I remember very clearly promising my father that, like him, I would guide scientists and researchers who came to work in our region. I kept this promise for a period of fourteen years and I am proud of my accomplishments. These years were indeed the highlight of my life, during which I learned much about my culture and traditions. And so it is a pleasure to tell you that my eldest daughter, Qulaut, who is named after my father, wishes to continue in her father's and grandfather's footsteps. She took an archaeology course last summer, given by Dr. Susan Rowley, and said she too would like to help researchers and scientists when she grows up. Time will tell if this is to be.

Once again I wish you a very happy birthday and many more to come.

Your Attiq, your namesake,

George Quviq Qulaut

Commissioner
Nuavut Implementation Commission
P.O.Box 147, Igloolik,
N.T., XOA OLO Canada

George's mother with him in the hood.
Photo: Jørgen Meldgaard, 1954.

A salute for you Jørgen on your 70th birthday

Jens Rosing

A legend among the Polar-Eskimos tells of two young men, who had an idea to visit the Inuit's many and distant settlements. For then there were many Inuit, and the two would seek out all their settlements - so that when they grew old, they would have something to tell.

The two were so young that they had only recently married; but neither of them had any children yet.

Before the journey they each took a horn from a musk ox and each carved a water scoop.

One couple headed west - the other east.

They drove their sleds as far as ice and snow would carry them. When the sun and the warmth melted the cold under the runners, they set up camp for the summer. When the cold tied the waters again - they hitched the dogs to the sleds and continued their long journey.

The years passed. They had children, and the children grew up - and had children.

One day when the travellers met - the old men were so worn by the years that they had to be led by the hard by their almost-grown grandchildren.

Deeply moved the two old men stood facing one another. Each each held out his water scoop for the other to feel. Practically only the handles were left - so many times had they been drinking water during their journey and scraped the scoops against the stony bottoms of rivers.

"Well, the countries are vast - and the places that are inhabited are many." That was what the two old men could tell each other.

Eskimo art

In 1959 Meldgaard took up a position as curator of the Department of Ethnography in the National Museum of Denmark. The same year, he published his thoughts on Eskimo art in a book entitled *Eskimo Sculpture* which was followed by an English edition (Meldgaard 1959, 1960). He thus revealed a new field of interest which he passed on to the public using wonderful language. The Greenlandic artist, Jens Rosing, played an important part in nourishing this interest. Meldgaard had met him in 1952 at Itinnera in Godthåbfjord, where Rosing had settled as a herdsman, with a herd of 264 reindeer which he had imported from North Norway the same year. Jens Rosing told Meldgaard about his childhood in Ammassalik, planting a seed in Meldgaard, who later wrote:

"When attempting to explain artistic endeavours in the dying Angmagssalik Culture, one must take into account the indigenous element of the rich Dorset Culture" (1959:31).

With his usual knack for seeing new perspectives, and presenting them clearly and simply, he drew the attention of the research world to a new problem. The following year he again put forward his hypothesis at the 25th Annual Meeting of the Society for American Archaeology: *"as I have phrased it before, several of these new traits in early Dorset smell of forest"* (1962:95).

Once again, on this occasion he turned Arctic archaeology in a new direction. This issue has since then occupied the minds of many, particularly in relation to immaterial aspects of culture (Carpenter this volume; Kleivan this volume; Petersen this volume; Sutherland this volume; Swinton this volume).

In 1960, he returned to Godthåb in order to investigate the Paleo-Eskimo caribou hunting ground which Jens Rosing had found in the fjord at Itinnera and, in 1958 attempted to excavate along with Helge Larsen (Meldgaard 1961; Møhl 1972). This was to be Meldgaard's last major Paleo-Eskimo excavation in Greenland for 21 years. Several researchers from abroad had already had an opportunity to take part in the fieldwork in Greenland (Laughlin this volume), and investigations at Itinnera continued in 1963, with participation from abroad (Giddings 1967:349). The finds from Meldgaard's excavations are still being used by new generations of researchers (Appelt this volume).

The Norse population and other Indo-Europeans

The Norse population was the focus of his museum work during the following years. During construction work at the Qassiarsuk settlement, known as Erik the Red's settlement Bratthlid, a skull had turned up. A preliminary test dig in 1961 established that a graveyard had been found, and traces of a small church building with peat walls were revealed. The following summer a more extensive excavation was initiated, and it became clear that they were faced with the remains of the oldest church in North America, Thjodhildes church (Meldgaard 1964, 1965, 1982, 1992).

The investigations continued for a number of years, and several of the participants of this first campaign have since then continued researching Norse Culture (Jones 1968, 1986; Krogh 1967, 1982).

Except for one detour to the Middle East, as head of the Danish Archaeological Expedition to Iran 1962-1963 (Meldgaard, Mortensen, & Thrane 1964), Meldgaard remained in the Arctic. In 1965 he was in Igloolik for the last time and in 1966 he was in Greenland to identify new research topics for the next generation of researchers. The topic was the cultural encounter between Eskimos and Europeans, which was to be examined through investigations in Upernavik (Hjarnø 1974) and in Godthåb (Gulløv & Kapel 1979). Meanwhile, Meldgaard was a research fellow at the National Museum of Canada between 1968-1969.

The new permanent Eskimo exhibitions in the National Museum of Denmark took place in the beginning of the 1970s taking stock of current research (Meldgaard 1975, 1977). At the same time he worked to establish an economically independent National Museum in Greenland. The latter became a reality in 1976 with Jens Rosing as its director for a two-year period. The museum's first major research project became the Inuit-Norse investigation of 1976-1977, conceived by Meldgaard (1976, 1977). Around 50 people from Greenland, Denmark, Norway, Canada, and the United States took part in the excavations during those two field seasons, with mutual pleasure and inspiration, and the effects of this 'cultural encounter' have been widespread (Arneborg this volume; Berglund this volumen; McGovern 1979, 1985).

Preservation, museums, and Home Rule

In 1977, in connection with the work of the Greenlandic committee on preservation, Meldgaard travelled through Holsteinsborg Municipality with the members of this committee. Using this Municipality as an example, the purpose of the trip was to evaluate the guidelines for future area-preservation in Greenland of areas of particular natural and cultural historic value (Meldgaard 1981). One of the outcomes was proof of the existence of an enormous caribou hunting site on the inland near Aasivissuit, which was later examined by archaeologists (Grønnow et al. 1983).

1979 was the centennial of Knud Rasmussen's birth and also the year in which Greenland won Home Role. Together with the Institute of Geography at the University of Copenhagen Meldgaard planned a memorial expedition to Kap Seddon, which lies halfway on the large sled-road going from Kap York via Melville Bay to Upernavik in West Greenland. Meldgaard took part in the preliminary research in 1978 and in the main investigations the following summer (Meldgaard 1980). En route they stopped at Qilakitsoq, where, in 1972, two ptarmigan hunters had found the interred and well-preserved bodies of eight Eskimos from the 15th century. This find has since become the focus of extensive research (Hart Hansen et al. 1985; Hart Hansen & Gulløv 1989).

Among the guests in Copenhagen at the centennial celebrations for Knud Rasmussen was Frederica de Laguna, who then did a "pilgrimage" to Upernavik, where she had worked as an assistant to Therkel Mathiassen half a century earlier. In her suitcase she carried a collection of photographs taken in 1929, and a piece of living history was revealed to the local population (de Laguna, this volume).

In 1981 the administration of cultural and educational affairs was transferred to Greenland's Home Rule. The creation of an independent Greenlandic board of museums had been prepared at a museum conference in Nuuk the previous year, and preservation efforts were now to be administered from Greenland (Kapel, this volume). Meldgaard took part in the ethnological-archaeological fieldwork that summer, which primarily was aimed at registering Eskimo folklore and sites in Jakobshavn and Uummannaq Municipalities. Cooperation with local museums and the local population as well as meetings with the local administration was an important part of the project. The results were filed in the archive of the Greenlandic National Museum in agreement with the new preservation act for Greenland and the law on museums in Greenland.

An old dream of visiting Qaaja, the old settlement halfway in the large Jakobshavn Isfjord came true in 1982. Meldgaard took up his work on the Paleo-Eskimos again on this site, which had midden deposits several metres deep as reported in 1870. The 77-year old Helge Larsen worked as his assistant. The excavations documented large amounts of well-preserved archaeological material, enough for many years of research for future generations, and a view into an enormous Paleo-Eskimo larder (J. Meldgaard 1983, 1996; Møhl, this volume; M. Meldgaard, this volumen).

The investigations at Qaaja were the beginning of a long series of locally initiated excavations of Paleo-Eskimo settlements along Greenland's coasts in the 1980s, and which are still being analyzed. Cultural encounters, Meldgaard's typology of harpoon heads, and his ethnographic and historical contributions to archaeology have found new relevance in Greenland as well as abroad (Andreasen this volume; Grønnov this volume; Gulløv this volume; Hansen this volume; McGhee this volume; Møbjerg this volume; Robert-Lamblin this volume).

Return to Greenland
Transfer of cultural property to Greenland has been a significant task for the National Museum of Denmark since 1982. Guidelines have been specified in a written agreement between the two countries. As a member of the Committee on Danish-Greenlandic Museum Coopera-

tion, Meldgaard has been responsible for choosing which ethnographic and archaeological collections will be nominated for transfer by the Committee. The transfer is expected to be completed by the end of the 1990s (Bahnson this volume; Grønlandssekretariatet 1985; Hart Hansen this volume; J. Meldgaard 1982; Schulz-Lorentzen this volume).

The ethical view on human remains is a significant aspect of this transfer process. In 1992 Meldgaard travelled to Thule on a research trip with the main purpose of bringing back and burying the human remains of a small group of Polar-Eskimos, whom Peary had taken to New York alive a century earlier (Gilberg 1994; Hart Hansen this volume; J. Meldgaard 1995). A shady chapter in the exploration of Greenland was hereby put to an end.

The newly renovated National Museum of Denmark was reopened to the public in 1992 after having been closed for over four years. Research proposals for projects in Greenland were put forward again, after the long period during which the museum had put all its energy into building up the Greenlandic museums system, and during which a new institution in Copenhagen, the Danish Polar Center, had been founded (1989) (J. Meldgaard 1993).

A new era
During this period Meldgaard also became Denmark's representative in a joint European-North American initiative, the outcome of which was the establishment of the International Committee for Archaeology in Chukotka. The opening-up of the former Soviet Union for international research projects has provided a fertile ground for new insights into the origins of Eskimo culture, and several new projects have seen the light in recent years (Fitzhugh this volume; Gulløv 1996; Müller-Beck this volume).

During his career as a curator Jørgen (himself) did not get an opportunity to visit this western part of the Eskimo Arctic, but in 1996 he prepared for his last season in the field at Disko Bay, where he was to verify new reports of Norse structures or Late Dorset long-houses. Investigations showed that the structures in question were built by Europeans in the 18th century. He ended, as he began in 1948, by sharing the joys of life in the field with his experienced colleague Hans-Georg Bandi (this volume).

Danish arctic research in the past half century can thus, be seen through the eyes of Jørgen Meldgaard. There is hardly a research topic that he has not touched. His effort spans from the earliest Paleo-Eskimo cultures, over the fabled Dorset Culture, to the whalers of the Thule Culture. But he has also explored the European presence in North America from medieval Norse settlements, via traces left by the whalers to colonial Greenland. For many years it was customary for foreign scholars to stop over in Copenhagen for inspiration from the Danish research environment, which was described as "the world centre of arctic anthropology". Meldgaard has been instrumental in maintaining this position.

For his efforts he has been awarded in Stockholm 1959 the 'Loubat-prize of the Royal Swedish Academy for History' and in Copenhagen 1976 the 'Antiquity and the Hans Egede-medal of Royal Danish Geographical Society'. In 1997 Meldgaard was awarded the Greenland Home Rule decoration given for meritorious services.

Jørgen Meldgaard (far right) together with the Khan of Hulailan in Luristan. Photo: Henrik Thrane, 1963.

Rolf Gilberg, curator, & Hans Christian Gulløv, curator, both at Department of Ethnograpgy, National Museum of Denmark, Copenhagen

References

Bandi, Hans-Georg & Meldgaard, Jørgen [1952]: **Archaeological Investigations on Clavering Ø, Northeast Greenland.** *Meddelelser som Grønland,* 126(4):85- (Copenhagen: Reitzel).

Fitzhugh, William W. [1972]: **Environment Archeology and Cultural Systems in Hamilton Intel, Labrador: A Survey of the Central Labrador Coast from 3000 B.C. to the Present.** *Smithsonian Contributions to Anthropology,* 16:1-299 (Washington DC: National Museum of the USA).

Giddings, J. Louis [1967]: **Ancient Men of the Arctic.** 409 p. (Lonson: Secker & Warburg).

Gilberg, Rolf [1994]: **Mennesket Minik (1888-1918). En grønlænders liv mellem 2 verdener.** 680 p. (Espergærde: ILBE).

Grønlandssekretariatet (editor) [1985]: **Gustav Holm Samlingen. Genstande indsamlet på konebådsekspeditionen til Ammassalik 1883-85 / The Gustav Holm Collection. Objects collected by the Umiak-Expedition to Ammassalik 1883-85.** 249 p. (Nuuk: Grønlands Landsmuseum, National Museum of Denmark & Grønlands Hjemmestyre, Pilersuiffik).

Grønnow, Bjarne, Morten Meldgaard & Jørn Berglund Nielsen [1983]: **Aasivissuit - The Great Summer camp. Archaeological, ethnographical and zoo-archaeological studies of a caribou-hunting site in West Greenland.** *Meddelelser om Grønland, Man & Society,* 5:1-96 (Copenhagen: The Commission for Scientific Research in Greenland).

Gulløv, Hans Christian [1983]: **Nuup kommuneani qangarnitsanik eqqaassutit - inuit-kulturip nunaqarfii / Fortidsminder i Nuuk kommune - inuit-kulturens bopladser.** 240 p. (Nuuk: Kalaallit Nunaata katersugaasivia & Copenhagen: National Museum of Denmark).

Gulløv, Hans Christian [1996]: **Ved porten til Den nye Verden. Nationalmuseet og de russiske udgravninger ved Bering Strædet. Summary: At the gateway to the New World. The National Museum of Denmark and the Russian excavations on the Bering Strait coast.** *Nationalmuseets Arbejdsmark,* 1996:163-175 (Copenhagen: National Museum of Denmark).

Gulløv, Hans Christian & Hans Kapel [1979]: **Haabetz Colonie 1721-1728. A historical-archaeological investigation of the Danish-Norwegian colonization of Greenland.** *Publications of the National Museum, Ethnograph-*

ical Series, 16:1-245 (Copenhagen: National Museum of Denmark).

Hart Hansen, Jens Peter, Jørgen Meldgaard & Jørgen Nordqvist (editors) [1985]: **Qilakitsoq. De grønlandske mumier fra 1400-tallet.** 216 p. (Nuuk: Grønlands Landsmuseum & Copenhagen: Christian Ejlers' Forlag) (English edition, London: British Museum Press 1991).

Hart Hansen, Jens Peter & Hans Christian Gulløv (editors) [1989]: **The mummies from Qilakitsoq - Eskimos in the 15th century.** *Meddelelser om Grønland, Man & Society,* 12:1-199 (Copenhagen: The Commission for Scientific Research in Greenland).

Hjarnø, Jan [1974]: **Eskimo Graves from Upernavik District.** *Meddelelser om Grønland,* 202(1):7-35 (Copenhagen: C. A.Reitzels Forlag).

Jones, Gwyn [1986]: **The Norse Atlantic Saga. Being the Norse Voyages of Discovery and Settlement to Iceland, Greenland, and North America.** 337 p. (New York: Oxford University Press) (Orginal 1968).

Krogh, Knud J. [1982]: **Erik den Rødes Grønland.** 266 p. (Copenhagen: National Museum of Denmark) (Original 1967).

Larsen, Helge [1953]: **Archaeological Investigations in Alaska since 1939.** *Polar Record,* 6(45):593-607 (*: *).

Larsen, Helge [1968]: **Trail Creek. Final Report on the Excavation of two Caves on Seward Peninsula, Alaska.** *Acta Arctica,* 15:1-79 (Copenhagen: Munksgaard).

Larsen, Helge & Jørgen Meldgaard [1958]: **Paleo-Eskimo Cultures in Disko Bugt, West Greenland.** *Meddelelser om Grønland,* 161(2):1-75 (Copenhagen: C. A. Reitzels Forlag).

McGhee, Robert [1996]: **Ancient People of the Arctic.** 244 p. (Vancouver: University of British Columbia Press 6 Hull: the Canadian Museum of Civilization).

McGovern, Thomas H. [1979]: **The Paleoeconomy of Norse Greenland: Adaptation and extinction in a tightly bounded ecosystem.** 395 p. Ph.D. Dissertation (Ann Arbor, Michigan: University Microfilms, Columbia University).

McGovern, Thomas H. [1985]: **Contributions to the Paleo-economy of Norse Greenland.** *Acta Archaeologica,* 54:73-122 (*: *).

Meldgaard, Jørgen - see list of publications.

Meldgaard, Jørgen, Peder Mortensen & Henrik Thrane [1964]: **Excavations at Tepe Guran, Lureistan. Preliminary Report of the Danish Archaeological Expedition to Iran 1963.** *Acta Archaeologica,* 34:97-133 (*: *).

Møhl, Ulrik [1972]: **Animal Bones from Itivnera, West Greenland. A Reindeer Hunting Site of the Sarqaq Culture.** *Meddelelser om Grønland,* 191(6):1-23 (Copenhagen: C. A. Reitzels Forlag).

Solberg, Ole [1907]: **Beiträge zur Vorgeschichte der Osteskimo. Steinerne Schneidegeräte und Waffenschärfen aus Grönland.** *Videnskabsselskabets Skrifter, II, Historisk-Filologisk Klasse,* 2:1-92 (Oslo: *).

Vebæk, C. L. [1992]: **Vatnahverfi. An inland district of the Eastern Settlement in Greenland.** *Meddelelser om Grønland, Man & Society,* 17:1-132 (Copenhagen: The Commission for Scientific Research in Greenland).

Some Personal and Biographical Notes on Jørgen Meldgaard

Klaus Ferdinand

Fig. 1: Meldgaard as a Mongolian gurtum (1946)

In the evening of October 23, 1946, Jørgen Laursen Meldgaard entered the assembly hall at the National Museum of Denmark with a sword in his hand, dressed in Mongolian silk robes, his face half covered by braids, streamers flowing down his back. "Melde", as he was called in the early years, came dancing as a shamanistic lama, a *gurtum*, in Henning Haslund-Christensen's show "One Night in Mongolia". Accompanied by the hollow sound of temple music, he - and other disguised Mongolians - stomped their way toward the shaman tent in front of the screen where Johannes Nicolaisen ("Nic") ferociously beating a drum, was in the midst of a shamanistic exercise, assisted by Martha Boyer and Halfdan Siiger. While Haslund, in his raspy voice, explained what was happening, the beautiful shaman drum ended up among the audience. It was a stunning performance and the response enthusiastic[1].

All young members of the staff of the museum were there that night. Matters were simpler then. The few employees all knew each other and the disciplines mixed both at the museum and outside working hours.

The years after the war were full of optimism and initiative; Helge Larsen had just returned from America, Werner Jacobsen ran off to Asia, Eigil Knuth was going to Peary Land, and Haslund was working in the collections preparing for his next large expedition. Melde and I were going to join him. Haslund incited us and had almost made us a promise[2].

In 1945 Melde had appeared and began studying archeology. At the same time Chief Curator Kaj Birket-Smith started ethnography as a discipline in Denmark[3]. Melde grew up in Glamsbjerg on the island of Funen, where his father worked as a school principal. He was an outdoor man, went on solitary archeological journeys and was an avid excavator. He had even worked for the National Museum of Denmark in Copenhagen during his school days. He also showed a keen interest in expeditions and voyages of discovery which he read diligently about. He had potential. At home he had his own archeological and zoological collections, meticulously systematized, which no one could touch while has was far away at high school. As many other provincial children who wanted an education, he had to leave home early and he attended high school at Rungsted Statsskole. He was, one presumes, an enterprising, ambitious and self-assertive loner; whose plans to become an archeologist were taken seriously at home! However, there were doubts about the future since he considered becomming a dentist to be able to study archeology in financial security.

That is what my sources from Funen have revealed. He had also considered studying architecture.

While a student Melde worked in the borderland between archeology and ethnography. That was where we met - sharing the dream of expeditions. Melde, however, was more cosmopolitan than the rest of us. He enjoyed a sumptuous lunch whilst reading the tabloid press, followed by a good cigar. We wondered how he could afford it but admired his style. He was respected for his work and was considered a clever student. His attitude towards reading, however, was not too obvious to us, perhaps even offhand.

One of his fellow students tells me that he never saw him sitting down reading. He would leaf through books or pace around the library looking up matters. Copenhagen grew too small for Melde. He had not, as the rest of us, passed the required Latin exam during his first year at university, and a dispensation had been refused. What did he do - the excellent strategist that he was? He transferred to the University of Aarhus where archeology had recently been established as a new discipline under Professor P. V. Glob. He got his dispensation and received the first Master's degree in Prehistoric Archeology and European Prehistory under Glob with a dissertation about the Ertebølle culture[4].

By the way, he was considerably late for one of the written tests. - We thought he had escaped the Latin, but he claimed that he had to sit through a harsh examination on the Gallic Wars by Professor of Classical Archeology, Poul Jørgen Riis! Melde is a true survivor!

We never got to go on an expedition together. We were supposed to join the most adventurous and demanding third leg of Haslund's Third Danish Central Asian Expedition - from India through Tibet to Inner Mongolia. Alas, no. That trip never took place. Jørgen joined Knuth's expedition to the North East Greenland through the assistance of Glob. That was in 1948 and marked the beginning of his connection to the Arctic area and his work together with H. G. Bandi and since then with many others.

We have since tried to cross paths. In collusion with others, but contrary to Glob's plans, Jørgen tried to get me to the National Museum of Denmark, and we have tried, in various ways, to persuade him to come to Århus and Moesgård. But, he was being awkward. He only wanted to make the move if he could have Bispegården ("the bishop's manor"), a beautifully situated farm close to Moesgård. It was almost like a Norse dwelling with its many buildings and the beautiful location, not unlike his farm (Skovgården) in Koblerne. But the farm was not even for sale! Jørgen!

Your visions and plans-stimulating, fantastic, and romantic - not unlike those of Glob - would have fitted well into the framework at Moesgård and enhanced it. However, it would hardly have given you the sense of "security" and "freedom" the National Museum of Denmark could offer you with its large staff and its ballast of world-famous collections and international status.

In 1962 we were to go to Luristan together, again arranged through Glob, but Kampsax would only pay for one person. Jørgen's two memorable and successful oriental expeditions with Henrik Thrane, Peder Mortensen, and several other excellent people became the result[5].

Since then, Janne and I have made several wonderful family journeys and trips to islands with Lissen and Jørgen (Meldgaard), Ida (Nicolaisen) and Nic. Tomorrow we set off again now with Bram (Professor Abraham Pais) and joined by your wonderful offspring.

Our two families also went to Perigor together where we saw cave paintings. Magnificent expressive and mellow images. But something bothered you; we were not the first, others had already been there! Yet, it triggered your urge to begin European paleolithic research. One cave looked untouched. Plans and dreams rumbled inside you with your ability to think big. You were wondering whether you could find an untouched cave - all to yourself. And then it happened.

One day you had to go off on your own - away from the rest of us. While Lissen, Janne and I went down to look at a famous "Black Madonna", you went off with a knapsack with food and a compass. Now was the time. Alone with nature or rather with the age old cultural landscape, hunting big for new discoveries. It did not happen that day, however! But the red wine and the food were excellent, when we met at our 16th century inn as planned. Jørgen was visibly impatient and grumbling when we arrived several hours after him!

Jørgen possesses many admirable qualities. He can be filled with enthusiasm, he is observant and incredibly creative if something catches his attention. He is hesitant but a survivor and a strategist. He is interested in quality, in solid and detailed knowledge and experiments, and last but not least the general outline, which he always manages to infuse with his own personal touch. Where knowledge and high quality reside, that is where one needs to be. Jørgen knows this and that has conveyed to him professional and personal authority and a lot of influence! This applies not only to his relation with archeology and cultural history (of which I do not intend to speak here) but to anything Jørgen ventures into, whether highland cattle, sheep, eels, hens or geese. He has an amazing intuition when he gets involved in anything. This is the case whether he interacts with people or animals, or when he touches and tells about a beautiful object or a well-made tool. Or when he chats with his animals at home. He exudes a gentle kindness.

Show him your new house or interior decor and he immediately graps the context. Well, well he says and then pronounces his verdict. He would have made an excellent interior designer or any kind of planner for that matter. It tickles his imagination and creativity. Just look at how he has transformed the landscape around his farm. Or developed the numerous exhibitions about the Arctic, Greenlandic art, and Persia, among other things, which he has designed or contributed to with interesting ideas, a brilliant idiom and his wonderful photographs. Professionalism, design, and creavity merged into a whole.

As to the recent birthday, I would like to say that there is no reason to despair. 70 is an arbitrary number and as to your retirement, life will provide much more freedom. I am speaking from my own experience. Work less and do only those things you like! You have talent! The most impressive of all your initiatives are the family expeditions, as for instance the "expedition" to Kárpathos in the Greek isles last summer. On this trip the next generations were to experience and learn. The expedition was planned in detail, maps were drawn, tasks delegated and presented to the various groups - dealing with archeology, history, zoology etc. - in writing, before we set out for this "almost unknown island", as Jørgen explained. The structure was clear. There was one - and only one - head of the expedition, he explained, him. He knows what he is worth! I didn't quite get Lissen's part but I think I know what it was! The expedition consisted of a carefully chosen group with children and no less than five grandchildren who were all thrilled! That is the way to pass it on!

And finally, do not dwell on the things you did not do. Here again I am speaking from my own experience. The material is there, and others which has already been demonstrated can continue your work and what you have started. Janne and I wish you all the best in the future and thank you for many years of friendship and wonderful times together with you and Lissen and your lovely family.

At the reception Jørgen Meldgaard resigned with "A few words about expeditions in the Pioneer Age and about the steps of growing old". Just as the person he is, with order and rational thought, it came:

"When I began my "career" here at the National Museum of Denmark fifty years ago we had a permanent notice on the noticeboard in the student lounge. The clas-

sical ladder illustrating the course of life, every step representing a decade, four steps to the top, four steps left until obliteration. The physical development towards absolute power in the forties, then decay, was clearly depicted through drawings. Development was predetermined for both matter and spirit, (70 was the year of dust) and the model was based on the experience and scientific research of generations. We believed it and lived according to it: we were busy. Life was so short, only the ascent represented life.

About a year ago, when I was at the lowest step, I bought a copy of the 'ladder' in the form of a reprint in the shop at the National Museum of Denmark. A depressing sight! However, shortly after that I came across some more recent research. Something negative, something positive for people in general and for museum staff in particular.

Our senses grow weaker - no doubt about that. The 70-year-old has lost 70% of his or her sense of taste and smell (measured by the loss of taste buds and olfactory cells). One's sight is reduced already at the age of 35 (however, this loss can be compensated through artificial means). Indeed, our senses grow weaker, yet we do not necessary become less qaulified as museum staff.

But the brain - 1997 is the year of the brain - and we are told now that the capacity to think, to perceive and elaborate ideas, increases till around the age of 50-60. (The exceptions being learning by heart and calenlation). Not till after the age of 60 is there a modest, measurable loss of capacity, and even at the age of 70-80 - at normal health - convolutions of the brain are comparable to the age of 20-30.

We have to change the structure of the age ladder, we need a new peak. Not necessarily a new structure for museum staff with retirement at 80, but a scaling down starting at around 60. For the benefit and happiness of all."

Meldgaard then presented a critical outline of his own professional life. The early years of powerful energy and curiosity, of impatience and new exciting challenges everywhere, of dangers and traps what he in a negative sense, as he put it, fell in with unfinished projects and an unfortunate lack of career ambitions. But, as he said, if one chooses to see it from a more positive perspective, he had passed on the challenges and put them in the hands of competent colleagues involved in the numerous projects he had worked on. Meldgaard concluded:

"Allow me to return to the ladder and the ages. I am very pleased that the museum is letting me retire gradually, giving me another step or two.

Even if my sense of taste and smell has been reduced by 70%, and I cannot fully enjoy my lunch, I believe it will be of mutual benefit. And hopefully I can continue research on and complete some of my old projects.

The age of "expeditions" is over. On the other hand there will be more time to spend at our home.

And together with the children, who in the good old days often came along on the expeditions - and who, probably for that reason are following in the footsteps of their father professionally, Dad and Mom will continue the expeditions. To warmer climates, however.

This is a piece of good advice to everybody: go on an expedition once a year with the entire family, regardless of age and numbers. Small clashes cannot be avoided but it creates unity.

This year I have invited my extended family on an expedition to Luxor, Egypt. We begin tomorrow.

The financial basis for this expedition are descendants of Red Erik and Tjodhilde, our Scottish highland cattle. I am selling Kraka and Freydis and others, and slaughter the young bulls, delicious meat at high prices. I am selling sixteen quarters after Easter - if anyone is interested."

Melde listening to the talks about himself as a staff member of The Department of Ethnography, in the National Museum of Denmark. Photo: Klaus Ferdinand, March 21, 1997.

Klaus Ferdinand, Professor Emeritus of Anthropology, Department of Ethnography and Social Anthropology, University of Aarhus, Moesgård, Århus

Notes

On Friday, March 21, 1997, Jørgen Meldgaard was celebrated at the National Museum of Denmark on the occasion of his 70th birthday and his retirement from the museum after four decades. Chief Curator Torben Lundbæk spoke on behalf of the Department of Ethnography and the National Museum of Denmark, he presented Meldgaard a large cardboard box containing two Canada geese, Meldgaard's favorite bird. The fox had eaten the last of his geese on his farm in Koblerne. Professor Henrik Thrane, University of Aarhus talked about their Iranian expedition. Curators Rolf Gilberg and Hans Christian Gulløv presented Meldgaard with a "first edition" of this Festschrift. I related some personal notes about Meldgaard and a life-long friendship and our shared professional dreams which we never got a chance to fulfil together. This is a revised version of the speech I gave at the reception.

(1) Henning Haslund-Christensen (1896-1948) was a reputed explorer and ethnographer having established the National Museum's Mongolian collections. Martha Boyer (1911-1995) was a student of ethnography and secretary and became curator at the Department of Ethnography and lecturer in East Asian studies at the University of Copenhagen. Johannes Nicolaisen (1921-1980) was student of ethnography and became the first professor of ethnography at the University of Copenhagen. Halfdan Siiger (1911-) was curator at the Department of Ethnography and became professor of Comparative Religions, Aarhus University. The Department of Ethnography, National Museum of Denmark has a fine series of photos of the dressed up Mongolians of that evening (Fig. 1).

(2) Helge Larsen (1905-1984) was curator, later Chief Curator at the Department of Ethnography. Werner Jacobsen (1914-1979) was archeologist having participated i Henning Haslund-Christensen's expedition to Mongolia 1938-1939, he undertook ethnographic studies in India and Nepal between 1948 and 1959, and became curator and head of the Department of Public Information Services, National Museum of Denmark. Eigil Knuth (1903-1996) was sculptor, author and arctic archeologist to be known for his Peary Land expeditions 1948 ff.

(3) Kaj Birket-Smith (1893-1977) continued in his position at the National Museum of Denmark. He did not want to become a professor.

(4) P. V. Glob (1911-1985) later became Director General of Antiquities and The National Museum of Denmark.

(5) Henrik Thrane (1934-) is a prehistoric archeologist, from 1996 professor at Aarhus University. Peder Mortensen (1934-) is near eastern archeologist, from 1996 director of the Danish Institute in Damascus.

Selected Bibliography

by Jørgen Meldgaard

Meldgaard, Jørgen [1949]: **Dødemandsbugten.** *Politiken*, Magasinet, 6. marts (Copenhagen).

Meldgaard, Jørgen [1952]: **A Palaeo-Eskimo Culture in West Greenland.** *American Antiquity*, 17(3):222-230 (Menasha, Wisconsin: Society for American Archeology).

Meldgaard, Jørgen & Hans-Georg Bandi [1952]: **Archaeological Investigations on Clavering Ø, Northeast Greenland.** *Meddelelser om Grønland*, 126(4):1-84 (Copenhagen: C. A. Reitzels Forlag).

Meldgaard, Jørgen [1953]: **Fra en grønlandsk Mumiehule.** *Nationalmuseets Arbejdsmark*, 1953:14-20 (Copenhagen: The National Mmuseum of Denmark).

Meldgaard, Jørgen [1955]: **Dorset Kulturen. Den Dansk-Amerikanske Ekspedition til Arktisk Canada 1954.** *Kuml*, 1955:158-177 (Århus: Jysk Arkæologisk Selskab).

Meldgaard, Jørgen [1955]: **Eskimoiske stenalderkulturer i Arktisk Canada.** *Polarboken*, 1955:113-127 (Oslo: Norsk Polarklub).

Meldgaard, Jørgen & Helge Larsen [1955]: **Archaeological Excavations in West Greenland, 1953.** *Polar Record*, 7(49):316 (Cambridge: Scott Polar Institute).

Meldgaard, Jørgen [1957]: **Eskimo-arkæologien i Etnografiens Tjeneste.** pp:25-39 in "Menneskets Mangfoldighed", editor: Kaj Birket-Smith, 206 p. (Copenhagen: E. Wangels Forlag).

Meldgaard, Jørgen [1958]: **Grønlændere i Tre Tusind Aar.** *Tidsskriftet Grønland*, 6(4):121-129 & 6(5):170-178 (Copenhagen: The Greenland Society).

Meldgaard, Jørgen & Helge Larsen [1958]: **Paleo-Eskimo Cultures in Disko Bugt, West Greenland.** *Meddelelser om Grønland*, 161(2):1-75 (Copenhagen: C. A. Reitzels Forlag).

Meldgaard, Jørgen [1959]: **Dyr i eskimoisk kunst.** *Naturens Verden*, 1959(juni):169-187 (Copenhagen: Rhodos).

Meldgaard, Jørgen [1959]: **Eskimo skulptur.** 48 p. (Copenhagen: J. H. Schultz Forlag).

Meldgaard, Jørgen [1960]: **Eskimo Sculpture.** 48 p. (London: Methuen).

Meldgaard, Jørgen [1960]: **Origin and Evolution of Eskimo Cultures in the Eastern Arctic.** *Canadian Geographical Journal*, 60(2):64-75 (Ottawa: Royal Canadian Geographic Society).

Meldgaard, Jørgen [1960]: **Prehistoric Culture Sequences in the Eastern Arctic as elucidated by Stratified Sites at Igloolik.** pp:588-595 in "Men and Cultures: Selected Papers of the Fifth International Congress of Anthropological and Ethnological Sciences", editor: A. F. C. Wallace, 810 p. (Philadelphia: University of Pennsylvania Press).

Meldgaard, Jørgen [1961]: **Afrikas sorte fortid.** *Naturens Verden*, 1961(2):33-69 (Copenhagen: Rhodos).

Melsgaard, Jørgen [1961]: **Tjodhildes Kirke på Brattalid.** *Skalk*, 1961(4):19-28 (Århus).

Meldgaard, Jørgen [1961]: **Fra Brattalid til Vinland.** *Naturens Verden*, 1961(december):353-385 (Copenhagen: Rhodos).

Meldgaard, Jørgen [1961]: **Om de gamle nordboer og deres skæbne.** *Tidsskriftet Grønland*, 9(3):93-102 (Copenhagen: The Greenland Society).

Meldgaard, Jørgen [1961]: **Saqqaqfolket ved Itivnera. Nationalmuseets undersøgelser i sommeren 1960.** *Tidsskriftet Grønland*, 9(1):15-23 (Copenhagen: The Greenland Society).

Meldgaard, Jørgen [1962]: **On the Formative Period of the Dorset Culture.** pp:92-95 in "Prehistoric Cultural Relations between the Arctic and Temperate Zones of North America", editor: John M. Campbell, *Arctic Institute of North America, Technical Paper*, 11:1-181 (Montreal: Arctic Institute of North America).

Meldgaard, Jørgen [1964]: **En landsby i Luristan.** *Skalk*, 1964(1):22-25 (Århus).

Meldgaard, Jørgen [1964]: **Krogh, Anders: Mand og Flint.** 62 p. (Copenhagen: Rhodos).

Meldgaard, Jørgen [1964]: **Tjodhildes kirke på Brattalid.** *Tidsskriftet Grønland*, 12(8):181-299 (Copenhagen: THe Greenland Society).

Meldgaard, Jørgen, Peder Mortensen & Henrik Thrane [1964]: **Excavations at Tepe Guran, Luristan.** Preliminary Report of The Danish Archaeological Expedition to Iran 1963. *Acta Archaeologica*, 34:97-133 (Copenhagen).

Meldgaard, Jørgen [1965]: **Nordboer i Grønland. En vikingebygds historie.** Søndagsuniversitetet 62:1-109 (Copenhagen: Munksgaards Forlag).

Meldgaard, Jørgen [1966]: **Hvem opdagede Amerika?** *Jordens Folk*, 2(1):200-204 (Copenhagen: Danish Etnographic Society).

Meldgaard, Jørgen [1966]: **Nordboernes Vesterbygd.** *Tidsskriftet Grønland*, 14:413-417 (Copenhagen: The Greenland Society).

Meldgaard, Jørgen [1967]: **Die Kunst der Grönländer.** *Dänische Rundschau*, 31:14-21 (Copenhagen: Danish Ministry of Foreign Affairs).

Meldgaard, Jørgen [1967]: **Die Wikinger in Grönland.** *Dänische Rundschau*, 31:27-35 (Copenhagen: Danish Ministry of Foreign Affairs).

Meldgaard, Jørgen [1967]: **Traditional Sculpture in Greenland.** *The Beaver*, Autumn:54-59, Magazine of the North (Winnipeg: Hudson Bay Company).

Meldgaard, Jørgen [1967]: **The Norsemen in Greenland.** *Danish Journal*, 58:15-22 (Copenhagen: Danish Ministry of Foreign Affairs).

Meldgaard, Jørgen [1971]: **50 året for Knud Rasmussens 5. Thule Ekspedition.** *Naturens Verden*, 1971(6-7):225-232 (Copenhagen: Rhodos).

Meldgaard, Jørgen [1971]: **Den 5. Thule Ekspedition 1921-1924.** *Tidsskriftet Grønland*, 18(10):303-314 (Copenhagen: The Greenland Society).

Meldgaard, Jørgen [1972]: **Om eskimoisk kunst i Canada og i Grønland.** pp:3-6 in "Inuit Skulpturer. Mesterværker i canadisk eskimokunst", katalog, editor: George Swinton & James Houston, 64 p. (Copenhagen: National Museum of Denmark).

Meldgaard, Jørgen [1973]: **The lost Vikings of Greenland.** *Natural History*, 92(5):36-43, 64-77 (New York: American Museum of Natural History).

Meldgaard, Jørgen [1974]: **Eskimo Masker.** Kalender for 1974. 12 p. (Copenhagen: A/B De Forenede Papirfabrikker).

Meldgaard, Jørgen [1974]: **Omkring Viborg og i Salling.** pp:269-294 in "Med Arkæologen Danmark rundt", Politikens Håndbøger (Copenhagen: Politikens Forlag).

Meldgaard, Jørgen [1975]: **Helge Larsen - Ipiutak and Other Arctic Adventures.** *Folk*, 16-17:5-11 (Copenhagen: Danish Etnographic Society).

Meldgaard, Jørgen [1975]: **Forhistorie og Nordboer.** pp:129-158 in "Grønland", editor: Palle Koch, 312 p. (Copenhagen: Gyldendal).

Meldgaard, Jørgen [1976]: **Grønlands Forhistorie.** pp: 129-159 in "Gyldendals Egnsbeskrivelse, Grønland", 312 p. (Copenhagen: Gyldendal).

Meldgaard, Jørgen [1976]: **Inuit-Nordbo undersøgelsen, 1976, en plan for arkæologiske udgravninger i Ameralik Fjorden.** *Tidsskriftet Grønland*, 24(2):33-44 (Copenhagen: The Greenland Society).

Meldgaard, Jørgen [1977]: **Inuit-Nordbo Projekt - Inugnik Qavdlunâtsianigdlo misigaauineq.** *Forskning i Grønland / Tusaat*, 2/77:3-7 (Copenhagen: Danish Polar Centre).

Meldgaard, Jørgen [1977]: **Inuit-Nordbo projektet. Arkæologiske undersøgelser i Vesterbygden i Grønland.** *Nationalmuseets Arbejdsmark*, 1977:159-169 (Copenhagen: National Museum of Denmark).

Meldgaard, Jørgen [1977]: **Inuit-Nordbo Projektet.** *Carlsbergfondets Årsskrift*, 1977:32-36 (Copenhagen: Rhodos).

Meldgaard, Jørgen [1977]: **Prehistoric Cultures in Greenland. Discontinuities in a Marginal Area.** pp:19-52 in "Continuity and Discontinuity in the Inuit Cultures of Greenland", Proceedings from Danish-Netherland Symposium 1976, editor: Hans P. Klystra, 125 p. (Groningen: Arctic Center, University of Groningen).

Meldgaard, Jørgen [1978]: **Das Eskimogebiet - Eskimokunst.** pp:246-251 in "Propyläen Kunstgeschichte, Kunst der Naturvölker", 307 p. (Berlin: Propyläen Verlag).

Meldgaard, Jørgen [1979]: **Da grønlænderne kom på Kunstkammer.** pp:42-47 in "Det Indianske Kammer", redaktør Torben Lundbæk og Henning Dehn-Nielsen, 71 p. (Copenhagen: The National Museum of Denmark).

Meldgaard, Jørgen [1980]: **Den forhistoriske bebyggelse.** pp:56-60 in "Holsteinsborg. Sisimiut kommune. Natur- og kulturforhold", 88 p. (Copenhagen: Ministery of Greenland and Institute of Geography).

Meldgaard, Jørgen [1980]: **Eskimoens kunst og hans liv.** *Vår Verden*, 3(3):4-10 (Trondheim: Samarbejdsprojektet Vår Verden).

Meldgaard, Jørgen [1980]: **Grønland / Greenland.** pp:1-16 in "Etnografiske genstande i Det Kongelige Kunstkammer 1650-1800 / Ethnographic Objects in The Royal Danish Kunstkammer 1650-1800", Nationalmuseets Videnskabelige Skrifter, Etnografisk Række 17:1-260, redaktion: Bente Dam-Mikkelsen og Torben Lundbæk (Copenhagen: Nationalmuseet).

Meldgaard, Jørgen [1980]: **Historien, Eskimoernes ferd gjennom tiden.** *Vår Verden*, 3(2):6-12 (Trondheim: Samarbejdsprojektet Vår Verden).

Meldgaard, Jørgen [1980]: **Melville Bugten. Arkæologiske og etnohistoriske undersøgelser på Knud Rasmussens Mindeekspedition 1979.** *Naturens Verden*, 1980 (1):1-14 (Copenhagen: Rhodos).

Meldgaard, Jørgen [1981]: **Den grønlandske dydige jomfru Maria og hendes præst. Historien bag Mathias Blumenthals maleri fra 1753.** *Nationalmuseets Arbejdsmark*, pp:70-75 (Copenhagen: The National Museum of Denmark).

Meldgaard, Jørgen [1981]: **Helge Larsen.** *Dansk Biografisk Leksikon*, 8:544-546, 3. edition, editor: S. Cedergreen Bech (Copenhagen: Gyldendal).

Meldgaard, Jørgen [1981]: **Rink-medaljen til Helge Larsen.** Det Grønlandske Selskabs 75 års jubilæumsfest 18. november 1980. *Tidsskriftet Grønland*, 29(1):2-7 (Copenhagen: The Greenland Society).

Meldgaard, Jørgen [1982]: **Aron, en af de mærkeligste billedsamlinger i verden / Kalaallit oqaluttuatoqaasa assiliartaat.** 112 p. (Copenhagen: The National Museum of Denmark).

Meldgaard, Jørgen [1982]: **Grønlandske akvareller: En kunst- og kulturskat er 1982 overført fra Nationalmuseet til Grønland.** *Naturens Verden*, 12:437-452 (Copenhagen: Rhodos).

Meldgaard, Jørgen [1982]: **Signe Rink, Kvinden bag Arons og Jens Kreutzmanns grønlandske akvereller.** *Nationalmuseets Arbejdsmark*, 65-72 (Copenhagen: The National Museum of Denmarkt).

Meldgaard, Jørgen [1982]: **Tjorhildes Kirke - den første fundberetning.** Tema: Nordboerne I. *Tidsskriftet Grønland*, 30(5-6-7):151-162 (Copenhagen: The Greenland Society).

Meldgaard, Jørgen [1983]: **Qajaa, en køkkenmødding i dybfrost. Feltrapport fra arbejdsmarken i Grønland.** *Nationalmuseets Arbejdsmark*, 1983:83-96 (Copenhagen: The National Museum of Denmark).

Meldgaard, Jørgen [1983]: **Signe Rink og de grønlandske akvareller.** *Tidsskriftet Grønland*, *(4):*-* (Copenhagen: The Greenland Society).

Meldgaard, Jørgen & Bent Gynther [1983]: **5 kapitler af Grønlands historie.** Elevbog, 112 p. (Nuuk: Pilersuiffik).

Meldgaard, Jørgen & Bent Gynther [1983]: **Kalaallit Nunaanni itsarsuup nalaaimmikkoortut tallimat.** 120 p. (Nuuk: Pilersuiffik).

Meldgaard, Jørgen & Bent Gynther [1984]: **5 kapitler af Grønlands historie / Kalaallit Nunaanni itsarsuup nalaaimmikkoortut tallimat.** Lærervejledning / ilinniartitsisunut ilisersuusiaq, 84/99 p. (Nuuk: Pilersuiffik).

Meldgaard, Jørgen [1984]: **Helge Larsen.** Nekrolog. *Nyt fra Nationalmuseet*, 23:16 (Copenhagen: The National Museum of Denmark).

Meldgaard, Jørgen [1984]: **Helge Larsen.** Nekrolog, *Politiken*, (Copenhagen).

Meldgaard, Jørgen [1985]: **Introduktion / aallaqqaasiut / Introduction.** pp:1-38 in "Gustav Holm Samlingen / Gustav Holmip Katersugai / The Gustav Holm Collection",

247 p. (Nuuk: Grønlands Landsmuseum, Nationalmuseet og Grønlands Hjemmestyre).

Meldgaard, Jørgen, Jens Peder Hart Hansen & Jørgen Nordqvist (editors) [1985]: **Qilakitsoq: De grønlandske mumier fra 1400-tallet**. 216 p. (Nuuk: Grønlands Landsmuseum & Copenhagen: Christian Ejlers Forlag).

Meldgaard, Jørgen, Jens Peder Hart Hansen & Jørgen Nordqvist (editors) [1985]: **The Mumies of Qilakitsoq**. *National Geographic Magazine*, 167(2):190-207 (Washington DC).

Meldgaard, Jørgen [1986]: **Dorset-Kulturen - udviklingstendenser og afbrydelser.** pp:15-32 in "Vort sprog - vor kultur". Foredrag fra symposium afholdt i Nuuk oktober 1981 arrangeret af Ilisimatusarfik og Kalaallit Nunaata Katersugaasivia. 220 p. (Nuuk: Pilersuiffik).

Meldgaard, Jørgen [1987]: **La découverte des Groenlandais de l'est: L'expédition Holm de 1883-1885.** *Swissair Gazette*, 1987(7):*-* (Zurich).

Meldgaard, Jørgen [1987]: **Vikings: The Norse Colonies. The Story of the Vanished Settlements.** *Swissair Gazette*, 1987(7):34-36 (Zurich).

Meldgaard, Jørgen, Jens Peder Hart Hansen & Jørgen Nordqvist (editors) [1987]: **De Mumies van Qilakitsoq.** 192 p. (Maastricht/Brussel: Natuur & Techniek).

Meldgaard, Jørgen [1988]: **Eskimokulturer og kolonisering.** pp:272-273 in "Historisk Atlas Danmark", editors: Jette Kjærulff Hellesen og Ole Tuxen, 303 p. (Copenhagen: G. E. C. Gad Forlag).

Meldgaard, Jørgen [1991]: **Bopladsen Qajaa i Jakobshavn Isfjord. En rapport om udgravninger i 1871 og 1982.** *Tidsskriftet Grønland*, 39(4-7):191-205 (Copenhagen: The Greenland Society).

Meldgaard, Jørgen [1991]: **Et Folk gennem 4000 År? Sarqaq-kulturen set i canadisk perspektiv.** *Tidsskriftet Grønland*, 39(4-7):210-213 (Copenhagen: The Greenland Society).

Meldgaard, Jørgen, Jens Peder Hart Hansen & Jørgen Nordqvist (editors) [1991]: **The Greenland Mummies.** 192 p. (London: The British Museum Press).

Meldgaard, Jørgen, Jens Peder Hart Hansen & Jørgen Nordqvist (editors) [1992]: **Qilakitsoq: De grønlandske mumier fra 1400-tallet**. Second edition, 192 p. (Nuuk: Grønlands Landsmuseum; Copenhagen: Christian Ejlers Forlag).

Meldgaard, Jørgen [1992]: **Fra Brattalid til Vinland.** *Naturens Verden*, 1992(6):201-240 (Copenhagen: Rhodos).

Meldgaard, Jørgen [1992]: **Vinlandsforskningen 1832-1992.** pp:5-12 in "Vikingernes sejlads til Nordamerika. 127 p. (Roskilde: Vikingeskibshallen).

Meldgaard, Jørgen [1993]: **Vinland Research 1832-1992.** pp:5-12 in "Viking Voyages to North America", 127 p. (Roskilde: Vikingeskibshallen).

Meldgaard, Jørgen [1993]: **Center for Grønlandsforskning på Nationalmuseet.** *Nationalmuseets Årsberetning*, 1993:40-41 (Copenhagen: National Museum of Denmark).

Meldgaard, Jørgen [1995]: **Eskimoer og Nordboer i Det yderste Nord.** *Nationalmuseets Arbejdsmark*, 95:199-214 (Copenhagen: National Museum of Denmark).

Meldgaard, Jørgen [1996]: **Pioneers: The Beginning of Paleo-Eskimo Research in West Greenland.** pp:9-16 in "The Paleo-Eskimo Cultures of Greenland", editor: Bjarne Grønnov, 334 p. (Copenhagen: Danish Polar Center).

Unpublished manuscripts

Meldgaard, Jørgen [1968]: **Dorset Culture Harpoon Head Chronology.** Unpublished manuscript.

Meldgaard, Jørgen [1980]: **Rink-medaljen til Helge Larsen. Tale holdt ved Det Grønlandske Selskabs 75 års jubilæums fest 18. november 1980.** 5 typed pages in Department of Ethnography, National Museum of Denmark, Copenhagen.

About Jørgen Meldgaard

Ferdinand, Klaus [1981]: **Meldgaard, Jørgen.** *Dansk Biografisk Leksikon*, 9:511-512 (Copenhagen: Gyldendal).

Jørgen Meldgaard. *Kraks Blå Bog* 1983:762 (Copenhagen: Krak).

Independence II in North East Greenland:
Some new aspects

Claus Andreasen

Introduction

The first major archaeological exploration in North East Greenland was carried out by members of the Danmark Ekspedition 1906-1908 (Thostrup 1911). Among the objectives of this first land based scientific expedition to North East Greenland was the collection of items relating to the Eskimo prehistory of the area. When they travelled north of Germania Land they found no ruins until they suddenly came upon Eskimo ruins at *Eskimonæsset*[1] on Holm Land (Thostrup 1911:205-208). On their travels further north a few more sites were found. In 1939 Knuth visited the area in the spring and excavated Thule Culture winterhouses on *Eskimonæsset*, Holm Land, and *Sophus Müller Næs*, Amdrup Land (Knuth 1942).

Later information from Knuth and others also proved the presence of Paleo-Eskimo settlements in the area. The information suggested the presence of Independence II of the same type as is known from the Peary Land area (Knuth 1984) and the Dove Bugt area (Andreasen & Elling 1995). However, the area was never thoroughly surveyed and information about the Paleo-Eskimo remains was extremely scarce and scanty up till 1993.

In order to get a preliminary framework for the cultural history in this region and its relationship to the North East Water-polynya through time, and to get a better understanding of the relationship between the Paleo-Eskimo Cultures in North Greenland and East Greenland, it was a major goal of the NEWland[2] 1993-Expedition to make a thorough survey inclusive excavations of Amdrup Land, Holm Land, and Henrik Krøyer Holme. This work turned up a large number of Paleo- and Neo-Eskimo sites

(Andreasen & Lange 1994; Andreasen 1997). During the NEWland 1996-project the coastal survey was completed, including the inland west of NEWland, and excavations were undertaken in the *Eskimonæsset* area. This article presents, in a preliminary form, some of the ideas provoked by the material found during this fieldwork[3].

NEWland

The coastal part of Amdrup Land and Holm Land (Fig. 1), is a flat, barren stone and gravel landscape consisting *"of sedimentary rocks - much of it limestone - of Upper Palaeozoic and Mesozoic age, in many places with a thin cover of Quarternary glacial and marine sediments"* (Hjort 1997). The foreland rises slowly to a height of 90 m to 100 m above sea level ca. 1 km to 10 km inland where ice-capped mountains rise to a height of between 400 m and 600 m above sea level The lowland is characterized as polar desert (Bay 1992:37) with a mean temperature in July and August of +1°C (Henrik Krøyer Holme), and with a very low precipitation. This easternmost fringe of the Inuit world borders the arctic ocean, here known as the North East Water: a huge polynya. According to ground-based reports[4] and satellite images (Toudal Pedersen et al. 1993) the sea-ice breaks up in early May, and in late June / early July the polynya has reached a considerable size; in late August / early September it freezes up again.

On the north side of Amdrup Land, the Antarctic Bay is icecovered for a longer period of the year, but a small secondary polynya occurs in the extreme southwest corner of the bay where the glacial melt water from Flade Isblink meets the sea. Available information indicates that

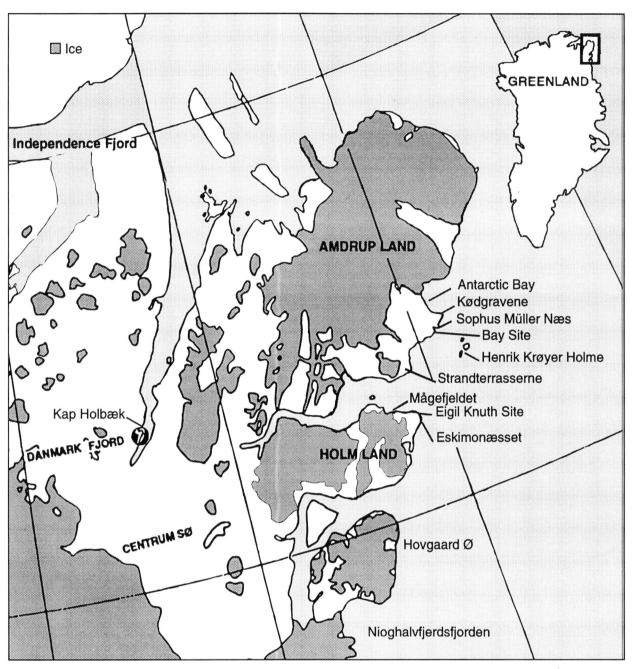

Fig. 1: North East Greenland with main names mentioned in the text.

the first areas to open close to the known settlements are the small polynya in Antarctic Bay and the one at the mouth of Ingolf Fjord (Weslawski & Wiktor 1994) right in front of the large Paleo-Eskimo site: *Eigil Knuth Site*[5].

The lack of vegetation has restricted the occurrence of terrestrial mammals to a few species: Lemmings (in some years), a few polar-hares, and maybe a few wolves (traces seen July 1996); neither muskox nor caribou can find a living here but small numbers of muskox are present in the icefree areas 25-30 km inland in Ingolf Fjord (the fjord between Amdrup Land and Holm Land).

The marine fauna seems most abundant in May and June with many walrus, bearded seal, and ringed seal. A few schools of narwhal may occasionally be seen in early summer. Whales have not been reported although several whale-crania, baleen, and ribs etc. are found on Thule sites. Polar-bears are frequently seen in early spring, with some also present during summer. Avian fauna comprises mainly gull, fulmar, tern, and eider.

In such an environment the prehistoric settlers in NEWland were restricted to a living based on marine mammals, probably supplemented by some bird-hunting.

Digging results

The archaeological survey in NEWland turned up three major settlement areas (Fig. 1):

(1) along most of the north coast of Amdrup Land from the secondary polynya in Antarctic Bay to *Kødgravene (the Meat Caches)* on the North East corner and a little further down the coast to the area around *Bay Site*.

(2) at the South East corner of Amdrup Land (the Kap Jungersen area with *Strandterrasserne*).

(3) at the North East corner of Holm Land (*Mågefjeldet, Eigil Knuth Site, Eskimonæsset*).

Outside these areas minor settlements are seen along the coast and on Henrik Krøyer Holme. These settlements are of both Paleo- and Neo-Eskimo origin.

According to artefacts, ruin-types, and a few ^{14}C-datings the prehistory in the area follows the general pattern of North Greenland's prehistoric development as established by Knuth during his almost 50 years of archaeological work in Peary Land (Knuth 1984): two Paleo-Eskimo horizons and at least one Neo-Eskimo horizon. In the latter the ^{14}C-datings and the inventory found in the four excavated winter houses[6] date the habitation to a late period around 1500-1600 A.D., but a few surface-finds of Thule 2-harpoonheads (*Sophus Müller Næs* and *Eskimonæsset*) suggest the presence of an earlier phase. Ruins from this early phase are still not found. During the 1996-season the first Late Dorset-ruin in North and East Greenland[7] was found on *Eigil Knuth Site*, thus adding a fourth - or rather a fifth - cultural component to the above-mentioned sequence.

Terminology

The terms 'Independence I' and 'Independence II' will be used for the material found in NEWland which in terms of typology and chronology can be related to the same periods in Peary Land as elucidated through Knuth's reports.

When mentioning features or periods further south on the east-coast I shall, however, use the terms 'Pre-Dorset' and 'Dorset' as denominators for the same periods as almost none of the ruins or artefacts found can be assigned specifically to either 'Saqqaq', 'Independence I', or 'Independence II'. Using terms like 'Saqqaq' or 'Independence I' for sites in East Greenland with just a few finds like a burin, a burinspall or a scraper would for the moment convey a wrong message of the supposed cultural relation of the few objects found.

Pre-Dorset

Recent ^{14}C-datings from sites in North East Greenland[8] have confirmed that the older ones are contemporary with Independence I in Peary Land meaning around 2500-2400 B.C. (calibrated). The chronological range of their stay in Peary Land seems restricted to about 500 years at

the most although a few dates indicate that some activities may have taken place up to around 1600 B.C. (calibrated). The length of their stay further south can not be assessed at the moment although some dates (two from NEWland[9] and six from Sønderland / Germania Land; Andreasen in press b) indicate the same chronological span as in North Greenland.

The surveys have shown that Pre-Dorset is present in this part of North East Greenland in a very marine environment compared to North Greenland while the topographical setting of the Pre-Dorset coastal sites further south on the eastcoast and in West Greenland normally are found in a more sheltered environment. Except for a single specimen of a small triangular Saqqaq-like biface found in Dove Bugt (Andreasen & Elling 1991) the few lithic artefacts can for the moment not be assigned to either Independence I or Saqqaq.

Independence II / Early Dorset

The available ^{14}C-datings from North and North East Greenland still point to a local, cultural discontinuity from Independence I to Independence II although two dates actually fall right between them; one from from Engnæs, ruin 1, Peary Land (K-1544; Knuth 1984:141) and another from *Kap Skt. Jacques*, Île de France (Knuth personal comment 1989). The rest of the dates from North and North East Greenland date this phase to:

About 850-450 B.C. (calibrated) in Peary Land (muskox-datings; Knuth 1984:141).

About 800-400 B.C. (calibrated) in NEWland (muskox- and corrected marine-datings).

About 500-200 B.C. (calibrated) in Sønderland/Dove Bugt (muskox-datings; Andreasen 1996).

Although caution should be taken when using the 'southern' dates as they mainly derive from one site they do suggest a possible relocation from north to south probably around 500-400 B.C. (calibrated).

The ruins in the Peary Land region are few: About 44 features of which only 24 are dwellings (Knuth 1981: 110). Another 29 dwellings are known from Peary Land down to Dove Bugt (Knuth 1983:8).

Since Knuth's finds at least another 100 dwellings in NEWland and almost 600 new dwellings and features (Andreasen & Elling 1995) have been added including the remarkable *Kap Skt. Jacques* site on Île de France. It is presently assumed that more than 400 ruins on *Kap Skt. Jacques* are dwellings of Independence II origin (Knuth personal comment).

Some large sites are found along the outer coastline where walrus may have been the main prey while a large number of minor sites are found in sheltered areas where seal-hunting must have been the major activity. The larger settlements are all situated at present-day large polynyas as in the NEWland-area and at *Kap Skt. Jacque*s or at small polynya-like situations.

Fig. 2: Ruin on Bay Site marked with small blacxk flags. (Photo: Claus Andreasen).

The Peary Land-sites show clear evidence of muskox hunting as do a few sites on the main coast and inland in Dove Bugt. Caribou bones have not been found at any of the sites.

The Eigil Knuth Site

In 1996 major excavations were undertaken at the *Eigil Knuth Site*. It is situated on the elevated beach-ridges on a gravel naze with the ocean to the east and Ingolf Fjord to the north. The features are found on most levels from about 1 m to 14 m above sea level with Thule features between 1 m to 5 m above sea level, Independence II features between 6 m to 12 m above sea level, and Independence I features and a single Late Dorset ruin lying at about 12 m to 14 m above sea level. Most of the Thule and Independence II features and the Late Dorset dwelling lie on the east side of the naze facing the sea, while the Independence I features primarily face the northern side towards Ingolf Fjord. A number of features were excavated with special focus on the spatial layout of the Independence II site, the layout of the individual features and the chronological span of the whole Paleo-Eskimo settlement period.

Independence II

Most of the Independence II features in the NEWland region have an axial arrangement built of thin, vertical slabs or marked by boulders. In northern Amdrup Land the features often have a stone periphery while this element is less pronounced on Holm Land. At *Eigil Knuth Site* most of the dwellings show an axial feature consisting of a rectangular group of smaller stones/cobbles often with charcoal and/or fat-staining between and around these and no clearly marked stone periphery. In a few cases small parts of upright slabs document that larger slabs once were part of the structure. Paving on one or both sides of the fireplace has not been seen.

A major reason to excavate the site was the presence of middens which are normally not seen on Dorset sites found between this area and 75°N. Most of the Independence II dwellings on *Eigil Knuth Site* and on the nearby *Mågefjeldet (Gull Mountain Site)* were associated with middens lying a few meters from the dwellings. The middens are circular to oval with a diameter of about 4 m to 5 m and are 5 cm to 10 cm deep. They show the same stratigraphy as the site itself: a top layer of coarse gravel turning into fine gravel further down. Bones, lithic and faunal debitage, and formed artefacts are found between the stones and on the fine gravel. Lichen-growth often revealed minor spots with organic dumps.

One element, however, stands out as extraordinary and characteristic of both the dwellings and the associated middens on *Eigil Knuth Site*: almost all of them were "marked" with a partial cover of small black flags, an element also known from some other sites in the NEWland area, but not known outside it[10] (Fig. 2).

The stones are small, local, smooth-edged, black, fist-to-palm sized flags that make each feature very visible in this bleak, gravel landscape consisting of eroded yellowish rock and chunks of coral.

Whenever even small collections of these flags were seen within the site area cultural debitage was associated with them. The flags probably derive from a few well-defined natural outcrops found just outside the site. At the dwellings and the middens the flags always lie on top of the feature, that is on top of the coarse gravel.

As a rule the flags do not touch each other except on sloping ground, that is primarily on the middens. Although the immediate impression is of a massive presence the total amount on each feature would hardly fill more than a few buckets. They do not give the impression of being used as cooking- or heating-stones. It seems clear that they were collected and carefully placed when the dwelling and the midden was left. Neither in the middens nor in the dwellings were any stratigraphic or other evidence of multiple occupations found, which on the other hand does not rule out that each ruin may have been in use for a number of consecutive years as part of a seasonal round within a larger subsistence area. The faunal, ecological, present zoological evidence, and lack of any kind of meat caches or meat graves suggest that the site was occupied during spring and early summer.

The flags mark the dwelling and the midden, but why: To attract heat to melt the snowcover earlier than on the surrounding area? To mark ownership to a site? Is it a sign to foreigners that the area is occupied?

Were they put there by newcomers to mark older features? Or were they placed each time a group left its dwelling just to be collected again when they returned? Or when people knew they were leaving the area for ever? Or by someone else? And why do we only find this element on certain sites in NEWland? No definite answer/s to any of these questions can be given yet but due to other elements found it might be tempting to see this element as an expression of some kind of regionalism or as a territorial marker.

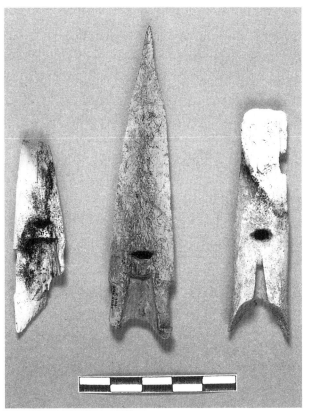

Fig. 3: Harpoon-heads from NEWland. Left and center: Open-socketed Indenpendence II harpoon-heads from Eigil Knuth Site. Right: Tyara-sliced harpoon-head fram Strandterrasserne. (Photo: Erik Holm).

Regionalism?

Although there is a general uniformity in the Independence II material in Peary Land and in NEWland, the black flags and a few other elements do point to some differences between these areas.

On the Peary Land sites the bulk of the faunal material is muskox- and seal-bones. Only a few artefacts made of walrus-tusk or walrus-bone have been reported: 11 pieces out of a total of 170 from the "Muskox Way", including Lonesome Creek (Knuth 1968:64).

Apart from the probably two Canadian pieces the rest derive from two sites in Jørgen Brønlund Fjord (*Deltaterrasserne, Vandfaldsnæs*) and one site in Independence Fjord (*Kap Ludovika*). As walrus has not been reported from these fjords the material is assumed to originate from the eastcoast and most probably from the NEWland area. Contrary to the Peary Land sites, the NEWland sites contain a large number of walrus-bones and only a few bones from muskox which is otherwise absent from the area. This distribution may be explained in at least two ways:

(1) It is the same group of people occupying both areas. During spring and early summer they hunt walrus at the coast and return to the inland in Peary Land for the fall and winter to fish and hunt muskox.

(2) Two regionally separate groups each occupying a specific territory, of which one might be mainly marine oriented (the NEWland group) and the other (the Peary Land group) has a more dual economy (muskox, fish and seal), being situated along the coasts of the Midsummer Lakes, Jørgen Brønlund Fjord, Independence Fjord and the southern part of Danmark Fjord. The two groups interact somewhere with each other to exchange commodities like tusk, and probably skins.

There are a number of problems inherent in each of these explanations and to examine them, an examination of all present material is needed. In case of the latter model, a movement of the hypothetical "Peary Land group" into the NEWland area might evoke the need to mark a territory or sites either by the local group or by the "intruders". Moving out from the inland could for example be caused by a climatic deterioration around 500-400 B.C. (calibrated) and/or if the muskox population had crashed or was depleted.

Peary Land and NEWland

The recent surveys have brought about a number of dwellings south of NEWland which have paved floors at one or both sides of an axial arrangement and is thus part of the interior architecture of the dwelling (Andreasen & Elling 1990:58). Sometimes only a circular-oval paving and no visible fireplace is found. From the Independence II sites in Peary Land Knuth has only reported *"structureless collections of flagstones with carbon layers and implements in front* [my underlining] *of the passage dwellings, particularly in front of such isolated hearth passage dwellings as lack the marking of a dwelling periphery."* (Knuth 1967:52).

Although some of his drawings do hint at the presence of interior paving he has not mentioned it as a specific type. The dwelling-type with interior paving has now been found in NEWland. One was found a few hundred metres south of *Eigil Knuth Site* no. 75. It exhibits the paving seen on the southern sites and also the wings normally associated with some of the Independence II sites in Peary Land (Knuth 1967:53-55) and with some of the sites in the Dove Bugt region (Andreasen 1996).

An additional 20-odd features were found by a survey-team on a very short ground-stop[11] at *Sommerterrasserne* on Amdrup Land on the north side of Ingolf Fjord. This site is almost 500 m from the coast situated at a little lake.

In dwelling 9 a harpoon-head closely resembling the Canadian "Tyara Sliced" harpoon-head was found (Fig. 3 right). This type is generally seen as a time-marker of Early Dorset in Canada (Maxwell 1985:167-168), but is not previously described as belonging to this group from

Fig. 4: Caribou hoof-miniature, Eigil Knuth Site, no. 20. Length: 3,0 cm. (Photo: Erik Holm).

Greenland. However, one harpoon-head of walrus-tusk reminiscent of this type is known from *Vandfaldsnæs* no. 9 (Knuth 1968:65), a feature which has produced four of the eight known harpoon-heads from the Peary Land and Danmark Fjord region.

Although Knuth never published detailed accounts of each site the published material seems to make *Vandfaldsnæs* special in Peary Land and interesting in relation to the two major Independence II sites on Holm Land: *Eigil Knuth Site* and *Mågefjeldet*. It is the only dwelling in Peary Land with an axial arrangement within a low gravel mound (Knuth 1967:55-56), an element which also seems to be present on *Mågefjeldet*. Apart from this it is *Eigil Knuth Site* no. 20, which attracts most attention in relation to *Vandfaldsnæs*.

In *Eigil Knuth Site* no. 20, an extraordinary piece of art was found at the northern edge of the fireplace: a beautiful cut miniature-replica of a caribou leg and hoof (Fig. 4). No other parts of adornments or amulets have been

Fig. 5: Two stuck, polished spall from a burin-like tool. Eigil Knuth Site, no. 20. (Photo: Erik Holm).

Fig. 6: Bifaces. Bottom: Mågefjeldet, no. 1. Top: Eigil Knuth Site, no. 20. (Photo: Erik Holm).

found on Dorset sites on the East coast and the piece is intriguing in showing a spiritual attachment to the caribou, the bones of which have never been found in an Independence II context in Greenland. On *Vandfaldsnæs* no. 9, Knuth (1968:67) found a few pendants and other artefacts cut in bone or muskox tooth which must also be related to personal adornments or to ritual purposes. No other Independence II ruin in Knuth's material has turned up such pieces. *Eigil Knuth Site* no. 20 also produced two very finely polished, struck burin-spalls (from two burin-like tools), the only indications of burin-like tools found in NEWland (Fig. 5). From Peary Land four examples of the burin-like tool are reported. Three of them were found on *Vandfaldsnæs* no. 10 and no. 11, whereas the fourth derive from Kap Holbæk (Knuth 1967:95). Knuth has published three ¹⁴C-datings of *Vandfaldsnæs* no. 9 all made on charred driftwood (Knuth 1984:141). One seems too old (K-933; 1230+/-110 B.C. uncalibrated) and two seem to be within the possible range, although at the older end of the supposed Independence II period at *Eigil Knuth Site* (K-934; 810 +/- 120 B.C. and K-934, 770 +/- 110 B.C., both uncalibrated).

Finally it should be mentioned that although bifaces form a large part of the lithic tools from the Independence II sites in North and North East Greenland no detailed study of these has been made yet. Knuth has only published a few of his bifaces and judging from these, two examples of a type slightly different from the present material known in North Greenland has now been found on Holm Land. One complete biface was found on *Mågefjeldet* no. 1, and in 1996 a basal fragment was found on *Eigil Knuth Site* no. 20 (Fig. 6). Both show a distinct bilateral notching with a more pronounced box-shaped basis than any other published or found in an Independence II or Dorset context from North and North East Greenland. The box-shaped base shows a similarity to the Canadian Grosswater Dorset-bifaces (see for example Taylor 1968; Plumet 1994: Fig. 14), although neither the box-shape nor the notching is as distinct as seen on the Canadian material.

These findings, summarized in Table 1, do suggest some kind of connection or interaction between some sites in NEWland and at least one site within the Independence II area in the Peary Land and Danmark Fjord re-

TABLE 1	*Vandfaldsnæs* no: 9, 10, 11	*Mågefjeldet* no: 1	*Eigil Knuth Site* no: 20	*Eigil Knuth Site* no: 75	*Sommerterrasserne* no: 9
Tyara Sliced-harpoonhead	X				X
burin-like tools /-spalls	X		X		
amulets/art	X		X		
gravel mound	X	X			
Grosswater Dorset biface		X	X		
paving				X	X
black flags		X	X	X	
walrustusk walrusbone	X	X	X		?

Table 1: Summary of elements mentioned in the text

gion. At the same time these elements set *Vandfaldsnæs* a little apart from the rest of the Peary Land group.

Apart from the above mentioned the NEWland-investigations have more than doubled the amount of Independence II harpoon-heads and cloven-hoof lances. This material, which mainly derive from *Eigil Knuth Site* and *Bay Site*, still awaits further analysis and a closer comparison with the North Greenland material.

Conclusion

The investigations in NEWland have brought about a number of features and objects which in many ways reflect the expected - and normal - picture of Independence II, but in other ways seem to make the Independence II in the survey-area a little different. A preliminary comparison with the contemporary Peary Land and Danmark Fjord sites has shown that at least one site, *Vandfaldsnæs*, has some elements in common with at least two sites in the NEWland region.

The distribution of faunal material and the presence of the black flags have raised the idea of possible local regionalism within Independence II in this region. Elements like the burin-like tool, the Tyara Sliced harpoonhead, amulet/art, and Grosswater Dorset-like bifaces seem to have a very restricted occurrence and to link one site in the Peary Land group in Jørgen Brønlund Fjord with a few sites in NEWland. Dwellings with interior paving are found in NEWland but not in combination with the black flags. This provides for the possibility of several - or at least two - Independence II groups which occasionally meet in NEWland where one of these groups for

some unknown reason, feels a need to mark a territory or its dwellings and middens with small black flags.

There is no doubt that the amount of Independence II sites and ruins on the northern part of the East coast far supercedes the Peary Land region and, in this sense, it no longer seems justifiable to perceive of Independence II in North Greenland as a culture relying primarily on muskox hunting supplemented by local sealing as reflected by the Peary Land settlement-pattern and faunal material. Taken as a whole the Peary Land material reflects either the presence of a small group, or simply the passing through of migrating Canadian Independence II people.

Finally, the possible difference between the two areas may instead be a simple reflection of seasonality with a strict segregation between objects relating to the main preys from the terrestrial respectively the marine world.

The occurrence of dwellings with a distinct interior paving and an axial arrangement is presently restricted to the area from NEWland and down to Dove Bugt. They too seem to be part of the Independence II and Grosswater Dorset architecture but judging from dates on Dorset material from Dove Bugt they belong to a slightly overlapping but mainly younger period than in North Greenland and NEWland where habitation seems to cease around 400 B.C. (calibrated).

In NEWland this type of dwelling is found outside the Independence II sites, and it is an open question whether they might represent another movement into the area of a Canadian Dorset group. In that case it might be their appearance which caused local people to mark their dwellings and middens.

Thus, although the NEWland area has confirmed the present general picture, it has in some ways also both expanded and blurred it. A number of questions relating to the cultural history of North and North East Greenland in the first millennium B.C. are raised by the material and so far none has been satisfactorily answered. There is, however, no doubt that when analyzed the material will provide a far more complex perception of this period than has been presented until now in most articles dealing with Independence II in this region.

Acknowledgements

Major funding was generously provided by the Danish Scintific Councils' Polar Science Initiative's (TUPOLAR) funding of the project: "Man, Culture, and Environment in Ancient Greenland". Important economic support was also received from the Winstedt Foundation, The Commission for Scientific Research in Greenland, the Greenland National Museum, and Canadian funds in order that Pat Sutherland, Museum of Civilisation, Ottawa, Canada and John Erwin, MA, Canada could participate. Sheila Coulson, ass. professor at the Institute for Nordic Archaeology, Art, History and Numismatics, University of Oslo, was kindly supported by her institution and by an Arctic Stipend from the Norwegian National Committee for Polar Research. Department of Prehistoric Archaeology, Aarhus University offered computerassistance and Tinna Møbjerg, same department, gave valuable comments on earlier drafts of this paper. I am gratefull to Hauge Andersson, the Danish Polar Center, for his cost-effective management of the logistical operations, and to the personnel at Station Nord for their practical support to the expedition and to the Sirius Patrol for allowing us to use their fine cabin "Eskimonæsset".

Finally, I am in deep debt to Jørgen Meldgaard for his constant support to me personally for almost 20 years and to his strong and never ending commitment to assisting museums in Greenland with information and all kinds of museum activities.

I am indebted to all the participants in NEWland 1996 for their commitment and discussions during fieldwork but the views and ideas expressed here remain the sole responsibility of the author.

Claus Andreasen, associated Professor; Department of Social and Cultural History, Ilisimatusarfik (University of Greenland).

Notes

(1): Names in italics are names of archaeological sites. In a few cases they are also official names.

(2): NEWland is an acronym for the coastal land-area bordering the North East Water (Nordøstvandet). This land comprise the coasts of Amdrup Land, Holm Land and the northeastern part of Hovgaard Ø.

(3): The participants were Claus Andreasen, Ilisimatusarfik (University of Greenland), Sheila Coulson, University of Oslo, Hans Lange, National Museum of Greenland, Tinna Møbjerg, University of Aarhus, Patricia Sutherland, Canada, the students Frederik Larsen and Grete Rendal, Ilisimatusarfik, and John Erwin, MA, Canada.

(4): The Danish Military's North East Greenland Dog-Sledge Patrol, The Sirius Patrol, has kindly given acces to their diaries to extract relevant information.

(5): In earlier reports this site has been called: *Nordre Eskimoæsset* (Andreasen & Lange 1994; Andreasen 1997), but was assigned its new name this year in honour of the work of the late count Eigil Knuth.

(6): Knuth has excavated one winterhouse on *Sophus Müller Næs*, and one on *Eskimonæsset* (Knuth 1942), Andreasen & Lange excavated one on *Sophus Müller Næs* in 1993, and Lange & Sutherland another house on *Eskimonæsset* in 1996.

(7): In North Greenland Late Dorset ruins were till now only known from the Thule District (Gulløv personal communication 1996, Knuth 1984:84 with references).

(8): The ^{14}C-datings will be published in "Grønlandsk Kultur- og Samfundsforskning 1997" (Nuuk: Ilisimatusarfik).

(9): *Kødgravene*, ruin 1 (AAR-1780), 100% marine carbon; radiocarbon years 4259+/- 90 B.P.; calB.C. 2404, and *Eigil Knuth Site*, ruin 32 (AAR-1773) 100% marine carbon, radiocarbon years 4060+/-90; calB.C. 2126.

(10): Taylor (1968:12-14) reported the occurence of a "... *scatter of from 15-200 granitic, and rarely limestone, pebbles or cobbles*" on each find spot at Arnapik. These pebbles are different as they are broken, angular chunks presumed to be hearth-stones or cooking-stones, an element also known from a number of other sites.

(11): Knuth may actually have found the site in 1939 although his description does not quite correspond to our findings. Furthermore his description points more to a Thule-house than to Paleo-Eskimo-dwellings.

References

Andreasen, Claus & H. Lange [1994]: **The Archaeology of Holm Land, Amdrup Land, and Henrik Krøyer Holme.** pp:163-165 in "Berichte zur Polarforshung. Reports on Polar Research 142/94. The 1993 North East Water Expedition Scientific cruise report of RV "Polarstern" Arctic Cruises ARK IX/2 and 3, USCG "Polar Sea" cruise NEWP and the NEWland expedition", editor: Hans-Jürgen Hirche & Gerhardt Kattner, 190 p. [Bremerhaven: Alfred-Wegener Institut für Polar- und Meeresforschung).

Andreasen, Claus & Henrik Elling [1995]: **Biologisk-arkæologisk kortlægning af Grønlands østkyst mellem 75°N og 79°30'N. Del 7: Arkæologisk kortlægning mellem Germania Land (76°30'N) og Lambert Land (79°30'N), sommeren 1990.** *Teknisk Rapport*, 25:1-60 (Nuuk: Grønlands Hjemmestyre, Miljø- og Naturforvaltning).

Andreasen, Claus [1996]: **A Survey of Paleo-Eskimo Sites in Northern Eastgreenland.** pp:177-189 in "The Paleo-Eskimo Cultures of Greenland - New Perspectives in Greenlandic Archaeology", editor: Bjarne Grønnow, 334 p., Publication 1 (Copenhagen: Danish Polar Center).

Andreasen, Claus [1997]: **The Archaeology of NEWland - An Archaeological Perspective.** *Journal of Marine Systems*, 1997(10):41-46 (Amsterdam: Elsevier Science).

Bay, Christian [1992]: **A phytogeographical study of the vascular plants of northern Greenland - north of 74° northern latitude.** *Meddelelser om Grønland, Bioscience*, 36:1-101 (Copenhagen: The Commission for Scientific Research in Greenland).

Hjort, Christian [1997]: **Glaciation, climate history, changing marine levels and the evolution of the Northeast Water Polynya - an overview.** *Journal of Marine Systems*, 1997(10):*-* (Amsterdam: Elsevier Science).

Knuth, Eigil [1947]: **Contributions to the Archaeology of North East Greenland.** Manuscript at Peary Land Fondation (Copenhagen: Danish Polar Center).

Knuth, Eigil [1967]: **Archaeology of the Musk Ox Way.** Contributions du Centre d'Études Arctiques et Finno-Scandinaves No. 5:1-70 (Paris).

Knuth, Eigil [1968]: **The Indenpendence II Bone Artifacts and the Dorset-evidence in North Greenland.** *Folk*, 10:61-80 (Copenhagen: Danish Ethnographical Society).

Knuth, Eigil [1981]: **Greenland News from between 81° and 83° North.** *Folk*, 23:91-111 (Copenhagen: Danish Ethnographical Society).

Knuth, Eigil [1983]: **The Northernmost Ruins on the Globe.** *Folk*, 25:5-21 (Copenhagen: Danish Ethnographical Society).

Knuth, Eigil [1984]: **Reports from the Musk-ox Way.** (compilation of Knuth's published articles and expanded with ^{14}C-dates). Private edition, 173 p. (Copenhagen).

Maxwell, Moreau S. [1985]: **Eastern Arctic Prehistory.** 327 p. (London: Academic Press Inc Ltd).

Pedersen, Leif Toudal, Preben Gudmandsen & Henning Skriver [1993]: **North-East Water. A remote sensing study.** 64 p. (Lyngby: Remote Sensing Unit, Electromagnetics Institute, Technical University of Denmark).

Plumet, Patrick [1994]: **Le Paléoesquimau dans la baie du Diana (Arctique Quebecois).** pp:103-144 in "Threads of Arctic Prehistory: Papers in honour of William Taylor, Jr.", editor: David Morrison & Jean-Luc Pilon, Archaeological Survey of Canada. *Mercury Series Paper*, 149:1-422 (Hull, Quebec: Canadian Museum of Civilisation).

Taylor, William E. [1968]: **The Arnapik and Tyara Sites. An Archaeological Study of Dorset Culture Origins.** Memoirs of the Society for American Archaeology. *American Antiquity*, 33(4)2:1-129 (Salt Lake City).

Thostrup, Christian Bendix [1911]: **Ethnographic Description of the Eskimo Settlements and Stone Remains in North-East Greenland.** *Meddelelser om Grønland*, 44(4):177-355 (Copenhagen: C. A. Reitzels Forlag).

Weslawski, J. M. & J. Viktor [1994]: **Marine shallow coastal ecology - with special reference to the plankton development.** pp:145-150 in "Berichte zur Polarforshung. Reports on Polar Research 142/94. The 1993 North East Water Expedition Scientific cruise report of RV "Polarstern" Arctic Cruises ARK IX/2 and 3, USCG "Polar Sea" cruise NEWP and the NEWland expedition", editors: Hans-Jürgen Hirche & Gerhardt Kattner, 190 p. (Bremerhaven: Alfred-Wegener Institut für Polar- und Meeresforschung).

The Construction of an Archaeological "Culture" Similarities and differences in early Paleo-Eskimo cultures of Greenland

Martin Appelt

Introduction

In recent years, scholars have questioned the division of North and North East Greenlandic Paleo-Eskimo cultures into two separate "cultures", which can be distinguished from the West Greenlandic Paleo-Eskimo cultures and the Pre-Dorset/Dorset continuum in other parts of the Eastern Arctic.

In relation to Greenland, it is the eskimologist Henrik Elling who has expressed this new view most clearly. He put it forward for the first time at the symposium entitled "The Paleo-Eskimo Cultures of Greenland - New Perspectives in Greenlandic Archaeology", held in Copenhagen in 1992. His views were also published in an article later that same year. After a thorough examination of the archaeological material from the Saqqaq Culture, Independence I Culture, Dorset Culture, and Independence II Culture Henrik Elling concludes that the distinction between the first two and the latter two cannot be maintained. Elling explains the differences which had previously been noted as "one culture's adaptation to various ecological, climatic, or geological conditions in the Pre-Dorset period" (Elling 1992:52, 1996).

The discussion which followed Elling's contribution at the above mentioned symposium gave an impression of general agreement with the views put forward by Elling.

This article will focus on the relationship between the Saqqaq and Independence I cultures and will offer a critical examination of Henrik Elling's arguments. Relations to Pre-Dorset outside of Greenland will only be touched on briefly. In this article I will attempt to demonstrate that there is still reason to consider the two early Paleo-Eskimo groups to be separate cultural manifestations.

History of Research

The "Saqqaq Culture" came into being, in the literature, in 1954 with Jørgen Meldgaard's excavations on the elevated beach terraces at Igloolik in the northern part of Foxe Basin (Meldgaard 1955). Here the excavation of several hundred ruins fully proved the existence of a culture similar to the "West Greenlandic Paleo-Eskimo culture", which Meldgaard had in 1952 already claimed existed based on material excavated by horticultural adviser Hans Mosegaard on the Saqqaq site in 1948. Meldgaard had to base his arguments on material which today is known to originate from very different times and places, such as stone objects from of the Pfaff and other museum collections from Disko Bay (Solberg 1907), Holtved's Dorset material from Thule (1944), Helge Larsen's Ipiutak objects from Alaska (1948), and Gidding's excavation at Cape Denbigh (1951). Comparisons led Meldgaard to conclude that the objects from the Saqqaq site belonged to a special phase in West Greenlandic Paleo-Eskimo culture which "*to some extent was influenced by Canadian Dorset*" (Meldgaard 1952:229). After his excavation in 1953 at Sermermiut Meldgaard's views were so well founded that he no longer talked about a Saqqaq "phase", but of a Saqqaq "culture" with a number of diagnostic artifact types.

At approximately the same time that Meldgaard defined his Saqqaq phase, Eigil Knuth was working in

Peary Land, where he found a number of Paleo-Eskimo ruins and stone objects. This new material was published in 1952 and was at that time tied to the Canadian Dorset Culture. However, in 1954, Knuth changed his mind and argued that this was an independent culture, which he named the *Independence Culture*. In the same article, he drew parallels between the Independence Culture and the "West Greenlandic Paleo-Eskimo Culture" but, because of the local connotations of the name, Knuth found that the material from North and North East Greenland could not be directly tied to the latter. In 1958, Knuth divided his material into an Independence I Culture and an Independence II Culture. Knuth writes about the former that it has strong similarities to the Pre-Dorset Culture which Meldgaard had recently isolated. However, at this point, the distinction between Saqqaq and Independence I was based on rather insubstantial evidence.

Over the following years, both Meldgaard and Knuth supplemented their material through excavations of other sites. Meldgaard summarized his work in an article from 1977. In this Meldgaard established that both the Saqqaq and Independence I Cultures originated in the Denbigh Culture, yet there were some differences between them. He emphasized triangular harpoon heads, knives with a transverse edge, long and narrow stone awls, and lamps, as particular Saqqaq types.

In 1978 Knuth published a similar review article, which primarily aimed at suggesting a tripartition of Greenland's prehistory into a Paleo-Eskimo, a Meso-Eskimo, and a Neo-Eskimo group. The Paleo-Eskimo group was, according to Knuth, characterized by a combination of many blades, burins, and burin spalls. The Independence I and Nuullit Cultures belonged in this group. In addition, there was a Pre-Saqqaq Culture consisting of the oldest Saqqaq sites in West Greenland (Tuapassuit in Godthåbs Fjord, dating from around 2000 B.C. (Knuth 1978)). The "Classic Saqqaq Culture" is characterized by the same features as the early group, but is distinguished by a lack of blades.

In the 1980s the circle of Greenland scholars working on the Paleo-Eskimo cultures of West Greenland and East Greenland expanded. The new research is mainly a continuation of Meldgaard's work, yet it differs on various points. Particularly important is a shift of emphasis from broad cultural-historic theories, encompassing large geographic areas, to examinations of an individual sites or a limited region. At the same time, ethno-historic sources come to play an important role in the development of models for the exploitation of Paleo-Eskimo resources (Gulløv 1983; Gulløv & Kapel 1988; Møbjerg 1981, 1986). This development within the discipline of archaeology also meant a refinement of excavation methods, particularly with regards to documentation. The 1980s brought an expansion of the geographical space within which the Saqqaq Culture could be documented. Møbjerg found several sites in Ammassalik (1988), which con-

tained Saqqaq objects. So did the Sandells in the Ittoqqortoormiit (Scoresbysund) region (Sandell & Sandell 1991), and Schledermann established the presence of Saqqaq Culture in Canada for the first time, on Ellesmere Island (Schledermann 1990).

Around 1990, the archaeologist Claus Andreasen and the eskimologist Henrik Elling directed the attention to North East Greenland again. The results of their investigations bring us right back to the point of departure for this article, namely the problem of classifying recently found material into the categories of the Saqqaq, Independence I, Dorset, and Independence II Cultures. Elling and Andreasen's area of interest lay between the hitherto known northern border of the Saqqaq Culture and the southern border of the hitherto known Independence I Culture, where the similarities of the diagnostic artifact types of these two cultures became more obvious (Andreasen & Elling 1991, 1995).

A discussion of the use of the term "culture" in relation to Paleo-Eskimo periods had already begun at the symposium "Paleo-Eskimo Research in Greenland" in 1987 (Møbjerg et al. 1988). Here it was suggested that "culture" be replaced by the term "group" to allow for more flexibility in the terminology. The outcome was a decision to use the "Saqqaq group", the "Independence I group", and the "Pre-Dorset group" in the future, and the "Arctic Small Tool tradition" as the umbrella term. Thus, a stand was not taken with regard to the basis for a separation, yet the need was expressed for a less pronounced separation between the two groups than the "culture"-suffix indicated.

In Canada this discussion began much earlier, with, among others, Irving's discussion (1962) of the use of "tradition", "complex", and "industry". McGhee (1976) took this discussion further by isolating a number of characteristics, which apparently distinguish Independence I from Pre-Dorset. Maxwell (1985) offers critical comments on this argument. Schledermann (1990), however, chooses to continue the interpretation of the two cultures as separate in his presentation of the extensive material from Ellesmere Island. Helmer (1994) attacks the problem from quite a different angle. His intention is to solve the "culture" problem by abandoning the problematic term "culture". Helmer's views are a direct extension of the recommendations of the Danish symposium in 1987 (Møbjerg et al. 1988).

Differences and similarities

Elling chooses to emphasize the similarities between the two rather than the difference, and this becomes the basis for his critique of the theory about two separate "cultures". Reviewing the differences emphasized by Meldgaard and Knuth, Elling finds that they can all be put down to differences in availability of various resources. In North and North East Greenland people have primarily had to base their existence on musk ox, whereas, in most other parts of Greenland, the variety of prey has been much greater. In the northern part of Greenland the soft siliceous slate was not available either, and therefore only a small amount of tools were polished. Finally, the blubber-lamp is not known from Independence I, a fact which is explained by the lack of soapstone. Furthermore, with reference to the "midpassage structure" which is now also known from the Saqqaq and Pre-Dorset Cultures (see Grønnow 1988; Maxwell 1985), he rejects the theory of difference in the construction of dwellings.

The questions which Elling does not pose are: how much of a difference should we expect to see? And, what should the character of this difference be before we can talk about two separate cultures?

In order to answer these questions we must look at the variations within in Saqqaq and Independence I respectively. Unfortunately, at this point in time, it is only possible to do so with respect to the Saqqaq Culture, as the condition of the Independence I material does not allow for detailed analysis. It should be noted, however, that Sutherland has worked on the problem in connection with her exploration of a number of settlements on Ellesmere Island (1996). She only succeeded to a small extent in showing variations among the tools at the Independence I sites.

Variations in the tools from the Saqqaq Culture

In recent years Grønnow and Kramer have attempted to break down the 1600-years time-span (Appelt 1995) of the Saqqaq Culture into chronological phases.

As the basis of his chronology Grønnow is using the large material from the Qeqertasussuk site (Grønnow 1987; 1990). In this material five horizons can be distinguished which together cover the period 2500-1400 B.C. Through these horizons the following trends in chronological development can be noted (Grønnow 1994):

1. Use of agate for the production of blades declines from 90% to around 25% from the oldest to the youngest phase. Agate is replaced by quartz.

2. Use of the particular dotted variant of killiaq (silicified slate) and of agate for the production of burins declines over time.

3. The width of the transition from the base of the burins to their distal end regularly decreases over time, from 14 mm to 11 mm.

Kramer's work on this material from more than 50 sites in the Sisimiut region which comprises most of the 1600-year period has led him to emphasize the following tendencies in the chronological development (Kramer 1996; Kramer & Jones 1992):

1. the oldest Saqqaq settlements lie 17-10 metres above sea level and the youngest 9-7 metres above sea level, while the Dorset sites are found at the beach.

2. In the oldest Saqqaq sites, silicified slate (killiaq) comprises between 90% and 70% of the lithic raw material used; in the younger Saqqaq phase the use decreases from 75% to 40%, and quartzite increases to more than 15%. In the Dorset sites, however, less than 40% killiaq is found.

3. The shape of projectile points changes from the oldest phase of the Saqqaq period to the youngest so that the transition between the distal end and the base becomes less marked.

4. Harpoon blades, and knives with a transverse edge, disappear in the younger phase of the Saqqaq period.

5. Soapstone lamps are added as a new element in the younger phase of the Saqqaq period.

If one tests the conclusions Kramer reached on grounds of the sites from the Sisimiut district, on the Saqqaq site Nunnguaq (Appelt 1995), from the Godthåbs Fjord, difficulties arise. Nunnguaq is dated to around 1800 B.C. (on charcoal of locally grown Alnus af. Crispa, Juniperus communis and Betula nana, calibrated $\pm$ 1 stand. dev. 1880 - 1790 B.C., K 6079). The relatively old date fits Kramers typological chronology with regards to the presence of harpoon endblades and "knives with a transverse edge". On the other hand the finds from Nunnguaq include several soapstone lamps, has killiaq frequencies lower than 70 %, was placed about two meters above sea level, and has projectile points with an indistinct transition point between stem and bladepart. Difficulties are also seen if one tests Nunnguaq against Qeqertasussuk as the "old" date from Nunnguaq is in conflict with the average width of the burins from Nunnguaq being 10.8 mm. (9.75 mm - 11 mm, n = 143). According to Grønnow's typology, Nunnguaq should thus be placed in the group of "younger" Saqqaq sites. A possible explanation for these difficulties may be that some of Grønnow's and Kramer's typological developments are restricted to a regional area and the specific activities on a given site or a given group of sites.

At present, the only variations that can be demonstrated within the 1600 year of chronological development in the Saqqaq Culture, seems to be a succession of very limited changes in preferences for different types of lithic raw materials. Possibly, the typical Saqqaq harpoon endblades and "knives with an transverse edge" disappear with the beginning of the younger Saqqaq Culture. The lamp may be a late phenomenon, in which case the transition from older to younger should be set at about 1800 B.C. According to Meldgaard (personal communication) the soapstone lamps are also found in the Igloolik area at the highest beach terraces, which means we are well inside the time period of older Saqqaq. All in all, the variations that can be demonstrated within the Saqqaq Culture seems limited and at present somewhat uncertain.

With these observations in mind, we will now return to the differences between the Saqqaq and Independence I Cultures which can be proved.

Differences between Saqqaq and Independence I

After reviewing the published work of Knuth and Meldgaard, Elling has created a list of features which supposedly distinguishes the two cultures:

1) dating,
2) raw materials used for the tools,
3) characteristics and size of the tools,
4) relative composition of equipment,
5) tools which are unique to one culture,
6) types of dwellings.

In what follows I will outline Elling's comments and discuss them point by point.

1. Dating the two cultures
In the past it has been argued that the Independence I Culture immigrated to the Eastern Arctic before the Saqqaq Culture. Elling has been able to reject this argument persuasively with reference to ^{14}C dating from Qeqertasussuk in recent years (Grønnow 1990).

2. Raw materials used for lithic tools
Elling believes that the difference between the two cultures in their use of raw materials for making tools is connected to the fact that killiaq has only been available in West Greenland. It should be noted, however, that recent investigations (Madsen & Diklev 1992) have proved the existence of killiaq or killiaq-like materials in Inglefield Land, Thule District, and Scoresbysund (Sandell & Sandell 1991). The Saqqaq people of West Greenland often travel far to obtain killiaq (Gulløv & Kapel 1988), and therefore, the fact that Independence I does not use killiaq is most likely caused by a preference for local materials.

3. Characteristics and sizes of the tools
Regarding the characteristics of the tools, Elling has particularly emphasized the different ways of using polishing and notching. The frequent occurrence of polished pieces in the Saqqaq Culture is explained by Elling through their use of the softer, and thereby more easily polished killiaq, whereas the use of notching in Independence I is explained through the adaptation of endblades for hunting musk ox. It must be noted, however, that softer types of stone can be found in Peary Land, immediately south of the core area of Independence I, and that the harder types of stone (that is agate) has been polished within Saqqaq

Culture (Appelt 1995). In his list of characteristics, Elling does not mention the far more frequent occurrence of deep serration among Independence I equipment. However, Elling proves very convincingly that the two cultures can not be separated on the basis of tool size.

4. The relative composition of equipment
Elling rejects the idea that the composition of tools in Saqqaq and Independence I, particularly in relation to burins and micro blades, indicates the existence of two separate cultures. It is true that the same number of burins have been found at several Saqqaq sites as at the Independence I sites. He is wrong, however, when he argues that the lower occurrence of blades among Saqqaq equipment is due to the widespread use of killiaq, as hard types of stone are available for micro blade production throughout the geographical area covered by the Saqqaq Culture. What we are talking about is rather differencies in activity patterns between Saqqaq and Independence I, leading to differencies in the use of particular artifact types.

5. Tools which are unique to one culture
Apparently, Elling can only identify two significant differences: the use of blubber lamps and triangular harpoon blades among the Saqqaq Culture, and the lack of those among Independence I. Elling explains the lack of blubber lamps in Independence I in two ways; soapstone is not available in the Independence I area and there is only a limited amount of seal blubber for fuel. I have a few objections to this argument: soapstone is, in fact, available in Inglefield Land (Madsen & Diklev 1992), and lamps could have been made from another material such as sandstone. Two lamps made of sandstone have been found at Nunnguaq in Godthåbs Fjord (Appelt 1996). Another explanation might be that the soapstone lamps were only used after the Independence I period as suggested above.

Elling explains the absence of harpoon blades, first and foremost, by arguing that people in Independence I were using self-bladed harpoons. However, among the very few harpoons known from an Independence I context, a harpoon head with bladeslit has been found (McGhee 1978).

Finally, we may wonder why Elling does not mention the narrow, symmetrical stone awls and the knives with transverse edges, which are exclusive Saqqaq types.

6. Types of dwellings
Elling also rejects the idea that the "midpassage structure" is specific to Independence I by referring to recent finds of such passages in both Saqqaq and Pre-Dorset contexts. 50 midpassage structures are mentioned in Knuth's material, which includes 131 ruins (Knuth 1978). I, on the other hand, have only been able to identify one possible "axial structure" in a Saqqaq context, at Qeqertasussuk in West Greenland (Grønnow 1990). That one is significantly shorter than the Independence I midpassage structures. It

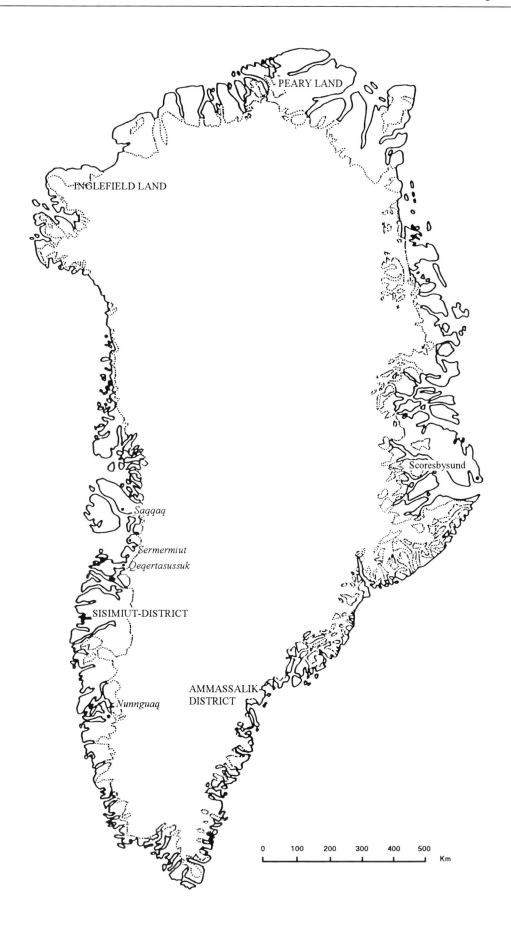

PEARY LAND

INGLEFIELD LAND

Scoresbysund

Saqqaq

Sermermiut
Qeqertasussuk

SISIMIUT-DISTRICT

AMMASSALIK-
DISTRICT

Nunnguaq

0   100   200   300   400   500
Km

is situated beside what we presume to be the entrance and consists of only two sections or rooms. Midpassage structures are also hard to find in Pre-Dorset contexts. Possible examples have been found at Uqalik (Mary-Rousellière 1976), but have not been described in detail or depicted. Several axial structures have been published in Labrador (for instance Cox 1978; Desroiers 1986), but none of these is built up of vertical slabs, nor does any of them have distinct room separations. This could be caused by a lack of slabs, but that is not likely.

Conclusion

Presumably, two groups of people living in significantly different environments, choosing different diets, organizing their dwellings in different ways, and designing their tools differently, have perceived themselves as belonging to two different "cultures".

We will probably never discover graves or clothing or learn about their language, their dances or any such thing, which would emphasize the "real" cultural differences or similarities. Therefore, in the future, the basis for assessing these relationships will mainly consist of analyzing minor variations in the lithic material, in the design of dwellings, and in the design and composition of fauna in the middens.

Acknowledgements

I am grateful to the Danish Research Counsil for the Humanities (Grant no. 9601947), whose financial support made development of this article possible. This article is built upon many years of discussion with Bjarne Grønnow, but it should be noted that the conclusions drawn here are my own. I wish to thank Bjarne Grønnow for his enthusiasm and patience.

Martin Appelt, Research Associate, Department of Ethnography, National Museum of Denmark, Copenhagen.

References

Andreasen, Claus & Henrik Elling [1991]: **De arkæolo-giske undersøgelser.** pp:54-65 in "Naturbevaring i Grøn-land", editor: Claus Andreasen, 132 p. (Nuuk: Attuak-kiorfik).

Andreasen, Claus & Henrik Elling [1995]: **Biologisk-Arkæologisk kortlægning af Grønlands østkyst mellem 75°N og 79°30'N. Del 7: Arkæologisk kortlægning mellem Dove Bugt (76°30'N) og Lambert Land (79° 30'N) sommeren 1990.** *Teknisk Rapport,* 25:1-60 (Nuuk: Grønlands Hjemmestyre, Miljø og Naturforvaltning.

Appelt, Martin [1995]: **Nunnguaq - en Saqqaqplads fra Godthåbsfjorden. En gammel udgravning i et nyt per-spektiv.** Unpublished MA-thesis submitted to Institute of Archaeology and Ethnology, University of Copenhagen, 87 p.

Appelt, Martin & J. Pind [1996]: **Nunnguaq - a Saqqaq Site from the Godthåbsfjord.** pp:129-142 in "The Paleo-Eskimo Cultures of Greenland - New Perspectives in Greenlandic Archaeology", editor: Bjarne Grønnow, 334 p. (Copenhagen: Danish Polar Center).

Cox, Steven L. [1978]: **Paleo-Eskimo Occupations of the North Labrador Coast.** *Arctic Anthropology,* 15(2): 96-118 (Madison: University of Wisconsin Press).

Desroiers, P. [1986]: **Pre-Dorset Surface Structures from Diana 1, Ungava Bay.** pp:3-25 in "Paleo-Eskimo Cultures in Newfounland, Labrador and Ungava", editor: *.*, *Reports in Archaeology,* 1:*-* (St.John's: Memorial University of Newfoundland).

Diklev, Torben & Bo Madsen [1992]: **Arkæologisk be-rejsning i Thule, 1991.** Unpublished report on file at Avernersuup Katersugaasivia, 42 p. (Qaanaaq: Thule Museum).

Elling, Henrik [1992]: **De palæoeskimoiske kulturer i Nordgrønland og Nordøstgrønland i relation til de vestgrønlandske.** pp:30-69 in "*", editor: *.*, 270 p. (Nuuk: Grønlandsk kultur- og samfundsforskning & Ilisamatusarfik).

Elling, Henrik [1996]: **The Independence I and Old Nuuliit Cultures in Relation to the Saqqaq Culture.** pp:191-198 in "The Paleo-Eskimo Cultures of Greenland - New Perspectives in Greenlandic Archaeology", editor: Bjarne Grønnow, 334 p. (Copenhagen: Danish Polar Cen-ter).

Giddings, James Louis [1951]: **The Denbigh Flint Com-plex.** *American Antiquity,* 16(3):193-203 (Menasha, Wis-consin: Society for American Archeology).

Grønnow, Bjarne [1988]: **Nye perspektiver i saqqaq-forskningen: en orientering om de tværfaglige under-søgelser på bopladsen Qeqertasussuk, Christianshåbs Kommune.** pp:21-38 in "Palæo-eskimoisk forskning i Grønland", editor: Tinna Møbjerg, Bjarne Grønnow & Helge Schultz-Lorentzen, 102 p. (Århus: University of Aarhus Press).

Grønnow, Bjarne [1990]: **Prehistory in Premafrost. Investigations at the Saqqaq-Site Qeqertasussuk, Disko Bay, West Greenland.** *Journal of Danish Archae-ology,* 7:24-39 (*: *).

Grønnow, Bjarne [1994]: **Qeqertasussuk - the Archaeol-ogy of a Frozen Saqqaq Site in Disko Bugt, West Greenland.** pp:197-238 in "Treads of Arctic Prehistory: Papers in honour of William E. Taylor, Jr.", editors: David Morrison & Jean-Luc Pilon, *Mercury Series paper* 149: 1-422 (Ottawa: Archaeological survey of Canada, Museum of Civilization).

Grønnow, Bjarne (editor) [1996]: **The Paleo-Eskimo Cultures of Greenland - New Perspectives in the Early Prehistory of Greenland.** 334 p. (Copenhagen: Danish Polar Center).

Gulløv, Hans Christian [1983]: **Nuup kommuneani qan-garnitsanik eqqaassutit - inuit-kulturip nunaqarfii / Fortidsminder i Nuuk kommune - inuit-kulturens bopladser.** 240 p. (Nuuk: Kalaallit Nunaata katersugaa-sivia & Copenhagen: National Museum of Denmark).

Gulløv, Hans Christian & Hans Kapel [1988]: **De palæoeskimoiske kulturer i Nuuk Kommune.** pp:39-58 in "Palæoeskimoisk forskning i Grønland", editors: Tinna Møbjerg, Bjarne Grønnow & Helge Schultz-Lorentzen, 102 p. (Århus: University of Aarhus Press).

Helmer, James W. [1994]: **Resurrecting the Spirit(s) of Taylor's "Carlsberg Culture": Cultural Traditions and Cultural Horizons in Eastern Arctic Prehistory.** pp:15-34 in "Threads of Arctic Prehistory: Papers in hon-our of William E. Taylor, Jr.", editors: David Morrison & Jean-Luc Pilon, *Mercury Series Paper,* 149:1-422 (Ottawa: Archaeological Survey of Canada, Canadian Museum of Civilization).

Irving, W. [1962]: **A provisional comparison of some Alaskan and Asian stone industries.** pp:55-68 in "Prehistoric Cultural relation between the Arctic and Temperate Zones of North America", editor: J. M. Campbell, *Technical Papers*, 11:1-181 (Calgary: Arctic Institute of North America).

Knuth, Eigil [1952]: **An Outline of the Archaeology of Peary Land.** *Arctic*, 5(1):17-33 (*: *).

Knuth, Eigil [1954]: **The Paleo-Eskimo Cultures of Northeast Greenland elucidated by three new Sites.** *American Antiquity*, 19(4):367-381 (Menasha, Wisconsin: Society for American Archeology).

Knuth, Eigil [1958]: **Archaeology of the farthest North.** pp:561-573 in "Proceedings of the 32nd Internatinal Congress of Americanists, 1956", editor: * *, * p. (Copenhagen: Munksgaard).

Knuth, Eigil [1978]: **The "Old Nûgdlit Culture" Site at Nûgdlit Peninsula, Thule District, and the "Mesoeskimo" Site Below it.** *Folk*, 19-20:15-48 (Copenhagen: Danish Etnographic Society).

Kramer, Finn Erik [1996]: **The Paleo-Eskimo Cultures in Sisimiut District, West Greenland. Aspects of Chronology.** pp:39-63 in "The Paleo-Eskimo Cultures of Greenland - New Perspectives in Greenlandic Archaeology", editor: Bjarne Grønnow, 334 p. (Copenhagen: Danish Polar Center).

Kramer, Finn & Hannah Jones [1992]: **Nipisat I - Nunaqarfik Saqqaq-kulturip kingusissuaneersoq / Nipisat I - en boplads fra den yngre Saqqaq kultur**. *Tusaat/Forskning i Grønland*, 1/92:28-32,33-38 (Copenhagen: Danish Polar Center).

Larsen, Helge & Froelich Rainey [1948]: **Ipiutak and the Arctic Whale Hunting Culture.** *Anthropological papers of the American Museum of Natural History*, 42:1-276 (New York: American Museum of Natural History).

Larsen, Helge & Jørge Meldgaard [1958]: **Paleo-Eskimo Cultures in Disko Bugt, West Greenland.** *Meddelelser om Grønland*, 161(2):1-75 (Copenhagen: C. A. Reitzels Forlag).

Mathiassen, Therkel [1958]: **The Sermermiut Excavations 1955.** *Meddelelser om Grønland*, 161(3):1-52 (Copenhagen: C. A. Reitzels Forlag).

Mary-Rousselière, Guy [1976]: **The Paleo-Eskimo in Northern Baffinland.** pp:40-57 in "Eastern Arctic Prehistory: Paleo-Eskimo Problems", editor: Moreau S. Maxwell, *Memoirs of the Society for American Archaeology*, 31:1-* (*: *).

Maxwell, Moreau S. [1985]: **Prehistory of Eastern Arctic.** 327 p. New World Archeological Record (New York: Academic Press Inc).

McGhee, Robert [1976]: **Paleoeskimo Occupations of Central and High Arctic Canada.** pp:15-39 in "Eastern Arctic Prehistory: Paleoeskimo Problems", editor: Moreau S. Maxwell, *Memoirs of the Society for American Archaeology*, 31:1-* (*: *).

Meldgaard, Jørgen [1952]: **Eskimo Culture in West Greenland.** *American Antiquity*, 17(3):222-230 (Menasha, Wisconsin: Society for American Archeology).

Meldgaard, Jørgen [1955]: **Dorset Kulturen. Den Dansk - amerikanske ekspedition til Arktisk Canada 1954.** *Kuml*, 1955:158-177 (Århus: Jysk Arkæologisk Selskab).

Meldgaard, Jørgen [1977]: **The Prehistoric Cultures in Greenland: Discontinuity in a Marginal Area.** pp:19-52 in "Continuity and Discontinuity in the Inuit Cultures of Greenland", editor: Hans P. Kylstra, 125 p. (Groningen: Arctic Center, University of Groningen).

Møbjerg, Tinna [1981]: **Den palæoeskimoiske ressource-udnyttelse, som den kommer til udtryk gennem bopladspalcering og knoglefund.** pp: *-* in "Vort sprog - vor kultur". Foredrag fra symposium afholdt i Nuuk oktober 1981 arrangeret af Ilisimatusarfik og Kalaallit Nunaata Katersugaasivia. 220 p. (Nuuk: Pilersuiffik).

Møbjerg, Tinna [1986]: **A Contribution to Paleo-Eskimo Archaeology in Greenland.** *Arctic Anthropology*, 23(1-2):19-56 (Madison: University of Wisconsin Press).

Møbjerg, Tinna (editor) [1988]: **Palæoeskimoisk forskning i Grønland.** Indlæg fra et symposie på Moesgaard 1987. 102 p. (Århus: University of Aarhus Press).

Sandell, H. & B. [1991]: **De palæoeskimoiske kulturer i Scoresby Sund.** *Tuusat/Forskning i Grønland*, 2/91:25-35 (Copenhagen: Dansk Polar Center).

Schledermann, Peter [1990]: **Crossroads to Greenland: 3000 Years of Prehistory in the Eastern High Arctic.** *Komatic Series*, 2:1-364 (Calgary: The Arctic Institute of North America of the University of Calgary).

Sutherland, Patricia [1996]: **Continuity and Change in the Paleo-Eskimo Prehistory of Northern Ellesmere Island.** pp:271-294 in "The Paleo-Eskimo Cultures of Greenland - New Perspectives in Greenlandic Archaeology", editor: Bjarne Grønnow, 334 p. (Copenhagen: Danish Polar Center).

Cultural Borders:
Reflections on Norse-Eskimo Interaction

Jette Arneborg

"The archaeological finds show that contacts [between Greenland Eskimos and Norsemen] were established, yet even more amazing is the lack of proof of mutual impact.

(De arkæologiske fund viser, at der har været kontakt [mellem eskimoer og nordboer i Grønland] men endnu stærkere taler manglen på vidnesbyrd om gensidig påvirkning)."

(Meldgaard 1977:162).

Ever since Hans Egede landed in Greenland in 1721 the nature of the culture contacts between the Norse population and the Eskimos in Greenland has been discussed lively. Many aspects have been discussed: Did they meet at all? If they did, where then did they meet? How did the meetings happen? How did the two Greenland populations influence each other, and if they did not, why not?

As Meldgaard's remark from 1977 indicates, it is today accepted that the Norsemen and the Eskimos in Greenland did know of each others existence even though we do not really know the nature of these contacts. Also emphasized by Meldgaard - the supposed meetings seem to have exerted remarkably little mutual influence on the two cultures. The Norse impact on the Thule Culture is still debated. The impact of the Thule Culture on the Norse Culture seems to have been absolutely absent.

The discussion about the mutual impact deserves more detailed analysis than I will be able to present here. However, a few reflections will be presented to stimulate future research. The discussion will have to take place in an interdisciplinary study. Nevertheless, being a medieval archaeologist, my point of departure here will be the Norse medieval society in Greenland.

The archaeological finds show that contacts were established...

Evidence of the culture contacts between the Norsemen and Eskimos in Greenland and in High Arctic Canada has been examined in several articles in recent years (Arneborg 1993, 1996; McGhee 1984, 1987). Here I will restrict myself to draw attention to a few points which I think are of importance to the discussion of Norse-Eskimo interaction.

The first known contacts between Norsemen and Eskimos are documented in the Norwegian history book "Historia Norvegiae" from the second half of the 12th century. The writer is supposed to have his information on Greenland from the Icelander Ari Frode Thorgilsson (Salvesen 1969), who mentions *Skrælings* in his "Islendingabók" from around 1130 A.D. However, not in relation to Greenland but in relation to Vinland (GHM I:171), and there may be some confusion and misunderstandings here, but still, if we rely on "Historia Norvegiae", Norse hunters may have become acquainted with *Skrælings* somewhere in Greenland around the year 1100 A.D., or perhaps even earlier.

The next time we hear about *Skrælings* is in the account of the Greenlandic priest Haldor who tells about Norse hunters who travelled far north around the year 1266 in order to search for *Skrælings*. It was the priests in the settlements who took the initiative to send an expedition to the north because returned hunters had told, that

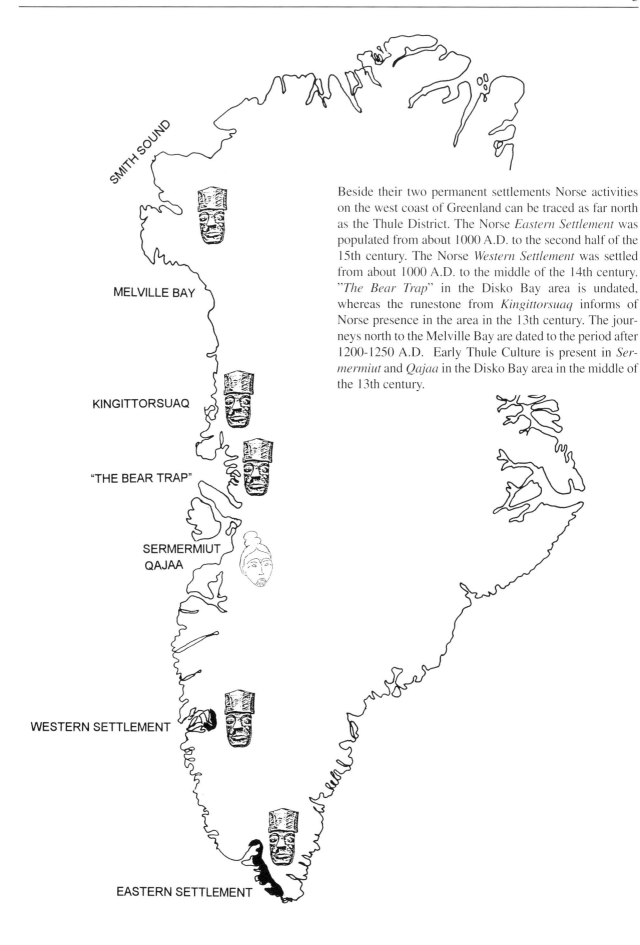

Beside their two permanent settlements Norse activities on the west coast of Greenland can be traced as far north as the Thule District. The Norse *Eastern Settlement* was populated from about 1000 A.D. to the second half of the 15th century. The Norse *Western Settlement* was settled from about 1000 A.D. to the middle of the 14th century. *"The Bear Trap"* in the Disko Bay area is undated, whereas the runestone from *Kingittorsuaq* informs of Norse presence in the area in the 13th century. The journeys north to the Melville Bay are dated to the period after 1200-1250 A.D. Early Thule Culture is present in *Sermermiut* and *Qajaa* in the Disko Bay area in the middle of the 13th century.

SMITH SOUND

MELVILLE BAY

KINGITTORSUAQ

"THE BEAR TRAP"

SERMERMIUT
QAJAA

WESTERN SETTLEMENT

EASTERN SETTLEMENT

they had not met any *Skrælings* in Nordseta. Unfortunately, we are not told why the Norsemen wanted to get in contact with the *Skrælings*. All we are told is that the new expedition only found the remains of *Skræling* habitation (GHM III:239-).

The archaeological record verifies that the Norsemen travelled north of the settlements. Artifacts made of tusk from walrus found in the Norse farms and bones of walrus, narwhal and polar bear in the middens give good evidence of that (McGovern 1985:81), because to catch walrus, polar bear, and narwhal the Norsemen had to travel to the Arctic waters north of the Western Settlement. There "The Bear Trap" on the Nuussuaq Peninsula in the Disko Bay has been explained as a Norse storehouse (Meldgaard 1995), and the runic stone from the small island of Kingittorsuaq north of Nuussuaq indicates that Norsemen visited the island somewhere in the 13th century (Stoklund 1993:533).

Supposedly somewhere in the 1370's the Norsemen did meet - very directly - with the Eskimos. "*Skrælings assaulted the Greenlanders and killed 18 man and captured two*". The information was written in an Icelandic annal in the year 1379 A.D. (Storm 1888). It is, however, only a brief mentioning which prodides no answers to questions such as where? and why?

The Disko Bay region has been escribed as the meeting point, and that is likely, even though we do not have any safe evidence of direct contacts between the two people there, yet (Arneborg 1991, 1993). The Thule Culture is now thought to have reached Thule in North Greenland from Canada in the 12th century (Meldgaard 1995:200), and the initial Thule Culture settlements at Sermermiut and Qaja in the Disko Bay are both radio carbon dated to the middle of the 13th century (Meldgaard 1995:208). The period of the Kingittorsuaq runic stone and the expedition of the priests.

In the High Arctic north of the Melville Bay Norse artifacts have been found scattered in Thule Culture houses on both sides of the Smith Sound indicating some kind of interaction, and here too the finds are dated to the 13th century (Schledermann 1993).

…yet even more amazing is the lack of proof of mutual impact.

Who exactly were the *Skrælings*, and how were they looked upon by the Norsemen?

According to "Ordbog over det Danske Sprog" the word *Skræling* means a weak, fainthearted, or even cowardice person, and from the written medieval sources we get an idea - though faint - of how the Norsemen looked upon the *Skrælings*. In "Historia Norvegiae" they are described as people who do not know of the use of iron; instead of iron they used stones and walrus tusks (Salvesen 1969:19). The description is in accordance with "Arí Frode Thorgilsson's Islendingabók", in which we are

for the first time introduced to the *Skrælings*. Here it is told that the first Norse settlers in Greenland found traces of habitation and stone artifacts:

"*…from which it may be seen that the same kind of people has passed that way as those who inhabited Vinland, whom the Greenlanders call Skrælings*" (Jones 1964:106).

In "Eirik the Red's Saga"[1] the *Skrælings* are described as:

"*…small ill favoured men, and* [they] *had ugly hair on their heads. They had big eyes and were broad in the cheeks*" (Jones 1964:182).

The description is not very flattering; we have to bear in mind however that the passage is about the *Skrælings* in Vinland who according to the story, through out the Norsemen of Vinland.

Besides the two mentioned sources we also have other late medieval descriptions in which the *Skrælings* are compared with trolls and pygmies, and it is difficult to distinguish reality from folktale (Arneborg 1991).

Both "Islendingabók" and "Eirik the Red's Saga" refers to events that took place around the year 1000 A.D. in Vinland, and here, according to McGhee (1984:9), the Norsemen most likely came into contacts with Port Revenge Indians of southern Labrador and Dorset Palaeo-Eskimos in northern Labrador. Still, the description of *Skrælings* in "Eirik the Red's Saga" may reflect the time the saga was written down, and, if so the "*small ill favoured men*" could be Thule Culture Eskimos.

The Vinland events are not quite dead when talking about "Historia Norvegiae", but if we decide to rely on the source the Norsemen met *Skrælings* in northern Greenland around the year 1100 A.D. or perhaps even earlier. At this time Thule Culture Eskimos had hardly crossed the Smith Sound from Canada, and we have to raise the question of who the *Skrælings* were, if they were not Thule Culture Eskimos. Were they then Palaeo-Eskimo Dorset?

To sum up: The Norsemen may have made contacts with at least three different people in Vinland and Greenland whom they called *Skrælings*. The meetings with the Labrador Indians and Dorset Eskimos must have been brief, whereas the contacts with the Thule Culture Eskimos can be documented archaeologically from about 1200-1250 A.D.

The existence of limited trade between Eskimos and Norsemen has been proposed (McGhee 1984 & 1987), and despite the poor historical and archaeological documentation and the hostile 1379-incident I will stick to this theory, at least as a working hypothesis. Even though the Norse settlers in Greenland were self-sufficient at a basic subsistence level, imports were necessary for the reproduction of the society, and the ties to Europe were from the very begining, based on the trade of Arctic commodities such as tusks and hides from walrus (Arneborg 1996).

The written accounts indicate that organized hunting parties went to the north to hunt Arctic animals, and I find

A Norse Greenlandic man with big eyes and a big flat nose. A beard and the long hair behind the ears. Stilistic the small figure falls in very well with Norwegian art tradition. Especially the long extended tongue is typical for Romanesque decoration.

These Greenlandic figures is made of soapstone and was originally the handle of a soapstone vessel. Found in 1922 in the Norse ruins at Igaliku Kujalleq at the Eastern Settlement (ruin group E56). Length: 9.5 cm. Belong to the National Museum of Denmark.

it most likely that the Norse hunters would also have tried to obtain the desired articles in some kind of exchange with the *Skrælings*. Just as the production of the North Scandinavian Saami population played an important part in the economy of the Norse North Scandinavian societies (Hansen 1990; Zachrisson 1993) I find it most likely, that the Norsemen would have tried to establish similar economical contacts with the *Skrælings* in Greenland (Arneborg 1996).

The motivation of the Norsemen is clear, and I would like to understand Haldor's account of the expedition to the far north in 1266 as a support to that idea. The Norsemen were searching for the *Skrælings*, who we may identify as Thule Culture Eskimos, to barter with them, and perhaps the account paints the picture quite clearly: nothing was formalized; contacts between the two groups were - as already stated by McGhee - sporadic and opportunistic (McGhee 1984:20-21).

In social anthropological terms the mode of exchange can be described as 'negative reciprocal'. 'Negative reciprocity' is the most impersonal kind of exchange between strangers and apart from 'barter' it also includes 'theft' (Sahlins 1972:195). But even in a negative reciprocal situation exchange of commodities does bring about some exchange of information also (Renfrew 1984:88).

Apparently the Norsemen did not distinguish the different people they met from one another. The Norsemen's

confusion does not give evidence of any great insight. On the other hand, the remarks on *Skræling* technology reflect some knowledge.

The fact that the Norsemen were unable to adopt Eskimo hunting technology has been pointed out as a fatal maladaptation to the Arctic conditions in Greenland. However, one could ask: Why should they? The amount of bones of sea mammals and caribou in the Norse middens (see McGovern 1985) indicates that Norse technology coped very well with the Greenlandic reality, and analysis of the δ ^{13}C contents of a number the bones of the Norsemen themselves support that idea. The δ ^{13}C value shows whether the diet has been predominantly terrestrial or marine, and from the last period of the Norse settlement in Greenland we have samples of buried Norsemen from *Sandnes Church* in the Western Settlement and from *Herjolfsnes Church* in the Eastern Settlement and from both sites the analysis indicate that marine diet had become predominant (manus in preperation). The δ ^{13}C values are similar to the values of Greenland Thule Culture Eskimos (Tauber 1989:137-).

Fundamental to the whole discussion of cultural impact is the concept of change and the Norse picture of the world. When the Norse colonists arrived in Greenland they came to unhabited land, which they incorporated into their Norse Scandinavian world. Even though at an early time, they may have obtained knowledge of

Skrælings far away from the settlements the premises of life in the new land were those of the Scandinavian social and economical reality.

In the world view of the Norsemen there was a clear cut distinction between 'inside' and 'outside', settled and unsettled, society and nature (Hastrup 1985:151-), and the *Skrælings* lived in and belonged to the unsettled, wild nature. Perhaps it is not accidental at all, that they were mixed with the trolls of the Scandinavian folktales. Despite the 1379-attack - which indicate an unpleasant kind of proximity - they formed part of the wild nature outside the settlements just like trolls.

It is, of course, nearly impossible to explain why specific changes did not occur in history. To the Norsemen nature was a resource, and may be we should discuss the exchanges with the *Skrælings* in that perspective.

Resources are socially defined and they do not exist without cultural acceptance and possibility to use them (Hastrup 1983:51). The Norsemen may have agreed to bartered with the *Skrælings*, but they never seem to have crossed the invisible border between the socialized 'inside' and the wild 'outside'. However, even though human behaviour is culturally dependent, people are not passively defined by their culture. They, too, define culture (Hastrup 1990:19). It would be a reduction merely to state that the culture of the Norsemen cut off the possibilities of cultural impact from the Eskimos. The lack of Eskimo influence on Norse Culture may simply be because the 'inside' side of Norse Culture to a certain - and yet undefined - point was able to respond to the objective changes in the environment. At a subsistence level, for instance, the Norsemen obviously did not need to adopt *Skræling* technology.

Still, we do not know for certain the reasons why the Norse settlements in Greenland were deserted after all. At a point the demands of the environment on the one side and of the social and economical structure on the other did not match, and the remaining population chose to set out. A final decision that would have fitted well into both the Norse and the Eskimo concept of life.

Notes

(1): **Eirik the Red's Saga** is preserved in two medieval editions from the 14th and the 15th centuries respectively. The saga is supposed to have been composed in the 13th century (Jones 1964:226).

Jette Arneborg, senior researcher, Department of Archeology and Early History, National Museum of Denmark, Copenhagen.

References

Arneborg, Jette [1991]: **Kulturmødet mellem nordboer og eskimoer**. Unpublished PhD dissertation (Copenhagen: University of Copenhagen.

Arneborg, Jette [1993}: **Contacts between Eskimos and Norsemen in Greenland.** pp:23-37 in "Tolvte tværfaglige Vikingesymposium", editor: E. Roesdahl & P. Meulengracht Sørensen, * p. (Århus: Aarhus Universitet).

Arneborg, Jette [1996]: **Exchanges between Norsemen and Eskimos in Greenland?** pp:11-21 in "Cultural and Social Research in Greenland 95/96. Essays in Honour of Robert Petersen", editor: Birgitte Jacobsen, 332 p. (Nuuk: Ilisimatusarfik/Atuakkiorfik).

GHM [1838-1845]: **Grønlands Historiske Mindesmærker** I-III (Copenhagen: *).

Hansen, Lars Ivar [1990]: **Samisk fangstsamfunn og norsk høvdingeøkonomi.** 275 p. (Oslo: *).

Hastrup, Kirsten [1983]: **Kulturelle kategorier som naturlige ressourcer. Exempler ra Islands historie.** "Samhälle och Ekosystem". *Forskningsrådsnämnden, rapport*, 83(7):40-54 (*).

Hastrup, Kirsten [1985]: **Culture and History in Medieval Iceland** . 285 p. [Oxford: Claredon Press).

Hastrup, Kirsten [1990]: **Nature and Policy in Iceland 1400-1800.** 367 p. (Oxford: Claredon Press).

Jones, Gwyn [1964]: **The Norse Atlantic Saga.** 246 p. (New York: Oxford University press).

McGhee, Robert [1984]: **Contact Between Native North Americans and the Medieval Norse: A Review of the Evidence.** *American Antiquity*, 49(1):4-26 (*).

McGhee, Robert [1987]: **The Relationship between the Mediaeval Norse and Eskimos.** pp:51-60 in "Between Greenland and America. Cross-Cultural Contacts and the Environment in the Baffin Bay Area", editor: *, *, * p. (Groningen: Arctic Centre. University of Groningen).

McGovern, Thomas H. [1985]: **Contributions to the Paleoeconomy of Norse Greenland.** *Acta Archaeologica*, 54(1983):73-122 (*).

Meldgaard, Jørgen [1977]: **Inuit-Nordbo projektet. Arkæologiske undersøgelser i Vesterbygden i Grønland.** *Nationalmuseets Arbejdsmark*, 77:159-169 (Copenhagen: National Museum of Denmark).

Meldgaard, Jørgen [1995]: **Eskimoer og Nordboer i Det yderste Nord.** *Nationalmuseets Arbejdsmark*, 95:199-214 (Copenhagen: National Museum of Denmark).

Renfrew, Colin [1984]: **Approaches to Social Archaeology.** 430 p. (Edinburgh: Edinburgh University Press).

Sahlins, Marshall [1972]: **Stone Age Economics**. 348 p. (London: *).

Salvesen, Astrid (translator) [1969]: **Norges Historie. Historien om de gamle norske kongene. Danernes færd til Jerusalem.** 136 p. (Oslo: *).

Schledermann, Peter [1993]: **Norsemen in the High Arctic?** pp:54-66 in "Viking Voyages to North America", editor: B. Laursen, * p. (Roskilde: The Viking Ship Museum).

Stoklund, Marie [1993]: **Greenland Runes: Isolation or Cultural Contact?** pp:528-544 in "The Viking Age in Caithness, Orkney and the North Atlantic. Select papers from the proceedings of the eleventh Viking Congress, Thurso & Kirkwall, 22 August - 1 September 1989", editors: C. Batey, J. Jesch & C. D. Morris, * p. (*).

Storm, Gustav [1888]: **Islandske Annaler indtil 1578**. 667 p. (Christiania: *).

Tauber, Henrik [1989]: **Age and diet of the mummified Eskimos from Qilakitsoq.** "The mummies from Qilakitsoq - Eskimos in the 15th century", editors: J. P. Hart Hansen & H. C. Gulløv, *Meddelelser om Grønland, Man & Society*, 12:137-138 (Copenhagen).

Zachrisson, Inger [1993]: **Mötet mellan skandinaver och samer.** pp:7-22 in "Tolvte tværfaglige Vikingesymposium", editor: E. Roesdahl & P. Meulengracht Sørensen, * p. (Århus: Aarhus Universitet).

Ancient Skin Clothing passing through Copenhagen

Anne Bahnson

The Collection

The world's most numerous and most varied collection of Inuit clothing is stored at the Department of Ethnography in the National Museum of Denmark, Copenhagen.

Some of the dresses, from Greenland, Canada, Alaska and Siberia, were collected for more than 150 years ago. However, most of the dresses were collected during the 1920s.

I have chosen to describe only a small part of this unique collection, namely skin clothing worn in West Greenland before 1900 A.D. Such costumes were made before trading companies supplied the Greenlandic women with large quantities of European articles such as sewing cotton, cloth made of silk, cotton and wool, small glass beads, artificial paint etc.

Continuity in Greenlandic Clothing before 1800 A.D.

Cut, pattern and materials used in West Greenland dresses are known as far back as the middle of the 15th century. Over a period of approximately 400 years - until the end of the 19th century - the basic patterns remained almost unchanged. However many minor differences can be seen with regard to the type of material employed over the years - and from one area to another.

Some of these differences served a functional purpose, for instance the hunter's adaptation to climatic conditions such as icy winds, snow and humidity. Other differences were created with style and fashion in mind, and the women obviously had a great desire to make beautiful garments. Especially with regard to women's clothing, the importance of fashion seems to have been prevalent.

Most important for the appearance of the dress are the differences caused by each woman's private choices and skills in skin composition and decoration.

Thus, both highly functional considerations as well as fashion were factors taken into consideration when the women designed costumes, - even under the most extreme climatic conditions.

Before going through the ancient skin clothing passing through museums in Copenhagen I would like to give a comprehensive description of the composition and appearance of the complete West Greenlandic clothing.

The Composition of the Dress

In the Arctic areas, it was essential for the people who lived there to protect the body from the harsh climate. In order to survive, clothing was required that could provide insulation from the cold, would allow movements and could prevent perspiration.

An Inuit fur dress consisted of two layers of skin, an inner coat with the hair against the body, and an outer coat with the hairy side out. The hair on the inner coat created a layer of insulating stationary air next to the body, a very good protection against the cold. The hair of the outer coat collected snow, rime and dirt, and was carefully beaten dry and clean, before it was carried into the warmth of the house.

The body of the person wearing the coat and the material of the coat would not be wet from perspiration, because the vapour would penetrate the hide. Furthermore, the dress had built-in air condition. After exertion the body perspired and the wearer would remove the hood. In this way the cold air would circulate inside the coat.

Men's clothing

Men's outer coats were most often made from sealskin. Three skins were required in order to make a coat, one for the front, one for the back and hood, and one for the sleeves.

The front of the body was continued in two shoulder-pieces, and the back was continued in the hood. Between the front and the back, two triangular pieces were inserted, in order to make the coat wider below. The early coats had both front- and backflaps, but the later coats were cut off straight at the lower edge. The sleeves were sewn to the trunk at right angles. The simple anorak-cut. The lower edge of the coat, the hood and the wrists usually had sealskin edges in different colors.

In areas where caribou hunting took place, the men often wore caribou skin coats in the winter. The pattern was almost the same as the pattern of the sealskin coat. Two skins were required for a coat, and the material used would preferably be autumn skins of young animals. The hood was made of the head skin of the deer.

Besides the ordinary coats made of haired skin, coats of waterproof skin were used particularly for kayak clothing. The cut of the kayak coat is similar to the cut of the ordinary coats. It is made of depilated sealskin, and the seams are ornamented with narrow stripes of depilated white skin. At the edge of the hood there is a drawstring to fasten around the face. Two smaller skin straps on each side of the hood are drawn behind thus serving to press the hood tighter round the head. There are drawstrings at the wristbands and at the lower edge of the coat with which the coat is drawn tightly round the kayak ring.

Inner coats of bird skins are the oldest type of inner coats. The common material was the skin of eiderducks, which had been plucked off its feathers so that only the down remained. Inner coats were also made of caribou skin, sealskin and dog skin.

The inner coat was made from a simpler pattern than the outer coat. The hood formed a separate part, and there were no shoulder pieces.

In the 17th century the men's trousers were rather short, reaching just below the knees, but later the legs of the trousers were made longer, and consequently the boots became shorter. The boots, as all Inuit boots, consisted of a sole and a top. The median seam running along the leg bended at the instep and ran down the side of the foot. The top was made of waterproof skin, and the sole of thick skin of bearded seal was gathered at heel and toe to fit the top. In front, at the edge of the sole, a hole was made on either side to keep the ankle band. This kind of lace was worn to fasten the boots.

Stockings were cut in the simplest manner possible, consisting of two pieces, the sole and the top. The materials used were seal and dog skin. The top of the stocking had a border of hairy sealskin to protect against snow and icy wind.

Fig. 1: The back of a woman's coat. The coat is made of caribou skin and richly ornamented with skin mosaic.
Photo: John Lee, National Museum of Denmark.

Women's clothing

The front piece of the women's sealskin coat was made out of one skin. The dark skin of the seal's back was running down the middle of the coat, and the light colored fur of the belly formed the sides. The front piece reached upwards to the breast, and ended downwards in a narrow pointed flap. Rather deep armholes were cut into the front. The back was divided in three sections, two sidepieces of light colored belly skin, and a five-branched center piece made of dark skin. One of the branches formed the back flap, which was longer and slightly wider than the front flap. At the top, two branches surrounded the base of the hood. The two small side branches were sewn to the shoulder pieces.

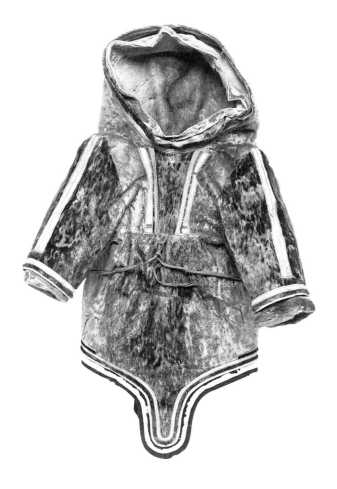

Fig. 2: The child-carrying coat, the amaat.

Photo: John Lee, National Museum of Denmark.

The sleeves were extremely wide by the deep cut armhole. The underside of the sleeves were considerably shorter than the top side. They were turned downwards and slightly forwards, following the women's horizontal movements.

The hood consisted of two symmetrical halves of light colored skin joined in the middle by an insertion of dark colored fur. The hood was very tall and extremely narrow.

On the caribou costume, the front skin was divided in the middle for an ornamental purpose. The front pieces continued in shoulder pieces and fit in the back piece. Under the neckline a rounded richly decorated piece and a rectangular piece with skin embroidery were inserted. The back was composed of the five branched middle piece

and two narrow side pieces (Fig. 1). All seams were decorated by insertions of strips and squares of white and brown skin. The hood was tall, and the smooth skin had been strengthened around the face by a string of baleen.

Women with babies wore the child-carrying coat, the amaat (Fig. 2). It mainly differed from the ordinary outer coat by its wide hood, and the wide back where the child was carried. To make an amaat, two sealskins or two caribou skins were required. The amaat was seen more often in North West Greenland.

In South Greenland it was worn until the middle of the 19th century, but later it almost disappeared and was replaced by anoraks made of cotton.

Women's inner coats were made of bird skins and cut like the outer coat, but in a simpler pattern.

Women's trousers were somewhat longer in the old days, and boots and trousers joined at the knee. One sealskin was required for a pair of trousers, and beautiful skin from a spotted seal was, and still is preferred. The sealskin trousers consisted of two symmetrical halves joined by a center seam. Each of these halves consisted of a front piece, a side piece and a back piece.

Along the upper edge there was a waistband made of depilated skin. In the northernmost districts the edge was made of hairy sealskin, in order to make it as warm as possible. Along the front of each leg was a rectangular piece, usually ornamented with artistic skin mosaic.

Trousers made of caribou skin were common in the central part of the west coast. The pattern used for this type of trousers was similar to that used for sealskin trousers. They were richly decorated with skin mosaic, too. The indoor-trousers, naatit, were made of short haired caribou skin or thin soft sealskin, tight and richly ornamented with leather bands or skin mosaics. During the 19th century this garment was no longer used in West Greenland. This was a result of the introduction of European underwear.

The oldest women's boots were short and very wide at the top. In the front, there was an insertion of a broad triangular piece.

In the days of Hans Egede women's boots were still rather short in agreement with the comparatively long trousers. In the last part of the 19th century the boots became longer, and reached far above the knee. At the upper edge of each boot there was a tongue-shaped knee piece. The early boots were made of waterproof skin and consisted of bootleg and sole. At the upper edge, the boot had a broad border of white depilated skin. The sole was gathered at the heel and the toe, and on both sides there was a hole cut for a strap. Later on when the boots became longer and more narrow, ankle bands were to be found, but they were very rare.

The stockings were made either of sealskin or caribou skin, worn with the fur side inward. The stockings were much longer than the boots, and edged at the top with a broad edge of black sealskin.

Fig. 3: The Ole Worm Museum around 1650 A.D.

Museum Wormianum

The oldest register of Greenlandic skin clothing in any Danish museum, comes from the museum "Museum Wormianum" founded by the Danish naturalist Ole Worm (1588-1654). He paid visits to several collections and well-known scientists in most of Europe and became greatly inspired.

In the middle of the 1620s he began to collect curiosities to his own museum. This collection was primarily being used as demonstration objects when he gave lectures for the medical students at the University of Copenhagen.

In the register from 1642 the following Greenlandic articles of clothing are described:

"Three Greenlandic shirts: Anorak made of sealskin, anorak made of bird skins, anorak made of fish entrails" ("3 grønlandske Skiorter: Anorak af Sælhundeskind, Anorak af Fugleskind, Anorak af Fiskeindvolde").

The frontispiece (Fig. 3) of the book "Museum Wormianum" from 1655 is showing the objects on view at the museum. The gutskin coat and the birdskin coat are hanging in the background just to the right of the window, while the figure on the back wall is carrying the sealskin coat. These old men's coats are all sewn in the typical pattern as descibed.

The museum of Ole Worm also contained other Greenlandic objects, a kayak hanging from the roof, walrus- and narwhal tusks near the window and paddles, bows and hunting weapons hanging on the back wall. The small shoes standing under the window could be a pair of the Greenlandic shoes, mentioned in the 'Kunstkammer'.

The 'Kunstkammer'

When Ole Worm died in 1654 the objects of the museum were handed over to the Royal 'Kunstkammer' of King Frederik III, located in the castle of Copenhagen. At this time, the interest in collecting exotic and curious objects was prevalent, and because of the large number of objects collected, it was decided to find a new and more spacious location for the 'Kunstkammer'.

In 1665 the new museum was founded. The entire collection was registered in 1673. This is actually the oldest catalogue at the Royal 'Kunstkammer'. Among the Greenlandic objects were: "*A picture of four Greenlanders, 3 Greenlandic shirts, 7 Greenlandic shoes and 2 Greenlandic hats*" ("Et Skilderie af fire Grønlændere, 3 grønlandske Skiorter, 7 grønlandske Skoe, 2 grønlandske Huer").

Finally, in 1675 the construction of the building for the new museum was completed and the objects moved to the new location. Today, the building contain the National Archives.

The picture mentioned (Fig. 5) was a large painting of four Greenlanders, a man, two women and a girl. In 1652 King Frederik III resumed the interrupted connection to Greenland and gave orders to the captains to enjoy and use "*whatever the land had been blessed with by God*".

They had this specific privilege for a period of 30 years. From 1652-1654 only three voyages took place. Captain David Dannel traded with the Inuit along the coast of West Greenland and acquired goods in demand such as hides from seal and caribou, ivory from whalrus and narwhal (unicorn) and several ethnographical objects. The latter were handed over to the 'Kunstkammer'.

During his last voyage Dannel captured four Greenlanders in the Fjord of Godthaab. On the way to Copenhagen, they sailed to Bergen, Norway where the picture was painted by a skilled portrait painter. Unfortunately, the painting was not signed, so the name of the artist remains unknown.

In fact, this painting is the oldest pictorial material of Greenlanders we have. It shows how people were dressed in the summer in West Greenland in 1654.

The man is wearing an inner coat, long sealskin trousers and boots of waterproof skin reaching the knees. He is holding his hunting tools, a bladder dart for seal hunting and bow and arrows for caribou hunting in his hands.

The women's coats are made of sealskin in the same cut as described above. They all wear short indoor trousers, probably due to the warm Danish summer as it would have been too hot to wear two layers of skin. Aparently, they wear the very wide boots without stockings, which seems to further indicate that it was too warm a climate for them to wear parts of their traditional clothing. The two women are beautifully tattooed in the face, a common tradition in use until Danish missionaries banned it during the 18th century.

In 1721 the missionary Hans Egede established the Hope Colony near the town presently called Nuuk, and the Danish colonization of Greenland began.

Along with the mission, the trade came to Greenland. It was not a profitable business in the beginning. The

Fig. 4: Grothschilling's painting of Pooq and Qiperoq, 1724. Original painting in National Museum of Denmark.

trade made by the trading company, *Det Bergen-Grønlandske Kompagni*, resulted in a large deficit. The missionary Hans Egede chose two native Greenlanders to do "sales promotion" for the Greenlandic articles. They set out on a journey to Copenhagen of their own free will to arouse interest in the mission and in trading with Greenland.

King Frederik IV welcomed Pooq and Qiperoq at the Royal castle of Frederiksborg in 1724. In the beginning of November the two Greenlanders, paddling in their kayaks became prominent figures of a magnificent colonial procession on the canals of Copenhagen attended by the King and most of the inhabitants of Copenhagen.

The trading company paid the famous painter B. Grothschilling to make an oil painting of Pooq and Qiperoq (Fig. 5) and gave it to the King. The painting was handed over to the Kunstkammer in 1725.

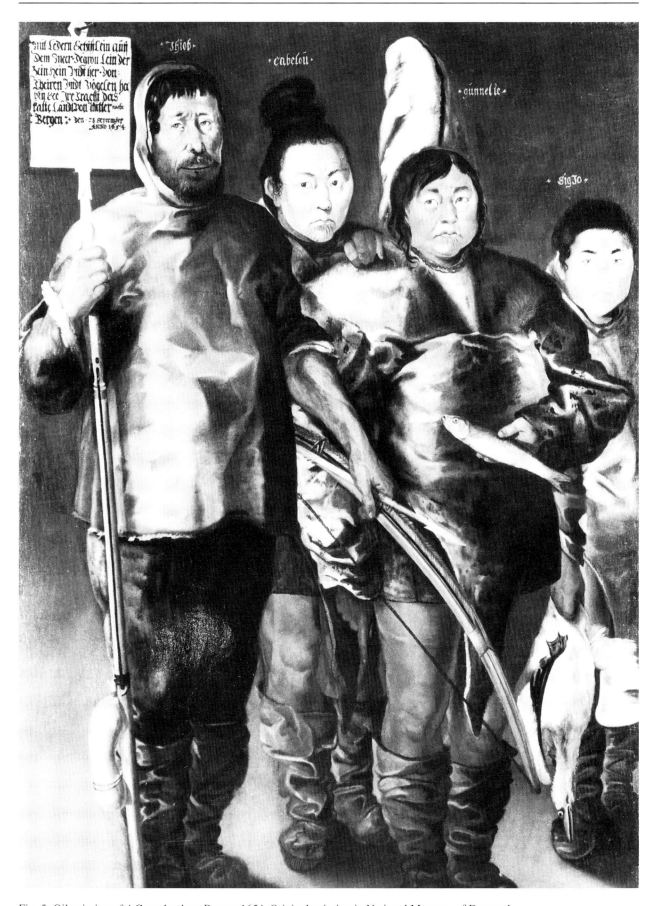

Fig. 5: Oil painting of 4 Greenlanders, Bergen 1654. Original painting in National Museum of Denmark.

At the painting Qiperoq is dressed in an inner coat with a light edging and an outer coat of depilated waterproof skin with front- and backflaps, sealskin trousers with white insertions in midfront of each leg and shoes of the same type as shown on the cover of Ole Worm's "Museum Wormianum". Pooq is dressed in an extremely beautiful and well-sewn dress consisting of a sealskin inner coat with long front- and backflaps and a waterproof kayak coat with insertions in white skin along all seams. He wears half-length trousers made of caribou skins decorated with skin embroidery in white and black, stockings, boots in waterproof skin with ankle bands with elegant buckles made of ivory. The boots are finished with edging at the top and the sole was nicely united at heel and toe.

Unfortunately, there are no women in the painting showing women's garments, but luckily, we know their garments from drawings and the description in Hans Egede's book, "Det gamle Grønlands nye Perlustration" (The new description of the old Greenland), published in 1741. He describes the dresses as follows: *"They have coats made of two layers of skin. The inner layer was made of caribou of which the fur was turned inside-out so that the hairy side of the skin was next to the body. The outer coat was also made of thin haired beautifully colored caribou skin. If caribou skin was not available, they would use sealskin, edged and decorated with white skin stripes between the seams. This looks very beautiful. The only difference between men and women's garments, is that the women's coats have wider and higher shoulders, and big, tall hoods"*

("De have dobbelte Peltze, en inden til nest Legemet af Rindsdyrs Skind, som Haarene vende ind paa, og en anden uden over, som ogsaa er af tynd Haared og smuk coleured Rinds-Skind, eller i dets mangel af Sælhunde-Skind, bebremmet og borderet med hvidt imellem Sømmene, som lader smukt. Qvindernes Klædedragt differerer fra Mændenes allene derudi, at de ere viide og høye paa Skuldrene, med store og høye Hetter").

Consequently, the cut described here is the same as was described earlier and as the coats of the captured women at the painting from 1654.

When the Nordic War ended (1700-1720), the number and variety of objects handed over to the 'Kunstkammer' grew. A considerable number of rarieties were given to the Kunstkammer from a collection at the castle of Gottorp. Among them a pair of Greenlandic boots and an old coat of sealskin. Therefore, the scientist decided to rearrange and build up the collection of archeological and ethnographical objects, natural products and curiosities in a more systematic way. The manager at the 'Kunstkammer' J. C. Spengler began to compile a scientific catalogue. At the same time, a scientific committee was set up to classify, number and describe all objects, and to separate those no longer suitable for the King's Royal 'Kunstkammer'.

When the members of the commitee carried out this work, they found the rooms of the 'Kunstkammer' to bee completely unsuitable to contain the collection. The roof was leaking, the windows were not tight and plaster and dirt sprinkled through the boards of the roof.

In order to save the collection, the paintings were placed elsewhere in Christiansborg. The considerable natural historic collection was scattered and placed in several scientific institutions. The prehistoric and ethnographic objects were gathered and placed as 'Kunstmuseet' in a building in Dronningens Tværgade. Those of the objects that were considered unsuitable to form part of the exhibition at the 'Kunstkammer' were sold at an auction August 31, 1824. Private collectors and institutions could buy exactly what they wanted from the objects put up for sale for instance: duplicates, shells, ivory from elephants and narwhales, antiquities, ethnographical objects, art, and some damaged objects. Among these objects were three Greenlandic coats, the shoes and the boots.

Christian Jürgensen Thomsen

In 1816 the young collector Christian Jürgensen Thomsen was appointed head of the Royal Museum of Nordic Antiquities. He worked very systematically and within a short time, he had registered all the objects at the museum. Furthermore, he arranged the exhibition in the three-periodic system: Stone, Bronze, and Iron Age, which is still being used today.

In 1839 Thomsen also became the curator at the 'Kunstmuseum', where Spengler worked as an assistant. The systematic work that Thomsen carried out also included the ethnographical material, so he and Spengler began to make a separate section for these objects.

As a result of the auction in 1824 there was apparently not a single Greenlandic costume left at the museum. In the beginning of 1839 Thomsen asked for permission to have objects sent from Greenland. In the spring of 1839, he sent a list of the objects he wanted to the Inspectors for Southern and Northern Greenland and to the Colonial Managers.

Later that same year, he and the geologist Pingel made a list describing the Greenlandic collection at the 'Kunstmuseum', and on this list were new objects, such as: *"Two complete women's dresses, one dress from the East Greenlanders, one Kapitek (kayak coat) and one whalehunting suit"* ("2 complette Fruentimmerdragter, 1 Østlænding Dragt, 1 Kapitek (halvpels) samt 1 Springpels") (Fig. 6).

All of the dresses were sent to curator Thomsen by Assistent Engholm in Holsteinsborg on the central west coast of Greenland.

Both inspectors and the colonial managers apparently started to collect objects for the museum in Copenhagen eagerly. The following year the collection already included several new objects, for instance: *"A woman's coat, a pair of white women's boots, a pair of waterproof*

boots with stockings and a pair of men's boots" ("En Fru-
entimmerpels, et par hvide fruentimmerstøvler, et par
vandskindsstøvler med strømper og et par mand-
folkestøvler"). These dresses came from manager Kielsen
in Julianehåb on the southern West Coast of Greenland.

In 1841 the number of objects sent was increased:
Funch, a missionary in Uummannaq, forwarded *"A
Greenlandic woman's dress for daily use*" ("En grøn-
landsk daglig Konedragt"), and from Holbøll, the Inspec-
tor in South Greenland, Thomsen received seven dresses.
In the letter enclosed Holbøll mentioned:

*"According to Mr. Thomsen's wishes I have acquired
some dresses. I have no doubt that you will also admire
the beauty of the skins and the sewing. However, I am
afraid that you might find that the prize is too high. ...
This is a complete set of dresses as they are used on land,
the dresses used at sea are associated with the kayak and
will be forwarded next year ...*" ("... Ifølge Hr
Justitsraadens Ønske har jeg anskaffet nogle Dragter, som
jeg hvad Skindenes Skiønhed og Syeningen angaar ikke
tvivler om vil finde Bifald, men derimod frygter jeg
meget for at Prisen muligen kan findes for høi. ... Dette
er nu en fuldkommen Svitte af Dragter saaledes som de
bruges paa Landjorden; Søedragten henhøre til Kajakken
og vil blive sendt med denne næste Aar ...").

In 1841 Thomsen opened his ethnographical museum
to the public with all the latest acquisitions and it, thus,
became the first public museum of its kind in the whole
world.

Caused by Thomsen's eagerness to collect itims, the
space at the Kunstmuseum soon became scarce. Therefore, that same year he made inquiries to have several
rooms at 'Prinsens Palais' at his disposal for The
'Kunstmuseum'. In 1842 a royal resolution was passed
stating that the 'Kunstmuseum' should be moved one
more time.

The number of Greenlandic objects grew steadily,
and in 1844 the Inspector of Northern Greenland, major
Fasting succeeded in getting hold of two men's and two
women's dresses from Aito near Holsteinsborg/Sisimiut
for the museum.

In 1845 Thomsen made a catalogue of the collection.
As one would expect, the items in the exhibition rooms
are thoroughly described.

Following the description of room no. XIII containing the Greenlandic objects, Thomsen expressed his gratitude to captain Holbøll, major Fasting, merchant Møller
and the physicians Rudolph and Lützen for the efforts
they had made to procure the Greenlandic objects for the
museum, mentioning the kayaks and the dresses, in particular.

It had been quite difficult for the colonial managers
to get hold of the dresses for the Ethnographical Museum.
In a letter of 16th of September 1841, the Inspector
of Northern Greenland, major Fasting wrote:

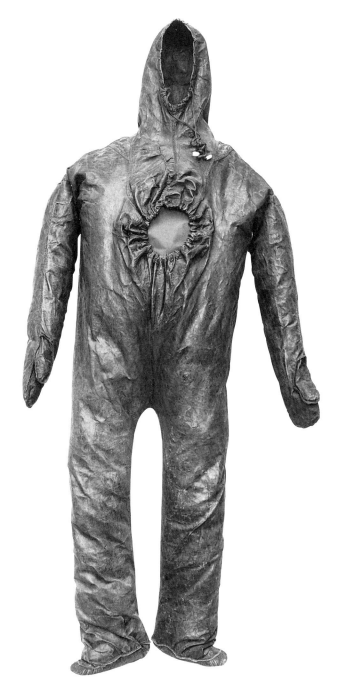

Fig. 6: Whale hunting suit from 1839. Original in National
Museum of Denmark.

"... You are disappointed that you have no daily garments. However, this is not so strange as the Greenlanders hardly have any themselves. It is a rare sight to see any Greenlander who has any clothing but what he is wearing. However, some of them have now started to smarten themselves up on Sundays and for solemn occasions. Besides the fur coat, they now use another type of jacket, - a custom they have learned from the Europeans. This jacket is called an anorak and is made of either linen or wool. These anoraks are easy to get, and the women often posses more than one. One of them will be the woman's favorite and be used for finery" ("... De klager over, at De ingen daglige dragter har; men det er ikke for underligt eftersom Grønlænderne ikke selv have sådanne. Det er sjældent, de har flere klæder end dem der hænge på kroppen; dog begynde enkelte nu at pynte sig om søndagen og ved højtidelige lejligheder. Derfor bruge de også nu en anden dragt foruden pelsen, hvilket europæerne have lært dem. Den hedder anorak, og består i et overtræk af linned ell. uldent tøj over underpelsen. Disse er lette at erholde. Derfor finder man også stunddom, at Fruentimmerne have flere af disse overtræk, hvormed de skifte, og hvoraf gerne Een anses for den smukkeste og bruges til stads").

At this time it was colonial policy to increase the prices for Greenlandic products and lower the price level for all European goods in the stores in order to raise the standard of living and simultaneously increase production. As a result of this procedure, a devasting situation occurred.

The Greenlanders sold everything necessary to maintain life, including skins for their dresses. This resulted in an enormous social distress. In a letter to Thomsen doctor Rudolph from Jakobshavn/Ilulissat described, among other things, a long and harsh winter in 1844 *"... it would not have been so terrible, if the Greenlanders had had clothing and blankets ... women, children and old people have been almost naked during this winter ..."* ("... som langt fra havde været så frygtelig, hvis Grønlænderne ikke saa aldeles havde været blottede for Klæder, baade Gang- og Brixeklæde ... Fruentimmer, Børn og gamle Folk har i Vinter saa godt som været nøgne ...").

The following years only a very few dresses were sent to the museum, and during the following 50 years, from 1850 to 1900, only eight women's and two men's dresses were registered.

The remaining old skin dresses at the Department of Ethnography

Unfortunately, the oldest skin clothings dating from before the colonization are no longer in the possession of the Department of Ethnography. As mentioned earlier, they were sold at an auction!

Several dresses from the 19th century were either destroyed due to the humid Danish climate and inadequate storing conditions or were infested with vermin.

Furthermore, several dresses were either exchanged with ethnographical and archeological museum objects from other museums abroad or repatriated to the National Museum of Greenland.

The only skin clothing from the 18th and 19th century remaining at the Department of Ethnography are three women's dresses, one man's dress, the whalehunting suit, kayak coats and some separate articles of clothing.

Changes in Greenlandic clothing after 1900

In the last part of the 19th century, the European cloth became very popular and was used instead of skin. The use of cloth formed a new tradition and particularly, in the case of the woman's dress, the modification was conspicuous.

The traditional cut of the coat with deep cut armholes, huge shoulders and high-cut at the hips, was very functional. It was an ideal clothing when the Greenlandic women carried out their daily tasks, such as standing in a stooping position and making horizontal movements while cutting and preparing the seal. The child carrying coat made a constant personal contact between mother and child possible, no matter what the woman's task was during the day.

This functional and characteristic design of the woman's coat made her look very beautiful and appear very feminine, accentuating the sex of the person wearing the coat. By the end of the 19th century the child carrying coat disappeared and the traditional woman's outer coat was replaced by the anorak made of cotton or silk. The cut of the woman's anorak was copied from the man's traditional outer coat.

The men's hunting garments also served a functional purpose and were extremely well adapted to the climatic conditions. Unfortunately, this type of traditional Inuit clothing had to give way to European cotton and woolen cloth too. However, the cut and material of the traditional skin clothing have never been surpassed by any modern type with regard to insulation capacity and utility.

Anne Bahnson, Assistant Curator, Department of Ethnography, National Museum of Denmark.

References

Bahnson, Anne [1996]: **Skinclothing in Greenland.** pp:60-88 in "Braving the cold, continuity an change in Arctic clothing", editors: C. Buis & J. Oosten, 213 p. (Leiden: Centre of Non-Western Studies).

Bahnson, Anne & Birthe Haagen [1994]: **Vestgrønlandske dragter.** 28 p. (Copenhagen: National Museum of Denmark).

Birket-Smith, Kaj [1924]: **Ethnography of the Egedesminde District.** *Meddelelser om Grønland,* 66:1-484 (Copenhagen: C. A. Reitzels Forlag).

Bruun de Neergaard, Helga [1962]: **Avigtat. Grønlandske skindmønstre.** 28 p (Copenhagen: Høst & Søns Forlag).

Dam-Mikkelsen, Bente & Torben Lundbæk (editors) [1980]: **Etnografiske genstande i Det kongelige danske Kunstkammer 1650-1800. Ethnographic Objects in The Royal Danish Kunstkammer 1650-1800.** *Nationalmuseets skrifter, Etnografisk række,* 17:1-260 (Copenhagen: National Museum of Denmark).

Egede, Hans [1741]: **Det gamle Grønlands Nye Perlustration.** 131 p. (Copenhagen: Johan Christoph Groth).

Hatt, Gudmund [1914]: **Arktiske Skinddragter i Eurasien og Amerika.** 255 p. (Copenhagen: J. H. Schultz Forlagsboghandel).

Liisberg, H. C. Bering [1897]: **Kunstkammeret. Dets stiftelse og ældste historie.** 192 p. (Copenhagen: Det Nordiske Forlag).

Rasmussen, Holger [1979]: **Dansk museums historie. De kulturhistoriske museer.** 226 p. (Copenhagen: Dansk kulturhistorisk museumsforening).

Unpublished letters from archives in The Department of Ethnograpy, National Museum of Denmark.

Arctic Prelude 1948:
A Summer Full of Experience in North East Greenland

Hans-Georg Bandi

When the fifty-year-old steamer *Godthaab* left Copen-hagen on June 6, 1948, two Arctic "greenhorns" were on board: Jørgen Meldgaard and myself (Fig. 1). The ship was loaded with provisions and materials for the "Dansk Peary Land Ekspedition" led by the inspiring Eigil Knuth. Kaj Birket-Smith, the grand old man of Eskimology, had made the necessary arrangements to give us two young archaeol-ogists - Jørgen was 21 years old whereas I would celebrate my 28th birthday during the trip - the exciting chance to spend the short summer on Clavering Ø (Clavering Island) in North East Greenland. We were supposed to complete Helge Larsen's important excavations at Dødemands-bugten. After a voyage of three weeks, including some days on Iceland, and a slowly crossing of the packice, we would stay for nearly six weeks on this island on 74°N and then return on board the *Godthaab* to Copenhagen, which took us one and a half week.

For both of us many aspects of this enterprise were new, interesting, and impressive, for me especially the great experience of the Danes in Arctic expeditions, their hospitality, life on a small ship and last but not least the wonderful wilderness of North East Greenland, rich in traces of prehistoric Eskimo populations. It was an excit-ing experience which definitively inspired our interest in Eskimo archaeology. For Jørgen and me it was the begin-ning of a life-time friendship.

For three weeks we were part of the 20 crew members on board the *Godthaab* which also carried a few passen-gers. The captain was a friendly, quiet man who offered me an akvavit each day for breakfast when he saw that the combination of the rolling ship and the herring salad was too much for my seasick stomach. Of great help to us was

Fig. 1: The *Godthaab* ready to leave Copenhagen June 6, 1948.

the first officer, Hemmike, who always had time to answer questions or discuss problems. All the sailors obviously liked the adventure of a Greenland expedition under rather primitive conditions. They were hard working and trained to set sail when the wind was strong enough to accelerate the slow steamer. There was plenty of nutritious food, but I had to accustom myself to Danish dishes. Given the size of the *Godthaab* the space for sleeping was rather narrow, the sanitary installations had to be called modest! The other passengers were four young British geologists and

Fig. 2 (above): Eigil Knuth in Iceland.

Fig. 3 (right): The *Godthaab* blocked by the packice.

glaciologists, three Danish students, as well as some Danes headed for trapping in North East Greenland.

After having left the Øresund the ship followed the Swedish coast because there was still a certain danger of mines in the Kattegat. Through the Skagerak we reached the North Sea, travelled between the Orkney and Shetland Islands and continued south of the Faeroe Islands in the direction of Iceland. A dense fog and the real danger of collision with other vessels forced the captain to be personally on the bridge all the time.

We reached Reykjavik on July 7, a Saturday evening - not the best time to enter a foreign city! The port authorities were not pleased to let the *Godthaab* dock because we had on board a considerable quantity of gasoline for the Catalinas of the "Peary Land Ekspedition", barrels of which were piled up near the caboose.

The stay in Reykjavik was needed to replenish the provisions on board the *Godthaab*. This gave us the opportunity to see some parts of Iceland, sometimes in the company of Eigil Knuth (Fig. 2) and other members of his Peary Land crew who had joined us with two PBY-5A Catalinas. When we left Reykjavik on Tuesday, July 13, we had additional passengers on board: 31 dogs belonging to three teams originating from West Greenland and supervised by the young Greenlandic hunter Karl Filemonsen, the first representative of the Eskimos I ever met.

The continuation of the journey toward North East Greenland was sometimes beautiful and exciting, sometimes slow and difficult. In the beginning we followed the West Coast of Iceland with its fjords and cliffs of lava and basalt, with thousands of sea birds and the reminders of Vikings who travelled here one thousand years ago.

Later we saw whales and the first icefloes appeared. Soon the *Godthaab* started to cross the packice. The nights became shorter and clear. Sometimes the ship stopped and we could go down on the ice (Fig. 3). Filemonsen used his kayak to hunt a seal (Fig. 4). We even met a polar bear. Eventually the silhouette of the Greenlandic coast could be seen for short moments. The navigators tried to locate Clavering Ø. Early in the morning of July 21 the *Godthaab* reached the island but the condition of the ice made it impossible to land at Dødemandsbugten. Therefore a small motor boat brought Jørgen and me with our equipment on shore at Kap Mary, near the southwest corner of Clavering Ø (Fig. 5). Unexperienced as I was, I had too much stuff in too big boxes. There we stood and waved good-bye to the crew returning to the *Godthaab*. It had been agreed that we would get transportation to Dødemandsbugten as soon as possible - whatever this meant! The *Godthaab* was supposed to go to Zackenberg on Young Sound, 37 km from Kap Mary as the crow flies. From there the material of the Peary Land expedition would be flown to the North by the Catalinas.

Kap Mary is a stony place where the small beach gives way to the steep slope of the Magnetikerbjærg, the summit of which reaches 563 m. It consists of reddish basalt. Jørgen had some information about prehistoric Eskimo settlements in this area and we actually found some house ruins, tent rings and other traces, partially already searched. We set up camp near the beach and while waiting to be transferred to Dødemandsbugten started to explore Kap Mary (Fig. 6). We also undertook small diggings. Our little radio transmitter was not strong enough to reach the *Godthaab* at Zackenberg. We saw some ships passing by and aircrafts flying over us. As we did not know when we would get transportation to Døde-mandsbugten, we had to be near the camp to get ready in a short time. The situation became even worse when on the sixth day of our "robinsonade" a mighty thunderstorm with heavy rain forced us to stay almost permanently in the tent (Fig. 7). Under these rather unpleasant auspices our activity was very much reduced.

But at least this gave us the opportunity to get to know each other better. Jørgen told me about his studies and his relations with the National Museum of Denmark in Copenhagen where Birket-Smith evidently had realized his capabilities. We spoke about our families, his parents and sister Else (Lissen, so important for his future life, was not yet in the picture!), my wife Regula and our two-year old son Till. I told him about my studies at the University of Fribourg during World War II when Switzerland was surrounded by Nazi-Germany and fascist Italy. The preparation of my Ph.D. defense had been interrupted by long periods of military service.

Jørgen was sometimes a little absent-minded, forgetting to eat when he read an interesting scientific report, but he had an exceptional gift for discovering archaeological traces in the field. I may have seemed meticulous to him, as I believed in military order in the camp and in an accurate timetable for our daily work. Nevertheless our mutual trust increased during those long days on Kap Mary. Also, we managed to walk to Kap Arnakke, 3 km to the east of Kap Mary with several winterhouse ruins, one of which we could investigate.

Eventually, after twelve days of waiting, a motorboat arrived belonging to the Lauge Koch geological expedition, which had agreed to give us a lift to Dødemands-bugten, 22 km further west on the south coast of Clave-ring Ø. On board were three Danes, one of them a son of Lauge Koch, and two Swedish geologists. In a hurry our material had to be placed in an attached jollyboat. After starting we took a zigzag course due to many icefloes in the rather calm sea. Half-way a breakdown of the engine

forced us to stay overnight in a primitive hunting lodge. The next day only two of the small crew continued with us to Dødemandsbugten. And then it happened: just before landing at Dødemandsbugten the Danish steersman Sybelius did not pay attention, the jollyboat rammed an icefloe, turned lop-side and most of our equipment slid down into the water, only a few things remaining in the flooded boat (Fig. 8, Fig. 9, Fig. 10).

At first we thought that our activity at Dødemands-bugten had come to an end before we could start it. But then we saw that our boxes and bags were floating, so that it was possible to recover most of them. On shore we came to realize that everything was wet and some things could not be used any more. For instance our little radio did not improve by its bath in salt water! In a case of emergency there would have been no chance to call for help. Our transportation crew left us soon afterwards and joined Lauge Koch's expedition ship *Gustav Holm* on its way to the rebuilt research station at Eskimonæs, 13 km west of Dødemandsbugten.

Anyway, we had finally reached our destination - Dødemandsbugten (Dead Man's Bay). A mournful and sinister name, yet a very apt one, as Helge Larsen wrote in 1934: "*For there, on the south coast of Clavering Island, lies the largest ruined settlement hitherto found in Greenland, its numerous house ruins, tent-rings and graves bearing witness to the death and extinction of a small tribe that once made a struggle for existence there.*" (Fig. 11).

Actually, Clavering Ø is the only place where natives have ever been seen by Europeans: Almost exactly 125 years ago, on August 23, 1823, Captain Douglas Charles Clavering met twelve Eskimos on the island that was later named after him. After some days of coexistence they left, probably scared by firearms. When the second German North Pole Expedition visited North East Greenland in 1869-1870 the Eskimos had completely disappeared from this area. It is not known whether the last tribes be-

Fig. 4: Karl Filemonsen using the break when the ship was stopped by ice to hunt a seal.

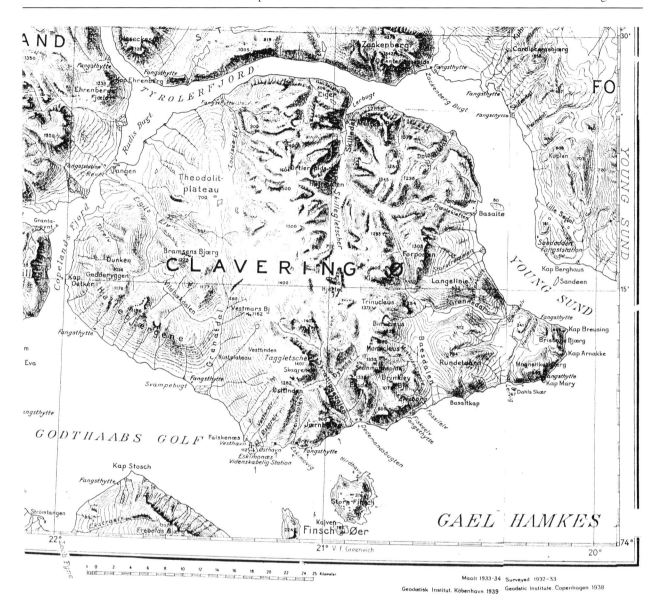

Fig. 5: Map of Clavering Island.

Fig. 6: Kap Mary on the south east corner of Clavering Island.

Fig. 7: Our camp at Kap Mary - Swiss invasion?

Fig. 8-10: Before, during, and after the 'shipwreck' off Dødemandsbugten.

Fig. 11: Dødemandsbugten on Clavering Island.

Fig. 14: Dødemandsbugten by night. Muskoxen are grazing between the house ruins.

Fig. 12: Our 'headquarter' at Dødemandsbugten.

Fig. 13: The beginning of a lifetime friendship. Bandi (left) & Meldgaard (right).

Fig. 15 & Fig. 16: A house ruin before and after excavation, seen from the front and from the back.

came extinct through starvation or disease, or whether they emigrated to the north coast or to the south for better hunting.

During World War II the presence of American soldiers left more recent traces in the vicinity of the Eskimo house ruins. The Germans had sent out a small group of meteorologists to North East Greenland to transmit regular weather reports about the situation in the North-Atlantic area. American bombers operating from Iceland and a ground crew were ordered to dislodge them. The Americans were supported by some Danish, Norwegian and Greenlandic trappers who had been hired by the U. S. Army to form a regular military patrol along the east coast of Greenland after the occupation of Denmark by Nazi-Germany. There are both American and German reports on these events (Balchen B. et al. 1945; Weiss G. 1949). Both show that on Clavering Ø there was quite a bit of military activity. Sledge teams must have passed near Kap Mary and Dødemandsbugten on their way to the well equipped Danish hunting and research station of Eskimonæs. This place was partially destroyed in 1943 by the Germans and later also bombed by American Flying Fortresses.

Jørgen and I were pleased to find a rather well-preserved wooden barrack at Dødemandsbugten (Fig. 12). It had probably been constructed by American troops. Since the end of the war it had evidently been used by trappers. It was very useful to us, especially as all our equipment was wet upon our arrival (Fig. 13). All over the place there was a lot of rubbish but also some useful goods such as canned food and barrels of gasoline.

The topographical situation at Dødemandsbugten is quite different from Kap Mary. The beach is about 2 km wide and represents the delta of a small river running down Skrælingedalen. It is a lovely setting which attracted quite a number of prehistoric Eskimo tribes to settle there. It must have been very well suited to their hunting.

From Helge Larsen's extensive report (1934) we know that he distinguished three different cultural stages: An earlier phase and two stages of the so-called mixed

culture of North East Greenland. Today it seems that the early phase corresponds to a Late Dorset II (Independence II?) mixed with early Thule Culture, all coming from the north; the mixed culture of which Larsen had found two stages at Dødemandsbugten is believed to be a mixture of this early phase with late Thule elements coming from the south. North East Greenland was evidently a melting pot which produced and domiciled several mixed cultures between the 14th century A.D. and the 17th-18th century A.D.

In his report Helge Larsen mentions 43 house ruins, of which he excavated 23, and furthermore a number of burials. Some ruins had been searched before his arrival, whereas others were probably used later by GIs as shelters for machine guns. But there were still six ruins which seemed untouched and some others only partially dug out.

We knew that we might stay about four weeks before the *Godthaab* could pick us up for the trip back to Denmark. Eventually we remained only a couple of days more than three weeks at Dødemandsbugten. Fortunately the weather was mostly good. So we could manage to finish the investigation at this interesting site, excavating most of the remaining houses and some burials. We even had time to make excursions to the east and west, investigating other parts of Dødemandsbugten.

The nights became darker, the moon reappeared and reached a giant size which was almost scaring. The temperature went down from +10°C to nearly zero. But the loneliness in the Arctic wilderness was very exciting. Our most interesting visitors were musk oxen which sometimes grazed between the house ruins (Fig. 14).

One day on an excursion we got the impression that an old male, probably eliminated by its herd, was getting ready to attack us. We shot him - but this is another story of which we are reminded in our homes by the skull at Jægerspris and the skin at Berne! Other events included the visit of the *Gustav Holm* on August 8, on board which we had the opportunity to personally meet the famous explorer Dr. Lauge Koch; the sudden arrival of

the *Godthaab* a week later, which came to Dødemandsbugten to fetch barrels of aviation gasoline and brought
us some provisions and, most importantly, mail from
home; or the short visit of some Norwegian hunters who
during the coming winter intended to stay in the barrack
we used during the short summer. But mostly, we were
quite isolated and dependent on each other. This deepened
our friendship.

We certainly did our best to bring as much information and as many finds as possible back to Europe (Fig.
15, Fig. 18). One of the house complexes we excavated
belonged to the oldest phase of the Eskimo presence at
Dødemandsbugten. Most of the other house ruins could
be dated by the aid of implements - carbon dating was not
yet feasible - to the end of a first phase of the North East
Greenland mixed culture. The few burials we investigated
were not of great interest (Fig. 17). But when we published
the results of our investigations at Dødemandsbugten,
including the diggings at Kap Mary and at Kap Arnakke, it
represented a useful supplement to Helge Larsen's earlier
report (Bandi & Meldgaard 1952).

Sunday, August 29, began as any other day except
that breakfast was rather late. During the day, we worked
in house ruins which had already been partially destroyed.

Fig. 19: One of us was proud of his beard...

At 7 p.m. we stopped and went to the barrack to prepare supper. Suddenly we saw the *Godthaab* approaching
the shore. Shortly afterwards Hemmike, the first officer
of the *Godthaab*, arrived with some others in a small
boat. Now we had to hurry to get our equipment ready
for loading. Only half an hour later we left Dødemandsbugten knowing that we would probably never reach this
place again. As soon as everything had been hauled on
board, the good old *Godthaab*, which has unfortunately
sunk since, it started the voyage back to Denmark.

Initially the ship sought its way through icefloes
which knocked loudly on the bow where Jørgen and I had
our bunks this time. The weather was changeable with
fog, sunshine and rain. Sometimes fair wind blew in the
sails and accelerated the ship. But huge waves also made
some of the passengers sea-sick. At night the ship made
its way through phosphorescent water. After seven days
we began to meet fishing vessels, soon also larger ships.
Two days later we saw the Norwegian coast far off. We
reached the Skagerak, entered the Kattegat and on September 9 at half past three p.m. we anchored in Copenhagen (Fig. 19, Fig. 20). Our exciting summer in North
East Greenland had come to an end, but our shared interest in Eskimo archaeology as well as our personal
friendship had been consolidated for life (Fig. 21). Jørgen
became an outstanding Eskimo archaeologist, investigating many places in the Arctic from Greenland to Alaska.
I had some opportunities to work in Alaska, especially on
St. Lawrence Island.

Fig. 20: ...and the other wants to look nice for the arrival at
Copenhagen: Jørgen Meldgaard's hairdresser is the late medical doctor J. J. Jensen.

Hans-Georg Bandi, Professor Emeritus, University of Bern,
Switzerland.

Abbreviation

PBY-5A Catalinas = long range recognition and bombing

References

Balchen B., C. Ford & O. La Forge O. [1945]: **War below zero. The battle for Greenland.** 125 p. (London: George Allen & Unwin Ltd).

Bandi, Hans-Georg [1969]: **Eskimo Prehistory.** 226 p. (College: University of Alaska Press).

Bandi, Hans-Georg & Jørgen Meldgaard [1952]: **Archae-ological Investigations on Clavering Ø, North East Greenland.** *Meddelelser om Grønland*, 126(4):1-84 (Co-penhagen: C. A. Reitzels Forlag).

Knuth, Eigil [1948]: **Haandbog Dansk Peary Land Ekspedition 1948-49-50.** 217 p. (Copenhagen: Dyra Bogtryk).

Larsen, Helge [1934]: **Dødemandsbugten, An Eskimo Settlement on Clavering Island.** *Meddelelser om Grønland*, 102(1):1-185 (Copenhagen: C. A. Reitzels Forlag).

Weiss, G. [1949]: **Das Arktische Jahr.** 168 p. (Braunschweig: Georg Westermann Verlag).

Fig. 17 (above) & Fig. 18 (below): A dead man from Døde-mandsbugten ... and a wooden doll (9.6 cm high) he might have carved.

Fig. 21: 48 years later on m.s. *Porsild* in the Disko Bugt area, West Greenland, Bandi (left) & Meldgaard (right).

Two Dogs and a Dragon

Joel Berglund

Zoomorphic representations have been one of mankind's preferred topics for the visual representations of situations or phenomenon and in rituals, magic, decoration, or simple creative zest. The other topic, anthropomorphic representations, will not be discussed here. Zoomorphic representations have been discovered in the form of plastic figures, carved or painted representations on rock walls or as elements in an ornamental whole, spanning the period from Paleolithic times until present day.

Ever since humans began to walk upright, animals and humans have been inseparable, but the relationship has always been on the humans' terms; animals could easily survive without humans, but not the other way around.

In hunter-gatherer societies, animals comprised the existential platform and relations between prey and hunter often turned into kinship relations, through which both parties could transform themselves into the shape of the other (Sutherland 1996:3). Later, when humans succeeded in controlling the food supply through agriculture, the role of animals decreased. However, certain species of animals entered into a closer relationship with humans through domestication.

Parallel to the fauna which existed in the known physical surroundings was another fauna, which one did not see often, but knew to be real from the myths. It existed in a realm inhabited by odd creatures, combinations of animals and humans and, interesting in this context, dragons. One characteristic of these creatures was their ability to enter into the human world without any problems and to intervene in human lives. It was furthermore significant that what one saw often was the expression of something else.

In Norse cultures the representations of animals peak during the period from the Germanic Iron Age to the Viking Age (Wilson 1995:33ff). However, they certainly do not disappear from the repetoir after that (Karlsson et al. 1995:7-26, 117-228; Augustsson et al. 1996:157-197). What happens is a change in the way animals are interpreted as agents of a deeper significance. The reason for this lies with the new world view which accompanies the transition from paganism to Christianity. As the world view changes, old models of interpretation are rejected and markers of value change from positive to negative; those which could not be changed were adopted and reinterpreted. At the same time, new styles and artistic ideals reach the North, that is the Romanesque style in the 11th century and the Gothic style in the mid 13th century (Lindgren et al. 1993:13, 52).

Zoomorphic Representations from "The Farm Beneath The Sand"

Zoomorphic presentations are not among the most frequently found objects in Norse excavations on Greenland. The best known examples are an etching of a dragon's head on a wooden chest board from Herojolfsnæs (Nørlund 1924:47), and a beautiful plastic work from Sandnæs (Roussell 1936:28) interpreted as being either an armrest for a chair or a tiller. Since then, three new examples have appeared. Between 1991 and 1996, Greenland's National Museum & Archives conducted an excavation of a Norse farm covered by sand, thus referred to as *The Farm Beneath The Sand*. It is situated in Nuup Kommunea on a plateau behind the innermost arm of the Ameralik Fiord, a very short distance from the ice cap (Anne-berg & Berglund 1993:7ff). In 1994, one zoomor-

Fig. 1: An animal figure on a wooden box.

the outline for a tail. The figure is 8 cm long, the head is 2.4 cm tall and 4 cm long. The snout, the forehead and the neck are clearly visible, whereas the chest and a front leg are merely outlined. There is no indication of eyes, mouth or ears on the head.

The cuts are robust and the intention is clear; the animals is intended to have this particular head shape, a strong neck and deep chest. The figure may have been carved while the box/chest was still in use because the figure is in an original position on the end piece of the box. In that case, its value would drop considerably since the carving would not have been made as a decoration, but as a pastime. However, surface burns inflicted after the ethcing was made suggest that the frame was taken apart and used to place hot items on. Several other delicate etchings made prior to the figure can be seen on the piece; this may also be the case with the curve above the head.

NKA 1950x3027

Fragment of a supply carved animal figure representing a creature with forepaws under its head (Fig. 2). Due to the missing hind section of the body and a visible fracture

Fig. 2: Carved animal figure.

phic re presentation was uncovered and in 1996, two additional examples appeared. Each of the three representations originates from a different place in the excavated settlement and each one is unique.

NKA 1950x1668

Animal figure (Fig. 1) partly carved, partly etched onto the end piece of a small box or chest. The side piece consists of a mortised frame around four sticks. The frame measures 22.2 cm x 15.7 cm. The animal figure is etched across three of the sticks and appears to be incomplete, showing only a rough outline consisting of head, neck and part of an upper body. A curve above the head may be

behind the upper portion of the front legs, the outline of the entire piece is unknown. The head has triangular eyes, one of which contains a pupil. The mouth is indicated on both sides by an open triangle, but no teeth are visible. Ears are placed where the back of the head meets the neck and back. The forehead, snout and lower jaw with drawn lips are clearly indicated. The legs show strong thigh muscles, but thin legs down to the toes. From the snout to the fracture the piece measures 9.5 cm, the head 2.7 cm, the thigh 1.5 cm, the front leg 3 cm, and the piece has an average depth of 1.2 cm. The shape is rounded, the carved parts are crudely cut with rather unclean V-shaped cuts and all surfaces of the piece have been polished.

Fig. 3 (on top) & Fig: 4 (below): decorated box cover with dragon head.

NKA 1950x3348

Delicately crafted, fully intact cover for a box 15 cm x 4 cm and 0.8 cm deep. On what must be considered the inner side is an unfinished representation of a dragon's head with its toothless mouth wide open and a rudiment of a chin as well as a neck, an ear and an eye (Fig. 3). Behind the neck is an elaborate inscription of knot runes covering the remaining surface of the cover. The rune inscription appears only as a preliminary dotted outline of the final carving and has been interpreted as the girl's name Biørk. The dragon's head is cut in a single, precise continuous line forming a V-shape. The front is beautifully decorated with three palmettoes and a cross braid (Fig. 4). As a whole, the piece was crafted with both skill and accuracy, revealing a broad knowledge of motifs common to Nordic cultures. It should be further noted, that none of the animals assume threatening positions.

The iconography and possible significance of the discoveries.

Humans live in what has been characterized as a socio-material world (Anderson 1979:35) and, among other things, what creates frames of reference and limitation are the physical points of reference of social phenomenon manifested in the physical world around us. For archeology, the socio-material world consists of those objects which have been unearthed. As the original meaning of an object cannot possibly disappear with age, the banal problem lies in retrieving the code. An object in itself is a concrete phenomenon, but as a 'sign' it has a referential purpose and is thus similar to a 'concept' in this respect. However, while the purpose of the concept can keep expanding, the purpose of the 'sign' is limited (Levi-Strauss 1987:30). Faced with the imagery of the past, we often find ourselves in an iconographical vacuum, unable to read the myriads of symbols and allegories which constitute texts within the text (Englund 1991:227).

The reason for this lies partly in the fact that the codes have been "forgotten" and that any interpretation of the past inevitably is rooted in the present (Hodder 1995: 151). When we are dealing with the iconography of the late Viking Age and the Middle Ages, however, the subject matter and the ways of expression are well known from various litarary sources and the history of Catholicism. The images vary from the most sublime art to hurried and sometimes awkward scribbles, but in both cases they are the expression of an intellectual action with an underlying meaning and an intention.

The first animal is a case of a hurried scribble, which may only have served to pass the time. It was never finished and possibly just tossed aside. Yet, the carving reflects the thoughts of that particular person. It seems to be a dog, but this is where the problem begins. Dog bones have been found at *The Farm Beneath The Sand*, but they point to a long-legged dog with a narrow snout (information from P. Gravlund, Zoological Museum). The carving, however, seems to suggest a stout dog with broad chest, strong shoulders, wide snout and a marked transition between the snout and the skull. These elements rather point to a Mastiff-type. However, this type has not previously been found in Greenland (McGovern 1992: 106; Degerbøl 1936:25ff) but is probably from Scandinavia (KHLNM 1982(7):64ff). The question is then, whether this type of dog actually existed, or whether the person who carved it had heard of such a dog or seen one when travelling outside of Greenland.

The next animal is a creature moving forward, its front legs pulled all the way up to its throat in the moment just before the next leap, its head streched forward, creating a straight line between the back and the head; the ears are flat pointing toward the rear, and the mouth is slightly open. Everything indicates that the animal is in full motion. It is difficult to determine what kind of animal it is, but presumably it is a dog, since it holds no significant similarities to known lions or dragons. It is no longer known what the animal was a part of, except that it served as an ornamental detail of a larger whole.

The last animal is very different from the two previous ones. We see the head and the neck of an animal with a wide open mouth forming the beginning of the girl's name Biørk written in the rare and very elaborate knot runes (Stoklund 1982:204). The upper line of the neck glides into the first letter so that there is no doubt that the animal and the name are tied together. Nor is there any doubt that the animal represents a dragon and apparently a very gentle dragon, very unlike the dragon from Herjolfsnæs which is baring its teeth (Nørlund 1924:47). In pre-Christian times, the dragon was a helper and a guardian of the ladies, but its role change with the advent of Christianity to become a symbol of evil and sin - at least in a Christian context, as for instance in the story of St. George and the dragon (KHLNM 1982(5): 268). In folkore, however, it retained its positive significance (Johansen 1996:88). It is, thus, obvious that the dragon and the girl are connected; the person who crafted the delicate cover wanted to pretect her symbolically. However, the small artwork was never finished and the girl's name never completed. What happened we can only guess, but a rejected marriage proposal is a likely guess.

The circumstances of the discoveries and their age

All these objects originate from the last developmental phase of the settlement and thus the last period in which the farm was in use. Object no. 1668 was found in the floor layer, which is dated to circa 1300 A.D. (year 1638), and the two other objects were found in the same layer, but in different parts of the settlement. The three zoomorphic representations were all discarded while the farm was still in use, and they ended up in the marsh under the cover of twigs and pieces of wood which onstituted the floor. None of these object show much resemblance to the dragon from Herjolfsnæs, which seems to date futher back, or the animal on the armrest of the chair from Sandnæs. Because of its lack of comparative elements, object no. 1668 escapes any attempt to categorize it stylistically, and may even be described as a timeless etching. The same cannot be said about object no. 3027 which, in its rather amputated appearance, indicates the Middle Ages. The position of the body parts and the animal's pose as well as the suggested movement point to a gothic style. Object no. 3348 is more inconclusive, but there is no doubt that it represents a dragon; the wide-open mouth gives it away. The plant ornamentation on the upper part of the cover may be interpreted as palmettoes showing features characteristic of the Roman lily motif, which may place it within the early Gothic phase, presumably around 1300 A.D.

However, one should be careful not to interpret these objects too narrowly in terms of style and chronology. We are dealing with rather rustic objects produced in the periphery of the Norse world and in an environment which would hardly have been influenced right away by changing fashions in design.

The physical location of the objects within the last phase of the farm settlement put a cap on the possible time of their production, and, in addition, the objects - except for no. 1668 - do not show traces of long-term use. Therefore, we can establish with a high degree of certainty that they were produced around the year 1300 A.D.

Behind the creation of an image or a figure lies a thought. The choice of creating an animals is obviously not random. The symbolic significance of the dragon as guardian of womankind is emphasized through incorporating the figure into the girl's name in such a way that the upper line turns into the first runic letter. Dogs had another meaning then which was hardly of a magical kind, but rather more terrestrial. They were close to their masters and were indispensable in a pastoral society for hunting and for herding sheep. There is good reason to believe that the dog was popular in the Norse farms and that it was therefore an obvious subject for artistic representations.

Joel Berglund, curator, Greenland National Museum, Nuuk

References

Andersen, Sten [1981]: **Positivism kontra hermeneutik.** 119 p. (Göteborg: Förlaget Korpen).

Arneborg, Jette & Joel Berglund [1993]: **Gården under sandet / naasorissaasup illua sioqqanik matusimasoq.** *Forskning i Grønland / tusaat*, 4:7-19 (Copenhagen: Danish Polar Center).

Augustsson, J. E, A-M. Blennow, J. von Bonsdorff, I. Estham, L. Karlsson, M. Nockert, A. Piltz, J. Svanberg, G. Tegnér, P. Tångeberg & M. Ullén [1996]: **Den Gotiska Konsten**. 543 p. (Lund: Signum).

Degerbøl, Magnus [1936]: **Animal Remains from the West Settlement in Greenland.** *Meddelelser om Grønland*, 88(3):1-55 (Copenhagen: C. A. Reitzels Forlag).

Englund, Peter [1995]: **Förflutenhetens landskap. Historiska essäer.** 281 p. (Stockholm: Atlantis).

Hodder, Ian [1995]: **Reading the Past.** 221 p. (Cambridge: Cambridge University Press).

Johansen, Peter [1996]: **The Transformative Dragon. The Construction of Social Identity and the Use of Metaphors during the Nordic Iron Age.** *Current Swedish Archaeology*, 4:83-102 (Stockholm: *).

Karlsson, L., M. Lindgren, M. Nockert, A. Piltz, J. Svanberg, P. Tåangeberg & M. Ullén [1995]: **Den Romanska Konsten.** 399 p. (Lund: signum).

KHLNM [1982]: **Kulturhistorisk Leksikon for Nordisk Middelalder.** 5:*-* & 7:*-* (Copenhagen: Rosenkilde & Bagger).

Lévi-Strauss, Claude [1987]: **Det vilda tänkandet.** 289 p. (Malmö: Moderna Klassiker). Orginal title: **Lan pensée sauvage**, Paris 1962.

Lindgren, M., L. Lyberg, B. Sandström & A. G. Wahlberg [1993]: **Svensk Konsthistoria.** 542 p. (Lund: Signum).

Nørlund, Poul [1924]: **Burried Norsemen at Herjolfsnes.** *Meddelelser om Grønland*, 67(1):1-270 (Copenhagen: C. A. Reitzels Forlag).

Roussell, Aage [1936]: **Sandnes and the Neighbouring Farms.** *Meddelelser om Grønland*, 88(2):1-219 (Copenhagen: C. A. Reitzels Forlag).

Stoklund, Marie [1982]: **Nordboruner.** *Tidsskriftet Grønland*, 30(5-7):197-206 (Copenhagen: The Greenlandic Society).

Sutherland, Patricia [1996]: **Lost Visions. Forgotten Dreams.** Exhibition katalogue, 24 p. (Hull: Canadian Museum of Civilization).

Vedbæk, Christian Leif [1992]: **Vatnahverfi. An Inland District of the Eastern Settlement in Greenland.** *Meddelelser om Grønland*, 17:1-132 (Copenhagen: C. A. Reitzels Forlag).

Wilson, David M. [1995]: **Vikingatidens Konst.** 238 p. (Lund: Signum).

Fig. A-C: Winter Island 1821-1822. Alaska State Museum, Anchorage. Artist unidentified. Engraved details appear in "The Private Journal of Captain G. F. Lyon" (1824).

19th Century Aivilik Iglulik Drawings

Edmund Carpenter

This is a fun essay. No novel theory underlies it. No massive documentation fills it. No grand conclusion caps it. It simply illustrates a handful of early Aivilik drawings from the many that lie forgotten in scattered archives. These are the sort of data Jørgen loves. I picture him coming upon them in a museum vault, opening their faded folders, examining each sketch, smiling from time to time, "Yes, yes," then, hours later, closing the last folder, "Well!"

Franz Boas asked George Comer, a Connecticut whaling master, to collect for the American Museum of Natural History. During seven wintering voyages to Hudson Bay, 1893-1912, Comer assembled over 2.000 ethnological specimens, compiled extensive records, made about 300 life-casts and 64 phono-recordings, and took many photographs. He was one of Boas' primary sources for "The Eskimo of Baffin Land and Hudson Bay", 1901[1].

Comer filled notebooks. In one, he spoke of a Netsilik: "*Old Sick Sick* ["Squrriel"] *told me* [1893] *that when he was a boy he went deer hunting with his father. They shot a deer and before they started to skin it, two very large men came to them and one of them put the deer on his back and then both went away.*

Sick Sick said they did not talk but were unusually large men. With a pencil he drew a rough sketch of the scene and then told me his legs shook till the two men were gone. His father offered no resistance.

I wondered at the time if these two men might not have been survivors of the Franklin Expedition as Sick Sick would then have been a boy about that time [1848]. *Sick Sick died at Lyon's Inlet about 1910.*"[2]

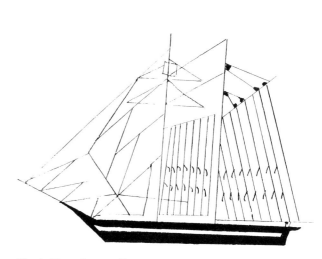

Fig. 1: The schooner *Era*

Comer appears not to have saved Siksik's drawing. But he saved others[3]. The artist who drew Fig. 1 remains unidentified, but the schooneer is unmistakably Comer's beloved *Era*. Note the attention to seam-lines in the sails. That same emphasis characterizes Aivilik drawings of garments and belongs to an ancient, widespread tradition where seams are not "thought away," as with us, but emphasized.

Fig. 2

"Jack" showed Comer how "Paddy" fell beneath his dog-traces (Fig. 2). Jack also sent him a note (Fig. 3), listing his pelts: 35 deer, 2 bear, 1 wolf, and estimating 8 days travel from camp to ship. Molihi [Maliki] requested matches, cartridges, needles and thread, file and cookies, with handshake as promise or reminder of friendship, and signed his name in alphabetic writing (Fig. 4). (The syllabic system, introduced by the Rev. E. J. Peck in 1894, occurs on later Aivilik drawings, for example those collected by K. Rasmussen in the 1920s).

Fig. 3   Fig. 4

Fig. 5:

In 1898, Comer asked Teseuke, one of his regular Aivilik whalers, to sketch Roes Welcome. Teseuke used the back of a 20"x30" chart of Bering Strait.

Fig. 5 served Comer as both map and notebook. Teseuke included islands, rivers, lakes, even a soapstone source; marked sled routes along the coast, as well as inland; represented musk ox herds as clusters of small dots; and drew minute figures of walrus hunters on the ice, shown here greatly magnified (Fig. 5a).

Fig. 5a

Comer added the locations of whales taken the five previous years; house ruins; food caches; and, just south of Cape Kendall, the entry: *"Natives in 1896. Not more than 20 natives and reported by them to be all there are now on Southampton Island. They say there used to be many more of them. Firearms unknown."* Another entry reads:

"Spirits is said to live here [Vansittart Island]."

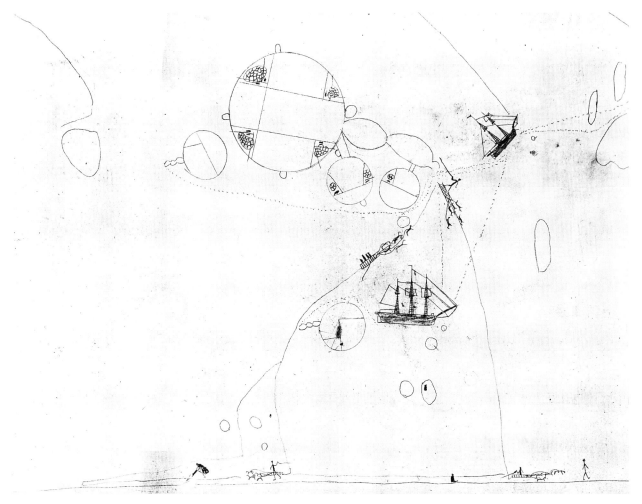

Fig. 6

That same year, Comer asked "Meliki" [Maliki] to draw a map of the winter quarters at Cape Fullerton. By then, Maliki had been regularly employed by whalers for over twenty years.

Fig. 6 includes Comer's Schooner *Era* and a larger ship, most probably the bark *A. R. Tucker*. Footpaths are rendered as dots, sled routes as continuous lines. Igloos are drawn disproportionately large.

For igloo templates, Meliki used cans. The custom became established. In 1921, Rasmussen asked Omowyuk (John "L", after John L. Sullivan) to help with a census by mapping igloos. Omowyuk knew Comer: His father, Arblick (Ben), and step-father, Eevarshar (Scotch Tom), aka Angutimarik (Real Man), worked for Comer; while his mother, Niviatsianaq (Shoofly), was Comer's mistress. Rasmussen got cans. When I arrived in 1950, the 61-year-old Omowyuk reached for cans.

Meliki provided further details in Fig. 7, including the sleeping places of Ben (1), Harry (2), Paul (3), Jack (4), Tupic Kenepeter (5), Stonewall Jackson (6) and himself (7).

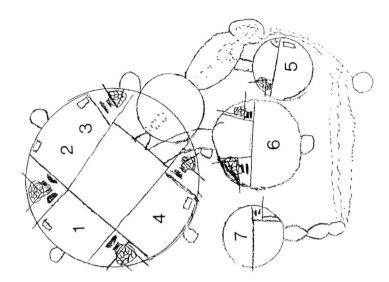

Fig. 7

Fig. 8 shows Meliki's plan of an igloo built in November, 1901, at Repulse Bay. Height inside: 14'; diameter: 27'; width of floor: 12'; height of sleeping platform: 2.5'.

"This is an unusually large one," writes Comer, "but few Natives can complete one of such size ... This house is used for all great times such as Anticooting [shamanistic performances] and dances."

Six families, including Teseuke's (about 23 people in all), lived in Room 1. Meliki's family of six lived in Room 2. Two families, totaling seven persons, occupied Room 3, while Room 4 housed a single family of six. About 41 people.

Small loops around the igloo peripheries represent storage areas within the igloo walls, accessible from within. Those marked "c" held clothing; "b," blubber; and "d," dogs, presumably pups.

"This is an unusually large one [igloo]," writes Comer, "but few natives can compelete one of such size ... This is used for all great times such as Anticooting [Shamanistic performances] and dances."

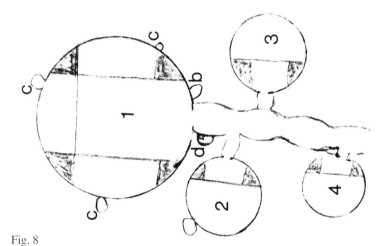

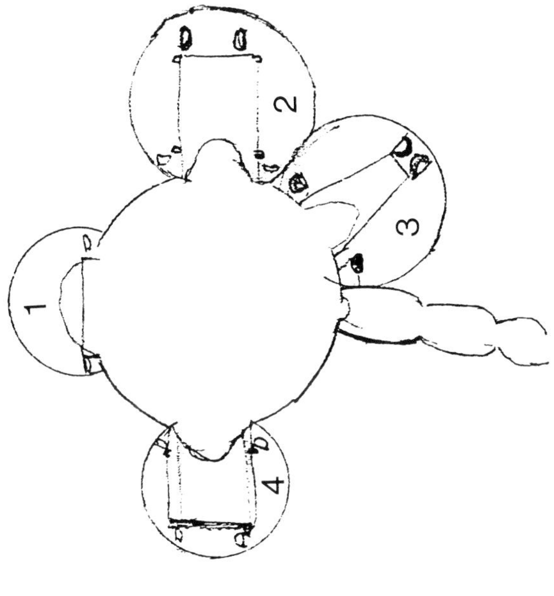

Fig. 8

Fig. 9 shows an igloo built December 17, 1901, at Repulse Bay. The central part was labeled "used for dances and anticooting" and identified "as a dance hall and for holding meetings to drive away sickness and killing evil spirits."

Room 1 held six people; room 2: 14 people; while room 3 and room 4 held eleven each. Total: 42 persons. Note the stone lamps.

Fig. 9

Fig. 10

Fig. 11

Fig. 12

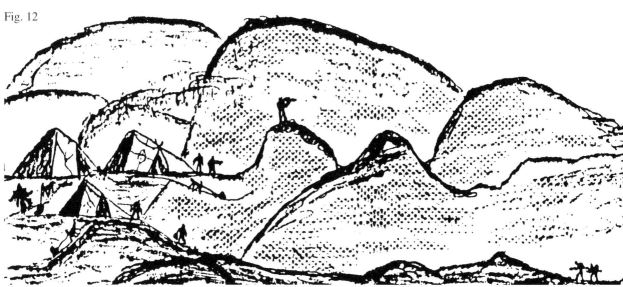

Figs. 10-11, illustrate three drawings by Teseuke (Harry), an Aivilik employed regularly by whalers since at least 1893.

Fig. 10 (circa 1898): shows, in Comer's words, *"the motion to indicate musk ox in sight."*

Fig. 11 (dated 1901): shows *"the man on the lookout signaling to the others that the deer are in sight by holding his arms up to represent horns."* Back at camp, dogs are tied to stones.

Fig. 12 (dated December 7, 1901): the hill-top hunter, *"on the look-out for deer,"* appears to be using a telescope. Camp *"dogs are tied to stones to keep them from going off or entering the tents."* At the lower right, hunters return, while in the lower left, a woman carries a pail of water.

"In making their tents, seal skin is used. The skins being split by the women who always use a knife which resembles a chopping knife. The outer half of the skin is used for the back part, while the inner part is used for the forward half of the tent, as this part is more transparent and admits the light, while the part over the back is dark."

Sketches collected by Charles Hall in the Frobrisher Bay area, in the 1860s, shade the rear half of tents, as in Fig. 12.

Teseuke darkened the hills to create the illusion of depth. He did so by placing the paper over a coarse fabric, perhaps sail cloth, then rubbing the hill sections with the flat edge of pencil lead.

Fig. 13: Teseuke's map of the headwaters of Wager River, effectively combines oblique and vertical perspectives. Clearly Teseuke suffered few inhibitions about shifting perspective when convenient.

Comer identified ponds (1); lakes (2); musk ox (3); musk ox in sight (4); dog team (5); head of Wager River (6); and the Wager River (7).

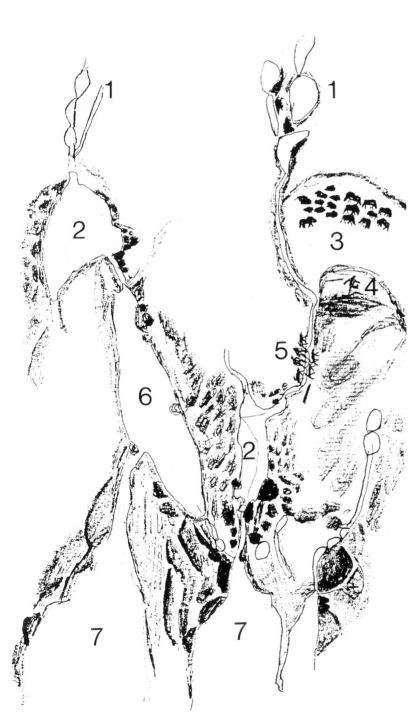

Fig. 13

Fig. 14

Fig. 14 shows seal-hunting on the ice. Faceless images also characterize Figs. 15-17.

Comer collected many such drawings, often of comparable quality. Garments, identifiably Aivilik / Iglulik, distinguish between sexes. The length of the rear flap on a woman's parka indicates the number of children she bore. Otherwise no hint of private identity marks these "corporate" figures.

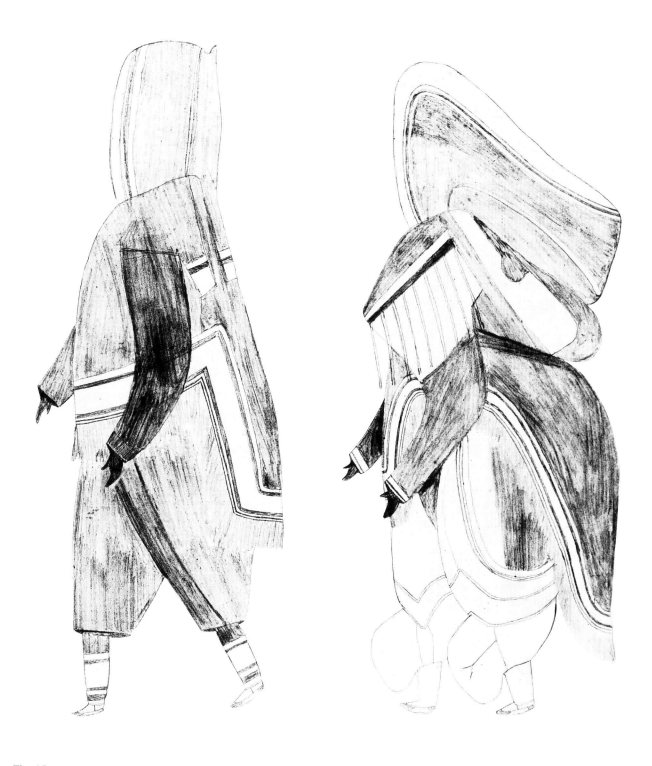

Fig. 15

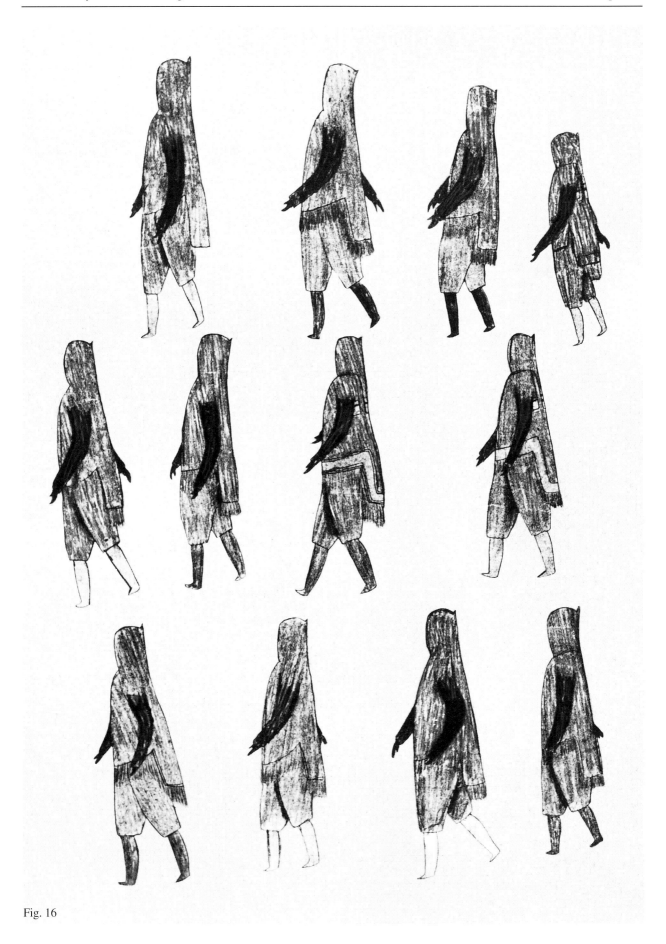

Fig. 16

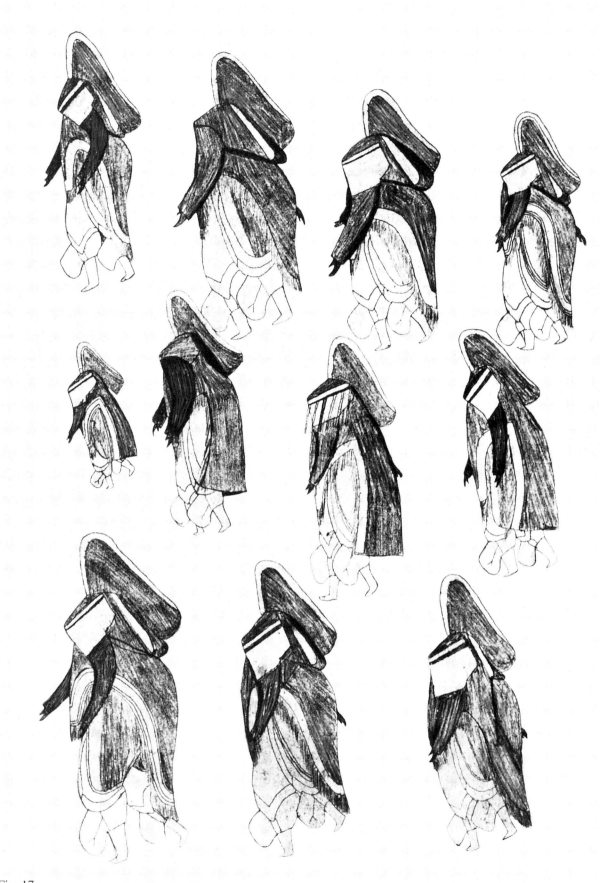

Fig. 17

The nine sheets of pencil drawings shown here as Fig. 18 - Fig. 29, come from Captain W. E. Parry's Arctic Expedition 1821-1823.

Captain George Lyon, a member of that expedition, added captions in ink and, possibly, brought them back with him to England.

In 1958, they were donated to the Scott Polar Institute[4].

Each measures 34 cm X 21 cm.

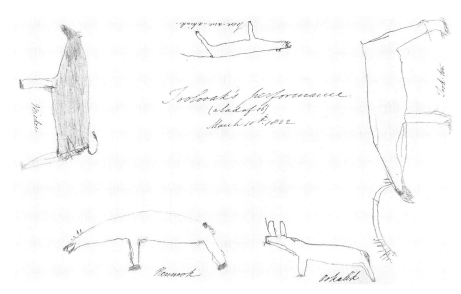

Fig. 18

Drawings appear on both sides of three of the nine sheets, so the total is twelve. Of these, Lyon identified six as the work of Toolooak.

He hat Fig. 18 labeled: *"Toolooak's performance"*, identified him as "a lad of 16", and dated the drawing *"March 10th, 1822"*, presumably at Winter Island.

The labels under its five figures read, clockwise:

"Nanook" (meaning bear); "Mickie" meaning 'small' and possibly refering to Lt. A. Reid's Scotch terrier, mentioned by Parry (1824) as "a great favorite with us"; *"Terre-awe-akuik"* (tereganniaq) meaning 'white fox'; *"Took-too"* (tuktu) meaning 'caribou'; *"Ooka-lik"* (ukalid) meaning 'Arctic hare'.

Fig. 19

Hopper shows *"Captain Parry in full uniform sitting down"* and *"Mr. Hopper (one leg wanting)"*. W. H. Hopper was the purser on the ship Fury.

Both drawings are captioned "Toolooak fecit".

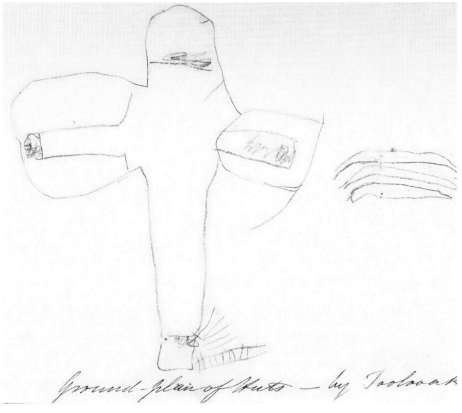

Fig. 20 shows the *"Ground-plan of Huts - byToolooak"* with a sled at the single entrance and three elevated kayaks to one side. The lines at the entrance may represent hunting weapons. Note the effort at shading(?) in the interior rooms.

Fig. 20

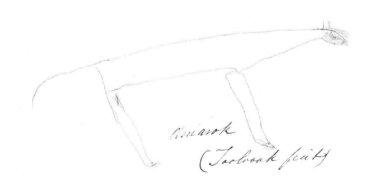

Fig. 21

Fig. 21 is identified as *"(Toolooak fecit)"* and shows an *"Amarok"* (amaruq) meaning (arctic wolf) and a *"Mouse"*, perhaps a lemming, more likely one of the stowaway mice infesting Parry's flour barrels.

Fig. 22 shows the *"Fury dismantled"* [Stripped of its sails] *(drawn by Toolooak).*

As with tent drawings, the Fury's stern is darkened. Note X-ray renderings of the masts below deck.

Fig. 22

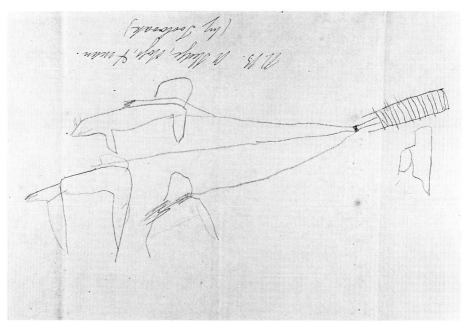

Lyon identified Fig 23 as *"N. B. A sledge, dogs, and man (by Toolooak)".*

Fig. 23

Fig. 24

The remaining drawings share certain details with one or another, but none with Toolooak's work.

I assume that Toolooak drew on only one side of the 6 sheets. The other artist(s) used three additional sheets, as well as the backs of three sheets already used by Too-looak.

Lyon captioned the figures in Fig. 24 from left to right: *"Kaoong-ut"* [elsewhere Ka-oog-ut]; *"Onng-a-luk"* [elsewhere Ayug-ga-look]; *"Okotook"; "Illigliuk"* [elsewhere Iigiuk]; *"Ayoket";* and below *"Siout-kuk"*. No personal detail, save name, marks any of these native figures. Yet Parry and Lyon describe many of them as physically distinctive. No hint of that appears here.

The artist who draw Fig. 25 (verso of Fig. 22) obviously and successfully employed a straight edge.

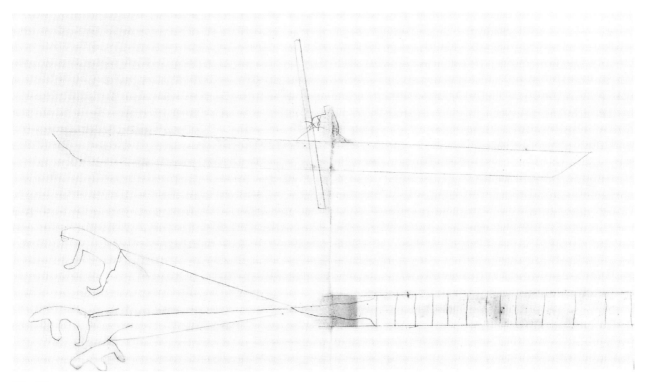

Fig. 25

In Fig. 26 (verso of Fig. 20) Lyon identified the two human figures as *"Hopper"* (left) and *"Parry"* (right). He also identified the animal, though I can't read his caption.

Over the back of this animal and over Hopper's head are light squiggles, as if the artist, unfamiliar with a pencil, had tested it.

Similar marks appear on other drawings whose crudity may lie primarily with the artists' unfamiliarity with pencils and drawing.

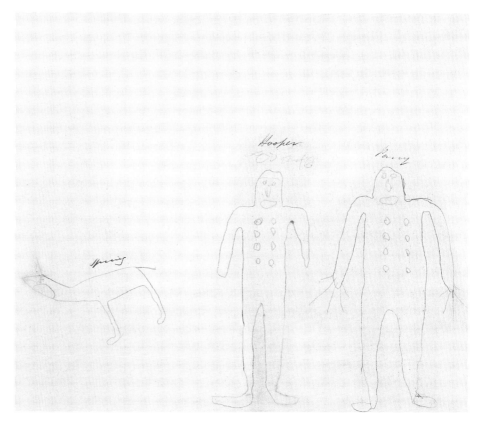

Fig. 26

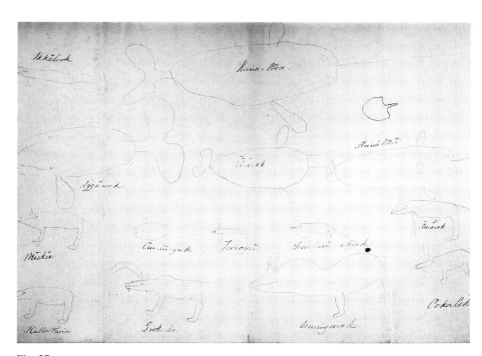

Note similarities between the animal drawings in Fig. 27 and those in Fig. 25, Fig. 26, and Fig. 29.

Fig. 27

Drawing #	Parry's Spelling (diacritics omitted)	Conventional Inuktitut (Igloolik Dialect)	Animal Type.
1	Ikalook	iqaluk	Fish (usually Arctic Char)
2	Keinalooa	qilalugaq	Beluga whale; narwhale
3	Aggawek	arviq	Bowhead whale
4	Eiuek	aiviq	walrus
5	Keinalooa	qilalugaq; qinalugaq	Beluga (white) whale; narwhale (narwhale is also termed *tuugaalik* = "the tusked one"
6	Mickee	Mickee (small?)	Name not recognized; might be an Inuktitut name for the Scotch Terrier which accompanied Parry's Expedition
7	Awinguk	avinngnaq	Lemming
8	Tirraga	tiriaq	Weasel
9	Tirreawakiuk (?)	tiriganniaq	White fox
10	Amarok	amaruq	Arctic wolf
11	Kableearioo	qavvigaarjuk; qavvik	Wolverine
12	Tooktook	tuktu	Caribou
13	Oomingmak	umingmak	Musk-ox
14	Ookalik	ukaliq	Arctic hare

John MacDonald, Nunavut Research Institute, Igloolik, NWT, Canada, kindly created the accompanying chart to go with Fig. 27.

I'm also greateful to him for correcting the spellings of various proper names.

Tribes in this area take their identity, their everlasting identity, from names believed to be periodically reincarnated. Many of the names recorded by Parry's 1821-1823 Expedition are still current among the Aivilik/Iglulik.

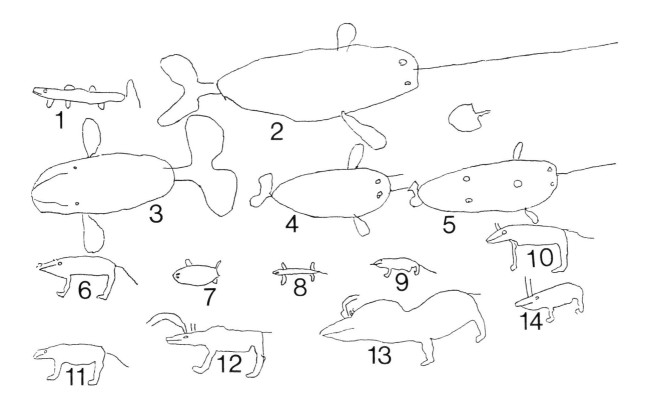

Fig. 27a

Lyon identified the naval
officer in Fig. 28 as simply
"Captain".

Fig. 29 (verso of Fig. 28)
shows fifteen fur-glad males
and one animal. Leah Otak,
Igloolik, believes that the
animal represents an arctic
hare.

In all of these drawings,
only Europeans are given
personal identities.

Fig. 28

Fig. 29

Fig. 30

Lyon identified Fig. 30 and Fig. 31 as the work of *"Eewinhraat"*, added captions in ink and took them back with him to England.

Each measures 31 cm X 24½ cm. Both sheets were donated to the Scott Polar Research Institute in 1944.

Each drawing employs a foreground line. Each also demonstrates an artistic skill absent in the other Parry Expedition drawings illustrated here. I wish we knew more of Eewighroot's familiarity with pencils.

Lyon captioned the figures, clockwise: *"Bear"; "Rein deer"; "Musk ox"; "Kablee-ghioo"* (quavvqaarjuk, qavvik) meaning 'wolverine'; and *"Eevighroot' dog"*.

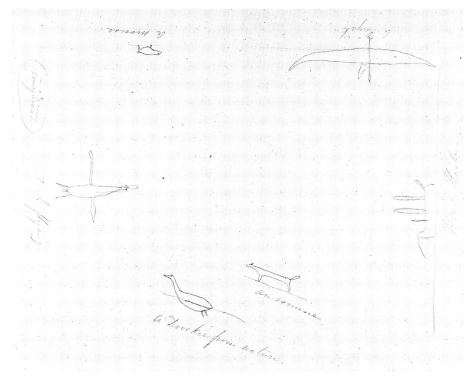

Fig. 31

Lyon labeled the images, clockwise: *"an ermine"; "a Dovekie from nature"; "Duck flying"; "a mouse"; "a kayak"; and "HMS Hecla"*.

At least five journals of Parry's 1821-1823 Expedition survived. Parry's and Lyon's are published.

Those by Francis R. M. Crozier, midshipman on the Fury, and W. H. Hopper, purser on the Fury, remain unpublished. So does most of the journal of William Mogg, clerk on the Hecla (?)6.

Mogg collected Fig. 32, which he labeled, *"Specimen of the Fine Art by a Native of Igloolik"* and *"Drawn by E-teo hi-tio* [Itikuttuk] *Igloolik 9 March 1823"*.

Its figures, Mogg wrote, were *"intented* [sic] *to represent"*

(1) *"a Wolf"*;
(2) *"[ditto] as seen in womb"*;
(3) *"Fox"*;
(4) *"Pigtails of Women"*;
(5) *"Esquimaux Man"*;
(6) *"[ditto] Woman"*;
(7) *"[ditto] man Protoookuloo"*;
(8) *"Esquimaux man"*
(9) *"Deer"*;
(10) *"Eteo-i-tio his Wife"*;
(11) *"Esquimaux man in indecent posture"*;
(12) *"Musk ox"*.

Human figures remain faceless. No mark of physique or garment - nothing - establishes private identity. Yet (7) and (10) are named.

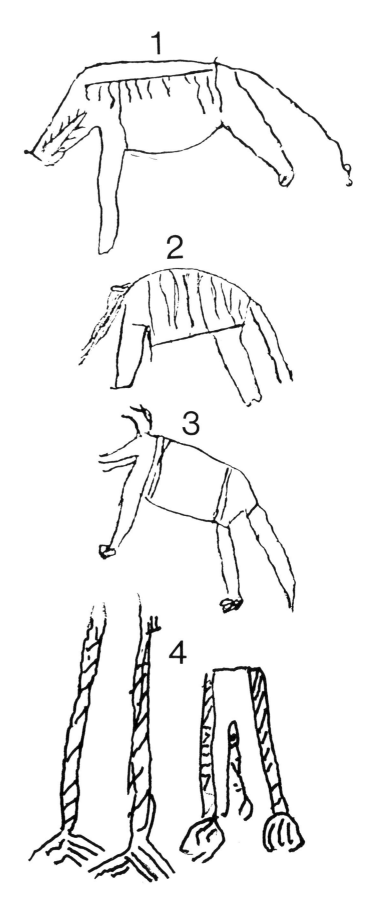

Fig. 32

Fig. 33

Notes

(1) For Comer's collecting activities, see **"An Arctic Whaling Diary: The Journal of Captain George Comer in Hudson Bay, 1903-1905",** edited by W. Gillies Ross, 1984. For two earlier diaries, see **"Manuscript Journal on Board the Era 1897-1899"** and **"Manuscript Journal on Board the Era 1900-1902",** both in the G. W. Blunt White Library, Mystic Seaport, Mystic, Conn.

I am indebted to Kelly S. Drake, Manuscript Assistant at that library, for sending me relevant passages from the 1897-1899 manuscript. Comer is always fascinating to read. He celebrated Christmas, 1897, by loading the yards with bags of presents donated by a Ladies Club, Andover, Massachusetts. Each ship member received a bag containing a button, thread, wax, thimble, comb, bandages & salve. Comer received, in addition, a box of candy.

Twenty-three local Eskimos came, plus five from Kenipithe. Comer gave each man a file, each woman a few yards of calico, each boy a jack-knife, and each girl enough calico for a dress, plus two spools of thread and a thimble.

He reckoned this as fifty presents, each accompanied by a bag of popcorn and peanuts. Second Mate Howland, *"rigged up for the occasion,"* acted as Santa Claus. Music, singing and dancing continued until 11 pm. "A goodly number" from the *A. R. Tucker* joined them.

(2) Comer's account of Siksik, comes from the **"Journal of George Comer",** 8:10, 1910-1911-1912; Anthropology Archives, American Museum of Natural History, New York.

(3) Fig. 1 to Fig. 17 come from the Anthropology Archives, American Museum of Natural History, except for Fig. 1, Fig. 9, and Fig. 12, now in the American Philosophical Society. Unlimited thanks to Barbara Conklin and Martha J. Harrison.

(4) Fig. 18 to Fig. 29 come by courtesy of the Scott Polar Institute, Cambridge University, Cambridge. 76/7/1-9.

(5) Parry, William Edward [1824]: **Journal of a second voyage for the discovery of a North-West Passage from the Atlantic to the Pacific; Performed in the Years 1821-1822-1823.** 384 p. (London: John Murray).

(6) Fig. 30 to Fig. 31 come by courtesy of the Scott Polar Research institute, Cambridge University, Cambridge. 76/6/1-2.

(7) Courtesy of the Archives and Special Collections, Hartley Library, University of Southampton, Southampton, England, MS 45,AO 183/2. See: Traverner, J. E. [1964]: **The ArcticWintering of H.M.S. Hecla and Fury in Prince Regent Inlet, 1824-1825, by William Mogg.** *Polar Record,* 12(76):11-28. (Cambridge: Scott Polar Institute).

References

Ross, W. Gillies [1984]: **An Arctic Whaling Diary: The Journal of Captain George Comer in Hudson Bay, 1903-1905.** * p. (*: *).

Parry, William Edward [1824]: **Journal of a second voyage for the discovery of a North-West Passage from the Atlantic to the Pacific; Performed in the Years 1821-1822-1823.** 384 p. (London: John Murray).

Traverner, J. E. [1964]: **The ArcticWintering of H.M.S. Hecla and Fury in Prince Regent Inlet, 1824-1825, by William Mogg.** *Polar Record,* 12(76):11-28. (Cambridge: Scott Polar Institute).

Edmund Carpenter

The Fate of Krueger's Expedition

Frederica de Laguna

"The Career and Disappearance of Hans K. E. Krueger, Arctic Geologist, 1886-1930" (Barr 1993)[1], has haunted me since I first saw it, because I had known Dr. Krueger over sixty years ago. I have read and reread this carefully researched account of his life, of the mystery surrounding the fate of his expedition, and of the heroic efforts of the parties that searched in vain for Krueger and his two companions. I have compared my impressions of him with what is here recounted, believing that in his complex personality lie the clues to understanding how he, his Danish assistant, Bjare, and his Inughuit (Polar-Eskimo) guide, Arqioq (or Akqioq) lost their lives. Of course, I do not know *where* or *how* Krueger's party died, but I can suggest *why*.

I met Dr. Krueger on board the *Hans Egede,* en route from Copenhagen to Greenland in June 1929, when I was assistant to Dr. Therkel Mathiassen, the Danish archaeologist. With Dr. Krueger were two other German geologists, whom I described as "old" Dr. H. Nieland and "young" Dr. F. K. Drescher, and a "young" Dane, Aage Rose Bjare. On this small vessel we were in close daily association for about three weeks until the Krueger party left the steamer at Umanaq, while Mathiassen and I continued on to our summer's work in Upernavik District. In the journal[2] I kept from our departure on 1 June until our return to Copenhagen on 2 November, I freely expressed my feelings about this wonderful adventure and the people I met. This was my first trip to the Arctic, fulfilling an ambition I had cherished since childhood, so I was prepared to enjoy everything and admire everyone connected with the north - including, at first, Dr. Krueger.

Although my comments and opinions were only those of a young women of twenty-two, they may be of interest in view of later events. I shall first give my youthful impression of Krueger and Bjare, quoting or summarizing from my journal, and later offer an interpretation of Krueger's personality.

In 1929 when we sailed from Copenhagen, I could read some German, but not speak it. Fortunately all the members of the Krueger expedition could speak English. I saw quite a bit of Bjare, who told me that he had lived for five years in Greenland. He was full of exciting stories, mostly about his wonderful dog team and an incredible journey they had made - ninety miles [144 km] in one day (!), although I wrote, "I suspect that he is straining the truth a bit to impress me." He was to be in charge of the non-scientific side of Krueger's expedition.

During the summer the four men were to travel about Umanaq Fjord in the motor boat which we carried on the fore deck of the *Hans Egede.* Then he and Krueger were to go on to Ellesmere Island. Their purpose, I understood, was to trace a particular geological formation which outcrops in West Greenland and on Ellesmere Island. (I learned only from Barr's article that Krueger's plans were far more ambitious).

The vast area in the High Arctic of Canada where they were going was completely uninhabited except for a few Royal Canadian Mounted Policemen at posts on Bache Peninsula and Craig Harbour. "Winter there," I wrote, "especially for two men, one of whom has never wintered in the Arctic, will be no joke." After a few days I could not envy Bjare, for I was beginning to form an unfavorable opinion of Dr. Krueger.

We soon ran into rough weather, which often prevented playing "tennis' with rope rings on deck. For amusement, I made a chess set out of cardboard, and "my efforts elicited many scornful wise-cracks from the others, especially from Dr. Krueger, who discovered a real set on board." But the latter was useless because the ship was pitching so badly, while my poor "non-skid chessmen could stand their ground except in the very worst weather."

Dr. Krueger was also scornful of the reading I had brought: Remarque's "Im Westen Nichts Neues," and the English translation, "All Quiet on the Western Front."

"It is still a fine book, in spite of what Dr. Krueger says. He claims that the writer has the "horizon of a little frog,' because he was always pitying the young men, whereas the older men were also unfortunate. Also Krueger criticized him for saying that no one knew why they were fighting. 'Maybe he didn't know,' Dr. Krueger burst out with astounding vehemence, 'but, by God, we knew!' But I don't think he did."

The stormy weather, including a "number ten gale, the real thing," lasted over two weeks. "Dr. Drescher, the poor young German, has been sick all this time. He never appears at meals, and as far as we can tell, has not been able to eat a thing. He used to lie out on deck in his sleeping bag. Once a big wave broke over the side and drenched him. He looks like a ghost, and we feel very sorry for him, also for old Dr. Nieland who shares his cabin. They are the two who are not going to Ellesmere Island." Seasickness for so long can be serious, yet, as I recall, Krueger, who never got seasick himself, seemed not to care. Fortunately, Drescher recovered in the calmer waters of Umanaq Fjord.

"I don't like Dr. Krueger. He thinks too much of himself, and is always putting other people in the wrong. He is a difficult person to get along with. His mouth is that of a spoiled child and he seems to cherish a sense of injury. I am glad that I don't have to spend the winter alone with him, and Bjare has to do. Bjare is really very sensitive and touchy, in spite of his affectation of boldness and his teasing manner. One really can't joke with him. I am afraid that he and Krueger will not get along well together. Krueger knows nothing about the Arctic winter, and it may get terribly on his nerves. Bjare will have a better time. If they take natives with them, as I suppose they will, Bjare can talk to them. He tells me that he loves the Arctic and would like to live there. But he and Krueger will be thrown too much on each other, and I should not be surprised if there were serious trouble, and I would not blame Bjare too much, either. I tried to find out what he thought of Krueger, but he was tight-lipped, and I was afraid to question him directly. One never sees them together, and there does not seem to be any spirit and enthusiasm in their expedition, as there is in ours. Mathiassen and I have devoted some pains to studying each other, in talking over our plans, and so on,

and in learning how to get along together, which we seem to do pretty well. But Bjare and Krueger will never really be friends."

It must be understood that I had known Mathiassen for only two months, and that he had asked me to go as his assistant after just one week's acquaintance. Yet everything went well for us, because we took pains that it should. Nor did the Arctic disappoint me.

"Miss Østerby [the nurse going to Umanaq] and Krueger play deck tennis together quite a bit, and he seems to like her a lot, but she does not care for him, and at night in our cabin we talk about pushing his face in [this childish expression due to language difficulties]. She seems to be the most popular person on the boat. I would give anything if she could only speak English a little better, for one can't make a man a confidant in everything."

We were at Umanaq for several days where Krueger's supplies and motor boat were unloaded. "Bjare rushed [into the main cabin], looking for his boss, Dr. Krueger. While they were testing [the motor boat], the screw had fallen off and now lay on the bottom of the harbor under fourteen feet of icy water, [deep in the mud]. It seems that the accident was due to a defect in the mechanism. The engine had reversed and just shot the propeller off. Bjare looked tired and dirty and almost ready to cry. He has had to take charge of the unloading of all the expedition's equipment. Coal dust from the hold and sweat were caked into his skin and he looked haggard. I could hardly bear to look at him; no man should look like that[3]. I guess Krueger has just about given him hell these last few days, and it did not help matters that Bjare and not Krueger had been on hand when the accident happened."

Fortunately at Umanaq there was Gabel Sørensen of the Royal Danish Geodetic Survey, a naval officer with experience in diving. The ship had a complete diving outfit, in case her own screw was broken in the ice, just as she carried a complete suit of sails. The first officer, also a diver, went down while Sørensen managed the air pipe and ropes in the barge. Then the first officer had to rest, and Sørensen made the next dive. "While he was down, there was only the second mate to take charge above, and one could not help wishing that there was someone as efficient as Sørensen in the barge. Krueger had been hovering around the barge, trying to help, but no one would let him touch anything. Bjare, however, seemed to be pretty useful." The screw was eventually recovered after repeated dives. During one of these, Sørensen, who had injured himself earlier but said nothing about it, nearly fainted. Fortunately he was able to give the emergency signal of three jerks on the line in time to be hauled up.

At the end of our summer's work, Mathiassen and I had to wait several days at Godhavn for the ship *Gertrude Rask* to take us back to Copenhagen. Dr. Alfred Wegener and the other members of his expedition, Drs. Ernst Sorge, Johannes Georgi, and Fritz Loewe, were also wait-

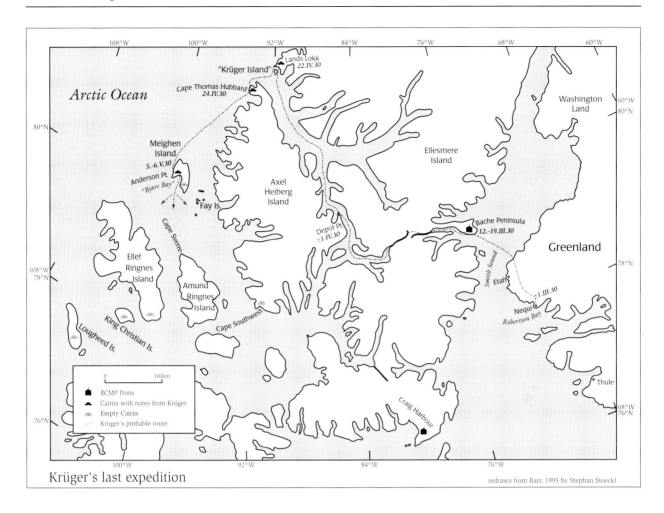

Krüger's last expedition

redrawn from Barr, 1993 by Stephan Stoeckl

ing for the ship. We had already heard much about Wegener's work, and now Sorge, who spoke excellent English, explained with enthusiasm their scientific accomplishments and adventures. Sørensen and four other members of the Geodetic Survey joined us before we left Greenland.

We celebrated Wegener's forty-ninth birthday on 1 November, just before reaching Copenhagen. "Everyone admired him. The spirit in his expedition could not have been finer. These four men were bound together by the strongest ties of mutual affection and respect. His men were devoted to Wegener and he to them. Perhaps the war produced such a fellowship; but war could not have inspired anything comparable to the loyalty to science that these men felt. They had, besides, that wealth of personal jokes and anecdotes that spring from happy days and hardships shared together.

No expedition could have offered a stronger contrast to that of Krueger. We asked Sørensen for news of him and Bjare, but he could not bring himself to speak of them. They had sailed north on the Canadian government supply ship [on July 27], and that was the last he had heard of them." My strong conviction that they would never return caused me to dream that the ship bringing

their supplies was unable to reach the rendezvous in time, thus dooming Krueger and Bjare to starvation. "I know that Sørensen had no hope for them, even at the start, and that was why he could say nothing."

It can be seen that not only I, but the Danes with whom I was associated, found Dr. Krueger disagreeable, opinionated, and unprepared to lead an expedition in the High Arctic. Can we reconcile that opinion with the very favorable impression that he evidently made on some, as indicated in Barr's account? The latter makes no judgmental statement, but the data are there. What was Krueger's real character?

Inspector A. H. Joy of the Royal Canadian Mounted Police (RCMP), who traveled north with Krueger on the supply ship (27 July to 4 August 1929), found in him "no pretence of egoism... [and] concluded that with the abundance of game in many places in the North, [Krueger] would be successful on his expedition under almost any circumstances. He impressed me as being a capable man and would give a good account of himself anywhere in the field of exploration" (quoted by Barr 1993:285).

Krueger was evidently rather good-looking[4], although I was not impressed, and could be charming and persuasive when he chose, but perhaps only to those from whom he expected benefits. He had at any rate so won the heart of young Baroness Hilda Schad von Mittelbiberach that she never recovered from his loss. He was well educated, clever, brave (though reckless), and had survived many dangerous adventures in German South West Africa (1910-1923).

During World War I he was a guerrilla leader of the Boers against the British, was captured and condemned to death, escaped, was recaptured but somehow obtained a pardon, how or why we are not told. Such an experience would have been enough to give him the illusion that he could live through anything. In 1923 he was contemplating British citizenship (He had lost his own in the transfer of his birthplace from former Prussia to Poland), which makes us question the depth of his loyalties.

In addition to other activities, for most of his 14 years in South Africa, Krueger had been a prospector in the deserts of Kalahari and Namibia and had managed a British vanadium mine, thereby gaining a practical knowledge of geology, and curiously enough, his first desire for Arctic adventure. It is with no surprise that I find in him many of the same traits that characterize the typical prospector, especially those who stampeded into Yukon Territory during the Klondike Gold Rush of 1897. Like them, did he not feel that grit and dogged endurance alone would enable him to surmount any obstacles? For him, scientific fame was like the gold that the prospector *knows* lies just over the next mountain and is determined to reach, no matter the sacrifices or the dying horses left along the Chilkoot Trail. I believe that Krueger must have been something of a charismatic leader, but one so blinded by his own ambition that he was ready to risk not only his own life, but was indifferent to the welfare of others.

Like the prospector who is secretive about his destination, lest others beat him to it, Krueger seems never to have been completely open about the plans for his last expedition, keeping some in reserve, or changing them. He was not really content to study rock formations on Ellesmere Island. Rather, he wanted go 200 miles out on the Polar Sea to discover the edge of the Continental Shelf, for he was astute enough to combine Wegener's theory of continental drift with the evidence of topography, noting that the northwestern edges of the Canadian Archipelago and northern Greenland lie on a southwest-northeast line, beyond which there could be no more land. Ultimately, perhaps, he would continue across the Polar Sea to Russia! (Barr 1993:287-89). In pursuit of these goals, Krueger, like the prospector, was laden down with murderously heavy gadgets: an echo sounder (which he later abandoned), a rubber boat, and fathoms of very heavy deep-sea sounding wire.

He was a hard worker and a quick learner. On his return to Germany from South Africa, he had systematically pursued studies of geology and of the Arctic. While

his Hessian West Greenland Expedition (late July to mid-November 1925) was inadequate preparation for the High Arctic, he was able to turn his geological investigations on this trip to good account. He obtained a Ph.D. from the University of Heidelberg, basing his doctoral dissertation on his fieldwork in Disko Bay and Umanaq Fjord. The Royal Geographical Society elected him a fellow. This honor and the 85 citations in his article (Krueger 1929)[5] on Arctic geology very favorably impressed the Canadian authorities and were instrumental in securing their help in 1929.

Like so many others, Krueger had been fired by Stefansson's books, especially "The Friendly Arctic", which made living off the country like a native seem so easy, and in 1924 began a correspondence with the author about his own plans to do the same while exploring the Canadian Arctic Archipelago. He does not seem to have taken seriously enough Stefansson's warning that not all parts of this region could support an expedition.

In 1924 (his plans changed later) his great expedition was to last 5 years: the first to be spent among the Inughuit (Polar-Eskimos) of Greenland to learn their skills, the second to practice them on Ellesmere Island, before doing the real work in the northwest part of the archipelago. Yet when he actually set off on his great expedition, Krueger's only experience of the Arctic had been 2½ months in West Greenland in 1925 and the July of 1929 before he went north. Although "fascinated by the superlative skills of the Greenlanders" (Barr 1993:283), which he briefly observed in 1925, there is no evidence that he tried to learn any directly from the Greenland natives. Did he believe himself so superior that this was not necessary?

If my recollection serves, Krueger actually contemplated beating them at their own game, for on the *Hans Egede* in 1929 he boasted about his sled, equipped with stainless steel runners despite the difficulties of boring holes through them for attachment. This would have been another example of a prospector's gadgetry. Yet I dare not stress this point without written confirmation in my journal, and in any case there is no evidence that such a sledge was actually used. Certainly those of the Inughuit would have been far superior because of their relative lightness and flexibility.

Like the typical prospector, Krueger was too impatient. As Constable N. M. McLean is reported to have remarked: Krueger was "the sort to whom 'you couldn't tell nothing' " (Barr 1993:289). McLean was in charge of the RCMP detatchment at Bache Peninsula, Ellesmere Island, the last outpost from which Krueger plunged into the unknown, and his opinion should carry weight.

What are the known facts?

The Canadian ship deposited Krueger and Bjare on 4 August at Neqe, an Inughuit settlement on Robertson Fjord in Greenland, between Thule and Etah. That fall (November?), they went alone on a major *"training trip"* to the northeast, without a guide and apparently without even the minimum of reasonable equipment or supplies. Overtaken on their way back by darkness and storms, without food, shelter, or fire, they had to hole up in the snow for many days, and survived only by eating raw their frozen dogs. They became sick soon after their return to Neqe. When the Danish administrator and the doctor from Thule saw them in late November, they had recovered somewhat, but were still emaciated and so weak they could scarcely walk, Krueger trembling all over. To Dr. Graham Rowley their reported symptoms suggested trichinosis from the raw meat.

None the less, in early March 1930, they set off across Smith Sound for Ellesmere Island, Krueger having persuaded Arqioq, a highly skilled, trusted and beloved Inughuk guide who knew the region well, to join him. With them were two other Inughuit, each driving a supply sled. They reached the RCMP post on Bache Peninsula on 12 March, their dogs already in poor condition and Krueger suffering from stomach cramps and vomiting.

On 19 March they were off again. Krueger left a note that they hoped to catch the supply ship at Bache that summer. If not, they would probably be at Dundas, the RCMP post on Devon Island, far to the south. Or, if held up elsewhere by open water, they would get to Bache after freeze-up and go south from Thule with the Greenland mail in February 1931. Lack of communication between posts and the multiple alternatives of this vague plan meant that no one had reason to suspect Krueger was missing until too late. Did he intend to keep his whereabouts secret?

On 11 April, the support sleds were back at Bache, having left their supplies at Depot Point, Axel Heiberg Island, where they parted from the expedition. Their Inughuit drivers would have had only bad news to report, if questioned *then*. They had left both white men in poor shape - Krueger with stomach cramps and in a bad temper, very irritable, because they and their dogs could hardly move their overloaded sled. When last seen, Krueger was leading, Bjare pushing from behind, while Arqioq was propping up the load from the side. The latter also sent back word to the administrator in Thule that he believed neither man could survive a long journey, for Krueger was spitting blood while climbing and Bjare had frozen his toes. But he, Arqioq, would not desert them. While the RCMP did not know about this at the time, the Inughuit at Bache and Neqe were already very worried.

On 22 April 1930, Krueger left a note in Peary's cairn at Lands Lokk on the west coast of Ellesmere Island, reporting one sledge, 17 dogs, and 3 men in good condition.

On 24 April, Krueger left a note in a cairn on Cape Thomas Hubbard on the west coast of Axel Heiberg Island that they had come from Lands Lokk and were on their way to Meighen Island.

Krueger's last message, dated 6 May 1930, in Stefansson's cairn on Anderson Point, Meighen Island, reported that his party had arrived on 5 May and were pro-

ceeding to Cape Sverre on Amund Ringnes Island. Like the previous notes, it was written in German by Krueger, and signed by all three men. No mention is made of their condition, although their rate of travel has been judged normal.

No further trace of them has ever been found despite years of searching. There is no evidence that they reached Amund Ringnes Island, and it is presumed they perished in the winter of 1930-1931.

Did Krueger deceive Arqioq about his ambitious plans? The drivers of the supply sleds thought that Krueger intended go all the way around Axel Heiberg Island, and so presumably did Arqioq. Such a route would have brought them past Cape Southwest on that island, and since no note from Krueger was found in any of the cairns on this prominent headland, it was assumed that the expedition had been lost before reaching this point. But as Osczevski[6] points out, it is more likely that Krueger wanted to winter on one of the islands from which he could more easily continue his search for the edge of the Continental Shelf the next year. He must have known that if they returned to Axel Heiberg Island it would be very difficult to dissuade Bjare and Arqioq from the temptation to continue on to Bache. Krueger would have kept them well to the west.

Stefansson believed that only a sudden catastrophe on the sea ice that left no traces could account for their disappearance. He suggested they had been poisoned by carbon monoxide from a faulty primus or stove, as were presumably Andrée and Strindberg on White Island near Spitzbergen in 1897.

Did Krueger actually reach Amund Ringness Island, but decide to go on beyond Cape Sverre before leaving a note? Perhaps his party turned aside to the outer Ringnes Island, Ellef instead of Amund, because the prospects for game seemed more favorable. Or, did they travel still farther to Lougheed Island where Stefansson had once found good hunting, and where Krueger had previously thought to winter? All these, and other possible destinations, have been considered.

But different years may bring vastly different conditions, and the plentiful game of one season may become scarce another year. Some areas of the sea and some islands are always devoid of game. Did Krueger's party die of starvation, as the Canadian Police officers and the Inughuit believed? Did the expedition push on to some remote outer island and there lose their lives because the hunting failed, their dogs died, they could therefore go no further? In the dark of winter, without matches or fuel, they could not even have melted ice for drinking water.

When they started from Depot Point with the overloaded sledge, both Arqioq and Bjare would have known that Krueger was leading them to ruin. Was it honor alone, having given their word, that bound them to him? And how could Krueger, sick as he was, still drive himself on and on, in vain pursuit of his dream?

Abriviations

RCMP = Royal Canadian Mounted Police

Notes

(1) Professor William Barr is Head of the Department of Geology, University of Saskatchewan, Saskatoon, Saskatchewan, Canada S7N 0W0.

(2) I quote from my original journal. A slightly shortened version is published as "Voyage to Greenland: A Personal Initiation into Anthropology". (de Laguna 1977). Reprinted 1995 with new preface and illustrations. The brief account of Wegener's death, based on a letter from Mathiassen in 1931, should be corrected (See Georgi 1935).

(3) Bjare already looks like an old man in the photograph (Barr 1993:286, Fig.7) taken in early August 1929, when they were put ashore from the Canadian supply ship at the Inughuit settlement in Robertson Bay, Northern Greenland.

(4) See the photograph taken in Darmstadt before his last expedition (Barr 1993:281, Fig.4). My journal contains surprisingly few descriptions of personal appearance, however.

(5) This seems to be a good, though rapid survey of circumpolar geological research, but I not a geologist. A large number of citations should not of themselves impress the scholar.

References

Barr, William [1993]: **The Career and Disappearance of Hans K. E. Krueger, Arctic Geologist, 1886-1930**. *Polar Record*, 29(171):277-304 (Cambridge: Scott Polar Institute).

de Laguna, Frederica [1977]: **Voyage to Greenland: A Personal Initiation into Anthropology**. 285 p. (New York: W. W. Norton), reprinted 1995 with new perface and illustrations (Prospect Heights, Illinois: Waveland Press).

Georgi, J. [1935]: **Mid-Ice: The Story of the Wegener Expedition to Greenland.** (New York: Dutton & Co).

Krueger, H. [1929]: **Recent Geological Research in the Arctic**, *American Journal of Science*, Series 5, 17:50-62 (New Haven, Connecticut).

Osczevski, Randall J. [1944]: "**The Disappearance of Hans Krueger**", *Polar Record*, 30(173):157-58 (Cambridge, England: Scott Polar Institute).

Frederica de Laguna, Professor Emeritus of Anthropology, Bryn Mawr College, Pennsylvania. Member Emeritus, National Academy of Sciences.

Searching for the Grail:
Virtual Archeology in Yamal and Circumpolar Theory

William W. Fitzhugh

*"One cannot but infer that the main features characteriz-
ing the [Western Maritime Barents/Kara Sea] culture are
also characteristic of the so-called "Thule culture"
identified by Therkel Mathiassen with data collected by
the [Thule] expedition in the North American Arctic and
in Greenland"* (Chernetsov 1935:131).

*"Let us pause to wonder why Eskimologists are so willing
to slog 3,000 miles overland across the forbidding ex-
panse of Siberia, where few if any convincing cultural parallels exist, and so reluctant to paddle half that distance
down the Pacific shore, where parallels are abundant. Is
this not a case of straining at a gnat and swallowing a
camel?"* (Chard 1958:86).

The search for common history and cultural links between
arctic peoples has been an early and persisting theme in
circumpolar anthropology and archeology. From a North
American perspective this idea is compelling because of
the widespread distribution and relative uniformity of Eskimo culture, biology, folklore, and linguistics. However,
the search for continuities in the Eurasian Arctic, and
therefore knowledge of Asian-American ties, has been
difficult because of a much greater ethnic diversity among
Eurasian Arctic Cultures; divergence between Eurasian
reindeer herding and North American hunting adaptations; convergence within Eurasia stimulated by a relatively recent spread of reindeer herding; political barriers
restricting archeological research and communication;
and lack of archeological data from much of the Russian

Arctic coast. This paper addresses the last of these issues,
the archeology of a portion of the West Siberian Arctic -
the Yamal Peninsula and lower Ob River region - that has
for 450 years figured in theories of Eskimo origins.

Yamal and the central Russian Arctic coast has had
an unusual role as a prospect for Eskimo origins. Early
reports of 16th-18th century explorers and travellers
in the Barents and Kara Seas reported an Eskimo-like
people living in coastal sites in pithouses who hunted
seals, polar bear, and walrus with harpoons in skin boats
resembling kayaks. These reports come from the English
explorer, Captain Stephen Burrough at Vaigach Island in
1556 (Hakluyt 1903); by the Dutch explorer Jan Guigen
Van Linshotten (1915) with the Barents Expedition in
1594-1595; and by La Martinier from a late 17th century
trip to the Pechora coast (La Martinier 1912). Crantz
(1767: 201,239) referring to these and other references
comments on theories of a possible Barents-Kara Sea origins of Eskimos but thought an Alaskan or northeast
Asian source was more likely considering closer biological and cultural ties. Most later theories proposed through
the 1930s were founded on similar concepts in which
interior peoples gradually adapted to coastal life in Arctic
zones. Hence, archeological theories first proposed origins from northward-moving European Paleolithic and
Mesolithic hunters who adapted to the Arctic coast
(Dawkins 1874; Sollas 1924), while later versions cited
locations such as Labrador (Strong 1930) or Bering Strait
(Mathiassen 1925, 1927; Collins 1937). Meanwhile a host
of theories elaborated reconstructive ethnographic models
involving coastal adaptation by interior hunting peoples in
various regions of North America (Boas, Steensby, Hatt,

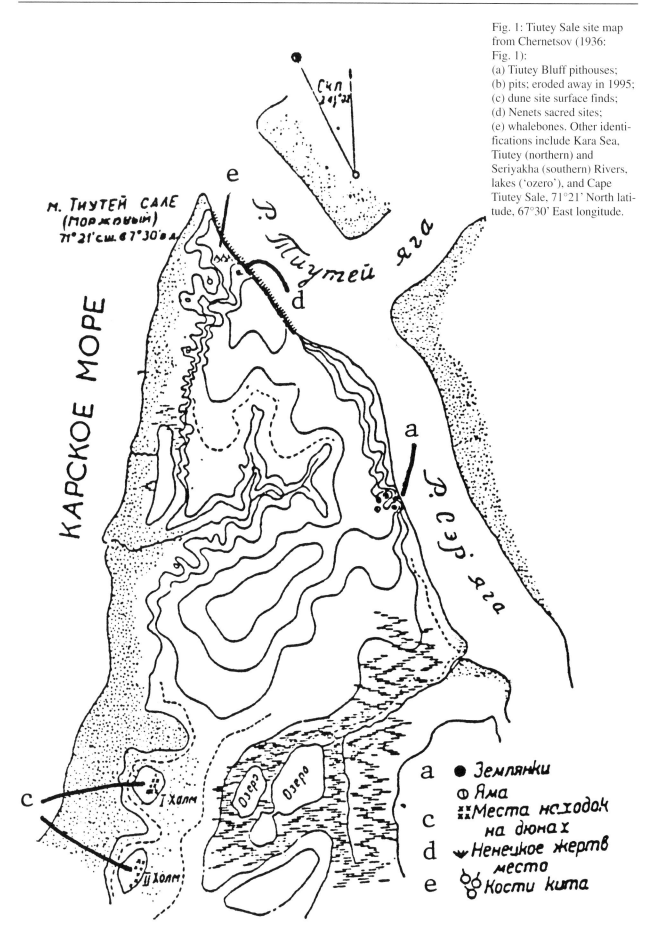

Fig. 1: Tiutey Sale site map from Chernetsov (1936: Fig. 1): (a) Tiutey Bluff pithouses; (b) pits; eroded away in 1995; (c) dune site surface finds; (d) Nenets sacred sites; (e) whalebones. Other identifications include Kara Sea, Tiutey (northern) and Seriyakha (southern) Rivers, lakes ('ozero'), and Cape Tiutey Sale, 71°21' North latitude, 67°30' East longitude.

Rink, Birket-Smith, and others). By 1930 most scholars believed that an ancient Eskimo-like culture would eventually be found to have circumpolar distribution, accounting for the many similar features known among northern ethnographic peoples (Bogoras 1929).

In this speculative era of Eskimology, Valerie Chernetsov's discovery in 1928 (but not published until 1935) of a possible early Eskimo-like culture at Tiutey Sale (Nenets for "Walrus Cape") on the Yamal Peninsula fulfilled many of these expectations. That his work coincided geographically with the early Samoyedic reference gave it additional credence. Although Chernetsov's claim was never fully developed and did not become known to most western scholars until cited by Larsen and Rainey in 1948, it was the single data point for early Arctic maritime adaptation in the unknown central Russian Arctic. It seemed highly unlikely that this area might contain the "holy grail" of Arctic archeology - the birthplace of Eskimo culture - but who could say it was impossible?

In similar fashion later archeologists have sought "virtual" solutions for the origins of Independence I and Pre-Dorset in pre-Saami cultures of Scandinavia and Western Siberia (Knuth 1967; McGhee 1983); Dorset origins in Subarctic Eastern North America (Meldgaard 1960, 1962); and later Eskimo origins sequentially from the Samoyeds, the European Paleolithic, and the Canadian Arctic barrens. Even after it became clear that Eastern Thule had its roots in Alaska, as Crantz, Rink, Steensby, and Mathiassen had predicted, and Jenness (1928) and Collins (1937, 1951) confirmed, speculation about Alaskan culture origins shifted further west into unknown Siberia and Eastern Asia. When Larsen and Rainey (1948) proposed the origins of Ipiutak burial ritual and art might be found in early West Siberian cultures, it was not a revolutionary claim.

This paper describes recent work in the Yamal region in relation to Chernetsov's (1935) and Larsen and Rainey's (1948) early proposals. For reasons noted above, these ideas have never been addressed directly with modern Siberian archeological evidence. Unconfirmed either way, the idea of a Yamal or central Russian Arctic role in circumpolar culture continuities has persisted. More than a century after Dawkins and others pointed out similarities in economy, technology, and art between European Ice Age cultures and Eskimo culture (de Laguna 1932-1933), we still lack archeological data to assess cultural history in the Eurasian arctic and boreal zones that Bogoras, Thalbitzer, Hatt, Rasmussen, Gjessing, Simonsen and others saw as central to questions of circumpolar contacts and development. However, as we shall see, Russian archeologists have for many years been making contributions to this subject that have not been widely known or appreciated in the West.

Tiutey Sale and Ipiutak

Larsen and Rainey's proposal was the first to call international attention to the archeology of the Trans-Ural and Yamal region as a potential source of Eskimo culture. After 50 years of theorizing about Eskimo origins from inland groups in northern Canada, and Collins' demonstration of 2,000 years of Eskimo history in the Bering Strait region where even the earliest phases were fully developed, the question of origins still remained unanswered. Larsen and Rainey proposed a West Siberian variant of the old inland origin idea at a time when Eurasian connections in circumpolar theory had gained considerable popularity. Solberg (1909) had speculated on Eskimo similarities in iron age cultures of northern Scandinavia; Collins (1937a, 1937b) had been writing about Asian elements in Eskimo culture since the 1930s; Gjessing (1944) had published his circumpolar stone age ideas; and American archeologists had begun to think about circumpolar and circumboreal contacts and diffusion (Spaulding 1946; Collins 1937b; Schuster 1951; Griffin 1953, 1960; Bryan 1957). Yamal and the lower Ob was the only location in the otherwise unknown Russian Arctic where archeology offered relevant evidence.

Since 1929 the work of Valerii Chernetsov and Wanda Moshinskaya had identified a series of archeological complexes and cultures in the lower Ob-Yamal region. One of these, the Ust-Poluy Culture or period (the usage varied), was particularly interesting since it was believed to date to the B.C./A.D. era, was an Arctic culture, and had Eskimo characteristics like semi-subterranean houses, harpoon technology, Arctic maritime faunal remains, and dog traction. Chernetsov (1974) and Mozhinskaya (1974) defined Ust-Poluy as a semi-sedentary Arctic hunting and fishing culture on the lower Ob that hunted reindeer with reindeer decoys, used dogs rather than reindeer for transport, and hunted seals and beluga with harpoons in riverine and coastal waters on a seasonal basis. While they argued strongly for the existence of Ust-Poluy as an indigenous Arctic culture (with addition of steppe elements and trade contacts to the south), their later works did not emphasize Arctic maritime adaptations, and in Chernetsov's final treatment of circumpolar issues (1970) Ust-Poluy and Yamal are barely mentioned. Only in Chernetsov's original 1935 paper is this issue raised, and only in terms of northern Yamal.

Ust-Poluy was the only tangible link between the early maritime cultures of northern Scandinavia and the White Sea and the western boundary of prehistoric Eskimo sites at the Bear Islands near the mouth of the Koly-ma River (Chard 1958). Yet from many points of view, descriptions of Ust-Poluy chronology, economy, settlement patterns, fortifications, ceremonial life, and external relationships were confusing or contradictory (for exsample Moberg 1960, 1975), and its relevance to the circumpolar discussion could be questioned. Compilation of various papers on lower Ob archeology in "The

Prehistory of Western Siberia" (Chernetsov & Mozhinskaya 1974, translated by Henry N. Michael from the original Russian edition of 1958) clarified but did not resolve many of these issues for western scholars.

The root of the issue has been Chernetsov's (1935) article "An Early Maritime Culture on the Yamal Peninsula" describing finds from his pioneering 1928-1929 survey in northern Yamal[1]. Actually, quite apart from evaluations in hindsight, this was a very fine paper indeed for a young anthropologist of his day, and re-reading it many times over continues to reap rewards. The conclusions reached, and these were actually advanced quite tentatively by the author, initially tantalized Russian Arctic scholars but remained largely unknown to western specialists because this paper was not included in Michael's 1974 edition, although reference to the Tiutey Sale sites occurs in several instances (Chernetsov & Mozhinskaya 1974:67).

Chernetsov's and Mozhinskaya's later work in the lower Ob in the 1930s, based in part on data collected by geologist V. N. Adrianov (who was purged in Salekhard in the 1930s (Krenke personal communication to Krupnik)), did nothing to confirm or deny the Ust-Poluy maritime issue and in fact failed to clarify whether the Tiutey Sale sites were part of the Ust-Poluy complex. For these reasons, the Yamal question receded in interest among Russian scholars, for whom there were more contentious issues about Ust-Poluy chronology, ethnicity, and typological relationships than its maritime or Arctic connections (Gryaznhov 1952; Mozhinskaya 1974:251-258; Shimkin 1960). Nevertheless, discussion of circumpolar issues continued (Chernetsov 1970; Lashook 1968; Mozhinskaya 1970; Simchenko 1976; Khlobystin 1982; Krupnik 1989 [1993]; Pitul'ko 1991; Golovnev 1992). Although considered in some of his other work these issues were barely referred to in Khlobystin's (1982) major synthesis of work along the Arctic coast from the Kara Sea to eastern Taimyr in the 1970s-1980s[2], possibly because these surveys produced generally negative results concerning Arctic maritime cultures and contacts.

In western literature, other than Larsen & Rainey (1948:158-161), there has been little awareness of the Siberian connection after 1948. Chard (1958) is the only archeologist who addressed the West Siberian and Yamal issue directly (see below). Seemingly unaware of Chard's publication, Moberg (1975) raised a number of questions about Ust-Poluy "cross-economy" southern contacts and called for new synthesis but did not evaluate its circumpolar connections. With all of the principals now dead, including Khlobystin, the matter of Yamal and Tiutey Sale, the "type site" for Chernetsov's Arctic maritime hypothesis, and its relationship to Ust-Poluy, remained unresolved. For westerners not conversant with Russian literature, Siberia in general and Yamal in particular remained an illusive strand of Arctic prehistory, while for Russians it seemed more illusory than illusive.

In 1994 an opportunity arose to collaborate with Russian colleagues in Yamal as part of a cultural heritage and conservation program funded by a grant from Amoco Eurasia Corporation. Working with Igor Krupnik of the Arctic Studies Center, Andrei Golovnev and Natalia Feodorova of the Urals Branch of the Russian Academy of Science, Vladimir Pitul'ko of the Institute of Material Culture Studies (formerly St. Petersburg Branch of the Institute of Archeology), and representatives of cultural and museum groups in Salekhard and Yar Sale, we have pursued a broad program of anthropological and cultural studies. This work, under the title, "Living Yamal", is now in its third year. Three research questions took prominence: evaluating the early maritime hypothesis; determining the ancient and recent history of reindeer herding; and exploring origins of modern ethnic peoples. In addition we promoted a broad range of cultural and heritage projects including museum displays, genealogical history, and educational programs for the benefit of all Yamal peoples (Golovnev 1995).

Modern Life and Culture

The study area - the Yamal-Nenets Autonomous Area - includes the lower region of the Ob River east of the northern terminus of the Ural Mountains, whose administrative center is the town of Salekhard (formerly the ancient town of Obdorsk, now in its 400th year as a Russian settlement), and extends north into the Yamal Peninsula. The latter is a 300 mile long and almost completely flat tongue of Arctic tundra, lakes, and meandering rivers between Ob Bay and Baydaratskaya Bay, extending north into the Kara Sea.

Today this area is occupied by Nenets (Samoyed), Khanty (Ostyak), and Komi peoples who share it with a large population of newcomers who are mostly ethnically Russian and Ukranian. Because of its political history as an early Gulag center, German, Baltic, and other peoples who were exiled here also contribute to the local population. However, north of Salekhard, the Nenets are the largest ethnic population (ca. 8,000) of which approximately 4,000 maintain a traditional life as nomadic reindeer herders despite the political upheavals and social and economic disruption of the 20th century (Krupnik 1996; Pika & Bogoyavlensky 1995; Osherenko 1995). These include Soviet attempts to collectivize and control their economy and movements, beginning in the 1930s; in the past 30 years, imposition in the midst of their summer reindeer pastures of massive oil and gas exploration and development; and finally, today, the collapse of the Soviet system which has left these people with little resources other than their own initiative.

The Nenets are believed to have moved into the Lower Ob and Yamal from homelands farther south and west, in the boreal forest or even forest-steppe zone. Oral history indicates they have been present in the Yamal for at least eight to ten generations, arriving probably not before the 17th century. (Prokof'yeva 1964; Golovnev 1992; Krupnik 1993:181).

In the lower Ob they encountered and to some extent merged with local Khanty, Komi, and Mansi groups who practiced intensive river fishing, hunting, and fur-trapping in the lower Ob and Ob Delta, and used a small-scale forest-type of reindeer herding. In the Yamal, which is one of the largest and most productive summer reindeer breeding pastures in all of the Russian Arctic, the Nenets replaced or assimilated a local indigenous group known in their folklore as *Sirt'ya* (or *Sikhirtya*), of whom only burial places and legends remain (Chernetsov 1935; Vasil'ev 1970, 1977). As noted by Golovnev (1992:101):

"According to [Nenets] legends, Sikhirtya lived in the underground where they "ride on dogs and herd mammoths." The places inhabited by the Sikhirtya, who are said to be ancestors of the Yaptik and Yavngad (sea hunter) clans, were called yan-tetto ("of earthern masters"), and were associated in the legends with the sea shore. Among their economic pursuits, sea mammal hunting was singled out."

Today about half of the Nenets people live a nomadic way of life, migrating 200-300 miles north and south each year from their winter camps in the northern forest fringe to summer pastures in central and northern Yamal. Their reindeer caravans, each with some 10-20 adults (joined by children after the end of the school year in June), are composed of 40-50 sleds, each drawn by 2-4 reindeer, accompanied by breeding herds of 500-1500 reindeer. The sleds are packed with the groups' entire possessions, personal materials, food, tentpoles and coverings, furniture, utensils, and other paraphernalia. Reaching central Yamal after 8-10 weeks, some groups establish base camps for the elders, women, and children near good fishing lakes, while the men proceed farther north with the herd, returning in the fall to pick up their families and head south to the forest. Other groups travel together without dispersing throughout the year. Increasingly, while parents and young men herd, children remain in the villages to go to school (September through June), where some older youth and young men also receive training in nursing and veternarian skills. While still formally designated as "brigades" as part of the government state farm or *sovkhoze* system, most groups spend much of their year outside of administrative control and at present receive little in the way of material goods from what is left of the threadbare Russian state economy in the north; and what they receive in the way of food, materials, and clothing is credited against delivery of reindeer meat to the state farms. Significant education and medical services are provided by local government administration. Recently a new cash economy has developed for the sale of reindeer antler to middlemen supplying the Asian medical trade.

Fig. 1: Khobka Vanuyto, Nenets elder, making reindeer sled at summer camp on West Seoyakha River, July 1994. (Photo by William W. Fitzhugh).

The Komi and Khanty practice another type of adaptation that may have deeper roots as a traditional way of life in the Lower Ob and Yamal region. Historically, the Komi are the most recent arrivals into the lower Ob region, where the Khanty have a deeper history (Krenke 1992; Murashko & Krenke 1996). Both today occupy semi-permanent residence places in villages, towns, and isolated hunting and fishing camps in the country and along the lower Ob and its tributaries, and in the channels of the Ob Delta. Those that still live as hunters, trappers, and fishermen use Russian-style log houses, and for summer fish camps may live in conical tents (chums) of the same type used by the Nenets throughout the year. Skin tent covers are still us use among the Nenets, and birch bark covers are seen on old abandoned Khanty sleds. Reindeer and horses are often used for transport in these activities, but Khanty do not maintain large numbers of reindeer. Both the intensive reindeer herding of the Nenets and the semi-permanent settlement patterns of the Komi and Khanty provide models for former subsistence strategies in the Lower Ob-Yamal region.

Ancient Times and Theories

From the legendary accounts of the *Sikhirtya* we have information about a people who lived on the Arctic coast in underground houses, used dogs rather than reindeer for transport, and hunted sea mammals long before the introduction of reindeer breeding. Such a description closely conforms to theoretical expectations for an early Eskimo-like culture and would agree well with Chernetsov's proposed hypothesis for an early maritime culture (Golovnev 1992).

Chernetsov's work at Tiutey Sale and Khaen Sale in 1929 was the first archeological work to be conducted in the Yamal (Chernetsov 1935, 1974:67). Near the mouth of the Tiutey River, at Tiutey Sale (in Russian *Morzhovaya*), about halfway up the west coast of Yamal, Chernetsov found the remains of three archeological sites. One was emerging from the sand dunes on the Kara Sea coast two kilometers south of Morzhovaya Cape. Another was a series of three pithouses dug into the crest of the bluff overlooking the Tiutey lagoon a kilometer from the cape on the south bank. A third was a "probable" housepit identified at the seaward end of the Cape. The dune site contained ceramics, stone tools, walrus and seal bones, but no metal and very few fox or reindeer bones. Chernetsov interpreted this as a seasonal summer camp of sea mammal hunters. The bluff site at the confluence of the Tiuteyakha and Seriyakha Rivers contained iron, bronze, and copper, together with abundant ceramics, stone, and wood artifacts, and a faunal assemblage including walrus, seal, whale, polar bear, reindeer, waterfowl, and rodents. Sea mammals, especially walrus, dominated the fauna. Permafrost conditions had preserved many of the finds, and the houses were described as pit dwellings seven meters in diameter with collapsed wood and sod roofs and ramp entryways. At the time of his visit Chernetsov found Nenets digging in one of the pits to recover copper and bronze, and other housepits were being used for trash disposal.

Chernetsov also reported finding several pithouses at a site at the northern tip of the Yamal, at Cape Khaen Sale on Malygin Strait, opposite Bel'yi Island. According to Nenets oral tradition, in the old days this was a favorite place for wild reindeer to cross to Bel'ye Island in their northern migration. Here Chernetsov found bones of seal, walrus, birds, polar bear, reindeer, and fox. The structure of some houses was still intact, and a human burial was found in one. Iron axes, iron arrowheads, a fragment of iron chain mail, a copper pot fragment, and a variety of wood and bone implements were found, including harpoon heads.

Chernetsov established a cultural sequence for these three sites based on typological comparisons to the south. At first he estimated that both the dune and bluff sites dated ca. 1000 A.D. based on ceramic and bronze ornament parallels, especially the "epaulette-like clasp of the Pyanobor type with an imprint of a bear" (Chernetsov 1935:123). However, of the two, he believed the dune site was older due to its lack of metal implements, and in later publications (Chernetsov 1974:68) he dated it by ceramics to the Iron Age without further definition. The Khaen Sale Cape site was dated to the 17th century by the typology of the iron axes and other materials. In his words:

"... we come to the conclusion that for a long period of time, various cultures existed on the Yamal Peninsula that were substantially different from the culture of modern Nentsy people, who are reindeer breeders. This culture was mainly based on sea mammal hunting and had settlements at the places that were most convenient for hunting walrus and seal....It is impossible to imagine that at some point in their existence in the Yamal, the Nentsy people lived in the pithouses, because their culture and whole way of life makes such a suggestion absurd. Being nomadic reindeer breeders, they had used totally different types of dwellings" (Chernetsov 1935:124).

Chernetsov then proceeded to recount the *Sikhirtya* legends that have been discussed by Golovnev, Vasil'ev, Lashook, and others about the existence of an earlier culture of pit-dwelling coastal sea mammal hunters who had preceded them in the Yamal.

Chernetsov's work was originally published in Russian in 1935, and his ideas about the settled life of an early sea mammal hunting culture in the Kara Sea did not become generally known in the West (though they were noticed by Scandinavians early on through a very brief French resume in Chernetsov's 1935 publication), until the appearance of Larsen and Rainey's Ipiutak report. In surveying the northern Eurasian literature for clues to the origins of Ipiutak, they cited Chernetsov's Yamal discoveries as of critical importance:

The discovery of an Eskimo-like culture so distant from the habitat of the present Eskimo is, of course, extremely significant. But Chernetsov's find contains one item which is of equal importance, a metal brooch or clasp of the Pyanobor type decorated with a bear's head held between the front legs. Its occurrence on the Yamal Peninsula indicates that the Arctic sea mammal hunters had some contact with the metal-using cultures farther to the south (Larsen & Rainey 1948:158).

In North America the search for the origins of Eskimo culture advanced substantially with Henry Collins' work on St. Lawrence Island in the 1930s. Collins' deep stratigraphic excavations revealed a sequential development of Eskimo cultures over 2,000 years in Bering Strait. But because his earliest Okvik cultures were fully "Eskimo" in nature, his work still begged the question of where these developments originated in the first place. Speculation that they lay in East Asia and Siberia rather than in Bering Strait was fueled by the belief that many of the innovations (for example armor, bow and arrow technology, metal, animal art, and so on) were of Asian origin.

A major development occurred with Larsen and Rainey's even more striking Eurasian parallels at Ipiutak. It became their opinion that Ipiutak burial ritual and shamanistic art was not just Asian-influenced, but of Asian origin (1948:157). They saw Ipiutak parallels in the first
millennium A.D. cultures of Western Siberia, especially in the lower Yenesei and Ob Rivers and northern Urals, whose peoples were familiar with bronze and iron, animal art of Permian and Ordos styles, and openwork art style. They believed these regions were the most logical places *"to search for the ancestors of the Ipiutak people"*, and that links between Ipiutak, early Alaskan Eskimo cultures, Yamal, and the Iron Age Scandinavian finds at Kjelmoy (Solberg 1909; Kleppe 1977) *"confirm our belief in an ancient circumpolar hunting culture"* (Larsen & Rainey 1948:160) of the sort proposed by Gjessing (1935, 1944, 1948, 1953).

"There can be no doubt that the finds described above are the remains of an ancient Arctic hunting culture, which at one time was probably circumpolar and of which the Eskimo cultures are the eastern branch. We have attempted to prove that the Ipiutak culture originated in Western Siberia, but whether all Eskimo-speaking peoples came from these [cultures] has yet to be decided. The Proto-Eskimo were probably reindeer hunters and fishermen who lived in the northern part of the forest zone of Eurasia and moved out to the Arctic coast in neolithic times. This movement probably occurred in Siberia, whence it spread westward to northern Scandinavia and eastward to America where we now find the Eskimo as the last survivors of an ancient circumpolar Arctic hunting culture" (Larsen & Rainey 1948:161).

Chester Chard (1958) was the first to respond critically to Larsen's and Rainey's Western Siberian Eskimo origin theory, believing that an East Asian origin for Ipiutak burial ritual, shamanism, and art was more likely, even though specific archeological comparisons were not yet available. He also questioned their supposition that early interior cultures of Siberia had moved north to the Arctic coast, developing an Arctic maritime culture that then spread west into Scandivania and east into Bering Strait and the New World. He pointed out that evidence of Eskimo culture did not extend into the East Siberian and

Laptev Sea west of Bear Islands and that maritime ecology of the central Eurasian Arctic coast was not conducive to development of intensive maritime economies. Further, he questioned the maritime hypothesis proposed by Chernetsov's for Tiutey Sale and of its importance in Ust-Poluy culture. Moberg's 1973 query (Moberg 1975) raised other issues noted above.

The latest contributions to this debate have come from discussion offered recently by Andrei Golovnev (1992) in response to Igor Krupnik's Russian publication (in 1989) of his dissertation (Krupnik 1993). Krupnik viewed the transition from Pre-Nenets to Nenets culture as a result of a complex of factors, mainly ecological, among which the onset of the Little Ice Age in the 16-18th century and increased external market influences were key factors; while Golovnev viewed the transformation from Pre-Nenets to Nenets more as an acculturative process in which the Nenets, as new arrivals in the Yamal, merged with preceding *Sikhirtya* peoples. As supporting evidence he cited oral historical data on an earlier tradition of sea mammal hunting, including of walrus, polar bear, and seals. In fact, there is nothing mutually exclusive in either view.

Yamal Archeological Survey

During July and early August of 1994 Andrei Golovnev, Sven Haakanson, Vladimir Pitul'ko, and I surveyed three regions of central and northern Yamal, assisted by helicopter support from Nadymgazprom and basecamp support from the Bovanyenkovo gas field stations and the Arctic Weather Station at Morzhovaya, north of Kharasavey (Fitzhugh 1994, 1995). This survey was part of the larger three year "Living Yamal" program developed by the Arctic Studies Center under the direction of Igor Krupnik and the author with funding from Amoco Eurasia Corporation and logistical support from Nadymgazprom[3].

We were not the first to explore the archeology of Yamal in recent years. For two years in the early 1990s a team from the Institute of History and Archeology (Ural Branch, Russian Academy of Science) excavated Yarte 6, a winter pithouse village on the Yuribei River in south-central Yamal. More recent work has been conducted here by Natalia Feodorova, Andrei Golovnev, and the author in 1995-1996. Although not yet reported, this site contained large amounts of reindeer bone from a series of pithouses similar to those described by Chernetsov from Tiutey Sale. On the basis of dendrochronology and pottery typology the age of the settlement has been determined as ca. 9th-11th century A.D. In addition to this work, an archeological survey of the lower Mordayakha River near Bovanyenkovo provided information on 20th century Nenets camps but recovered little evidence of earlier occupations. Other excavations in the vicinity of Novi Port and Yar Sale produced information on sites dating from the Neolithic to the present day, but they too remain mostly unpublished (Lashook 1968; Kosinskaya & Feodorova 1994). However, by far the most interesting work accomplished to date in Yamal is a culture contact and change study of 19th century cemetery remains excavated in 1909 by D. T. Yanovich from Khalas-Pugor, a small Khanty fishing village in the Ob Delta, conducted by Nikolai Krenke and Olga Murashko (Krenke 1992; Murashko & Krenke 1996).

Our first survey region was along the upper reaches of the Western Seoyakha River from its Neyta Lake source to the oil development at Bovanyenkovo, a distance of some 150 km. The Seoyakha drains the spine of the Yamal, in two branches, both rising in the Neyta Lakes. The West or "muddy" Seoyakha, which we surveyed, drains west through Bovanyenko to the Kara Sea, while the "clear" East Seoyakha drains east into Ob Bay. By using these routes one can, with a short portage across the Neyta Lake isthmus, cross the Yamal peninsula and reach the Yenesei without risking a boat voyage being blocked by sea ice in the passage between northern Yamal and Bel'yi Island. The Neyta route was routinely used by Russian cossacks and fur traders in the early 1600s.

During our survey we found wild animal resources almost totally lacking in the Yamal interior. Although the Seoyakha has a few fish, it is the abundance of whitefish in the nearby lakes that makes human survival possible during the summer season today. Wild reindeer were still present in Yamal during Chernetsov's visit in 1928-1929 but became extinct shortly afterward. We saw no wild reindeer. It appears that these animals are now totally absent, and we saw few signs of fox and no wolf tracks. The primary summer resource, other than fish, are molting geese, which are found in small nursing flocks on the river and in flocks of thousands on the larger lakes.

Nine Nenets camps dating to the past few decades of the 20th century were found along the West Seoyakha. These sites (Haakonson 1994) are generally placed on 20 m to 50 m above the river in places that provide some relief from thick clouds of mosquitos. They were marked by scattered remains of worked antlers, bundles of willows and alder brush gathered for firewood; fish and reindeer bone (much of the latter worked), artifacts ranging from glass beads to lawn chairs, and trash consisting of tin cans, bottles and other "outside" consumables, toys, and so on.

The ubiquitous features observed on all sites were hearth pits consisting of shallow 20 cm to 30 cm diameter circular or square depressions dug 5 cm to 10 cm through the vegetation into the sand. Each had been the central hearth of a Nenets tent. Revegetation patterns indicating differential ages permits these hearths to be assigned to various age classes and gives an indirect means for estimating occupancy duration and group size, based on numbers of chums of a given age. Sven Haakanson is studying data from these sites. In addition to his contribution to the 1994-1996 archeological projects, he has lived

and travelled with Nenets and is making important contributions to ethnography, ethno-archeology, and ritual landscape studies for his Harvard University dissertation.

Many 20th century Nenets sites also contain remains of earlier occupations dating to a time when ceramics had not been replaced by metal pots, which in central Yamal occurred around 15th-17th centuries. Charcoal, pottery, food bone, and occasionally metal artifacts were often found at sites showing enriched vegetation growth, beneath which were organic-rich deposits about 10 cm to 30 cm thick. Since these sites also contain numerous reindeer bones, they appear to be the remains of reindeer hunters or herders whose settlements had longer periods of local residence than Nenets chum camps do today. Modern Nenets camps are occupied for only a few days (or weeks if they are base camps for women, children and elders) and do not develop buried organic soil horizons. Having allocations of ca. 2,000 reindeer, such groups must move constantly to find sufficient forage. But even as recently as 1940-1950 Nenets lived in smaller groups with only a few hundred reindeer and could afford to occupy camps for longer periods of time before forage was depleted (Krupnik, personal communication). This pattern may also explain the more settled life indicated for the ceramic period sites which we found in the same areas as Nenets camps today. Charcoal from ceramic components at three of these sites, West Seoyakha 1 (Nenets 3), Tusida Hill (Nenets 4), and Ngynzito (Nenets 8) produced uncalibrated radiocarbon ages of 290+/-50 B.P., 390+/-70 B.P., and 1070+/-100 B.P. respectively (Table 1).

Our second survey was at Tiutey Sale, a prominent Cape in northwestern Yamal with a rich local marine ecology. In spring and summer months, Tiutey is visited by seals, waterfowl, walrus, polar bear, has a year-round fish resource, and is also an important summer pasture for reindeer. Among the several recent Nenets sites found on the Tiuteyakha and Seriyakha Rivers were two which also contained earlier ceramic components. One, Eryapthayakha 1, produced a radiocarbon age of 400+/-70 B.P. on charcoal. Returning to Morzhovaya Station, we relocated Chernetsov's dune and river bluff sites, but found that his Cape site with its possible pithouse had been destroyed by erosion. The Dune site was buried beneath a two meter high sand dune. Ceramics, fire-cracked rocks, and bones were present, exactly as described by Chernetsov. People must have camped here to ambush walrus and seals that even today occasionally haul out on this beach in the late summer and early fall.

Our 1994 results showed the Tiutey Sale Bluff site also conformed to Chernetsov's description, being located on the high bank overlooking the lagoon. We found the site in a final state of destruction from riverbank erosion some seventy years after Chernetsov had also noted extensive damage. Worked wood, bone, ceramics, brass and copper ornaments, charcoal, and other remains were streaming down the melting permafrost face of the melt-

Table 1. Radiocarbon Dates from the Living Yamal Project, 1994-1995 Field Seasons

Site	provenience	sample	lab no.	mat'l	identif.	BP	calib @	intercept
Nenets 8	Test Pit 1	94-2	B-79112	char	willow	1070 +/- 100	AD 770-1195	AD 990
West Seoyakha 1	Nenets 3, L1	94-9	B-79113	char	birch	290 +/-50	AD 1475-1675*	AD 1645
Seriyakha R. 2	Test Pit	94-42	B-79117	char	conif.	modern		
Eryaptayakha 1	Test pit	94-35	B-80860	char	con/will	400 +/- 70	AD 1415-1655	AD 1470
Tousida Hill	L4, south ridge	94-46	B-80861	char	bir/con?	390 +/- 70	AD 1420-1655	AD 1475
Tiutey Sale 1	eroding bank	94-13	B-79114	char	conif.	1480 +/-60	AD 440-665	AD 605
Tiutey Sale 1	Test Pit 1	94-25	B-79115	char	conif.	790 +/- 60	AD 1165-1300	AD 1260
Tiutey Sale 1	L1, timber	94-29	B-79116	char	larch	1370 +/- 50	AD 615-770	AD 665
Tiutey Sale 1	L1, Sq.4a, fl. 1	95-1	B-91284	char	conif.	1640 +/- 50	AD 330-550	AD 420
Tiutey Sale 1	L1, Sq.4a, fl. 2	95-2	B-91285	char	conif.	770 +/- 90	AD 1040-1400	AD 1270
Tiutey Sale 1	L1, H3 floor	95-3	B-91286	char	conif.	1450 +/- 50	AD 540-670	AD 630
Tiutey Sale 1	L2, 26W/16S#	95-4	B-91287	char	conif.	1230 +/- 60	AD 670-970	AD 790
Tiutey Sale 2	Sq.3	95-5	B-91288	char	conif.	540 +/- 60	AD 1300-1455	AD 1415
Yarte 6	Sq. 1, L6	95-6	B-91289	wood	hrdwd$	890 +/- 70	AD 1010-1275	AD 1175

@ Stuiver and Becker calibration program (University of Washington Quaternary Isotope Laboratory, version 1.3); all ranges are 2 sigma and means are intercept point.
* Additional calibration ranges are AD 1775-1800 and AD 1945-1950.
# L2C hearth
$ hardwood twigs: willow, heather, alder, birch, and bark fragments

ing mud cliff from one-meter thick cultural deposits buried beneath the sod above. One of these sod blocks contained part of a ceramic cricible, indicating that even at this far northern location, Tiutey people were producing metalwork, apparently with charcoal produced from driftwood, which is found here in abundance. The presence of axe-cut logs and buried cultural deposits one meter below the surface in the Locality 1 cut suggested buried house structures, and at Locality 2 a test pit in the middle of a shallow depression six meters in diameter was found to contain a 10 cm to 20 cm level of frozen cultural deposit containing masses of cut wood debitage, ceramics, charcoal, and bone. This feature certainly was a house pit. Walrus, seal, polar bear, reindeer and other animal bones were recovered. (Later, in 1995, Feodorova's excavations recovered similar fauna but failed to find evidence of harpoons or any other evidence of maritime technology (Feodorova 1996)). Radiocarbon ages of 1480+/-60 B.P. and 1370+/-50 B.P. were returned from samples taken from the L-1 eroding bank in 1994, and another of 790+/-60 B.P. from the L-2 house pit floor described above. The amount of wood and bone, the large numbers of artifacts, and the depth of the floor deposits all suggested a multi-house settlement, whose economic focus was primarily sea mammal hunting, although small amounts of fox, reindeer (wild or domestic), and waterfowl bones were also present.

It appears that Tiutey Sale Bluff site contains several sequential occupations of different ages. According to Chernetsov, Nenets were using the house pits for dumps or caches in the 1920s. Judging from the presence of a fresh reindeer skull on the surface during our visit, present-day Nenets herders continue to use the site for ritual sacrifices and have been observed in this practice at the Cape by the Morzhovaya Weather Station personnel. While they used to stay here to hunt walrus for extended periods in the 19th century to the early 20th century, as shown by faunal remains and boat parts at historic period Nenets camps, they no longer do so today because walrus are so rare as to be unobtainable. However, within the main archeological deposit a sequence of pithouse constructions over a several hundred year period between 6th-9th century A.D. is evident. Faunal remains indicate a mixed marine mammal and terrestrial subsistence of certain spring thru fall residence; but it is difficult to establish the fact of winter residency because there are few indicator species on which this determination can be made, and results of reindeer antler and teeth sectioning are not yet complete. The middens are composed of masses of wood chips and grass, rather than bone-rich deposits, that could mark relatively brief occupations. By contrast, middens found in north Scandinavian and North American and East Siberian Sea maritime sites contain masses of bone in greasy black middens.

The question of reindeer economy at Tiutey Bluff remains difficult to assess until the completion of Feodorova's report. A few reindeer remains were found in our 1994 survey and 1995 excavations, as well as training harness parts (Feodorova 1996), so domestic animals were present, but probably not in numbers needed for a domesticated food source. The small numbers of these remains might suggest that reindeer were hunted using tame

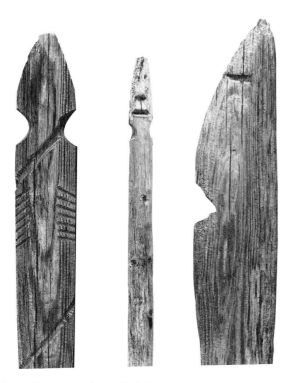

Fig. 3: Representations of siadeis, or helpingspirits, found at Drovyanoy 3 chache dating about late 1930s.
(Courtesy of Yar Sale Museum; photo by Adelaide de Menil).

decoy reindeer. There is no indication of a major dependence on hunted reindeer occurred at the interior site, Yarte 6, which contained masses of reindeer bones. It would appear that the Tiutey Sale people kept small numbers of animals for transport or use as decoys but depended for primary sustenance on marine products. Tiutey Bluff people certainly did not have large herds and cannot have practiced an intensive settlement and subsistence herding system of the Nenets type of ca. 17th-20th centuries. It is possible that the abandomment of the Tiutey Sale marine-oriented subsistence and settlement system resulted from decline of marine mammal populations, especially of walrus and polar bear, in the Kara Sea as market-oriented commercial hunting expanded in the late Viking and medieval period (Hofstra & Samplonius 1995). Excavations conducted with Feodorova, Golovnev, Haakanson and others in 1995 (Feodorova 1996; Fitzhugh 1995) will produce a definitive published work on the "last remains" of this important site in the near future.

Our radiocarbon dates from both the 1994-1995 seasons now show the chronology of the Seoyakha and Tiutey Sale sites (with their ceramics, subsurface house pits, mixed maritime and terrestrial economy, including, possibly, limited reindeer herding) to fall into the period 500-

1700 A.D. Only after this date does the ethnographic Nenets pattern of fully nomadic, large-scale reindeer herding become established, as stated by Krupnik (1977, 1993) based on his analysis of historical records. Chernetsov's ideas for a Tiutey Sale Bluff site at ca. 1000 A.D. is within the range of our radiocarbon date ranges for this site, ca. 5th-12th century A.D.; but our radiocarbon date for the dune site, ca. 1300-1400 A.D., conflicts with Chernetsov's 1935 views based on ceramics. Further work is needed here, as this site has barely been tested to date.

Our last survey location was at Drovyanoy Factoria [trading post] at the northeastern tip of the Yamal Peninsula. Here we found different kinds of archeological sites. The most recent and dramatic was a Russian radar base that had been abandoned precipitously by the military in 1991, with everything left intact. This became our 'luxurious' home. On the south side of the stream was the ruin of a Russian trading post dating to the early 1900s. A kilometer to the south along the north side of a small stream we found numerous mid-late 20th century Nenets camps. And several hundred meters west of the military post, we recovered the remains of a Nenets cache consisting of a tool or work box containing a 3-kopek coin pendant dated 1934. The remains included three carved wood *siadeis*, or helping spirits, ornaments and jewelry, fragments of glass, cloth, odd-shaped mineral-bearing rocks, a polar bear tooth, and other materials, including a tin figure of a person and miniature bows and arrows made of wire. The materials appear to have been left purposefully and may represent a shaman's death cache. To Golovnev, some of these artifacts suggested Khanty or Mansi styles more than Nenets. This collection (Golovnev 1995) has been donated to the Yar Sale District Museum in the town of Yar Sale in southern Yamal and will be described in an English publication in the future.

The presence of polar bear bones and teeth at Yamal ritual sites, even ones far from the coast, suggests the former importance of these animals in the ritual life of Nenets, who today rarely, if ever, hunt or encounter them during their summer herding cycle. Another important feature of 20th century Nenets settlement patterns was the presence at or far removed from dwelling sites, of many sacred sites and burials containing sacrificed reindeer remains, ritual deposits of vodka bottles, sacred power stones, and other ritual paraphernalia. It is clear from these remains, scattered everywhere throughout the country, that Nenets continue to see themselves as inhabiting a highly sacrilized landscape whose geographic dimensions are physically marked by ritual behavior. The common presence of polar bear skulls and teeth indicates the continuing importance of an Arctic marine component in ideology if not in contemporary subsistence, now that sea mammal hunting is no longer actively practiced by Nenets, as it was in earlier days. Vestiges of a formerly more intensive hunting life, including maritime hunting, still exists in the life of modern Nenets from the Seoya-kha village region and at other locations in northern Yamal where groups of Nenets remain in the North, some tending herds, some hunting during the winter, while others travel south with their herds (Dektor 1996). Finally, symbolic and real human burials in sacred sleds with sacrificed reindeer and the person's personal possessions were frequently encountered in our Yamal surveys. These sites, especially the larger cemeteries on the main migration routes, continue to be used by Nenets today. Full results of our Yamal surveys and excavations are being prepared for publication, together with historical, ethnographic, and cultural studies, as part of the "Living Yamal" project with Feodorova, Golovnev, and Krupnik.

An East Kara Sea Survey

In August of 1994 our field team was picked up at Drovyanoy Cape by a Russian hydrographic ship *Jacob Smirnitskii* on which we spent the next four weeks conducting surveys in the Kara Sea whenever we could convince the crew to let us ashore. We surveyed portions of Shokalski Island, selected regions of the lower Yenesei, and Zveroboy Island off the mouth of the Pyasina River. Very little of archeological interest was found along these low and rapidly eroding shores. Our voyage took us to the western end of Vilkitski Straits at the northern tip of Taimyr, where our vessel, under contract with Texas A and M University, became beset in thick ice. Eventually we were placed in tow by the Russian nuclear-powered icebreaker *Vaigach*, which attempted to force a passage through Vilkitski Strait to the ice-free Laptev Sea, but our propeller was damaged by ice, and we were forced to turn back, leaving our aspirations for a Laptev Sea survey for a future date.

Despite its lack of tangible results, the survey produced interesting conclusions bearing on circumpolar archeology, several of which are briefly noted here:

(1) As stated by Bogoras (1929) and repeated by Chard, *"the Arctic coast of Siberia between (roughly) the Kolyma and the Ob is unsuited for sea-mammal hunting and of little use to humans, in marked contrast to the American Arctic ... none of the historical inhabitants of this area, such as the Yukagir and Yakut, make any use of the sea, ... the population of the coastal zone, such as it is, centers on the rivers. The northern part of the vast Taimyr Peninsula, for instance, is completely uninhabited"* (Chard 1958:84). In fact, they are biological unproductive zones, with shallow, turbid, largely brackish water and have few fish or marine mammals. Similar observations have been made by others (Lashook 1968:192; Kosarev 1984:80; Golovnev 1992:96). Wild reindeer occasionally visit some of these coastal regions and islands, and we encountered a group of 6-8 animals on Zveroboy Island. We also saw large numbers of wild reindeer migrating south in scattered groups along the east bank of the Yenesei at ca.

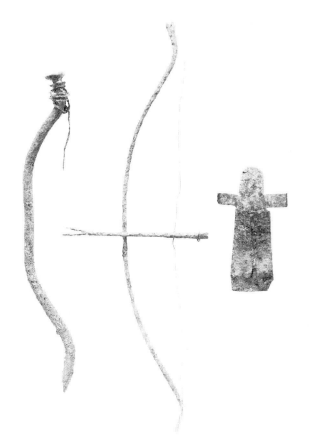

Fig. 4: Sheet iron image of shaman and shaman's iron nail bows and arrow from Drovyanoy 3 cache. (Courtesy of Yar Sale Museum; photo by Adelaide de Menil).

latitude 71° North, north of Noril'sk. The other major summer resource of this region is whitefish, many species of which can be caught in large numbers in the rivers and lakes. Foxes, geese, ducks, and a variety of raptors were also noted during our helicopter flight between Dikson and Noril'sk. It is difficult without archeological evidence to ascertain the degree to which these conditions may also have existed in the past, for Russian expansion (northern sea route, industrialization, and so on) may have had a negative impact on the ecology of even this northernmost region. Nevertheless, there is good reason to believe that the Taimyr coast represents the nadir of marine biological potential in the Russian Arctic when viewed from the perspective of the more productive Barents and Chukchi Sea regions.

(2) No recent ethnographic camps were noted, except on Shokolskii Island, where a Nenets family lived, subsisting on the local wild reindeer herd, earlier in the 20th century.

(3) Historic and modern use of these coastal regions is largely for fox trapping and hunting by the "Old Settlers" of Pomor origin of the predominately European Russian Arctic.

(4) Driftwood is a major resource along the Kara Sea coast and islands, and is delivered in huge quantities yearly by the Ob, Yenesei, Pyasina and other large north-flowing rivers. That this driftwood was a crucial necessity for life on the treeless Russian Arctic tundra coast is seen by its massive presence at Zhokov Island in the northern Laptev Sea (Pitul'ko 1993).

(5) No traces of ceramic or earlier sites were found during our brief passage along the Arctic coast of the Yamal. Nor does it appear likely that there was ever much occupation of these coasts, at least in recent millennia, because of the low volume of resources and scarcity of marine mammals. Rather, it appears that riverine fishing and interior hunting and herding in the country extending as far north as the forest edge, provided the primary economic opportunities during recent times.

(6) The severe erosion of the low frozen mud coasts of the Kara Sea, which are undergoing submergence today and probably have been for millennia, militates against site preservation in these areas. Prospects of discovering archeological sites of coastal peoples dating before the past 1500 years here are poor. On the other hand, Neolithic sites such Khaodimka near Yar Sale in southern Yamal, and others reported by Khlobystin (1982), Pitul'ko (1991) and others from Vaigach in the West Kara Sea, dating from the Neolithic to the present, are known, giving hope that more intensive survey may eventually provided a larger database. At present, other than at unique situations like Zhokov Island (Pitul'ko 1993), evidence for Mesolithic and early Neolithic occupations of the central Russian Arctic coast is lacking.

Early Yamal

The data gathered in our brief survey of the Yamal points toward a final resolution of the debate over the Chernetsov proposal, an idea that both he and other Russian archeologists of his era also acknowledged as having been a provisional hypothesis. The question now is not whether early inhabitants of the Yamal hunted sea mammals, for it is clear from Tiutey Sale and other sites that they did; it is rather the extent of maritime adaptation achieved, the season period of use, the duration of occupancy on the coast, and the type of technology and adaptation employed (Golovnev 1992:97). A separate but related issue is the question of early Holocene sites: whether in earlier Holocene times with higher sea levels and more moderate climate there may have existed a more bountiful maritime ecology with corresponding cultural development in the central Russian Arctic. The latter topic cannot be addressed here but needs consideration.

Previous theories of Pre-Nenets settlement patterns cover a wide range of potentialities. Chernetsov (1935) believed people remained in northern Yamal throughout the year, living in pithouses and hunting marine mammals

from sites like Tiutey Sale during the winter and fall, spending summers hunting and fishing on the interior. Lashook (1968:192) proposed a settlement model with coastal residence based on marine hunting in the fall. Golovnev (1992) proposed settlement throughout the year in northern Yamal, with summer hunting of marine mammals and winter fishing and reindeer hunting on the interior. Mozhinskaya (1953:82,101) and Krupnik (1981:71; 1989:181) proposed a dual model that had groups of northern settlers residing permanently in the north hunting marine mammals and reindeer at suitable locations, while migratory hunter/herders hunted at the coast only during the summer after their herds had arrived in these regions.

Our 1994 data provide broader archeological support for earlier conclusions by Russian archeologists (Chernetsov 1935; Lashook 1968) and ethnologists (Vasil'ev and Dolgikh) indicating that the "Pre-Nenets" peoples of Yamal dating to ca. AD 500-1700 were not intensive, migratory reindeer herders like the historic Nenets. Rather, finds at Tiutey Sale and the early components found along the Seoyakha suggest a more settled way of life that involved shallow pithouse structures and longer periods of occupation, possibly including winter camps, at advantageous fishing and reindeer hunting sites. In addition to interior hunting and fishing, marine mammal hunting and acquisition of other seasonal maritime resources was conducted seasonally, but in a far less intensive way than occurred at Eskimo sites or Younger Stone Age and Iron Age sites in northern Scandinavia. Tiutey Sale site midden depth is shallow and bone concentrations are low compared to even lightly-used coastal sites from other Arctic regions, and there is no evidence of specialized maritime hunting technology like toggling harpoons. It seems likely that most sea mammals hunted in early times at Tiutey Sale were clubbed at beach haul-out sites or taken from boats with spears and clubs, since no barbed harpoons have been found in our excavations. In fact, the Tiutey Sale technology seems more terrestrial than maritime. However, even in the early 20th century Nenets hunted marine mammals and fished with lap-straked wood boats off Tiutey Sale, as indicated in the diaries and photographs of Vladimir Evladov who visited this region in 1928-1929 (Evladov 1992). Remains of their boats are still found here on the beaches and in coastal Nenets sites. Whether decline of sea mammal populations or intensification of reindeer herding resulted in elimination of this component of the Nenets subsistence base, or both, is still open to discussion. However, history and Nenets tradition tells of groups of Nenets herders who were forced to abandon herding by the loss of their animals and survived with small numbers of transport or decoy reindeer as hunters, fishermen, and trappers, living in locations where animal resources permitted. Such a life would produce an archeological record like that noted at Tiutey and at the Seoyakha ceramic period sites. For this reason it seems necessary to caution against allowing the intensive herding life of modern Nenets people to serve as the only model of even recent cultural adaptations in the Yamal region. A more diversified economy and settlement pattern is indicated even in oral history, Russian records, 17th century archeological remains, and photographs. As Krupnik and Golovnev have concluded (Krupnik 1977/ 1993:183; Golovnev 1992:99) local extermination of the wild reindeer (which is a common consequence of intensified reindeer economies) and decimation of marine mammals by commercial hunting may have made year-round occupation by small "hunter" groups impossible in northern Yamal, effectively forcing most Nenets people into the "all-or-nothing" intensive migratory pattern known today.

These conditions could account for two alternative pre-17th century reconstructions:
(1) a specialized sea mammal hunting culture with permanent year-round residence in northern Yamal at sites like Tiutey Sale at which these resources were concentrated, with summer reindeer hunting and fishing on the interior (the Chernetsov/Golovnev perspective); or
(2) a dual economy in which some parts of a local group tended small reindeer herds as they migrated between the forest and northern Yamal, while others maintained a sedentary life hunting sea mammals and land game in northern Yamal (the Mozhinskaya/Krupnik perspective).

In either case, it is certain that both domestic and wild reindeer existed in the Yamal prior to 1700 A.D. and that the Early- or Pre-Nenets residence pattern was more sedentary than the modern Nenets pattern; was composed of smaller numbers of tents and individuals, for example 2-3 dwellings per camp; and occurred at locations that continued to be used by Nenets on coast and interior but were rarely reoccupied for more than a single season. Radiocarbon dates suggest that this early, more diversified adaptation continued for more than a millennium prior to the beginning of historical records ca. 1500 A.D. Chernetsov's and Golovnev's views of a permanent maritime-based culture during medieval times in northern Yamal is not supported by our 1994 archeological evidence or by Feodorova's 1995 Tiutey Sale excavations.

The historical and ethnographic information presented by Vasil'ev, Golovnev, and others about sea mammal hunting by early Nenets peoples in northern Yamal raises the possibility that the contrast between the late historic Nenets (that is migratory reindeer herding) adaptation and the more economically-diverse life of "Pre-Nenets" people may be over-drawn. Early Nenets (that is small group herders and hunters) moving into northern Yamal may have adopted sea mammal hunting from an earlier population or may have merged with another ethnic group with local experience in sea mammal hunting. Thus Nenets may have balanced their more specialized herding pattern with a sea mammal hunting component that provided them with products like ivory, blubber, skins, and thong, materials that had great value not only to their herding brethren but to the external southern markets upon which the Siberian "metal age" was increasingly dependent. Cast bronze ornaments and ritual objects of ancient traditional pattern have been an important part of lower Ob and Yamal cultural life from 2,000-3,000 years ago virtually until the present day (Feodorova 1994) and are found at cemeteries and in many ritual and sacred sites. In any case we need to be wary of over-reliance on the modern Nenets ethnographic model. Thus we find our current preliminary conclusions in relative agreement with a recent assessment by Pitul'ko (1991:30), who reported:

"Krupnik distinguishes two variants of maritime hunting in the West Arctic: the culture of settled hunters, and the seasonal hunting of the nomadic tribes of the tundra (Krupnik 1989:181). Archeological results, however, show that the Far Northeast of Russia in Europe and the northern parts of West Siberia never attained a level permitting the formation of settled maritime cultures. It is more probable that, throughout the history of the area, mari time hunting was mainly seasonal, and correspondingly less successful ... It is clearly obvious that indigenous maritime hunting never resulted in the formation of settled cultures, similar for example to those of the Eskimos."

However, I do not believe, like Krupnik and Pitulko, that the decline of maritime hunting in the West Russian Arctic can be linked primarily to ecological effects of the Little Ice Age. Rather I would put the emphasis (which they consider to be secondary forces) on market effects resulting from commercial sea mammal hunting and the intensification of reindeer herding that brought with it the destruction of the wild reindeer stocks that would have been critical to the survival of the coastal-dwellers may have been equally important if not dominant in this process.

Most "Eskimologists" now agree that the 'holy grail' of circumpolar archeology is not likely to be found in the Ob-Yamal or trans-Ural region but closer to the current Eskimo homeland in Northeastern Siberia or along the North Pacific or Bering Sea coast.

The Arctic Sea Hunting Cultures

The new Yamal data contribute a new perspective to the on-going discussion about circumpolar culture contacts and relationships, in several ways. First, it needs to be pointed out that Chernetsov never intended his Tiutey hypothesis, based on survey data only, to assume the status of a fully-developed argument for early Eskimo-like cultures in northern Yamal. And although he developed the "Eskimo" connection carefully, citing features from early historical accounts, geneaological and linguistic data, oral history and folklore, ecology, and archeological data noted above, he never repeated it in later publications, probably upon reconsideration of the evidence. The Tiutey bluff site was already badly damaged and many of the finds were from eroded surface deposits. The same circumstances obtained at the beach site. Even with completion of our recent excavations it is difficult to make categorical statements about the bluff site from the limited data available. That Chernetsov failed to include Tiutey as part of the Ust-Poluy complex and never elaborated his claims for its Arctic maritime status also argues for moderation in critiquing the maritime hypothesis in what was one of his earliest - and excellently reasoned - professional papers. Rather more attention should be given to Larsen and Rainey as promoters of Chernetsov's early views in their forceful argument for Ipiutak contacts.

Second, Russian data discussed by Krupnik, Khlobystin, Shumkin, Pitul'ko, and others concerning maritime culture developments in Kola and the West Siberian Arctic zone indicate that this region saw its greatest maritime culture specialization during the early metal culture period about 4,000-3,000 years ago, with subsequent decline attributed by most specialists to climatic cooling and ecological change after that (Pitul'ko 1991:24). There is some belief that maritime specialization may have roots in even earlier times. Khlobystin's (1982) data for Taimyr does not include maritime features, and data for the Laptev and East Siberian Seas are lacking or poorly known until the appearance of Eskimo-related sites about 1,000-1,500 years ago. Whether or not earlier maritime cultures could have existed is an open question, but is unlikely except in conjunction with reindeer hunting, as indicated at Zhokov, an 8,000 year old Mesolithic site in the northern Laptev Sea (Pitul'ko 1993).

Today a thorough review of Larsen and Rainey's views is both needed and overdue. Their suggestion of trans-Uralian and Permian stylistic ties, citing Tallgren's work primarily, may still be partially correct from an art-stylistic point of view, although it now seems unlikely that a Tiutey Sale or Ust-Poluy culture connection was the mechanism for dispersal; and certainly this dispersal must have been through culture contacts rather than by a migration of Arctic-adapted people from the Ob and Kara Sea to Beringia. It is here that Spaulding's (1946) departure from Gjessing's circumpolar diffusion route has a distinct advantage (see also Bryan 1957; Simonsen 1972). Considering the suggested biological impoverishment of the Central Siberian high Arctic coast and waters, contacts would have been more likely to have occurred along the northern forest fringe or mainland river valleys (Taimyr) where the hunting of wild reindeer and lake and river fishing provided a more stable subsistence base, as well as forest shelter. A second channel in this diffusion zone might have existed in the steppes to the south, where animal-style art occurs across great distances from the Black Sea to Mongolia and northern China. The distribution of Siberian shamanism and its artistic trappings, animal-style art, the use of death masks known from Eastern Asia, and other elements of Asian spiritu-alism and technology (armor, bow technology) must then have reached Bering Strait through various channels along the North East Asian/Russian Pacific coastline.

During a recent Fulbright research visit to the Smithsonian, Natalia Feodorova, my Yamal partner in archeology and a specialist on later prehistory of the trans-Ural region, lectured on the Uralic Bronze and Iron Age traditions to art historians of the Freer Gallery of Asian Art. Her presentation was illustrated with numerous examples of cast bronze figures and ornaments found throughout the northern and central Urals and Ob Basin (Feodorova 1994) dating to the last 2,000 years. None of this material was considered by the Freer experts as related in any significant way with the Scythian or East Asian animal style art traditions.

This is not the place to evaluate these broader issues, but to note that when very little was known about archeology of eastern Siberia and Asia, Larsen and Rainey led a way toward new understanding of northern cultures. While they probably attached too much attention to Arctic coast distribution, they envisioned the spread of concepts through art, ritual, and belief systems as sub-components of northern cultures and thus reoriented former arguments of circumpolar culture theory away from the study of comparative technology and adaptation, which had been emphasized previously by Gjessing and perhaps overly-so also in my own work (Fitzhugh 1974, 1975a, 1975b). Certainly, the appearance of Ipiutak does not result from a migration of Asians into Alaska from the Yamal or the Urals, as hypothesized by Larsen and Rainey but results from processes of culture contact and exchange of ideas, beliefs, and artistic and ritual practices with Asia, facilitated by small-scale movements of people bearing a pan-Siberian shamanistic complex like that recovered at Ipiutak.

Yamal is therefore an instructive case in the history of circumpolar archeological thought, for it points out the need for sharing and publication of archeological materials and the pitfalls of isolation and reliance on secondary or preliminary reports. From today's perspective the emphasis on Uralic prototypes for Ipiutak ritual imagery seems somewhat far-fetched considering the lack of detailed data from crucial intervening regions of Eastern Siberia and northern China and Mongolia, where early elements of Eskimo art seem likely to be found as Chard has consistently argued. On the other hand, it appears that East Asian elements such as animal-style and transformation art appear strongest in the Okvik and Old Bering Sea Traditions, whereas trans-Siberian shamanistic art and paraphernalia seem more closely connected to the Ipiutak ritual complex. If the later should prove to be linked to boreal and Arctic complexes, and Okvik/OBS to the Western Pacific/East Asian complexes this would not be too surprising given the geographic distribution of these cultures (Gerlach & Mason 1992). After so much attention to early cultural developments in the Lena basin by Yuri

Mochanov, Svetlana Fedoseeva, and others, it would now be instructive to pay more attention to the last 5,000 years of time here and in the Okhotsk-Amur region where parts of our "grail" may be found.

This paper suggests it would be more profitable to turn our attention to southern contacts to find the formative and transformative features of Central Russian Arctic cultures, as envisioned by the later works of Chernetsov and Mozhinskaya, Khlobystin, Pitul'ko, Feodorova, and others like Larsen and Rainey, Spaulding, Chard, Griffin, Moberg, to investigate cultural processes between the Arctic and Subarctic or steppe regions. In the Eurasian Arctic, especially in its central Siberian zone between the Yenesei and the Lena rivers, Arctic coasts are not likely to be east-west highways that they have been in Beringia and the North American Arctic. Food and driftwood, two scarce necessities for Arctic life from the Indigirka to the White Sea, are found in the river systems and deltas, and its seems unlikely that lateral contacts across the central Siberian Arctic coast ever had formative roles in the distribution of cultures or cultural elements following the classic circumpolar model. This does not mean that early peoples may not have developed ingenious adaptations to high Arctic conditions, as evidenced by the Zhokov Island site, a reindeer and polar bear hunting site dating 8000 B.P. (Pitul'ko 1993). Living in driftwood dwellings hundreds of miles from the forest at the edge of the continental shelf near is not what one would imagine of Mesolithic hunters. Strange things also seem to have happened also to mammoths on Wrangel Island (Vartanyan & others 1993). And who can say if bones of Scottish highland cattle will not be found at Igloolik or Thule.

Fig. 5: 1994 Yamal survey team (left to right): Vladimir Pitul'ko, Andrei Golovnev, Sven Haakanson, William W. Fitzhugh.

Acknowledgments

This work has been conducted by the Smithsonian's Arctic Studies Center in collaboration with the Institute of History and Archeology (Ural Branch) of the Russian Academy of Science, with support from Amoco Eurasia and their Russian partners, Nadym Gazprom, the Rock Foundation, and the Smithsonian. I thank James Quigel of Amoco Eurasia corporation for the faith he had in Krupnik's "Living Yamal" proposal, and the personnel of Amoco's Nadym field office for support and assistance; Vladimir Penkin and Rustam Zakiev of Nadymgazprom for their logistics support and hospitality; and Adelaide de Menil and Ted Carpenter and the Rock Foundation which provided crucial support for the *Jacob Smirnitski* cruise, together with cruise organizer James Brooks of the Geochemical and Environmental Research Group (GERG) of Texas A&M University. I especially want to thank my collaborators for the opportunity to be able to undertake exciting work in a new field area, in Russia. I could not have asked or hoped for a more generous, congenial, or dedicated team. Sven Haakanson has assisted the author in so many ways since the inception of "Living Yamal" that he must be specially acknowledged, and he has contributed valuable suggestions to this paper. As a near constant field companion, translator, and stimulating friend and colleague, he has greatly enriched my experiences as a neophyte Russian fieldworker. The same has to be said of Andrei Golovnev, who initiated me into the Yamal world in 1994 with his characteristic skill and elan. His knowledge and travel experience in Yamal is legendary, and he has been an colleague with whom I have spent many fascinating and entertaining hours during the 1994 and 1995 field seasons. Two others must also be mentioned. Natalia Feodorova assumed the lion's share of organizing the 1995 and 1996 archeological expeditions in Yamal. Those field seasons were as pleasurable as they were scientifically rewarding and gave me a chance to learn esoteric Russian field techniques (for example *grieby* cleaning) first-hand. Vladimir Pitul'ko has also taught me much about Russian Arctic archeology over the past several years, in Yamal, on *Jacob Smirnitski*, and in Antonov-2's. I have come to respect the fine accomplishments of Russian archeologists (far too little known in the West) even though I have not been able to learn from their literary work directly due to my minuscule capacity in Russian language. Natalia also bore the brunt of my nasty brush with tularemia in Yamal in 1996. Finally I owe the greatest debt to my co-Director of "Living Yamal" Igor Krupnik, whose genius for organization and unparalleled knowledge of the Russian Arctic studies has made this program a delight to be associated with. Krupnik's and Pitul'ko's careful reading and contributions to an earlier version of this manuscript also made an indelible mark, for which I am grateful, as always.

An earlier version of this paper co-authored with Sven Haakanson, was presented at the Alaskan Anthropological Association meetings in Anchorage in March 1995.

This paper is dedicated to the Danish scholars who have, for more than two centuries, been leaders in developing the field of "Eskimology" and circumpolar studies, not only in Greenland but throughout all regions of the Arctic. In a more personal way, Jørgen, I wish to acknowledge your encouragement and stimulation since the very start of my career, when we crossed paths with my request for information about your 1956 fieldwork at Eskimo Island in Hamilton Inlet, Labrador, and your informative reply of 5 March 1968. Since then, your introductions to Danish and other Scandinavian scholars, your family's always gracious hospitality, and the visit of a Meldgaard of the Morten variety for a season of archeological work in northern Labrador with me in 1980, have enriched my life and career. Nakumik!

Notes

(1) English translation by Ludmila Bonnichson on file at Arctic Studies Center, for inclusion in "Classics of Yamal Anthropology" to be published as part of the "Living Yamal" project.

(2) Khlobystin's "The Archaeology of Taimyr and the Problems of the Origins of Archaeological Cultures of the Eurasian Far North" (1982), has been translated into English with the assistance of Vladimir Pitulko, Leonid B. Vishnyatsky, Knut Helskog, and others and is being edited for publication by the Arctic Studies Center at the Smithsonian.

(3) The "Living Yamal" program has been organized as a joint American-Russian partnership to explore the heritage and cultures of the Yamal region. Originally planned by Igor Krupnik, the author, and Andrei Golovnev, in 1993, the program later expanded to include a number of other American and Russian researchers including Sven Haakanson, Vladimir Pitulko, David Dektor, Alexander Pika, Natalia Feodorova, Bruce Forbes, and others. Feodorova and the author conducted two major archeological expeditions, in 1995 to excavate the Tiutey Sale and Yarte 6 sites and in 1996 to survey the lower Ob Delta region and continue excavations at Yarte 6. Krupnik has organized work on Yamal ethnohistory, ethnography, and museology. Funding and logistics for many of these projects have been provided by Amoco Eurasia Corporation and Nadymgazprom in an effort to mitigate the impact of oil and gas development on the cultures, peoples, and archeological resources of Yamal.

William W. Fitzhugh, Arctic Studies Center, Department of Anthropology, Smithsonian Institution, Washington D.C. 20560, USA

References

Bogoras, Waldemar [1929]: **Elements of the culture of the circumpolar zone.** *American Anthropologist*, 31(4): 579-601 (Menasha, Wis.: American Anthropologist Society).

Bryan, Alan [1957]: **Results and interpretations of recent archeological research in Western Washington with circum-boreal implications.** *Davidson Journal of Anthropology*, 3(1):1-16 (*: *).

Chard, Chester [1958]: **The western roots of Eskimo culture.** pp: 2:20-27 in "Actas del XXXIII Congresso Internacional de Americanistas", San Jose, Costa Rica, 20-27 July, 1958. * p. (Costa Rica: *) (reprinted in Shimkin, "Western Siberian Archaeology").

Chernetsov, Valeri N. [1935]: **An Early maritime culture on the Yamal Peninsula**. *Sovetskaya Etnografiya*, 4-5:109-133 (*: *) (in Russian); English translation by Ludmila Bonnichson on file at Arctic Studies Center.

Chernetsov, Valeri N. [1970]: **On the question of the ancient substratum in the cultures of the circumpolar region.** pp:260-267 in "Selected Papers of the VIIth International Congress of Anthropological and Ethnological Sciences, 1964", editor: *, *, * p. (Moscow: Nauka).

Chernetsov, Valeri N. [1974]: **The Early History of the Lower Ob Region.** *Translations from Russian Sources*, 9:1-74, editor: Henry N. Michael, original in: V. N. Chernetsov & W. Mozhinskaya: "The Prehistory of Western Siberia", 377 p. (Montreal/London: Arctic Institute of North America/McGill-Queen's University Press).

Collins, Henry B. [1937a]: **Archeology of St. Lawrence Island, Alaska.** *Smithsonian Miscellaneous Collections*, 96(1):*-* (Washington: National Museum of the USA).

Collins, Henry B. [1937b]: **Culture migrations and contacts in the Bering Sea region.** *American Anthropologist*, 39(3):375-384 (Menasha, Wis.: American Anthropologists Society).

Collins, Henry B. [1951]: **The origin and antiquity of the Eskimo.** *Smithsonian Institution Annual Report for 1950*:423-467 (Washington DC: Smithsonian Institution).

Crantz, David [1767]: **The history of Greenland: containing a description of the country, and its inhabitants; and particularly, a relation of the mission carried on for above these thirty years by the Unitas Fratrum, at New Herrnhut and Lichtenfels, in that country.** 2 vols. * p. & * p. (London: Printed for the Brethren's Society for the Furtherance of the Gospel among the Heathen, & sold by J. Dodsley).

Dawkins, Boyd [1874]: **Cave hunting. Research on the Evidence of Caves Respecting the Inhabitants of Europe.** * p. (London: MacMillan and Company).

Dektor, David [1996]: **Nenets in Yamal: opportunities in cultural continuity and preservation of tradition.** 29 page manuscript in Russian at Arctic Studies Center.

DeLaguna, Frederica [1932-1933]: **A comparison of Eskimo and Paleolithic art.** *American Journal of Archaeology*, 36(4):477-511; 37(1):77-107 (*: *).

Evladov, Vladimir P. [1992]: **Across the Yamal tundra to the Byel'yi Island. An expedition to northern Yamal in 1928-1929**. [in Russian] Editor: Alexander Pika, * p. (Tyumen: Institute of the Problems of the Peoples of the North).

Feodorova, Natalia V., A. P. Zykov, S. F. Koksharov, & L. M. Terekhova [1994]: **Ugrian Heritage: West Siberian antiquities from the collection of the Urals University**. * p. (Ekaterinburg: "Tyumentransgas" and Urals State University, History and Archaeology Institute, Russian Academy of Sciences) [Rusian/English].

Feodorova, Natalia V. [1996]: **Tiutey Sale, a site in northern Yamal: on the issue of the circumpolar maritime adaptation.** 45 p. Manuscript in Russian on file at the Arctic Studies Center (Washiongton DC: National Museum of the USA).

Fitzhugh, William W. [1974]: **Ground Slates in the Scandinavian Younger Stone Age with reference to circumpolar Maritime adaptations.** *Proceedings of the Prehistoric Society*, 40:45-58 (*: *).

Fitzhugh, William W. [1975a]: **A comparative approach to northern maritime adaptations.** pp:1-18 in "Prehistoric Maritime Adaptations of the Circumpolar Zone", editor: William W. Fitzhugh, * p. (The Hague: Mouton).

Fitzhugh, William W. [1975b]: **A comparative approach to northern maritime adaptations.** pp: 339-386 in: "Prehistoric Maritime Adaptations of the Circumpolar Zone", editor: William W. Fitzhugh, * p. (The Hague: Mouton).

Fitzhugh, William W. [1994]: **"Living Yamal": Preliminary field report for 1994.** 40 p. (Washington: National Museum of Natural History, Smithsonian Institution, Arctic Studies Center).

Fitzhugh, William W. [1995]: **Archeological excavations in Yamal, 1994-1995: the "Living Yamal" Project.** 65 p. (Washington: National Museum of Natural History, Smithsonian Institution, Arctic Studies Center).

Gerlach, Craig S. & Owen K. Mason [1992]: **Calibrated radiocarbon dates and cultural interaction in the Western Arctic.** *Arctic Anthropology*, 29(1):54-81 (Madison: University of Wisconsin Press).

Gjessing, Gutorm [1935]: **Fra Steinalder til jornalder i Finmark.** * p. (*: *).

Gjessing, Gutorm [1944]: **The Circumpolar Stone Age.** *Acta Arctica*, 9(2):1-70 (Copenhagen: Ejnar Munksgaard).

Gjessing, Gutorm [1948]: **Some problems in Northeastern archeology.** *American Antiquity*, 13:298-302 (*: *).

Gjessing, Gutorm [1953]: **The Circumpolar Stone Age.** *Antiquity*, 107:131-136 (*: *).

Golovnev, Andrei V. [1992]: **An ethnographic reconstruction of the economy of the indigenous maritime culture of northwestern Siberia.** *Arctic Anthropology*, 29(1):96-103 (Madison: University of Wisconsin Press).

Golovnev, Andrei V. [1995]: **A Shaman's sledge at the Drovanoy-3 site.** pp:*-* in "Peoples of Siberia - Rebirth and Development". Integration of Archaeological and Ethnographic research. Materials of the Third all-russian Scientific Seminar dedicated to the 110th anniversary of S. I. Rudenko's birth, editor: *, * p. (Omsk: *) [in Russian. English translation by Mila Bonnichson for "Living Yamal" program on file at Arctic Studies Center, Washington DC: National Museum of the USA].

Griffin, James B. [1953]: **A preliminary statement on the pottery from Cape Denbigh, Alaska.** pp: 40-42 in: "Asia and North America: trans-pacific contacts", editor: Marion W. Smith, *Memoirs of the Society for American Archaeology*, 9:1-* (Salt Lake City: *).

Griffin, James B. [1960]: **Some prehistoric connections between Siberia and America.** *Science*, 131(3403):801-812 (*: *).

Gryazhnov, M. P. [1952]: **Some results of three years of archaeological work on the upper Ob.** [in Russian] *Brief reports of the Institute of Material Culture Studies*, 48:93-102 (*: *).

Haakanson, Sven [1994]: **Yamal Field report**. pp:*-* in: "Living Yamal: preliminary field report for 1994", * p.

(Washington: Arctic Studies Center, National Museum of Natural History).

Hakluyt, Richard [1903]: **The principal navigations, voyages and discoveries of the English nation.** [1589]. 2:324-344 (Glascow: James MacLehose and Sons).

Hofstra, Tette & Kees Samplonius [1995]: **Viking expansion Northwards: Mediaval sources.** *Arctic*, 48(3):235-247 (Calgary: Arctic Institute of North America).

Jenness, Diamond [1928]: **Archaeological investigations in Bering Strait, 1926.** *Annual Report of the National Museum of Canada for the Fiscal Year 1926, Bulletin*, 50:71-80 (Ottawa: National Museum of Canada).

Khlobystin, Leonid [1982]: **Taimyr Archaeology and the Problems of the Origins of Archaeological Cultures of the Eurasian Far North.** PhD dissertation submitted to the Institute of Archeology. ... where?

Kleppe, Else Johansen [1977]: **Archaeological material and ethnic identification: A study of Lappish material from Varanger, Norway.** *Norwegian Archaeological Review*, 10(1-2):32-59 (Oslo: *).

Knuth, Eigil [1967]: **Archaeology of the Muskox Way.** *Contributions du Centre d'Etudes Arctiques et Finno-Scandinaves*, 5:*-* (Paris: *).

Kosinskaya, L. & Natalia Feodorova [1994]: **An archeological inventory of the Yamal-Nenets Autonomous Area.** [in Russian] 114 p. (Ekaterinburg: Russian Academy of Sciences).

Krenke, Nikolai [1992]: **Archaeological evidence of cultural interaction in the Ob Delta region in the 19th century.** *Kontaktstencil*, 36:131-140 (Turku: *).

Krupnik, Igor [1993]: **Arctic Adaptations: Native Whalers and Reindeer Herders of Northern Eurasia.** * p. (Hanover: Dartmouth College, University Press of New England) [1977 PhD thesis published in Russian in 1989].

Krupnik, Igor [1996]: **Northern peoples, southern records: the Yamal Nenets in Russian population counts, 1695-1988.** pp:67-91 in "Northern peoples, southern states: maintaining ethnicities in the circumpolar world", editor: Robert P. Wheelersburg, * p. (Umea: Cerum).

Larsen, Helge & Froelich Rainey [1948]: **Ipiutak and the Arctic Whale Hunting Culture.** *Anthropological papers of the American Museum of Natural History*, 42:*-* (New York: American Museum of Natural History).

Lashook, L. P. [1968]: **The "Sirtya" - early inhabitants of the Subarctic.** pp:*-* in "Problems in the Anthropology and Historical Ethnography of Asia", * p. (Moscow: Nauka) [in Russian].

McGhee, Robert [1983]: **Possible Pre-Dorset culture connections to Scandinavia.** Presented at the Annual Meeting of the Canadian Archaeological Association. * p. (Halifax, Nova Scotia).

Martinier, P.M. De La [1912]: **Puteshestviye v severnye strany** [A trip to the North]. *Zapiski Moskovskogo Arkheologicheskogo Instituta*, 15:*-* (Moscow: *) [in Russian], Translated from the French, "Voyages des pays septentrionaux", Paris 1671].

Mathiassen, Therkel [1925]: **Preliminary report of the Fifth Thule Expedition: Archaeology.** pp:206-215 in "Proceedings of the 21st International Congress of Americanists, 1924" (Goteborg: *).

Mathiassen, Therkel [1927]: **Archaeology of the Central Eskimos, the Thule culture and its position with the Eskimo culture.** *Report of the fifth Thule Expedition, 1921-1924*, 4(1):1-327 & 4(2):1-208 (Copenhagen: Gyldendal).

Meldgaard, Jørgen [1960a]: **Prehistoric Cultural Sequences in the Eastern Arctic as elucidated by Stratified Sties at Igloolik.** pp:588-595 in "Selected Papers of the 5th International Congress of Anthropological and Ethnological Sciences, 1956", 810 p. (Philadelphia: University of Pennsylvania Press).

Meldgaard, Jørgen [1960b]: **Origin and evolution of Eskimo cultures in the Eastern Arctic.** *Canadian Geographical Journal*, 60(2):64-75 (Ottawa: Royal Canadian Geographic Society).

Meldgaard, Jørgen [1962]: **On the formative period of the Dorset culture.** pp:92-95 in "Prehistoric cultural relations between the Arctic and temperate zones of North America", Technical Paper 11, editor John M. Campbell, 181 p. (Montreal: Arctic Institute of North America).

Moberg, Carl-Axel [1960]: **On some Circumpolar and Arctic Problems.** *Acta Arctica*, 12:67-74 (Copenhagen: Ejnar Munksgaard).

Moberg, Carl-Axel [1975]: **Circumpolar adaptation zones east-west and cross-economy contacts north-south: an outsider's query, especially on Ust'-Plouy.** pp:101-110 in "Prehistoric Maritime Adaptations of the Circumpolar Zone", editor: William W. Fitzhugh, 405 p. (The Hague: Mouton).

Mozhinskaya, Wanda [1970]: **The Iron Age in northwestern Siberia and its relation to the development of circum-polar region cultures.** pp:*-* in "Proceedings of the VII International Congress of Anthroplogical and Ethnological Sciences, Moscow, 1964", editor; *, *, * p. (Moscow: Nauka).

Mozhinskaya, Wanda [1974]: **Archaeological antiquities of the northern part of Western Siberia.** *Translations from Russian Sources*, 9:251-325, editor: Henry N. Michael, originally in: V. N. Chernetsov & W. Mozhinskaya: "The Prehistory of Western Siberia", * p. (Montreal/London: Arctic Institute of North America & McGill-Queen's University Press).

Murashko, Olga & Nikolai Krenke [1996]: **Burials of indigenous people in the Lower Ob region: dating, burial ceremonies, and technical interpretations.** *Arctic Anthropology*, 33(1):37-66 (Madison: University of Wisconsin Press).

Osherenko, Gail [1995]: **Property rights and transformation in Russia: institutional change in the Far North.** *Europe-Asia Studies*, 47(7):1077-1108 (*: *).

Pika, Alexander & D. Bogoyavlensky [1995]: **Yamal Peninsula: oil and gas development and problems of demography and health among indigenous populations.** *Arctic Anthropology*, 32(2):61-74 (Madison: University of Wisconsin Press).

Pitul'ko, Vladimir [1991]: **Archeological data on the Maritime Cultures of the West Arctic.** *Fennoscandia Archaeologica*, 8:23-34 (*: *).

Pitul'ko, Vladimir [1993]: **An early Holocene site in the Siberian High Arctic.** *Arctic Anthropology*, 30(1):13-21 (Madison: University of Wisconsin Press).

Prokofyeva, E. D. [1964]: **The Nentsy.** pp:547-570 in "The Peoples of Siberia", editors: M. G. Levin & L. P. Potapov, 948 p. (Chicago: Chicago University Press).

Schuster, Carl [1951]: **A survival of the Eurasiatic animal style in modern Alaskan Eskimo art.** pp:35-45 in "Selected Papers of the 29th Congress of Americanists. New York, 1949", editor: Sol Tax, * p. (Chicago: University of Chicago Press).

Shimkin, D. B. [1960]: **Western Siberian archaeology (an interpretive summary).** pp:*-* in "Men and Cultures: selected papers of the 5th International Congress of Anthropology", * p. (Philadelphia.: *).

Simchenko, Yuri B. [1976]: **Culture of the reindeer hunters of Northern Eurasia: an ethnographic reconstruction.** [in Russian] * p. (Moscow: Nauka).

Simonsen, Povl [1972]: **The cultural concept in the Arctic Stone Age.** pp:163-169 in "Circumpolar Problems", editor: G. Berg, * p. (New York: Pergamon Press).

Solberg, O. [1909]: **Eisenzeitfunde aus Ostfinmarken.** * p. (Christiania: *).

Sollas W. J. [1924]: **Ancient hunters and their modern representatives.** 3rd edition, * p. (New York: MacMillan Company).

Spaulding, Albert C. [1946]: **Northeastern archaeology and general trends in the northern forest zone.** pp:3:143-167 in "Man in Northeastern North America", editor: Frederick Johnson, Papers of the Robert S. Peabody Foundation, * p. (*: *).

Strong, William D. [1930]: **A stone culture from northern Labrador and its relation to Eskimo-like cultures of the Northeast.** *American Anthropologist*, 32:126-144 (*: *).

Van Linshotten, * [1915]: **Dutch expeditions to the Arctic coast of Russia in 1594-1595.** *Zapiski po giografi*, 39(3-4):*-* (St. Petersburg: *) [in Russian].

Vartanyan, Sergei L., V. E. Garutt & Andrei V. Sher [1993]: **Holocene dwarf mammoths from Wrangel Island in the Siberian Arctic.** *Nature*, 362:337-340 (*: *).

Vasil'ev, Valerii [1970]: **Siirtia - legenda ili real'nost'** [Siirtia: Legend or reality]. *Sovetskaya ethnographiya*, 1:151-157 (*: *) [in Russian. English translation on file at Washington DC: Arctic Studies Center, National Museum of the USA].

Vasil'ev, Valerii [1977]: **Nenets historical legends as a source for studies of the ethnogenesis and ethnic history of the northern Samoyedic peoples.** pp:113-126 in "Ethnic History and Folklore", editor: R. Lipets, * p. (Moscow: Nauka) [in Russian, translated into English by Ludmila Bonnichson for "Living Yamal" program, manuscript on file at Washington DC: Arctic Studies Center, National Museum of the USA].

The Saqqaq Harpoon:
An Analysis of Early Paleo-Eskimo Harpoon Heads from Qeqertasussuk, West Greenland

Bjarne Grønnow

Introduction

Due to their complex designs and archaeological contexts harpoon heads are loaded with information on culture chronology, culture contacts, diffusion, migrations, hunting economy, et cetera. In short, harpoon heads form the 'back bone' of our present version of the prehistory of the Arctic. The Thule Culture harpoon chronology constructed on typological grounds by Therkel Mathiassen is the classical example (Mathiassen 1927). Jørgen Meldgaard's sequence of Paleo-Eskimo harpoon heads from his excavations at Igloolik is another classical example (Meldgaard 1955, 1960). Jørgen broke new grounds due to the fact that his 'type lines' representing over 3,000 years of harpoon head history were results - not from a supposed 'evolution' of types - but from direct chronological observations on the archaeological sites on fossil beach ridges. Although not yet published in full Jørgen Meldgaard's harpoon types have since formed the 'classical' sequence against which finds of Paleo-Eskimo harpoons are evaluated (for example Maxwell 1985).

Since Jørgen's excavations in the 1950s and early 1960s a comparatively rich material of Dorset harpoons has been found in the Eastern Arctic. But until recently only a handfull of the earliest Paleo-Eskimo harpoons was known outside the Igloolik region due to lack of sites with preserved organic materials. However, the few finds showed that the Igloolik sequence did only cover part of the variation of the earliest Eastern Arctic harpoons. For example 'male' or tanged types were found in the eastern High Arctic Canada in Pre-Dorset and Independence I

context (for example McGhee 1979; Helmer 1991; Schledermann 1990) and in West Greenland in Saqqaq context (Meldgaard 1961, 1983).

Spurred by Jørgen Meldgaard, the renewed interest during the 1980s in the earliest West Greenland cultures has resulted in a remarkable increase of data on the organic artifacts of the Saqqaq Culture (summary in Grønnow 1996:1-6). In particular the excavations at Qajaa (Meldgaard 1983, 1991) and Qeqertasussuk (Grønnow 1994, 1996) in Disko Bugt as well as the Nipisat site in Sisimiut Municipality (Kramer 1994, 1996) have added to the picture of the diversity of the earliest harpoons. In sum, excavations on the two permafrozen sites from Disko Bugt have produced about seventy Saqqaq harpoon heads - the hand full has now turned into a bag full.

In the present paper the fifty harpoon heads found in stratigraphical contexts at Qeqertasussuk form the basis of analyses. A deliberately simple typology is introduced and chronological information is gained from the stratigraphy at the site. New information on the 'life circle' of the Saqqaq harpoons, the raw material preferences and their role in the hunting strategy is presented. Finally some symbolic aspects of the harpoon heads will be touched upon.

The Qeqertasussuk Harpoon Heads

The stratigraphical context

The archaeological investigations at the Qeqertasussuk site have been presented in several papers (M. Meldgaard

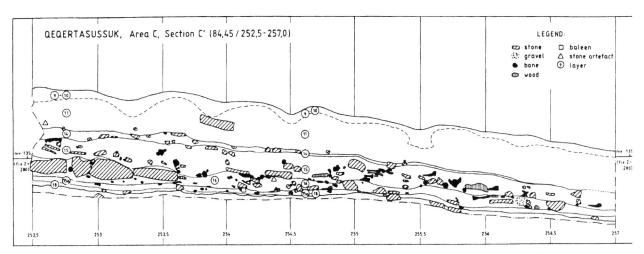

Fig. 1: Section C' representing 4.5 m of the main section at Qeqertasussuk. Layer 15a and layer 18 contains artifacts of Component 5. Layer 16 contains Component 4. Compoment 5 and Component 4 are dated to the period about 3900 B.P. to 3700/3650 B.P. Layer 15 contains Component 3 (3700/3650 B.P. to 3500 B.P.). Layer 14 contains Component 2 (3150 B.P. to 3400/3300 B.P.). Layer 11 contains Component 1 (3150 B.P. and later). The time frames of the artefact components of the different layers are based on ^{14}C-dating of the turf layers (Grønnow 1994).

1991, Grønnow 1994, 1996). Here I will limit the presentation of the site to the following facts, which are relevant for the the chronology of the site:

The Qeqertasussuk site is a relatively small (in area) and 'uncontaminated' Saqqaq site with almost full organic preservation in permafrozen culture layers. Qasigiannguit Museum's excavations during the years 1984-1990 of a few midpassage dwelling floors and heavy midden layers have produced several thousand artifacts of stone and organic matter as well as a comprehensive faunal material. Through analyses of the complex series of culture layers in the dwelling area as well as in the midden areas it is possible to define five artifact components. They are covering the time span from about 4000 B.P. to at least 3100 B.P. Harpoon heads have been recovered from permafrozen layers containing artifacts belonging to Component 5 through to Component 2. The layers defining Component 1, the latest and very rich phase as measured in number of stone artifacts, are above the permafrost table. Accordingly, the harpoon heads and other artifacts of organic material belonging to Component 1, have not been preserved. The time frames of the different artifact components based on ^{14}C datings of the defining layers at Qeqertasussuk is shown in a cross section (Fig. 1).

The harpoon heads

56 artifacts from Qeqertasussuk are classified as harpoon heads. Seven of these are pre-forms or blanks. Like the other artifacts of organic material from the site the harpoon heads from the earliest layers (containing artifact Components 5, 4 and 3) are generally in a better state of preservation than those of the upper layers, Component 2.

As mentioned above no harpoon heads are preserved in the uppermost sequence of layers containing the artifacts of Component 1.

The majority of the harpoon heads belongs to Component 5 and 4 (33) whereas only three and six have been recovered from layers containing Component 3 and 2 respectively (Table 1).

component	number
2	6
3	3
4	16
5	2
1/5	1
2/3	2
3/5	2
4/5	11
Total	56

Table 1: The number of harpoon heads of the artefact components.

component	ivory	antler	wood	total
2		6		6
3		3		3
4	3	12	1	16
5		2		2
1/5		1		1
2/3		2		2
3/5	1	10		11
4/5		13	2	15
total	4	49	3	56

Table 2: The raw material preferences relating to the harpoon heads.

Raw material preferences and 'life circle'

Table 2 clearly shows that antler was by far the dominating raw material chosen for harpoon heads. But ivory and drift wood was used as well.

Every detail of a Saqqaq harpoon head is made with care. In particular the heads made of ivory are small masterpieces. The wooden harpoon heads are large and hardened by scorching.

The quite comprehensive assemblage forms a basis for observations concerning the 'life circle' of a Saqqaq harpoon. Fig. 3:11 and Fig. 4:6 illustrates two blanks of antler representing different stages of the manufacture proces of the male, tanged head. The antler was softened, probably by boiling, and roughly shaped probably by means of a small adze (Fig. 4:6). The roughout was then worked with a knife with a sharp and even edge, that is the edge of a micro blade. Details such as the barb, the distal blade slot and the line hole were probably carved by means of a burin (Fig. 3:11) whereas the spurs were shaped by grinding. The beautiful finish was obtained by polishing the piece, probably with a fine grained sand stone. Finally the scratches on the harpoon base were made either by sawing or by cutting.

During hunting the harpoon heads were damaged. Typically the male heads mounted with a small triangular end blade broke through the blade slot when the point hit a hard bone. The end blade was pushed downwards with great force and cut away part of the distal end of the harpoon head (Fig. 3:6; Fig. 3:7; Fig. 3:9). The harpoon heads of Type Qt-D (see below) with a long proximal tang apparently had a week point just below the lateral barb (for exemple Fig. 5:3; Fig. 5:4; Fig. 5:6).

The selfbladed harpoon heads were frequently resharpened by grinding or cutting. Thus, in my oppinion almost all the toggling heads recovered at Qeqertasussuk are completely worn down pieces (for example Fig. 2:4 - Fig. 2:9). Originally they must have been about 8 cm long (Fig. 2:1; Fig. 2:2), but during their 'life circle' they were damaged and reduced to 4 cm to 6 cm. The resharpening process removed the lateral barbs and probably also changed the function of the heads.

Damages like broken line holes might be expected. The narrow, elongated holes are typically carved only a couple of millimetres from the edge of the piece. However, none of the line holes are damaged. Accordingly the pull of the line has been 'soft' and the impact of the pulling forces has mainly been parallel to the longitudinal axis of the harpoon base. In this connection the small dimensions of the line holes must be mentioned. The average size is a mere 6,6 mm by 2,5 mm (measured on 42 heads).

Typology

The comprehensive assemblage of harpoon heads from Qeqertasussuk provides a basis for a typological classification based on morphological and metrical analyses.

At first glance a characteristic 'Saqqaq style' is seen: The small dimensions, the 'aerodynamic' outlines, carefully made details such as blade slots shaped as a pair of tweerzers and characteristic bifurcate barbs.

There is great variation within this frame of 'Saqqaq style'. The assemblage is devided into two main categories according to the shape of the proximal end: Toggling harpoon heads with an open socket (Type Qt-A, 'female') and tanged harpoon heads (Types Qt-B, Qt-C and Qt-D, 'male').

Type Qt-A: Type Qt-A comprises 15 heads (including 2 roughouts) (Fig. 2). As mentioned above I consider only few of these complete - that is not resharpened (for example Fig. 2:1 & Fig. 2:2). They are selfbladed and they are provided with a single distal lateral barb.

The shape of the proximal spur varies. Five heads have a single spur, four are provided with two deeply cut proximal spurs ('cloven foot like'). Finally, four heads have two or three small proximal spurs.

The open sockets of Type Qt-A are narrow. The average maximal width of the socket measured on ten heads is 6,0 mm (range: 5,5 mm - 7,6 mm). All the Type Qt-A heads are provided with an incised zone providing a firm base for the lashing around the open socket.

The position of the line hole in relation to the open socket varies: in some cases the line hole is cut in direct connection with the distal end of the socket (Fig. 2:7). In other cases the elongated line hole is placed 5 mm to 10 mm above the socket (Fig. 2:6). Typically, the line hole is perpendicular to the 'flat side' of the head. In only two cases the line hole is parallel to this side (for example Fig. 2:2).

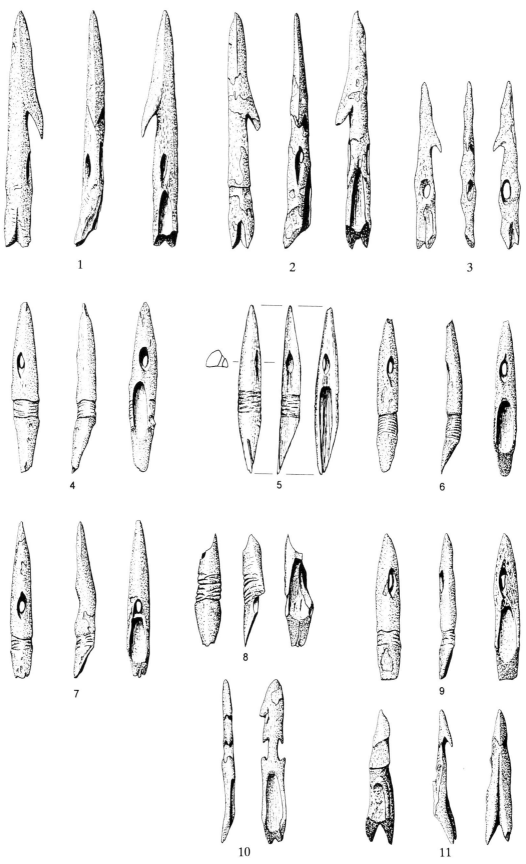

Fig. 2: Harpoon heads, Type Qt-A. Fig. 2:1 is 79 mm long. Fig. 2:8 is of ivory, the others are of antler.
(Drawings by Lars Holten (LH) and Eva Koch Nielsen (EKN, Fig. 2:5)).

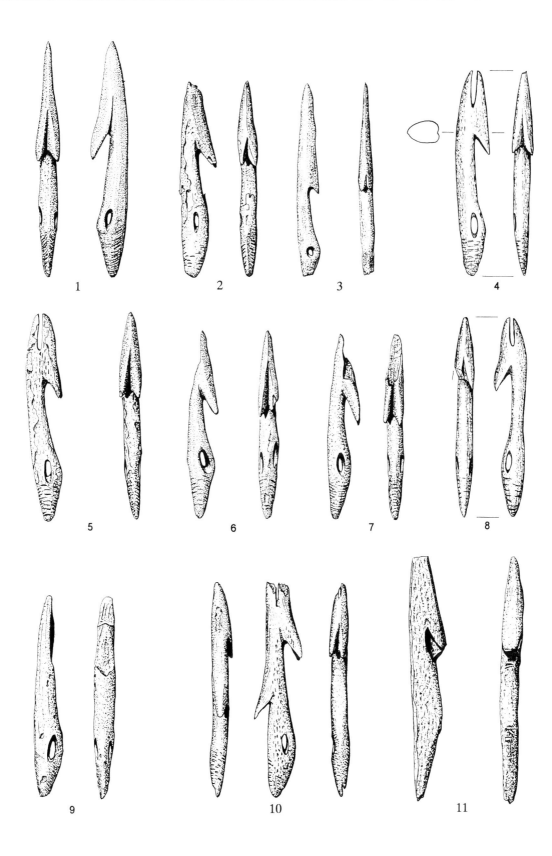

Fig. 3: Harpoon heads, Type Qt-B. Fig. 3:1 is 78 mm long. Fig 3:1, 3:7 and 3:9 are of ivory. The others are of antler. 3.11 is a preform. (Drawings by LH and EKN (fig. 3:4 and 3:8).

Type Qt-B: Type Qt-B is a male harpoon head with a tapering tang. The tanged proximal end has an asymmetrically placed line hole (Fig. 3). 19 of the heads in the assemblage are classified as Type Qt-B (plus four preforms) making it the most common Saqqaq harpoon head of Qeqertasussuk. 13 Type Qt-B heads are provided with a distal slot for an end blade, whereas only six (including the two wooden heads) are selfbladed (for example Fig. 3:1 to Fig. 3:3).

The tapering tangs are always scratched, sometimes with very fine cutmarks. The line holes are carved. They are elongated except for two, which are almost round (for example Fig. 3:3). All complete antler and ivory heads of Type Qt-B have a distal barb which is typically devided into two prominent spurs.

Type Qt-C: Type Qt-C is a male head with a tapering tang. The line hole is placed in the centre line of the flat side of the tang.

Type Qt-C comprises five heads (and one pre-form) (Fig. 4). Two heads are complete and quite spectacular due to the number and composition of barbs (Fig. 4:1; Fig. 4:4). Two other fragmented pieces have probably had a distal end like the majority of Type Qt-B (a distal barb with two spurs) (Fig. 4:2; Fig. 4:3). Finally a tang fragment probably represents a large harpoon head of Type Qt-C (Fig. 4:5).

Type Qt-D: Type Qt-D is characterized by the position of the line hole above a lateral barb half way between the tang and the distal end of the harpoon head. Thus the proximal end of the Type Qt-D harpoon is remarkably long in comparison with the other types. Type Qt-D comprises six heads of which only two are complete (Fig. 5).

All Type Qt-D harpoon heads have a distal blade slot and a distal barb with two spurs. Only in one case does the lateral barb below the line hole have two spurs (Fig. 5:4).

Finally a couple of atypical harpoon heads have been found.

Metrical analyses

The Saqqaq harpoon heads from Qeqertaussuk are extremely light compared to the harpoon heads of the Dorset and Thule Cultures. The average length of the complete specimens (39 heads, all types) from the site is a mere 64,7 mm (range: 45 mm to 126 mm).

The 17 intact, non-resharpened harpoon heads of Type Qt-B form a basis for an analysis of length (excluding the wooden harpoon heads) - a frequency distribution of length (Fig. 7). Table 3 shows that Type Qt-B typically is between 52 mm and 76 mm long with a marked peak around 64 mm to 67 mm. Separate speciments - very short and very long heads - are around 46 mm to 49 mm and 79 mm to 82 mm long, respectively.

Measurements of the blade slot were taken on all types. The average length of the blade slot is 10.1 mm (18 heads, range 6,9 mm to 13,2 mm) and the average width is 5,3 mm (16 heads, range 4,6 mm to 6,0 mm). As expected,

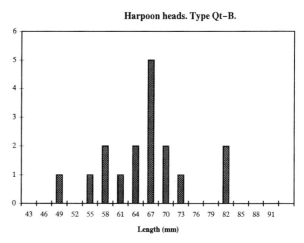

Fig. 6: Frequency distribution of length of harpoon heads of Type Qt-B.

Number of heads, type Qi-B	17
average length in mm	64.3
var	72.2
std	8.5
minimum length in mm	45.0
maximum length in mm	79.0

Table 3: Metric analysis of length of Qt-B-harpoon heads.

these blade slot dimensions confirm that the small triangular bifaces with ground sides served as end blades for harpoons.

Chronology

Most of the harpoon heads from Qeqertasussuk have been excavated in a stratigraphical context. Thus there is a basis for a relative and absolute chronology of the earliest harpoon heads of West Greenland.

Harpoon heads of Type Qt-A, the open socketed harpoons, have mainly been found in layers of the earliest phases at the site. These heads belong to Component 5 and 4. However, a single Type Qt-A head (Fig. 2:2) belongs to Component 2 (Layer 14a [Area C]). This is one of the latest layers with organic preservation. No significant chronological tendencies can be observed in relation to the different variants of the Type Qt-A. Heads with one, two or three proximal spurs are found in the same layers. The limited number of Type Qt-A-heads does not allow further chronological conclusions.

The Type Qt-B-heads - the typical Saqqaq harpoon head - show the same chronological pattern as Type Qt-A. They are found in a series of layers reaching from the earliest culture layers (Layer 15a [Area C] and Layer 6 [Area B]) to one of the uppermost layers (Layer 14 a) below the permafrost level. Thus Type Qt-B spans from Component 5 and 4 (17 pieces) over Component 3 (two pieces) to Component 2 (one piece). The variants of Type Qt-B are not chronologically significant.

Only one of the five Type Qt-C-heads have been found in a context which represents only one component: Fig. 4:1 belongs to Component 4. The others (mainly from test pits) are spanning from Components 4/5 to 2/3. Finally, the Type Qt-D-heads represent an unambiguous chronological trend. Three of the six heads belong to Component 2 and one belongs to Component 3. The last two are from test pits and cannot be determined to a single component. Thus, it is quite clear that the characteristic Type Qt-D is a relatively late type. It was introduced to the site during the period represented by the artifact assemblage of Component 3. It must be emphasized again that due to lack of organic material in the uppermost layers nothing can be said about the harpoon heads of the latest phase at Qeqertasussuk represented by the Component 1 artifact assemblage. This component is by far the most comprehensive in terms of number of stone artifacts.

In conclusion, the main harpoon types have been used during very long time spans. Based on ^{14}C datings from Qeqertasussuk this corresponds to the period about 4000 B.P. until at least 3100 B.P. The Type Qt-D-heads, however, show a distinct chronological trend. This type is relatively late at the site (Component 3 and 2), that is from about 3650 B.P. to at least 3400 B.P.

Early harpoon heads in Greenland and Canada: Comparative observations

Only a limited number of early Paleo-Eskimo sites with organic preservation is known from the Eastern Arctic. Accordingly finds of harpoon heads from the Independence I, Saqqaq and Pre-Dorset cultures are very rare.

From Greenland early harpoon heads have been found at Itinnera (Meldgaard 1961; Gynther & Meldgaard 1983), Nipissat (Kramer 1994, 1996), Qajaa (Meldgaard 1991; Møhl 1986:85) and in the Thule area (Diklev & Madsen 1992 and personal communication). Most of the published pieces from these sites have typological parallels in the Qeqertasussuk material. For example two harpoon heads from Qajaa (Meldgaard 1991:200; Møhl 1986:Fig. 5C) are typologically equal to Type Qt-C at Qeqertasussuk. These two heads from Qajaa have been ^{14}C dated to 1820 (+/-80) B.C. (calibrated) (comparable to Component 4 at Qeqertasussuk). The Qajaa head (Møhl 1986:Fig. 5B) also belongs to Type Qt-C whereas the open socket head Fig. 5A from the earliest layers at Qajaa has no parallel.

The harpoon heads of the late Saqqaq site, Itinnera (dated to about 3000 B.P.) and the fragment from Nipissat (Kramer 1994:221) add to the information from Qeqertasussuk: The common Type Qt-B-head, was used during the whole time span of the Saqqaq Culture. Finally, it must be mentioned that a large Type Qt-B ivory head with slot for an end blade and probably also a slot for a side blade was collected by hunters on Kronprinsens Ejlande in Disko Bugt (Gynther & Meldgaard 1983:36). None of the heads from Qeqertasussuk have slots for side blades. And no bifacial side blades are found among the several thousand stone artifacts of this site.

From Eastern Arctic Canada finds of early Paleo-Eskimo harpoon heads have been reported from Ellesmere Island (Schledermann 1990, 1996), Devon Island (McGhee 1979; Helmer 1991), Baffin Island (Mary-Rousseliere 1976), and Igloolik (Meldgaard 1960; S. Rowley personal communication).

In the present paper a brief overview of the most striking parallels to the Qeqertasussuk material will be presented.

The fragment illustrated in Schledermann (1990:88), Plate 8A from the Bight Site, Feature 2 on Ellesmere Island is a Type Qt-A harpoon (it resembles Fig. 2:1). Feature 2 belongs to the Saqqaq Complex of Ellesmere. It is dated to 3840 +/- 70 B.P. (To 1556) (contemporary with Component 5 at Qeqertasussuk). However, Schledermann (1990:85) considers this absolute dating of Feature 2 several centuries too early.

The Devon Island sites at Port Refuge and at Icebreaker Beach have produced a dozen early Paleo-Eskimo harpoon heads which all have counterparts in the Qeqertasussuk material. The two tanged heads from Upper Beach, Feature 6 (McGhee 1979: Plate 4q, 4s) are Type Qt-B-heads and the two open socketed heads from the Cold Component (Plate 4f, 4u) are Type Qt-A-heads. They are dated mainly through context to the Independece I Culture. This is contemporary with Component 5 at Qeqertasussuk.

Parallels to the two heads of the Gull Cliff Component (McGhee 1979: Plate 12a, 12b) are found in Components 5 to 3 in the Qeqertasussuk material.

The harpoon heads from the North Devon Island sites belonging to the Icebreaker Beach complex (Helmer 1991:305-308) include three Type Qt-B heads and three Type Qt-A-heads. The similarities between these heads and the ones from Qeqertasussuk are striking. The Icebreaker Beach Component is dated by ^{14}C to about 3850 B.P. to 3700 B.P. (Component 5 and 4 at Qeqertasussuk).

Included in the assemblage from the middle Pre-Dorset Twin Ponds Complex, which is dated to 3650 B.P. to 3300 B.P., is an open-socketed toggling harpoon head (Helmer 1991: Fig. 11). This piece seems to be similar to the head (Fig. 2:7) and thus it confirms the wide time range of the Qt-A type as observed at Qeqertasussuk.

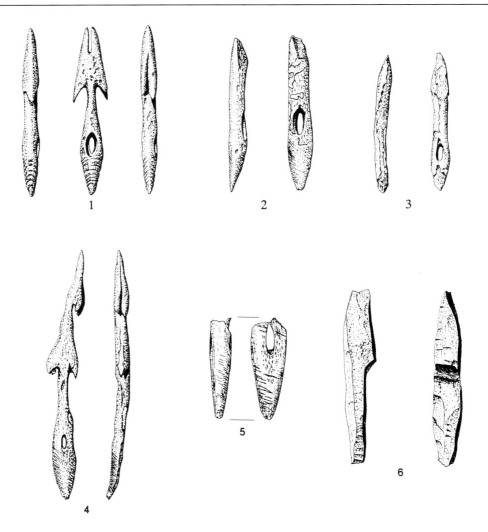

Fig. 4: Harpoon heads, Type Qt-C. Fig. 4:1 is 56 mm long. All heads are made of antler. Fig. 4:6 is a pre-form. (Drawings by LH and EKN (Fig. 4:5)).

Finally, the investigations by Meldgaard 40 years ago and, recently, by Susan Rowley on the famous sites of Igloolik in central High Arctic Canada have produced early harpoon heads of great interest in this context. The Qt-A harpoons of Qeqertasussuk fit into Meldgaard's earliest Pre-Dorset type-states of Type Line A (Meldgaard personal communication). However, the Igloolik heads are considerably heavier and more elaborate than their Greenlandic counterparts. The same goes for two recently found tanged ivory heads from the Pre-Dorset beaches at Igloolik (Susan Rowley personally communication). They belong to Type Qt-C in Qeqertasussuk terminology.

Toggling Type Qt-A-like heads are found further West in the Canadian Arctic, for example at early Paleo-Eskimo sites on Victoria Island and Banks Island (for example Maxwell 1985: Fig. 5:2, Fig. 5:C, Fig. 5:D). In contrast the tanged Types Qt-B, Qt-C, and Qt-D have, to my knowledge, only been found at the sites mentioned above. These harpoon are 'markers' of the true Eastern Arctic pioneers.

The Saqqaq harpoon as a hunting weapon

Reconstructing the Saqqaq harpoon
Not only the harpoon heads but also several other components of the Saqqaq-harpoon complex have been found at Qeqertasussuk.

The small triangular end blades with ground sides have been mentioned above (Fig. 7:1 - Fig 7:4). The end blade was wedged tight in the slot. Neither lashing nor 'glue' was used.

The foreshafts for the toggling harpoon heads are known from Qeqertasussuk and other sites (Fig. 7:5 - Fig. 5:6) whereas no foreshafts for the male harpoons have been identified in the material.

The harpoon shafts are probably represented through a class of shaft fragments measuring about 12 mm to 20 mm in cross section diameter. This is the same 'caliber' as leister shafts, bird spears, light lances and light spears (Grønnow 1994:220).

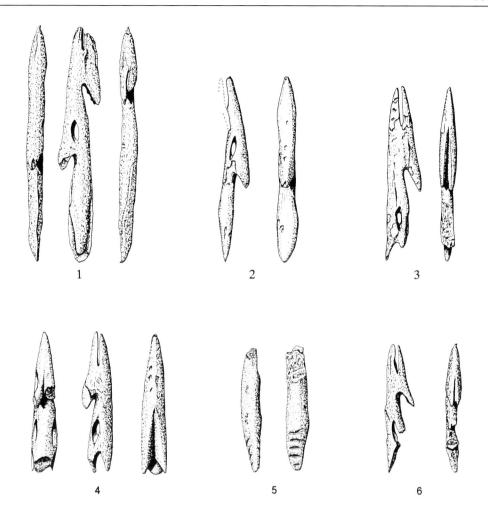

Fig. 5: Harpoon heads, Type Qt-D. Fig.5:1 is 7.9 mm long. All heads are made of antler. Fig. 5:5 is a proximal end fragment. Drawings by Lars Holten.

One piece (Fig. 7:7) is probably a harpoon line buckle. Apart from this no other artifact among the houndreds of bone and antler objects can with certainty be related to harpoons. There are no finger rests and no mouth pieces or other indication of bladder technology at all.

No atlatls or throwing boards have been found at Qeqertasussuk, but these are known from a few other early sites in Greenland and Arctic Canada (Møbjerg 1995: Fig. 10; Meldgaard 1991:200; Helmer 1991: Fig. 8h). Like most of the Saqqaq hunting gear the atlatls are very light. The groove in which the proximal end of the harpoon shaft rested measures 10 mm to 13 mm (maximum diameter).

Finally, it should be mentioned that the Qeqertasussuk material includes a number of line fragments of baleen, seal skin and senew (Grønnow 1994:218-219). Some of these could have been harpoon lines.

The harpoon and the game

This information on the different components of the early Paleo-Eskimo harpoon adds to the picture of a remarkably well equipped and highly mobile Saqqaq seal hunter using extremely light weapons in comparison with later cultures (Grønnow 1994:225).

The Saqqaq hunter hunted from his boat (Grønnow 1994:216), from land or from the floe edge on fairly long distances - probably up to 20 m to 30 m - with his light throwing harpoons tipped with tanged harpoon heads. In contrast, the thrusting harpoon provided with a long shaft and toggling head was probably the primary weapon for seal hunting on ice during winter (breathing hole hunting of ringed seal) and spring (utoq hunting).

Hunting of a wide range of game species in all size-classes is documented through the comprehensive fauna material from Qeqertasussuk (Grønnow 1994:218). The light harpoons could have been used not only for small seals but also for catching large fish like salmon and cod (Grønnow & Meldgaard 1991:132-133) and for different sea birds, for example great auk. Information on the role of the Saqqaq harpoon in whale hunting and walrus hunting is lacking. As mentioned before, none of the harpoon heads found at Qeqertasussuk seem to be heavy enough to meet the demands of marine 'big game hunting'.

The terrestrial predator

Like its historic counterpart an important hunting tool like the Saqqaq harpoon head must have been loaded with symbolic meanings. Through the choices of raw material, design and combination of barbs the Saqqaq harpoon head must have carried 'coded' messages to the spiritual beings providing the game as well as more profane signals to fellow hunters, such as ownership marks. Much of this information cannot be read and translated today due to culture and time barriers. Here I will limit the discusion on the symbolic aspects of the harpoons to a few subjective remarks.

Even if the Saqqaq style is clearcut, each individual harpoon head has its own 'personality'. The number and position of the barbs as well as differences in the details of the spurs could be a sort of ownership marks. This is at least the case for the barbed Thule Culture arrow heads (for example Grønnow et al. 1983:30-31).

In my oppinion, the Saqqaq harpoon heads demonstrate a relationship to the terrestrial sphere rather than the maritime world.

Firstly, the by far preferred raw material is antler.

Secondly, the shape of the basal spur of some of the heads is that of a realistic 'cloven foot' inspired by the shape of the clovens of caribou or musk ox. This element from the terrestrial sphere is well known in Paleo-Eskimo (Transitional or Independence II) contexts from the socalled cloven foot lances (for example Knuth 1978:69; Claus Andreasen personal communication).

Thirdly, the shape of the distal end of most of the tanged heads can be seen as associated with the head of a terrestrial predator: In my interpretation the spurs are shaped like the conical ears of an attacking animal and - in this line of thought - the blade slot could symbolize the mouth of a wolf or a fox.

These terrestrial connotations of the Saqqaq harpoon heads used for hunting marine game emphasize the opposition between the worlds of the land and the sea. This must be seen in contrast to the marked references to maritime game inscribed in the shape of harpoon heads of the later cultures, in particular the Thule Culture (for example Rosing 1986:77). The Saqqaq hunter with his 'terrestrial' harpoons and elaborate equipment for land hunting - advanced bows and arrows and light throwing spears (Grønnow 1994:225) - might have felt himself more dependant on the powers of terrestrial rather than maritime spirits.

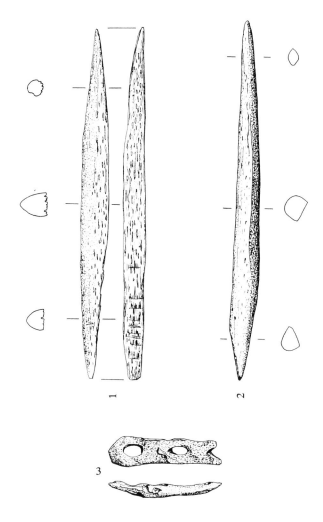

Fig. 7: Fig. 7:1 to Fig. 7:4: A selection of small triangular harpoon end blades of killiaq. Fig. 7:5 to Fig. 7:6: Foreshafts of whale bone. Fig. 7:5 is 137 mm long. Fig. 7:7: Harpoon line buckle (?).
Drawings by Eva Koch Nielsen and Lars Holten.

Summary and Conclusions

About 50 harpoon heads from the Qeqertasussuk site, Disko Bugt, were analyzed. They represent by far the largest assemblage of early Paleo-Eskimo harpoon heads from the Eastern Arctic. Furthermore, most of the harpoon heads were found in stratigraphical context. It is possible to date the different types of heads relatively as well as absolutely.

A simple morphological division of the heads were suggested resulting in the definition of four main types based on the shape of the proximal end and the position of the line hole:

Qt-A: toggling harpoon head ('female') with open socket.

Qt-B: tanged harpoon head ('male') with the line hole placed in an asymmetrical position at the end of the tang.

Qt-C: tanged harpoon head ('male') with the line hole in a symmetrical position on the tang.

Qt-D: tanged harpoon head ('male') with the line hole placed in front of a lateral barb half way between the tang and the distal end of the head.

The types Qt-A, Qt-B, and Qt-C (Qt-B being by far the most common Saqqaq type) were found in all layers with preserved organic materials, that means that these types were used from the earliest artifact component, Component 5, through to Component 2. This means that the main harpoon heads of the Saqqaq Culture in Disko Bugt were used at least in the time period 4000 B.P. to 3100 B.P. No organic material is preserved from the latest phase at Qeqertasussuk (Component 1), but a few finds from other sites in Greenland suggest that at least Qt-A, Qt-B and some varieties not found at Qeqertasussuk were used also during the late Saqqaq Culture. At present the Qt-D-type is exclusively found at the Qeqertasussuk site. It was introduced during the time of Component 3 and was found also in Component 2 context (c. 3650 B.P. to 3400 B.P.), so it represents a relatively late development at the site.

Metric analyses showed that the harpoon heads were remarkably small (average length of intact heads is 64,7 mm) in comparison to harpoon heads of the later cultures. None of the harpoon heads seem to be heavy enough to meet the demands of 'big game' hunting. On the contrary, the Saqqaq hunter based himself on extremely light weight equipment and, apparently, the bladder hunting technology was not known at all.

A brief overview of early Paleo-Eskimo harpoon heads from Greenland and Arctic Canada showed that the combination of female Type Qt-A and male Types Qt-B and/or Qt-C is known from Igloolik to North West and West Greenland. The cultural context is primarily Pre-Dorset and Saqqaq.

The typical 'life circle' of a harpoon head from the pre-form to the worn out and discarded state could be traced in the material. The most important observation was that almost all selfbladed toggling harpoon heads found represented broken or heavily resharpened pieces which probably had changed function during their 'life time'.

Caribou antler were, by far, the prefered raw material for the harpoon heads, but ivory and even drift wood were used as well. This raw material preference and stylistic elements, for example the 'cloven foot' proximal ends, led to a brief discussion of the possible terrestrial connotations of the Saqqaq harpoon heads. Do these symbolic aspects of the harpoons, contradicting the maritime world in which they were used, mean that the Saqqaq man saw himself as primarily a terrestrial hunter - even if marine game, sea birds and fish formed the main resource base of the Saqqaq Culture in West Greenland?

Acknowledgements

I would like to thank Jørgen Meldgaard warmly for introducing me as a quite young student to arctic archaeology 20 years ago. Jørgen has always been a most inspiring mentor, colleague and friend.

Bjarne Grønnow, Director of Historical-Archaeological Experimental Centre, Lejre, Denmark.

References

Diklev, Torben & Bo Madsen [1992]: **Arkæologisk berejsning i Thule, 1991.** Unpublished report on file at Avernersuup Katersugaasivia, * p. (Qaanaaq: Thule Museum).

Grønnow, Bjarne, Morten Meldgaard & Jørn B. Nielsen [1983]: **Aasivissuit - the Great Summer Camp. Archaeological, ethnographical and zooarchaeological studies of a caribou-hunting site in West Greenland.** *Meddelelser om Grønland, Man and Society*, 5:1-96 (Copenhagen: *).

Grønnow, Bjarne & Morten Meldgaard [1991]: **De første vestgrønlændere. Resultaterne af 8 års undersøgelser på Qeqertasussuk-bopladsen i Disko Bugt.** *Tidsskriftet Grønland*, 39(4-7):103-144 (Copenhagen: Det Grønlandske Selskab).

Grønnow, Bjarne [1994]: **Qeqertasussuk - the Archaeology of a Frozen Saqqaq Site in Disko Bugt, West Greenland.** pp:197-238 in "Threads of Arctic Prehistory: Papers in honour of William E. Taylor, Jr.", editors: D. Morrison & J.-L. Pilon, *Mercury Series, Paper* 149:1-422 (Ottawa: Archaeological survey of Canada).

Grønnow, Bjarne (editor) [1996]: **The Paleo-Eskimo Cultures of Greenland. New Perspectives in Greenlandic Archaeology.** 334 p. (Copenhagen: Danish Polar Center).

Grønnow, Bjarne [1996]: **The Saqqaq Tool Kit - Technological and Chronological Evidence from Qeqertasussuk, Disko Bugt.** pp.17-37 in "The Paleo-Eskimo Cultures of Greenland. New Perspectives in Greenlandic Archaeology", editor: Bjarne Grønnow, 334 p. (Copenhagen: Danish Polar Center).

Gynther, Bent & Jørgen Meldgaard [1983]: **5 kapitler af Grønlands forhistorie.** 113 p. (Nuuk: Pilersuiffik).

Helmer, James [1991]: **The Paleo-Eskimo Prehistory of the North Devon Lowlands.** *Arctic*, 44(4):301-317 (Calgary: The Arctic Institute of North America).

Knuth, Eigil [1978]: **The Independence II Bone Artifacts and the Dorset-evidence in North Greenland.** - *Folk*, 19-20:61-88 (Copenhagen: Dansk Etnografisk Forening).

Kramer, Finn E. [1994]: **På sporet af forhistorien.** *Tidsskriftet Grønland* 42(7):217-225 (Copenhagen: Det Grønlandske Selskab).

Kramer, Finn E. [1996]: **Akia and Nipisat I: two Saqqaq sites in Sisimiut District, West Greenland.** - pp:65-87 in "The Paleo-Eskimo Cultures of Greenland. New Perspectives in Greenlandic Archaeology", editor: Bjarne Grønnow, 334 p. (Copenhagen: Danish Polar Centre).

Mary-Rousselière, Guy [1976]: **The Paleo-Eskimo in Northern Baffinland.** pp:40-57 in "Eastern Arctic Prehistory: Paleoeskimo Problems", editor: Moreau S. Maxwell, *Memoirs of the Society for American Archaeology*, 31:1-* (Salt Lake City: Society for American Archaeology).

Mathiassen, Therkel [1927]: **Archaeology of the Central Eskimos, I-II.** *Report of the Fifth Thule Expedition 1921-24*, 4(1-2):1-327 (Copenhagen: Gyldendal).

Maxwell, Moreau S. [1985]: **Prehistory of the Eastern Arctic.** 320 p. (New York: Academic Press Inc.).

McGhee, Robert [1979]: **The Paleo-Eskimo Occupations of Port Refuge, High Arctic Canada.** *Mercury Series, Archaeological Survey Paper*, 92:1-176 (Ottawa: National Museum of Man).

Meldgaard, Jørgen [1955]: **Dorsetkulturen. Den Dansk-Amerikanske ekspedition til Arktisk Canada 1954.** *Kuml*, 1955:158-177 (Århus: Jysk Arkæologisk Selskab).

Meldgaard, Jørgen [1960]: **Origin and Evolution of Eskimo Culture in the Eastern Arctic.** *Canadian Geographical Journal*, 60(2):64-75 (Ottawa: The Canadian Geographical Society).

Meldgaard, Jørgen [1961]: **Saqqaqfolket ved Itivnera. Nationalmuseets undersøgelser i sommeren 1960.** *Tidsskriftet Grønland*, 9(1):15-23 (Copenhagen: Det Grønlandske Selskab).

Meldgaard, Jørgen [1983]: **Qajaa, en køkkenmødding i dybfrost. Feltrapport fra arbejdsmarken i Grønland.** *Nationalmuseets Arbejdsmark*, 1983:83-96 (Copenhagen: The National Museum of Denmark).

Meldgaard, Jørgen [1991]: **Bopladsen Qajaa i Jakobshavn Isfjord. En rapport om udgravninger i 1871 og 1982.** *Tidsskriftet Grønland*, 39(4-7):191-205 (Copenhagen: Det Grønlandske Selskab).

Meldgaard, Morten (editor) [1991]: **Qeqertasussuk. De første mennesker i Vestgrønland.** *Tidsskriftet Grønland*, 39(4-7):*-* (Copenhagen: Det Grønlandske Selskab).

Møbjerg, Tinna [1995]: **Sidste nyt fra Nipisat I - en Saqqaq boplads i Sisimiut Kommune, Vestgrønland.** *Tidsskriftet Grønland*, 43(2):45-54 (Copenhagen: Det Grønlandske Selskab).

Møhl, Jeppe [1986]: **Dog Remains from a Paleo-Eskimo Settlement in West Greenland.** *Arctic Anthropology*, 23 (1-2):81-89 (Madison: University of Wisconsin Press).

Rosing, Jens [1986]: **Havets enhjørning.** 83 p. (Århus: Wormianum).

Schledermann, Peter [1990]: **Crossroads to Greenland: 3000 Years of Prehistory in the Eastern High Arctic.** *Komatic Series*, 2:1-364 (Calgary: The Arctic Institute of North America of The University of Calgary).

Schledermann, Peter [1996]: **Voices in Stone. A Personal Journey into the Arctic Past.** *Komatic Series*, 5:1-221 (Calgary: The Arctic Institute of North America of the University of Calgary).

The Soul of the Prey

Hans Christian Gulløv

The harpoon head has always been known as one of the most important diognostic types in Eskimo archaeology. This can hardly be disputed and it is precisely on this group of objects that our basic chronologies of the North American Arctic are based. Further discussion within the disciplines of eskimology and Arctic archaeology no longer seems relevant, as this topic is already so well understood. Yet, the 'sensitive and speaking harpoon heads' continue to fascinate archaeologists who intuitively sense that there is more to them than what can be described as design and type (Meldgaard 1986:31).

Since early colonial times in Greenland we have known that each harpoon head has its own soul. We know that the seal was fond of beautiful hunting tools which it sought out in order to be hit; and as long as the hunter respected existing taboos, the harpoon would enter the animal without causing pain. However, if for some reason the animals failed to come, the harpoon head had to be changed. A different kind of wood or bone was chosen 'and the structure thoroughly changed' (Dalager 1915:47; Glahn 1771:347).

For the Greenlandic hunter in the 18th century the significance of the harpoon head was thus closely tied to the soul of the prey. Even in the 20th century this relationship could be described in the Eastern Arctic where "*the soul of a seal resides in the harpoon head for one night after the seal has been killed*" (Rasmussen 1929:185).

These two perceptions of design and content each present a way to think about the concept of time. However, the archaeologist's diachronic presentation of typological change is essentially different from the hunter's synchronic perception of the object endowed with a soul, which is here a medium for the continued existence of the living (Rasmussen 1929:60-61). With this view we have an explanation for a change which does not only tell of failure of hunting but which could indicate a change in attitude which is expressed in relation to others, for instance in connection with an encounter between cultures. In what follows I will give a few examples of how this may be described archaeologically, well aware that my point of departure is hypothetical, as I presuppose a cultural continuity which ensures that the soul of the prey can reside in the harpoon head. In other words, I want to point to two periods and geographical scenarios in which archaeology can presumably contribute information about cultural encounters and climatic changes. I have chosen the Thule Culture at the arrival to Greenland in Thule District and the Thule Culture in West Greenland in the 17th and 18th centuries, a period which is described as the Little Ice Age.

The Beginning at Smith Sound in Thule

The gateway to Greenland is situated at Smith Sound, where archaeological investigations on both sides of the sound have taken place since the 1930s (Holtved 1944, 1954; McCullough 1989). The earliest investigations on the Greenlandic side of the sound clearly showed that the architecture on the small Ruin Island off the coast of Inglefield Land differed significantly from other investigated ruins in the area and that the types of harpoon heads found on Ruin Island could also be found unchanged at the Bering Strait. The characteristics of Ruin Island were also established in other sites during Holtved's continuous investigations, and since 1978 they have occurred at Ellesmere Island, where the finds seem to represent the earliest phase of the Thule Culture: the Ruin Islanders (Holtved 1944, 1954).

However, Holtved's archaeological observations from Greenland continue to raise doubts about whether the Ruin Island phase is, in fact, the earliest Thule Culture, and no other investigations which might disprove his archaeological findings have yet been conducted. Yet, we may conclude that the Ruin Islanders were, if not the first, then at least early representatives of the Thule Culture in the High Arctic, who also had access to objects originating from the Norse population in South West Greenland. In the Smith Sound region we find the largest number of Norse objects ever recorded in an Eskimo context. They occur primarily in the ruins of the Ruin Island phase, which on both shores of the Smith Sound have been ^{14}C dated to 1200-1400 A.D. (Gulløv 1993; McCullough 1989).

Comparing harpoon heads from the Ruin Island phase found on Ellesmere Island with those from Greenland, it is apparent that the classical types Thule-2, Thule-3, and Thule-4 are found in both places. On the Greenlandic heads we also see vestigial barbs and grooves for sideblades, characteristics which are particularly known from Alaska (see Fig. 1). In the Greenlandic material we also find the well known flat Thule-5 type, which Collins in the 1930s pointed out as specific to the Eastern Arctic with pronounced Dorset features of shape and linehole (1937:316).

Examples of these types are shown to the right in Fig. 1. They were all found in the same ruin from the Ruin Island phase on the classic Uummannaq settlement (today Dundas) in the heart of Thule District. The following types were found there: Thule-2 with vestigial barbs, Thule-3 with vestigial sideblade grooves and spurs, the keeled Thule-4 type, Thule-4 with a Norse iron point, Thule-5, and a piece of industrial copper of Norse origin (Holtved 1944(I):132ff).

With the flat Thule-5 harpoon head, a new type was introduced whose origin has been debated for more than 60 years. Despite decades of archaeological efforts the occurrence of an encounter between the Thule and Dorset Cultures has not been proved, and the question is still the focus of much research (see Park 1993). On the other hand, investigations of the Late Dorset Culture have been intensified during recent decades resulting in a narrowing of the gap between the end of this phase and 1200 A.D., from which time there is strong evidence of the Thule Culture in the High Arctic. It has even been argued that Thule Culture winter dwellings could have been constructed very shortly after the Dorset site had been left, "perhaps even in the same season" (McGhee 1996:218).

These events take place shortly after 1000 A.D., when, it can be established, there was a climatic change in the northern hemisphere. The 12th century becomes an important period in Greenland, when the change from Paleo-Eskimo to Neo-Eskimo Culture takes place in the northern part of the country, and a reduction of the Norse range

lands can be established in the southernmost part (Vedbæk 1992:108). During this period a new type of harpoon head, Thule-5, is introduced in the Ruin Island phase of the Thule Culture. Why?

In order to answer this question it is important to stress that the choice of the Thule-5 type was not a random choice. It was introduced at a time of climatic changes, and in a society in which almost two thirds of the prey consisted of smaller seals (McCullough 1989: Table 11). The relationship between the hunting tool and the prey described above is also reflected in the introduction of Thule-5, which I will describe as a response to an ecological challenge. The fact that the prototype of this design existed in the Dorset Culture indicated that they too knew how to handle the challenge of satisfying the soul of the prey. That is why they chose a type whose effect they already knew.

There are, however, several different variations of the design which were probably used for specific prey. But what they all have in common is the fact that their prototypes exist in Late Dorset. The choices among the spectrum of harpoons in the Dorset Culture were many, when the first pioneers from the Thule Culture came to the Eastern Arctic. But Late Dorset was chosen and a tradition was passed on through the Thule Culture. This is evident from Fig. 2 which at the top shows the Dorset types F, Ha, G, and E and below the derived types from Thule Culture in Canada, the Smith Sound region, and East and West Greenland. The Western Eskimo tradition with open sockets is primarily found in Canada and West Greenland, whereas all East Greenlandic types have closed sockets (Gulløv 1993).

The flat Dorset derived types make up a significant group in Greenland after the 1200-1400 A.D. period (see Jordan 1979) and occur together with a continued use of western Eskimo types.

In Greenland these occurrences may be described as "parallel traditions". Yet the introduction of these at Smith Sound can only be understood through the remarkably close relations between Late Dorset and Early Thule Cultures. This is as far as I can go on the basis of existing Greenlandic source material, which does, in fact, contain evidence of an exchange of ideas that is not accidental. But this suffices to ensure the continued existence of the soul of the prey.

The End in West Greenland

"*In the Thule District there is a remarkable lack of finds from around 1500 (maybe 1600) to around 1800 ... From the 1600s and 1700s I cannot point to a single house ruin*" (Meldgaard 1986:29). This comment is based on Holtved's archaeological work from the 1930s the chronology of which has been established "*with some reservation for the 17th-18th centuries which are only poorly represented, if at all*" (Holtved 1944(II):40).

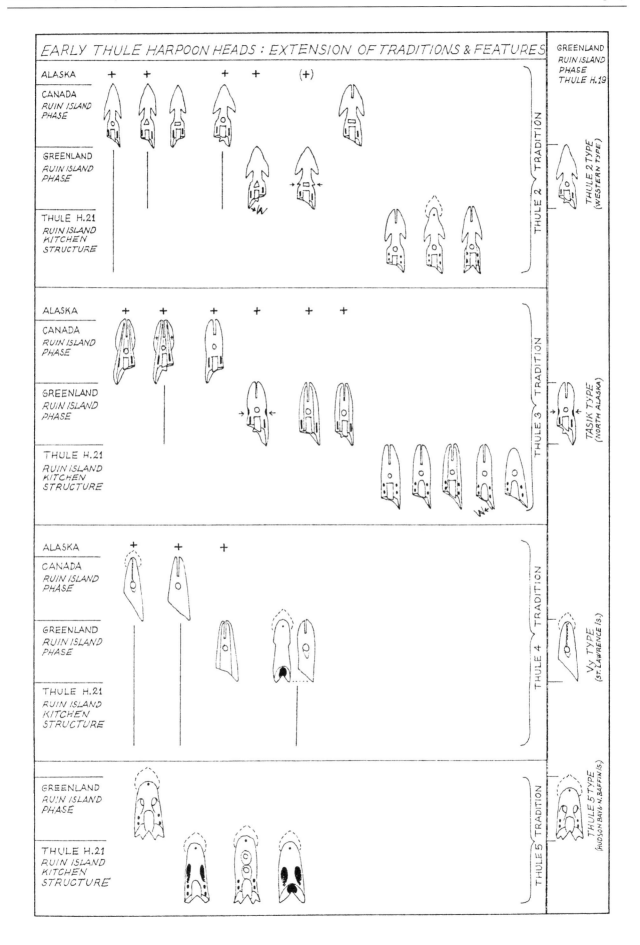

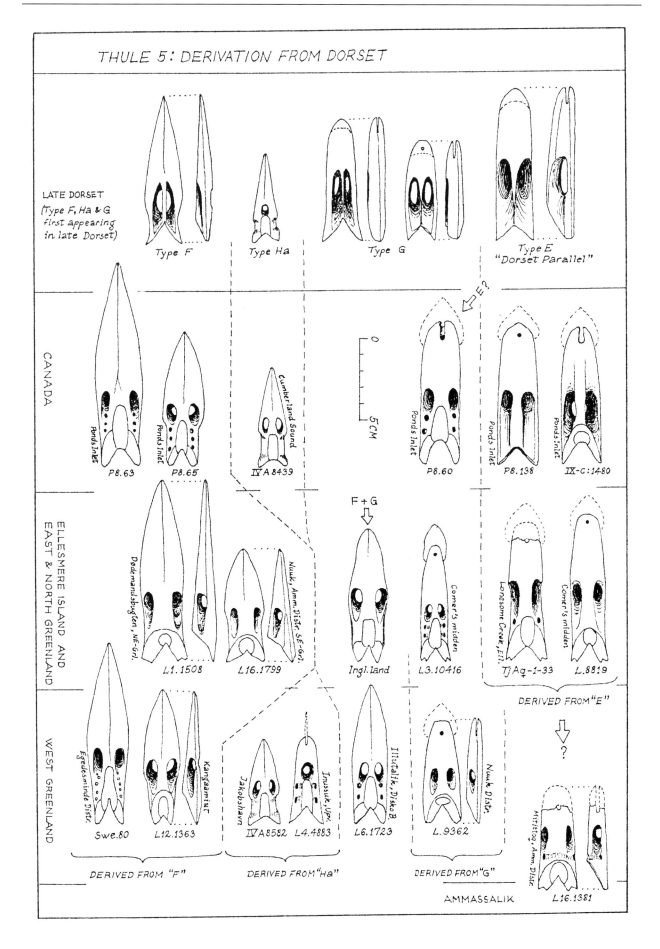

THULE 5: DERIVATION FROM DORSET

LATE DORSET
(Type F, Ha & G
first appearing
in late Dorset)

Type F   Type Ha   Type G   Type E "Dorset Parallel"

CANADA

Ponds Inlet P8.63   Ponds Inlet P8.65   Cumberland Sound IV A 8439   Ponds Inlet P8.60   Ponds Inlet P8.138   Ponds Inlet IX-C:1480

ELLESMERE ISLAND AND EAST & NORTH GREENLAND

Dødemandsbugten, NE-Grl. L1.1508   Nuuk, Amm.Distr. SE-Grl. L16.1799   F + G Ingl.land   Comer's midden L3.10416   Lonesome Creek, Ell. TjAq-1-33   Comer's midden L.8819

DERIVED FROM "E"

WEST GREENLAND

Egedesminde Distr. Swe.80   Kangaamiut L12.1363   Jakobshavn IV A8582   Inussuk, Upv. L4.4883   Illutalik, Disko B. L6.1723   Nuuk Distr. L.9362   ?   Mitivttoq, Amm. Distr. L.16.1381

DERIVED FROM "F"   DERIVED FROM "Ha"   DERIVED FROM "G"

AMMASSALIK

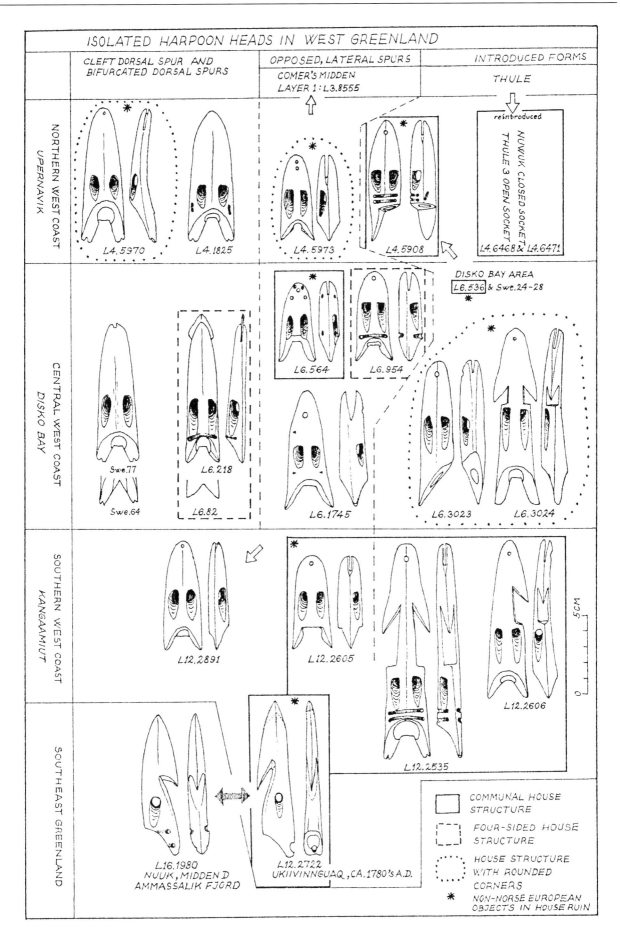

ISOLATED HARPOON HEADS IN WEST GREENLAND

In other words, the Thule Culture exists for approximately 300 years at the Gateway to Greenland. After that this population can only be found in the eastern and southwestern areas of the country. This is the Post Norse period, in which the majority of Eskimo sites are concentrated in the southern part of the country. In particular, there is a growth in the population along the coast of the Davis Strait, whose open streches of ice-free coastline were, by the 16th century, already attracting European explorers and whalers.

The "parallel traditions" can still be proved in the country through the flat, Dorset derived harpoon heads and the thin heads of western Eskimo origin. Among the latter, particular the Thule-4, which include the socalled "inussuk" variety, are dominant (see Jordan 1979). Harpoon heads with open sockets became obsolete when the region around the Gateway to Greenland became depopulated. West Greenland was thus, after the 16th century, a somewhat isolated area in the Eastern Arctic, where *the Europeans intervene in history; and consequently, the development here would have followed the prehistoric model with serious times of need for the West Greenlander*" (Meldgaard 1986:29). However, a look at the West Greenlandic harpoon spectrum from this period paints another picture of Eskimo society than indicated by the doomsday prophecy above.

Firstly, an influence into isolated West Greenland can be established. This influence is evident in the north in Upernavik through a reintroduction of harpoon heads with open sockets which have been found in house ruins and late pagan graves (Hjarnø 1974); in the south an East Greenlandic influence is detected (Gulløv 1995, 1996). Secondly, the Eskimo economy proved flexible in relation to European whaling and did not collapse until the missions made the population sedentary, thereby putting an end to the long trading expeditions (Gulløv 1985).

Until then, that is until the mid-18th century, communications between various groups of people far from each other had taken place, but around 1800 A.D. the connection to Thule via Melville Bay and to South East Greenland via Kap Farvel were cut off. However, it is the situation in West Greenland before the colonial freeze which is reflected in the flat hybrid harpoon heads in Fig. 3.

The majority of the West Greenlandic harpoon heads from this period are flat, and derived from Thule-5 (Dorset E and G). The spurs are either placed dorsally or laterally. The latter type seems to originate in Disco Bay and have later been found in larger house ruins with rounded corners from Disco Bay and Upernavik as well as in the upper layers of Comer's midden in Thule.

This type has also been found in a vast area from Kangaamiut in the Southwest to Upernavik in the North, in rectangular communal houses, a type of dwelling which was introduced by the southern Greenlanders, with the intention of showing people up north how to build houses (Mathiassen 1931:50).

Among the re-introduced types in the northern parts of West Greenland were the thin harpoon heads, Thule-3 and Thule-4 ('Nuwuk', see Ford 1959:94), found in communal houses from the 18th century (Fig. 3). This happened at a time when "the newcomers at Upernavik seem to have retained a stronger East Greenlandic phonological substrate than those in the southwest, which may have something to do with relative size of population, life-style more or less contrasting with that of west coast neighbors, or date of arrival in the respective confrontation areas" (Fortescue 1986:416). Linguistic influences are also evident in the southern part of West Greenland stemming from the arrival of travellers from the southeast coast (Fortescue 1986:416). Their arrival also made its mark on harpoons in the identical thin and flat barbed heads (Fig. 3) which are used on both coasts (H. C. Gulløv 1995:22, 1996:100).

Harpoon heads with dorsal spurs, closest to Thule-5(G), seem to be the oldest of the variants described in Fig. 3. They are only found on the northern west coast. In Upernavik they are even found in the same archaeological context as the re-introduced western Eskimo types. This tradition is a result of the increased travel activity which began in the 17th century. The "parallel traditions" can still be read in the hybrids which came about as the result of the encounter between the original Thule Culture of West Greenland and the immigrants from the north and the south. In this West Greenland scenario we may detect an interesting parallel to the transition from Pre-Dorset to Dorset which was "*characterized by quick changes of types, some disappear completely, new paths are sought, and at the same time the design becomes less fixed, the variations increase. I will call it a period of stress*" (Meldgaard 1986:24).

Precisely during the 17th and 18th centuries a significant change in the resources of Greenland took place. This period was later to be called the Little Ice Age, during which the West Greenlandic communities showed great creativity in an attempt to cope with the ecological challenge (Gulløv no date A). Our earliest ethno-historical sources originate from this period. They tell about the necessity to change the design of the hunting tools if for some reason the prey failed to come. Just as it was the case at the Gateway to Greenland half a millenium earlier, this process of change was not characterized by random choices, but was deeply rooted in a tradition which determined the design.

In the Post-Norse period of West Greenland it was the recent immigrants from the north and the south who sparked innovation by introducing new varieties of the hunting equipment which had proved efficient in the areas they came from (Gulløv 1996). The 17th and 18th centuries comprise a true period of stress in the Meldgaardian sense (Meldgaard 1986). But times of deprivation did not occur, as long as the seals approved of the beautiful hunting tools whose myriad possibilities of design during this

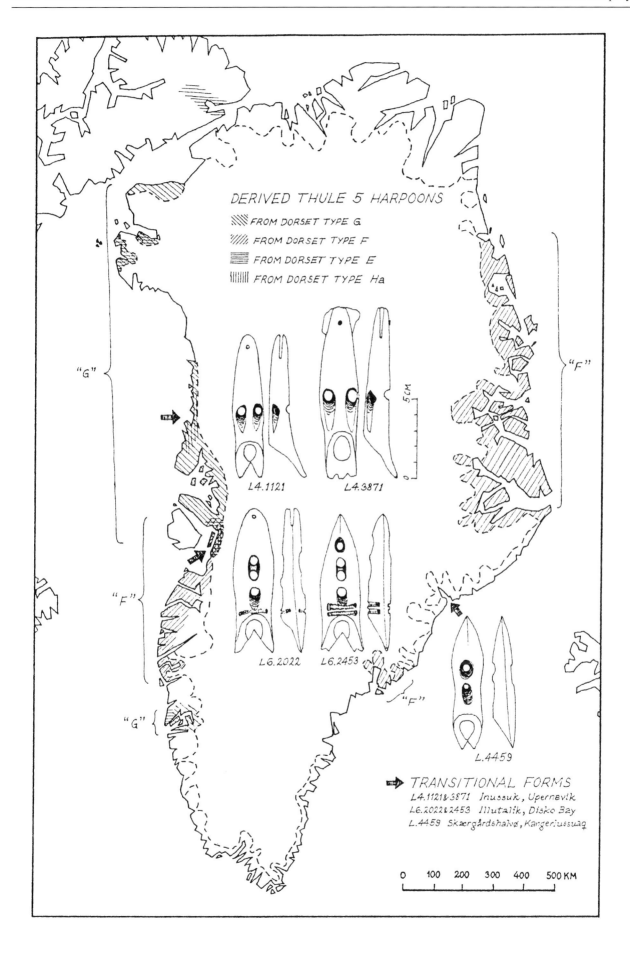

DERIVED THULE 5 HARPOONS
FROM DORSET TYPE G
FROM DORSET TYPE F
FROM DORSET TYPE E
FROM DORSET TYPE Ha

"G"

"F"

L4.1121   L4.3871

L6.2022   L6.2453

"F"

"G"

"F"

L.4459

TRANSITIONAL FORMS
L4.1121&3871 Inussuk, Upernavik
L6.2022&2453 Illutalik, Disko Bay
L.4459 Skærgårdshalvø, Kangerlussuaq

0   100   200   300   400   500 KM

period seemed *legio*. Difficulties arose, however, when the West Greenlandic society was locked into the colonial economic structure and industrially manufactured harpoon heads were to satisfy the soul of the prey (see Gulløv & Kapel 1979:75).

Discussion

My point of departure was two different perceptions of the concept of time as they are expressed through the design and the content of the harpoon head. The diachronic presentation of the archaeologist forms the skeleton of the discipline of cultural history, whereas the hunter's perception of content reflects ecological circumstances. But despite these different perceptions, determined by different purposes, there is a common thread running through them. The soul is the element of continuity of living beings and the harpoon head is its medium. Regarding this harpoon head *"the archaeologist must be permitted to speak about kinship and to claim that the hunters have had exactly the same thought about this object"* (Meldgaard 1986:31).

The choice of geographic scenarios describes the beginning and the end of the Thule Culture in Greenland. This opens up for a cognitive-processual archaeological interpretation of the material object as a symbol within processes of cultural change (see Renfrew & Bahn 1991: 432). This presupposes that the communicative significance of the chosen object as described by the Greenlandic hunters of the colonial period was the same meaning it held at the Gateway to Greenland centuries earlier. This was my hypothesis which I believe to have proven in the above account. Archaeologically speaking, the harpoon head is part of the described scenarios, but it should also be considered an ethno-historical source, and *"by reading these and especially the well known diagnostic types, the harpoon heads, as symbols of the relation between nature and society, we get a new kind of cognitive map with localities that speak of meetings, hunting and trade"* (Gulløv 1996:102).

During the 15th and 16th centuries a depopulation of northern Greenland and the Gateway to Greenland occurred. After that, the "parallel traditions" are seen in the southern part of the country, Thule-5(G) being the preferred type along the West Coast and Thule-5(F) along the East Coast (Fig. 4). But archaeology shows that, early on, there was experimentation with the line hole. Thus, in Upernavik, in the northernmost part of West Greenland, the Thule-4 type becomes a flat hybrid in the 15th century (Mathiassen 1930: pl.5), while the types from the lower cultural layers in the middens of Disko Bay from the same period use a different principle (Mathiassen 1934: pl.3). In Southeast Greenland, an influence from the north can be seen in the 16th century (Gulløv 1995: 27), and in the region around Kangerlussuaq, where narwhal hunting was good, line hole innovation also occurred (Fig. 4).

These types can thus be read as ethno-historical sources on hunting grounds, where the ecological challenge put high demands on the hunting tools which did not always satisfy the soul of the prey and where societies had succumbed even though *"the hunting of seals, narwhals and polar bears in any case usually has been good"* as told from Southeast Greenland (Degerbøl 1936:47).

By perceiving the archaeological data as ethno-historical sources, the character of the data changes. Instead of having an objective existence independent of theory, it becomes an element of significance in Eskimo society. In 1752 the lack of success in hunting in Southwest Greenland was, thus, still explained through the fact that the tools "had been bewitched" (Dalager 1915:47) and therefore, they had to be changed. An irrational explanation, thus, became rational.

Conclusion

I have chosen the relationship between hunter and prey as the determining factor in my description of the possibilities which Jørgen Meldgaard's intuitive archaeologal explanations open up. I have shown that a cultural encounter between the Dorset and Thule Cultures is more than likely, and that the basic idea behind the design of a harpoon head is contextual rather than functional. I have demonstrated a potential for interpretation which still exists in the field of Greenlandic archaeology, and shown that an object can be regarded as an ethno-historic source. (For a more extensive discussion of this view and the continuity of Greenland's Thule Culture, see Gulløv no date B) But first and foremost, like Meldgaard I have believed in "the sensitive and speaking harpoon heads".

Hans Christian Gulløv, curator
Department of Ethnography, National Museum of Denmark

References

Collins, Henry B. [1937]: **Archaeology of St. Lawrence Island, Alaska.** *Smithsonian Miscellaneous Collections*, 96(1):1-431 (Washington DC: Smithsonian Institute Press).

Dalager, Lars [1915]: **Grønlandske Relationer ... sammenskrevet ved Friderichshaabs Colonie i Grønland Anno 1752.** editor: Louis Bobé, *Det grønlandske Selskabs Skrifter*, 2:1-94 (Copenhagen: The Greenland Society).

Degerbøl, Magnus [1936]: **The Former eskimo Habitation in the Kangerdlugssuak District, East Greenland.** *Meddelelser om Grønland*, 104(10):1-48 (Copenhagen: C. A. Reitzels Forlag).

Ford, James A. [1959]: **Eskimo Prehistory in the Vicinity of Point Barrow, Alaska.** *Anthropological Papers*, 47(1):1-272 (New York: American Museum of Natural History).

Fortescue, Michael [1986]: **What Dialect Distribution can tell us of Dialect Formation in Greenland.** *Arctic Anthropology*, 23(1-2):413-422 (Madison: University of Wisconsin Press).

Glahn, Henric Christopher [1771]: **Anmærkninger til de tre første Bøger af Hr. David Crantzes Historie om Grønland.** 388 p. (Copenhagen: Gerhard Giese Salicath).

Gulløv, Hans Christian [1985]: **Whales, Whalers, and Eskimos: The Impact of European Whaling on the Demography and Economy of Eskimo Society in West Greenland.** pp:71-96 in "Cultures in Contact. The European Impact on native Cultural Institutions in Eastern North America 1000-1800 A.D.", editor: William W. Fitzhugh, Anthropological Society of Washington Series, 320 p. (Washington, DC: Smithsonian Institution Press).

Gulløv, Hans Christian [1993]: **In Search of the Dorset Culture in the Thule Culture.** pp:201-214 in "The Paleo-Eskimo Cultures of Greenland: New Perspectives in Greenlandic Archaeology", editor: Bjarke Grønnow, *Proceedings from a Symposium, May 1992*, 334 p. (Copenhagen: Institute of Prehistorical Archaeology, University of Copenhagen.

Gulløv, Hans Christian [1995]: **"Olden times" in Southeast Greenland: New archaeological investigations and the oral tradition.** *Inuit Studies*, 19(1):3-36 (Quebec: Départment d'anthropologie, Université Laval).

Gulløv, Hans Christian [1996]: **Reading the Thule Culture - History between Archaeology and Ethnography.** *Cultural and Social research in Greenland*, 95/96:90-106 (Nuuk: Ilisimatusarfik/Atuakkiorfik).

Gulløv, Hans Christian [in print a]: **Ice summers and long-distance journeys - an Inuit perspective on the Little Ice Age.** In "Proceedings from a Seminar on Climate and Man in the Arctic, March 1996" (Copenhagen: Danish Polar Center).

Gulløv, Hans Christian [in print b]: **From Middle Ages to Colonial Times. Archaeological and Etnohistorical studies of the Thule Culture in Southwest Greenland, 1300-1800 A.D.** In *Meddelelser om Grønland* (Copenhagen: Ther Commission for Scientific Research in Greenland).

Gulløv, Hans Christian & Hans Kapel [1979]: **Haabetz Colonie 1721-1728. A historical-archaeological investigation of the Danish-Norwegian colonization of Greenland.** *Etnografisk Række*, 16:1-245 (Copenhagen: The National Museum of Denmark).

Hjarnø, Jan [1974]: **Eskimo Graves from Upernavik District.** *Meddelelser om Grønland*, 202(1):7-35 (Copenhagen: C. A. Retizels Forlag).

Holtved, Erik [1944]: **Archaeological Investigations in the Thule District, I-II.** *Meddelelser om Grønland*, 141(1):1-308 & 141(2):1-184 (Copenhagen: C. A. Reitzels Forlag).

Holtved, Erik [1954]: **Archaeological Investigations in the Thule District, III: Nûgdlît and Comer's Midden.** *Meddelelser om Grønland*, 146(3):1-135 (Copenhagen: C. A. Reitzels Forlag).

Jordan, Richard H. [1979]: **Inugsuk Revisited: An Alternative View of Neo-Eskimo Chronology and Culture Change in Greenland.** pp: 149-170 in "Thule eskimo Culture: An Anthropological Retrospective", editor: A. P. McCartney, *Mercury Series*, 88:1-569, Archaeological Survey of Canada (Ottawa: National Museum of Man).

McCullough, Karen M. [1989]: **The Ruin Islanders - Early Thule Culture Pioneers in the Eastern High Arctic.** *Mercury Series*, 141:1-347, Archaeological Survey of Canada (Ottawa: Canadian Museum of Civilization).

McGhee, Robert [1996]: **Ancient People of the Arctic.** 244 p. (Vancouver: University of British Columbia Press).

Mathiassen, Therkel [1930]: **Inugsuk - a mediaeval Eskimo settlement in Upernavik District, West Greenland.** *Meddelelser om Grønland*, 77(4):147-340 (Copenhagen: C. A. Reitzels Forlag).

Mathiassen, Therkel [1931]: **Ancient Eskimo Settlements in the Kangâmiut Area.** *Meddelelser om Grønland*, 91(1):1-150 (Copenhagen: C. A. Reitzels Forlag).

Mathiassen, Therkel [1934]: **Contributions to the Archaeology of Disko Bay.** *Meddelelser om Grønland*, 93(2):1-192 (Copenhagen: C. A. Reitzels Forlag).

Meldgaard, Jørgen [1986]: **Dorset-Kulturen - udviklingstendenser og afbrydelser.** - pp:15-31 in "Vort sprog - vor kultur", Foredrag fra symposium afholdt i Nuuk i oktober 1981 arrangeret af Ilisimatusarfik og Kalaallit Nunaata Katersugaasivia, 220 p. (Nuuk: Pilersuiffik).

Park, Robert W. [1993]: **The Dorset-Thule Succession in Arctic North America: Assessing Claims for Culture Contact.** *American Antiquity*, 58(2):203-234 (Salt Lake City: American Society for Archeology).

Rasmussen, Knud [1929]: **Intellectual Culture of the Iglulik Eskimos.** *Report of the Fifth Thule Expedition 1921-1924*, 7(1):1-308 (Copenhagen: Gyldendal).

Renfrew, Colin & Paul Bahn [1991]: **Archaeology. Theories, Methods, and Practice.** 543 p. (London: Thames and Hudson Ltd).

Vebæk, Christian Leif [1992]: **Vatnahverfi. An inland district of the Eastern Settlement in Greenland.** *Meddelelser om Grønland, Man & Society*; 17:1-132 (Copenhagen: The Commision for Scientific Research in Greenland).

Repatriation of Ancient Human Remains
Recent Cases from the Arctic Region

Jens Peder Hart Hansen

Introduction

Since the late 1960s, when interest in preserving ethnic and cultural heritage grew internationally as a corollary of newly achieved independence and nationalism in Third World countries, ethical, legal, and moral questions about cultural property, cultural sensitive objects, and human remains have proliferated (Frisbie 1993).

A 1970 UNESCO convention provides for the return of cultural property between nations. An example has been the return of approximate 1,800 medieval Icelandic manuscripts from Denmark to Iceland. Iceland was since 1918 under Crown Union with Denmark, its old colonial master, and became an independent republic in 1944. The manuscripts had been collected in Iceland in the 17th and 18th century and they would probably all have perished if not brought to Denmark. The manuscripts are widely regarded as Iceland's main cultural heritage. The repatriation took place 1971-1997 according to Danish legislation from 1961.

Since the end of World War II the Arctic region has witnessed an increasing pressure from the local Inuit populations for political independence. Regional political structures have been created, for example Inuit Circumpolar Conference, and local self government has been established, for example Home Rule in Greenland 1979.

This paper will report three recent cases of repatriation of ancient human remains in the Arctic region involving institutions in Denmark and Greenland and will briefly describe the return of parts of the Greenland collections of ethnographic and archaeological objects in the National Museum of Denmark.

5th Thule Expedition 1921-1923 - revisited

In early 1990 the Inuit politician Peter Ernerk from Repulse Bay raised the issue in the legislative assembly of the Northwest Territories (NWT), Canada, in Yellowknife that human remains and grave gifts collected by the Fifth Thule Expedition in the areas of Naujat-Repulse Bay, Pond Inlet and Arctic Bay in Canada ought to be repatriated. He labelled the excavations in 1922 and 1923 as outright grave robbery and both the archaeologist, Therkel Mathiassen, and the leader of the expedition, Knud Rasmussen, were later accused of grave robbery in the local media.

Peter Ernerk claimed that in addition to 3,000 artifacts the remains of 64 bodies were taken to Denmark. The NWT minister for culture and communication, Titus Allooloo, initiated official investigations and it was clarified that the ethnographic and archaeologic objects from the Fifth Thule Expedition were in the collections of the National Museum of Denmark and the skeletal material in the Laboratory of Biological Anthropology, University of Copenhagen (LBAUC).

Accordingly, the administration of the government of the NWT officially approached the LBAUC, where the skeletal material had been stored since the return of the expedition in 1924, requesting repatriation for reburial. No mentioning was made of grave gifts and artifacts. Before this approach inofficial contacts had been made and it was decided to keep the issue on a low level in Denmark and to solve the problem administratively. The Canadian federal authorities did not seem very enthusiastic during the inofficial contacts and were never officially involved.

The ownership of the material in the traditional sense was not evident. The Fifth Thule Expedition was primarily financed by the Thule Station (founded 1910 by Knud Rasmussen, and runned by Peter Freuchen) in Greenland and was administered in Copenhagen by Rudolf Sand, brother-in-law of Knud Rasmussen, and not by the National Museum of Denmark or the University of Copenhagen. The material was delivered to the LBAUC in 1924 for scientific examinations, the results of which were published in 1937 (Fischer-Møller 1937).

The LBAUC holds large collections of prehistoric skeletons of Danish and foreign origin and is depository for prehistoric human remains from Greenland. The collections are securely stored and are only for scientific and educational use. Skeletal remains received from museums and likewise institutions after excavations are regarded as deposited and as legally belonging to the depositing institution. The LBAUC can not interfere with such material without permission. Material received from other sources is regarded as the property of the Laboratory, which is part of the University of Copenhagen. It was the opinion of the LBAUC that the material from the Fifth Thule Expedition belonged to this group.

Due to the age of the collections (often more than 100 years) there are uncertainty about the ownership in quite a few cases. However, in the actual case Danish ownership as such was contested by the Canadian claim.

The Fifth Thule expedition was carried out in agreement with the Canadian authorities. The expedition raised, however, some concerns for the Canadian government (Zaslow 1988). The plans about the expedition made some governmental officials suspicious that it might be an attempt to usurp Canadian authority in the Arctic. Danish authorities were, however, able to convince that the purpose of the expedition was purely scientific.

The expedition brought back to Denmark several thousand archaeological specimens and some skeletal remains (Mathiassen 1927). No laws at that time were addressing such activities in the NWT. A means for issuing permits for scientific expeditions in the NWT was not instituted until 1926 (Scientists and Explorers Ordinance, Northwest Territories Council, 23 June 1926) and not until the enactment of the Eskimo Ruins Ordinance on 5 February 1930 were permits required specifically for the purposes of excavating archaeological sites or removing artefacts from the NWT (Arnold 1992).

The purpose of the expedition was to study the Inuit groups of North America. The skeletons were from the period 1200-1700 A.D., which means that they are the remains of the so-called *Thule Culture People*. This designation was proposed by Knud Rasmussen and is internationally recognized.

According to the inventory lists of the LBAUC and scientific publications the material from the mentioned localities comprised crania and other skeletal remains from 34 individuals.

The authorities in the NWT were asked about the possible relationship between present day inhabitants of the localities mentioned and the requested skeletal material. The supposition made that the material represents the ancestors of the present day Inuit of the region, at least from a cultural point of view, is actually a result of the work of Therkel Mathiassen.

The scientific importance of the material is today restricted, and after negotiations between the University of Copenhagen and the National Museum of Denmark it was agreed that the museum had the right of deciding over the material. The museum wanted to repatriate in order to obtain good-will and probably hinder new claims, particularly for artifacts. In consequence, the museum accepted the claim of a direct link to the present inhabitants of the three communities. The museum stated that it was sympathetic toward the reasoning in the communities where the inhabitants felt that their ancestors deserved a proper burial in their rightful burial ground.

The National Museum of Denmark therefor consented to the wishes of the inhabitants of Naujat-Repulse Bay, Pond Inlet, and Arctic Bay for the return of the skeletal remains for reburial. It was also expressed that it was a Danish wish that the public accusations of Knud Rasmussen and Therkel Mathiassen as grave robbers stopped. Their activities were according to the habits of those days and they had not violated any regulations.

As stated the scientific importance of the material was restricted. Therefor, the LBAUC and the University could accept that the skeletal material was handed over for human reasons. It was the opinion that the material ceased to be scientific from the moment of handing over. From then the material was plain human remains with known origin and affiliation to identified present day persons. The remains were then only aimed for reburial. Possible scientific investigations could be carried out before the handing over, and Canadian scientists were welcomed. It was a precondition for the handing over that the material would be reburied and that it was neither put up for exhibition in any context nor made the object of scientific investigations. With Canadian approval minor specimens were secured for future elementary, DNA and possible other analyses.

The practical arrangements after handing over were coordinated by Charles D. Arnold, Director of the Prince of Wales Northern Heritage Centre in Yellowknife, NWT. The bones were buried 18 September 1991 under a rock cairn at the Naujan site with about 60 residents of Repulse Bay in attendance (Arnold 1992). The local lay minister said that he would not bless the bones as his ancestors had already done that in their own way when the bodies were first put in their graves. Instead he proceeded to bless the ground on which the bones now lay.

Fig. 1: Four of the six Polar-Eskimos Peary brought to New York photoed December 11, 1897 in Bronx. From left: Nûtaq, Uisâkavsak, Minik, and Qissuk. Courtesey of the Peabody Museum, Havard University. Photo by Hillel Burger.

Thule-New York 1897
and back 94 Years later

Another famous explorer, Robert E. Peary, was also accused of improper behaviour in relation to humans beings in the Arctic. In 1897 he brought 6 Polar-Eskimos from Thule, North Greenland, to New York for exhibition in order to raise money for new expeditions. Four died within 8 months, a child was adopted by an American family after the death of his father, and one returned to Greenland.

The bodies of the four dead persons were in some cases given fictitious burials and were later skeletonized for scientific purposes. In one case for a time one skeleton might have been on show in the American Museum of Natural History in New York. The adopted Eskimo child

named Minik had later the experience of finding the skeleton of his father in the exhibition halls of the museum, at least according to a local newspaper.

Minik returned for a period (1909-1916) to Greenland but came back to the U.S.A. in 1916 and died in 1918. He was buried in New Hampshire. The dramatic story of this group of Polar-Eskimos and particularly of the child, Minik, has been told in popular (Harper 1986; Lauritzen 1987) and scientific books (Gilberg 1994).

Danish scientists tried during the later half of this century to obtain admission to the skeletal remains of these persons but without luck. The bones were locked up in the museum, probably due to earlier public criticism of the behaviour of Peary and the museum with regard to the bringing of the Polar-Eskimos from Greenland with promises by Peary which were not fulfilled and to the role of the museum in securing the bodies after their death for scientific purposes. In some cases the museum even denied the existence of the bones.

With the U.S. federal *Native American Graves Protection and Repatriation Act* (NAGPRA) of 1990 started extensive repatriations of artifacts and ancient human remains from museums and other institutions in the U.S.A. to native populations groups and societies in the U.S.A., most often for reburial. The NAGPRA requires all agencies of the US government and any museum receiving federal funding to identify all human remains, funerary and sacred objects and other items of cultural patrimony in their collections.

Thus, U.S.A. museums have completed inventories of artifacts and human remains taken or purchased from Indian and other native tribes and through the years several cases of repatriation have taken place. Possibly influenced by this trend in the U.S.A. and by the diminishing scientific importance of the material the American Museum of Natural History took the initiative in 1992 to repatriate the remains to Greenland. The community of Qaanaaq (Thule) was contacted but expressed no wish to receive the bones. The bones were from individuals who were identified by names but no descendants were known. No claims for repatriation were raised by Greenland authorities or possible family members.

Through negotiations between the American Museum of Natural History and the National Museum of Denmark (Jørgen Meldgaard) and the National Museum of Greenland (Emil Rosing) transferral of the material from New York to Thule in North Greenland was organized. The transferral was financed by private U.S.A. sources. On 1 August 1993 the remains were buried in the cemetery of Qaanaaq (Thule) and a memorial service was held. It was recognized that the remains were of pagans who were not christened and without any known present day relatives.

Repatriation of Alaskan Chugach Remains from Denmark

In May 1996 three solid cases were delivered by air freight to the Chugach Heritage Foundation in Anchorage, Alaska. The sender was the National Museum of Denmark. The content of the cases was 24 small carefully sealed boxes each holding the remains of one individual from the prehistoric Chugach people of Alaska from the 17th and 18th century (Hansen 1997).

The remains, mostly skeletal material, were removed in 1933 from their resting places in Prince Williams Sound for scientific purposes by a Danish-American Expedition following the habits of those days. The villages of the Chugach region comprise an area which encompasses Prince William Sound from Icy Bay near Yakutat to Port Graham on the Kenai Peninsula. These villages are Tatitlek, Eyak, Port Graham, English Bay, Chenega and Nuchek.

The leaders of the expedition were dr. Frederica de Laguna, archaeologist from the University of Pennsylvania, and dr. Kaj Birket-Smith, ethnographer from the National Museum of Denmark. The cultural remains were divided among the universities of Pennsylvania and Washington and the National Museum of Denmark. Some of the skeletal material was deposited in the University of Pennsylvania Museum. One coffin with a skeleton was, however, in 1938 brought to the National Museum of Denmark and exhibited 1938-1968. Birket-Smith made another deposit of further skeletal material from the expedition at the LBAUC.

The skeletal material in the LBAUC has been inventoried. Some of the material has been included in earlier anthropological studies. In agreement with the Chugach Heritage Foundation small specimens have been secured for DNA-analyses which may point to the ethnic background of the individuals, affinities with other Alaskan and North American population groups, and direct kind ship among the individuals. The results of these tests will be submitted to the Chugach community.

The ethnological results of the expedition were published in Copenhagen (Birket-Smith 1938, 1953) while the archaeological results were published in Seattle in 1956 (de Laguna 1956).

In 1992-1993 artifacts and skeletal remains belonging to the Chugach community were repatriated from the Smithsonian Institution and from the University of Pennsylvania, and several reburials took place. The Chugach Heritage Foundation was also aware of the material in Copenhagen and approached the National Museum of Denmark with a request for repatriation. It was stated that "*the Chugach people feel that their ancestors' spirits were taken from their homeland and that the spirits are not at peace until they are returned from the museums' storage boxes to their original villages and graves with dignity and respect*" (Johnson 1997). This request was received positively and the practical arrangements were carried out by John F. C. Johnson, Chugach Heritage Foundation, and Jørgen Meldgaard, National Museum of Denmark.

The transportation with the Scandinavian Airlines System from Copenhagen to Seattle and on with Alaskan Airlines to Anchorage was smooth and uneventful. The travel documents stated the content and no one wanted to test the statement and open the cases. The Anchorage customs officer wanted only to be made sure that the remains were not bringing contagious diseases from abroad into Alaska. He was convinced, without inspection, that any contagious disease these people may have suffered from had their origin in Alaska and gave permission to the repatriation of possible ancient germs.

On 26 September 1996 a memorial service was held at Saint Michael's Russian Orthodox Church in Cordova.

Fig. 2: From left: Matrona Tiedeman, Makari's daughter and interpreter; Chief Maraki Chimovitski, oldest Aleut in 1930 and main storyteller; Dr. Frederica de Laguna, anthropologist from the University of Pennsylvania; Dr. Kaj Birket-Smith, anthropologist from the National Museum of Denmark, who recorded stories told by Makari; Norman Reynolds, research assistant from the University of Washington. Photo taken at Palugvik, Prince William Sound, 1930s. Courtey of Frederica de Laguna.

The *Ancient Ones* were treated with dignity and respect as if they had died the day before (Johnson 1997). A large group of elders attended and the next day the remains were reburied at four different locations.

The spirits and remains of the Ancient Ones are now back at home after an extended stay on foreign soils. The prehistoric villages and burial groups are the foundation of our cultural existence. They are places of strength and power of an unknown force that must be treated with dignity and respect forever (John F. C. Johnson, Cultural Resource Manager, Chugach Heritage Foundation).

Discussion

The NAGPRA has had great influence in the U.S.A. with regard to the fulfilment of wishes of Indigenous groups and tribes for the return of cultural heritage and human remains from museums and other institutions.

Museums do have a fiduciary responsibility to the public for their collections. When those collections in the U.S.A. include American Indian human remains, sacred and ceremonial items, and items of cultural patrimony, which under the NAGPRA are no longer even arguably owned by the museum, however, the museum's trust is no longer a public one. It is one owed directly and solely to the sources of the collections and to their descendants (Downer 1993).

Another core repatriation issue relates to the meaning of *ownership*. Among traditional peoples many cultural materials or remains cannot be owned, except perhaps in a collective sense. This idea is surprisingly similar to museum concerns about maintaining a collective, public world heritage (Zimmerman 1993). Modern technics of copy making and improved conditions for communication and travel diminish the claim that original scientific basic material is present in all relevant research institutions.

Alone the Smithsonian Institution (National Museum of Natural History) has been the depository of approximately 18,500 North American human remains.

One of the most important repatriations has been the Larsen Bay agreement (Bray & Killion 1994) which was significant in that the Alaskan village's remains were one of the largest collections of the Smithsonian Institution and that the return was initially contested by the institution.

The NAGPRA acknowledges a museum's *right of possession* to an object, even a sacred object, if the museum acquired the object with the voluntary consent of an individual or group that had authority of alienation.

Fig. 3: In 1993 four boxes with bones from the American Museum of Natural History were burried at the churchyard at Qaanaaq, North Greenland. Courtesy of Adelaide de Menil.

Native Americans may not like the fact that their ancestors voluntarily transferred possession of these objects to museums, but NAGPRA does not mandate that they be repatriated (Merrill et al. 1993).

The repatriation of ethnographic and archaeologic relicts and ancient human remains has been used by radical politicians and by reactionary groups as a means to attract public attention to their cause. It is important that curation and ownership of museum collections not become political tools, either as an example of oppression of and insensitivity to minority cultures or as an insular antipathy to scientific research (Zimmerman 1993). It is, however, important to note that political front persons may in these cases take guidance from spiritual leaders and elders. Politics are involved in the sense that repatriation is a contest for control over cultural matters and intellectual property rights about them, and in some cases there has indeed been open pursuit of publicity and power (Zimmerman 1993).

The value of multi- and interdisciplinary investigations of ancient human remains for obtaining information about the cultural past and cultural identity of prehistoric population groups by applying the methods of modern natural and medical sciences has sometimes been forgotten in the political fight.

With regard to ancient human remains it must be stressed that much information on ancient man, his life ways and cultures, and diseases has been obtained by investigating ancient archaeological human remains (Ubelaker & Grant 1989; Alexandersen et al. 1992).

This is also the case in the Arctic region. The loss of potential knowledge seems to be greater in the case of losing admission to prehistoric skeletal materials than to ethnographic objects. Skeletal materials represent one of

a very limited array of sources of knowledge about prehistoric people and their lives, and their potential for revealing additional information increases with each advance in biomedical technology, e.g. DNA analysis. Ancient human material may also be valuable reference sources for evaluation of present or future environmental conditions of importance to the living population (AMAP 1997).

Within the Arctic region there has been political pressure for repatriation of ancient human remains in Alaska and Northern Canada. Traditionally, ancient human remains from the past of Greenland are stored in the LBAUC, in recent years deposited by the National Museum of Greenland. Multi- and interdisciplinary investigations have been carried out on skeletal material and mummified bodies in close cooperation between Greenlandic and Danish institutions (Hansen et al. 1985, 1991; Hansen & Gulløv 1989).

Greenlandic politicians have expressed their interest in such investigations and supported them recognizing the necessity to utilize all means to obtain a detailed knowledge of the past, particular when no written history is available. No wishes have been expressed to have Greenlandic human remains returned from institutions in Denmark or abroad for reburial.

The situation is another with regard to ethnographic and archaeologic specimens. Greenland is within the Danish realm and attained Home Rule in 1979. Greenland has approximate 55,000 inhabitants of which around 87% are of Inuit descent. The responsibility for the cultural sector was transferred to Greenland in 1981 and Greenland has its own legislation in the field: the Protection of Historical Sites and Buildings Act and the Greenland Museum Ordinance.

Through generations the National Museum of Denmark has been accumulating Greenlandic collections. The idea of transferring parts of these collections to museums in Greenland is not new. Already in 1961 the National Museum of Denmark agreed to contribute to the collections of a planned Greenland National Museum. This transfer of ethnographic and archaeologic objects started in 1982 on the occasion of the 1000th anniversary of Eric the Red's settlement in South Greenland. The socalled *Aron collection* consisting of 204 original watercolours made in the years 1858-1868 by the seal hunter Aron of Kangek (Meldgaard 1982; Kaalund 1997) was the first item to be handed over.

Since 1984 a joint Danish/Greenlandic Museum Commission has been sharing the vast archaeologic and ethnographic collections of the National Museum of Denmark collected through centuries. Thousands of important objects have been repatriated to the Greenland Museum in full agreement and to the satisfaction of everybody. A re-registration of the Greenland collection of the National Museum of Denmark, some 15,000 ethnographical and 100,000 archaeological objects, has taken place (Schultz-Lorentzen 1988).

Already in 1913 it was suggested that Greenland should have a museum of its own (Schultz-Lorentzen 1988). It was, however, only in 1956 that a museum association was formed and in 1966 a museum was opened in the Ny Hernnhut mission building in the capital Nuuk / Godthaab. In 1972 it was specified in the Danish Museum Act that the Greenland Museum was a regional museum. With the transferral of cultural affairs to the Homerule Government of Greenland in 1981 and with the Greenland Museum Ordinance the Greenland Museum in effect became the National Museum of Greenland. The museum system in Greenland has since been developed with the building of a new museum so that collections can be transferred from Denmark without risk of damage. Several local museums have also been founded. Thus, important cultural and historical material has been repatriated during recent years from Denmark to Greenland on the basis of objective criteria and in a friendly atmosphere without emotional discussions.

Jens Peder Hart Hansen, MD, DMSc
Department of Pathology, Gentofte Hospital, University of Copenhagen, DK-2900 Hellerup, Denmark

Abbriviations

LBAUC = Laboratory of Biological Anthropology, University of Copenhagen
NAGPRA = Native American Graves Protection and Repatriation Act
NWT = Northwest Territories, Canada

References

Alexandersen, Verner, Pia Bennike, Jens Peder Hart Hansen & Niels Lynnerup [1992]: **Biological Anthropology: prospects for a bio-cultural discipline.** *Arkæologiske Udgravninger i Danmark*, 1992:60-67 (Copenhagen: Det arkæologiske Nævn).

AMAP [1997]: **Arctic Pollution Issues: A State of the Arctic Environment Report.** 188 p. (Oslo: Arctic Monitoring and Assessment Programme).

Arnold, C. [1992]: **Repatriation of Skeletons to the Northwest territories: Past and Present.** *Information North*, 18(3):1-4 (Calgary: Arctic Institute of North America).

Birket-Smith, Kaj & Frederica de Laguna [1938]: **The Eyak Indians of the Copper River Delta, Alaska.** 592 p. *Det Kgl. Danske Videnskabernes Selskab.* (Copenhagen: Levin & Munksgaard).

Birket-Smith, Kaj [1953]: **The Chugach Eskimo.** *Nationalmuseets Skrifter, Etnografisk Række*, 6:1-262 (Copenhagen: National Museum of Denmark).

Bray, T. L. & T. W. Killion (editors) [1994]: **Reckoning with the Dead.** The Larsen Bay Repatriation and the Smithsonian Institution. 194 p. (Washington DC: Smithsonian Institution Press).

de Laguna, Fredericka [1956]: **Chugach Prehistory. The Archaeology of Prince William Sound, Alaska.** * p. (Seattle: University of Washington Press).

Downer, Alan S. [1993]: Comments to "The Return of the Ahayu:da. Lessons for Repatriation from Zuni Pueblo and the Smithsonian Institution" by William L. Merrill, Edmund J. Ladd, & T. J. Ferguson. *Current Anthropology*, 34:556-557 (Chicago: University of Chicago Press).

Fischer-Møller, K. [1937]: **Skeletal Remains of the Central Eskimos.** *Report of the Fifth Thule Expedition 1921-1924*, 3:1-104 (Copenhagen: Gyldendal).

Frisbie, Charlotte J. [1993]: Comments to "The Return of the Ahayu:da. Lessons for Repatriation from Zuni Pueblo and the Smithsonian Institution" by William L. Merrill,

Edmund J. Ladd, & T. J. Ferguson. *Current Anthropology*, 34:558 (Chicago: University of Chicago Press).

Gilberg, Rolf [1994]: **Mennesket Minik.** 680 p. (Espergærde: ILBE).

Hansen, Jens Peder Hart, Jørgen Meldgaard & Jørgen Nordqvist (editors) [1985]: **Qilakitsoq. De grønlandske mumier fra 1400-tallet.** 216 p. (Nuuk: Grønlands Landsmuseum; Copenhagen: Christian Ejlers' Forlag).

Hansen, Jens Peder Hart, Jørgen Meldgaard & Jørgen Nordqvist (editors) [1991]: **The Greenland Mummies.** 192 p. (Nuuk: The Greenland Museum; Copenhagen: Christian Ejlers' Forlag; London: The British Museum).

Hansen, Jens Peder Hart & Hans Christian Gulløv (editors) [1989]: **The Mummies from Qilakitsoq - Eskimos in the 15th Century.** *Meddelelser om Grønland, Man & Society*, 12:1-199 (Copenhagen: The Commission for Scientific Research in Greenland).

Hansen, Jens Peder Hart [1997]: **Chugach Remains Repatriated From Denmark.** *Newsletter*, Spring 1997:5-10 (Anchorage, Alaska: Keepers of the Treasures).

Harper, Kenn [1986]: **Give Me My Father's Body.** 275 p. (Frobisher Bay: Blacklead Books).

Johnson, John F. C. [1997]: **Ancient Chugach Native Remains are Back Home Again.** *Newsletter*, Spring 1997:3-4 (Anchorage, Alaska: Keepers of the Treasures).

Kaalund, Bodil [1997]: **Aron fra Kangeq 1822-1869.** 126 p. (Copenhagen: Brøndum).

Lauritzen, Philip [1987]: **Myten om Minik.** 138 p. (Copenhagen: Gyldendal).

Mathiassen, Therkel [1927]: **Archaeology of the Central Eskimos.** *Report of the Fifth Thule Expedition 1921-1924*, Descriptive Part, 4(1):1-327; The Thule Culture and its Position within the Eskimo Culture, 4(2):1-208 (Copenhagen: Gyldendal).

Meldgaard, Jørgen [1982]: **Aron - en af de mærkværdigste Billedsamlinger i Verden.** 112 p. (Copenhagen: National Museum of Denmark).

Merrill, William L, Edmund J. Ladd, & T. J. Ferguson [1993]: **The Return of the** `Ahayu:da`. *Current Anthropology*, 34:523-567 (Chicago: University of Chicago Press).

Native American Graves Protection and Repatriation Act (P.L. 101-601; 104 State 3048; 25 U.S.C. 3001-3013) November 16, 1992.

Schultz-Lorentzen, Helge [1987]: **Tilbage til Grønland - det dansk-grønlandske museumssamarbejde.** *Nationalmuseets Arbejdsmark*, 1987:177-192 (Copenhagen: National Museum of Denmark).

Schultz-Lorentzen, Helge [1988]: **Return of Cultural Property by Denmark to Greenland: From Dream to Reality.** *Museum International*, 160:200-205 (Paris: Unesco).

Ubelaker, D. H. & L. G. Grant [1989]: **Human Skeletal Remains: Preservation or Reburial?** *Yearbook of Physical Anthropology*, 32:249-287 (New York: Wiley Uss).

Zaslow, M. [1988]: **The northward expansion of Canada 1914-1967.** * p. (Toronto: McClelland & Stewart).

Zimmerman, Larry J. [1989]: **Human bones as symbols of power: Aboriginal American belief systems towards bones and "grave-robbing" archaeologists.** pp:211-216 in "Conflict in the archaeology of living traditions", editor: R. Layton, * p. (London: Unwin Hyman).

Zimmerman, Larry J. [1993]: Comments to "The Return of the Ahayu:da. Lessons for Repatriation from Zuni Pueblo and the Smithsonian Institution" by William L. Merrill, Edmund J. Ladd, & T. J. Ferguson. *Current Anthropology*, 34:562 (Chicago: University of Cicago Press).

Jigs from Greenland

Keld Hansen

In his book "Eskimo Sculpture" (1959) Jørgen Meldgaard wrote about the specialized Inuit tools and weapons such as harpoons and arrowheads, that in the making of these *equal attention was payed to beauty and efficiency - the two concepts were two sides of the same thing to the Inuit. The game animal also valued a handsome weapon and preferred to be killed by this.*

As I hope to show in the following pages, one may elaborate on Jørgen Meldgaard's words and claim that the same observation is valid for the fishing gear of the Inuit. And as for the fish, they too, failing a choice in the matter, may have preferred to be hooked on an imaginative, beautiful, and functional jig.

For hundreds, not to say thousands, of years the people of Greenland, Canada, Alaska, and Siberia have known and used a number of highly specialized methods of fishing. The most commonly used was probably to catch salmon and trout with a 'fish-lure' and a fishingspear or leister. In many places the so called *saputit*, stone-weirs, were maintained for centuries by the collective effort of the people. A stone-weir is a system of stone fences in the rivers which block the passage of the fish, making it possible at low the water to spear an amount of fish large enough to last the hunting families through the long, dark winter.

Harpoons for fishing, snares and traps, and in more recent times nets and "longlines" have all been used in Arctic waters, but to claim as many early writers have done that jigging was only for poor hunters or women and children does not seem probable, as one observes the ingenuity and amount of work put into the preparation of the fishing tackle in many museum collections. To utilize all available natural resources on a year round basis is a well known characteristic of Inuit society, and fish must have been a welcome variation as well as a necessary vitamin supplement to the usual diet of land and sea mammals. It is difficult to imagine why there should ever have been anything unpleasant, not to say degrading, in providing the household with a catch of fresh fish, when the occasion rose.

The archaeological find material

Arhaeological investigations in West Greenland, for instance at Qajaa and Qerqertarssusuk in the Disko Bay area show that 4.000 years ago the Saqqaq people were capable of catching deep sea fish like cod (Gadus morhua), Greenland halibut (Reinhardtius hippoglossoides) and Norway haddock (Sebastes marinus). Unfortunately their fishing gear have not been found, but fishbones were excavated and analyzed by archaeologists and biologists and determined to be of the species mentioned above personaly communication with Morten Meldgaard). There were, of course, many more bones from seal, whale and reindeer, but this could very well be a case of the fishbones quite literally having 'gone to the dogs', as they still do. Some of the fishbones could have been from cod which in certain periods of the year swim into shallow water where they can be speared from the shore. In other instances they can be interpreted as a secondary catch. During a hunting trip in Melville Bay in the summer of 1967 I personally experienced, for instance, how one can land Greenland halibut from a depth of 400 metres without any fishing gear. I was manouvering a small cutter around the icebergs and managed to harpoon and shoot a 2.5 m long hooded seal, while three hunters from the village of Nuussuaq were hunting narwhal from their kayaks near my boat. These experienced hunters immediately questioned me about the behaviour and movements of the hooded seal on the ice when I shot it. I answered to the best of my ability and was very surprised when the men declared that in that case we were going to eat Greenland halibut. I watched them cut open the seal, heat up a pot of saltwater on the stove and put in large pieces of fresh, undigested Greenland halibut taken from the stomach of the seal - more than enough for four hungry men.

Fish-jigs are not found in archaeological excavations of sites earlier than the 17th century Thule Culture. From approximately the same period there is a number of historical records.

Early historical descriptions

The English explorer John Davis wrote after his voyage in 1586 that Greenlanders on the west coast offered him cod, but unfortunately he did not think to ask them how they cought the fish. Olearius on the other hand in 1656 gives a description of Greenland fish-hooks:

"They are not made of iron, but from fish-bone, that is seal-bone, which they know how to shape with care."

In the beginning of the 17th century the nobleman Jens Bielke wrote a long poem about conditions in Greenland, probably on information given to him by the members of the Lindenov expedition, led by James Hall, who had returned in 1605. The sixth treaty of the poem says:

"From birds claws were the hooks with which they went fishing, ... "

These hooks made of birds claws may have existed. But in that case the bird must have been an eagle, unfortunately such 'fishing claws' have not been found in any archaeological sites. More likely the description in the verse refers to jigs fitted with a fish-lure made from the red feet of the black guillemot, or in the case of sea scorpion jigs with a lashed-on breastbone from a bird.

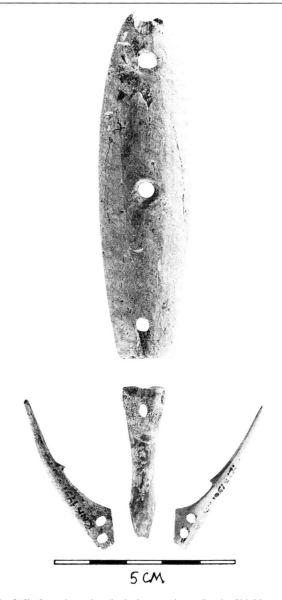

Fig. 2: Jig from the archaeological excavation at Sønder Skjoldunge in East Greenland. The sink is of soapstone, the two barbs of bone are fastened to a toe-bone from a seal.

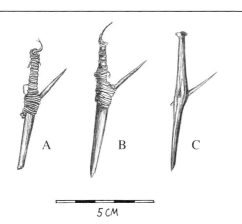

Fig. 1: Fishing hooks from the 18th century. A from Thule (Holtved). B & C from Inugsuk north of Upernavik (Mathiassen).

From the description of Greenland given by Peder Hansen Resen in 1687 we learn that a Daniel Dannel in 1652 at 63°N, 65°N and 67°N (that is between Nuuk and Sisimiut) met many natives and bought from them various kinds of fish, among which were bream, large halibuts and a small unknown fish that was dried in the wind and sun.

Large halibuts (Hippoglossus hippoglossus) and *ammassat* (mallotus villosus), the small fish unknown to Europeans, are correctly described, but the freshwater bream would hardly have been for sale at the latitudes in question. Dannel may have been referring to halibut, wolf fish (Anarrhichas minor), or lumpfish (Cyclopterus lumpus).

On his second journey in 1653 Dannel reports large amounts of cod and big halibuts, while on his third journey in 1654 the crew sailed out to fish at the mouth of the Godthåb fjord *where they found much fish at a shallow outside Balravier, and also in the same place saw a mermaid with flowing hair and very lovely.*

Here too we accept the information on cod and halibut, but do not really believe in the lovely mermaid. The same report understandably omits to mention that four adult Greenlanders were captured and taken back to Europe as showpieces.

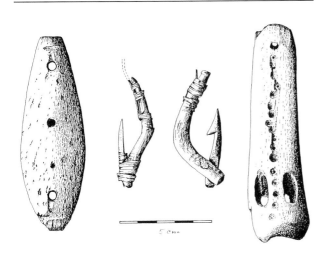

Fig. 3: Sinks of soapstone (A & D) and two fishing hooks. (B) has a barb made of the breastbone from a seabird. (C) has a barb made of antler. Drawing by H. C. Gulløv.

In 1722 the priest Hans Egede writes in his Relations from Greenland:

Their fishing gear are long straps of sealskin or pieces of baleen from the whalefish with hooks of bone or the iron, they buy from us. Generally speaking their tools, boats and other things are done in a pretty and clever manner, even though it is slow work and there is a lack of convenient tools.

We must bear in mind that the man writing this is an efficient, rational European missionary, and even Hans Egede, were he alive today, would have to admit that most of the traditional tools and weapons from Greenland, harpoon heads, knives, arrows, fishing tackle etc. for thousands of years had been made without the help of 'convenient tools'. That it may have taken many a long winter's night for a hunter and fisherman to make exactly the jig he wanted and knew would bring him a catch, would just enhance his pleasure in the tool and his belief in its ability to make the fish want to be hooked especially by his jig. His children, the future hunters and fishermen, certainly would admire this handmade tool more so than had it been bought readymade from a European.

Many years later Hans Egede did admit that the Greenlanders' fishing tackle were both efficient and functional, when he wrote, that the Greenlanders could catch fish with their lines of baleen more easily than European fishermen with their lines of hemp.

In 1724 Poul, one of Hans Egede's sons, wrote after an incident where a native family had cut up one of his Latin books and remodelled it as a useless white anorak:

My dividers, which I had also lost, I later found by a grave together with the other tools belonging to the deceased, and both the legs were bent like the hooks they use for catching sea scorpion and fastened to a line made of baleen.

Poul Egede continues, that at the icefjord between Jakobshavn and Claushavn he was given a 364 fathoms long line made of baleen.

Finally we have the description of a Greenland fishing hook written in the beginning of the 18th century by Zorgdrager, the captain of a Dutch whaler:

A fishing line of 7-8 fathoms made of baleen in one end in a loop hangs a stone with three or four hooks fastened above and below two or three white beads or some other milkywhite piece.

In 1812 the missionary and ethnographer Otto Fabricius gives a very detailed description of the Greenlandic fishing tackle. He makes a distinction between jigs for sea scorpions used from a kayak or from the ice, with the same type of short line as the one on a fishing rod used from land, and the deep sea line used for fishing for halibut, Greenland halibut, catfish and cod. Fabricius writes of the sea scorpion jig:

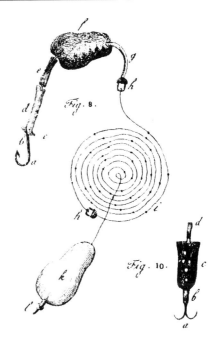

Fig. 4: Jig for sea scorpion. Original plate from Fabricius 1812 (Fabricius 1962).

Fig. 5: Small jigs, to a minimum weight of 150 gram, are used especially for fishing sea scorpion in shallow water, where it is often possible to see the fish in the clear water.

Fig. 6: Larger jigs, up to one kilogram in weight, are used in deep water and strong currents. Cod, wolf fish, and, as shown on the drawing, halibut and redfish are often caught at a depth of several hundred metres.

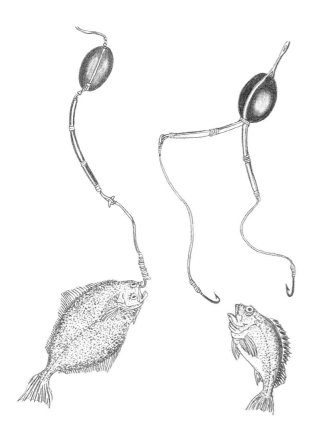

No live bait is used with these jigs, they are just moved about in the water, attracting the fish from the deep by their glittering stone.

He says further that the constantly moving jig should be held just over the seabed, and when the fish is just above it with its mouth gaping, the fisherman jerks the line. The hook will catch the fish, in the mouth or elsewhere.

Jigs from the present century

Today one can observe a great number of handmade and imaginative jigs in museums in Denmark and Greenland. The largest collections, of course, are in the National Museum and Archives of Greenland in Nuuk and the National Museum of Denmark in Copenhagen. There is still hope, however, for those of you who have not acquired your own jig. With a bit of ingenuity and experience it is possible to fish without equipment. Along the streams in Greenland one can often watch how children as well as adults, at the sight of a trout among the stones in the ice cold water, in a split second will grab and land the large fish with their bare hands. And I have once seen an old woman take a safety pin out of her collar, bend the end of the pin a little, fasten it to a piece of string and lower the whole thing into the water and a few minutes later to land a big, fat and kicking trout on the heather by her kamiks.

In Hans Lynge's memoirs of his childhood in Nuuk he writes about catching sea scorpion (Cottus scorpius L.) without hooks or jigs:

As far back as I can remember we fished. When our mother forbade us to fish because there were fish every-where and our clothes smelled of fish, and she would refuse to give us money to buy hooks at the shop, we would get hold of some old string and bind the live bait to one end. Then we would go down to the coast, lie on our stom-achs on a protuding rock and fish for sea scorpion. The idea was to let the fish swallow the bait and as much of the line as possible before one gently pulled it out of the water. If it began spitting out one had to give out some line. A sel-frespecting sea scorpion would not let go of the bait that easy, and with a bit of patience it would swallow the line so thoroughly that one could pull it out.

When it comes to making a jig the technical knowl-edge of the children equalled that of the grown men. Most of the jigs illustrated here were no doubt made in the man-ner which Hans Lynge describes in detail, telling us how as a boy he used the melting pot where his father melted lead for rifle bullets and shot cartridges:

I got hold of a piece of cork which I pierced and then fitted two jigs crossed like an anchor through the hole. Then I made a cylinder of old newspaper and lashed the cork with the jigs tightly at one end. A fire of heather was lit between three boulders placed so the melting pot could rest on them without turning over. I enjoyed the dangerous job and was rather proud of the good result. No adult would forbid a young Greenland boy to do this. At the age of ten we had been taught how to help our father load his

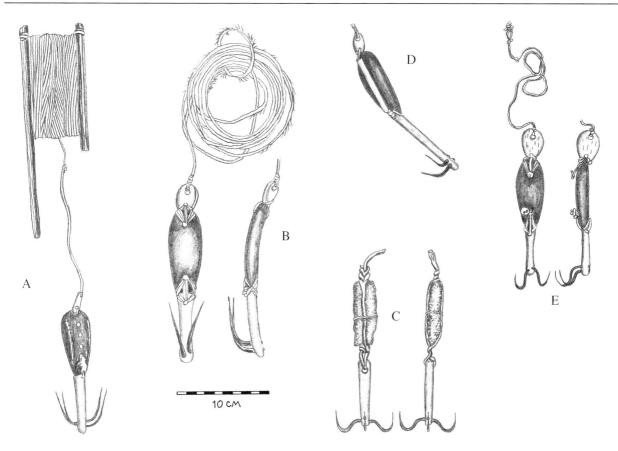

Fig. 7: A selection of jigs for sea scorpions from West Greenland. The small empty holes in the soapstone sinks were probably meant for small pieces of cloth that attracts the fish.

(A) and (D) still has the stem of a feather attached. On (E) one can see a couple of mother of pearl buttons from the local shop. The sinks are usually made of soapstone, but one can also find granite used as in (C).

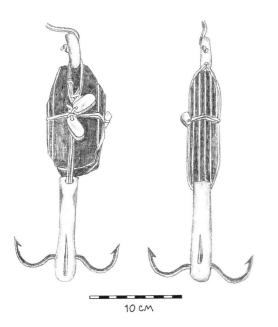

Fig. 8: In this case the sink is made of 7 hoops bound together with ivory beads.

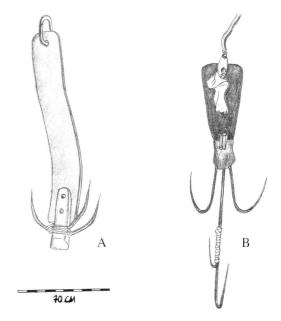

Fig. 9: Upernavik jig. (A) is made of a thick brass plate with sharpened nails as babs fastened to a piece of reindeer antler. The piece of cloth in (B) is red silk, which is very common in all surviving traditional jigs sinks.

cartridges, an even more dangerous job. I then flattened the tip of the cylindrical plummet which was now melted to the jigs, and scraped the surface of the lead to make it shine.

In this article there has been space to illustrate only a small selection of Greenland jigs, which over time have been used from land, kayaks, umiaqs, dinghies, larger boats or through a hole in the winter ice along the coasts of Greenland. One thing all these jigs seem to have in common is the fact that they are rarely used with live bait, but the fish are attracted by a 'lure', a different one for each kind of fish, which is fastened to the line above the jig or jigs. The hook is pulled up into the fish and out of its rightful element it comes. A fish-lure can be various forms of beads made of tooth or bone, glimmering fishbone or split bones from birdwings. In more recent times we also see porcelain buttons or little red pieces of cloth. Like the Spaniards, who think that the bull charges at the sight of red, the Inuit of the Arctic seem to think that red is the very colour with which to catch fish. Before the arrival of European merchants with red cloth for sale they would use the red feet of the black guillemot in Greenland or as in Alaska a little red spot on the beak of crested auklet.

The jigs illustrated in this article clearly show that all Arctic hunters throughout time have employed the same accuracy, ingenuity and craftmanship in the making of their functional and often beautifully designed fish-hooks, as they did with their harpoon heads and other hunting equipment designed for the larger and more prestigious mamals.

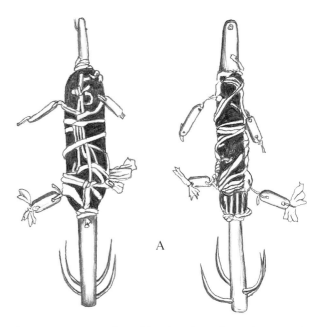

Fig. 11: Two heavy jigs with a lot of small attachments. (A) with beads of walrus tusk and small red pieces of cloth. (B) has pieces of cloth fastened with small wooden pins in the two hollows on the front.

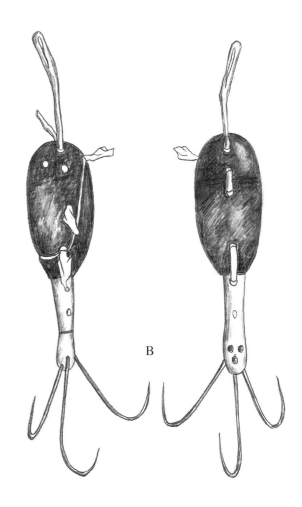

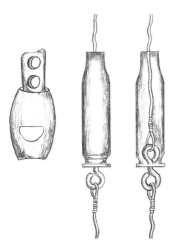

Fig. 10: To prevent the line from twisting when fishing it is very useful to have a whirl on it. Left: 18th century whirl of bone. Right: 20th century whirl made from a cartridge-case.

Keld Hansen is curator at the Viking Ship Museum in Roskilde.

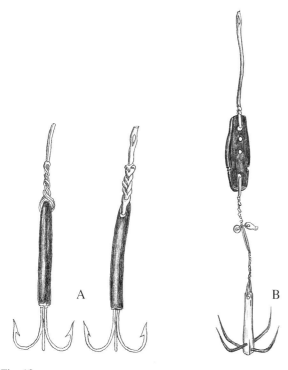

Fig. 12: Two jigs for sea scorpions. (A) is the type Hans Lynge made as a child, with a lead sink. The sink on (B) is a flat piece of soapstone, probably reused from a pot or a lamp.

Fig. 13: Jig for sea scorpion with red and white pieces of silk tied to a sink of soapstone. Notice that the upper part of bone or tusk, as on all jigs, is fastened at an angle. When fishing, this jig goes through the water in a curve making it easier to hook the fish.

Fig. 14: Wolf fish (Anarhichas minor) jigged 1961 in a fjord in West Greenland. The jig was bought at the local shop.

Fig. 14

Fig. 12

5 CM

Fig. 13

References

Birket-Smith, Kaj [1924]: **Ethnography of the Egedesminde District.** *Meddelelser om Grønland*, 66:1-484 (Copenhagen: C. A. Reitzels Forlag).

Egede, Hans [1925]: **Det gamle Grønlands Nye Perlustration eller Naturel-Historie 1741.** *Meddelelser om Grønland*, 54:1-442 (Copenhagen: C. A Reitzels Forlag).

Egede, Paul [1988]: **Efterretninger om Grønland 1721-1788.** *Det grønlandske Selskabs Skrifter*, 29:1-204 (Copenhagen: Det Grønlandskle Selskab).

Fabricius, Otto [1962]: **A Precise Description of the Hunting of Terristrial Animals, of Fowling and Fishing by the Greenlanders.** *Meddelelser om Grønland*, 140(2):67-96 (Copenhagen: C. A. Reitzels Forlag).

Gulløv, Hans Christian & Hans Kapel [1979]: **Haabetz Colonie 1721-1728.** Etnografisk Række, 17:1-245 (Copenhagen: The National Museum of Denmark).

Hansen, Keld (editor) [1971]: **Grønlandske fangere fortæller.** 207 p. (Holsteinsborg: Nordiske Landes Forlag).

Holtved, Erik [1944]: **Archaeological Investigations in the Thule District.** *Meddelelser om Grønland*, 141(1):1-308 & 141(2):1-184 (Copenhagen: C. A. Reitzels Forlag).

Lee, Richard B. [1968]: **What Hunters Do for a Living, or, How to Make Out on Scarce Resources.** pp:30-48 in "Man the Hunter", editor: Richard B. Lee & Irven DeVore, 415 p. (Chicago: Aldine Publishing Company).

Kisbye Møller, J. [1985]: **Jens Bielkes grønlandsberetning 1605.** *Tidsskriftet Grønland*, 33(5-6-7):117-192 (Copenhagen: Det Grønlandske Selskab).

Lynge, Hans [1981]: **Grønlands indre liv. Erindringer fra barndomsårene.** 106 p. (Nuuk: Det grønlandske Forlag).

Mathiassen, Therkel [1930]: **Inugsuk.** *Meddelelser om Grønland*, 77:148-337 (Copenhagen: C. A. Reitzels Forlag).

Meldgaard, Jørgen [1959]: **Eskimo Skulptur.** 48 p. (Copenhagen: J. H. Schultz Forlag).

Nationalmuseets Spørgeliste nr. 5. Fiskeri. (Copenhagen 1960: The National Museum of Denmark).

Zordrager, C. G. [1723]: **Alte und neue Grönländische Fischerei.** * p. (Leipzig).

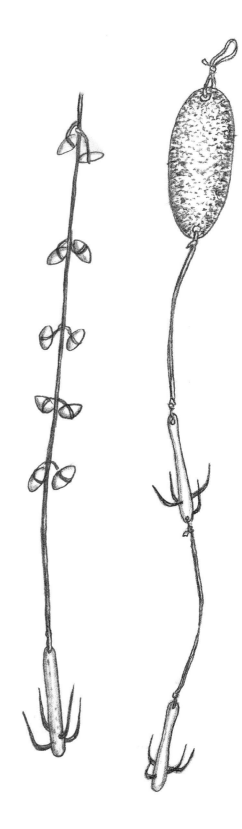

Fig. 15: Most places in West Greenland a jig is called qasorsaq, a kind of arrow (qarsoq). The verb qarsorsarpaa means 'to get it with a hook' or 'to hook it'. A hook is called oqummersaq (oqummiaq is 'something in the mouth', and oqummisserpoq is 'stick something in your mouth').

Pioneer Settlements of the Belcher Islands, N.W.T.

Elmer Harp, Jr.

The first reference to the archaeology of the Belcher Islands occurs in the reports of the Fifth Thule Expedition (Mathiassen 1927). In 1922 Knud Rasmussen had purchased a collection of specimens that was said to have come from graves in the Belchers, and when Therkel Mathiassen analyzed these finds he attributed them to the Thule Culture. However, at that time Mathiassen had not yet accepted the validity of Dorset Culture, recently identified by Diamond Jenness as a stage that preceded Thule Culture (1925), and he did not recognize that the Belchers collection contained a mixture of Thule and Dorset elements. After that brief exposure to the scholarly world the Belchers receded into eclipse for fifteen years.

Then George Quimby (1940) and Jenness (1941) described new collections that had been gathered there by local Inuit, and by that time scientific interest in Dorset Culture had grown stronger, despite the fact that all of these early collections completely lacked any provenience data.

(In 1974 I discovered on northern Flaherty Island what I believe to be the general site area where the natives dug up some or all of these last collections: it was a clustered array of thirty house rings and pits from 80-90 feet above sea level, but twenty-five of them had been severely vandalized so I elected not to investigate further).

Quimby's report proclaimed a new manifestation, 'Manitunik', which he interpreted as a 16th century occupation; he believed the primary culture base of Manitunik had been Thule, with a secondary overlay of Dorset influence. Jenness's descriptions, on the other hand, included some unmistakable Dorset types, such as flaked stone triangular harpoon points with concave bases, ground and polished nephrite gravers with bevelled edges and single side notches, facet-ground slate knives with side notches, and realistic ivory carvings of animals and human beings. (I found many identical or similar specimens in Dorset sites at low elevations, such as Kingaaluk, although unfortunately there were no associated organic remains).

Once more the Belchers subsided into archaeological obscurity, until 1954 when Claude Desgoffe initiated a field campaign there. Sadly, however, Desgoffe and his two Inuit companions perished in a boating accident that summer, but his collection of artifacts and field notes was retrieved and deposited in the National Museum of Canada. Still later, in 1970, these materials were turned over to Joseph Benmouyal, a graduate student at the University of Montreal. Mr. Benmouyal's study and analysis of the Desgoffe collection became the substance of his Master's thesis at Montreal (1972), and I am indebted to him for an opportunity to study this excellent and thorough document.

Benmouyal's descriptions affirm that the Desgoffe collection derives mainly from Thule Culture: it may have contained several items of more recent vintage, as well as a few Dorset specimens, but these were minor aberrants. Hence, Benmouyal concluded that the Manitunik culture, as defined by Quimby, had not existed, and he believed that the collection studied by Quimby was a mixture of specimens from sites of three different cultures, for example Thule, post-contact Inuit, and also probably Dorset.

Incidentally, all of Desgoffe's collections derived from seven coastal sites scattered through the archipelago, so he was apparently unaware of the fact that earlier sites existed at higher interior levels.

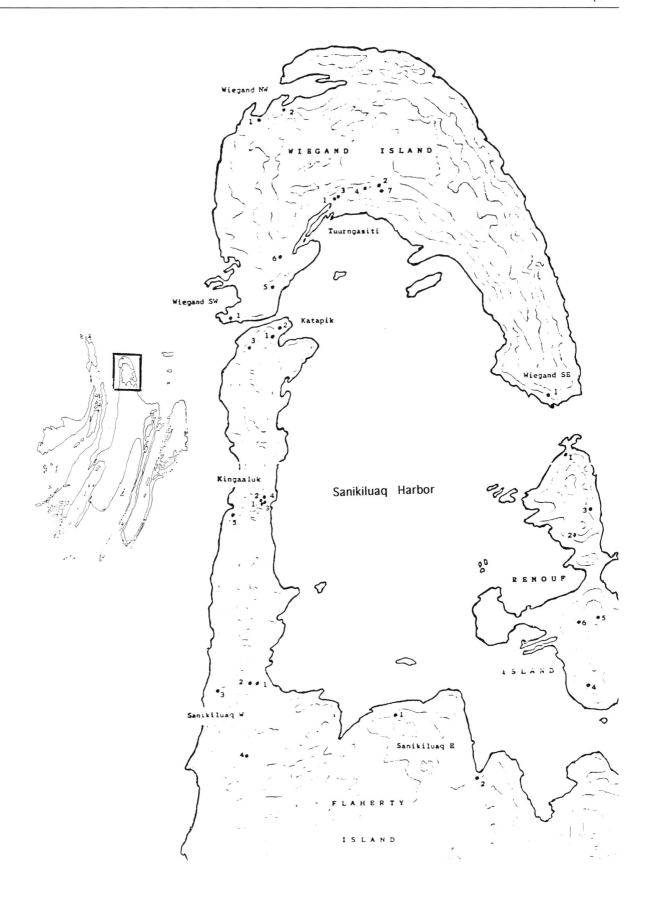

Fig. 1: The Becher Islands, Northwest Territories, Canada.

Fig. 2: The High Sites at Tuurgasiti.

a: View of T-2 looking south over Sanikiluaq Harbor.

b: T-4, House-2

On the basis of my reconnaissance in the Belchers in 1974 and 1975 I agree with him about the nonexistence of a significant, discrete Manitunik entity. However, in earlier phases of the culture sequence there I discovered a number of Pre-Dorset sites that bear a notable resemblance to the Independence Cultures of northern Greenland (Knuth 1967), and, of all the prehistoric sites in the Belcher Islands known to me, they occupy the highest positions, upwards of 100 feet (30½ m) above sea level. Dorset sites occurred from 100 feet to 50 feet (30½ m to 15 m) above sea level, Thule sites from 50 feet to 30 feet (15 m to 9 m), while recent and modern sites are normally found below 30 feet (9 m). Due to space limitations here I cannot present all of these matters in comprehen-

sive detail, but I trust the following minimal descriptions, photos, and field sketches pertaining to the highest sites will suffice for this brief paper about the pioneer hunters who first came to the Belchers.

As representative examples of these high sites I have chosen Tuurngasiti-2 (T-2) and Tuurngasiti-4 (T-4) on Wiegand Island, and Renouf-2 (Fig. 1).

'Tuurngasiti' is a name told to me by the local people, who said that it means 'the land of many ghosts'. The Inuit of Sanikiluaq apparently have definite notions about that upland site area embedded in their folk-lore, but at the time of my investigations none of them knew anything about the early sites that lay underfoot, and they expressed great surprise upon viewing my excavations.

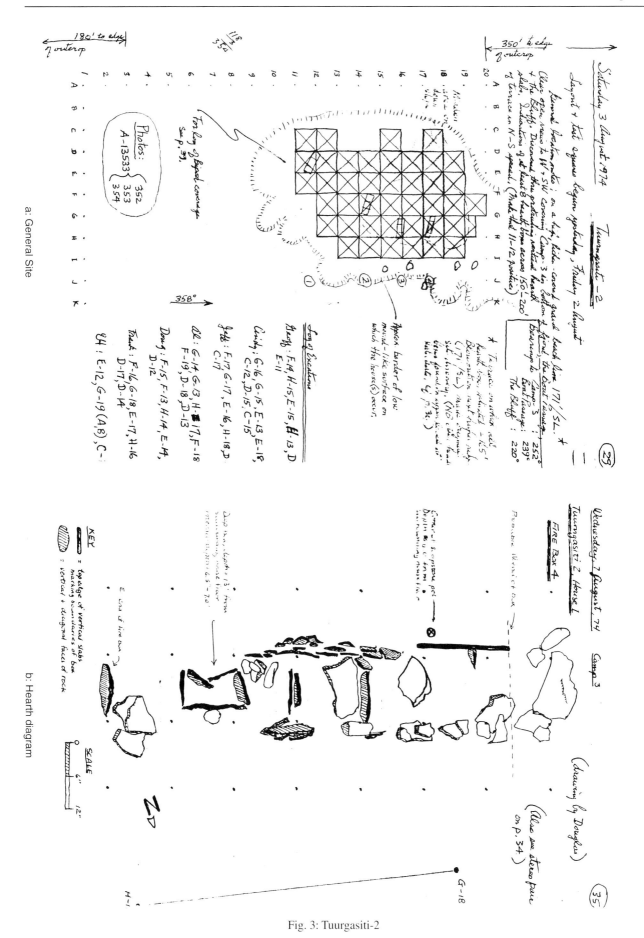

a: General Site

b: Hearth diagram

Fig. 3: Tuurgasiti-2

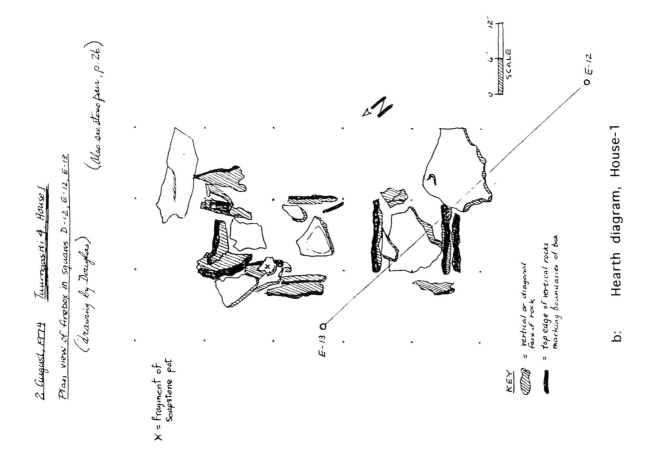

2 August, 1974   Tuurgasiti-4 House

Plan view of firebox in squares D-12, E-12, E-13

(drawing by Douglas)

(Also see stereo pair, p. 26)

X = fragment of soapstone pot

KEY   ▨ = vertical or diagonal face of rock

       ▬ = top edge of vertical rocks marking boundaries of box

b: Hearth diagram, House-1

a: Hearth box in House-1

Fig. 4: Tuurgasiti-4

Fig. 5: Heart Boxes before excavation.

a: T-6, House-7

b: Renouf-2, House-1

Fig. 6: Renouf-2, House-!.

a: During excavation

b: Excavation completed

These sites share similar high barrens on Wiegand and Renouf Islands, and very few other hilltops in the archipelago reach the same or higher elevations. T-2 is 171 feet (52 m) high, T-4 is 127 feet (39 m) high, and Renouf-2 is 123 feet (37½ m) above sea level. The occupation areas are situated on low, gently curving terraces that are contained within shallow swales which, in turn, are bordered at varying distances by Pre-Cambrian outcrops that are capped by heavily glaciated basalt flows (Fig. 2). These dry upland surfaces are covered with a thin growth of lichen and mosses, and they bore no immediate evidence of human activity, past or present: There were no stone rings or surface structures, no excavated house floors, only a scattering of small ruptures in the turf and very shallow blowouts.

However, one of these blowouts offered the first clue to a hidden site, a sparse sprinkling of chert flakes. A trial excavation around that small patch of debitage then exposed a rectangular hearth box, the first that I had seen in the Belchers. It was like numerous others to follow in the high sites, and each of these submerged structures consisted of thin rock slabs set vertically into the ground to form a square, hollow box, sometimes with double walls, and usually near one or both ends of an elongated hearth trench (Figs. 3:4). These structures very closely resemble the hearth boxes of the Independence I Culture of Peary Land, as described by Knuth (1967), and also those from the Port Refuge site on Devon Island described by McGhee (1976). At Tuurngasiti, more painstaking surface exploration taught us that portions of the edges of these vertical slabs sometimes protruded slightly through the natural camouflage of moss and lichens, and when we found two or more edge segments appearing either in parallel or rectangular formation this anomaly unerringly signaled a buried hearth and a house floor (Figs. 5:6). That early lesson learned at T-2 led to the discovery of 15 other house locations in that one site alone.

These were probably skin-covered spring or summer dwellings, although I saw no traces of structural members or roofing materials. The house floors were barely covered by the scanty tundra vegetation, and those that stood apart as single lodges were circular and about 15 feet (4½ m) in diameter, as defined roughly by an area that was relatively free of stones (Fig. 2b).

In T-2 the first four hearths that we excavated formed a slightly curved alignment that faintly suggested a larger communal structure (Fig. 3a), but that speculation was not further substantiated. The longitudinal axes of the central hearth pits pointed in most cases toward the sea front, but there were no clear indications of a doorway facing in that direction. There were no raised platforms, and the major spaces on either side of the central hearth were the essential unpaved living areas.

Chipped stone tools and scrap flakes, generally few in number, were scattered randomly about the floor of the dwellings, although in two houses a small cache of im-

plements had been stowed in one of the hearth boxes. Organic debris was totally absent in most houses, but we did find two small unproductive patches of bone fragments in middens on the slope below the houses. Steatite was very rare in the high sites and our finds consisted only of several fragments of shallow blubber lamps and one complete specimen lying fully exposed amidst the surface lichens on the periphery of T-2.

There was no sign of deep, rectangular cooking pots, and I believe their absence helps to explain the function of the slab rock boxes: The hunters who briefly occupied these high sites were travelling light, without the burden of heavy and fragile stone cooking pots; second, although I observed steatite veins in outcrops at low coastal elevations, no source of potstone may have been available close to the high sites. Fragments of charcoal were occasionally localized in the middle segments of the hearth pits, together with firecracked rocks, but not in the hearth boxes at either end of the trenches. Moreover, I did not observe substantial fire signs, such as blackening or carbonized deposits, on the interior surfaces of most boxes. Therefore, I think the square hearth boxes might have been draped with raw animal skins and used with heated rocks as food-boiling pots. (Compare the carefully paved hearth box in Renouf-2, House-1: Fig. 6).

The specialized hearth boxes occurred only in the shallow tent circles in the high sites, and I did not find any associated with semi-subterranean winter dwellings in lower sites.

In addition to these hearth structures, the high Belcher sites yielded rather thin, inconsistent inventories of flaked stone and slate artifacts (Figs. 7:8) that differed markedly from collections made in the Dorset winter houses at lower elevations, approximately 50 feet to 100 feet (15 m to 30½ m) above sea level. In regard to the few projectile points from the high sites, those with basal side notches were most common, followed by long isoscelene shapes with straight bases; only one site yielded serrated-edge points, and simple stemmed points did not occur at all. Side blades were plentiful in two sites, and bevelled slate points with single or double side notches occurred in three sites; they were very numerous in T-5.

In general, weapon points seem to have been a minor component of material culture, whereas fabricating tools were more numerous, particularly asymmetric biface knives and end scrapers. Occasional ground and polished gravers occurred in several sites at different levels, but only in the high sites did we find true burins, especially in the lodges of T-2, together with a high incidence of burin spalls and retouched prismatic blades (Fig. 7). These latter traits, together with the hearth boxes, establish a clear cultural difference between the high sites and the Dorset and Thule sites at lower levels, while most other elements of the tool and weapon inventory occurred sporadically in various of the lower sites and are therefore less determinative of cultural identity.

site	house	date	sample
Tuurngasiti 2	6	1170 B.C.	SI-2564
Tuurngasiti 2	10	965 B.C.	SI-2565B
Tuurngasiti 2	5	725 B.C.	SI-2563A
Tuurngasiti 2	8	580 B.C.	SI-2565A
Tuurngasiti 2	10	175 B.C.	SI-2566
Tuurngasiti 2	11	145 B.C.	SI-2567
Tuurngasiti 4	1	350 B.C.	SI-2142
Kingaaluk-1		605 B.C.	SI-2129
Kingaaluk-1		380 A.D.	SI-2130
Kingaaluk-1		890 A.D.	SI-2132
Renouf-2	no date available		

As for the time of these occupations, there is a broad sequential fit from high-early to low-late sites, but major inconsistencies do occur, presumably because of humic contaminants and other environmental irregularities that must have affected the dating samples. The following brief table shows the spread of radiocarbon dates from the high Tuurngasiti-2 and 4 sites to Kingaaluk-1, which is arbitrarily selected as a representative of the low-late Dorset occupation. Otherwise, the mid-level early Dorset sites are omitted because they lie beyond our detailed consideration.

Dates for the high sites must be accepted leniently. I regard the earliest at 1170 B.C., and probably the latest two at 175 B.C. and 145 B.C. as extreme. Those in the middle range (see table 1) might more reasonably be grouped together in comfortable moderation. The basic problem here is lack of sufficient data: the inventory from the Belchers is still very limited, and beyond the linkages that burins and structured hearth boxes establish between the Belcher Islands high sites and some ancestral arctic expression of Independence I, we are driven to conjecture.

At the low-late end of the occupation sequence, as at Kingaaluk-1, there are comparable problems. The two latest dates are supportable because of associated Dorset artifacts, and the suspiciously early 605 B.C. date is also accompanied by late Dorset artifacts. However, that particular dating sample was found close beside a crude three-sided firebox made of vertical slabs, which faintly resembled the more elegant hearth boxes of the high sites. In spite of this anomaly it seems reasonable to assume that the Dorset and Thule sites in the Belcher Islands were generally occupied within the first millenium A.D. I am unable to separate other earlier or Pre-Dorset stages from the Belchers sequence, and I have no positive explanations for the deviant combinations noted above.

Originally, I thought that Dorset Culture in the Belcher Islands might have its most direct and closest affinities with late Dorset sites that I have investigated in Richmond Gulf and the Nastapoka Islands off the east coast of Hudson Bay. All of these sites fall within a comparable range of elevation above sea level, and there are numerous generic similarities in their artifact assemblages. However, there are differences in house design and artifact types such as burins, side blades, and a preponderance of ground and polished slate weapons which are associated only with the Belcher Islands. Add to these the structured hearth boxes and we see a complex that seems to relate more directly northward, into the core area of Dorset Culture through Taylor's Tyara site in northeastern Hudson Bay (1968), through Maxwell's early Dorset sites at Lake Harbour, Baffin Island (1973), through Meldgaard's series at Igloolik (1962), and ultimately to the remote time of Knuth's Independence I Culture stage in North East Greenland.

In this brief paper I have not had an opportunity to honor sufficiently the great contributions to Dorset studies that Jørgen Meldgaard has made over many years. All of us with an interest in arctic prehistory are indebted to him for his long, dedicated involvement in the archaeology of Greenland and the eastern Arctic, and for the excellence of his resultant oeuvre. I have known him since the early years of his career, and I am honored to be able to count him as a friend. He is a true exemplar of a gentleman and a scholar.

Elmer Harp, Jr., Professor, Dartmouth College, USA.

Fig. 7: Various types from Tuurngasiti.

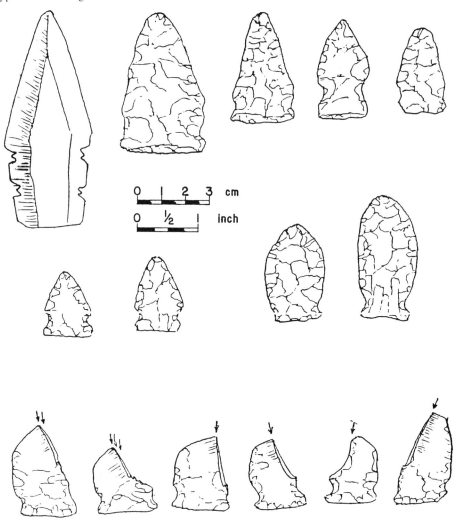

T-2: Points, Knives, Burins

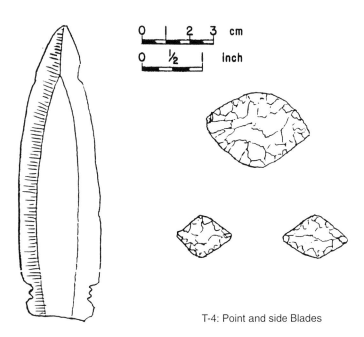

T-4: Point and side Blades

Fig. 8: Tuurngasiti Types.

a: T-2 Various   b: T-4 Various

c: Renouf-2 Various   d: T-4 Steatite lamp

Acknowledgement

This research was generously supported by the National Science Foundation under grants GS-42889 and SOC74-13294 A01, for which I have been continuingly grateful.

References

Benmouyal, Joseph [1972]: **Etude Archeologique de sites Eskimo aux Iles Belcher, T.N.O.** Dissertation submitted to the Graduate Faculty of the Department of Anthropology, University of Montreal, in partial fulfillment of the requirements for the degree of Master of Arts. Manuscript.

Jenness, Diamond [1925]: **A New Eskimo Culture in Hudson Bay**. *The Geographical Review*, 15:428-37 (New York: *).

Jennes, Diamond [1941]: **An Archaeological Collection from the Belcher Islands.** *Annals of the Carnegie Museum*, 28:189-206 (Pittsburgh).

Knuth, Eigil [1967]: *Archaeology of the Musk-Ox Way. Contribution*, 5:1-70 (Paris: Ecoles Pratiques des Haute Etudes, Sorbonne, Centre d'Etudes Arctiques et Finno-Scandinaves).

Mathiasson, Therkel [1927]: **Archaeology of the Central Eskimos.** *Report of the Fifth Thule Expedition 1921-1924*, 4(1):1-328 & 4(2):1-208 (Copenhagen: Gyldendal).

Maxwell, Moreau S. [1973]: **Archaeology of the Lake Harbour District, Baffin Island.** *Archaeological Survey of Canada, Mercury Series*, Paper 6. * p. (Ottawa: *).

McGhee, Robert [1973]: **Paleoeskimo Occupations of Central and High Arctic Canada.** pp:15-39 in "Eastern Arctic Prehistory: Paleoeskimo Problems", editor: Moreau S. Maxwell, *Memoirs of the Society for American Archaeology*, 31:15-39 (Washington DC).

Meldgaard, Jørgen [1962]: **On the Formative Period of the Dorset Culture.** pp:92-95 in "Prehistoric Cultural Relations between the Arctic and Temperate Zones of North America", editor: John M. Campbell, *Arctic Institute of North America, Technical Paper*, 11:1-181 (Montreal: Arctic Institute of North America).

Quimby, George I., Jr. [1940]: **The Manitunik Eskimo Culture of East Hudson Bay.** *American Antiquity*, 6: 148-165 (Washington DC: Society for American Archeology).

Taylor, William E., Jr. [1968]: **The Arnapik and Tyara Sites; an Archaeological Study of Dorset Culture Origins**. *Memoir*, 22:*-* (Washington DC: Society for American Archaeology).

He who opens an Old Grave also raises a Storm[1]
Preservation Activities in Greenland seen in Historical Perspective

Hans Kapel

It was less than 100 years ago that the effort to secure the part of Greenland's cultural heritage represented by old settlements, graves, hunting grounds, and historical buildings began. The preservation idea was put forward and debated in a political forum for the first time in 1913.

This article describes the long bureaucratic road from the birth of the idea, expressed in the first declarations of intent, to the passing of the present Home Rule Act on preservation in 1980.

To bring the events into a historical context, the development of the Danish preservation efforts has been explained in brief. Finally, the establishment of the cultural-historic index on preserved relics of the past, and its adjustment to EDB, is mentioned.

The preservation issue on the agenda

At the provincial council's meeting in Nanortalik on August 30, 1913, it was discussed by what means one could preserve the Greenlandic cultural heritage and protect archaeological finds and relics for posterity. The question was dealt with as item eleven on the agenda provided.

Leading catechist Josef Kleist, member for the 1st district (Nanortalik), found it unreasonable that grave finds were exported from the country, since the Greenlanders had no other history than what was found in the graves.

This view gained support, among others from the photographer John Møller, elected for the 8th district (Nuuk), who, with regret, concluded that previously used hunting tools were now almost impossible to obtain as a consequence of the extensive grave robberies in recent years.

Member for the 3rd district, hunter Gerhard Hansen (Alluitsup Paa) emphasized the fact that Greenlanders were not to blame for the unfortunate conditions, and the council's chairman, Ole Bendixen, could confirm that the plunderings had been systematized by Danes. The problems, he said, were biggest in the districts of Sukkertoppen and Holsteinsborg, where the local population - to some extent - had been tempted to take part in the destruction[2].

The reason why this question was considered in the Provincial Council in 1913, was a notice issued two years earlier by the leader of the National Museum of Denmark, Sophus Møller, to the Greenland Administration, with a request for arrangements to be made to preserve Greenland's cultural treasures. The delayed response to this request was undoubtably due to the change in systems in 1912, when the provincial councils of North and South Greenland respectively were established, and could therefore take a political stand in the issue.

The letter from the National Museum of Denmark was partly a reaction to several years of systematic destruction of graves and ruins, as mentioned especially concentrated around Sukkertoppen and Holsteinsborg. It was here that Reverend V. C. Frederiksen over a period had gathered a substantial collection of object, with the aim to supply the museum in Svendborg with a representative Greenland collection.

The move made by the National Museum of Denmark was probably caused by the fact that valuable museums object were seen to bypass the country's central museum, and part of V. C. Frederiksen's collections

Fig. 1: The Provincial Government for South Greenland photographed after the first election in 1911. Rear, from left: Johannes Josefsen (Qaqortoq); Josva Kleist (Frederiksdal); Jens Hansen (Nanortalik); Jacob Hegelund (Paamiut); Otto Egede (Narsaq); Peter Rosing (Kangaamiut); Hans Motzfeldt (Qeqertarssuatsiaat); Gerhard Hansen (Sydprøven). Sitting, from left: Nathan Lyberth (Maniitsoq); govenor Ole Bendixen; Carl Sivertsen (Sisimiut); John Møller (Nuuk). Photo by John Møller (Photoarchive NKA).

were thus "taken home" a few years later, from Svendborg to the National Museum of Denmark. But we must also keep in mind that right around the turn of the century, conservation efforts intensified in Denmark, as a consequence of a long-standing systematic destruction and plundering of grave mounds around the country. The Danish conservation work will be firefly mentioned in the following section.

The Provincial Council's discussion in 1913 was not only the first time that the thought of establishing a museum in Greenland was put forward: it was also the starting point of a long and laborious process, which did not result in an actual conservation act applicable for Greenland until 1974, an act which - following the Home Rule's implementation in 1980 - was replaced by the present legal foundation.

Danish conservation efforts over 200 years

In Denmark, it was acknowledged very early that the law and royal resolutions had to be applied if one wanted to preserve cultural relics such as castle mounds, castle ruins, megalithic graves, and the like. Already in 1666, King Frederik III sent out "The Royal Proclamation on Old

Monuments and Antiquities". Many of the country's most outstanding relics were saved on that account.

Many individual finds, which turned up as arable land was cultivated, were protected by *Danefæloven* (The Danish Treasure Trove Law), which was published in 1752. This law was aimed not only at the king's proprietary right to finds which represented a certain economic value; it also had to protect object which, because of their age and rarity, could cast light on our mutual past.

In the time leading up to the year 1800, the awareness of the value of these relics as identity-creating elements was increased. At the same time, there was a tendency, not only in Denmark, but in the whole of Europe, to include "the antique" as an element in the romantic and nationalistic ideas which characterized this age. Similar efforts to secure more humble cultural traces in the open landscape - especially grave mounds - was intensified, and the Danish criminal code, which took effect in 1866, determined a penalty for *"he who on purpose or as accomplice takes part in removing or destroying public monuments"*, a code, though, which had only minor effect, faced with the extensive destruction following the drastic expansion of agriculture through the 19th century.

Fig. 2: The ruins at Igaliku, the Gardar of the Norse. Copperplate from a drawing made by Th. Groth during G. F. Holm's reconnaissance in 1880. (The Norse Arcgive, National Museum of Denmark).

The work to secure the *in situ* relics in particular was institutionalized in 1807 with the foundation of "The Commission for the Conservation of Antiquities", on whose initiative lists of protected premises, in situ relics, as well as ruins and a few standing buildings, were regularly drawn up. In 1848, inspector of antique monuments, J. Worsaae's tasks were set in a royal order, in which he, among other things, is directed

"To institute and in the future guard the protection and conservation of the most important antique relics of the past in our kingdom and in our duchies, such as stone circles, cairns, passage graves, grave mounds, runic stones, castle mounds, castle ruins, old churches and similar architectonic monuments, as well as other curious relics from older times."

The National Museum of Denmark did not launch a systematic registration of the country's relics before 1873, a project which stretched over more than 60 years, while simultaneously, the first recorded protections were established based on the principle of voluntary preservation. A large number of grave mounds and megalithic layouts were, as mentioned, continuously destroyed as agriculture progressed, and the need for a more efficient kind of protection - through a special legislation on relics and ruins - was acknowledged.

In 1912, a provision was introduced into the new criminal code, saying that *"he who violates a specifically recorded relic can be sentenced to imprisonment for a maximum of three years, ordinary imprisonment, or - under mitigating circumstances - fined"*. This was a clear increase, compared to the 1866 code.

But many years were to pass before the thoughts of a specific legislation in this field could be realized. The first bill in a conservation act was put forward in January 1916. The case was sent on to commissions, and not until the passing of the "Nature Conservation Act of 1937", containing a special paragraph on *in situ* relics and ruins, was the necessary legal basis secured. The 1937 Act simply determined that all antique relics were automatically protected. Thus, the principle of voluntary preservation was overruled.

This was in due time. The country was once again widely travelled, and in the beginning of the 1950s the number of preserved monuments of the past totalled 27,774 - about a third of those previously known (Ebbesen 1985).

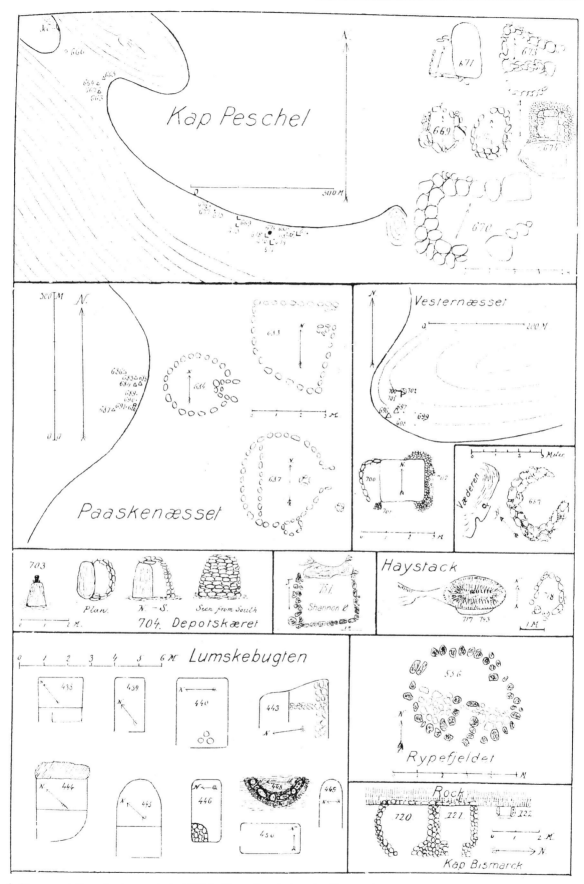

Fig. 3: Documentation of ruins made in 1907 in Dove Bay during the "Danmark Expedition 1906-1908" headed by Chriustian Bendix Thostrup.

The Relics of Greenland and their Conservation

It began with the Norsemen

It can be said that the interest in the visible evidence of the Norse settlement in Greenland began already at the beginning of the 18th century with Hans Egede's attempt to locate and investigate the ruins. The Greenlanders Hans Egede met knew most of the locations of the ruins. His interest in them and his efforts to seek them out, sprang from his expectations to find descendants of "*the old Norwegians*". Apart from visiting parts of the ruins in the fjords around Godthåb, Hans Egede made several smaller excavations in both the West and the East Settlements (Vester- og Østerbygden)[3].

With the foundation in the 1830s of The Royal Nordic Society for Ancient Manuscripts, investigations of the extensive written source material - casting light on the 500-year old history of the settlements - were systematized. The result of this work was the publication of *The Historic Relics of Greenland*, published between 1838-1845.

In 1878, the Commission for the Administration of Geological Investigations in Greenland was established. This was changed the following year to the *"Commission for the Administration of Geological and Geographical Investigations in Greenland"*. One of the commission's most important tasks was to carry out a nationwide mapping - geologically, topographically, and archaeologically.

The first goal-oriented exploration of the ruins in the East Settlement (Østerbygden) was initiated in 1880 by first lieutenant Gustav F. Holm, whose results were published in *Meddelelser om Grønland* (Bruun 1894, 1917), the first systematic record of the Norse ruins in Greenland was made, an index whose ruin numbering is still in use, even after the introduction of new conservation numbers in 1978.

The involvement of the Inuit relics

At the same time, the interest in the early history of the Inuit population was more limited. It is true that, as early as the 18th century, 'Kunstkammeret' in Copenhagen had received a good deal of material revealing the Greenlanders' way of life, but this was predominantly of an ethnographic nature.

Not until H. J. Rink's pioneer work in the latter part of the 19th century (Rink 1866, 1871a, 1871b) was the interest in the origin of the Inuit people awaken. In many ways, Rink was a foresighted man, and one might expect that he had already seen the necessity of protecting the old settlements and similar cultural treasures, by law or other public regulations To my knowledge, however, nothing on such matters written from his hand exists.

Around the turn of the century, it became common practice that the by now numerous expeditions exploring unknown areas of the country took care of archaeological,

Fig. 4: Sophus Müller drawn by P. S. Krøyer in 1888 when he was 42 years old.

as well as primary tasks, and a great number of settlements relics and other prehistoric artifacts, were located and mapped (see Ryder 1895; Amdrup 1909; Thostrup 1922; Thomsen 1917). The location and sometimes very detailed descriptions of the finds have been of decisive importance in subsequent archaeological research, in spite of the fact that the work was often carried out by people without an archaeological background.

Greenlandic archaeology is generally considered to have been founded in 1929, when Therkel Mathiassen initiated his investigations, and since that time, systematic explorations were made in large parts of Greenland.

Fig. 5: Igaliku. The structure in the background was built with stones from the ruins. Many prehistoric sites such as this were used as quarries, even after the circular of 1916 had taken effect. (Photo: P. Nørlund, 1926, the Norse Archive, National Museum of Denmark).

The First Preservation Provisions are hatched

The circular of April 19, 1916

As initially mentioned, the letter sent by Sophus Møller in 1911 to the Greenland Administration, contained a suggestion for the protection of treasures in Greenland[4]. As a consequence of the aforementioned debate in 1913, the Provincial Council could recommend that the Administration draft a bill for the Ministry, although with minor changes, aimed at establishing a museum in Greenland.

During the next couple of years the case was presumably suspended, perhaps because of the changes suggested by the Provincial Council. The National Museum of Denmark did not wish to renounce its sovereign and proprietary right to potential archaeological finds in Greenland.

However, in a letter of April 10, 1915, Sophus Møller, along with Daugaard Jensen (the previous inspector of North Greenland, who in the meantime had become director of the Administration of the Greenland Colonies) brought up the case again. The reaction came promptly, as Daugaard Jensen had already on May 17 of the same year responded by returning the final draft for the conservation provisions, which in content was very close to Sophus Møller's original proposal.

The proposal was adopted and announced under the title:

"Ordinary circular of April 19, 1916 from the Home Ministry concerning Measures for the Protection of Cultural Relics in Greenland" (See appendix I).

As shown, Sophus Møller had succeed in maintaining the sovereign authority of the National Museum of Denmark when it came to sanctioning archaeological investigations and retaining the right to control all finds brought out of Greenland. It would be too simplified to see this attitude as an expression of cultural imperialism. The same attitude was displayed towards the many local museum hatched during these years in Denmark. The National Museum of Denmark reserved unlimited rights to confiscate all finds deemed fair to include in the national collections.

On the contrary, one must probably consider the last item of the circular as a helping hand to the Provincial Council of South Greenland's desire to found a Greenland Museum - perhaps a compromise accomplished by Daugaard Jensen's intervention in the negotiations.

The Regulation of April 10, 1937

The plans for the Greenland Museum were not realized at this stage, and during the following years, nor did the conservations efforts leave visible traces in the archives. Per-

Fig. 6: Garden surrounding a longhouse from the 1500 years at Nuumiut near Narsaq. (Photo: Hans Kapel, 1993).

haps this has to do with the bitter rift which arose in Denmark between the National Museum of Denmark and the Danish Society for the Conservation of Natural Amenities, each accusing the opponent of betraying national values for fear of losing the right to excavate.

The reason for this division was the Act on Natural Conservation proposed in 1916. This proposition broke the principle of voluntary preservation. The National Museum of Denmark opposed this very strongly. They thought good relationships with the plot owners were a condition for archaeological research and the preservation of relics of the past.

Certain concrete preservation provisions, however, were carried out in Greenland. Thus, in 1913: "Provision on Preservation of the cairns etc. put up by surveying expeditions from The Geodetic Institute" and in 1933: "The Regulation concerning Cemeteries in Greenland".

So, the making of laws had not died out completely. Concurrently with the reading of the Danish Natural Preservation Act, the Greenland Administration co-operated with the National Museum of Denmark (Johannes Brønsted & Therkel Mathiassen) on an updating and improvement of the preservation provisions. Finally, in 1937, this lead to the publication of: "Regulation concerning the Protection of Relics in Greenland", which took effect as of January 1, 1938[5].

The provisions in this regulation create an opportunity to protect areas which "*for historical, ethnographic, archaeological, or similar reasons would preferably be preserved untouched*". Various restrictions are established in connection with the public's access to and use of these areas, and a penalty is fixed for violating these regulations.

The "forgotten" preservations

Together with the regulation of April 10, 1937, the Administration published a list of 39 sites, which were protected in accordance with §1 of the provisions.

The sites in questions are all well-known historically and archaeologically. Two of them are situated in East Greenland, while the rest are distributed over West Greenland (see Appendix II).

These preservations seem to be forgotten in more recent times, where a great deal of energy has been spent carrying through with the preservation of areas such as the Sermermiut settlement at Ilulissat.

The regulation of 1948

For many years following, the 1937 rules were in force. But in 1948, there was a need to insert a sentence in §4, which was apparently found to be too weak. The problem was the Norse ruins, which were not treated with due respect[6]. The appendix reads:

"In certain cases - and according to the chief administrative officer's provisions - it may be prohibited to used ruins for cultivation, as a compost heap, stable, or storage house. At inhabited settlements, each Norse ruin must be marked by a preservation pole."

One may say that what was in question was a specification rather than a tightening, as §2 of the regulation already prohibited "... *any enterprise which may damage the special character of the place*" It was, thus, illegal to "*put up tents or houses, light bonfires, dig, and remove stones, peat, or vegetation*".

The general formulation of these provisions also shows how, at this time, the Norse relics were still given first priority. Many Inuit ruins in South Greenland have - until a few years ago - supplied the soil for village gardens, or have been directly used in the cultivation of vegetables.

These revised provisions, which i wording are almost the same as the regulation of 1937, took effect as of January 1, 1949[7].

The administration of the preservation provisions

Now there was a tool to secure the relics of the past, but how were the provisions administered?

Through the 1940s, C. L. Vebæk worked very hard at investigating and preserving the Norse relics in South Greenland, as well as in fjord systems around Nuuk. During this period, the sheep trade expanded extensively, and the task was not always easy. Thus, during these years, several dispensations have been given which have led to the demolition of ruins that were a hindrance to development. The antiquarian work in Greenland was not overseen by any stable administration at this time, and therefore the is no exact account of how many and which ruins were affected[8]. However, in connection with the present efforts to establish an EDB-based preservation index, this information will be consolidated.

Therkel Mathiassen's long term work in Greenland has been especially important in terms of protecting Inuit relics. It was he who was responsible for pointing out the 39 sites that were preserved on the basis of the 1937 regulation. Furthermore, Therkel Mathiassen tried to leave the settlements which he excavated in such a state that the ruins were accessible and attractive to future visitors.

But the provisions in force were not always sufficient. In 1950 a circular was sent out which outlined particular preservation provisions for the church ruin at Qa-qortoq and the Sissarluttoq ruins in Igaliku Fjord[9]. In 1954, an area preservation of the ruin vicinity around the Moravian Brethren mission station Ny Herrnhut in Nuuk was put into effect[10].

The realization of the old dream - the creation of a Greenland museum - in the 1950s once again gave life to efforts to improve the preservation provisions. Many wished to replace the many regulations with an actual law

Fig. 7: Therkel Mathiassen during his fieldwork in South Greenland in 1934. His diaries and topographical notes have served as the basis for the preservation of prehistoric sites in large parts of Greenland. (Photo: Erik Holtved, Department of Ethnography, National Museum of Denmark).

especially for Greenland. In a letter from the National Museum of Denmark to the ministry, signed by Jørgen Meldgaard, a proposition for such a bill was set out.

The proposition was in every way more substantial than the provisions in the existing regulations. Where it previously said that areas *could* be protected according to a special administration provision, the proposition's §1 establishes the fact that a number of exemplified relics *are* protected by definition.

The reaction from the ministry, however, was long in coming. In 1967, the permanent secretary, Eske Brun, took up the case in the Commission for Scientific Project in Greenland, and pressure was also brought to bear on the ministry by the Nature Conservation Board. Finally, in 1969, the ministry established a committee under the direction of Supreme Court Judge J. Trolle.

After five years of committee work the new preservation act was ready to be passed in 1974.

The Preservation Act of 1974

The provisions in the Preservation Act of 1974 in many ways maintained a satisfactory protection of the Greenlandic relics, although, unfortunately, one must conclude that the possibilities it contained - especially in terms of preserving buildings - were only exploited to a very small extent.

The Act was based on the extensive work which in 1967 lead to the revision of the Danish preservation act, and the content broadly corresponds to this. As a curiosity, it may be mentioned that the Danish Act's paragraph on outdoor advertising was included. These provisions have hardly been relevant in Greenland.

The Keeper of National Antiquities (= Rigsantikvaren), who at the time was also the leader of the National Museum of Denmark, still had the authority to administer the paragraphs on relics and archaeological finds, but he was placed under the ministry for Greenland, to which possible complaints might be directed.

Certain authorities belonged to the governor's office (= Landshøvdingeembedet). This particularly applied to the provisions on area preservation based on facts other than purely archaeological ones.

"As a rule, finds must remain in Greenland. The Keeper of National Antiquities may appoint local representatives, who may receive reports on finds and store delivered object until their destination has been decided upon."

However, the basic point of view was still that archaeological finds belonged to the National Museum of Denmark in Copenhagen. Yet, the change of wording reflected the situation around the Greenland Museum (= Grønlands Landsmuseum), which in 1966 had become a government-approved, subsidized museum. Besides, the Committee had seen the writing on the wall. The political development clearly pointed to home rule, which was introduced in 1979.

The administration of cultural matters is transferred to Greenland. The preservation act of 1980

In October 1980, the 'Landsting' decree on museum systems was adopted, thereby passing the responsibility for Greenland's cultural heritage to Greenland. The decree was directly followed by the "Landsting act no. 5 of October 16 on preservation of *in situ* relics and buildings". The basis for the antiquarian work was hereby created, and is today handled by the Greenland National Museum & Archive (= Grønlands Nationalmuseum & Arkiv).

The most important aim of the act was, of course, to establish the change of competence in the field. The paragraph on *in situ* relics was kept almost unchanged, but otherwise the content was in many ways new. A division according to subjects has been made:

Chapter I: *In situ* relics
Chapter II: Buildings, church yards, parts of buildings, and cairns
Chapter III: Cultural-historic areas

Chapter II brings together subjects which were previously included in separate circulars and orders. Earlier provisions on landscape preservation were excluded, and covered in a special nature preservation act.

The Antiquarian Work under Home Rule

Relics of the past and the physical planning

With the implementation of home rule, a massive boom took place in the development project which is to turn Greenland into a modern society. Already in 1979, a major expansion of sheep farming was planned with the aid of EEC funds. The National Museum of Denmark became involved in this work, and in 1980 carried out extensive research in an attempt to ensure that the development would respect the many Norse ruins in the area. This project has been continued through preservation tours on an almost annual basis.

Since then, the Greenland Museum - now the Greenland National Museum & Archive - has taken part in physical planning in many other fields. Through the 1980s there has been a centralized effort through the Fiscal Committee's Office for Physical Planning to improve the basis of the planning on both a national and a local level. This has increasingly implicated the museum in the treatment of cases involving apportionment of land, urban development, the establishment of airports, etc.

In the mid-1970s, preliminary investigations began in a number of areas which could provide opportunities to develop water power. In 1982, the Greenland Museum joined this endeavour and has since carried out research in six of the suggested areas. In the course of two field seasons, in 1990-1991, archaeological excavations were made prior to the establishment of a hydroelectric power station in Bukse Fjord, a task which was accomplished within a budget of one million Danish kroner.

Similarly, the increasing activity in the hunt for minerals in Greenland has left its mark on the antiquarian work. All concession cases are presented to the museum, which then estimates whether cultural-historic interests might be influenced by construction work or other projects necessary for investigations or a possible utilization.

The antiquarian work field has, thus, been expanded dramatically within the last 15 years. The preconditions for an acceptable administration of the preservation act is a basic mapping of the country's relics. This task, however, is so extensive and resource-demanding that completion in the near future is unlikely. But a great deal of work is being done - not least by the local museums - to register the relics in their respective areas. All information on new finds is now registered in a central relic index.

Establishing the preservation archive

A sketch plan, proposed by Jørgen Meldgaard in 1961 to a museum in new buildings, held a detailed plan for the administrative structure of such a museum. A "topographical archive" was part of the proposition, and the idea was that the National Museum of Denmark establish the archive based on already existing material.

The building project was never realized, though, and it was not until 1969, with the appointment of the new committee, that a new initiative was taken towards establishing a preservation archive. Jørgen Meldgaard made index cards for the registration of both Norse and Inuit relics, but instead of co-operating, the National Museum of Denmark's Second Department (the medieval collections) preferred to carry through with a reorganization of Daniel Bruun's old registrant on Norse ruins.

The cataloguing of the Inuit relics was never really set to work, and it took an outsider's appeal to get the case revived.

In 1977, the act on area application, town development, and settlement was passed. The following year, the Greenland national planning committee (= landsplanudvalget) addressed the National Museum of Denmark (via the National Association of Local Authorities in Denmark) in an appeal to set up a preservation archive. At the beginning of 1981, the financial basis for the beginning phase had been established, and the work began.

Already in May, an inventory could be made. At this point, an archive existed, containing more than 200 map sheets covering all of Greenland, on which known relics had been marked. The archive part consisted of a matching card index, in which approximately 2,500 sites were described.

The job was far from done, though, since at the National Museum of Denmark alone, there was a substantial amount of archival material, which had not yet been looked at. Added to this was a continuous updating of the archive, as a consequence of an increasing number of reports on new ruin finds. From 1981, the Greenland Museum launched systematic preservation tours, and several local museums made investigations in their areas on their own initiative.

The Agreement on Cooperation and the Greenland Secretariat

The economic foundation for the further development of the archive was insufficient, though, and the work was basically at a standstill until 1984, when the agreement on cooperation between the Greenland Museum and the National Museum of Denmark on remittance of cultural treasures was agreed upon.

It was natural to regard the knowledge of archaeological relics, gathered by the National Museum of Denmark through 100 years of research, on equal terms with museum objects. With this background, it was decided that the future work on the preservation archive was to be transferred to the Greenland Secretariat.

The entries to the archive were still growing, and by 1985 it included more than 6,000 sites. This made the idea of changing the archive to EDB relevant. In the period 1987-1990, a data structure for the future "cultural-historic register" was drawn up, and about a quarter of the card index was entered. Since then, difficulties with software and other problems have made it necessary to reorganize the database. But today it has been completed, and the further work on entering and updating data is well under way.

To make the Greenland National Museum capable of handling the antiquarian tasks as they are defined in the preservation act, the archive has from the beginning been made out in two copies, and the material in Nuuk has been updated.

As presumed in the agreement on cooperation, the register will be handed over to Greenland once the present updating and revision has been completed, and Greenland must then take care of the database maintenance and the registration of new discoveries of relics on its own.

Hans Kabel, curator at Greenland Secretariat, National Museum of Denmark, Copenhagen.

Notes

(1): An old omen from the Frederikshåb area, written down by Knud Rasmussen (Rasmussen 1924).

(2): Meeting summary in: Reports and Notifications Concerning the Administration of Greenland. No. 2, 1914.

(3): Hans Egede among other things made smaller excavations in the church ruins "Hvalsey" at Qaqortoq and "Anavik" in the Godthåb Fjord.

(4): The letter from Sophus Møller may seem surprising. The National Museum of Denmark had until then shown little interest in archaeological material from Greenland. Thus, around 1880 the museum had been offered an extensive collection, collected by district medical officer Christian Pfaff from excavations and collections from graves in Disko Bay. The very same Sophus Møller, who was then a newly hatched museum assistant, had refused the offer. This decision was later on sharply criticized by Kristian Bahnson, William Thalbitzer and others, who thought it was time to collect material from West Greenland.

(5): The regulation was signed by Stauning and published in "Beretninger og Kundgørelser", 1937 (3):1006-1008.

(6): As a notable example of an overruling of the preservation provisions, the Norse farms at Igaliku and Qassiarsuk may be mentioned. Here stones from the ruins were used as building material, and some of the ruins were used as chicken farms, gardens, etc.

(7): Regulation concerning preservation of relics in Greenland. The Prime Minister's Department, The Greenland Administration, November 11, 1948.

(8): However, a summaric list made by Vebæk does exist. It includes 29 sites i 'Østerbygden' and one in 'Vesterbygden', in cases where dispensation has been given or where preservations have been completely or partially revoked.

(9): Circular of May 20, 1950, concerning the preservation of the Aqaortoq church ruin and the Sigssardlugtoq ruin. "Beretninger og Kundgørelser" (= Accounts & Announcements) 1959, pp:205-206.

(10): An order concerning the protection of areas at Ny Herrnhut. "Kundgørelser vedrørende Grønland" (= Announcements concerning Greenland) 1954, paragraph 27, group 9, lb.no.1.

APPENDIX I

Ordinary Circular of April 19, 1916, from the Minister of the Interior concerning Measures for the Securing of Cultural Relics in Greenland.

After Negotiation between the National Museum of Denmark and the Administration concerning Precautions to Secure Cultural Relics in Greenland - a case also debated in the South Greenland National Council at a meeting in 1913 - the Ministry of the Interior has determined the following Provisions to be studied for the Securing of the Relics mentioned:

1. Danes and foreigners who have received Permission for Travels and Sojourns in Greenland will be informed that they must refrain completely from Excavation in the Inuit and Norse Settlements and Graves, unless they have obtained special Permission to do so.

2. All employees under public, ecclesiastical, or temporal Authorities in Greenland - Europeans as well as Greenlanders - are requested to refrain from all Investigations and, as far as possible, all Disturbances in Eskimo and Norse settlements and in Graves, unless this takes place in accordance with a specific Agreement with the National Museum of Denmark.

3. The native Population is informed of the desirability not to dig in the old Settlements or Graves, and is urged to leave these relics of past life in peace.

4. The export from Greenland of old Eskimo and Norse objects can only happen via Copenhagen, and only on the Condition that, on Arrival, they are inspected by the National Museum of Denmark, whose Right it is to take what is necessary for a Completion of the Collections in question in return for Refunding the Expenses for these objects and their Transportation or suitable Remuneration of their Value. If Agreement cannot be reached on the amount of the Remuneration, the case will be decided on by the Administration.

5. For the observance of this Provision, it is put upon the Colony Administrators to file Report to the Administration, each time old Eskimo or Norse objects, including the yield of Excavations and Collections performed with the Permission of the Ministry, are exported from Greenland, whether or not the Consignment takes place for some Person living in Greenland or is brought by Travellers, who have only stayed in the country temporarily. It is therefore imposed on the Shipmasters to take care that such Goods are only discharged in Copenhagen.

6. If a Folklore Collection were to be established, the National Museum of Denmark is responsible - at abovementioned Investigations - for taking out such objects as may be of value to such a Collection, all according to explicit agreements with the Administration.

APPENDIX II

Preserved areas in accordance with paragraph 1 in "Regulation of April 10, 1937 concerning Securing Relics of the past in Greenland.

Julianehåb District:
Tugtutup Isua. The whole settlement. Since all ruins here are exposed, it is a primary concern that this settlement should be preserved.
Igdlutalik at Narsaq. The unexcavated ruins.
Unartoq. The unexcavated ruins.
Kangeq at Nanortalik.
Anordliuitsoq. The whole settlement.
Frederikshåb District:
Ukivik north of the colony. The whole area.
Natdla.
Godthåb District:
Utorkait. The unexcavated ruins.
Kekertarmiut at Agpamiut. The unexcavated part.
Sarkarmiut at Kangarmiut. The whole area.
Ingik at the colony. The whole area.
Umanaq south of the colony.
Holsteinsborg District:
Kekertarmiut near the colony. The whole area.
Nipisat.
Egedesminde District:
Ikeransanguaq near Niakornarsuk. The unexcavated ruins.
Simiutalik.
Christianshåb District:
Kaja at Jakobshavn Isfjord.
Tugssaq in Southeast Bay (Sydostbugten)
Jakobshavn District:
Kilersiut. The whole area.
Sermermiut. The whole area.
Rittenbenk District:
Kagdlo. The whole area.
Igdluluarssuk at Sarqaq. The whole area.
Igdlutalik at Torssukatak. The great ruin, graves, and nangissat.
Ilerfit. The whole area.
Saputit. The reindeer fence (Rengærdet).
Godhavn District:
Perdlertut in Nordfjord. The whole area.
Umanaq District:
All ruins on the island **Igssua.**
Eqaluit. The whole area.
Nugssuaq. The Bear Trap (Bjørnefælden).
Nussaq. The whole area.
Upernavik District:
All ruins north of Nugssuaq (Kraulshavn).
Inusuk. The unexcavated part of the compost heap.
Gl. Skibshavn. The whole area.
Bruuns Ø. The whole area.
Ungarssuk in Umiarfik Fjord. The whole area.

Angmagsalik District:
Upernavik in Sermiligak. The whole area.
Kulusuk. The reindeer fence (Rengærdet).

References

Amdrup, G. [1909]: **The former Eskimo Settlements on the East coast of Greenland between Scoresby Sund and the Angmagsalik District.** *Meddelelser om Grønland*, 28(4):285-328 (Copenhagen: Retizels Forlag).

Ebbesen, K. [1985]: **Fortidsminderegistrering i Danmark.** 150 p. (Copenhagen: Fredningsstyrelsen).

GHM [1838-1845]: **Grønlands Historiske Mindesmærker I-III.** I: 797 p., II: 791 p., III: 950 p. (Copenhagen: Det kongelige Nordiske Oldskrift-Selskab).

Grønlands Landsmuseum [1983]: **Fredning i Grønland.** Fortidsminder og bygninger. Materiale fra et seminar om den nye fredningslov afholdt i Nuuk, november 1982 (Nuuk: Grønlands Landsmuseum).

Nielsen, I. (redaktør) [1987]: **Bevar din arv.** Udgivet af Skov- og Naturstyrelsen i anledning af 100-året for 1937-lovens vedtagelse. 367 p. (Copenhagen: Skov- og Naturstyrelsen).

Rasmussen, Knud [1924]: **Myter og Sagn fra Grønland: Vestgrønland.** 2:1-354 (Copenhagen: Gyldendal).

Rink, Henrik J. [1866]: **Eskimoiske Eventyr og Sagn.** 376 p. (Copenhagen: *).

Rink, Henrik J. [1871a]: **Eskimoiske Eventyr og Sagn.** Supplement. 279 p. (Copenhagen: *).

Rink, Henrik J. [1871b]: **Om Eskimoernes Herkomst.** *Aarbog for Nordisk Oldkundskab og Historie*, *(*):269-302 (Copenhagen: *).

Ryder, C. [1895]: **Om den tidligere Eskimoiske bebyggelse af Scoresby Sund.** *Meddelelser om Grønland*, 17(6):281-374 (Copenhagen: C. A. Reitzels Forlag).

Thomsen, Thomas [1917]: **Implements and Artefacts of the North East Greenlanders - finds from graves and settlements. Danmarks-ekspeditionen til Grønlands Nordøstkyst, 1906-1907.** *Meddelelser om Grønland*, 44(5):357-496 (Copenhagen: C. A. Reitzels Forlag).

Thostrup, Christian Bendix [1911]: **Ethnographic Deschription of the Eskimo Settlements and Stone Remains in North East Greenland.** *Meddelelser om Grønland*, 44(4):277-355 (Copenhagen: C. A. Reitzels Forlag).

Developments in Labrador Inuit Archaeology Research

Susan A. Kaplan

Social scientists working in Labrador, Canada, have been investigating how various indigenous groups have adapted to Labrador's geography and environment, responded to climate change, and dealt with each other and westerners. Over the last 25 years, scholars have established a broad overview of the Labrador Inuit's culture history using archaeological and ethnohistorical data, and have identified environmental and socio-economic factors that may have affected the course of Labrador Inuit cultural development.

According to our present understanding, the Labrador Inuit of the 13th to 16th centuries lived in small, single family semisubterranean sod houses. Sod house settlements, inhabited by three to five families (25 to 35 people), were located on outer islands where groups principally exploited marine mammal resources.

The extent and nature of a regional and interregional trade is unknown, though researchers believe that nephrite, fine grained slates, and soapstone were among the items exchanged (Fitzhugh 1994; Kaplan 1983; Taylor 1984).

During the 18th century, Labrador Inuit lived in "communal houses," large, rectangular, semisubterranean sod structures with multiple sleeping platforms and lamp stands, each house inhabited by an extended family, averaging 20 people (Taylor 1974, 1984). Large fall and winter sod house settlements were located in inner island and fjord regions (Kaplan 1983, 1985). People hunted a variety of marine and terrestrial animals, including large baleen whales. Leadership extended beyond the household and settlement level, and was associated with extensive trade networks that linked regions economically. Animal-derived materials moved south and European-made goods moved north along the coast

(Jordan 1978; Jordan & Kaplan 1980; Kaplan 1985; Taylor 1974, 1984).

Scholars have differing hypotheses concerning what factor(s) might have triggered the societal changes between the 16th and 18th centuries, including environmental change, population growth, European contact, and trade. While not agreeing about causes, all have noted that the 18th century represents an interesting case of the evolution of an egalitarian hunting culture. Whether the Labrador Inuit culture changed in response to stress or as a result of success has remained in dispute. This paper reviews the progress being made as researchers try to resolve this question.

Early Research

The first scholarly publication concerning Labrador Inuit prehistory was written by Junius Bird (1945), who spent the summer of 1934 excavating 22 sod houses at five sites in the Hopedale region. He identified three semisubterranean sod house forms, and seriated these from smallest to largest and from single sleeping platform to multiple sleeping platforms, and suggested that the seriation represented a chronological sequence from oldest to youngest. He equated the size of a house with the composition of a residential unit, and concluded that Labrador Inuit social organization had changed over time.

Bird was particularly intrigued by the Inuit's adoption of large rectangular semisubterranean houses. He dated these structures to the 18th century based on the European-derived materials recovered from them. Bird proposed that the structures were adopted by the Inuit as a defense against hostile Europeans, noting that during this period " ... *white contacts frequently were dangerous and perhaps provided [the Inuit] a motive for banding more closely together*" (Bird 1945:179). His proposal was never taken seriously by other researchers, perhaps because they immediately understood the tactical disadvantage of housing numbers of people in one structure that had a single, constricted exit.

The most detailed description of the social organization, and subsistence and settlement patterns of the 18th century Labrador Inuit was written by J. Garth Taylor (1974), almost 30 years after Bird published his work, and after explorers, adventurers, and professional archaeologists collected additional information about the prehistory of the area. Taylor, using 18th century Moravian missionary documents, described the composition of residential groups occupying communal houses and examined how ecological and social factors affected settlement size. In the 1974 work and subsequent studies, he described the roles of individuals identified as leaders, the practice of having multiple wives, the long-distance baleen trade, the effects of the introduction of the rifle on Inuit hunting practices, and social, economic, and ceremonial aspects of the 18th century Labrador Inuit whaling tradition (Taylor 1974, 1984, 1985, 1988, 1990; Taylor & Taylor 1977).

Ongoing Debate

In the 1970s, Peter Schledermann and Richard Jordan engaged in a debate regarding the nature of 18th century Labrador Inuit society. Peter Schledermann excavated sod houses in Saglek Fiord and identified three house forms, including a large rectangular structure with multiple sleeping platforms, which he called a "communal house". He dated this large house to the 1700-1850 A.D. period (Schledermann 1972).

Schledermann recognized that a changing environment, as well as contact with Europeans, could have affected the economic activities of the Labrador Inuit. He suggested that the presence of Europeans in southern Labrador might have attracted native groups to that portion of the coast. He went on to hypothesize that the severe environmental conditions of the Little Ice Age may have caused whales to move south and resulted in a southern shift of Inuit dependent on these large marine mammals.

In 1974 Richard Jordan undertook the excavation of sod houses on Eskimo Island, Hamilton Inlet. These houses were first reported by Jørgen Meldgaard in 1968 and had been investigated by William Fitzhugh (Fitzhugh 1972). Jordan noticed that different sized houses had markedly different types and amounts of European goods in them. Of particular interest were the quantities of artifacts recovered from a communal house, including thousands of glass beads, numerous clasp knives, European fish hooks, shot, and spoons; and ceramic, glass, and kettle fragments (Jordan 1974). On the basis of architectural and ethnohistorical data, Jordan reconstructed a three-stage Labrador Inuit occupation using the character of Eskimo-European interaction and the nature of the Inuit economy as organizing principles. He suggested that contact with Europeans, not climatic factors, accounted for the changes evident in Labrador Inuit culture history.

Schledermann further refined his discussion of the effects of the Little Ice Age on Inuit occupations of eastern Canada, citing the climatological work of Bryson and Wendland (1967), Dansgaard (Dansgaard and Johnsen 1971), and others. He developed a model of how game would have been affected by the different environmental conditions and correlated architectural and settlement distribution changes with the changing environmental conditions. He noted that the climate between 1600-1850 A.D. was particularly severe, and linked it with the adoption of the rectangular communal houses in Labrador and the clover-leaf shaped houses in Cumberland Sound, Baffin Island. He proposed that the communal house was an Inuit adaptive response to worsening climate conditions. He argued that during this period resources were scarce and communal living was adopted to conserve fuel for heating and cooking, and to facilitate resource sharing (Schledermann 1976a, 1976b).

In his discussion of the relationship between environment and culture Schledermann was not alone. North American archaeologists, including Arctic researchers (see for instance McGhee 1972; Fitzhugh 1972) were liberated from a descriptive, culture historical focus through adoption of ecological concepts that grew out of Julian Steward's work and began to embrace ideas now identified with environmental archaeology.

Jordan (1977, 1978), who had adopted a similar ecological approach to his work on the evolution of Maritime Archaic cultures in Labrador, took issue with Schledermann's environmentally based model as it applied to this later time period and argued that the communal house was an economic unit that functioned around a whaling crew. Taking a cue from Taylor's ethnohistorical work and North Alaskan anthropologists ethnographic discussions of North Alaskan whaling communities (see for instance Rainey 1947; Spencer 1959), he hypothesized that a communal house was headed by an individual who controlled whaling as well as access to European goods moving through trade networks. Both Schledermann and Jordan were employing a systems theory approach in their work, though one was arguing that the culture's response to the environment triggered the societal changes, the other that culture contact was responsible for the culture's evolution.

Regional Surveys

In the late 1970s the Smithsonian Institution and Bryn Mawr College conducted broad regional surveys of northern Labrador (Torngat Archaeological Project) designed to explore the changing subsistence-settlement patterns of the region's prehistoric peoples. Environmental and geographical considerations were important components of this work (Fitzhugh 1980). More localized surveys in northern and central Labrador followed in the 1980s. These investigations and the Labrador Inuit Association's land claims work (Brice-Bennett 1977) resulted in the identification of over 200 Labrador Inuit sites, as well as associated Moravian Mission stations and Hudson Bay Company posts, between Hamilton Inlet and the Button Islands, and provided the groundwork for Susan Kaplan's synthesis of Labrador Inuit culture history.

Kaplan examined how factors in the geography (a mountainous, deeply indented coastline made up of fiord and island systems), ecology (seasonally available resources, a system prone to cyclical crashes of key terrestrial mammals and sensitive to climatic changes), and the complex and long Inuit-European contact history (with Basque, Dutch, French, and British groups) affected the Inuit. She argued that the social and economic organization of Inuit society had changed repeatedly over a 600 year period in response to changes in resource availability, demography, and the character of European-Inuit contact. She also discussed the rise of the 18th century Inuit entrepreneur, and the development and elaboration of leadership and interregional trade, arguing that they were prompted by increases in population size and density, and Inuit exploitation of a European presence in the south (Kaplan 1980, 1983, 1985). In this work Kaplan developed a multi-causal framework to address questions of culture change, trying to dovetail long-term processual ecological models of change with short-term models of rapid change that was triggered by unique historical events.

Current Research

Since the early 1980s, work on Labrador Inuit culture has taken place on a smaller scale, with Callum Thomson's excavations in Saglek Fiord, Fitzhugh's investigation of a Staffe Island sod house site (1994), Kaplan's work on boulder structures and sod houses in the Nain and Okak regions, Réginald Auger's research in the Strait of Belle Isle region (Auger 1985), and Stephen Loring's work on a Moravian Mission midden in Nain. The key issues that arose in the 1970s and 1980s have remained unresolved. The subsistence economy of the Labrador Inuit population has been poorly understood since few large faunal collections have been recovered. Archaeological interpretations have relied on surveys bolstered by a rich ethnohistory, and the paleoenvironmental discussion has not been developed using Labrador-based work. Rather, people have relied on analogies concerning the prehistory and the paleoclimate developed elsewhere.

Current research underway in Labrador is designed to address gaps in data and involves intensive excavations of sod houses, direct involvement of an archaeozoologist excavating associated middens in an effort to recover large, controlled faunal collections with which to better understand the economy of the Inuit, and development of more detailed and sophisticated paleoenvironmental models.

This work suggests that the sod house sequence proposed by Bird and modified by later researchers is not as straight forward as first reported.

Iglosiatik Island 1 is located on an outer island south of Nain, in the Voisey Bay area. The site consists of 15 sod houses built into the sand bank of a fossil cove. The site dates between the late 1400-1600s. A number of the houses are small, rectangular, semisubterranean structures, each with a single sleeping platform along the rear wall, and a long entrance passage containing a paved and edged cold trap. The floors in these houses are tightly paved and rest on sterile sands. The houses resemble the early form described in the Bird, Schledermann, and Jordan sequences.

House 15 consists of a large, rectangular room with a small oval room off of it. The house dates to the early or mid-1600s. In addition to a well-defined rear sleeping platform in the main room, a U-shaped hearth and raised platform were uncovered in the small room. The kitchen has yet to be located, though there is reason to believe it is adjacent to the entrance passage at the front of the house, an area that has not been excavated. Slate, nephrite, soapstone, along with iron artifacts and a copper pendant were recovered from the house.

The relationship of this large two-room structure to single room and later communal houses is not yet clear. Whether it is organizationally similar to the clover-leaf shaped structures of Baffin Island remains to be determined.

Uivak Point is a sod house site located on the mainland, on the southwestern shore of Uivak Point, a peninsula directly north of the Okak Islands. The hills surrounding the sod houses offer a panoramic view of the open Atlantic, as well as the protected waters of the inner bay. Moravian descriptions of the community began in 1773, when Jens Haven reported the occupation of two winter houses (Taylor 1974:11). The missionaries reported three houses occupied by 73 people in 1777-1778, the site unoccupied in 1779-1780, and 65 people living at the settlement in 1781 (Taylor 1974:17). Taylor (1990) has written about the kashims, or dance houses, associated with whaling successes, built at the site. According to the missionaries, the inhabitants of Uivak Point and other Okak settlements pursued large baleen whales.

Kaplan, Jim Woollett an archaeozoologist, high school students from Labrador, and undergraduate and graduate students from Canada, the United States, and the United Kingdom have spent three seasons excavating House 7 and its associated midden. The excavation of a 7 m by 2 m midden area down-slope from House 7 has been completed, and 32 1-m^2 units within the house have been excavated to floor level. Also, the house and midden have been linked with a 15 m long trench.

The sheet midden varies in depth from 15 cm to 80 cm and was excavated in arbitrary 5 cm increments following the contour of the slope. All soil was dry screened to maximize recovery of small animal and artifact remains. The bottom 15 cm consisted of frozen deposit with hair, feathers, baleen, hide, bone, and wood preserved.

The excavation of the 12 m by 8 m rectangular house proceeded differently. Units were excavated to the first pavement and architectural features were mapped. Whale bones, used in the construction of walls and platforms, were recovered along with quantities of timber.

Many artifacts of traditional Inuit Culture were found, including bone toggles for dog harnesses, ivory harpoon heads, ivory combs, a faceless wooden doll, a wooden toy bear, bone knife handles with baleen lashings, and drilled ivory and whale bone. The ceramics, metal objects, glass fragments, and glass beads are of a uniform 18th century date and resemble those recovered from 18th century contexts at Eskimo Island, though they do not appear in the same quantities.

The midden yielded a rich macrobotanical assemblage, including quantities of crowberry and blueberry seeds, indicating the importance of such foods in Inuit subsistence, and also the likelihood that the highly organic midden includes human waste. Preliminary analyses suggest that small marine mammals comprise over 69% of the midden, with ringed and harp seals accounting for most of the fauna. Whales are not well represented in the midden assemblage. This is not surprising, given the probability that the whales were butchered off site and whale bones transported to the house for specific purposes (Woollett 1996). The large number of dogs represented in the midden and the significance of molluscs in the Inuit diet are among the questions Woollett is addressing as he seeks to understand the nature of 18th century Inuit economy.

The need to re-examine the question of the nature and impact of the climate on 18th century Labrador Inuit is obvious. There is reason to believe that significant advances can now be made in this area. The Greenland Ice Sheet Project (GISP2) recovered an ice core that has great stratigraphic integrity. Scientists are compiling proxy records of climate change with seasonal to millennia scales of resolution. These records reveal much more than temperature trends. For instance, scientists can discuss the amount of precipitation that fell (Meese et al. 1994) and whether storms were prevalent during a certain period (Buckland et al. 1996). Kaplan's work with Hudson's Bay Company records has revealed that factors such as the distribution of fast ice and pack-ice, and the frequency of storms were critical in Labrador. Starvation occurred when weather conditions, strong winds in particular, destroyed the fast ice and prevented people from hunting or traveling to cached food supplies (Kaplan 1983).

Jacoby and D'Arrigo's work with tree ring sequences in Quebec/Labrador provide the possibility of understanding more directly local climatic conditions (Jacoby & D'Arrigo 1989; D'Arrigo & Jacoby 1993). They have shown that limits of tree growth and growth rates of individual trees are influenced by the thermal effects of air masses sweeping across northern boreal forests and forest-tundra ecotones. This work, along with information concerning pack-ice conditions, being gleaned from historic sources (Teillet 1988; Wilson 1983), suggest that archaeologists should be able to fine-tune the environmental picture and better understand the challenges and opportunities presented to the 18th century Inuit population.

Resolution of those questions will not be the sole keys to understanding the cultural developments seen in the 18th century in Labrador. Barnett Richling (1993) has called attention to the need to consider carefully assumptions about how the Labrador Inuit responded to abundance and scarcity, as applied to critical resources as well as rare objects of European manufacture. In a critique concerning approaches to the study of Labrador communal houses, Richling questions whether European-made objects were private property, as the existing archaeological explanations would suggest, and therefore excluded from the customary forms of reciprocity. Referring to the work of Riches (1982), in which motives and mechanisms of sharing are examined in Canadian Inuit Cultures, Richling argues that exotic material culture may not have been considered private property, and would have been shared according to customary practices. Since these items were rare, he argues they would have fallen into the patterns of sharing observed when a community faces scarce food resources. During periods of scarcity, people living under one roof will better communicate the "special extent to which they are prepared to subscribe to the ideals of rendering support and succor" (Riches 1982:185; Richling 1993:74). In the end, Richling focusses on scarcity as an explanation for architectural and social developments seen in the 18th century.

Richling's critique deserves careful consideration, for it is a cautionary tale reminding archaeologists that they must be well-acquainted with the ethnographic literature and socio-cultural work.

His proposal needs to be examined further, given the work George Wenzel has done in the Clyde River community. Some of Wenzel's observations support Richling's observations. For instance, store bought foods are incorporated into the traditional foods distribution systems. However, Wenzel reports practices among younger men who are protecting certain high-value items, such as snow mobiles, from being incorporated into the traditional on-demand distribution network in which older hunters gain access to goods based on kinship and partner relationships (Wenzel 1995). Whether certain European-made items were similarly protected by 18th century Inuit entrepreneurs is worth considering.

The above survey suggests that archaeological and paleoenvironmental research projects are beginning to generate the data with which researchers should be able to answer the questions that have lingered in the communal house debate. In the 1980s, when trying to dovetail ecological and historic models of change, Kaplan had difficulty dealing with the different temporal scales employed by the models. This problem may finally be solved as well, given the increased ability of environmental researchers to examine the climate record using a variety of temporal scales of resolution. Both the environment and European contact had effects on Labrador Inuit, and to seek the primacy of the one over the other is an outdated approach. To understand how together these factors might have dampened or exaggerated change is now the challenge before researchers.

Susan A. Kaplan, Director of The Peary-MacMillan Arctic Museum, Bowdoin College, Brunswick, Maine 04011, USA.

References

Auger, Réginald [1985]: **The Inuit in the Strait of Belle Isle.** *Archaeology in Newfoundland and Labrador, Annual Report*, 5:272-298, editor: J. Sproull-Thomson, 249 p. (St.John's, Newfoundland: Historic Resources).

Bird, Junius [1945]: **Archaeology of the Hopedale Area, Labrador.** *Anthropological Papers of the American Museum of Natural History*, 39(2):121-186 (New York: American Museum of Natural History).

Brice-Bennett, Carol [1977]: **Land Use in the Nain and Hopedale Regions.** pp:97-203 in "Our Footprints are Everywhere", editor: Carol Brice-Bennett, 381 p. (Nain: Labrador Inuit Association).

Bryson, Reid A. & W. M. Wendland [1967]: **Tentative Climatic Patterns for Some Late Glacial and Post- Glacial Episodes in Central North America.** pp:271-298 in "Life, Land and Water", editor: W. J. Meyer-Oakes, 416 p. (Winnipeg: University of Manitoba Press).

Buckland, Peter C., et al. [1996]: **Bioarchaeological and Climatological Evidence for the Fate of Norse Farmers in Medieval Greenland.** *Antiquity*, 70:88-96 (*: *).

D'Arrigo, Rosanne & Gordon Jacoby [1993]: **Secular Trends in High Northern Latitude Temperature Reconstructions Based on Tree Rings.** *Climatic Change*, 25:163-177 (Boston: Reidel Publishing Co.).

Dansgaard, W. & S. J. Johnsen [1971]: **Climatic Record Revealed by the Camp Century Ice Core.** pp:37-56 in "The Late Cenozoic Glacial Ages", editor: K. K. Turekian, 606 p. (New Haven: Yale University Press).

Fitzhugh, William W. [1972]: **Environmental Archaeology and Cultural Systems in Hamilton Inlet, Labrador.** *Smithsonian Contributions to Anthropology*, 16:1-299 (Washington DC: Smithsonian Institution Press).

Fitzhugh, William W. [1980]: **Preliminary Report on the Torngat Archaeological Project.** *Arctic*, 33(3):585-606 (Calgary: Arctic Institute of North America).

Fitzhugh, William W. [1994]: **Staffe Island 1 and the Northern Labrador Dorset-Thule Succession.** pp:239-268 in "Threads of Arctic Prehistory", editors: David Morrison & Jean-Luc Pilon, 422 p. (Quebec: Canadian Museum of Civilization).

Jacoby, Gordon & Rosanne D'Arrigo [1989]: **Reconstructed Northern Hemisphere Annual Temperature Since 1671 Based on High-Latitude Tree-Ring Data from North America.** *Climatic Change*, 14:39-59 (Boston: Reidel Publishing Co.).

Jordan, Richard [1974]: **Preliminary Report on Archaeological Investigations of the Labrador Eskimo in Hamilton Inlet in 1973.** *Man in the Northeast*, 8:77-89 (*: *).

Jordan, Richard [1977]: **Inuit Occupation of the Central Labrador Coast since 1600 A.D.** pp:43-48 in "Our Footprints are Everywhere", editor: Carol Brice-Bennett, 381 p. (Nain: Labrador Inuit Association).

Jordan, Richard [1978]: **Archaeological Investigations of the Hamilton Inlet Labrador Eskimo: Social and Economic Responses to European Contact.** *Arctic Anthropology*, 15(2):175-185 (Madison: University of Wisconsin Press).

Jordan, Richard & Susan Kaplan [1980]: **An Archaeological View of the Inuit/European Contact Period in Central Labrador.** *Etudes/Inuit/Studies*, 4(1-2):35-46 (Québec: Départment d'anthropologie, Université Laval).

Kaplan, Susan [1980]: **Neo-Eskimo Occupations of the Northern Labrador Coast.** *Arctic*, 33(3):646-658 (Calgary: Arctic Instutute of North America).

Kaplan, Susan [1983]: **Economic and Social Change in Labrador Neo-Eskimo Culture.** Ph.D. dissertation, Department of Anthropology, Bryn Mawr College.

Kaplan, Susan [1985]: **European Goods and Socio-Economic Change in Early Labrador Inuit Society.** pp: 45-69 in"Cultures in Contact: The European Impact on Native Cultural Institutions in Eastern North America, A.D. 1000-1800", editor: W. Fitzhugh, 320 p. (Washington DC: Smithsonian Institution Press).

McGhee, Robert [1972]: **Climate Change and the Development of Canadian Arctic Cultural Traditions.** pp: 39-60 in "Climatic Changes in Arctic Areas During the Past Ten Thousand Years", Acta Universitatis Ouluensis, Serie A, Geologica 1, editors: Y. Vasari et al., * p. (Oulu: *).

Meese, D. A. [1994]: **The Accumulation Record from the GISP2 Core as an Indicator of Climate Change Throughout the Holocene.** *Science*, 266:1680-1682 (*: *).

Rainey, Froelich G. [1947]: **The Whale Hunters of Tigara.** *Anthropological Papers*, 4(2):231-283 (New York: American Museum of Natural History).

Riches, David [1982]: **Northern Nomadic Hunters-Gatherers: A Humanistic Approach.** 242 p. (New York: Academic Press).

Richling, Barnett [1993]: **Labrador's "Communal House Phase" Reconsidered.** *Arctic Anthropology*, 30(1): 67-78 (Madison: University of Wisconsin Press).

Schledermann, Peter [1972]: **The Thule Tradition in Northern Labrador.** M.A. Thesis, 147 p. (St.John's: Memorial University of Newfoundland).

Schledermann, Peter [1976a]: **Thule Culture Communal Houses in Labrador.** *Arctic*, 29(1):27-37 (Calgary: Arctic Institute of North America).

Schledermann, Peter [1976b]: **The Effect of Climatic/Ecological Changes on the Style of Thule Culture Winter Dwellings.** *Arctic and Alpine Research*, 8(1):37-47 (*, Colorado: Institute of Arctic & Alpine Research).

Spencer, Robert F. [1959]: **The North Alaskan Eskimo: A Study in Ecology and Society.** *Bureau of American Ethnology Bulletin*, 171:1-490 (Washington DC: U.S. Government Printing Office).

Taylor, J. Garth [1974]: **Labrador Eskimo Settlements of the Early Contact Period.** *Publications in Ethnology*, 9:1-102 (Ottawa: National Museum of Man).

Taylor, J. Garth [1984]: **Historical Ethnography of the Labrador Coast.** *Handbook of North American Indians, Arctic*, 5:508-521, editor: David Damas, 829 p. (Washington DC: Smithsonian Institution Press).

Taylor, J. Garth [1985]: **The Arctic Whale Cult in Labrador.** *Etudes/Inuit/Studies*, 9(2):121-132 (Québec: Départment d'anthropologie, Université Laval).

Taylor, J. Garth [1988]: **Labrador Inuit Whale Use During the Early Contact Period.** *Arctic Anthropology*, 25(1):120-130 (Madison: University of Wisconsin Press).

Taylor, J. Garth [1990]: **The Labrador Inuit Kashim (Ceremonial House) Complex**. *Arctic Anthropology*, 27(2):51-67) (Madison: University of Wisconsin Press).

Taylor, J. Garth & Helga Taylor [1977]: **Inuit Lane Use and Occupancy in the Okak Region, 1776-1830.** pp:59-81 in "Our Footprints are Everywhere", editor: Carol-Brice Bennett, 331 p. (Nain: Labrador Inuit Association).

Teillet, John V. [1988]: **A Reconstruction of Summer Sea Ice Conditions in the Labrador Sea Using Hudson's Bay Company Ships' Log-Books, 1751 to 1870.** M.A. Thesis, 161 p. (*: University of Manitoba).

Wenzel, George [1995]: **Ningiqtuq: Resource Sharing and Generalized Reciprocity in Clyde River, Nunavat.** *Arctic Anthropology*, 32(2):43-60 (Madison: University of Wisconsin Press).

Wilson, C. [1983]: **Some Aspects of the Calibration of Early Canadian Temperature Records in the Hudson's Bay Company Archives.** pp:144-202 in "Climate Change in Canada 3", editor: C. R. Harrington, * p. (Ottawa: National Museum of Natural Sciences).

Woollett, Jim [1996]: **Zooarchaeology and the Paleoeconomy of Uivak, Northern Labrador.** Paper presented at the Canadian Archaeological Association, Halifax, Nova Scotia.

Poetry, Politics, and Archaeology in Greenland

Inge Kleivan

In his contribution on Dorset Culture to a symposium in Nuuk in 1981, Jørgen Meldgaard quotes extracts of a poem by the Greenlandic politician and poet Aqqaluk Lynge (Meldgaard 1986:15-16). A reproduction of the illustrated poem was hanging on the wall which Meldgaard had in front of him while he was sitting writing his paper. It was not a poetic picture of the life of the distant ancestors of the Greenlanders that have fascinated him. It was an ironic poem dealing with scientists in the Arctic. This article discusses two such poems and their historical context. The following is a translation based on the Danish version of "Til Hæder og Ære" (= In Honour and Glory) included in a bilingual collection of Lynge's poem.

All quotations are withhout regard to whether they are written in Greenlandic and/or Danish rendered in English translation.

"They travelled and travelled / in a country where they thought / that no human beings could settle and live - They travelled and travelled / and when they arrived they found people / who did not know anything else / about human beings than themselves. - They travelled and travelled / and the hospitality was big / the curiosity without limits / but the guests could not be satisfied. - They travelled and travelled / and everywhere they came / people were examined / their clothes, sledges and equipments were bought up. - They travelled and travelled / to a country so big / that there cannot be people enough / to name that many places. - They travelled and travelled / and each island or fjord / headland or mountain was named / in honour of this or that or themselves. - They travelled and travelled / and returned with maps of the country, and the way of life described - to gain honor and

glory / medals et cetera / for having travelled in a country where people are settled and living." (Lynge 1982:11-12).

The poem was reproduced as a piece of visual art handwritten in Danish in a way that caught the eyes, and illustrated by the Greenlandic artist Anne-Birthe Hove (born 1951). In the center of the drawing are two blond Danes with beards, one is holding a rod while the other is reading the figures. A little further back to the left is a Greenlander returning, carrying a burden with a long piece of equipment, probably for catching trout. To the right is a Greenlandic woman attending to the cooking pot over the fire, while another blackhaired Greenlander is sitting resting on a stone. Fish are spread out for drying. The contrast between the people who are familar with the landscape and its resources and the two scientists is emphasized by the numerous placenames, named after Danes which the mountain scenery in the background is supplied with.

The poem combined with the drawing was included as an illustration in the proceedings of the conference where Jørgen Meldgaard gave his paper on "The Dorset Culture - tendencies of development and interruptions". Meldgaard's only comment was: *"And I recognize, slightly upset, myself"* (Meldgaard 1986:15).

Some years later another Greenlandic poet, Ole Korneliussen, published a poem with even stronger attacks on archaeologists and other scientists. The poem was called:

"Videnskabsmændenes Sang" (= The song of the scientists):

"This country could be / very lovely / very exciting / if it had been unpopulated. - This country could / be very

HVOR MENNESKET LEVER OG BOR.

DE REJSTE OG REJSTE I ET LAND, HVOR DE TROEDE, AT INGEN MENNESKELIGE VÆSENER
KUNNE LEVE OG BO.
DE REJSTE OG REJSTE OG DA DE KOM, FANDT DE NOGLE SOM IKKE KENDTE ANDET TIL
MENNESKER END SIG SELV.
DE REJSTE OG REJSTE OG GÆSTFRIHEDEN VAR STOR, NYSGERRIGHEDEN UENDELIG;
MEN GÆSTERNE VAR IKKE TIL AT MÆTTE.
DE REJSTE OG REJSTE, ALLE VEGNE HVOR DE KOM BLEV MENNESKER UNDERSØGT,
DERES KLÆDER SLÆDER OG UDSTYR BLEV OPKØBT.
DE REJSTE OG REJSTE TIL SÅ STORT ET LAND KAN DER IKKE VÆRE MENNESKER NOK
DE REJSTE OG REJSTE TIL AT NAVNGIVE SÅ MANGE STEDER.
OG HVER EN Ø ELLER FJORD, ET NÆS ELLER FJÆLD BLEV DER GIVET NAVNE
TIL ÆRE FOR DENNE OG HIN —— OG DEM SELV.
DE REJSTE OG REJSTE OG REJSTE TILBAGE MED KORT
OVER LANDET...... BESKEVET TIL HÆDER OG ÆRE,
MEDALJER MED MERE FOR AT HAVE BEREJST ET LAND
HVOR MANGE MENNESKER LEVER OG BOR.

DIGT AF:
ARQALUK LYNGE

exciting / be very lovely / if we depopulated it. - These people would / be exciting would be / rare / if only they lived / like they used to do in the past. - To hell / with motorization / wage system / old age provision. - The greedy sheep-breeders / have built houses / close to the lovely ruins / How are we then / to examine them and show off. - This country could be / very exciting / if it were unpopulated / All the exciting things / we could examine / are being spoilt by those idiots / It would be wonderful / if they still used / their kayaks / or were lying in their graves." (Korneliussen 1993:47).

The political mobilization of young Greenlanders in Denmark in the seventies

To use poetry and music in a political discussion was nothing new in Greenland, for example Greenland's national anthem "Nunarput utoqqarsuanngoravit" (= Our country you have grown old) written 1912 by Henrik Lund (1875-1948), was part of a public debate where he encouraged his countrymen to take part in the modern development of their country.

In the seventies several young Greenlanders in their creative writings and in other ways expressed deep dissatisfaction with the modernization of the Greenlandic society and the Danish dominance. In 1973 the first Greenlandic rock music long-playing record appeared produced by a group of young Greenlanders who were studying in Denmark. It was very well received both in Greenland and Denmark. The songwriter was Malik Høegh (born 1952). The group called themselves *Sume* (= Where) and the record "Sumut" (= Where to).

Some of these young people got an organizational and political training during their years as students in Denmark that prepared them for their future roles in Greenland. Greenlandic youth in Denmark formed their own voluntary association *Unge Grønlænderes Råd* (= Young Greenlanders' Council - later changed into Greenlandic: *Kalâtdlit inûsugtut ataqatigît*). Lynge was a member of the board from its start in 1970 and chairman 1974-1976. Young Greenlanders became part of the Danish Youth Rebellion and questioned the role of both Danish and Greenlandic authorities. Lynge and other young Greenlanders were invited to deliver speeches at demonstrations organized by the Danish left wing against the war in Vietnam, the World Bank, and the like (Langgård 1990:25). Greenlanders began to see their situation in an international perspective. Aqqaluk Lynge became a member of the board of Inuit Circumpolar Conference in 1980 and was vice-president 1983-1992.

At The Arctic Peoples' Conference in Copenhagen 1973 the differences in political views expressed by Lynge and Lars Chemnitz, chairman of the Provincial Council of Greenland, were a foretaste of the formation of the Greenlandic political parties *Inuit Ataqatigiit* and *Atassut* (Kleivan 1992:231). It was, however, a third poli-

cal movement, *Siumut* which became the leading party. Ever since Home Rule came into effect in Greenland on May 1, 1979 Siumut has had the political power alone or in coalition with either Atassut or Inuit Ataqatigiit. The Greenlandic political parties are not affiliated to political parties in Denmark, but Siumut is comparable with a social democratic party, Atassut with a liberal party and Inuit Ataqatigiit with a left wing socialist party.

Two young Greenlandic poets

Aqqaluk Lynge and Ole Korneliussen were born half a century ago in 1947, Lynge in Aasiaat, Korneliussen in Nanortalik. Tremendous changes have taken place in Greenland during their lifetime, politically, economically, educationally etc. They both spent their final years of schooling in Denmark and both started at the University of Copenhagen but did not finish their studies.

Lynge, however, finished another education and returned to Greenland in 1976 as a social worker. He has also worked as a journalist at Kalaallit Nunaata Radiua (Radio Greenland) in Nuuk. Aqqaluk Lynge's name has since the early seventies primarily been connected with policy.

Ole Korneliussen, however, stayed on in Denmark but is considered one of Greenland's most interesting poets.

Both Lynge and Korneliusen wrote poems at an early age. A Greenlandic anthology "agdlagarsiat" edited by Jens Poulsen (1970) includes several brief poems written by Lynge between 1964 and 1969 (Poulsen 1970:19-22). At that time he used his Christian name Knud which he later as part of the political and cultural mobilization replaced with his Greenlandic name, Aqqaluk (a girl's little brother).

The poem quoted above gave name to his bilingual collection of poems: "Til Hæder og Ære / Tupigusullutik angalapput" (Lynge 1982). Most of the poems were probably written in Danish and addressed to Danes. Several of them were written to be used in a Danish television production in eight parts "In the trail of Knud Rasmussen's sledging" (I Knud Rasmussen's slædespor, 1978). Hove gave the mountains Danish names in her illustration of the poem "Til Hæder og Ære" (= In Honour and Glory), but the scientists who travelled and travelled may rather refer to the Fifth Thule Expedition to Arctic Canada and Alaska.

Included in the collection of poems was also "Ode til Danaidernes kar" (= Ode to the vessel of the Danaids), about imperialism and capitalism in Greenland, perhaps the best known poem by Aqqaluk Lynge. It was published already in 1972 in the Danish newspaper "Politiken" with an illustration by the Danish artist Bodil Kaalund showing the worship of the Golden Calf (Smidt 1972).

Somewhat ironical Lynge's collection of poems was published by a Danish publisher, Brøndum, who had specialized in beatifully printed books primarily with original works by Danish lithographic artists to new poems by Danish poet or poems translated into Danish. It was illustrated in a non-political way by one of the finest Greenlandic artists, Aka Høegh (born 1947).

One of Korneliussen's earliest poems "Muren" (= The wall) is dated East Berlin Easterday 1970. He published his first collection of poems in Greenlandic in 1973. It was called "Putoq" (= The hole). "Putoq Nutaaq" (= The new hole) appeared in 1991 and in Danish as "Glamhuller" (= sound-holes) in 1993. ("Galmhuller" is a rarely used word for the holes in church towers made so that the sound of the bells can get out).

"Putoq Nutaaq" and "Glamhuller" were illustrated by the Greenlandic artist Jessie Klemann (born 1959). Some of Korneliussen's later poems in "Glamhuller" were as he says in the preface thought in Danish and written in Greenlandic, others were thought in Greenlandic and written in Danish, and still others were thought in Danish and written in Danish. He has cooperated with the Danish poet Vagn Steen about the present linguistic form of the poems.

Writings by Lynge and Korneliussen have been included in several anthologies, magazines and newspapers in Greenlandic and Danish. Some of Lynge's poems have even been published in Norwegian, Swedish, Icelandic, English, French, and Russian (Ramlau-Hansen 1994).

Korneliussen has also published a collection of short stories in Greenlandic, "Uumasoqat" (= Cohabiter) (1992), whereas Lynge has published a book about Inuit Circumpolar Conference (1993).

Poems as comments on archaeological and other scientific investigations

The two poems quoted here are sarcastic poems with the object of ridiculing foreign scientists and exposing their motives. By using third person in the plural *they* Lynge is distancing himself from the scientists and identifying himself with the inhabitants of the country. He uses sarcasm to describe the foreigners who gain glory by travelling in an inhabited country. The message is spelt out: you gain honour by returning home and telling about what is new to you but what we are familiar with. But reality is not that simple. The self-evident cultural knowledge is not the same as a genuine anthropological understanding (Hastrup 1993:156) or archaeological or other scientific understanding.

Korneliussen has chosen to use first person in the plural *we* and to pretend to know the innermost thoughts of the scientists. He is obviously overshooting the mark when he presents their wishful thinking: Greenland would be a very interesting country for scientists if only it were uninhabited or if only the Greenlanders lived in their old traditional way. These stereotypes tell something about concepts that Greenlanders, or some Green-

landers, have or have had. The stereotype that anthropologists and eskimologists are only interested in the traditional culture has been very persistent, even among Greenlandic politicians.

In his poem, Korneliussen comments on the different interests that sheep breeders and archaeologists have in the area where the medieval Norsemen used to live.

Since the beginning of the twentieth century Greenlandic sheep breeders have settled in the southern part of Greenland in the municipalities of Nanortalik, Qaqortoq, Narsaq, and Paamiut. Naturally, Norsemen and the modern sheep breeders in many cases choose the same green pastures for their sheep. The still visible ruins of the Norsemen's houses, stables, churches etc. have, however, caused some trouble for the modern utilizers of the area.

Norsemen, archaeologists and sheep breeders

Ever since Hans Egede, the first missionary of the Greenlanders, initiated the Danish-Norwegian colonization in 1721, Europeans in Greenland have had an interest in the fate of the Norse population and in the ruins that testified where they once lived. Naturally the big ruins have also fascinated Greenlanders who told legends about the Norsemen. In addition to some Greenlandic school books some popular scientific books on the Norsemen have been published in Greenlandic (Kleivan 1991b:242-243). As a reaction to the celebrations in South Greenland in the summer of 1982 of the arrival of the Norsemen to Greenland 1000 years earlier, a national day of Greenland was introduced in 1985, a day when the Greenlandic nation, as Jonathan Motzfeldt, Siumut, put it, could celebrate "*its national and cultural values*" (Kleivan 1991a:9).

In a report based on visits to a number of sheep breeders in 1978 the Greenlandic cultural-historian H. C. Petersen stressed that the sheep breeders on the one hand appreciated the historial significance of some ruins, but on the other hand they wanted to get rid of most ruins that were in their way (Petersen 1978:34).

The find of an archaeological site may put a temporary or permanent stop to building plans as it happened in Qassiarsuk, the Norsemen's Brattahlid, in 1961. The archaeologists got involved when Meldgaard got a visitor at the National Museum of Denmark in Copenhagen who came to see him "about the skull of Erik the Red", the initiator of the Norse colonization in Greenland. Then he placed a skull in pink tissue paper on Meldgaard's table. It came from Qassiarsuk where a hostel for school-children from the outlying farms was going to be build. The same day the excavation started, however, some skulls appeared. The Greenlandic catechist Lars Motzfeldt who had himself pointed out the site which had a fine view of the fjord and the mountains realized that it might be an old Norse buriel place and stopped the work. It was established that the skull had belonged to a Norseman, and during the archaeological excations in the following summers, the ruins of a church surrounded by a grave-yard became visible (Meldgaard 1982). The hostel had to be built elsewhere.

Archaeology and tourism

Qassiarsuk is not far from Narsarsuaq, the airport of South Greenland, and quite a number of tourists have vis-ited the Norse ruins since tourism in 1959 began for real with the first charter flight to Narsarsuaq. Tourism as an industry, however, developed only slowly, but the Home Rule Parliament has decided that tourism is to become a major industry. Tourism is expected to bring both foreign currency to Greenland and to create jobs. In the coming years a considerable number of visitors to Qassiarsuk are going to have a look at the excavated ruins of the first Christian Church, not only in Greenland, but in the New World.

Archaeologists are well aware that it is necessary to cooperate with local politicians and local politicians are well aware of the value of archaeological sites for tourism. When the preliminary results of the interdisci-plinary investigations of a Saqqaq Culture settlement on the island of the Qeqertassuk were published in 1991 in Greenlandic and Danish in connection with a travelling exhibition the mayor of Qasigiannguit/Christianshåb was asked to write the preface. He stressed that it was impor-tant that children got an insight into the life of their ancestors, but even if the inhabitants and the municipal council were very interested in the past, they had to face the future:

"With the growing flow of tourists to the town hope-fully a museum telling about the first Greenlanders will contribute to non-local and foreign visitors finding Christianshåb worth a visit, preferably a long visit." (Lyberth 1991:2-3).

Archaeology and the Home Rule Government

There has for many years been an interest in the many ruins of the Inuit Cultures in Greenland, especially since Therkel Mathiassen in 1929 started his systematic exca-vations. Some of his results were published in Green-landic in 1936.

Meldgaard who later demonstrated that Greenland had a much longer prehistory than one previously had realized (Meldgaard 1952) has been co-author of a school book on Greenland's prehistory prepared for the Greenlandic school in both a Greenlandic and Danish edition and a bilingual teachers' guidance (Gynther & Meldgaard 1983, 1984). A cast of a number of character-istic prehistoric objects were taken in 1979 to be used for demonstration in the classroom.

Both politicians and archaeologists have realized the importance of informing the population. The text of the Law of Protection of October 16, 1980, passed by the Home Rule Parliament, was included as an appendix in a survey of all registered Inuit ruins and the like of the past in the municipality of Nuuk published by the National Museum of Denmark and the National Museum of Greenland (Gulløv 1983).

The bilingual book includes maps of about 350 local-ities and more than 1000 Inuit ruins with information about which sites are protected. In the preface Jørgen Meldgaard and Claus Andreassen emphasize that the sur-way is based on the detailed knowledge of many local people, and that more information is wanted by the muse-ums in Greenland. They suggest that the book might serve as a guide for local citizens and tourists, and even be used in the schools.

Archaeological excavations may cause ethical prob-lems, and archaeologists may be seen as intruders. Since January 1, 1981, however, the Home Rule Government has been responsible for laws concerning museums and cultural preservation regulations (Andreasen 1986 and Schultz-Lorentzen this volume).

Greenlandic students and employees at museums participate in the excavations of the prehistoric sites of their country and in 1992 the first Greenlandic archaelo-gist graduated at the University of Copenhagen. The cru-cial questions of where and when to dig, who are to do the excavations and write and publish the results, and where the excavated things are to be exhibited and kept do not seem to cause big problems.

"The quiet life of a revolution"

The development taking place in the years following the implementation of Home Rule in Greenland May 1, 1979 has been called "The quiet life of a revolution" (Brein-holt-Larsen 1992). The modernization process initiated by Danish politicians was continued by Greenlandic politicians.

At the first election of the Greenlandic Parliament (Inatsisartut/Landsting) Siumut won 46,1% of the votes, Atassut 41,7% and Inuit Ataqatigiit 4,4%. Inuit Ataqatigiit won no seats. But at the next parliamentary election in 1983 Siumut won 42,3%, Atassut 46,6%, and Inuit Ataqatigiit 10,6% of the votes. Two seats were won by Inuit Ataqatigiit, one of them by Aqqaluk Lynge. He was minister for social affairs, housing, technology and environment 1984-1988. At the two most recent elections in 1991 and 1995 Siumut won 37,3% and 38,4% of the votes, Atassut 30,1% and 30,1%, and Inuit Ataqatigiit 19,4% and 20,3% (Kalaallit Nunnaanni Naatsorsueqqis-saartarfik/Grønlands Statestik 1996:33). Inuit Ataqatigiit increased its votes in 1995 but Aqqaluk Lynge was not reelected.

In an interview just after the election he explained his defeat by referring to his work with reconstituting the Home Rule owned KNI (Kalaallit Niuverfiat (= Green-land Trade)) and that he as chairman of KNI Holding A/S had had to be responsible for necessary, but unpopular decisions (Anonymous 1995).

Criticism of the political leaders

Some of the young Greenlandic politicians who were politically active at the beginning of the seventies and who implemented Home Rule in 1979 are still active, among them the present Prime Minister Lars Emil Johansen, Siumut, (born 1946) and the former Prime Minister Jonathan Motzfeldt, Siumut, (born 1938). Generally speaking Home Rule in Greenland is considered a success even if it has to be admitted that there are economical and educational problems. A few political leaders, however, have caused popular discontent. An editorial in the Greenland newspaper Atuagagdliutit/Grønlandsposten (A/G) in 1994 under the heading "Fornyelse" (= Replacement) argued that most of the Greenlandic politicians from the seventies "were used up". The occasion was an approaching election to the Danish Parliament in 1994. Since 1953 when Greenland according to an amendment to Danish constitution was included as a "province" of Denmark Greenland has elected two members of the Danish Parliament (Folketing) out of 179.

Before the election took place a Greenlandic reader of Atuagagdliutit/Grønlandsposten in a letter to the editor strongly supported the editorial which suggested replacement of the old politicians. She wrote under the heading "Burnt out politicians" that the Greenlandic politicians either needed replacement or to wake up and look critically at themselves so that the new generation should not loose faith in them. She included a poem to the newspaper, published both in Greenlandic and Danish, which she had written when Home Rule celebrated its 10th anniversary in 1989. It was a paraphrase of Aqqaluk Lynge's poem quoted above and was called "Til politikernes hæder og ære" (= In honour and glory of the politicians):

"They travelled and travelled / in a country where they thought / that no human beings / would ask questions. - They travelled and travelled / and came nowhere / they did not know anything / but to take themselves into consideration. - They travelled and travelled / everywhere they arrived / people became at a loss / their clothes, sledges, and equipment became superfluous. - They travelled and travelled / to so many countries / that people at home / did not know why. - They travelled and travelled / to conferences and meetings / to name associations / in honour and glory of this and that and themselves. - They travelled and travelled / and returned / with contracts drawn up on everything / and rules described / that others were to observe / and got their pockets filled / at the expense of others in a country / where people are settled and living." (Møgeltoft 1994).

The sarcasm is now turned against the Greenlandic politicians. It is now they who gain glory and honour by travelling and many of these travel do not seem to be necessary. They are even accused of getting rich through their position as politicians. Møgeltoft's poem was illustrated by a photo of Greenlandic politicians with Aqqaluk Lynge in the foreground sitting with papers and microphones before them. Aqqaluk Lynge was one of three candidates nominated for an electoral pact between Siumut and Inuit Ataqatigiit in the hope of getting both seats in the Danish Parliament.

The pact, however, won only one seat whereas the other seat was won by Atassut. The old politicians were reelected i 1994: Hans Pavia Rosing, Siumut, who had been a member of the Danish Parliament since 1987 and Otto Steenholdt, Atassut, who had been a member since 1977.

By being published in the newspaper Atuagagdliutit/Grønlandsposten Møgeltoft's poem reached a large number of readers. It had no decisive influence on the fact that Lynge was not elected, but it was one of many small pushes that contributed to his defeat in the elections to the Greenlandic Parliament in 1995. At that time he had already lost his position as leader of Inuit Ataqatigiit. It is, however, difficult to imagine that an outstanding political personality like Aqqaluk Lynge has had his day in domestic policies. In 1995 he fought hard to get the job as president of Inuit Circumpolar Conference but had to withdraw after three inconclusive ballots and became one of the vice-presidents. In 1997, however, the president resigned and Aqqaluk Lynge was made president.

Two mature Greenlandic poets

In an interview in Atuagagdliutit/Grønlandsposten in 1994 Aqqaluk Lynge spoke about how he himself and his poems had changed over the years:

"From writing powerful poems about oppression and dependence, I have passed on to writing more about love. I think it is a natural development I have gone through. You think differently when you grow older. You are no longer so categorical. You have your corners rubbed off. Today I look more at the beautiful things in life, whereas in my youth I regarded it as an honor to fight for the right to be ourselves. What I wrote in my early youth was in a way negative, whereas today I look more ahead - look at things in a more grown-up way." (Ramlau-Hansen 1994).

In 1995 Lynge was elected president of the small Greenlandic Society of authors, Kalaallit atuakkiortut.

Ole Korneliussen, who settled in Denmark, has not been a public figure like Aqqaluk Lynge, even if he on several occasions has read his poems to audiences both in Denmark and Greenland.

By not being a politician and being without political ambitions he has felt free to make critical comments on Greenlandic politicians from a distance. In the poem called "Kommunernes magt" (= "The power of the municipalities" he makes sarcastic remarks about the many meetings, sometimes without many results, held by local politicians. Just like in Møgeltoft's poem he makes a dividing line between *them*, the politicians, and *we*, the people. They are inside, we are outside:

"*On the sheltered side of the meeting room / it smells / of tobacco / cigars / and coffee*."

The concluding lines run: "*They hold a meeting / they hold a meeting / and resolve / to hold a meeting again.*" (Korneliussen 1993:48).

The poem "Medaljerne" (= The medals) is a paraphrase of a traditional song which is well-know in Greenland. It makes fun of the politician who is getting thicker: "*The anorak begins to tighten*" and who gains glory and honor. The last vers runs: "*Our former masters thank me very much / aaja ajja jaa / I thank very much for their medals / aaja ajja jaa / My cassock is now quite heavy / The medals have become so many / aaja ajja jaa / With age comes stiffness / aaja ajja jaa / I cannot wear the medals any more.*" (Korneliussen 1993:45-46).

So that no one should be in doubt who is talking Korneliussen has supplied the poem with a note:

"*Greenland's first Prime Minister, Jonathan Motzfeldt, who is a clergyman, got an unbelievable number of medals.*" (Korneliussen 1993:71).

Korneliussen's poems - most of them are non-political - are highly appreciated by young Greenlanders. A lecturer at Ilisimatusarfik, the University of Greenland, in Nuuk explains it by referring to the fact that the poems (in "Putoq" (1973)) are different in form and content from other Greenlandic poems. They ask existential questions without in any way suggesting the answers.

"*It is probably the only book that really fascinates young readers.*" (Langgård 1990:27).

Concluding remarks

Verbal art and visual art are sometimes able to comment more powerful on a subject than any other form of documentation or analysis. That explains why a poem may find its way into a scientific article. Political poems reflect what is going on in a society, even it differences are exaggerated and stereotypes florish. Like the poems dealt with in this article they are products of a historical situation. From the inception of Home Rule Greenlandic politicians have had the responsibility of the development and that have made them a more obvious target than Danes in the Greenlandic society of the recent years.

Inge Kleivan is a retired lecturer at the Department of Eskimology, University of Copenhagen, Denmark

References

Anonymous [1994]: **Fornyelse / Nutarterineq.** *Atuagagdliutit/Grønlandsposten*, 134(71):5 (Nuuk).

Anonymous [1995]: **Aqqaluk Lynge vil med i landsstyret / Aqqaluk Lynge naalakkersuinermi suleqataarusuppoq.** *Atuagagdliutit/Grønlandsposten*, 135 (19):10-11 (Nuuk).

Andreasen, Claus [1986]: **Greenland's Museum Laws: An introduction to Greenland's Museums under Home Rule.** *Arctic Anthropology*, 23(1-2):239-246 (Madison).

Breinholt-Larsen, Finn [1992]: **The quiet life of a revolution: Greenlandic Home Rule 1979-1992.** *Études/Inuit/Studies*, 16(1-2):199-226 (Quebec).

Gulløv, Hans Christian [1983]: **Nuup kommuneani qangarnitsanik eqqaassutit inuit-kulturip nunaqarfii / Fortidsminder i Nuuk Kommune - inuit-kulturens bopladser.** 239 p. (Nuuk).

Gynther, Bent & Jørgen Meldgaard [1983]: **5 kapitler af Grønlands forhistorie.** 113 p. (Nuuk: Pilersuiffik) (Greenlandic edition 1983).

Gynther, Bent & Jørgen Meldgaard [1984]: **5 kapitler af Grønlands forhistorie / Kalaallit Nunaanni itsarsuup nalaa immikkoortut tallimat. Lærervejledning / Ilinniartitsisunut ilitsersuusiaq.** 84/99 p. (Nuuk: Pilersuiffik).

Hastrup, Kirsten [1993]: **Native Anthropology: A Contradiction in Terms?** *Folk*, 35:147-161 (Copenhagen: Danish Ethnographical Society).

Kalaallit Nunaanni Naatsorsueqqissaartarfik / Grønlands Statestik [1996]: **Grønland 1996 Kalaallit Nunaat.** Statistisk Årbog. Ukiumoortumik paasissutissat (Nuuk).

Kleivan, Inge [1991a]: **Greenland's national symbols.** pp:4-16 in "Greenland: Nationalism and Cultural Identity in Comparative perspectiv", editors: Susanne Dybbroe & Poul Brøbech Møller, *North Atlantic Studies*, 1(2):3-71 (Århus).

Kleivan, Inge [1991b]: **Historie og historier i Grønland.** pp:234-258 in "Klaus Khan Baba: En etnografisk kalejdoskopi tilegnet Klaus Ferdinand den 19. april 1991", editors: Susanne Dybbroe et al., 398 p. (Århus: Aarhus University).

Kleivan, Inge [1992]: **The Arctic Peoples' Conference in Copenhagen, November 22-25, 1973.** *Études/ Inuit/ Studies*, 16(1-2):227-236 (Québec).

Korneliussen, Ole [1992]: **Uumasoqat.** 86 p. (Nuuk: Atuakkiorfik).

Korneliussen, Ole [1993]: **Glamhuller.** 68 p. (Nuuk: Atuakkiorfik). (Greenlandic editions: Putoq 1973 and Putoq nutaaq 1991).

Langgård, Per [1990]: **Grønlandsk litteratur i 70-erne og 80-erne.** *Nordica - tidsskrift for nordisk teksthistorie og æstetik*, 7:15-37 (Odense: Odense Universitetsforlag).

Lyberth, Christian [1991]: **Indledning. Tema: Qeqertasussuk. De første mennesker i Vestgrønland.** *Tidsskriftet Grønland*, 39(4-5-6-7):98-99 (Copenhagen: The Greenland Society). (Greenlandic edition 1991).

Lynge, Arqaluk [1982]: **Til hæder og ære. Grønlandsdigte / Tupigusullutik angalapput.** 84 p. Grafiske arbejder af Aka Høegh (Copenhagen: Brøndum).

Lynge, Aqqaluk [1993]: **Inuit. Inuit Issittormiut kattuffiata oqaluttuassartaa / Histoire de la Conférence Circumpolaire Inuit / The Story of the Inuit Circumpolar Conference.** 123 p. (Nuuk: Atuakkiorfik).

Mathiassen, Therkel [1936]: **kalâtdlit oqalugtuagssartáinik ilisimassavut.** atuagâraq 9, 32 p. (Nûk: kalâtdline qáumarsautigssîniaqatigît naqitertitât).

Meldgaard, Jørgen [1952]: **A Palaeo-Eskimo Culture in West Greenland.** *American Antiquity*, 17(3):222-230 (Salt Lake City).

Meldgaard, Jørgen [1982]: **Tjorhildes Kirke - den første fundberetning.** Tema: Nordboerne I. *Tidsskriftet Grønland*, 30(5-6-7):151-162 (Copenhagen: Det Grønlandske Selskab).

Meldgaard, Jørgen [1986]: **Dorset-Kulturen - udviklingstendenser og afbrydelser.** pp:15-32 in "Vort sprog - vor kultur". Foredrag fra symposium afholdt i Nuuk oktober 1981 arrangeret af Ilisimatusarfik og Kalaallit Nunaata Katersugaasivia. 200 p. (Nuuk). (In Greenlandic 1986).

Møgeltoft, Kista [1994]: **Udbrændte Politikere "Til politikernes hæder og ære" / "Tupigisaallutik angalapput".** *Atuagagdliutit / Grønlandsposten*, 134 (74):16 (Nuuk).

Petersen, H. C. [1978]: **Rapport fra rejse til fåreholdersteder i Sydgrønland 5.-26. juni 1978.** 41 p. (Manuscript in Danish Polar Center, Copenhagen).

Poulsen, Jens (editor) [1970]: **agdlagarsiat.** 156 p. (Godthåb: Kalâtdlit-nunane naqiterisitsissarfik / Det Grønlandske Forlag).

Ramlau-Hansen, Laila [1994]: **Takorloortarpaa atuakkiortunngornissi / Drømmen om at skrive.** *Atuagagdliutit/Grønlandsposten*, 134(15):10 (Nuuk).

Smidt, Poul [1972]: **Grønlandsk bitterhed i politisk digtning.** *Politiken*, 22 October (Copenhagen).

Danish Arctic Scholarship with a Foreign Accent

William S. Laughlin

"When working in the Igloolik area the archaeologist cannot help developing into an evolutionist." (Meldgaard 1962:92).

The Linguistic Sources of Inspiration

While a first year graduate student at Haverford College I was permitted to take a year long seminar in ethnology with Frederica De Laguna at nearby Bryn Mawr College. During the winter of 1941-1942 she announced that Paul-Emile Victor would give a lecture on Greenland at the University of Pennsylvania. His lecture was skillfully illustrated with chalkboard illustrations in the same graphic style as those illustrations in "La Civilisation du Phoque" (Victor & Robert-Lamblin 1989). He pointed out that the word for the direction north and right, and for the direction south and left, had been employed in West Greenland with the assumption that the man was seated in his kayak and faced out to sea. However, in East Greenland the terms are preserved, but south is north and north is south. He drew the conclusion from this evidence that the West Greenlanders had migrated around Cape Farvel and thence to their known distribution on the east coast.

My Oregon experience prompted my interest in origins of the Native Americans. In particular the Athabaskan speakers of Oregon such as the Chetco and Khustenete on the southwest coast. Sapir (1916) had called attention to the large number of unrelated languages in Oregon and is quite well known for calling attention to linguistic diversity and origins, particularly in reference to the origin of Eskimos. A. L. Kroeber's "Cultural and Natural Areas of Native North America" (1939) was extraordinarily useful, both for this treatment of the Kalapuya, confined to the Willamette Valley, and of the Aleut and Eskimo world, as were his studies of the Polar-Eskimos who came to New York[1].

Hrdlicka and the Eskimo Origin

Among other precursor events leading to my desire to go to Denmark and Greenland was first a summer with Ales Hrdlicka of the Smithsonian that took me to Kodiak, the Aleutian Islands and the Commander Islands in 1938. He had a proclivity for mummy caves and deep sites such as Larsen Bay, Kodiak Island, and Chaluka, Umnak Island, but failed to recognize the significance of the blade and core industry of Anangula, memorialized in the Aleut (Unangan) name for this large, old (9,000 years B.P.) and rich site, the *"place for making blades (knives)"*.

Hrdlicka's 1930 map of the entry of Native Americans into the New World (Fig. 1) illustrates his belief in a late entry into the New World. He repeatedly estimated the arrival of either Koniags or Aleuts as somewhere around the time of Christ, unaware of the superb example of divergence provided by the Aleuts and Koniag Eskimos now dated by radiocarbon and various genetic materials to be in the 9,000 year B.P. range. He also overlooked the publication on the amber mining operation on Umnak Island. He knew the limitation on long distance travel in skin boats prevented the introduction of amber or "magical whale poison" from Kamchatka. The 1930 map and Hrdlicka's authority have distracted attention from discovering who discovered America, when, and by what route. The Aleuts (Unangan) are superb observers. They named him "Dead-Man's Daddy" because he came every summer and collected the dead people.

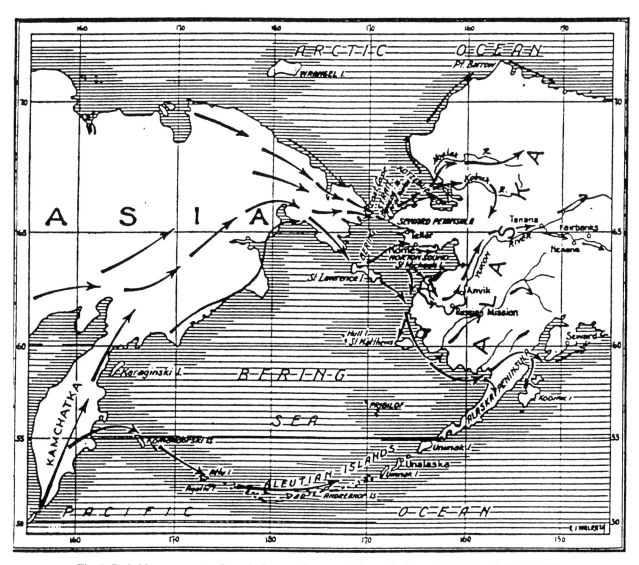

Fig. 1: Probable movements of people from northeastern Asia to Alaska and in Alaska (Hrdlicka 1930).

His low opinion of the female component of our single species did not prevent him from excavating females though he much preferred male skeletons.

The Anaktuvuk Detour

I had agreed to study the Anaktuvuk Eskimos with the aim of determining if they were Eskimos or Athabaskan Indians. The blood group data, together with the genealogies was sufficiently clear to remove any ambiguity, a proper concern of the Arctic Aeromedical Laboratory which had invested years of sophisticated research in these and other peoples native to Alaska. The hitch with the research operation (necessarily a tandem hitch) lay in the fact that I could only perform the research in December of 1955, owing to my plans for residence and study in Denmark on a Fulbright scholarship.

My guide in Anaktuvuk, a thoroughly experienced Arctic expert, Warren O. Tilman, showed me his missing toes. Consequently, I lost no time finding an Eskimo lady who would make me a pair of soft-soled caribou boots. Another lady made me a large, also beautiful, pair of wolf mittens. Shotgun barrels had long been used for scraping caribou, wolf, bear and other skins but the supply was limited. Tilman brought two sizes of airplane frame tubing, with beveled scraping end, larger and smaller. The ladies were delighted, and very helpful to me. In order to enlarge my sample I arranged to be driven to Tulugak, some 12 miles northeast of Anaktuvuk Pass to collect the blood of several people wintering there, Simon Paneak among them. The first driver turned back in the face of a storm. The driver who took me the next day was named Lazarus, and quite properly for he brought us back from the dead. We spent a lot of time looking for sled tracks of others, without success. At midnight he told me he had seen the same willow bush three times. I asked if we were lost and he thought yes.

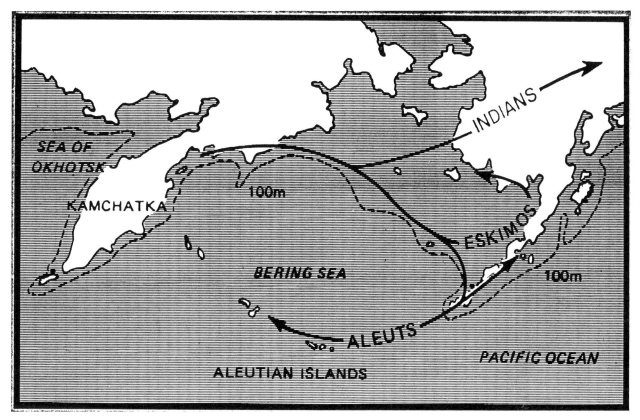

Fig. 2: (C. G. N. Mascie-Taylor & G. W. Lasker)

We had no food, no sleeping bags or heater and the temperature was obviously much lower than the minus 40°C back in Anaktuvuk. We turned the sled on its side and the dogs promptly burrowed into the snow bank. Lazarus and I kicked out a hole in the snow and lay on the bottom for the night. The next day we made it back to Anaktuvuk shortly after dark.

My genealogical data was of some use to verify kinship data assembled by Leopold Pospisil (Pospisil and Laughlin 1963). We spent Christmas at Bettles, my frost bitten face was photographed in color at the Aeromedical Laboratory.

Study in Denmark

It had become obvious that study in Denmark and in Greenland was indispensable to understanding the origin of Aleuts and Eskimos, and that an understanding of the origin of Aleuts and Eskimos was the key to understand-

ing the arrival and success of all Native Americans. Accordingly, I applied to the Fulbright scholarship program and received support and accreditation to the Anthropology Laboratory of the University of Copenhagen and the Department of Ethnography in the National Museum of Denmark. I spent mornings doing research in the Laboratory of Anthropology, and bicycled into the Museum on a bicycle loaned to me by Fred Milan, for lunch and a study of archaeological collections in the afternoon.

Lunch was held in the library and was ultimately pleasant and informative. Kaj Birket-Smith, Helge Larsen, Jørgen Meldgaard, and other curators and visiting guests were in frequent attendance. Eigil Knuth queried me on whether cleft hoof or cloven hoof was the better term for harpoon types. He had already noted similarities between early Anangula and Peary Land (Knuth 1954). I appreciate the information awarded me in conversations,

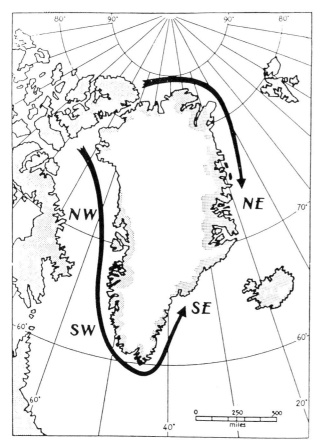 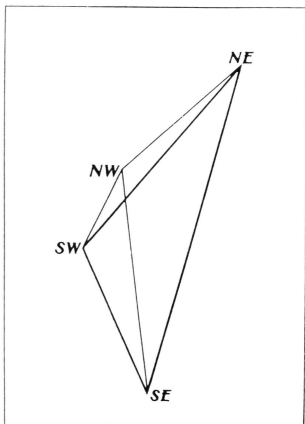

Fig. 15 (left). Migration of the Eskimos about Greenland. The migration was confined to the coasts because of the inland ice. It moved in two directions, with the result that the terminal isolates (the Northeast and the Southeast), separated for the longest period, show the greatest morphological differences. Fig. 16 (right). Geometric representation of the relative degrees of similarity between the four Greenland Eskimo isolates. The difference between the Northeast and the Southeast isolates is greater than the difference between any other two contiguous isolates. Though geographically as far apart as the Northeast and Southeast isolates, the Northwest and Southwest isolates exchanged mates more frequently and are much more similar to each other. [Courtesy of L. S. Penrose (43)].

and of course the opportunity to see original specimens, such as the Lagoa Santa crania. It is now possible to grasp in greater perspective the shared traits between early Native Americans and later groups in time that Birket-Smith had commented on (Birket-Smith 1948).

In Greenland

There are many precursor observations that can now be collected and used to illustrate the abundant evidence for a single migration into the New World, with subsequent divergence. The distribution of the Four Founding Lineage Haplotypes in Native Americans clearly favors a single migration into the New World (Merriwether, Rothhammer, & Ferrell 1995).

The eminent Russian scholar, Waldemar Jochelson, remarked in 1925 that the various data he had unearthed in his Aleutian researches of 1910: "... *fail to give us a definite measure of time which could be expressed in figures; nevertheless, they show clearly that the Aleut came to the islands many centuries ago, if not during the earliest period of the peopling of Northwestern America.*"

Soon after the arrival of Meldgaard and I in 1956 at Sønderstrømfjord Air Force Base in West Greenland we walked to a burial crypt near the Inland Ice. Upon removing some of the roofing stones we found a very young child, fully clothed. Upon replacing each of the stones in their original position Jørgen took a few samples of the moss that had been used to chink the spaces between the stones. He pointed out that it would be examined by a botanist on the off chance that it had been brought back from a Viking voyage to the New World.

The next few weeks I collected blood for typing. I lived in the old Post Office building, formerly a whale look out. An old style telephone made in Horsens (also the birthplace of Vitus Bering), had been used to phone whale sighting information down to the boats below. The medical doctor was busy inoculating the people against polio. This required visiting small as well as large living places. I wrote an article for the *Fulbright Monitor* which contains identification of the various personnel involved and direct observations on the assiduous work of Meldgaard and his impressive range of knowledge, and fuller identification of the Institute of Forensic Medicine.

Isolation or Contact

Greenland presents an uniquely defined area in which to study the direction of human migration because of the limited options imposed by the marine coast and the Inland Ice. The unique and remarkable crossing from the south west to the east coast in 1936 by a Danish-French team comprised of Eigil Knuth, Robert Gessain, Paul-Emile Victor[2], and Michel Perez, their sleds and a carefully selected dog team.

Jørgen Balslev Jørgensen and I chose to study the direction of migration around Greenland, based on frequency data of discrete traits of the cranium and mandible. Thus, it was possible to include the north east isolate though it's last living members passed away over a century ago.

The difference between the two terminal isolates, the North East and the South East is greater than the differences between any other two contiguous isolates. L. S. Penrose (1954) suggested that the North East isolate had separated before entry into Greenland and thus has considerable relevance to the researches of Eigil Knuth. Our study of the direction of migration in Greenland has recently been confirmed by Bruno Frohlich and P. O. Pedersen (1992) as well as others.

My next trip to Greenland[3], in 1963, took me and Balslev Jørgensen to Qaanaaq where we joined the Gilberg family in a study of the Polar-Eskimo, many of whom had been moved from Thule town in 1953 to Qaanaaq. Aage Gilberg, a medical doctor, and his wife Lisbet had previously known many of the people when Aage Gilberg was the health officer in Thule (Gilberg 1978).

The Alaskan Border

Ales Hrdlicka demonstrated a true cline of reduced cranial index from the lower to the upper Kuskokwim River. First, he compared the head form of the burials finding that those at the mouth of the Kuskokwim were broader than those further upstream. He compared skeletal materials with living people and found the same signal feature, the heads at the mouth of the Kuskokwim were broader than those upstream. He remarked that the closer the Eskimos (Yuit) were geographically closer to the Athabaskans, the greater the differences became, good evidence that intermixture could not be detected.

Hrdlicka's demonstration of this cline accomplished still another purpose. There were no broadheaded Yuit north of the Kuskokwim, meaning that the broadheads were moving in from the south. This alone should have alerted him to the fact that Bering Strait was not an entry zone from Siberian Eskimos (Yuit). It is one of the finest studies that Hrdlicka ever did for it demonstrated that Eskimos did not originate in Siberia and it detected a basic and common trend in our single human species. Tragically he impeached his valid findings in favor of a two strain hypothesis (Hrdlicka 1933).

There is no detectable cline on Kodiak Island for the good reason that it is possible to walk across Kodiak rather than being confined to the coast as in Greenland. The overall distribution of Aleuts and Eskimos is in itself highly informative and yields a full record of its origin and direction of migration.

The materials we have to work with are the genetics, medical examinations, photon measurements of bone mineral content in skeletal and living persons, linguistics, radiocarbon dates, material culture including excavated artifacts in context, house features, uplifted terraces, and contemporary material culture. This is here the richest coalescence of divergence data of any population system in the world.

We may begin a contemporary analysis of the origin of the Aleuts (Unangan) and the Kodiak Eskimos (Sugpiak or the larger linguistic category Yuit) by noting that genetic analysis using thirty-eight loci found a substantial difference between Aleuts and Kodiak Eskimos (Majumder, Laughlin, & Ferrell 1988).

DNA analysis of the same two groups using mitochondrial DNA revealed a significant difference between Aleut speakers and Eskimo speakers indicating an early separation of these two groups who cannot speak to each other (Merriwether, Rothhammer, & Ferrell 1995). All four haplogroups were found in all three major linguistic groups nominated by Greenberg and supported by C. Turner and Steven Zegura (Greenberg, Turner & Zegura 1986).

A Single Wave

The overall distribution is powerful evidence of a single wave of migration into the New World. It is obvious that the entry route into the New World followed the southern coast of the Bering Land Bridge, the Bering Sea was, of course, significantly warmer than the Arctic Ocean and rich in marine birds, sea mammals, fish, kelp, drift whales and drift wood. The Bering Strait region was primarily polar desert. Though the possibility that ancestors of the Athabaskans might have worked their way up the Yukon River when it emptied into the Bering Sea south of St. Lawrence Island cannot yet be ruled out.

Obviously, the greatest diversity indicates the area of origin (Sapir 1916). Clearly, the greatest linguistic barrier in the continuous distribution lies between Aleut (Unangan) ands Eskimo (Yuit), and the next but lesser barrier lies in Norton Sound, between Yuit and Inupiat-Inuit. Obviously, within the last four thousand years or slightly earlier, Yuit speakers decided to occupy both sides of Bering Strait. Thus, it appears that Old Bering Sea / Okvik, Punuk, Ipiutak and Birnirk were contemporaneous. The contemporaneity of these cultures indicates that distinctive artifact and ornamentation styles served as social boundary markers rather than evolutionary ancestral and successive descendant styles (Gerlach & Mason 1992).

Extension of
the Arctic Small Tool Tradition

Another significant development has been the increasing recognition of the Pre-Arctic Small Tool tradition in the Aleutian Islands, which in retrospect had been indicated in 1954 by the late Eigil Knuth, "The Paleo-Eskimo Culture of North East Greenland Elucidated by Three New Sites", in which he noted that examination of material from North East Greenland established the particular stamp of the Independence culture:

"*A purer Paleo-Eskimo character, and more distinct perspectives to the core and lamellar flake culture of Alaska than is the case for the west Greenland finds.*" (1954:378, for which he cited Laughlin 1951; Laughlin, Marsh & Leach 1952).

Size measurements suitable for comparative studies are a relevant concern. Thickness appeared to be the only dimension not affected by edge retouch. Accordingly, we compared the thickness of 713 specimens parsed into five kinds of stone. The Analysis of Variance showed significance when limy chert and cherty shale were combined into one group, and compared with chert, cherty shale, and basalt and andesite, a significant difference emerged, a difference that would be expected in less than 1% of cases on the basis of chance. Thus, the relationship between hardness and size was evident, and a factor to consider wherever small tools are found.

Interestingly, I joined Richard A. Knecht, Museum Project Director, Unalaska, Richard S. Davis of the Department of Anthropology, Bryn Mawr College and several persons with much past experience in the excavation of the Margaret Bay site, Unalaska, radiocarbon dated to 5,700 Years B.P. It had proved to be rich and contained a house feature reminiscent of the ellipticaldouble platform dwelling No. 11 from the site "Deltaterrasserne", North Greenland (Knuth 1954:372). Parallel stone walled chambers are outstanding features in each case. Related structures are seen in Independence I and Independence II ruins (Knuth 1967, plate 7 & 8).

Knecht's recognition of real similarities between Unalaska and Independence I likely has an earlier antecedent on Umnak Island. In 1974 A. P. Okladnikov and I excavated a large slab stone feature on a hill overlooking Chaluka and Nikolski Bay. It was completely empty. The Russian archaeologists overlooked nothing and further, there was a Dane, Bruno Frohlich, surveying and photographing.

In 1948 our Peabody Museum-Harvard team had found a unique six sided stone slab box, with a burial inside. Richard A. Knecht, who is familiar with Chaluka and Sandy Beach on Umnak, and with the Anangula Early blade and later Transition cultures, has the necessary information to probe in detail the connection which Knuth had noted many years ago.

Mapping the Origin

Anangula has yielded several of the diagnostic traits usually cited as evidence of the Arctic Small Tool tradition, as has Margaret Bay. The angle burin (Fig. 5) differs from the Arctic Small Tool tradition in that it is much earlier than those to the North, including Greenland. Accordingly, Richard A. Knecht and I have labelled this older, ancestral form the Pre-Arctic Small Tool tradition.

The evidence that Eskimos originated in the South and migrated North is both adequate and overwhelming. Hrdlicka's 1930 map of migrations to the east in Siberia, converging at Bering Strait and then trickling down to areas of highest numbers contributed to a long and unnecessary delay in recognizing the southern origin of Aleuts within the Aleutian chain and some portion of the Alaska Peninsula, and the northward migration of the Eskimos from South to North, then to Chukotka and to Greenland.

Aleuts have long been appended to Eskimos by a hyphen, suggesting that they were country cousins of dubious lineage. Hrdlicka[4] did many fine things in his researches, of which the Kuskokwim study is one of the finest for he published the hard data though overlooking the significance of the differences between the three intercepts in the Kuskokwim cline. He had at his command adequate data to demonstrate the origin of the Aleuts and Eskimos and the northward expansion of the Eskimos.

The Aleut-Eskimo distribution is valuable for many reasons. First, it is parsed into three sequenced divisions arranged in a linear fashion, with two critical linguistic and archaeological partitions demarcating the three related populations. The Aleuts cannot understand the Koniag Eskimos, they have been separated much too long.

Using the excellent genetic studies of E. M. Scott, which sampled all eight Athabaskan groups in Alaska, Inupiat-Inuit, Siberian Yupiq of St. Lawrence Island and coastal Siberia, and Koniag Eskimos (Sugpiaq) of Kodiak Island and the Alaska Peninsula, and Aleuts (Unangan), Harper's analysis is richly informative:

"*While between-group differences reflect the bifurcation point between two groups, the within-group differences provide an estimate of the precursor time available to accumulate and organize genetic variation.*" (Harper 1980).

Three time estimates of major relevance: 19,000 years B.P. is the Origin of Native Americans, 15,000 years B.P. is the divergence of Athabaskans, and 5,100 years B.P. marks the divergence of Yuit, and Inupiat-Inuit. The branch points are based on the within and between group diversity scaled to the divergence of Aleuts (Unangan) and Yuit (Eskimos), 9,000 B.P. (see Fig. 4).

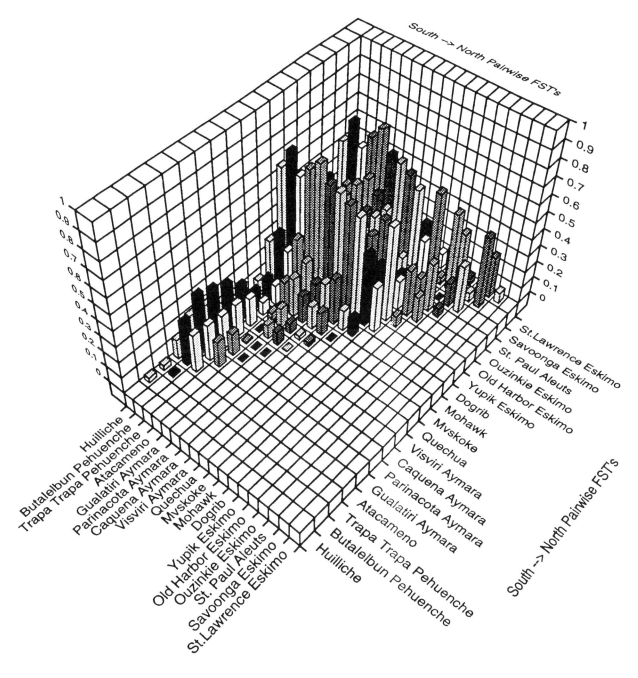

Fig. 4.   Pairwise FSTs for the populations typed in this paper. Populations are arrayed in geographic order from south to north on the X axis (which proceeds diagonally to the right) and from north to south on the Z axis (which proceeds diagonally to the left). The Y axis (the height of the bars) indicates the FST values for each pair of populations. The actual values and the variances appear in Table 3.

Fig. 4: (Merriwether et al 1995:422).

Fortunately, the Aleutian Islands are not a crossroads but rather a rich 'cul-de-sac', a permanent home for marine birds, drift whales and drift wood, many species of fish and invertebrates. Sea otters of course were useful for warm clothing but the arrival of the cossacks denied this resource[5].

Final Remarks

There are several insightful passages in Froelich Rainey's, "Reflections of a Digger" relevant to the peopling of the New World and directly based on his own experience in Arctic Research. Thus, *"seven years of searching in the Arctic proved nothing about those hypothetical Bering Strait migrations that are supposed to have peopled America at an unknown time in the past"* (1992: 85).

Cultural, linguistic, genetic, and archeological evidence prove that Yuit speaking Eskimos migrated over to the Siberian coast. The micro-blades, reminiscent of the ones found at Denbigh but not Ipiutak, appear at Onion Portage and at Anangula in the Aleutian Islands about 6,000 B.C. and at the Trail Creek site on the Seward Peninsula about 7,000 B.C. (Rainey 1992:91).

Obviously the hypothetical picture of origins and arrivals presented by Hrdlicka in 1930, is seriously in error and should be replaced with factual evidence concerning origins, divergence, direction of migration, the significance of the largest divergence in the Aleut-Eskimo world, and the later divergence at Norton Sound. The increasing likelihood is that there was only one migration from Siberia, across the North Pacific Coast of the Bering Land Bridge, well endowed with drift wood and drift whales, as well as sea lion, sea otters, walrus and probably sea cows (see Fig. 2).

The Canadian coast is rich in resources, occupied by several distantly related persons and characterized by marine hunting and fishing peoples, often divergent from each other, superb boats and other necessary material adaptations to a marine and resource rich coast. The high population densities, given in Kroeber (1939), confirmed or enlarged in more recent studies, reflect the early development of the technology and knowledge to exploit the rich resources of land and sea. A newer and more factually founded picture of the great event, the investiture of the inhabitants or the New World, is slowly taking form and articulate expression.

Fig. 5: Angle burin.

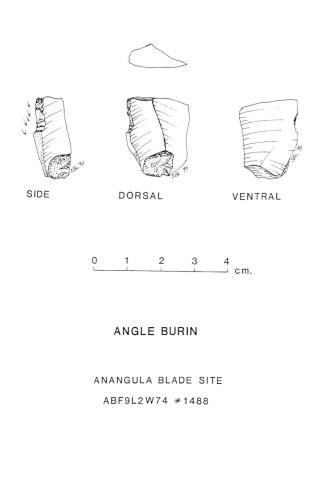

ANGLE BURIN

ANANGULA BLADE SITE

ABF9L2W74 #1488

Acknowledgements

I am indebted to Danes, Russians, Japanese and Japanese Americans, French, Canadians, Norwegians and others, including Finns and Germans, with whom I have worked. There is an Arctic legacy that guarantees good reception, facilitation of research, both basic and applied. The Aleuts (Unangan), and Koniags (Alutiiq) are now directly involved in research and museums for display and for analysis.

William S. Lasughlin, Professor, Ecology and Evolutionary Biology, University of Connecticut, Storrs, USA.

Notes

(1) Gilberg has published the definitive work on the Polar-Eskimo who came to New York, based on extensive field work and a thorough command of all existing sources (Gilberg 1994).

(2) Years later Victor received training in parachute jumping at a U. S. Forest Service jumper school at Seeley Lake, Montana, and trained several dogs to jump as well. He directed a search and rescue squad to rescue Soviet and American pilots lost in north Alaska and in the Aleutian Islands.

(3) A part of our funding was from the World Health Organization, and a part came from the Wenner-Gren Foundation, at the instance of Paul Fejos, a former long term inhabitant of Copenhagen where he made many films (Dodds 1973).

(4) A useful mnemonic device that observes alphabetic tradition appropriate to evolutionary divergence, is contained in the first name of Ales Hrdlicka: thus AL for Aleut, precedes ES for Eskimos.

(5) Genetic Distance Analysis shows considerable genetic differentiation between Aleuts and Kodiak Island Eskimos. (Majumder, Laughlin, & Ferrell 1988:481-488) (Merriwether, Rothhammer, & Ferrell 1995:311-430).

References

Birket-Smith, Kaj [1948]: **Kulturens Veje.** 728 p. (Copenhagen: Jespersen og Pios Forlag).

Dodds, John W. [1973]: **The Several Lives Of Paul Fejos.** * p. (New York: The Wenner-Gren Foundation).

Frohlich, Bruno & P. O. Pedersen [1992]: **Secular Changes Within Arctic and Sub-Arctic Populations: A Study of 632 Human Mandibles From The Aleutian Islands, Alaska and Greenland.** *Arctic Medical Research*, 51:173-188 (Oulu: Nordic Council for Arctic Medical Research).

Gerlach & Mason [1992]: **Calibrated Radiocarbon Dates and Cultural Interaction in the Western Arctic.** *Arctic Anthropology*, 29(1):54-81 (Madison: University of Wisconsin Press).

Gilberg, Aage, Lisbet Gilberg, Rolf Gilberg & Mogens Holm [1978]: **Polar Eskimo Genealogy. Appendix: Polar-skimo Genetical and Anthropological Markers.** *Meddelelser om Grønland*, 203(4):1-197 (Copenhagen: C. A. Reitzels Forlag).

Gilberg, Rolf [1994]: **Mennesket Minik (1888-1918). En grønlænders liv mellem 2 verdener.** 680 p. (Espergærde: ILBE).

Greenberg, J. H., C. G. Turner II & Steven L. Zegura [1986]: **The Settlwement of the Americas: A Comparison of the Linguistic, Dental and Genetic Evidence.** *Current Anthropology*, 27(5):477-497 (Chicago: University of Chicago Press).

Harper, Albert B. [1980]: **Origins and Divergence of Aleuts, Eskimos, and American Indians.** *Annals of Human Biology*, 7(6):547-554 (*: *).

Hrdlicka, Ales [1930]: **Anthropological Survey In Alaska**. *Forty-Sixth Annual Report Of The Bureau Of American Ethnology.* * p. (Washington, D.C.: Smithsonian Institute Press).

Hrdlicka, Ales [1933]: **The Eskimo of Kuskokwim.** *American Journal of Physical Anthropology*, 18(1):93-145 (New York: American Association of Physical Anthropologists).

Jochelson, Waldemar [1925]: **Archeaological Investigations In The Aleutian Islands.** Publication 367. * p. (Washington, D.C.: Carnegie Institution).

Knuth, Eigil [1954]: **The Paleo-Eskimo Culture of Northeast Greenland Elucidated By Three New Sites.**

American Antiquity, 4:367-381 (Washington DC: Society for American Archeology).

Knuth, Eigil [1967]: **Archaeology of the Musk-Ox Way**. Contributions de Centre d'Etudes Arctiques Finno-Scandinaves 5, 70 p. (Paris: Ecole Pratique Des Hautes Etudes-Sorbonne).

Kroeber, A. L. [1939]: **Cultural and Natural Areas of Native North America**. * p. (Berkeley: University of California Press).

Laughlin, Marsh & J. W. Leach [1952]: **Supplementary Note On The Aleutian Core And Blade Industry.** *American Antiquity*, 18(1):69-70 (Washington DC: Society for American Archeology).

Laughlin, William S. [1951]: **Notes On An Aleutian Core And Blade Industry.** *American Antiquity*, 17(1):52- 55 (Washington DC: Society for American Archeology).

Laughlin, William S. [1956]: **Isolate Variation in Greenlandic Eskimo Crania.** *Acta Genetica et Statistica Media*, 6:3-12 (*: *).

Laughlin, William S. [1956]: **Anthropological Researches in Greenland.** *Fulbright Monitor*, 4(7):13-16 (*: *).

Laughlin, William S. [1963]: **Eskmos and Aleuts: Their Origins and Evolution**. *Science*, 142:633-645 (*: *).

Laughlin, Sara B. [1990]: **Diagram of Angle Burin excavated from Anangula Blade Site 1974**. * p. (*: *).

Laughlin, Willam S. & A. B. Harper [1988]: **Peopling of the Continents: Australia and America**. pp.14-40 in "Biological Aspects Of Human Migration", editors: C. G. N. Mascie-Taylor & G. W. Lasker, * p. (New York: Cambridge University Press).

Majumder, P. P., William S. Laughlin, and R. E. Ferrell [1988]: **Genetic Variation in the Aleuts of the Pribilof Islands and the Eskimos of Kodiak Island.** *American Journal of Physical Anthropology*, 76:481-488 (New York: American Association of Physical Anthropologists).

Meldgaard, Jørgen [1962]: **On The Formative Period Of The Dorset Culture.** In "Prehistoric Cultural Relations Between The Arctic And Temperate Zones Of North America", *Technical Paper*, 11:92-95. (Calgary: Arctic Institute of Northe America).

Merriwether, D. A., F. Rothhammer, and R. E. Ferrell [1995]: **Distribution of the Four Founding Lineage Haplotypes in Native Americans Suggests a Single Wave of Migration for the New World.** *American Journal of Physical Anthropology*, 98:411-430 (New York: American Association of Physical Anthropologists).

Penrose, L. S. [1954]: **Distance Size and Shape.** *Annals of Eugenics*, 18:337-343 (*: *).

Pospisil, L. & William S. Laughlin [1963]: **Kinship Terminology And Kindred Among The Nunamiut Eskimo.** *Ethnology*, 11(2):180-189 (Pittsburgh: Department of Anthropology, University of Pittsburgh Press).

Rainey, Froelich [1992]: **Reflections of a Digger**. * p. University Museum Publications, (Philladelphia: University of Pennsylvania).

Robert-Lamblin, Joelle [1982]: **An Historical and Contemporary Demography of Akutan, An Aleution Village.** *Etudes/Inuit/Studies*, 6(1):99-126 (Québec: Département d'anthropologie, Université Laval).

Robert-Lamblin, Joelle [1979]: **Endogamy and Exogamy in two Arctic coummunityies: Aleut and East Geenlandic Eskimo.** pp:293-307 in "The First American: Origins, Affinities and Adaptations", editors: William S. Laughlin & A. B. Harper, * p. (New York: Gustav Fisher).

Sapir, Edward [1916]: **Time Perpective In Aboriginal American Culture: A Study in Method.** Memoir 90, Anthropological Series 13:*-*, Department of Mines, Geological Survey (Ottawa: Government Print Bureau).

Victor, Paul-Emile & Joelle Robert-Lamblin [1989]: **La Civilization du Phoque.** * p. (*: Armand Colin and Raymond Chabaud).

The Canadian Arctic in Transition: Pre-Dorset to Dorset

Moreau S. Maxwell

It has now been four decades since Jørgen Meldgaard at Igloolik and Henry Collins on Southampton Island, each through fieldwork, recognized the Dorset Culture and a cultural complex which preceded it. Meldgaard (1960) labeled his earlier complex Sarqaq (current spelling Saqqaq) in recognition of its similarity to the Greenlandic Saqqaq which had been discovered shortly before (Meldgaard 1952). Collins (1956) designated his 'Pre-Dorset', noting only that it preceded Dorset without implying any nexus between them. Later, Taylor (admittedly with scanty data), demonstrated the sequential nature of the two and elevated Pre-Dorset to upper case. Building on this, subsequent scholars have effectively reified this concept of sequence. But within these four decades there has been no clear explanation of the nature of the sequence. The problem reduces to three possibilities:

(1) There was a simple development in which one phase (Pre-Dorset) evolved over time into the other (Dorset);

(2) There was a significant change between the two such as might have been caused by a drastic shift in climatic conditions or animal populations which evoked major economic change.

(3) A third complex, neither Pre-Dorset nor Dorset, and possibly carried by some different ethnic group, which intervened between the two.

The fact that this is a current and recurring problem in Eastern Arctic prehistory is apparent from a number of recent papers discussing the issue (Nagy 1994; Helmer 1994; Le Blanc 1994; Renouf 1994) and from the plethora of taxa that have been used for this time frame - Independence II, Groswater, Terminal Pre-Dorset, Tran-

sitional Dorset, the 'transitional stage', and the 'transitional horizon'. Saqqaq probably belongs with this group of terms. It will be treated later, but for now it is important to note that according to current evidence it is at this time period that Saqqaq apparently terminates, leaving West Greenland a cultural void until later in the Dorset series.

In discussing the nature of the relationship between Pre-Dorset and Dorset, I want to return to two of Meldgaard's statements based on his work at Igloolik. The first was a suggestion that Dorset "*had the smell of the forest*" (Meldgaard 1960). The second, in a letter to me in 1977, suggested that on the 23 m and 22 m terraces at Igloolik when Pre-Dorset would have been evolving into Dorset, the people appeared to have been 'stressed'.

The premise behind the first statement was a sound one. To Meldgaard, familiar with Greenlandic and traditional Inuit, the Dorset appeared ill-equipped for Arctic survival. They lacked dogs for breathing hole hunting or bringing bears to bay; they had no bows or arrows, or throwing boards for harpoons or bladder darts; drills which are so much a part of daily Inuit living were absent and their house structures hardly seemed adequate for Arctic winters. The answer had to be that Dorset was an intrusive culture emanating from south of the treeline. Subsequent research has revealed that there was no woodland Amerindian group which could have been responsible for this intrusion but the fact remains that there were important cultural elements in Pre-Dorset that were absent in Dorset. It may be important now to return to Meldgaard's premise and to consider the differences between Pre-Dorset and Dorset. Nagy (1994:4) points out that several authors (myself included) have emphasized the sequence or transition between Pre-Dorset and Dorset while simultaneously stressing cultural distinctions between the two. This has effectively negated the concept of transition. Now to emphasize differences between Pre-Dorset and Dorset rather than similarities requires a closer look at what was going on culturally in the intervening time period between the two.

The best evidence of this is still the work that Meldgaard did at Kapuivik on Jens Munk Island near Igloolik. Here remains from the 23 m and 22 m terraces should fall into this time frame from about 850 B.C. to 400 B.C. Recovered material shows very rapid changes in artifact styles. Harpoon heads, which both before and after conformed to only a few styles, went through a dramatic series of changes according to a suite of line drawings that Meldgaard kindly sent to me and to others. Within this assemblage of harpoon heads were a number of very large heads with transverse line holes and side blade inserts. These large heads had not appeared in earlier sites, nor did they appear in later ones. In Meldgaard's view, in this short period in which the land rose and the seas subsided a meter - perhaps only a century or two - the people *"were highly stressed"*. They were rapidly experimenting with new artifact designs, possibly within the span of a single generation. It is within this short period that bows and arrows and the bow drill were abandoned, not to appear again in the Eastern Arctic for at least 1.500 years.

Cultural changes on the south coast of Baffin Island at this time were more dramatic but only because there was no organic preservation in Pre-Dorset sites and complete preservation in the permafrost of Dorset ones. Here the beginning of Dorset marks the sudden appearance of sled shoes, small model sleds, snow knives, ice creepers and magical art. It is impossible to say whether these traits might have occurred earlier had there been organic preservation.

On Baffin Island's south coast only minor traits distinguish the stone tools of the transitional period. Pre-Dorset burins had their working edges spalled whereas the working edges of Dorset ones were first flaked and then ground and polished. Several burins from transitional sites had the working edge first spalled and then ground and polished. This same distinctive burin type appears on the 23 m terrace at Igloolik and in Groswater sites on coastal Labrador. The interim period also marks the first appearance of nephrite and rectangular soapstone vessels at Igloolik and on southern Baffin and nephrite in a Groswater site on the Lower North Shore of Quebec (Pintal 1994, Fig.6a). This suggests an increase in interregional exchange.

More important than stylistic and material changes in artifact complexes is the evidence of drastic cooling of the environment. The Tanfield site on the south coast of Baffin Island dated to earliest Dorset times by the presence of Tyara Sliced harpoon heads, was clearly occupied

shortly after the onset of permafrost. Organic materials including feathers and sinew were perfectly preserved; there had been no formation of humus and no indication of water sorting. On the other hand, the adjacent Avinga site in the same valley and only 2,4 m higher above sea level, had clearly been occupied before the onset of permafrost. In the midden there was no trace of bones or organic artifacts; 30 cm of humus had formed and there was clear evidence of water sorting of stone artifacts.

The majority of artifacts recovered from the site were similar to Dorset ones from Tanfield, but some showed vestiges of terminal Pre-Dorset such as the distinctive spalled and then ground burin and triangular end blades with fine serrations along lateral edges. Surely, if the transition was a period of such marked and sudden climate change as suggested by the above evidence it would have had major effect on the available prey animals. It may be this, in part, that accounted for Meldgaard's 'stress' which was then countered by the people with frantic stylistic experimentation in an effort to restore the previous balance of man and nature.

Of the various cultural complexes identified in the transition period of about 2800 B.P. to 2200 B.P., the best defined is Groswater (Cox 1978; Fitzhugh 1980). Distinctive settlement systems and subsistence activities have been ascribed to it in addition to distinctive characteristics in artifact traits. Harpoon heads (Renouf 1994) are less like either Pre-Dorset or Dorset and more closely resemble those of Independence II.

The cultural difference between Groswater and Dorset is most clearly seen in the Newfoundland sites of Phillip's Garden East and Phillip's Garden West which both straddle the Phillip's Garden site. Both outer sites have artifact assemblages characteristic of Groswater, whereas the inner site is clearly Dorset (Renouf 1994). Two of these, Phillip's Garden East and Phillip's Garden serve well to highlight a comparison between Groswater and Dorset settlements and subsistence activities. Although both are located in the same spot for harvesting migrating harp seals, the Groswater site was only occupied seasonally but the Dorset one through many seasons. This distinction is characteristic of the more mobile Groswater bands and the Dorset ones which were more sedentary and focused on marine resources.

In an attempt at standardizing culture-classificatory terminology in the Eastern Arctic, Helmer (1994) has grouped the North Devon Lowlands and Cape Hardy Complex; Bache Peninsula and Three Sisters Complex, and Port Refuge and Lower Beaches Complex into a Regional Phase of a Transitional Horizon. He has named this Regional Phase: "Central High Arctic Transitional Dorset". Shortening this to "Central High Arctic Transition" would strengthen the proposition that these complexes are neither Pre-Dorset nor Dorset but an intermediate collective. It is significant that the distinctive spalled and polished burin I have described appears in both the Cape Hardy Complex of North Devon (Helmer 1991: Fig. 16:o, Fig. 16:aa) and in the Grave Rib and Skræling Island ASTt 5 sites of Ellesmere Island's Bache Peninsula (Schledermann 1990: Plate 23d, Plate 28f). In fact, the closest resemblance of the Cape Hardy artifacts is in the transitional Killilugak assemblage of South Baffin Island.

This transition time was clearly marked by regional variation in population and intensity. Groswater on Labrador and Newfoundland appears to have been expanding as Dorset was penetrating from the north. Populations declined on north and south Baffin Island and on the north Devon shore but appear to have increased on Ellesmere Island and northeastern Greenland (letter from Andreasen to Maxwell 1991). The most dramatic decline was on the west coast of Greenland where Saqqaq, formerly a complex and stable culture, dissappeared in about 2700 B.P. (Grønnow 1994).

In conclusion it would appear that there is now enough evidence to recognize a third cultural complex, neither Pre-Dorset nor Dorset, that developed in the Eastern Arctic between the calendar years of 850 B.C. and 250 B.C. I would like to suggest that this complex either be called simply 'Transition' or 'Groswater'. Following Helmer (1994) it could then be regionally divided into:

(1) Labrador Groswater - Labrador, Newfoundland;

(2) Central Groswater - North and South Baffin Island, Igloolik 23m terrace;

(3) High Arctic Groswater - North Devon Island and West Ellesmere Island.

It may be that Port Refuge, northern Ellesmere, northeastern Greenland and the Ile de France off the eastern Greenland coast all belong to a separate transitional period complex - 'Independence II'.

There is little doubt that the evolution of Dorset owes its ultimate roots to Pre-Dorset but these wide-spread 'Groswater' and 'Independence II' complexes certainly contributed to its development. The causes of the 'stresses' of the transition are less apparent. A major change in climate with its concomitant imbalance of man and nature has been suggested. Grønnow (1994:234) in looking for causes of the apparent collapse of Saqqaq, suggests *"drastic changes and decline in the resource base due to changing sea currents and ice conditions"*. Consequent reduction in prey animals might have caused abandonment of some regions and a consequent break in important social and exchange networks.

Whatever the causes, it is important to remember that there are few places in the world where the balance between humans and animals is so critical. It would take little to upset this balance.

Moreau S. Maxwell, Professor Emeritus of Anthropology, Michigan State University, USA.

References

Collins, H. B. [1956]: **Archaeological Investigations on Southampton and Coats Islands, N.W.T.** Annual Report of the National Museum of Canada for 1954-55. *National Museum of Canada Bulletin*, 142:*-* (Ottawa: *).

Cox, Steven L. [1978]: **Paleo-Eskimo Occupations of the North Labrador Coast.** *Arctic Anthropology*, 15(2): 96-118 (Madison: University of Wisconsin).

Fitzhugh, William W. [1980]: **Preliminary Report on the Torngat Archaeological Project.** *Arctic*, 33(3):585-606 (Calgary: The Arctic Institute of North America).

Grønnow, Bjarne [1994]: **Qeqertasussuk - The Archaeology of a Frozen Saqqaq Site in Disco Bugt, West Greenland.** pp:197-238 in "Threads of Arctic Prehistory: Papers in honour of Willam E. Taylor, Jr.", editors: David Morrison & Jean-Luc Pilon, *Mercury Series Paper*, 149:1-422 (Hull, Québec: Canadian Museum of Civilization).

Helmer, J. W. [1991]: **The Palaeo-Eskimo Prehistory of the North Devon Lowlands.** *Arctic*, 44(4):301-317 (Calgary: The Arctic Institute of North America).

Helmer, J. W. [1994]: **Resurrecting the Spirit(s) of Taylor's "Carlsberg Culture": Cultural Traditions and Cultural Horizons in Eastern Arctic Prehistory.** pp:15-34 in "Threads of Arctic Prehistory: Papers in honour of William E. Taylor, Jr.", editors: David Morrison & Jean-Luc Pilon, *Mercury Series Paper*, 149:1-422 (Hull, Québec: Canadian Museum of Civilization).

Le Blanc, R. J. [1994]: **The Crane Site and the Lagoon Complex in the Western Canadian Arctic.** pp:87-102 in "Threads of Arctic Prehistory: Papers in honour of William E. Taylor, Jr.", editors: David Morrison & Jean-Luc Pilon, *Mercury Series Paper*, 149:1-422 (Hull, Québec: Canadian Museum of Civilization).

Meldgaard, Jørgen [1952]: **A Palaeo-Eskimo Culture in West Greenland.** *American Antiquity*, 17(3):222-230 (Menasha, Wis.: Society for American Archeology).

Meldgaard, Jørgen [1960]: **Prehistoric Culture Sequences in the Eastern Arctic as Elucidated by Stratified Sites at Igloolik.** pp:588-595 in "Selected Papers of the Fifth International Congress of Anthropological and Ethnological Sciences 1956", 810 p. (Philadelphia: University of Pennsylvania Press).

Nagy, M. [1994]: **A Critical Review of the Pre-Dorset/Dorset Transition.** pp:1-14 in "Threads of Arctic Prehistory: Papers in honour of William E. Taylor, Jr.", editors: David Morrison & Jean-Luc Pilon, *Mercury Series Paper*, 149:1-422 (Hull, Québec: Canadian Museum of Civilization).

Pintal, J-Y. [1994]: **A Groswater Site at Blanc-Sablon, Quebec.** pp:145-164 in "Threads of Arctic Prehistory: Papers in honour of William E. Taylor, Jr.", editors: David Morrison & Jean-Luc Pilon, *Mercury Series Paper*, 149: 1-422 (Hull, Québec: Canadian Museum of Civilization).

Renouf, M. A. P. [1994]: **Two Transitional Sites at Port au Choix, Northwestern Newfoundland.** pp:165-196 in "Threads of Arctic Prehistory: Papers in honour of William E. Taylor, Jr.", editors: David Morrison & Jean-Luc Pilon, *Mercury Series Paper*, 149:1-422 (Hull, Québec: Canadian Museum of Civilization).

Schledermann, Peter [1990]: **Crossroads to Greenland: 3000 Years of Prehistory in the Eastern Arctic.** *Komatik Series*, 2:1-364, (Calgary: Arctic Institute of North America).

Meetings Between Dorset Culture Palaeo-Eskimos and Thule Culture Inuit: Evidence from Brooman Point

Robert McGhee

The archaeological work undertaken by Jørgen Meldgaard at Igloolik, in the eastern Canadian Arctic, shed light on several diverse aspects of Arctic prehistory. One such question involves the nature of contact between the Palaeo-Eskimo people of the Dorset Culture and the ancestors of the Inuit. Meldgaard (1960a, 1960b) noted several types of evidence which suggested that contact had occurred in the Igloolik area: the adoption of Thule-derived elements such as the cold-trap entrance and rear sleeping platform in houses built during the final phases of Dorset occupation; the finding of a number of Thule Culture artifacts in these same Dorset houses; and a new interpretation regarding the legends of the Tunit.

The Tunit stories are a part of Inuit oral history throughout the Eastern Arctic, and tell of a people who occupied the country before ancestral Inuit arrived. Archaeologists had generally assumed that, if the stories referred to an actual population in the past, these people were likely to have been either Indians or early Inuit of the Thule Culture.

The stories which Meldgaard learned from the people of Igloolik, however, suggested an alternative identification. According to Meldgaard's Igloolik friends, the Tunit had lived in rectangular houses with open hearth and short sleeping bench, made stone tools, hunted caribou with spears, had no dogsleds, and used small round lamps. All of these characteristics were reminiscent of the Dorset Culture as reconstructed from the archaeological remains which Meldgaard was excavating.

As Meldgaard (1960a:594) reported "... *it was an important additional result of the field work in 1954 to give a new identification of the Tunit ... it became obvious to us that the Tunit had nothing to do with the Thule Culture - they were the Dorset people.*"

The identification of Dorset Culture Palaeo-Eskimos with the Tunit of Inuit legend is compelling evidence that the two groups had come into contact, probably during the initial phase of Inuit expansion into the Eastern Arctic. This historical evidence supported the tenuous archaeological indications of contact between Dorset and early Inuit. Many archaeologists of the past several decades have accepted Meldgaard's identification of the Tunit with the Dorset population, and have rather uncritically assumed that some form of contact must have occurred between peoples of the Dorset and Thule Cultures. This general assumption has recently been questioned by Park (1993), whose detailed analysis led him to reject the evidence which has been adduced in favour of Dorset-Thule contact. Indeed, his study of the evidence led him to propose that, in fact, the Dorset people were likely to have been extinct before the eastward movement of Thule Culture Inuit.

Park's arguments include rejection of the scattered radiocarbon dates which suggest Dorset survival in some regions of Arctic Canada until as late as the 15th century A.D., while indicating that the Thule expansion occurred prior to the 11th century. Some of the early dates related to Thule occupation, and some of the late Dorset dates are rejected on the basis of questionable materials or association (Park 1993:206-208). An entire large suite of dates from several sites in the Labrador/Ungava peninsula, proposed as evidence of Dorset survival in this area until the 15th century, are questioned on the grounds that the Dorset ascription of the associated remains is mistaken, and the dates actually relate to Thule Inuit occupation of the area. Park interprets several reports of Dorset artifacts found in early Thule dwellings in two ways. Most frequently, he suggests that mistaken associations have resulted from the fact that Dorset midden deposits are frequently incorporated into the construction materials of Thule houses. Secondly, and more interestingly, he suggests that such mixtures may be evidence that Thule people characteristically collected archaeological material from Dorset sites, either out of curiosity, to use the objects themselves, or as models for their own artifacts.

The second explanation for mixed assemblages leads to an alternative explanation for the Tunit legends. Rather than deriving from a people actually encountered in the Eastern Arctic, Park suggests that the legends are based on archaeological reconstructions of predecessors whose remains were examined and systematically interpreted by the Inuit of the Eastern Arctic. Such a situation, Park argues, would be consistent with the Tunit ascription of the Dorset Culture settlements indicated by Meldgaard's Igloolik informants, as well as of Thule Culture settlements in other regions of the Eastern Arctic.

Park's stimulating arguments and provocative conclusions have yet to be challenged in the literature of Arctic archaeology. The present paper has been developed in response to his conclusions, but does not pretend to be a comprehensive rebuttal of his arguments. Indeed, his interpretation of much of the evidence related to Dorset-Thule contact is persuasive. The numerous problems associated with the use of the radiocarbon dating technique in an Arctic context, for example, preclude its use to provide a convincing temporal support for Dorset-Thule contact. Most of the reported cases of Dorset artifacts recovered from Thule winter houses (with the implication that Palaeo-Eskimo Dorset people were occupying these distinctively Inuit structures) are most economically explained as mixed assemblages resulting from the incorporation of Dorset midden deposits in Thule houses.

Some of the evidence for a late Dorset survival in the Labrador-Ungava area is quite likely, as Park (1993:213) suggests, a result of misinterpretation of mixed Dorset and Thule assemblages in a region where poor organic preservation results in the destruction of most evidence of Thule occupation. Park's (1993:224-225) argument that the "flat" styles of Thule harpoon heads could have been patterned on archaeological specimens, is plausible. These objects are the elements of Inuit technology which are most convincingly modeled on Dorset styles, and other suggestions of technological continuity from Dorset to Thule Culture are not compelling.

On the other hand Park's contention that there was a clear temporal break between Dorset and Thule occupations of the Eastern Arctic is no more convincing than are the arguments for contemporaneity. Both views are based on interpretations of radiocarbon dates which require a degree of precision beyond the capability of current techniques. As Park (1993:206) notes, a few of the late radiocarbon dates on Dorset assemblages in the Central Arctic and High Arctic cannot be easily rejected. Some of the late Dorset dates from the Labrador-Ungava region appear more reasonable, when one considers the few pieces of smelted metal which have been associated with Dorset assemblages in the region. These objects almost certainly originated in the Norse colonies in Greenland, and could have reached the Dorset people no earlier than the eleventh century (McGhee 1984a). On the basis of the evidence related to dating, one cannot reject a scenario involving an eastward thrust of Thule Inuit people beginning in the 10th and 11th centuries, while Dorset populations continued to survive in some regions of the Eastern Arctic until significantly later.

Park assembles convincing arguments against a significant degree of acculturation having occurred between Dorset and Thule peoples. However, the absence of acculturation cannot stand as evidence against contact having taken place between the two groups. One would expect evidence of acculturation or the transfer of technology if close and long-lasting relationships were established, or if a significant proportion of one population had been incorporated into the other group. However, if contacts were sporadic, ephemeral, or hostile, we might not expect to find this sort of evidence. I would suggest that the nature of contact between Dorset Palaeo-Eskimos and Thule Inuit was more likely to have been of the latter kind, and that we should perhaps consider the sort of evidence which we would expect to survive as witness to such encounters. The archaeological remains from Brooman Point, on Bathurst Island in the central High Arctic, provide a possible example of such evidence.

The Thule village at Brooman Point consists of 20 large winter houses, which appear to have been occupied relatively early in the Thule period (McGhee 1984b). Although no acceptable radiocarbon dates were obtained on this occupation, the styles of artifacts suggest temporal equivalence to sites which have been ascribed to the 12th and 13th centuries A.D. The sequence of house construction at Brooman Point suggests use of the site over a period of at least several decades. A few small and lightly-built winter houses, without flagstone flooring or raised sleeping platforms, were found stratigraphically beneath the large houses which produced early Thule artifacts. These small structures, one of which produced an early harpoon head resembling the Alaskan Sicco type, may relate to an initial Thule occupation of this site and of this region of the High Arctic.

On the outskirts of the Thule village lie the remains of a few small Late Dorset dwellings: shallow sub-rectangular pits 10 cm to 15 cm deep, with no defined internal structure and few associated artifacts. The midden associated with these dwellings is thin and sparse. A longhouse structure and separate hearth-row lies a few hundred metres away, and were probably associated with the same Late Dorset occupation of the site.

Numerous Late Dorset artifacts were recovered during excavation of the Thule winter houses and the middens which surrounded them. The houses seem to have been built on the central portion of the Dorset occupation site, and the Dorset artifacts accidentally incorporated into the Thule structures with the gravel and turf matrix used as construction material. All structural evidence of Dorset use of this portion of the site seems to have been destroyed by the Inuit construction projects. It also seems likely that Dorset specimens were collected either as curiosities or as functional artifacts, in the manner suggested by Park. The best evidence for such activity is in the form of a large whale bone lance head of characteristic Thule type, which was tipped with a chipped stone point identical to those associated with the Dorset component of the site. The point was most likely collected from the surface of the site, where similar specimens can be found today.

Other circumstances, however, suggest a closer connection between the Dorset and Thule occupants of the site. The Late Dorset dwellings and middens outside the Thule village are not associated with the development of a significant surface deposit of turf, and consequent raising of permafrost to incorporate the artifacts and refuse associated with the Dorset occupation. The bone, antler, and ivory artifacts found in these areas of the site show significant weathering: bleached and cracked surfaces on artifacts exposed directly to the weather, or a brown patina marked with root-etchings on artifacts buried in the dry and shallow soil. However, the Dorset artifacts found in Thule houses or in the humid and frozen midden deposits associated with the Thule village are remarkably well preserved. These artifacts appear to have been incorporated in Thule structures or middens before any deterioration occurred, and most are as perfectly preserved as the majority of Thule specimens which were directly deposited into this environment. A few specimens of relatively fragile organic material could not have survived for long in a Dorset deposit before incorporation into the heavily-frozen Thule houses. These include a Dorset harpoon head with preserved leather thong attached; another harpoon head with well preserved sinew lashing; and a small basket woven from plant roots, which contains a few Dorset artifacts.

Although contemporaneity cannot be proven on the basis of this evidence, temporal proximity can be suggested. The degree of preservation of Dorset artifacts such as these strongly suggests that the construction of Thule winter houses at this site occurred very shortly after its abandonment by Dorset Culture occupants. Other evidence provides supportive hints that actual contact may have occurred.

One such hint is provided by a characteristic Thule artifact, the bone handle of a man's knife, which was recovered from the buried floor deposit of one of the small Dorset dwellings located at a distance from the Thule village. The provenience of the find argues against its having been accidentally incorporated into the dwelling deposits during the subsequent Thule occupation of the locale. It seems probable that the Dorset occupants of the dwelling either obtained the artifact directly from a Thule individual, or picked it up from an unoccupied Thule settlement. There is no further evidence of Thule artifacts having been in possession of Dorset inhabitants of the site, but such evidence could have been lost in the subsequent incorporation of the central portion of the Dorset settlement into the houses and middens of the Thule people. Meldgaard (1960a:590) reported recovering a number of Thule artifacts from the Late Dorset houses at Alarnerk. In both cases, the finds suggest that the last Dorset inhabitants of these areas probably knew of the Thule people and their technology.

Evidence of Dorset acculturation to Thule technology at Brooman Point is limited to a few circular perforations which have been used in the manufacture of Dorset artifacts recovered from the site. These apertures contrast with the elongate gouged perforations which are characteristic of most Dorset technology, and suggest an imitation of the bow-drilling technique used by the Thule people. Similar circular perforations, apparently made by a twisting motion of a hand-held tool rather than with a bow-drill, are seen on occasional artifacts in several Late Dorset assemblages in the Canadian Museum of Civilization. These artifacts hint at a more widespread but somewhat perfunctory imitation of the technology brought by newcomers to the Dorset homeland.

The slight evidence in the Brooman Point collection relating to possible contact between Dorset and Thule people, appears to reflect a situation of ephemeral or hostile interaction between two groups whose occupation of the local area slightly overlapped in time.

Such interaction would seem to be predicted from what we know of the very significant social, cultural and technological differences which must have existed between the two groups. For example, it is virtually certain that Dorset and Thule people spoke languages which were not mutually comprehensible. Even if the languages of both people were derived from the Eskimoan family, the time-depth of the isolation between Alaskan Eskimos and the Palaeo-Eskimos of Arctic Canada strongly suggests that the two languages would have changed to a degree that mutual comprehension would not have been possible. Current thinking places the ancestry of the Palaeo-Eskimos in Siberia and removes them from the Eskaleutian speech community which had developed in southern Alaska (Dumond 1987:155), so that any possible linguistic relationship between Dorset and Thule speech would have been extremely distant.

Communication difficulties must have been compounded by the very different social communities from which the two groups derived. We know practically nothing of the social organization of the Dorset people, except that in most areas (including the Brooman Point region) Dorset communities were small, scattered and isolated: the social organization of these small communities must have been relatively simple, flexible, and deriving most of its elements from kinship. Thule Inuit social organization, on the other hand, can probably be best reconstructed as similar to that of the historic North Alaskan Inuit, whose ancestors produced the Thule Culture and its eastern expansion into Palaeo-Eskimo territory. On the basis of this reconstruction, the Thule Inuit must have had a social pattern based in large communities with relatively complex authority structures, and a heritage of inter-community warfare. Armed with superior weapons in the form of the sinew-backed bow, with hunting and transportation technology capable of providing for relatively large groups of people, and the aggressive social qualities characteristic of Alaskan Inuit society, the Thule people must have been formidable competitors for the territories occupied by small and isolated Dorset communities.

The traditional histories of the Inuit generally portray the Tunit as a timid people who were easily put to flight, and who retreated or were driven from their homelands by the Inuit newcomers (Rasmussen 1929:257; 1931: 425). If Meldgaard is correct in ascribing a Dorset identity to the Tunit, such a description of Dorset-Thule interaction fits well with what we might expect on the basis of the social differences described above. The fact that many early Thule villages are built on the remains of late Dorset communities indicates that both groups were attracted to the same locales because of the economic advantages of such sites. At Brooman Point, for example, both groups seem to have been attracted to a location which provided access to the concentrated sea mammal resources of a small polynia. Direct competition for such locales might be expected to have usually led to the sort of rapid displacement of Dorset people that is described in the stories of the Tunit.

The repetition of many such small-scale local events, with the Dorset Palaeo-Eskimos retreating continually to more isolated and less economically viable areas, would have eventually resulted in the disappearance of the Dorset way of life without the development of significant contact or cultural exchange between the Palaeo-Eskimos and their Inuit supplanters. Such a process, based on a relationship which began in fear, aggression and mutual disdain, might have continued over several centuries without leaving significant archaeological evidence of contact between the two groups. We might recall that a similar lack of archaeological evidence regarding acculturation characterizes the relationships between the Thule Culture Inuit and the Greenlandic Norse, groups whom we know to have interacted over a period of centuries (McGhee 1984a).

The evidence recovered from Brooman Point would seem to be compatible with such a reconstruction of interactions between the Dorset and Thule populations. Park (1993) is probably correct in rejecting most of the evidence which has been adduced to suggest that a significant degree of acculturation occurred between the two groups. On the other hand, his view that Dorset and Thule people never encountered one another, and that therefore the eastward expansion of Thule Inuit was not implicated in the disappearance of Dorset Culture, cannot be easily accepted. We should perhaps consider an alternative to the questions posed by Park (1993:203) as the central issue of his paper: "*did the Thule encounter and learn from people of the Dorset Culture, or had the small and scattered Dorset population died out prior to their arrival?*"

A third scenario, comprising sporadic and ephemeral contact over a period of generations, but resulting in no significant transfer of knowledge or technology between the two groups, would seem to be more consistent with the present archaeological evidence as well as with our reconstructions of the societies and cultures of the peoples involved. Perhaps future archaeological evidence of Dorset-Thule interaction should be expected to resemble that recovered from Brooman Point: slight, ambiguous, difficult to interpret, but compatible with the Inuit historical accounts relating to the disappearance of the Tunit, the people whom Meldgaard first clearly identified with the people of the Dorset Culture.

Robert McGhee is a curator at the Canadian Museum of Civilization, Ottawa, Canada.

References

Dumond, Don E. [1987]: **The Eskimos and Aleuts**. (Revised Edition). 180 p. (London: Thames and Hudson).

McGhee, Robert [1984a]: **Contact Between Native North Americans and the Mediaeval Norse: a Review of the Evidence.** *American Antiquity*, 49(1):4-26 (Salt Lake City: *).

McGhee, Robert [1984b]: **The Thule Village at Brooman Point, High Arctic Canada.** *Mercury Series Paper* 125:1-158 (Ottawa: Archaeological Survey of Canada, Canadian Museum of Civilization).

Meldgaard, Jørgen [1960a]: **Prehistoric Culture Sequences in the Eastern Arctic as elucidated by Stratified Sites at Igloolik.** pp:588-595 in "Men and Cultures: Selected Papers of the Fifth International Congress of Anthropological and Ethnological Sciences", editor: A. F. C. Wallace (Philadelphia: University of Pennsylvania Press).
Meldgaard, Jørgen [1960b]: **Origin and Evolution of Eskimo Cultures in the Eastern Arctic.** *Canadian Geographical Journal*, 60(2):64-75 (Ottawa).

Park, Robert [1993]: **The Dorset-Thule Succession in Arctic North America: Assessing Claims for Culture Contact.** *American Antiquity*, 58(2):203-234 (Salt Lake City: *).

Rasmussen, Knud [1929]: **Intellectual Culture of the Igloolik Eskimos.** *Report of the Fifth Thule Expedition 1921-1924*, 7(1):1-304 (Copenhagen: Gyldendal).

Rasmussen, Knud [1931]: **The Netsilik Eskimos: Social Life and Spiritual Culture.** *Report of the Fifth Thule Expedition 1921-1924*, 8(1-2):1-542 (Copenhagen: Gyldendal).

Fig. A: Blond shaman - Self-portrait.
Foto: Jørgen Meldgaard, August 1954.

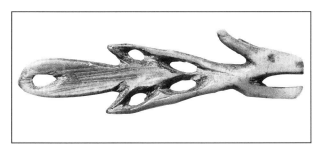

Fig. B: Flying fox ear ring. 3,8 cm long.

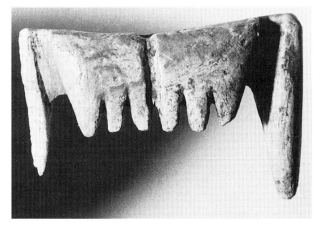

Fig. C: Ivory teeth. 3,5 cm long.

Fig. D (center): The naturalistic carving of a fox was excavated by Jørgen Meldgaard at Graham Rowley's Abverdjar site. [14]C date: c. 700 A.D. - 900 A.D. (4.0 cm long).

Fig. E: Sewing needles. Photo: Jørgen Meldgaard, 1954.

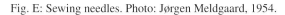

Foxes and the Blond Shaman

Ivory carvings representing the fox are found in the Dorset Culture, Iglulik area, Arctric Canada. Jørgen Meldgaard considered some of them to be the equipment of shamans. In his tent at Alarnerk he took a photograph of the awe-inspiring shaman. (Fig. A).

The objects shown above are from Alarnerk, house 1501, c. 200 A.D. - 300 A.D. (Fig. B & Fig. C).

In the Iglulik area Jørgen Meldgaard found that in the Pre-Dorset/Dorset Culture sequence bones of foxes were relatively frequent in the early Dorset Culture. And it was similart with the bone needles. Fox hunting was likely undertaken primarily to secure skins for garments. He suggested that the very special type of Dorset sewing needle - so unlike "ordinary" forms in the Eskimo world - indicated that the Dorset woman had to pull (not to press) her needles through the skin.

Local informants participating in the excavations were astounded at these awkward needles. They were no good for seal skins. Fox skins were proposed!

Sisikasiit:
the Place with the Fox Holes

Morten Meldgaard

"The fox is probably the most clever of all our countrys animals, but man must be more clever and able to out-smart his game - even if it is clever and shy" (Josefsen et al. 1964).

So introduce the West Greenland hunters Nathan Josefsen, Mikael Lynge, Sebulon Egede, Amos Egede and Enok Motzfeldt their description of fox hunting techniques used in the early part of this century.

Working with the fox bones from the 4000 year old Saqqaq Culture site Qeqertasussuk, in Disko Bay, it was useful to have the knowledge of such experienced hunters in mind. However, we were also able to make our own observations on fox behaviour because a fox family excavated a den in sand and gravel deposits in the middle of the archaeological site.

The fox family of seven was mainly active during the night, a fact we encountered every morning before starting excavations. The strings that formed the carefully set grid system were aiways neatly severed by sharp teeth, and the markers that carried the essential coordinates were scattered all over the terrain (Fig. 1).

More problematic, however, was the foxes' habit of marking smelly items with their own smelly items. Because of the excellent preservation condotion in the frozen soil, animal bones, bird feathers, fossil excrements, etc. still, carried a strong four thousand year old odour. Any plastic bags with bones or other artifacts left

Fig 1. Two arctic fox pups (photo: Aurora Foto, Thomas Berg).

---

on site could therefore be found clearly marked with fox excrements in the morning. This could quite easily be dealt with, but more problematic was the foxes' habit of polluting our small insect traps, dug down in the soil surface.

The fox denning area on the Qeqertasussuk site was extensive and gave the impression of having been in use for centuries. It was an intriguing thought that the charming rascals that living our midst could well be descendents of the foxes that were hunted by the inhabitants of the site 4000 years ago.

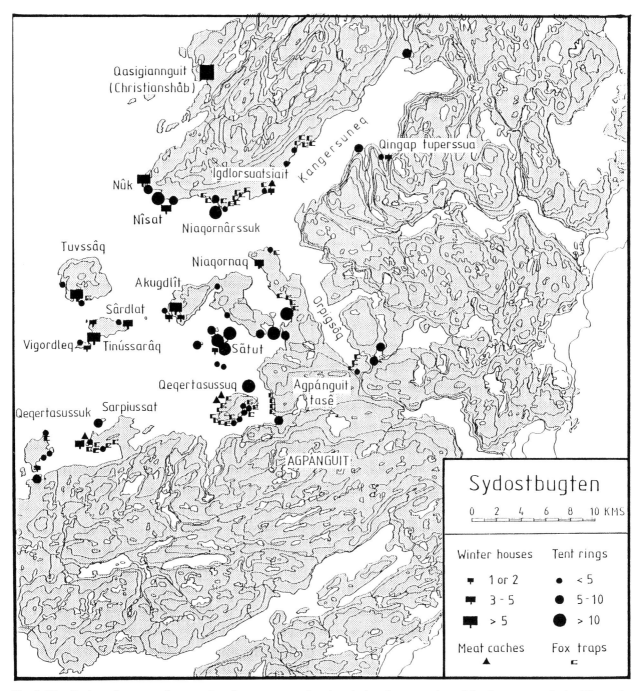

Fig. 2: Distribution of stone set fox-traps based on surveys undertaken during the excavation of the Qeqertasussuk site. The settlement of Akulliit, from where most of the fox traps were operated, was abandoned in 1963.

Not suprisingly, the presence of foxes on this site has earned it the Greenlandic name Sisikasiit - the place with the fox holes. This name is not on the official geodætic map, but was related to Emil Rosing in 1981 by Frederik Jensen, who had for many years been the manager of the village of Akulliit, and by Villads Olsvig, also a former inhabitant of Akuliit, during an interview in 1983. Unfortunately, we did not know of this name until after the archaeological site had been named Qeqertasussuk, from the name of the island on which it is situated.

The Arctic Fox

The Qasigiannguit district has always been known as a fine fox district, probably the best in West Greenland. Moreover, foxes can be found in most parts of the district, in the interior, along the coasts, and on most islands. In winter they also explore the sea ice. An active scavenger, the Arctic Fox can often be found eagerly searching the coastline for carrion during low tide, browsing through willows for birds nests, or poking around the kitchen tent in an archaeological camp.

Fig. 3: Stone set fox-trap in use. The photo was taken near Aasiaat in the early part of this century.
(Photo by Kaj Birket-Smith, National Museum of Denmark).

In winter they tend to follow tidal cracks in the sea ice or search the ice-edge, where there is a likelihood of coming across a dead bird, left-overs from a hunting expedition, or other edible items (Birks & Penford 1990; Müller 1906:314; Ostermann 1921:111; Porsild 1921: 101; Rosendahl 1942:56).

The Arctic Fox occurs in a white and a blue phase. In the Qasigiannguit district these are almost equally represented, but approximately every fourth year large white foxes from Baffin Island invade the central parts of West Greenland, and the percentage of white foxes increases significantly. Besides these changes in color frequencies, the West Greenland Fox populations also experience large population fluctuations approximately every tenth year (Braestrup 1941; Vibe 1967).

Historically, the Arctic Fox was valued for its fur which was an important source of income. Intensive hunting was carried out in the southern part of Disko Bay, along with every other place on the west coast of Greenland. Stone set fox traps that were in use until the 1960s

Fig. 4: Cranium of Arctic Fox. Note that the occipital part of the cranium has been smashed either to get at the brain or as a result of the method of hunting or killing the animal. The foxes from the site are significantly larger than modern foxes in the area. This could be a result of better growth conditions 4000 years ago.

Fig. 5: An articulated fox-paw can be seen to the left. A fox-jaw protrudes from the permafrozen soil to the right.

are still found on almost every promontory and small island in Sydostbugten (Fig. 2 & Fig. 3), and the hunters from Akulliit relate that especially good hunting grounds were found along the coasts of Kangersuneq, Orpisooq, and Sydostbugten (M. Meldgaard unpublished).

The fox bones

The conditions for preservation in the permafrozen midden deposits were excellent and the bones were mostly in perfect shape. Often fox limbs and vertebral columns were found neatly articulated, and in some cases the feet were preserved with hair and claws still in place (Fig. 4 & Fig. 5). The high concentrations of fly puppae in the cavities of many of the fox crania together with the high frequency of articulated bones, gives the impression of a camp with recurrent periods of successful hunting and conditions of surplus.

More than 100,000 animal bones were excavated at the Qeqertassusuk site. About 60% are mammal bones, and of these, fox represent around 11%. Based on an estimate of "minimum number of individuals", and based on our knowledge of the midden's total volume, it can be calculated that a minimum of 945 foxes were caught at the site, most of them between c. 2400 B.C. and 2100 B.C. (M. Meldgaard unpublished) (Fig. 6).

Based on tooth-sectioning it turned out that almost 60% of the foxes were immature animals less than 1 year old while 2, 3, 4 and 5 year old foxes each represented about 10% of the sample. Only 2 individuals reached an age of 6 and 7 years, respectively, and both of them had extremely worn teeth (Fig. 7). It is not surprising that there is such a high percentage of juvenile foxes in the sample.

In addition to constituting a large part of the natural population, young-of-the-year are less shy and less wary, making them easier to approach and trap compared to older more experienced foxes (Müller 1906:314; Rosendahl 1942:56).

Because the growth rate of foxes is high during their first year of life, as is the case with juvenile animals in general, it is possible to relate specific growth intervals to monthly time intervals.

Thus the relative pulp cavity width of juvenile fox canines, as elucidated by X-ray investigations, has proven to be a reliable indicator of season of death (Fig. 8).

The data show that most of the juvenile foxes were killed in late fall and winter, with a slight peak in November, and that a few animals were killed in early fall and in spring or early summer.

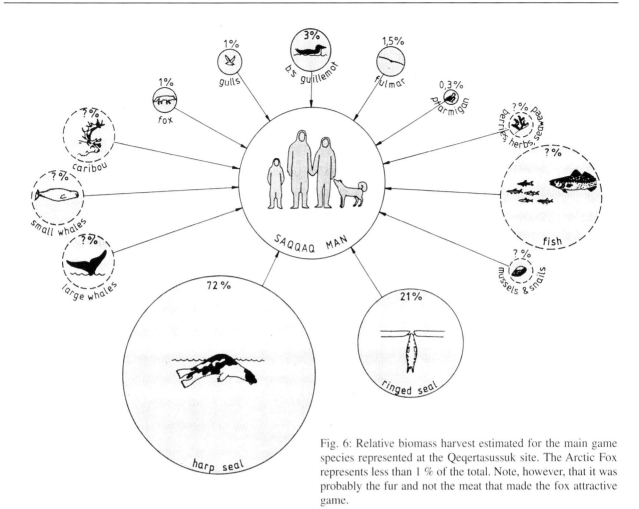

Fig. 6: Relative biomass harvest estimated for the main game species represented at the Qeqertasussuk site. The Arctic Fox represents less than 1 % of the total. Note, however, that it was probably the fur and not the meat that made the fox attractive game.

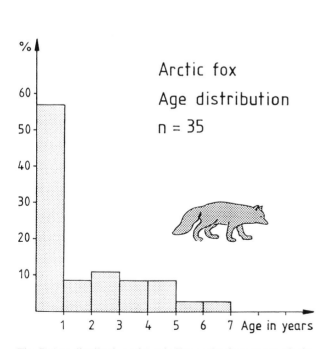

Fig. 7: Age distribution of Arctic Fox at the Qeqertasussuk site based on tooth sectioning.

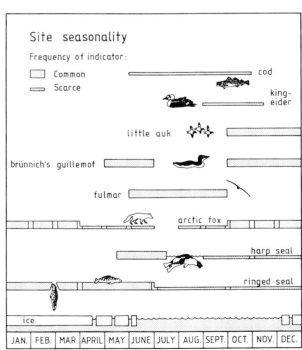

Fig. 8: The canine teeth of juvenile foxes provided the most precise seasonal dating of all seasonal indicators at the site.

Fox fur

It is quite understandable that the Saqqaq inhabitants at Qeqertassussuk preferred winter foxes over summer foxes. Winter fox fur is simply of much better quality. The Arctic Fox develops a winter coat in October, juveniles a little earlier than adults. From November to February the fur quality is best. Molting occurs in April, at which time the fur is shaggy and completely useless (Vibe 1981). Consequently, there is a general correspondance between the season of the Saqqaq fox hunt at Qeqertasussuk and the season of optimal fur quality. Thus fox hunting was likely undertaken primarily to secure skins, probably for garments.

The assumption that fur was the main product of fox hunting is supported by the large number of articulated fox feet, limbs and vertebra that were found, indicating that these parts were discarded on the midden following butchering, and that they were not cooked and eaten.

Fox hunting

Numerous fragments of hunting gear were excavated at Qeqertasussuk, including remains of bow and arrow and of dart and spear, all of which could have been used to kill foxes (Grønnow 1988). However, from ethnographic and historic sources it is evident that small individualistic carnivores like the Arctic Fox are most easily caught in traps. This could also have been the case in Saqqaq times but unfortunately, we have no archaeological proof of fox traps contemporary with the site, at or near Qeqertasussuk. But perhaps some of the many recent stone set fox traps, placed on sites that have always attracted foxes, contain stones from much older traps?

Warm fur and well made clothes

Delicate needles, fine sinew thread, and preserved fragments of skin work and kamiks exhibiting an eloquent sewing technique, all point to a well developed tradition for skin treatment and tailoring. Fox skin is very practical for warm winter clothes, and from experiments we know that the Arctic Fox, because of its highly insulating fur, can withstand temperatures of ÷40°C without even raising its metabolism (Gordon 1977:405). Fox skin was undoubtedly an important component in the winter clothing of the Saqqaq people that lived at Qeqertasussuk, and surely the garments presented themselves beautifully - but we still need to prove it archaeologically.

Morten Meldgaard, Ph.D., zoology,
Director, Danish Polar Center

References

Birks, J. D. S. & N. Penford [1990]: **Observations on the ecology of Arctic Foxes Alopex lagopus in Eqalummiut Nunaat, West Greenland.** *Meddelelser om Grønland, Bioscience*, 32:1-26 (Copenhagen: The Commission for Scientific Research in Greenland).

Braestrup, F. W. [1941]: **A study on the arctic fox in Greenland.** *Meddelelser om Grønland*, 131(4):1-101 (Copenhagen: C. A. Reitzels Forlag).

Gordon, M. S. [1977]: **Animal Physiology: Principles and Adaptations.** 699 p. (New York: MacMillan Publishing Co., Inc.).

Grønnow, Bjarne [1988]: **Prehistory in Permafrost. Investigations at the Saqqaq Site, Qeqertasussuk, Disco Bay, West Greenland.** *Journal of Danish Archaeology*, 7:24-39 (Odense: Odense University Press).

Josefsen, N., M. Lynge, S. Egede, A. Egede & E. Motzfeldt [1964]: **Rævejagt.** pp:30-34 in "Lærebog i fangst for Syd- og Nordgrønland", editor: H. C. Christiansen, 132 p. (Copenhagen: Den Kongelige Grønlandske Handel).

Müller, R. [1906]: **Vildtet og Jagten i Sydgrønland.** 519 p. (Copenhagen: H. Hagerups Boghandel).

Ostermann, H. [1921]: **Landjagten.** pp:110-113 in "Grønland i tohundredeaaret for Hans Egedes landing", editors: G. C. Amdrup, L. Bobé, A. S. Jensen & H. P. Steenby, *Meddelelser om Grønland*, 60:1-567 (Copenhagen: C. A. Reitzels Forlag).

Porsild, M. P. [1921]: **Dyrelivet.** pp:101-104 in "Grønland i tohundredeaaret for Hans Egedes landing", editors: G. C. Amdrup, L. Bobé, A. S. Jensen & H. P. Steenby, *Meddelelser om Grønland*, 60:1-567 (Copenhagen: C. A. Reitzels Forlag).

Rosendahl, Phillip [1942]: **Jakob Danielsen en grønlandsk maler.** 80 p. (Copenhagen: Gyldendal).

Rosendahl, Phillip [1961]: **Grønlandsk jagt- og fangststatistik.** *Geografisk Tidsskrift*, 60:16-38 (Copenhagen: Det Kongelige Danske Geografiske Selskab).

Vibe, Christian [1967]: **Arctic animals in relation to climatic fluctuations.** *Meddelelser om Grønland*, 170(5): 1-227 (Copenhagen: C. A. Reitzels Forlag).

Vibe, Christian [1981]: **Pattedyr.** pp:364-459 in "Grønlands Fauna. Fisk, Fugle, Pattedyr", editor: Finn Salomonsen, 463 p. (Copenhagen: Nordisk Forlag).

A Heavy Duty Chopping Tool
from a Birnirk House in Ekven, Chukotka

Hansjürgen Müller-Beck

In the summer of 1996, despite all financial problems, a limited excavation was continued at house 18 in Ekven, Chukotka (Fig. 1). This is the first settlement structure which was discovered at this site during excavations from the State Museums of Oriental Art (Dneprovsky 1996) by a transnational team (Blumer 1996) as part of an INTAS-projekt (No. 94-964). Dr Jøgen Meldgaard participated as an advisory member of the International Commitee for Archaeology in Chukotka, alongside the Danish archaeologists Dr. Hans Kapel and Dr. Hans Christian Gulløv, and three Russian, one Swiss, and two German excavators, who were employed in the field.

At the same time, the Ekven cemetery was also excavated. This location has been the focus of research since 1993 (Leskov & Müller-Beck 1993; Dneprovsky 1996). In the winter of 1995-1996 the archaeological materials were completely conserved, analysed, and documented by means of drawing and photographing. An analysis of the faunal remains of house 18 was also done in this period by Dr. A. B. Savinetsky from the Group of Historical Ecology in the Svertsov Institute of Ecology and Evolution of the Russian Academy of Sciences in Moscow (Director: Dr. L. G. Dinesman). All these works were supported by the INTAS-project mentioned above.

Both at the Svertsov Institute of Ecology and Evolution and in Copenhagen radiocarbon datings were conducted. Here I just want to mention the result of the datings in Moscow, based on grass which was obtained from the sleeping platform: 1430 ± 200 B.P. (IEMAE-1197). This date is in accordance with the arguments of R. Blumer (1996) and it supports the identification as Early Birnirk (Stanford 1976; Morrison 1991).

According to the arrangements between Anadyr and Moscow, 50% of the archaeological materials of the 1995 campaigns from the cemetery were brought back to Chukotka. They will be distributed between the regional museum in Anadyr and the recently extended museum in Lawrentiya. The selection was first made by the museum in Moscow alone, because the proper commission could not hold a meeting in the capital. An exchange, possibly demanded later by Chukotka, is nevertheless still possible.

In the summer of 1996 the excavation was focused on the central and northeastern sections of house 18 including the entrance area. The work was done by four Russian, one Swiss and three German archaeologists; the financial means were provided by the SMOA in Moscow, the SLSA in Bern and Vaduz, and by the DFG in Bonn. Under surprisingly good weather conditions and despite the considerably increased costs and a more difficult supply situation, the team could finally put in 120 days of work, which was 25% more than in 1995. The morphochronologically discernable finds could be stylistically recognised as widely known Birnirk forms.

After the recovery the surprisingly rich material was subjected to a first conservation and extensive cataloging. It is now in Moscow for the final conservation, documentation and analysis. According to the present arrangements (which have recently been disputed in Chukotka), the material is to be divided up between the museums in Moscow and Chukotka. How this can reasonably be achieved is still an open question. It mainly requires an extension of the small depot in Anadyr and the establishment of facilities in Chukotka for the preparation and

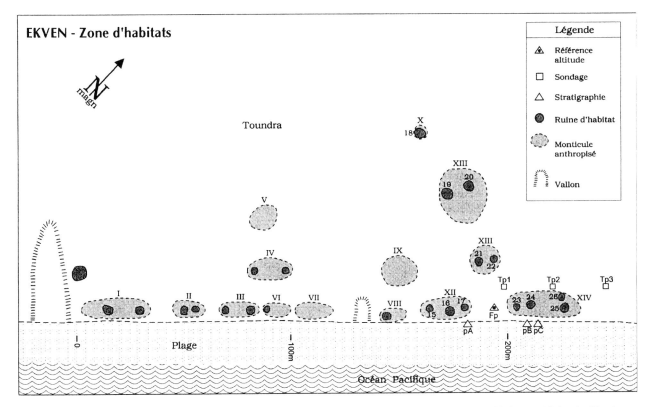

Fig. 1: The Ekven settlement with house 18 in the Northeast (Blumer 1996).

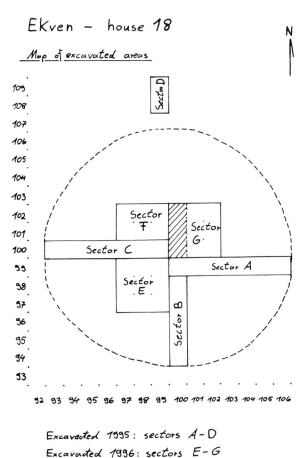

Fig. 2: Excavations in house 18 in Ekven 1995 (Blumer 1996).

supervision of the finds. This will also be relevant for the presumably larger inventories of future salvage excavations in areas of beach erosion. These excavations are becoming more and more urgent because of a loss of up to a meter of sediment due to storms every year. The difficulties that would arise during excavation because of permafrost can be solved.

In 1997 house 18 will be completely excavated in a campaign lasting at least two and a half months. The area comprises about 400 m² if all marginal working places are included. At least 12 excavators will be employed, tents will be used as well. A test excavation will be undertaken in house 25 (Fig. 1). Additionally, test trenches to the west of the settlement will be excavated, supplemented by a drainage system to avoid erosion (as in high profiles in gravel- or sand-pits).

Nevertheless, it remains an open question how the erosion, which is caused by storms and which has been becoming more serious in the last decades, can be prevented. Considering the tremendous forces that are involved, breakwater elements weighing one to ten tons might have no effect at all. It would be ideal (and hopefully not completely utopian) to anchor available, discarded ships of the Russian or American navy permanently or temporarily near the coastline as part of the general conversational arrangements in Beringia.

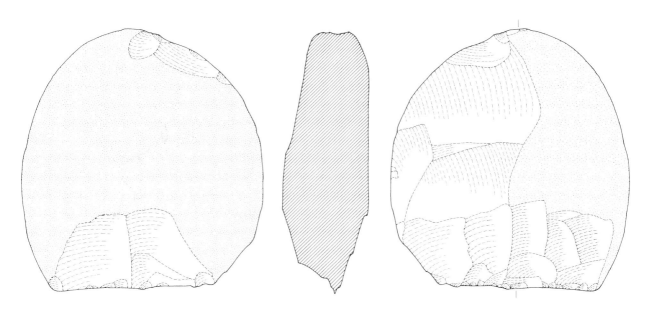

Fig. 3: The chopping tool (F-162) from documentation level 14 at the centre of house 18, excavation 1996:
(a) Face A, (b) Face B, (c) section. Pencil original Müller-Beck, Ink Frey., 16,5 cm maximum breath.

An urgent requirement is also the establishment of a new excavation camp. Within ten minutes' walking distance of the western part of the settlement an ideal location above the cliff is available. This might at the same time reduce the threat to the settlement caused by passing track vehicles. Apart from being used during archaeological campaigns, such a camp could be used as a station for other research as well. Also, the logistics have to be planned more realistically.

By western-European standards this would still be relatively cheap and be of considerable and not only symbolic significance for the cultural policy of Chukotka which is in a difficult position between the two great powers of Russia and the United States. If nothing is done now, important sources for the transnational research in the Arctic will be lost. Also the indigenous population needs to be convinced that archaeological and ecological projects are more than just campaigns to provide museums with objects. Research could contribute to a renewed appreciation of a better and extensive usage of the ecosystem by controlled hunting and controlled utilisation of animal products such as ivory, whale bones, and reindeer antlers.

The range of the technological observations, which are not only of specific scientific value will be illustrated here with a more or less unexpected find. Subsequently, it is attempted to formulate some of the wide-ranging problems of the developments of the Eskimo cultures to which the unusually rich Birnirk findings in house 18 might offer some solutions.

The stone tool may be regarded as "timeless". It is a heavy chopping tool (Fig. 3:a-c), made from a greywacke.

It was found in the central sector F in documentation horizon 14, on the floor of the central room of house 18. It carries field number F-162. Maximal length is 17,7 cm, the maximal breath is 16,5 cm, and the maximal thickness is 6,0 cm. The cutting edge, which was prepared by skillful bifacial strokes has a breath of 11,7 cm.

Because of its size far above the average, such an object would even attract attention in the early Old Pleistocene African pebble tool industries of the Oldowan, 1.900.000 years ago (Leakey 1971), or in the Middle Pleistocene Ting-ts'un complex in China (Aigner 1981).

With regard to its dimensions it can only superficially be distinguished from recent Australian pebble tools (Tindale 1941). It differs only in a more careful preparation of the cutting edge (Fig. 4).

Heavy chopping tools are used in Australia without any additional shaft for the felling of trees. In the context of the Old-Bering-Sea and of the later Birnirk we know of skilfully shafted axes which of course were also

Fig. 4: Whale bones from the central construction of house 18, Ekven 1996. (Photo B. Seif), scale 2 meter.

applicable for the procurement of wood and large bones. But the traces at the shortened whale bones which were used for the construction of house 18 (Fig. 4) show the employment of a heavy duty tool. And here the utilisation of such rough forms certainly makes sense. In the reduction of the whale ribs as constructive parts that needed to be equally long because of static reasons and were visible above ground before the excavation, heavy duty tools are perfectly reasonable. The distal ends of the ribs were cut off. The broader proximal end piece, which was seldom fully preserved, was more suitable to carry the upper parts of the roof construction.

After a precise determination of the length of the single ribs it should be possible to reconstruct the heights of the poles and subsequently the height of the whole construction, that is, the former house. The heavy weight of the tool was the main presupposition of its effectiveness. The precise scope of the shortened ribs was not important so the construction of a shaft, that could have resisted the powers involved, would have been an unnecessary investment; a relation that was also observed in Australia.

From a constructional-morphological point of view this nearly atavistic form was an optimal solution. This took place at a time when the Palaeo-Eskimo microblade technique was already left behind and replaced by a skillful polishing of stones – following the old techno-logical definition – a "neolithic" technique. This was surely also the time and place when iron, exchanged over large distances, was already utilised for precision tools. Consequently, because of its simplicity, the recovered chopping tool represents convincing evidence for the pragmatic technology of the Eskimo whale hunters in Beringia 1400 years ago.

Around this time the Arctic cold phase of the last millenium had already passed and the warmer period of the medieval Viking age had begun (McGhee 1987). Out of the traditions of the Old-Bering-Sea complex and before the flowering of the Thule industries, Birnirk had developed as an intermediary stage. The "genetic" role of the Punuk style remains unclear, despite the association with Birnirk into one chronological stage by McGhee (1987). He regards the spread of the Birnirk elements simply as an adoption of new Siberian techniques in Alaska.

Both solutions are possible because of the blurred transition between Old-Bering-Sea and Birnirk in western Beringia and also in Ekven. Whether linguistic entities or skeletal-morphological differentiable populations can be correlated with the genesis of new techniques (for example developed maritime hunting with floatgear) is rather doubtful, especially after experiences with similar attempts in Central Europe.

Abbriviations

SMOA: State Museum of Oriental Art

SLSA: Schweizerische-Liechiensteinische Stiftung
        Für Archäologische Forschungen in Ausland

INTAS:

IEMAE: Moscow Radiocarbon Laboratorium number

DFG: Deutsche Forshungs-Gemeinschaft

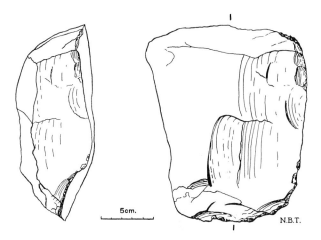

Fig. 5: Australian hand axe from 1935 (Tindale 1941).

This could also mean that we may imagine the spread of the Birnirk-Punuk-Thule techniques with the changes in the corresponding ornamental styles up to Greenland as a diffusion of cultural elements without any extensive migrations. This would, in any case, be a model which would allow an assimilation of the different older Eastern Dorset populations into a new synthetical Thule as a "general culture". Additionally, this might also do more justice to the archaeologically accessible sources of which language does not form a part. And cultural behaviour is mainly influenced and largely determined by the technological basis anyway.

It will be exciting to conduct more specific analysis on the levels of influence involved in these relations. House 18 in Ekven will contribute to this task with its rich materials, ranging into areas of non-pictorial art, which will be dealt with more extensively in another place.

Hansjürgen Müller-Beck, Emeritus Professor, Universität Tübingen, Schweiz

References

Aigner, J. [1981]: **Archaeological Remains in Pleistocene China.** *Forschungen zur Allgemeinen und Vergleichenden Archäologie*, 1:197-219, editor: H. Müller-Beck, 351 p. (München: Beck).

Blumer, R. [1996]: **Première Expédition Archéologique Internationale en Thoukotka, Sibérie nord-orientale. Rapport de la contribution suisse aux travaux de l'été 1995.** Jahresbericht 1995:110-154 (Bern & Vaduz: Schweizerische-Liechtensteinische Stiftung für archäologische Forschungen im Ausland).

Dneprovsky, K. A. [1996]: **Archaeological Expedition in Chukotka of the State Museum of Oriental Art (Moscow).** 3 p. in "International Conference on Barents Spitsbergen Arctic 1996, Abstracts", * p. (Barentsburg).

Leakey, M. D. [1971]: **Olduvai Gorge.** 3:1-39 in "Excavations in Beds I and II, 1960-1963". 306 p. (Cambridge: Cambridge University Press).

Leskov, A. M. & Hansjürgen Müller-Beck [1993]: **Arktische Waljäger vor 3000 Jahren.** 208 p. (Mainz: Hase & Koehler).

McGhee, R. [1987]: **Peopling the Arctic.** pp:*-* in "Historical Atlas of Canada, Vol. I: From the Beginning to 1800, Plate 11", editors: R. C. Harris & G. J. Matthews, 69 plates (Toronto: University of Toronto Press).

Morrison, D. [1991]: **The Diamond Jenness Collections from Bering Strait. Archaeological Survey of Canada.** *Mercury Series Paper* 144:1-171 (Hull: Canadian Museum of Civilisation).

Stanford, D. J. [1976]: **The Walpaka Site, Alaska. Its place in the Birnirk and Thule Cultures.** *Smithsonian Contributions to Anthropology*, 20:96-114 (Washington DC: The National Museum of America).

Tindale, N. B. [1941]: **The Hand Axe Used in the Western Desert of Australia.** *Mankind*, 3(2):37-41 (London: *). Kraus reprint 1971 (Nekdeln, Liechtenstein).

New aspects of the Saqqaq Culture in West Greenland

Tinna Møbjerg

Less than 50 years ago the Saqqaq Culture was defined as a separate phase of the Paleo-Eskimo cultures in Greenland. Not until the excavation at the stratified site at Sermermiut (Larsen & Meldgaard 1958, Mathiasen 1958) was it possible to separate the Saqqaq and the Dorset Cultures.

Since that time many investigations at Paleo-Eskimo sites have taken place all over Greenland (Gulløv 1986). But still, the knowledge of the early prehistory of Greenland is so scarce that nearly every new excavation brings important new data for understanding the Saqqaq Culture. That happened at the excavations on Qaaja (Meldgaard 1983, 1991) and Qeqertasussuk (Grønnow 1988, 1994, 1996; Grønnow & Meldgaard 1991). This was also the case when the curators from the museum of Sisimiut established a systematic investigation of Paleo-Eskimo sites in the municipality of Sisimiut between 1985-1995. More than 100 Paleo-Eskimo sites were registered and, as usual the Saqqaq sites were more numerous than the Dorset sites. On three of these Saqqaq sites extended excavations took place between 1989-1995[1].

Description of the sites

Akia (SIK 491)

Akia is situated just north of Sisimiut (Fig. 1). 127 m^2 were excavated between 1989 and 1991 (Kramer 1996a, 1996b). The site is located 40 m from the present coast at a height of 12 m above sea level. The excavation showed three different settlement areas called A, B, and C. Only area A contains a dwelling structure - a ring of stones surrounding a box hearth. In addition, there was lot of fire cracked stones west of the dwelling and northwest of it was an outdoor box hearth.

No organic material besides charcoal was preserved. 444 tools and 5.831 flakes were recovered. All artefacts were types well-known from the Saqqaq Culture. Burins were the most common tool type together with burin spalls. Other artefact types were sidescrapers, endscrapers, microblades, arrowpoints, lancepoints, bifaces with transverse edge, triangular harpoon points, adzes, strike-a-light, and pieces of pumices with grinding grooves. No sherds of soapstone were found at all.

The dominant raw material was killiaq and only a few artefacts, especially microblades and sidescrapers were made from other raw materials as rock crystal, agate and quartzite.

There is only one ^{14}C dating form Akia, which dates the site to the oldest sequence of the Saqqaq Culture (see table 1).

Asummiut (SIK 173, 899, 900, and 901)

Asummiut is located only a few kilometers west of Akia. The area was investigated in 1995 as a salvation program in connection with establishing a new airport in Sisimiut[2].

All together four discrete settlement units were recovered at different distances from the present coast (Møbjerg & Grummesgaard-Nielsen 1996; Grummesgaard-Nielsen 1995).

SIK 173.

This site was the largest and well-known from a survey in the area before the excavation in 1995 (Kramer 1996b; Meldgaard 1980).

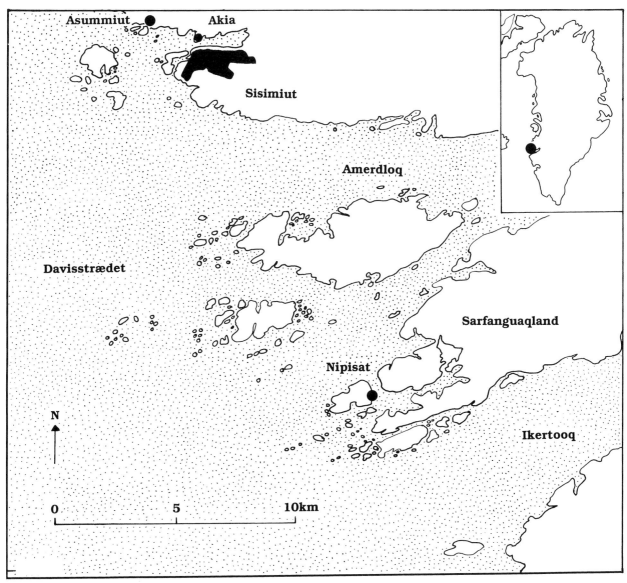

Fig. 1: Sketch map of the Sisimiut district with the three sites: Asummiut, Akia, and Nipisat marked with dots.

The site is situated 80 m from the coast at an elevation of 12 m to 13 m above sea level. 159 m² were excavated which makes up half the settlement area. The excavation recovered eight more or less well-defined dwelling structures with a central hearth. Because of repeated use of the site many of the dwelling structures were disturbed. Besides charcoal very little organic material was preserved.

The more than 500 artefacts primarily consisted of burins, burin spalls, and many pieces of pumice with grinding grooves. Less numerous were arrowpoints, denticulated small triangular harpoonpoints, knife blades, endscrapers, sidescrapers, polished stone awls, strike-a-light, and adzes.

No sherds of soapstone were recovered. The raw material was mainly killiaq. That means that the artefact

material from SIK 173 looks very much like the material from Akia.

Three charcoal samples from a profile section have been dated at the AMS Laboratory at the University of Aarhus. These datings place the site in the oldest sequence of the Saqqaq Culture (see table 2).

SIK 900

The site is situated 140 m west of SIK, 173 m and 120 m from the present coast line at an elevation of 14 m above sea level. 29 m² were excavated and a dwelling structure 3 m in diameter with the midpassage marked by small pebbles was recovered. Besides charcoal no organic material was preserved. The excavation recovered several hundred flakes and 150 stone artefacts consisting of burins, knife blades, points, endscrapers, and pumice

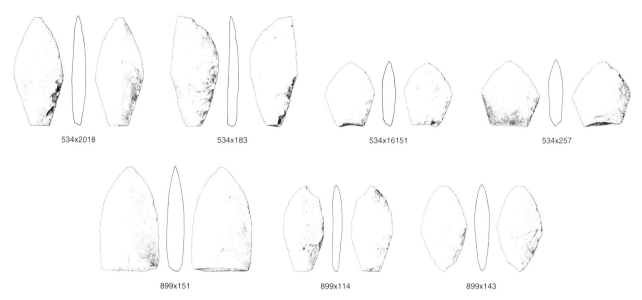

534x2018   534x183   534x16151   534x257

899x151   899x114   899x143

Fig. 2: Polished and bevelled tools made of killiaq. Upper row: Nipisat. Lower row: Asummiut SIK 899. (Photo draw by Jørgen Holm).

with grinding grooves. No sherds of soapstone were recovered. Killiaq was the dominant raw material and only few pieces were made from other materials.

A sample of charcoal was dated at the AMS laboratory and this date is about the same age as the two oldest from SIK 173 (see table 2).

SIK 899
This site is situated 40 m southeast of SIK 900 at an elevation of 11,5 m above sea level. A settlement unit, remarkably different from SIK 173 and SIK 900, was recovered. The number of stone artefacts from the 30 m² excavated area is only 60 (flakes are not included) but, in addition, there are several hundred small soapstone chips. Noteworthy, too, is the presence of bevelled and polished tools (Fig. 2). The site is interpreted as an activity area for manufacturing soapstone. Unfortunately the amount of charcoal was too small for ¹⁴C dating.

SIK 901
The last settlement unit at Asummiut is situated 40 m south of SIK 899 and 60 m from the coast at an elevation of 10,5 m above sea level. The excavation of 23 m² shows the cultural deposit lying directly on the bedrock. The site is interpreted as a dumping area because no dwelling structures were seen. No organic material was preserved but more than 50 stone artefacts and many flakes were recovered and all were well-known Saqqaq types. In addition, three sherds of soapstone were revealed. Unfortunately, no material for ¹⁴C dating was preserved.

Nipisat
The site is situated on a small island 15 km south of Sisimiut (Fig. 1). The settlement area lies 50 m from the present coast at an elevation between 9 m and 13 m above sea level. Today the settlement area is covered with dense vegetation and nothing could be seen on the surface when curator Finn Kramer visited the place in 1989. However, a test pit 10 cm below recent sod revealed some well-preserved bones together with stone artefact types from the Saqqaq Culture[3]. (Kramer & Jones 1992; Kramer 1994, 1996a, 1996b).

Nipisat is outstanding in two ways. First of all, several separated layers have been found at a Saqqaq site in Sisimiut municipality, and the preliminary analysis has clarified that these chronological differences are reflected morphologically. Second thick deposits of crushed shells over- and underlaying the cultural layer give excellent preservation conditions for bone, antler, and ivory. More than 200 m² have been excavated in the period from 1989 to 1994 recovering 15.000 bone fragments (Gotfredsen 1992, 1996), more than 1.000 artefacts and several thousands of flakes (Møbjerg 1995a, 1995b).

The investigation has shown that the site has both horisontal and vertical stratigraphy. In the southwestern part of the site two main cultural layers could be identified (layer 2 and layer 2K), separated by thick layers of crushed shells. In addition, smaller lenses with bones and artefacts were identified above and below layer 2K. It seems that layer 2 continued towards the northeast as a

Site no	Site Name	Laboratory no.	^{14}C age BP	Calibrated age BC	Cal ± 1 stdv.	Dated on:
SIK 491	Akia area A	K-5788	3790±85	2200	2400-2050	Charcoal/Salix sp. & bet. nana
SIK 534	Nipisat layer 2 1990	K-5864	2860±80	1000	1130-910	Bone from Rangifer. tarandus
SIK 534	Nipisat layer 2 1989	K-5584	2940±80	1130	1260-1000	do
SIK 534	Nipisat layer 2 1994	K-6460	2910±60	1110-1060	1200-1000	do
SIK 534	Nipisat layer 2 1993	K-6194	2670±85	810	900-790	Bone from Rangifer.tarandus
SIK 534	Nipisat layer 2 1993	K-6193	2920±85	1120	1260-950	do
SIK 534	Nipisat layer 2 1992	K-6198	3180±125	1430	1590-1310	Charcoal/Salix sp. & bet. nana
SIK 534	Nipisat layer 2 1993	K-6192	3670±90	2030-1990	2180-1910	Bone from Rangifer tarandus
SIK 534	Nipisat layer 2K 1994	K-6459	3010±95	1260-1230	1390-1080	Bone from Rangifer tarandus
SIK 534	Nipisat layer 2K 1993	K-6195	3310±85	1600-1530	1680-1470	do
SIK 534	Nipisat layer 2K 1992	K-6031	3490±80	1860-1790	1890-1690	do
SIK 534	Nipisat layer 1B 1993	K-6196	3300±85	1530	1680-1460	Bone from Rangifer tarandus

Table 1: ^{14}C dates from Akia and Nipisat from the ^{14}C Laboratory at the Nationalmuseum of Denmark, listed as conventional ^{14}C ages BP (Before Present=1950). Copenhagen. The ^{14}C dates are calibrated according to Stuiver and Pearson 1993 (Kramer 1996b)

Site no	Site Name	Laboratory no	^{14}C age BP	Calibrated age BC	Cal ± 1 stdv.	Dated on
SIK 173	Asummiut layer 2A	AAR-3028	3370±65	1670	1740-1530	Charcoal/ Salix species
SIK 173	Asummiut layer 2B	AAR-3029	3575±65	1900	2010-1780	Charcoal/Betula nana
SIK 173	Asummiut layer 3A	AAR-3030	3605±65	1940	2030-1880	Charcoal/Betula nana
SIK 900	Asummiut layer 2	AAR-3027	3630±80	1970	2130-1880	Charcoal/Salix glauca

Table 2: ^{14}C dates from Asummiut from the AMS laboratory at the University of Århus, Denmark (Heinemeier et al. 1993) listed as conventional ^{14}C ages BP (Before Present=1950). The ^{14}C dates are calibrated according to Stuiver and Pearson 1993

Fig. 3: Needles from Nipisat. Upper row: the needles are
made of bird bone. Below: a large antler needle.
(Photo: P. Delholm, Moesgård.

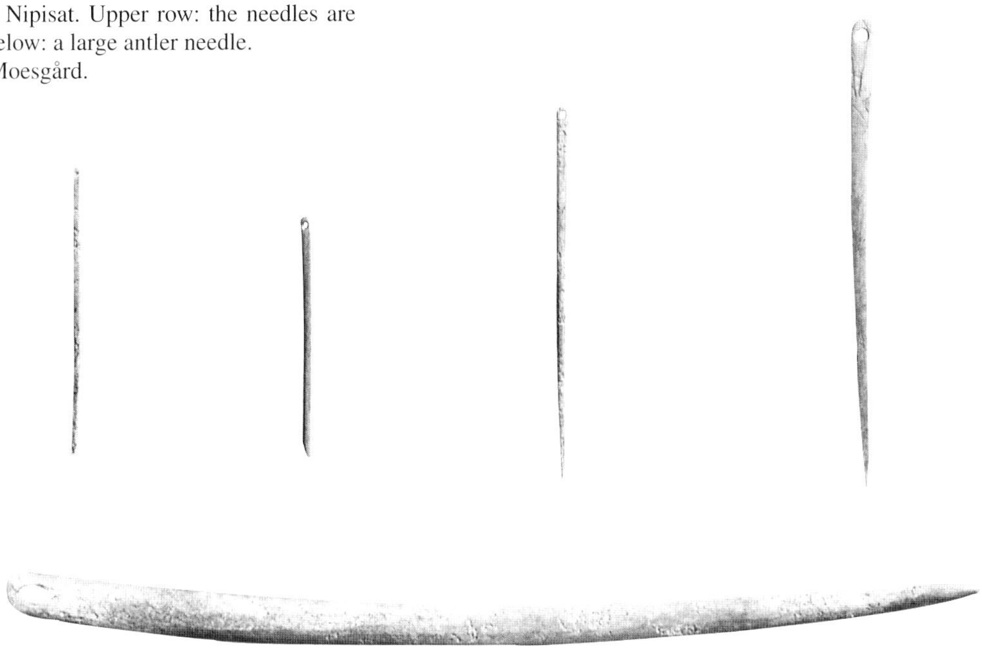

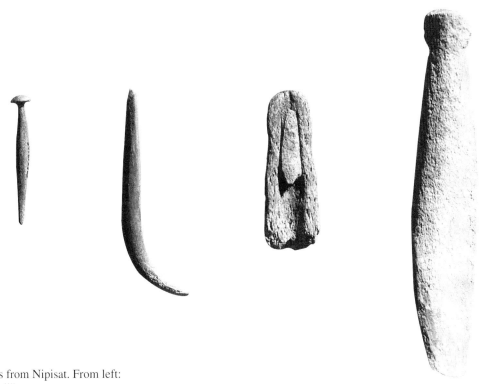

Fig. 4: Tools from Nipisat. From left:
1) ivory "nail"
2) antler implement with an eye.
3) fragment of a throwing board made of whale bone
   with a little inserted hook of antler
4) implement of antler
(Photo: P. Delholm, Moesgård)

Fig. 5

Fig. 6

Fig. 5: Leister or bird dart made of ivory, notice the nice inci-
sion shaped as an Y below the last hook. 16,5 cm.
(Photo: Gert Brovad, Zoologiscal Museum, Copenhagen).

Fig. 6: Fargment of an antler "leister or bird dart", 10,4 cm.
Notice the incised line and the hook shaped as a caribou hoof.
(Photo: Gert Brovad, Zoologiscal Museum, Copenhagen)

very massive layer overlaying directly a very thin and
decomposed layer 2K in this area. Layer 2 and layer 2K
were not separated by shell layers in this area.

However, surpassing bedrock disturb the stratigraphy and the layers have been interrupted in such a way
that we cannot be sure that layer 2 in the northeastern part
is identical with layer 2 in the southwestern part of the
site.

As seen from table 1 there is great variability in the
^{14}C datings. Noteworthy is the fact that the three datings
coming from layer 2 in the northeastern area are young,
ranging from 1130 B.C. to 1000 B.C. Compared to that
the eight datings from the main settlement area in the
southwestern part of the site had a larger variaty, especially K-6192 from layer 2 seems to be too old and K-
6459 seems to be too young. Further analysis and more
datings will elucidate this problem.

The stone artefacts from the oldest layer (2K) are of
the well-known types from the Saqqaq Culture. But, in
addition, many different tools of bone, antler, and ivory
were recovered. Needles (Fig. 3) and pressure flakers
were predominant. A fragment of a throwing board made
of whale bone with an inserted hook of antler was one of
the more spectacular objects together with the little ivory
"nail" (see Fig. 4:3 & Fig. 4:1). The bevelled implements
(see Fig. 2) were only registered from the youngest layer

(2) together with objects of soapstone such as gambling
pieces and sherds from cooking pots and lamps. Leisters
and bird darts with ornaments (Fig. 5 & Fig. 6) also came
from the latest occupation. A special kind of lance heads
(see Kramer & Jones 1992: Fig. 6) was recovered from
the same layer. Maybe it has been used for walrus or
whale hunting.

Looking at the stone artefacts, killiaq has been the
predominating raw material, especially in the oldest layer
(2K). In layer 2 the number of artefacts made of different
raw materials such as agat, quartzite, and rock crystal
was higher.

The faunal material of more than 15.000 bones represents about fifty species. An interesting feature is the
large number of caribou bones, which shows that the distribution of caribou was different from today's, at that
time they must have lived closer to the coast. Common
seal, harp seal, hooded seal, bearded seal, walrus, and
porpoise are also represented in the material in such large
numbers that they must have been hunted from boats.
The bird bones similarly provide new information. The
great auk was identified in the oldest layers, and the oldest swan discovered in Greenland was found at Nipisat.
The large number of goose bones is also striking. Finds
of caribou calves, half-grown seals, and unfledged eider
young and goose suggest that the site was occupied from

June to September. But the analysis is still preliminary and future analysis will show, whether there are changes in resource exploitation over time (Gotfredsen 1992, 1996, in press).

Different dwelling structures were recovered, most of them single box hearths. But in 1994 a dwelling structure consisting of a diffuse ring of stone (3 m to 4 m) with a very well-defined box hearth was recovered (Fig. 7). Therefore, it is possible to elucidate the infrastructure at the site. This structure belongs to the oldest occupation phase and maybe K-6192 is related to this structure. An AMS dating of charcoal will properly clarify this problem.

Discussions

The preliminary results from the three different sites, Akia, Asummiut, and Nipisat, show some new trends. At least two different phases of the Saqqaq Culture can be seen in the Sisimiut area as proposed by Kramer (Kramer 1996a, 1996b). The oldest phase is represented at Akia, Asummiut (SIK 173 and SIK 900), and Nipisat layer 2K. No soapstone objects or bevelled tools are recovered, and killiaq is predominant as raw material. There are also differences in resource exploitation. The great auk is only known from the oldest layers at Nipisat.

From Akia and Asummiut this phase is dated between 2200 B.C. - 1670 B.C. (calibrated). The datings from Nipisat are more complex and layer 2K is dated between 1860 B.C. - 1230 B.C. (calibrated).

The youngest phase is represented in Asummiut (SIK 899 and SIK 901) and Nipisat layer 2 and dated between 1430 B.C. - 810 B.C. (calibrated) at Nipisat. In addition, to well-known artefact types from the Saqqaq Culture a new tool type is represented, namely the polished and bevelled tools (Fig. 2). This kind of objects have been recovered earlier from Disko Bugt, but had been registered as Dorset tools (see Larsen & Meldgaard 1953: plate 5.26). That was the reason behind Finn Kramer's proposal that the youngest phase of Nipisat was an transitional phase between Saqqaq and Dorset Cultures (Kramer & Jones 1992:29).

Killiaq is still the dominant raw material of the younger phase but other materials such as agate, quartzite, and rock crystal are used too. Noteworthy, too, is the appearance of a great number of sherds and objects of soapstone.

In addition to sherds of the circular lamp known from Ittinera (Meldgaard 1961) and Nunguaq (Appelt 1995) gambling pieces, sinkers, and thick sherds, indicate new types as big cooking pots, were found. Apparently, there is an older phase of the Saqqaq Culture in which the use of soapstone was not yet known. Sites which were occupied before 1400 B.C. do not have traces of soapstone. It is valid for the Disko Bugt area, Maniitsoq (Petersen 1988), Sisimiut and Nuuk (Gulløv 1983; Gulløv & Kapel 1988). There is a problem with one date from Nunguaq,

1880 B.C. - 1790 B.C. (calibrated), but from the other artefact types at the site, Appelt chose to place Nunguaq in the younger part of the Saqqaq Culture (Appelt 1995).

Looking at the artefacts made of organic material such as bone, antler, and ivory many new types are recovered, particularly from the youngest phase. Frames of reference for the material from Nipisat are very scarce. One reason is that the preservation conditions are only good on a few sites from the Saqqaq Culture. However, three can be mentioned namly Qaaja (Meldgaard 1983, 1991), Qeqertasussuk (Grønnow 1988, 1994, 1996; Grønnow & Meldgaard 1991), and Ittinera (Meldgaard 1961). Compared to the bone and wood artefacts from Qeqertasussuk in Disko Bugt, there are great differences, caused by differences in resource exploitation, enviroment, or chronology.

Qeqertarsussuk is dated between 2550 B.C. - 1430 B.C. (calibrated), which means that Qeqertasussuk was abandoned at the same time as the youngest habitation on Nipisat started. Today the closest parallels to the Nipisat material of organic materials are from Taylors excavation in 1965 on Banks and Victoria Island (McGhee personal communication 1996). The datings from Wellington Bay, Menez, Buchanan, and Umingmak (Müller-Beck 1977; Taylor 1967) are very close to the youngest occupation on Nipisat. But why do we not find any parallels from the area between West Greenland and the Arctic Archipelag in Canada? We do not have any answers yet.

Currently we don't know what happens around 1600 B.C. to 1500 B.C., when the younger phase of the Saqqaq Culture begins. If we look at the northern part of Alaska we have the same change in the Arctic Small Tool tradition. The Denbigh Flint Complex changes to Choris between 1600 B.C. to 1400 B.C.

In addition to chipped biface, ground slate knives (presumably for cutting through the skin and blubber of sea mammals) are introduced together with ceramic. Artefacts such as heavy notch stones-indicating netfishing are registered at the same time (Anderson 1984:86; Giddings 1964). From Nipisat tools as the objects (see Fig. 3:4) can be used for net making (Plumet personal communication 1996) and one piece of soapstone has notched as if it was used as sinkers. To this tool kit the bevelled and polished tools can be added.

The existence of contacts between Alaska, the Canadian High Arctic, and Greenland cannot be settled based on the above mentioned data alone. It is noteworthy, however, in that connection that Grønnow (1994:210) finds the closest parallel for the tool kits of organic materials from Qeqertasussuk between the Inuit from the 19th century in the Bering Straits (Nelson 1889) and not from the Thule Culture (the ancestors of the Greenlanders).

From the palynological studies in Greenland (Fredskild 1973) we know that the climate changed during the same periods. Optimal conditions in Greenland started around 2500 B.C. and reached a peak at about 1600 B.C.

By 750 B.C. the climate had again become colder and more humid (Maxwell 1985:103) corresponding to the upcoming of Dorset Culture.

The results from the analysis of the Sisimiut material[4] are still very preliminary. To further elucidate what triggers changes all over the Arctic at the same time we need a much closer international cooperation from Greenland to Sibiria.

Tinna Møbjerg, Department of Prehistoric Archaeology, University of Aarhus, Moesgård, DK-8270 Højbjerg

Abbriviations

AMS: accelerator-massespektrometri

SIK: Sisimiuni Katersugaasivik
    (= Holsteinsborg Museum)

Notes

(1): The author is very gratefull to the curators of Sisimiut Museum: Finn Erik Kramer, Anne Mette Olsvig and Søren Thuesen for a fine cooperation which has given me the opportunity to work with the Paleo-Eskimoic materials from 1993 up to present.

(2): The investigation was financed by the Greenlandic Air Service and the excavation was carried out by Stig Grummesgaard-Nielsen for the National Museum of Greenland.

(3): Curator Finn Erik Kramer was in charge of the excavation from 1989 to 1993 and the author was in charge of the last field season in 1994.

(4): The author is very gratefull for a grant from 1995 to 1997 under the program: Men, Culture and Enviroment in Ancient Greenland from the Danish Research Council's special program for supporting Arctic Research: TUPOLAR.

Fig. 7: Close up of the box hearth in the midpassage structure at Nipisat. (Photo: Stig Grummesgaard-Nielsen).

References

Anderson, Douglas D. [1984]: **Prehistory of North Alaska.** pp:80-93 in "Handbook of North American Indians", Arctic, 5:1-829, editor: David Damas (Washington DC: Smithsonian Institution).

Anderson, Douglas D. [1988]: **Onion Portage: The Archaeology of a Stratified Site from the Kobuk River, Northwest Alaska.** *Anthropological Papers of the University of Alaska*, 22(1-2):1-163 (Fairbanks, Alaska: University of Alaska Press).

Appelt, Martin [1995]: **Nunnguaq - en Saqqaq - plads fra Godthåbsfjorden. En gammel udgravning i nyt perspektiv.** 85 p. Unpublished master thesis from Department of Ethnology and Archaeology. University of Copenhagen.

Fredskild, Bent [1973]: **Studies in the vegetational History of Greenland. Paleobotanical investigations of some Holocene lake and bog deposits.** *Meddelelser om Grønland*, 198(4):1-245 (Copenhagen: C. A. Reitzels Forlag).

Giddings, James L. [1964]: **The archaeology of Cape Denbigh.** 331 p. (Providense, Rhode Island: Brown University Press).

Gotfredsen, Anne Birgitte [1992]: **Nyt fra Saqqaq kulturen.** *Tusaat/Forskning i Grønland*, 1:39-45 (Copenhagen: Danish Polar Centre).

Gotfredsen, Anne Birgitte [1996]: **The Fauna of the Saqqaq Site Nipisat I, Sisimiut District, West Greenland: Preliminary results.** pp:97-110 in "The Paleo-Eskimo Cultures of Greenland - New Perspectives in Greenlandic Archaeology", editor: Bjarne Grønnow, 334 p. (Copenhagen: Danish Polar Centre).

Gotfredsen, Anne Birgitte [in press]: **Sea Bird Exploitation on Coastal Inuit sites, West and Southeast Greenland.** *International Journal of Osteoarchaeology.*

Grummesgaard-Nielsen, Stig [1995]: **Arkæologiske undersøgelser i forbindelse med anlæggelsen af en lufthavn ved Sisimiut.** Unpublished report at the National Museum of Greenland. 23 p. (Nuuk).

Grønnow, Bjarne [1988]: **Nye Perspektiver i Saqqaqforskningen.** pp:21-98 in "Palæoeskimoisk forskning i Grønland", editor: Tinna Møbjerg et al, 102 p. (Århus: Aarhus Universitets Forlag).

Grønnow, Bjarne [1994]: **Qeqertasussuk- the Archaeology of a Frozen Saqqaq Site in Disko Bugt, West Greenland.** pp:197-238 in "Treads of Arctic Prehistory. Papers in honour of William Taylor, jr., editors: David Morrison & Jean-Luc Pilon, *Archaeological Survey of Canada. Mercury Series paper* 149:1-422 (Ottawa: Museum of Civilization).

Grønnow, Bjarne [1996]: **Driftwood and Saqqaq Culture Woodworking in West Greenland.** pp:73-89 in "Cultural and social research in Greenland 95/96. Essays in Honour of Robert Petersen", editor: Birgitte Jacobsen, 332 p. (Nuuk: Ilisimatusarfik/Atuakkiorfik).

Grønnow, Bjarne & Morten Meldgaard (editors) [1991]: **Qeqertasussuk. De første mennesker i Vestgrønland.** *Tidskriftet Grønland*, 39(4-7):97-224 (Copenhagen: Det Grønlandske Selskab).

Gulløv, Hans Christian [1983]: **Fortidsminder i Nuuk Komune - Inuit kulturens bopladser.** 245 p. (Nuuk: Grønlands Nationalmuseum; Copenhagen: National Museum of Denmark).

Gulløv, Hans Christian [1986]: **Introduction.** *Arctic Anthropology*, 23(1-2):1-18 (Madison: University of Wisconsin Press).

Gulløv, Hans Christian & Hans Kapel [1988]: **De palæoeskimoiske kulturer i Nuuk Kommune.** pp:39-58 in "Palæoeskimoisk forskning i Grønland", editors: Tinna Møbjerg et al. 102 p. (Århus: Aarhus Universiitets Forlag).

Heinemeier, Jan, S. H. Nielsen & N. Rud [1993]: **Danish AMS datings, Århus 1992.** Arkæologisk udgravninger i Danmark 1992:291-304 (Copenhagen: Det Arkæologiske Nævn).

Kramer, Finn Erik [1994]: **På sporet af Forhistorien.** *Tidsskriftet Grønland*, 42(7):217-226 (Copenhagen: Det Grønlandske Selskab).

Kramer, Finn Erik [1996a]: **Akia and Nipisat I: two Saqqaq sites in Sisimiut District; West Greenland.** pp:65-96 in "The Paleo-Eskimo Cultures of Greenland - New Perspectives in Greenlandic Archaeology", editor: Bjarne Grønnow, 334 p. (Copenhagen: Danish Polar Centre).

Kramer, Finn Erik [1996b]: **The Paleo-Eskimo Cultures in Sisimiut District, West Greenland. Aspects of Chronology.** pp:39-64 in "The Paleo-Eskimo Cultures of Greenland - New Perspectives in Greenlandic Archaeology", editor: Bjarne Grønnow., 334 p. (Copenhagen: Danish Polar Centre).

Kramer, Finn & Hannah Jones [1992]: **Nipisat I - en boplads fra den yngre Saqqaq kultur**. *Tusaat/Forskning i Grønland*, 1/92:28-38 (Copenhagen: Danish Polar Centre).

Larsen, Helge & Jørge Meldgaard [1958]: **Paleo-Eskimo Cultures in Disko Bugt, West Greenland**. *Meddelelser om Grønland*, 161(2):1-75 (Copenhagen: C. A. Reitzels Forlag).

Mathiassen, Therkel [1958]: **The Sermermiut Excavations 1995**. *Meddelelser om Grønland*, 161(3):1-52 (Copenhagen: C. A. Reitzels Forlag).

Maxwell, Moreau S. [1976]: **Eastern Arctic Prehistory. Paleo-Eskimo problems**. *Memoirs of the society for American Archaeology*, 31:*-* (*).

Maxwell, Moreau S. [1985]: **Prehistory of Eastern Arctic**. 170 p. New World Archeological Record (New York: Academic Press).

Meldgaard, Jørgen [1961]: **Sarqaq-folket ved Itivnera. Nationalmuseets undersøgelser i sommeren 1960**. *Tidsskriftet Grønland*, 9(9):15-23 (Copenhagen: Det Grønlandske Selskab).

Meldgaard, Jørgen [1980]: **Den forhistoriske bebyggelse**. pp:56-59 in "Holsteinsborg. Sisimiut kommune. Natur- og kulturforhold", 88 p. (Copenhagen: Ministeriet for Grønland/Geografisk Institut).

Meldgaard, Jørgen [1983]: **Qajâ, en køkkenmødding i dybfrost. Feltrappport fra arbejdsmarken i Grønland**. *Nationalmuseets Arbejdsmark*, 1983:83-90 (Copenhagen: National Museum of Denmark).

Meldgaard, Jørgen [1991]: **Bopladsen Qajaa i Jakobshavn Isfjord. Rapport om udgravninger 1871 og 1982**. *Tidsskriftet Grønland*, 39(4-7):191-205 (Copenhagen: Det Grønlandske Selskab).

Müller-Beck, Hansjürgen [1977]: **Excavations at Umingmak on Banks Island, N.W.T. 1970 and 1973**. Preliminary report. Urgeschitliche Materialhefte no. 1, * p. (*: Universität Tübingen).

Møbjerg, Tinna [1995a]: **Sidste nyt fra Nipisat I**. *Tidsskriftet Grønland*, 43(2):45-54 (Copenhagen: Det Grønlandske Selskab).

Møbjerg, Tinna [1995b]: **Nipisat I. A Saqqaq site in Sisimiut District, West Greenland**. pp:88-94 in "Archaeological Field Work in the Northwest Territories, in 1994 and Greenland in 1993 and 1994", editor: Margeret Bertulli, Joel Berglund & Hans Lange, *Archaeology Reports*, 16:1-109 (Prince of Wales: Northern Heritage Centre).

Møbjerg, Tinna, Bjarne Grønnow & Helge Schultz-Lorentzen [1988]: **Palæoeskimoisk forskning i Grønland. Indlæg fra et symposium på Moesgård 1987**. 102 p. (Århus: Aarhus Universitetsforlag).

Møbjerg, Tinna & Joëlle Robert-Lamblin [1990]: **The settlement Ikaasap Ittiva, East Greenland. An ethno-archaeological investigation**. *Acta Archaeologica*, 60:229-262 (Copenhagen: Munkdgaard).

Møbjerg, Tinna & Stig Grummesgaard-Nielsen [1996]: **Excavations at Asummiut, West Greenland**. pp:55-59 in "Archaeological Field Work in the Northwest Territories, in 1994 and Greenland in 1993 and 1994", editor: Valovie Kenny, Margeret Bertulli, & Joel Berglund, *Archaeology Reports*, 17:1-76 (Prince of Wales: Northern Heritage Centre).

Nelson, E. W. [1889]: **The Eskimo about Bering Strait**. *Eighteenth annual report of the Bureau of American Ethnology, 1896-97*, 997 p. (Washington DC: Smithsonian Institute).

Petersen, Robert [1988]: **Palæoeskimoiske fund i Maniitsoq Kommune**. pp:59-68 in "Palæoeskimoisk forskning i Grønland", editors: Tinna Møbjerg et al., 102 p. (Århus: Aarhus Universiutets Forlag).

Stuiver, M. & G. W. Pearson [1993]: **High-precision bidecadal calibration of radiocarbon time scale, A.D. 1950-500 B.C. and 2500-6000 B.C.** *Radiocarbon*, 35(1): 1-24 (Tucson: The University of Arizona Press).

Taylor, William E. jr. [1967]: **Summary of Archaeological Field work on Banks and Victoria Islands, Arctic Canada, 1965**. *Arctic Anthropology*, 4(1):221-243 (Madison: University of Wisconsin Press).

Greenland - A Quaternary Zoological View

Jeppe Møhl

Introduction

The analysis and description of earth finds of animal bones have been a tradition at the Zoological Museum in Copenhagen for over 150 years. The first publications on the subject were by J. H. Reinhardt in the 1820s, and with his successor, Japetus Steenstrup, Quarternary Zoology came into its own.

Over the years large quantities of bone finds have been received from the Danish peat bogs and archaeological excavations. But also from Arctic regions: Greenland, Canada, and Alaska, the Zoological Museum has received bone finds in connection with archaeological excavations.

The first bone finds from Greenland originate from Qajaa, an Eskimo settlement on the south side of Jakobshavn's Isfjord on the west coast of Greenland. It was the zoologist Japetus Steenstrup who in his investigations of Danish Stone Age settlements and their piles of mollusc shells, coined the term "Køkkenmøddinger" (= kitchen middens). It was in connection with these investigations and the heated debate about them, that Steenstrup, to support his theories, sought material from the Greenlandic kitchen middens. Carl Fleisher, son of the colony leader in Jakobshavn, took this as a challenge, and with this in mind carried out the first excavation of a settlement in Greenland in 1871 (Meldgaard 1983). His interest in the archaeology and prehistory of Greenland resulted in a fine excavation and a careful description of the layers. Fleisher concludes inter alia that there are several cultural layers, with the Eskimo Stone Age lowest! In this respect he was unbelievably farsighted, as three quarters of a century would pass before the archaeologists acknowledged that there had been a Stone Age - a Paleo-Eskimo Culture preceding the present Thule Culture.

In 1953 Jørgen Meldgaard, then a trained archaeologist, took part in the excavation of the Semermiut midden at Jakobshavns Isfjord and helped to document the presence of Paleo-Eskimos in Greenland.

With Meldgaard's involvement in Arctic archaeology, and thanks to his special ability to explore especially exciting prehistoric finds, a large quantity of bone finds were sent to the Museum.

Meldgaard's father, who was a principal at Søllested School, nurtured his son's interest for prehistory, among other things by building up a large collection of geological, archaeological, and zoological objects. It is from this collection that the Zoological Museum's beautiful specimen of a Stone Age European pond tortoise (*Emys orbicularis*) originates.

As a schoolboy Meldgaard in 1943 took part in an archaeological excavation at Bukkerup on Funen. Among the bone material sent in from this excavation were 13 skeletons of extremely small Medieval cattle with a shoulder height of about 100 cm (Hatting 1993).

After Meldgaard became employed by the Department of Ethnography in the National Museum of Denmark, the real collaboration between him and the Zoological Museum began. At that time Ulrik Møhl was in charge of the daily work of identification of skeletal material.

It led to a long and warm friendship between the Meldgaard and Møhl.

It would of course take too long to name all the different excavations and bone finds which over the years have been worked up and stored at the Museum. However, to give an idea of the extent of this material, it is here relevant to point out that the Greenlandic bone material up to now comprises 540 single finds and altogether

Table 1. Species composition of excavated bones in Igloolik material, eastern arctic Canada.

Species of vertebrates	Pre-Dorset or Saqqaq	Dorset		
		Oldest Phase	Middle Phase	Youngest Phase
Mammals:				
Arctic fox (*Alopex lagopus*)	X	X	X	X
Polar bear (*Ursus maritimus*)		X	X	
Wolverine (*Gulo gulo*)			X	
Reindeer (*Rangifer tarandus*)		X	X	X
Musk ox (*Ovibos moschatus*)			X	
Walrus (*Odobenus rosmarus*)	X	X	X	X
Ringed seal (*Phoca hispida*)	X	X	X	X
Bearded seal (*P. barbata*)	X	X	X	X
Whale, unidentified				X
Birds:				
Eiders (*Sommateria* spp.)	X	X	X	X
Old-squaw (*Clangula hyemalis*)			X	X
Gulls (*Larus* spp.)			X	X

takes up about 50 m³. Everything is registered in an electronic database, and most of it is sorted and identified by species. A huge number of analyses have been carried out, of which the ¹³C/¹⁴C analyses are especially important. Also numerous articles have resulted from this work.

Examples of Meldgaard's most significant finds

During 1954, 1957, and 1965, Meldgaard worked in Arctic Canada and found an exciting Paleo-Eskimo settlement at Igloolik (Table 1).

The settlement itself lies on terrain that slopes gently towards the sea. Following the glacial period, this part of the land gradually rose, which meant that the Eskimos, who preferred settlements very close to the coast, had to move downwards towards the retreating coastline.

Therefore, the ruins are found situated down the slightly sloping terrain, with the oldest settlements above and the youngest ones farthest down. Meldgaard could therefore study and show variation in the cultures and development of hunting implements in a way never seen before.

In a letter accompanying the bone material from the 1954 Igloolik excavation, he wrote in 1955 to U. Møhl:

*"The entire material has been excavated in connection with Paleo-Eskimo ruins in the Igloolik area, (69°-*70° *North, 80°-81° West). Up to now no bone material older than* [that of] *the Thule Culture has been excavated in Arctic Canada or Greenland, and furthermore it proved possible in the Igloolik area to show two Paleo-Eskimo Cultures; the older can tentatively be called "Pre-Dorset Culture", the younger is the "Dorset Culture", wi despread in Canada and Greenland, which at Igloolik could be divided into 5 phases. The division is mainly based on the height of the ruins over the sea, as Dorset was found at heights of 8 meters to 22 meters over the sea, Pre-Dorset 37 meters to 53 meters over the sea, distributed on a richly developed system of raised beach ridges. ¹⁴C material was included for dating of the different levels, but the results are not yet available. A preliminary archaeological dating is given as: Dorset about 700-2000 years old, Pre-Dorset about 3000-5000 years old."*

The skeletal material from Igloolik is extremely interesting, but unfortunately still unpublished. In U. Møhl's list of bones (Table 1) for eksemple, he notes that: *"The main part of the material is 'seen from an edible* ["meat"] *point of view' very clearly walrus and seals, but fox and eiders are found in conspicuous numbers."*

At the excavation of a Dorset settlement on Inglefield Land, North Greenland, in 1996, well preserved faunal material was obtained with a species composition like that of the material from Igloolik

Table 2. Vertebrate species identified in excavations at Itinnera, Inner Godthåbsfjord, West Greenland. Number of bone fragments that could be accurately identified, with total numbers of fragments for Arctic fox, seals, reindeer and birds.

Mammals

Arctic fox.. 6

    Harp seal (*Phoca groenlandica*).. 14
    Bearded seal... 2
    Unidentified seals.. 110
        Total number of seal bones... 126

Reindeer 6,140

Birds

Cormorant (*Phalacrocorax carbo*).. 1
Arctic eider (*Somateria mollisima borealis*) 45
Glaucous gull (*Larus hyperboreus*).. 1
Iceland gull (*L. glaucoides*) 3
Brünnich's murre (*Uria lomvia*) 56
Great auk (*Pinguinus impennis*).. 6
Unidentified birds 70
Total number of bird bones 182

Of 6,458 fragments, the 6,140 reindeer bones made up ca. 95%, seal bones only 2%, bird bones 3%.

Itinnera, an inland Paleo-Eskimo reindeer hunting ground (95% reindeer) at the inner of the Godthåbsfjord, excavated 1960, Jørgen Meldgaard, dated to 1400±1200 B.C. (Fig. 1, Table 2).

Based on the studies of teeth in the lower jaws of reindeer it can be shown that the settlement was seasonal, used only from late June to early August.

Furthermore, the bone material revealed that the marrow-splitting technique used by these Saqqaq people had a greater similarity with European reindeer hunting grounds than with those of the subsequent Thule Culture (Møhl 1972).

The mammals and birds identified in the material from Itinnera, together with the total number of identified bones of each species, are listed in Table 2.

From a zoological point of view it is interesting to note that the large reindeer material originates exclusively from the "little caribou" (the European reindeer, *Rangifer tarandus pearyi*) which weighs only half as much as the present-day, large Greenland reindeer (the Greenland caribou, *R. t. groenlandicus*; Meldgaard 1986). Fig. 1 shows the different parts of the skeleton from which the excavated bone fragments originate.

Among the remains of the few other animal species which occur in the faunal material were bones of the Great Auk, which earlier was known only from a few finds in the Thule Culture (Meldgaard 1988).

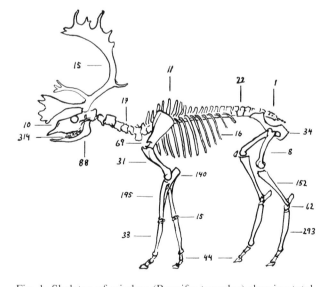

Fig. 1: Skeleton of reindeer (Rangifer tarandus) showing total number of bone fragments found in excavations at Itinnera, West Greenland. Right and left bones of paired structures (for example ribs, legs) were not differentiated.

Fig. 2: Fig. 2. Qajaa, West Greenland, July 1982. View of the settlement of Qajaa (foreground) looking north. Deposits of the Paleo-Eskimo Period extend for about 50 m along the coast, as can be seen in the foreground of the photo. (Photo by Jeppe Møhl).

Qajaa. An Inuit settlement with Saqqaq, Dorset, and Thule Cultures in the Jakobshavns Isfjord, excavated 1982 by Jørgen Meldgaard, oldest culture layers dated to 1975±80 B.C. (Fig. 2, Fig. 3; Table 3).

Qajaa, a typical Eskimo seal-hunting ground with a massive midden sealed by permafrost, gave possibilities for exciting, well preserved organic finds. An aerial view of the site is shown in Fig. 2.

During the summer's work it soon became apparent that Qajaa offered something most unusual about Greenland's first population. The permafrozen midden-layer up to 1.20 m thick, contained well preserved deposits from the Saqqaq Period, with a wealth of bones from the prey, together with implements of wood and bone. Especially striking were the finds of fine and beautifully carved walrus tusk harpoon heads, shafted awls and knives, together with wooden parts of various harpoon shafts, bows and arrows and much more. Earlier finds from the Saqqaq Period had up to then only yielded very thin layers in which organic materials were lacking. As a result implements of wood and bone were, therefore, essentially unknown (Meldgaard 1983). The bone material is extremely interesting and elucidates very clearly the faunal composition of this period (Fig. 3, Table 3).

Table 3 shows for the first time the species richness in the faunal material formed by Greenland's first inhabitants.

A more simplified version is given in Fig. 3, showing which species have been crucial to these Saqqaq people in precisely this part of Greenland. Moreover, for the first time the dog is shown from this earliest Eskimo culture in Greenland (Møhl 1986).

Among the excavators was Helge Larsen, who despite risking gangrene in his feet worked with unbelievably good humor and energy:

He brought forth from the frozen earth objects up to then unknown from Greenland's oldest Paleo-Eskimo hunting community, the Saqqaq Culture. "Old Helge's" unusual vitality and willingness to tell about similar experiences from the "cradle" of the Eskimo Culture in Alaska inspired and enthused all of us during this unusual excavation.

Tabel 3. Vertebrate species identified from the Saqqaq horizon, Qajaa site, West Greenland.

Species of vertebrates	No of bones or bone fragments
Mammals, domestic:	
Dog (*Canis familiaris*)	18
Mammals, wild:	
Arctic hare (*Lepus arcticus*)	1
Arctic fox	22
Reindeer	10
Harbor seal (*Phoca vitulina*)	1
Ringed seal	119
Harp seal (*Pagophilus groenlandicus*)	339
Seals, unidentified (ringed + harp seals)	13,491
Bearded seal (*Erignathus barbatus*)	1
Narwhal (*Monodon monoceros*)	2
Whales, unidentified	1
Birds:	
Fulmar (*Fulmarus glacialis*)	15
Eiders (*Sommateria* spp.)	76
White-fronted goose (*Anser albifrons*)	1
Ptarmigan (*Lagopus mutus*)	32
Glaucous gull + Iceland gull	775
Black-legged kittiwake (*Rissa tridactyla*)	4
Dovekie (*Plotus alle*)	2
Brünnich's murre	82
Black guillemot (*Cepphus grylle*)	35
Raven (*Corvus corax*)	16
Birds, unidentified	108
	Total 15,151

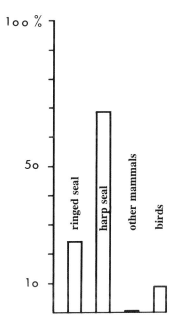

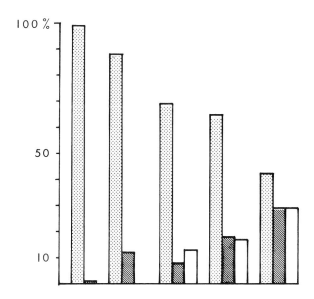

Fig. 3. Qajaa, West Greenland. Relative abundance of bone fragments of ringed seal, harp seal, other mammals, and birds. See also Table 3.

Fig. 4. Relative abundance of bone fragments of the three dominant mammal types (seals, reindeer and domestic animals: dogs, pigs, sheep, goats, cows, horses) found in excavations at five different sites in West Greenland.

The Inuit-Norse Project 1976-1977. Inner Godthåbs-fjord, Jørgen Meldgaard.

Besides the different Eskimo cultures' presence in the Arctic, the fate of the early Norsemen has also had Meldgaard's attention. On several occasions his trowel has uncovered new aspects of these Vikings, hunters, and farmers from the Far North.

The first encounter between the Eskimo and the Norse Cultures was the subject of a very large investigation started by Meldgaard in 1976. Three Norse settlements and two Eskimo ones were chosen as the objects of the summer's investigations. There were participants from Denmark, Greenland, Norway, Canada, and the U.S.A. The excavations were arranged as workshops. This form of excavating, with many people with very different backgrounds, was extremely productive, both of energy to dig and of scientific ideas and discussions. The main objective of this summer's investigations was to throw light on the question of the Norsemen's disappearance from the Western Settlement at the same time as the arrival of the Eskimo, and the possible cultural interactions between them. Unfortunately, the attempts to excavate the Eskimo sites, which were contemporary with the Norsemen's last occurrence there, did not succeed.

Lack of Eskimo sites from this period is perhaps due to the isostatic movements in the area, so that sites, then located close to the coast, have simply sunk into the sea. Nevertheless, the enormous material of objects and fauna which was unearthed that summer contributes a great deal to a further understanding of and debate about two so different cultures.

As can be seen in Fig. 4, the two Eskimo sites, Umi-ivik and Tuperluk, are typical seal-hunters' sites with a certain input from reindeer. The three Norse settlements have also utilized the seal resources to a marked degree, but, understandably, these resources were less important for the farms further inland (Møhl 1982).

Conclusions

The results of these many bone analyses are still growing, and the picture of the past continues to become more and more refined. The absence or presence of a given animal species or the relationships between them can tell much about the climate and utilization of resources in earlier times. Seasons can often be determined with reasonable certainty through showing the presence of certain species or by studying the growth rings in mammal teeth. ^{14}C analyses of bones have given numerous datings which have made important contributions to dating the different finds. Other isotope analyses (^{13}C and ^{15}N) of bones are just beginning and appear to be a further illumination of the diet of the period investigated.

Acknowledgements

Dr. Mary E. Petersen, Zoological Museum, University of Copenhagen, translated the manuscript to English and provided helpful discussion of the text.

Jeppe Møhl, Zoological Museum, University of Copenhagen, Universitetsparken 15, DK-2100 Copenhagen Ø, Denmark

References

Hatting, Tove [1993]: **Oksefund fra Bukkerup og Turup.** *Fynske Minder*, 1993:93-98 (*: *).

Meldgaard, Jørgen [1983]: **Qajaa, en køkkenmødding i dybfrost.** *Nationalmuseets Arbejdsmark*, 1983:83-96 (Copenhagen: National MUseum of DEnmark).

Meldgaard, Morten [1986]: **The Greenland caribou - zoogeography, taxonomy, and population dynamics.** *Meddelelser om Grønland, Bioscience*, 20:3-88 (Copenhagen: The Commission for Scientofic Research of Greenland).

Meldgaard, Morten [1988]: **The Great Auk, Pinguinus impennis (L.) in Greenland.** *Historical Biology*, 1:145-178 (London: Harwood Academy).

Møhl, Jeppe [1982]: **Ressourceudnyttelse fra norrøne og eskimoiske affaldslag belyst gennem knoglemateri-alet.** *Tidsskriftet Grønland*, 30(8-9):286-295 (Copenhagen: The Greenland Society).

Møhl, Jeppe [1986]: **Dog remains from a Paleoeskimo settlement in West Greenland.** *Artic Anthropology*, 23(1-2):81-89 (Madison: University of Wisconsin).

Møhl, Ulriuk [1972]: **Animal bones from Itinnera, West Greenland.** *Meddelelser om Grønland*, 121(6):1-22 (Copenhagen: C. A. Reitzels Forlag).

On "smell of forest" in the Greenlandic Myths and Legends

Robert Petersen

You would need a more sensitive olfactory organ than a butterfly's to be able to smell the forest in treeless Greenland. Jørgen Meldgaard, who in the High Arctic Alarnerk/Alarniq could sense the "scent of forest" (Meldgaard 1955:171, 1962:75), was closer to the forest than if he were in Greenland.

Some archaeological surprises

Meldgaard's statements were due to some finds from early Canadian Dorset, where many found implements and house utensils had different shapes and sizes and were made from other materials than the almost simultaneous Pre-Dorset finds from the same area (Meldgaard 1960b, 1962). It was, in fact, a break with tradition.

As I may evaluate, Meldgaard's statements were based on, among other things, soapstone dishes with a rectangular ground plane that might indicate former materials such as wood or birch bark, unfortunately perishable materials. I suppose that artifacts of imperishable material copied from original ones of perishable material may sometimes give archaeologists interpretation problems, especially when they are found in another area.

Bone needles pointed at both ends, with flattened cross section, and with oblong, dug out eyes (Meldgaard 1962:93) are a typological mutation, and in fact, they indicate that a Dorset woman had to hold her needle in a different way than a Pre-Dorset woman (see page 214). The way of digging out holes resembles the Maritime Archaic tradition from Labrador 7500 B.C. - 3000 B.C. (compare Tuck 1976:27, 37, 43, illustrations), even if the time gap between Maritime Archaic and Dorset was not closed. Another resemblance is found in the use of red ochre, probably for ritual purposes (Meldgaard 1959:18;

Tuck 1976:23). These facts probably indicate contacts towards the south. One is reminded of Beothuck "red indians", who might have shared Newfoundland with the Dorset people, at least during part of their stay there (compare Tuck 1976:70). In this regard we might also note that the prehistory of the Beothuck was probably longer than the 1000 years previously estimated (Tuck 1976:64). Despite the limited evidence, it is reasonable to assume that the Beothuck Culture was a branch of development from Maritime Archaic. Meldgaard himself pointed to the Archaic and Woodland Cultures as possible origins of the peculiarities of the Dorset Culture within an Eskimo context (Meldgaard 1962:75).

The rapid change of material culture, from late Pre-Dorset to early Dorset, can undoubtedly be explained by the local development. Still, I miss some kind of a catalyst that would explain the abruptness of the changes. Furthermore, I feel the recent literature on Dorset Culture lacks the aforementioned "smell of forest". The suddenness of the development might indicate that there were cultural influences from several sides at the same time. I do not intend to raise doubts about the fact that the basic roots of Iglulik Dorset stem from Iglulik Pre-Dorset. But I do feel that a theory of rapid, local cultural development from Pre-Dorset is not a sufficient explanation. Regrettably, this common insufficient interpretation is not necessarily due to lack of found artifacts, but rather that some finds were left out of the leading theories.

While both Pre-Dorset and Thule migrated eastward in warm climatic periods, it is worth remembering that the most simple migrations caused by climatic changes, go in the south-north direction, also in the eastern part of Canada. In fact, the Iglulik-Dorset expanded either southward or northward from their nuclear area several times (Meldgaard 1986:19-20).

Some examples of factors in cultural change

1. **Changed conditions:** such as climatic change or migration to new environments.
2. **Specialization:** Compare the difference between harpoon heads used for walrus hunting and those used for narwhals. Thus, specialized tools can introduce new functional elements outside the area for which they were first created.
3. **Material:** Utilization of a new material or lack of traditionally used materials, for example the earlier lack of wood in Thule. Qillarsuaq's groups used the qarmat in Thule until the lack of wood forced them to adopt the local tradition.
4. **Contact with people with other traditions:** The social position of the two groups may be a more decisive factor in determining the extent of cultural change resulting from an encounter than the relative size of the groups. How many original cultural elements survive the cultural change may also depend on this. (Compare Malmberg 1965:169). Furthermore, it is accepted that the presence of another language in one's home area strengthens the speed of a process of linguistic change. Similar observations may be valid for other cultural elements beyond the linguistic ones. Not least the speed of cultural change may be influenced by the presence of a group with other traditions.
5. **Fashion:** Why did long-tailed garments once become common in Arctic Canada? And: Why did the Qillarsuaq-group adopt a short-tailed cut when they came to Thule? It was hardly due to the availability of material alone.

On some peculiarities in the Greenlandic folklore

Not only within archaeology, but also in other areas of cultural history, do we find peculiarities which are difficult to explain. To my knowledge, these matters were not often included in the discussion of Dorset questions.

As a starting point, I want to postulate that Greenland holds some traditions that deviate from the rest of the eastern Thule Culture area. These deviations emerge in the stories about the encounters between Inuit and *Tornit* (the Greenlandic plural of Tuneq) or *Tuniit* (the Canadian plural of Tuniq). These stories are rather detailed and so consistent that I am willing to regard them as seriously as excavated archaeological finds in context. I am not thinking of isolated accidental things that are as difficult to deal with as loose surface finds. I am thinking of "finds" that are part of a larger pattern. I am thinking of things

that I have to regard as being older than the Thule Culture in Greenland. If this is true, it would indicate that the influence from Dorset Culture upon Greenlandic traditions may be greater than we imagined. The only alternative I see is to deny them.

The problem that emerges is that changes in the Dorset ornamentation pattern only appeared in Meldgaard's phase III (Meldgaard 1955:169-172, 175). If we presume that these ornamental patterns had magical significance, they were not adopted, just because somebody had seen them somewhere. They were developed in one area together with their magical explanations, and others had to learn their symbolic content, before they adopted them along with their ideological background (H. C. Petersen 1986:72, 74, note 19).

One of the concepts that attracted my attention was the West- and East Greenlandic view of deranged persons as cannibals (R. Petersen 1964:78). In East Greenlandic stories deranged persons are described as being in an early stage of cannibalism (compare Sandgreen 1987:224), and in several West Greenlandic legends insane persons turn into cannibals (Rink 1866:70-73, 1871:17-22). Also, historical incidents have been recorded in which insane persons were killed or buried alive because they threatened to eat their housemates (compare Gad 1974:166). In several stories it was mentioned that cannibals ate their house fellows or claimed to have done so - even if the housemates had, in fact, fled in time (Rink 1866:72).

In other words, it was thought that insane persons were cannibals, and that starvation cannibals would turn insane. In these stories a person turned insane after having been served meat rubbed with human fat from a grave. These stories deal with a non-ceremonial cannibalism (R. Petersen 1990:100). This view which connected insanity with cannibalism was missing among the Inughuit (Polar-Eskimos) and in eastern Arctic Canada. Another interesting thing in this context is that the development of the illness among different groups suited the local perception of insanity. But despite the fact that "piblortok", *pillerortoq/perlerortoq* in Thule, lacked cannibalistic contents, there may be an etymological connection, as *perlertoq* means 'one starved to death'. Thus, a basic connection between insanity and starvation may exist.

In fact, it is among the boreal Indians that we again find the connection between insanity and cannibalism. Here a human windigo/witiko was considered insane and cannibal at the same time. There were stories of people, who in a state of insanity bit through their tongue, and who were therefore feared to be cannibals, and were killed. The insane person saw his/her fellows as beavers (compare Landers 1938:37). There is similarly a Greenlandic story about an insane man who saw his house fellows as amulets (Nielsen 1955:200; H. Lynge 1955:58). A common trait is that the house fellows were seen as something other than human beings.

Greenlandic stories about *Tornit* may be divided into two groups. In one group Tornit are described - like other inland dwellers - as a spirit people with strong magical abilities. They are described with few details. Instead, the stories focus on their gigantic size and supernatural abilities. In the other group of stories, there are detailed narratives of inland human beings without bow and arrows, without dogs, and maybe without vessels. They had houses with a *paaq*, an entrance passage without a cold trap (K. Lynge 1978:105), and with a large smoke hold at the top of the house. It was through a similar hole that people peeped into the house (Rasmussen 1924:162). Besides, Tornit spoke an understandable, but phonetically peculiar language. There is no doubt that the legends tell about an Eskimo dialect, which would be difficult for some local Inuit to understand.

If we look at the legend of *Aqissiaq* (Rasmussen 1924:101-133; K. Lynge 1978:78-119), it tells about Inuit and Tornit in Greenland. In Greenland it is a narrative about human beings and their experiences, but its contents are unique among the Greenlandic legends. The environment, the games, etc. are those of Greenland. But even if the animals are those of Greenland, they remind me of animals in many Indian myths: raven, fox, bear, halibut, whale, salmon species, and one gigantic "worm", known in Greenland as a mythical animal. In fact, they occur in natural context, but the three last mentioned animals, plus one kayaker, killed by Aqissiaq, - whose name means 'Young ptarmigan' - remind me of the four figures killed by the Thunderbird: a gigantic salmon, a whale, a war canoe, and various manifestations of a serpent that also appear in its own shape - and only in this way they have something to do with each other in the legend of Aqissiaq.

In the legend, the whale was lured up a river with a magic song normally used for brook trout, and according to some versions all these animals were cut into two pieces lengthwise, in a left and right half like some details in the serpent myths and pictures as part of dualistic cosmology (Locher 1932). It is also peculiar that in the Aqissiaq legend, travel directions - the four cardinal points - are mentioned in connection with Aqissiaq's adventure with the four beings from the underworld. In those adventures, Aqissiaq first climbed an enormous mountain, and then went down a deep slope, that in the worm motif is edged with dead human bodies (B. Lynge 1951:97).

It was the way to the Land of the Dead in the Underworld. Thus, the Aqissiaq legend contained elements of a cosmological myth with an Upperworld, this world, and an Underworld. A line from this world to the Underworld can for example take the shape of a fishing line of baleen strips tied together (Rasmussen 1924:112).

Even if the story itself is Greenlandic, the scenery, in fact, is different from that of the Inuit as we are accustomed to seeing it.

Another peculiarity of the Aqissiaq legend is its use of repetition. As I have already pointed out, the four cardinal points were mentioned in connection with Aqissiaq's encounter with the four beings from the Underworld. A lot of the actions happen in four stages, or are repeated so that they occur four times, eight times, twelve times etc. Some peculiar expressions are also repeated. For instance, the phrase *"he looked back over his shoulder"* occurred 8 times, and *"when he had said this, he then said"* occurred 32 times.

Repeated expressions occurred either 8, 12, 16, 20, 28, or 32 times. It is probably no accident when a certain act of revenge in one variation of the legend is committed by three persons in four stages (Rasmussen 1924:106), and in another variation by four persons in three stages (Anonymous 1861:30). This use of numbers is non-Greenlandic and the number four is not a common element in Greenlandic or any other Thule Culture legends. Inuit do not play with numbers in this way. Many other elements of Indian cosmology occur in this legend which are otherwise unknown in the Thule Culture area.

If we refuse to accept this as accident, we have to find parallel examples elsewhere, and we find them in Indian areas, the best evidence occurring among the Northwest Coast Indians. There we find cosmological myths with an Upperworld, this world, and an Underworld. We find a Thunderbird that killed four central Underworld figures, namely a serpent that my appear as a salmon, a whale, and a war canoe (compare Locher 1932). We also find the four cardinal points, the number four, and all kinds of multiples of four. In this connection the number four has a basic importance. There are elements in these Indian cosmological myths that are missing in the story of Aqissiaq, and probably, it was necessary to leave them out. The thunderbird killed the four figures by his bow and arrows, but Aqissiaq had to stab them with a spear, harpoon them, or kill them with a stone.

In several Indian legends we find a ladder from a lower world to a higher one. Aqissiaq, being a Tuneq, could not use it, so he had to be our first alpinist, but a line from this world to the Underworld made of baleen strips tied together occurs, and we find the world slope even five times, four times in connection with Aqissiaq's fight with the four central Underworld figures, the fifth being a counter-action in which Aqissiaq's life was brought into serious danger by a blizzard that turned anti-clockwise. The translation of this cosmological myth obvious passed through the Dorset Culture.

The problem of the cosmological myth and the holy number four is rather complex. It is probably based on the axes of the daily and yearly movements of the sun. It is clearly a cosmological idea from the geographical zone where the sun rises and sets every day, and goes from east to west via the south. In Greenland it is reduced to only the yearly axis of the sun, south and north, probably because the migration route from Canada to Greenland went through the High Arctic, where the sun could be seen both night and day for months, and correspondingly, was below the horizon during an equivalent period of time in the winter. Thus, Indian prayers were said four times, once towards each cardinal point, while the Greenlandic spells were said only twice, towards the south and the north.

Another serious problem is that suiting myth cycle probably had disappeared from the eastern boreal area of North America, where contact with the roots of Dorset Culture was possible. According to Hatt's theories, myth cycles of older layers were replaced in those parts of North America by Asiatic motifs (Hatt 1949). That must have been the case with this kind of cosmological myth cycle in the boreal area. I cannot see another explanation, even if it were a simplified model, or the myth of Aqissiaq is impossible in Greenland. So, we lack real proof, but have a lot of strong presumptions.

As we lack variations of the Aqissiaq legend/myth among the Inuit west of Greenland, we might, of course, regard this legend as an impossible story. The way from Greenland to the Indian cosmology is Blocked by Inuit originated from the Thule Culture, and a time gap of about 2000 years. In fact, it is impossible, in view of the prehistory, which shows no direct influence from Dorset on to Thule Culture. It does not fit into current views of Greenland's prehistory, yet it cannot be explained away.

The details I mentioned, both the cosmological elements and the play with numbers, are as real as archaeological typological elements. When we are convinced that the peculiarities in this legend are not accidental traits, then it will be necessary to give Greenland's prehistory a reinterpretation. It is my hope that archaeologists will include these aspects when reevaluating the Dorset problem.

The details brought up in this paper need not necessarily disturb the archaeological findings, but they may change the interpretations. In fact, the *"smell of forest"* clings to some artifacts from Alarniq in 1954 and some from Qalirusiq and Kapuivik from 1957. They too cannot be explained away.

Aqissiaq himself must be allowed to have the final words. When an old man got a whale to swim up a river by singing a magic song, Aqissiaq said: *"This is hard to believe!"*. Indeed, it is hard to believe it. Aqissiaq said these words *four* times.

Robert Petersen, emeritus professor of Eskimology, Ilisimatusarfig/University of Greenland, Nuuk, Greenland.

Photos: Jørgen Meldgaard & Robert Petersen, 31 July 1957.

A smell of forest?

Robert Petersen and Jørgen Meldgaard carried out field-work in the Iglulik area, Arctic Canada, in the summer of 1957. The main purpose was excavations of Dorset and Pre-Dorset sites - supplemented with collection of legends about the prehistoric poeple: the Tuniit/Tornit.

The "smell of forest", which Jørgen Meldgaard perceived in the artifacts of early Dorset Culture, was thinned and very faint during the nine days and nights they spent drifting in the ice of Fox Basin in an attempt to reach the Kapuivik settlement on Jens Munk Island.

However, Robert Petersen may have felt a scent of Indians - supporting speculations about contacts towards South - intensified by studying the Tuniit stories in Knud Rasmussen's book "Intellectual Culture of the Iglulik Eskimos" - as documented in these photographs.

References

Anonymous [1861]: **Kalâdlit Okalluktualiait** II. Noungme.

Bugge, Aage & Augustinus Lynge [1951]: **Atuainiutitât** II. 254 p.(Nûk: Grønlandsdepartementip naqitertitai).

Gad, Finn [1974]: **Fire detailkomplekser i Grønlands historie.** 283 p. (Copenhagen: Nyt Nordisk Forlag, Arnold Busch).

Hatt, Gudmund [1949]: **Asiatic Influence in American Folklore.** *Historisk-Filologiske Meddelelser,* 31(6):1-122 (Copenhagen: Kgl. danske videnskabernes Selskabs).

Landes, Ruth [1938]: **Ojibwa Woman.** * p. (New York: Columbia University Press).

Locher, G. W. [1932]: **The Serpent in the Kwakiutl Religion.** * p. (Leiden: Rijksuniversität Leiden).

Lynge, Bendt [1951]: **Aqigssiap oqalugtuai.** pp:91-97 in "Atuainiutitât II", editors: Bugge & Lynge, 254 p. (Nûk: Grønlandsdepartementip naqitertitai).

Lynge, Hans [1955]: **Inegpait.** *Meddelelser om Grønland,* 90(2):1-187 (Copenhagen: C. A. Reitzels Forlag).

Lynge, Kristoffer [1978]: **Kalâtdlit oqalugtuait oqalualâvilo** I-III. 360 p. (Nûk: Det grønlandske Forlag).

Malmberg, Bertil [1965]: **Sproget og mennesket.** 197 p. (Copenhagen: J. H. Schultz Forlag).

Meldgaard, Jørgen [1955]: **Dorset Kulturen. Den Dansk-Amerikanske Ekspedition til Arktisk Canada 1954.** *Kuml,* 1955:158-177 (Århus: Jysk Arkæologisk Selskab).

Meldgaard, Jørgen [1959]: **Eskimo Skulptur.** 48 p. (Copenhagen: J. H. Schultz Forlag).

Meldgaard, Jørgen [1960a]: **Prehistoric Culture Sequences in Eastern Arctic Elucidated by Stratified Sites at Igloolik.** pp:588-595 in "Selected Papers of the Fifth International Congress of Anthropological and Ethnological Sciences 1956", editor: Anthony F. C. Wallace, * p. (Philadelphia: University of Pennsylvania Press).

Meldgaard, Jørgen [1960b]: **Origin and Evolution of Eskimo Cultures in the Eastern Arctic.** *Canadian Geographical Journal,* 60(2):64-75 (Montreal).

Meldgaard, Jørgen [1962]: **On Formative Period of the Dorset Culture.** *Technical Paper,* 11:92-95 (Montreal: Arctic Institute of North America).

Meldgaard, Jørgen [1977]: **Prehistoric Cultures in Greenland. Discontinuities in a Marginal Area.** pp:19-52 in "Continuity and Discontinuity in the Inuit Cultures of Greenland", Proceedings from Danish-Netherland Symposium 1976, editors: Hans P. Kylstra & Lies H. Liefferink, 125 p. (Groningen: Arctic Center, University of Groningen).

Meldgaard, Jørgen [1986]: **Dorset-Kulturen - udviklingstendenser og afbrydelser.** pp:15-32 in "Vort sprog - vor kultur". Foredrag fra symposium afholdt i Nuuk oktober 1981 arrangeret af Ilisimatusarfik og Kalaallit Nunaata Katersugaasivia. 220 p. (Nuuk). (In Greenlandic 1986).

Nielsen, Martin [1955]: **Sîmuk qaersormio.** *Avangnâmioq,* 42:200-206 (Qeqertarssuaq: Avangnäta naqiterivia).

Petersen, H. C. [1986]: **Indtryk fra forskellige grønlandske indsamlingsstudier omkring ressourceudnyttelse og kulturkontakter.** pp:63-76 in "Vort sprog - vor kultur", editors: Robert Petersen & Rischel, 220 p. (Nuuk: Ilisimatusarfik & Kalaalit Nunaata Katersugaasivia).

Petersen, Robert [1964]: **The Greenland Tupilak.** *Folk,* 6(2):73-102 (Copenhagen: Danish Ethnographical Society).

Petersen, Robert [1990]: **On the Material Element in the Supernatural Aspect of the Former Greenlandic Religion.** *Temenos,* 26:95-103 (Helsinki: Finnish Society for the Study of Comparative Religion).

Rasmussen, Knud [1924]: **Myter og sagn fra Grønland II: Vestgrønland.** 356 p. (Copenhagen: Gyldendalske Boghandel Nordisk Forlag).

Rink, Hinrich J. [1866-1871]: **Eskimoiske Eventyr og Sagn I-II.** 376 p, & 259 p. (Copenhagen: C. A. Reitzels Forlag).

Sandgreen, Otto [1987]: **Øje for øje, tand for tand.** 457 p. (Bagsværd: Otto Sandgreens Forlag).

Tuck, James A. [1976]: **Newfoundland and Labrador Prehistory.** 127 p. (Ottawa: National Museum of Man).

L'Importance Archéologique de la Région de Kangirsujuaq au Nunavik (Arctique québécois): Un centre chamanique dorsétien?

Patrick Plumet

L'intérêt archéologique de la région de Kangirsujuaq fut signalé pour la première fois par l'ethnologue Bernard Saladin d'Anglure au début des années soixante. Il venait d'y découvrir les seuls pétroglyphes dorsétiens connus jusqu'à maintenant. Il nota également la présence de nombreux habitats anciens, attribués aux Tunnit, où il ramassa en surface quelques objets, surtout dorsétiens (Saladin d'Anglure 1962; Taylor 1963).

Chargé d'enseignement au Département d'anthropologie de l'Université de Montréal en 1966-1967, Saladin d'Anglure incita l'un de ses étudiants, Georges Barré, à entreprendre pour sa maîtrise une reconnaissance archéologique préliminaire de la région. La préhistoire de l'Arctique québécois était alors très peu connue.

Cette reconnaissance eut lieu au cours de l'été 1967, mais en raison des conditions climatiques difficiles, Barré ne put accéder aux pétroglyphes. Il pratiqua des sondages restreints assortis de relevés stratigraphiques et de schéma topographiques dans quelques-uns des sites indiqués par Saladin d'Anglure.

Ce travail révéla l'importance de l'occupation paléo-esquimaude et néo-esquimaude. Par la suite, en 1977 et en 1979, lors d'une reconnaissance générale de la rive sud du détroit d'Hudson effectuée dans le cadre du programme de recherche Tuvaaluk[1], cette importance se confirma et l'originalité de certains sites par rapport à ceux de l'Ungava occidental apparut. Mais il devint aussi manifeste que, depuis leur découverte, les pétroglyphes subissaient des dégradations dues à l'homme (voir les photos).

Deux projets d'opérations de sauvetage et de mise en valeur, l'un purement québécois, soumis dès 1978, l'autre québéco-danois, ébauché en 1994, n'aboutirent pas[2]. Pourtant entre les deux projets, le développement du tourisme, et en particulier des croisières qui déposent leurs clients sur le principal site de pétroglyphes, contribue à l'accélération des dégradations. Celles-ci ont commencé à inquiéter des spécialistes de l'Arctique aussi bien aux États-Unis qu'au Danemark. De plus, depuis 1980, aucune recherche thématique importante n'a été entreprise dans cette région, pourtant l'une des plus riches de l'Arctique québécois[3]. Puisse cet article, écrit en hommage au spécialiste du Paléo-esquimau et de l'art qu'est Jørgen Meldgaard, inciter une équipe de recherche, éventuellement internationale, à travailler dans la région de Kangirsujuaq. Elle pourrait y examiner l'opportunité de faire classer les sites contenant des pétroglyphes, afin de leur assurer à la fois une meilleure protection et un minimum de mise en valeur.

Explorations et données ethnohistoriques
(Carte 1)

En 1884, la Première expédition canadienne de la baie d'Hudson déposa Robert Frederik Stupart dans la baie qui devait porter son nom, juste au sud du cap du Prince de Galles. Il était chargé des relevés météorologiques et de l'observation des glaces. L'année suivante, la seconde expédition du même nom amena Frank F. Payne, qui prit la relève de Stupart. Chacun d'eux publia une description des Inuit de la région (Stupart 1887; Payne 1889).

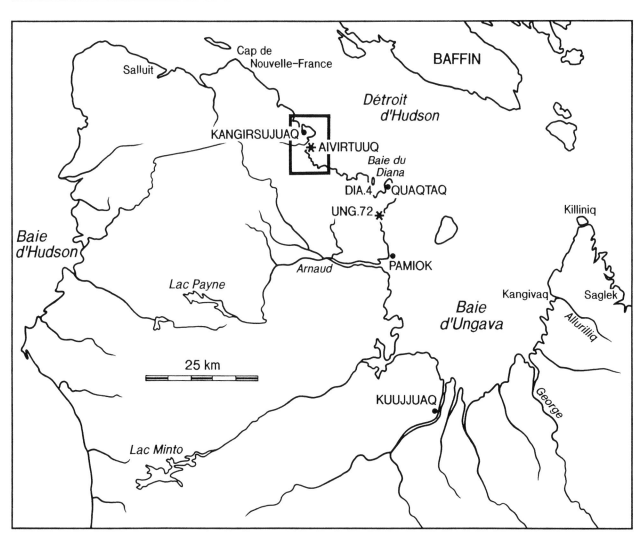

Carte 1: Carte générale de l'Arctique québécois et emplacement des principales localités mentionnées dans le texte.

C'est le géologue Albert P. Low qui donna le nom de Wakeham à la baie où se trouve le village inuit de Kangirsujuaq. Au cours de l'expédition canadienne de 1897 dans le détroit d'Hudson, dirigée par William Wakeham, Low avait exploré le secteur de côte compris entre Douglas Harbour, 50 km au nord-ouest sur la rive sud du détroit, et le George, au fond de la baie d'Ungava. Le navire de l'expédition, le *Diana,* devait laisser son nom à une autre baie beaucoup plus grande, *Tuvaaluk* pour les Inuit, qui s'ouvre juste à l'ouest de la baie d'Ungava. La présence de sites archéologiques dans cette baie fut également signalée par Saladin d'Anglure, qui tenta de détourner les femmes de Quaqtaq d'une entreprise de pillage collectif d'un ancien village thuléen à Opingivik (Site DIA. 7). Ses observations orientèrent les recherches que j'y entrepris à partir de 1968[4]. Wakeham Bay fut ensuite francisé en *Maricourt* par les Québécois, avant que le nom inuit ne soit devenu officiel vers 1980.

Dès la fin du 18e siècle, Jens Haven avait recueilli des renseignements sur cette région auprès d'Inuit de la baie d'Ungava qui connaissaient la côte depuis Saglek, au Labrador, jusqu' # à la baie de Stupart, juste au sud du cap *Prince of Wales* près de Kangirsujuaq (Carte 1, Haven 1973a, 1973b, in Taylor 1975:270). *Tuaq,* c'est-à-dire Tuvaaluk, la baie du Diana, et *Aiviktok,* aujourd'hui transcrit Aivirtuuq (le lieu où il y a beaucoup de morses), situé à la pointe Frontenac, environ 18 km au sud du cap *Prince of Wales,* étaient deux localités comptant respectivement 10 et 30 iglous de neige selon ces informateurs. Les autres localités pour lesquelles le nombre d'habitations était indiqué sont toutes autour de la baie d'Ungava. Elles ne comprenaient pas plus de 10 iglous de neige, sauf "Kangivaq" sur la côte est, qui est sans doute la région du cap Qarmait (site archéologique UNG.3 dans Plumet & Gangloff 1990) et d'une île proche de l'embouchure de l'Allurillik (ou Alluviaq). Une maison d'hiver et 20 iglous de neige y sont signalés. G. Taylor (Plumet & Gangloff 1990:270 & table 1) évalue la population totale d'Aivirtuuq, qu'il estime répartie sur 30 km de côte, à 300 personnes, soit 100 de plus que dans les

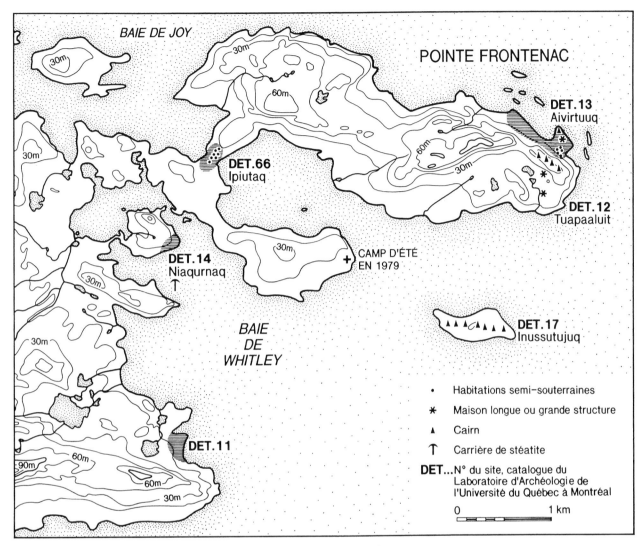

Carte 2: La région d'Aivirtuuq et de la pointe Frontenac, au sud de Kangirsujuaq.

localités les plus peuplées de l'Ungava. Au 18e siècle, la région s'étendant au sud de Kangirsujuaq aurait donc été le plus gros centre de peuplement à la fois du Labrador, de l'Ungava et de la partie sud-est du détroit d'Hudson (à l'est du cap de Nouvelle-France) et l'un des trois secteurs de côte le plus densément occupé (10 personnes au mille, soit 6,25 au kilomètre). Par ailleurs Tuvaaluk et Aivirtuuq furent, toujours selon Haven (1773b, cité par J. G. Taylor 1975), des lieux de chasse à la baleine exceptionnels, Aivirtuuq étant même *the most famous place in all Labrador for whales*!

Les vestiges archéologiques
(Cartes 2, 3 et 4)

Les vestiges archéologiques les plus nombreux et les plus importants sont concentrés entre le cap du Prince de Galles, au nord, et la pointe Bégon, au sud, éloignés l'un de l'autre d'une quarantaine de kilomètres à vol d'oiseau. Ces vestiges sont répartis dans les baies de Joy et de Whitley que séparent le cap Frontenac, où se trouvent

plusieurs sites de différentes périodes, dont Aivirtuuq. La baie de Wakeham elle-même comprend au moins deux sites. L'un, Qarmait, est juste au sud du village actuel, l'autre, Niaqunguut, sur le cap qui commande l'entrée du fjord. Chacun d'eux regroupe au moins 6 ou 7 habitations semi-souterraines, dont certaines pourraient être dorsétiennes, et des dizaines d'emplacements de tentes de toutes les périodes. Pour trouver une autre concentration de sites comparable, il faut aller bien à l'ouest du cap de Nouvelle-France, dans la région de Salluit ou, vers l'est, dans la baie du Diana puis le long de la côte ouest de la baie d'Ungava.

Dans la baie de Joy, c'est l'île Ukiivik qui présente le plus d'intérêt (DET. 56 à 62 sur la carte 3). Saladin d'Anglure (communication personnelle) y observa un affleurement de quartz laiteux exploité intensivement par les Dorsétiens et dont on semble retrouver les produits jusqu'au fond de la baie d'Ungava. Il nota également que le détroit séparant l'île du continent constituait un piège, autrefois exploité par les Inuit, où les baleines se retrouvaient prisonnières lorsque la marée descendait. Barré distingua à Ukiivik sept concentrations principales d'habitations réparties sur différents niveaux de plages entre 4 m et 30 m d'altitude. Chacune de ces concentrations compte de 1 à 56 structures. En plus des nombreux emplacements de tente, 95 habitations semi-souterraines ont été répertoriées dans l'île. Plusieurs d'entre elles sont certainement dorsétiennes. Tupirvikallak (DET. 63), sur la terre ferme le long de de la côte nord de la baie, comprend également sept maisons semi-souterraines apparemment thuléennes, mais associées à un outillage essentiellement dorsétien ou non identifiable culturellement.

Barré (1970:95) considère que ce site pourrait être important pour comprendre la transition Dorsétien-Thuléen. Dans l'île Qikirtalualuk, la plus grande de la baie, ce sont des emplacements de tente, mais aussi une habitation semi-souterraine dorsétienne isolée à 450 m du rivage qui furent observées. La toute petite île voisine, Ujaragittuq, recèle trois autres habitations semi-souterraines dorsétiennes associées à du matériel également dorsétien et, selon Barré (1970:99) c'est l'un des rares sites purement dorsétien de la région. Si nous laissons la pointe Frontenac de côté pour l'instant, nous rencontrons sur la terre ferme, dans la baie de Whitley, le dernier habitat d'hiver important à la latitude de Qajartalik, le principal site de pétroglyphes. C'est Illuluarjuit (DET. 67), dont les 11 maisons semi-souterraines typiquement thuléennes sont alignées face au rivage et à la petite île de Tilligarvik, où les Inuit de Kangirsujuaq installaient leur camp d'hiver jusqu'en 1958.

Les sondages pratiqués dans ces maisons ont livré un matériel essentiellement dorsétien. Un autre habitat, plus petit, se trouve encore plus au sud-est, dans l'île qui prolonge la côte sud de *Burgoyne Bay*. Il contient au moins cinq habitations d'hiver apparemment thuléennes et des emplacements de tentes. Beaucoup d'autres sites, jusqu'au sud de la pointe Bégon, ne contiennent que des structures de surface témoignant de camps de printemps ou d'été, les plus visibles étant les plus récents.

Le centre de cette région est la pointe Frontenac où se trouve Aivirtuuq (Carte 2, Photo 1). Elle est reliée à la terre ferme par une sorte de tombolo relique large de plus de 250 m, dont les sédiments s'insèrent entre les affleurements rocheux. Sa forme allongée est à l'origine du toponyme inuit *Ipiutaq*, camp d'hiver jusqu'en 1958 et important site archéologique comprenant au moins une douzaine de maisons, peut-être quinze, la plupart typiquement thuléennes et quelquesunes peut-être dorsétiennes. Elles se trouvent sur la crête de la partie sédimentaire du tombolo, entre 5,50 m et 10 m d'altitude. La vingtaine d'objets lithiques ramassés par Barré en surface et dans différentes maisons de type thuléen témoigne principalement du Dorsétien (8 objets), mais aussi du Thuléen (3 objets). Les autres sont culturellement indéterminés (Barré 1970:34 & 96-97). L'importance de la fréquentation du lieu, en particulier pour le passage

vers Aivirtuuq, est attestée par deux sentiers, l'un arrivant du sud-ouest et s'arrêtant avant les habitations, l'autre partant du rivage sud et se dirigeant vers le nord en passant à l'est du groupe principal de maisons. Mais l'un d'eux peut être une piste de caribous, comme un affût ancien l'indiquerait. Ipiutak est une situation privilégiée en raison de la proximité des deux petites anses bien abritées, l'une s'ouvrant dans la baie de Joy et l'autre dans celle de Whitley.

Enfin, c'est l'extrémité orientale de la pointe Frontenac qui correspond au lieu-dit *Aivirtuuq* (DET. 13). L'endroit est, avec Ukiivik, le point de terre le plus proche de la limite des glaces côtières d'hiver comme de printemps. Encore très fréquenté au printemps, c'était traditionnellement un lieu de chasse au morse en hiver (Saladin d'Anglure 1967:68).

Les restes de structures diverses en pierres sont extrêmement nombreux sur les larges plages sou-levées qui entourent la petite crique. Celle-ci est délimitée à l'est par une croupe rocheuse marquée d'un cairn (1,40 m de hauteur et <0,90 m de diamètre). Quatre autres cairns, de 0,70 m à 1,15 m de hauteur et <50 cm de diamètre, jalonnent la ligne de crête rocheuse juste au sud, à près de 80 m d'altitude. Ces repères témoignent de l'importance de l'endroit que confirme l'imbrication de caches, d'habitations diverses en surface et d'autres structures sedondaires. À 125 m à l'est de la crique, dans les aires de dépôts sédimentaires les plus élevées, entre 10 m et 15 m d'altitude, au moins cinq dépressions irrégulièrement circulaires, bien visibles, indiquent des habitations. Deux d'entre elles ont probablement un couloir d'entrée. Trois paraissent dorsétiennes. D'autres se devinent sous la tourbe. Le sondage restreint pratiqué par Barré devant l'une des habitations dorsétiennes, tout comme les ramassages de surface, n'ont livré que des objets dorsétiens ou culturellement indéterminés (Barré 1970:34, 97-98 & Fig. 60).

Un peu plus bas vers le nord, enfoncés dans des sédiments de plage couverts de graminées, des blocs demi-métriques et métriques délimitent une structure allongée de 12 m de longueur et 4 m de largeur. Elle inclut au nord une dalle sur chant et, à son extrémité est, deux blocs métriques en place (voir Plumet 1985:330). Ce sont là toutes les caractéristiques d'une petite maison longue dorsétienne ressemblant à celle d'Imaha III à Pamiok, dans la baie d'Ungava (Lee 1968, Plumet 1985: 305).

Sur le versant sud de la pointe Frontenac, en retrait de la grève Tuapaaluit, le site DET. 12 contraste avec le précédent et paraît dépourvu de vestiges récents. Il est face à l'îlot Inukshutuijuk (Inussutujuq), bas et couvert d'un champ de blocs, mais sur lequel on devine des sépultures et des caches (DET. 17, Carte 2 et Photo 3). Saladin d'Anglure, qui signale aussi de nombreuses sépultures, n'en rapporta que des objets néo-esquimaux (Saladin d'Anglure 1962; Taylor 1963:34). Au moins sept grands cairns en forme de tour, couverts de lichen

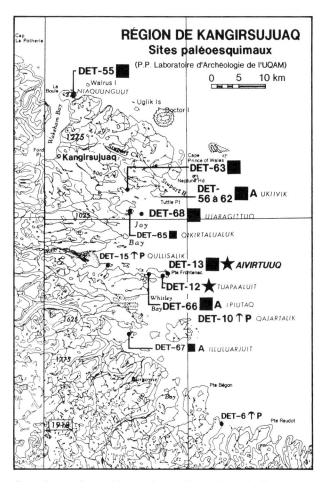

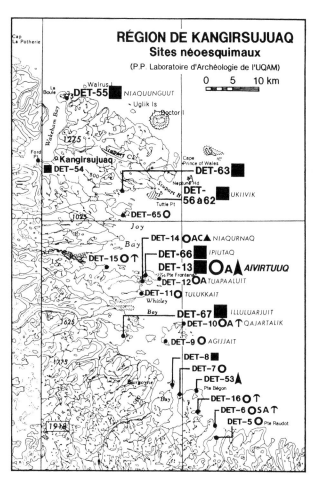

Carte 3: Les sites paléo-esquimaux de la région de Kangirsua-juaq.

Carte 4: Les sites néo-esquimaux de la région de Kangirsujuaq.

noir, et d'une hauteur maximale de 1,70 m, sont alignés le long de la crête. Serait-ce l'important lieu d'inhumation décrit par Payne?[5] Quant au site DET.12, il occupe un étroit cordon de plages soulevées qui s'élève jusqu'à une vingtaine de mètres. La plage de 8 m supporte une grande maison longue dorsétienne bien caractéristique de celles de l'Ungava (25,7 m x 7 m). Plusieurs fosses s'alignent à l'extérieur le long des murs et deux caches anciennes ont été aménagées à l'intérieur en récupérant des blocs, peut-être dès le Dorsétien, mais après l'abandon de la maison. Dans l'épaisseur des murs, qui incluent de gros blocs métriques dressés, il est possible de deviner l'emplacement de niches latérales abritant sans doute les foyers domestiques, comme les niches dégagées dans la maison longue de Qilalugarsiuvik (Plumet 1985). En dehors d'une autre structure circulaire incomplète en gros blocs jointifs, peut-être dorsétienne, la partie inférieure du site ne laisse pas apercevoir d'autres vestiges importants et ne semble pas avoir été très fréquente après les Dorsétiens (Photo 2).

■ Habitation(s) semi-souterraine(s)

O Structure(s) d'habitation en surface

★ Maison longue ou grande structure

▲ Cairn(s) balise(s)

C Structure reliée à la chasse au caribou (affût, mur, leurre...)

A Autres structures: caches, abris...

↑ Carrière de stéatite

P Pétroglyphes

Photo 1: Aivartuuq (DET 13), partie est, vue vers le nord. Au premier plan, emplacements d'habitations semi-souterraines sans doute dorstiennes. (Cliché: Patrick Plumet).

Photo 2: La maison longue du site Frontenac (DET.12) vue vers le sud-ouest. On aperçoit les grands blocs métriques dressés, surtout à l'extrémité est, mais aussi à l'ouest; on devine deux séparations intérieures. Des fosses extérieures sont visibles surtout le long du mur sud. (Cliché: Patrick Plumet).

Par contre, sur les plus hautes plages qui forment un vaste champ de blocs parsemé de flaques d'eau, on peut difficilement discerner diverses structures de surface, sans doute plus nombreuses qu'il n'y paraît, mais on remarque clairement un grand enclos ovale, d'environ 13 m x 6,50 m, délimité par des blocs demi-métriques et métriques entassés (Photo 3).

L'intérieur est recouvert de graminées et deux structures secondaires, apparemment des caches, occupent chacune des extrémités. La seule autre grande structure analogue que je connaisse dans l'Arctique est celle du site Saint-Onge (UNG.72) dans l'Ungava, qui mesure 9,50 m x 5 m. Elle est également au-dessus d'une grande maison longue (Plumet 1985:329, Photo 146) et à l'écart de tout vestige du Néo-esquimau.

Le site DET.12 semble donc l'un des rares sites purement ou principalement dorsétien de la région.

Interprétation préliminaire

Au moins 100 maisons semi-souterraines et de nombreuses constructions de surface ont été recensées entre Kangirsujuaq et la pointe Bégon. Elles s'ajoutent aux maisons et aux autres structures visibles dans les deux principaux sites de la baie de Wakeham, Qarmait (DET. 54, Carte 4) et Niaqunguut (DET. 55, Carte 4). Un petit nombre d'entre elles seulement peuvent, avant la fouille, être considérées comme dorsétiennes en s'appuyant sur l'expérience acquise dans la baie d'Ungava. Par contre, la plus grande partie du matériel recueilli en surface ou dans les sondages est dorsétien. En Ungava oriental et dans la baie du Diana, la pauvreté en outillage des sites du Néo-esquimau a déjà été remarquée. Elle s'explique en partie par le rôle moins important de la pierre à cette époque. Par contre les habitats du Paléo-esquimau sont presque toujours installés à des endroits différents de ceux du Néo-esquimau, ce qui pourrait se comprendre si, comme je le pense, Thuléens et Dorsétiens coexistèrent régionalement jusque vers le 15e siècle (Plumet 1994). Le long du détroit d'Hudson, par contre, il est clair que les habitats néo-esquimaux sont installés dans les mêmes sites que ceux du Paléo-esquimau et souvent creusés dans des gisements dorsétiens, entraînant le mélange d'objets des deux périodes. Or cela ne peut s'expliquer ni par une stabilisation ancienne du niveau marin relatif, ni par une subsidence comme le long de la côte orientale de la baie d'Ungava et dans la région de Killiniq (Plumet & Gangloff 1991; Clark & Fitzhugh 1991). Le fait que pratiquement tous les sites contiennent du matériel dorsétien, souvent d'aspect tardif, dans la région de Kangirsujuaq, atteste que celle-ci eut aussi une très grande importance au Paléo-esquimau. L'altitude élevée de certains habitats permet de croire qu'un Dorsétien ancien, voire du Groswatérien et du Pré-dorsétien, pourraient être trouvés. Cette importance n'était peut-être pas seulement économique comme le laissent croire les pétroglyphes. La maison longue et le grand enclos, que je crois dorsé-

tien, du site UNG. 12, près d'Aivartuuq, sans doute des lieux de regroupement cérémoniels comme ceux de l'Ungava ou de la Terre d'Ellesmere (Schledermann 1990), confirment aussi le rôle social et sans doute religieux que pouvait avoir cette localité avant l'arrivée des Thuléens.

L'archéologie, qu'il reste à entreprendre, de la région de Kangirsujuaq, pourrait faire apparaître un autre type de relations interethniques entre Dorsétiens et Thuléens que celui suggéré par les données de Tuvaaluk (la baie du Diana), ou du moins les compléter. Pour que les Thuléens se soient installés régulièrement aux mêmes endroits que les Dorsétiens, il fallait soit que ceux-ci aient déjà quitté la région, soit qu'il se laissent exterminer, ou encore qu'il y ait une fusion des deux populations. Nous n'avons pas de date pour l'arrivée du Thuléen à Kangirsujuaq. Mais nous savons qu'il se manifestait à l'île aux Iglous, dans la baie du Diana, dès le milieu du 12e siècle ou le début du 13e (Plumet 1994:138) et que le Dorsétien s'y distinguait encore clairement à la fin du 15e siècle dans l'habitation semi-souterraine A, mi-dorsétienne mithuléenne, du site Tuvaaluk (DIA. 4-A), dont la structure intégrait des os de grande baleine (Plumet 1979). À propos de ces os, tout comme Barré en 1967, je n'en ai pas remarqué dans les structures, même thuléennes, des baies de Joy et de Whitley, en dépit de leur importance comme centre de chasse aux grands cétacés. Par contre Saladin d'Anglure en a observés le long des côtes, particulièrement à Ukiivik.

Les carrières de stéatite et les pétroglyphes
(Cartes 2, 3 et 4)

Lorsqu'en juin 1961 Saladin d'Anglure commença ses recherches à Kangirsujuaq, les Inuit lui relatèrent qu'ils avaient vu des "faces de diable" sur un affleurement de stéatite émergeant de la neige. Celui-ci venait d'être découvert quelques jours auparavant à Qajartalik (DET. 10) et les sculpteurs du village souhaitaient en exploiter la pierre, qui était de bonne qualité. Conduit sur les lieux, l'ethnologue prit une première série de photos, puis y retourna en septembre pour compléter les observations. Il compta un minimum de 44 faces qu'il répartit dans deux grandes catégories opposées, celle des faces allongées et celle des faces rondes, mais 26 représentations se rapprochaient à la fois des deux catégories (Saladin d'Anglure 1963).

Il attribua toutes ces figures au Dorsétien (Photo 4). De plus, divers signes, qui n'ont pas beaucoup retenu l'attention, parsemaient les parois. En raison du grand intérêt de cette découverte, le Musée national du Canada confia en 1965 à Saladin d'Anglure le mandat d'effectuer des relevés, des moulages et, si possible, de rapporter des échantillons qui permettraient une analyse lichénométrique (Saladin d'Anglure 1965). Il retourna donc à Qajartalik avec quatre Inuit et réalisa avec eux les relevés, mais, en raison de problèmes de transport, les moulages ne furent entrepris que l'année suivante. En

Photo 3: La grande structure ovale de la partie supérieure du site Frontenac (DET. 12) vue vers le sud-ouest. L'île allongée qui traverse la photo est Inussutujuq (DET. 17, Carte 2), dont les cairns de la crête ne sont pas visibles car la photo est prise de haut, de sorte qu'ils ne se détachent pas sur l'horizon. (Cliché: Patrick Plumet).

1966, constatant qu'un bloc de stéatite, portant une face gravée et du lichen, avait commencé d'être détaché à la scie et à la hache par les Inuit, il se mit d'accord avec eux pour que ce bloc soit prélevé et envoyé au Musée[6].

Il expliqua, par contre, l'importance qu'il y avait de préserver les autres pétroglyphes (Saladin d'Anglure, communication personnelle 1996)[7]. Lors de la même mission, il fut possible d'examiner à Upirngivik (DET. 6), au sud de la pointe Bégon, une autre carrière, contenant de 13 à 15 pétroglyphes, et de rechercher vainement une troisième dans la baie de Joy, près de Nuvukallak.

C'est au cours de la mission de 1977 du programme Tuvaaluk et grâce aux enquêtes de Monique Vézinet, que celle de Qullisalik (DET. 15) fut retrouvée. De plus, deux autres carrières, apparemment dépourvues de gravures, furent échantillonnées la même année: DET. 14 (Niaqurnaq) et DET. 16 au pied de la pointe Bégon. Il y avait donc, à ce moment-là, au moins cinq carrières, dont trois conservaient encore des faces gravées, à 25 m d'altitude à Qajartalik et à 20 m à Upirngivik. D'autres auraient été découvertes depuis. La comparaison des photographies prises par Saladin d'Anglure en 1965 avec celles de 1977 montre que de nouvelles dégradations étaient survenues entre ces deux moments: des faces avaient été maladroitement regravées avec un trait plus fin, peut-être par un Inuk qui aurait également gravé deux caractères syllabiques ou par un photographe de Montréal (Photo 5). Comme nous l'avons mentionné, ces dégradations se sont poursuivies depuis.

Il n'est pas utile ici de présenter de nouveau les pétroglyphes dont certaines photographies sont connues, en particulier celles de Fred Bruemmer (1972) qui, malheureusement, repassa au charbon de bois les figures pour qu'elles soient plus visibles! Aucune étude spécialisée n'a encore pu en être réalisée. Il n'est plus besoin de souligner la ressemblance des faces gravées sur la stéatite avec certains petits masques en ivoire et surtout avec les nombreuses figures grimaçantes des multifaces dorsétiens (Photo 4).

Ces pétroglyphes seraient-ils, comme on le pense pour l'art dorsétien, associés à des pratiques chamaniques? Pourquoi ne se trouvent-ils que dans la région de Kangirsujuaq et dans un secteur de côte dont les points extrêmes, Qullisalik au nord et Upirngivik au sud, éloignés de 36 km, encadrent Aivirtuuq? Cet endroit aurait-il été un centre chamanique dorsétien, dans lequel les deux grandes structures de Tuapaaluit (DET. 12) auraient eu une fonction? Il existe d'autres carrières dorsétiennes dans l'Arctique, dont une très importante à Fleur-de-Lys (Terre-Neuve). Aucune gravure n'y a été observée. Des analyses des concentrations en éléments des terres rares ont été effectuées sur les échantillons des cinq carrières et sur ceux prélevés dans des fragment de lampes ou de récipients dorsétiens de l'Ungava et du Labrador. Les résultats semblent indiquer qu'il pouvait y avoir des relations entre ces carrières, difficiles à différencier entre elles par les analyses, et des habitats de la baie du Diana, mais aussi de Killiniq au nord du Labrador (Archambault 1981). Aivirtuuq rayonnait-il déjà aussi loin au temps des Dorsétiens?

Conclusion

Espérons que les Inuit du Nunavik, le territoire de l'Arctique québécois qui leur a été reconnu, établiront un jour une politique de l'archéologie et du patrimoine équivalant à celle qui est pratiquée au Groenland, par exemple. La collaboration, qui semble harmonieuse, entre archéologues danois et archéologues groenlandais a permis ces dernières années de renouveler les perspectives de la préhistoire paléo-esquimaude au Groenland et de réaliser un remarquable travail de mise en valeur auquel se consacra en partie Jørgen Meldgaard. Dans l'Arctique québé-

Photo 4: Quelques uns des pétroglyphes de Qajartalik. Les gravures représentent des faces rondes, sans doute des masques, très proches de ceux trouvés dans certains sites dorsétiens. En haut et à gauche, un visage allongé, le plus grand des trois, semble avoir un front cornu, comme la masquette en ivoire trouvée par Meldgaard près d'Igloolik. On remarquera la fente qui apparaît à plusieurs reprises sur le front des figures gravées, tout comme sur celui de certaines figurines humaines ou animales dorsétiennes. Sur cette paroi, quelques unes des figures de droite, d'ailleurs plus effacées et peut-être plus anci-ennes, semblent tracées par une main différente que celle des figures de gauche. Au moins deux styles sont représentés. Plusieurs signes, difficiles à interpréter, sont également visibles, en bas, sous le masque vers le milieu de la photo, et entre celui-ci et le visage le plus creusé, au dessus et à gauche, dont le menton est paré de 4 poils de barbe.

Tous ces visages joufflus, dont la bouche est relativement petite, donnent l'impression que le personnage souffle, peut-être comme un chamane lors de certaines cérémonies? (cliché Patrick Plumet).

cois, depuis 1980, malgré les nombreuses reconnaissances d'Avataq et les fouilles entreprises par cet organisme dans un très important site groswatérien découvert par l'équipe du programme Tuvaaluk, aucune donnée nouvelle n'a encore été publiée. Le territoire du Nunavik est pourtant d'une richesse exceptionnelle[8]. La région de Kangirsujuaq, en relation avec les recherches effectuées jusqu'à 1980 dans la baie du Diana, permettrait d'étudier la transition entre le Paléo-esquimau et le Néo-esquimau.

Une partie des habitations semi-souterraines de cette région, considérées comme thuléennes, pourraient très bien être Dorsétiennes et témoigner d'une acculturation des dorsétiens, comme celle du site Tuvaaluk et peut-être comme celles, non encore fouillées, de la Pointe aux Iglous, sur la rive nord de l'Arnaud (ARN. 2). La recherche des sources des matières premières lithiques et l'étude de celles-ci, en particulier du quartzite ferrugineux, très noir, qui apparaît aussi en grande quantité à l'embouchure de l'Arnaud, étendrait notre connaissance du réseau spatial paléo-esquimau et serait un moyen de vérifier si les liens avec le Labrador étaient vraiment aussi forts et exclusifs qu'il m'a semblé à partir des données de l'Ungava. Contrairement au Néo-esquimau, les relations avec la partie du détroit d'Hudson qui s'étend à l'ouest de la Pointe de Nouvelle-France restent très faiblement attestées au Paléo-esquimau. Par ailleurs, à partir des mêmes sites occupés au Dorsétien et au Thuléen, il serait facile de comparer les modes de subsistance des deux cultures et peut-être de discerner leurs interactions. Enfin, des fouilles effectuées au pied des parois de stéatite gravées seraient l'occasion de retrouver quelques outils et peut-être des ébauches de récipients situant les pétroglyphes dans la chronologie dorsétienne. Mais de nouveaux relevés des gravures et une entreprise de conservation devraient ête confiés à une équipe pluridisciplinaire très expérimentée.

Photo 5: Ce visage allongé, plus difficile à voir, a été regravé entre 1966 et 1977. Le trait récent, plus fin, s'inscrit à l'intérieur et au fond du trait d'origine, nettement plus large et dont la surface ne se distingue pas de celle du rocher. Deux autres figures voisines ont subi le même traitement. Du côté opposé au doigt, à la hauteur de la joue gauche du visage, il est intéressant de remarquer le début de deux caractères syllabiques gravés apparemment avec le même outil que celui utilisé pour redessiner le pétroglyphe. Sur la photo, la deuxième partie de l'inscription se perd dans l'ombre. (Cliché: Patrick Plumet).

Abréviations

DET. xx, DIA. xx, UNG. xx indiquent les numéros des sites dans les séries régionales de la baie du Diana, de la rive québécoise du détroit d'Hudson et de la baie d'Ungava. Numérotation dans le catalogue du laboratoire d'archéologie de l'Université du Québec à Montréal.

Patrick Plumet, Laboratoire d'archéologie, Département des sciences de la terre, Université du Québec à Montréal, Canada

Notes

(1): Programme de recherche pluridisciplinaire suventionné par le Conseil de Recherches en Sciences Humaines du Canada, le fonds Formation des Chercheurs et d'Actions Concestées du Québec et l'Université du Québec à Montréal. Il se déroula dans l'Arctique québécois de 1975 à 1980 et étudia principalement la mise en place du peuplement préhistorique de l'Ungava.

(2): Le premier projet avait été considéré comme prioritaire par la Direction générale du patrimoine du Ministère des affaires culturelles du Québec. Son financement était assuré à la fois par cet organisme, par la Commission archéologique du Canada et par le Laboratoire d'archéologie de l'Université du Québec à Montréal grâce au programme Tuvaaluk. Il ne put se réaliser en raison de dissensions à l'intérieur de la communauté de Kangirsujuaq, dont une partie était en faveur du projet et l'autre contre. Il faut dire qu'en 1978, chez les Inuit du Nouveau Québec commençait à se manifester une opposition, encouragée du sud, contre l'affirmation culturelle, linguistique et politique du Québec.

Le second projet, d'envergure internationale, fut proposé en 1994 à Daniel Gendron, étudiant de second cycle en archéologie et seul responsable de l'archéologie à l'Institut culturel Avataq. Son élaboration faisait suite aux inquiétudes exprimées par plusieurs collègues et à leur étonnement que le Québec n'ait pas encore pris les mesures nécessaires pour protéger ces sites exceptionnels. Hans Kapel, archéologue danois spécialiste de l'art rupestre et de l'Arctique devait y participer, accompagné d'archéologues Groenlandais impliqués dans la mise en valeur et la protection des sites. Alan Watchman, spécialiste de la datation des rupestres, Gilles Tassé, également spécialiste de l'art rupestre au laboratoire d'archéologie de l'Université du Québec à Montréal et les spécialistes d'archéométrie du Département des sciences de la terre (Université du Québec à Montréal) faisaient également partie du projet. Les participants danois offraient d'assurer une part importante du financement, le reste devant être demandé à différentes sources publiques et privées. Seuls le transport et la logistique sur le terrain revenaient à Avataq. Ce projet de deux ans pouvait être pour les Inuit du Québec une occasion de se former à la mise en valeur avec des congénères du Groenland et offrait aux scientifiques la possibilité d'entreprendre une étude approfondie de toutes les carrières de stéatite connues de la région. En dépit d'un premier accueil apparemment favorable, aucune réponse définitive n'a été donnée par Avataq à la proposition, mais il semble qu'au cours de l'été 1996, Gendron organisa au principal site de pétroglyphes une petite expédition s'en inspirant. Elle ne comportait aucun spécialiste affirmé de l'Arctique (Voir Plumet 1996 et la réponse de Gendron et al. 1996).

(3): En dehors d'une école de fouille pour les Inuit organisée dans la baie du Diana, des études de potentiel et des opérations d'urgence supervisées ou réalisées par Avataq (mais qui n'ont donné lieu a aucune publication depuis 15 ans), Yves Labrèche, du laboratoire d'archéologie de l'Université du Québec à Montréal, a entrepris pour son doctorat, surtout avec les Inuit de Kangirsujuaq, des recherches "géo-archéologiques" et "ethnoarchéologiques" sur les modes de subsistance et d'entreposage des périodes récentes (Labrèche 1988, 1991, 1992).

(4): La baie du Diana devint le centre du programme Tuvaaluk.

(5): *"The favorite place of burial is an island [...], and near Cape Prince of Wales an island about ten acres in area was seen literally covered with graves; and monuments ten feet high were erected here and there throughout it."* (Payne 1889:16).

(6): À cette époque, les îles côtières de l'Arctique québécois qu'aucun estran ne reliait à la terre ferme à marée basse, relevaient des Territoires du Nord-Ouest. Le Musée national du Canada était donc en droit de faire effectuer un tel prélèvement. Aujourd'hui, ces îles, longtemps réclamées par le Québec, sont officiellement reconnues comme une partie du Nunavik, le territoire des Inuit du Québec.

(7): Lors de la négociation de la première mission de sauvetage envisagée en 1978, le groupe de Kangirsujuaq qui s'y opposait utilisa l'argument qu'une face avait été enlevée dans la carrière et était détenue dans le sud, mais sans jamais faire référence à Saladin d'Anglure. Or la communauté était au courant de ce prélèvement. Il est possible toutefois que d'autres prélèvements sauvages aient eu lieu, des rumeurs désignant nommément des personnes du sud qui furent en poste à Maricourt entre 1966 et 1977. Un musée privé aurait même été constitué avec des objets de la région. Aujourd'hui, le Musée canadien de la Civilisation a retourné à Kangirsujuaq la face qu'elle conservait, mais si une ou plusieurs autres manquent elles ne sont pas près de revenir. Cela montre cependant combien il est urgent que des mesures de protection soient prises et qu'une formation à la conservation du patrimoine soit dispensée dans le nord du Québec pour contrer la commercialisation des biens archéologiques, qui n'est pas seulement le fait des Blancs.

(8): J'ai pu examiner quelques-unes des collections d'Avataq et j'ai eu l'impression qu'elles pourraient apporter des éléments nouveaux, en particulier sur le Paléo-esquimau inférieur dans l'Ungava oriental, sur le Groswatérien dans l'Ungava occidental, sur l'occupation paléo-esquimaude de la côte est de la baie d'Hudson et plus généralement sur les habitations du Paléo-esquimau.

Références

Archambault, M. F. [1981]: **Essai de caractérisation de la stéatite des sites dorsétiens et des carrières de l'Ungava, Arctique québécois.** *Géographie physique et Quaternaire*, 35(1):19-28 (Montréal.: *).

Barré, G. [1970]: **Reconnaissance archéologique dans la région de la Baie de Wakeham (Nouveau-Québec).** 107 p. (Montréal: La Société d'Archéologie Préhistorique du Québec).

Bruemmer, Fred [1972]: **Les faces du diable.** *Perspectives*, 20 mai 1972:10-11 (Montréal: *).

Clark, P. U., & William W. Fitzhugh [1991]: **Postglacial relative sea level history of the Labrador coast and interpretation of the archaeological record.** pp:189-213 in "Paleoshorelines and prehistory: an investigation of method", editor: L. L. Johnson, 243 p. (Boca Raton, Fl: CRC Press).

Gendron, Daniel, Daniel Arsenault & Louis Gagnon [1996]: **A propos du sauvetage des pétroglyphes dorsétiens de Qajartalik dans le Nunavik: réplique de l'Institut culturel Avataq à la lettre de M. Patrick Plumet.** *Études/Inuit/Studies*, 20(2):117-122 (Québec: Départment d'anthropologie, Université Laval).

Haven, J. [1773a]: **A brief account of the dwelling places of the Eskimos to the north of Naghvakh to Hudson Strait, their situation and subsistence.** Manuscrit inédit, * p. (London: Archives of the Moravian Church).

Haven, J. [1773b]: **Extract of the voyage of the sloop George to reconnoitre the northern part of Labrador in the month of August and September 1773.** Manuscrit inédit, * p. (London: Archives of the Moravian Church).

Labrèche, Y. [1988]: **Histoire de l'utilisation des ressources naturelles par les Inuit dans les estuaires de Kangiqsujuaq: perspective ethnoarchéologique.** pp:512-516 in "Les recherches des étudiants dans le Nord canadien", editors: W. P. Adams & P. G. Johnson, 596 p. (Ottawa: Association Universitaire Canadienne d'Études Nordiques).

Labrèche, Y. [1991]: **Provisions, traditions et peuplement de la côte sud du détroit d'Hudson.** *Études Inuit Studies*, 15(2):85-105 (Québec: Départment d'anthropologie, Université Laval).

Labrèche, Y. [1992]: **Suite des fouilles sur l'île Ukiivik et entrevues à Kangiqsujuaq (1989).** pp:227-228 in

"Recherches archéologiques au Québec 1990", editors: A.-M. Balac et al., 241 p. (Québec: Association des archéologues du Québec).

Lee, T. E. [1968]: **Archaeological discoveries, Payne Bay region, Ungava, 1966.** 2e édition, 1970, Travaux divers 20. 169 p. (Québec: Centre d'études nordiques, Université Laval).

Nagle, Christopher [1982]: **1981 field investigations at Fleur de Lys soapstone quarry, Baie Verte, Newfoundland.** pp:102-129 in "Archaeology in Newfoundland and Labrador 1981", editors: Jane Sproull Thomson & Callum Thomson, Annual Report 2, 237 p. (St. John's: Historic Resources Division, Government of Newfoundland and Labrador).

Payne, F. F. [1889]: **Eskimo of Hudson's Strait.** *Proceedings of Canadian Institute*, ser. 3, 6:213-230 (Toronto: Clark).

Plumet, Patrick [1979]: **Thuléens et Dorsétiens dans l'Ungava (Nouveau-Québec).** pp:110-121 in "Thule Eskimo culture: an anthropological retrospective", editor: A. P. McCartney, *Mercury Serie* 88, 586 p. (Ottawa: Musée National de l'Homme, Commission archéologique du Canada).

Plumet, Patrick [1985]: **Archéologie de l'Ungava : le site de la Pointe aux Bélougas (Qilalugarsiuvik) et les maisons longues dorsétiennes.** Préface de José Garanger, annexes de M.-F. Archambault & de M. Julien, *Paléo-Québec*, 18:1-471 (Montréal: Laboratoire d'archéologie, Université du Québec à Montréal).

Plumet, Patrick & P. Gangloff [1990]: **Contribution à l'archéologie et l'ethnohistoire de l'Ungava oriental: côte est, Killiniq, îles Button, Labrador septentrional.** *Paléo-Québec*, 19:1-286 (Québec: Presses de l'Université du Québec).

Plumet, Patrick [1994]: **Le Paléoesquimau dans la baie du Diana (Arctique québécois).** pp:103-143 in "Threads of Arctic prehistory: Papers in honour of William E. Taylor, Jr.", editors: D. Morrison & J.-L. Pilon, *Mercury Series* 149, 422 p. (Hull: Archaeological Survey of Canada, Canadian Museum of Civilization).

Plumet, Patrick [1996]: **A propos du sauvetage des pétroglyphes dorsétiens de Qajartalik dans le Nunavik (Arctique quiébécois). Questions et réflexions sur la politique de l'archéologie dans le Nunavik.** *Études/Inuit/Studies*, 20(2):112-116 (Québec: Département d'anthropologie, Université Laval).

Saladin d'Anglure, Bernard [1962]: **Découverte de pétroglyphes à Qajartalik sur l'île de Qîlertaaluk.** *North*, 9(6):34-39 (Ottawa).

Saladin d'Anglure, Bernard [1963]: **Discovery of petroglyphs near Wakeham Bay.** *The Arctic Circular*, 15(1):7-14 (Montréal).

Saladin d'Anglure, Bernard [1965]: **Rapport succinct sur le travail effectué au cours de l'été pour le Musée national du Canada.** 15 p. Rapport déposé à la Commission archéologique du Canada (Ottawa).

Saladin d'Anglure, Bernard [1967]: **L'organisation sociale traditionnelle des Esquimaux de Kangirsujuaaq (Nouveau Québec).** *Travaux divers*, 17:1-204 (Québec: Centre d'Études Nordiques, Université Laval).

Schledermann, Peter [1990]: **Crossroads to Greenland: 3000 years of prehistory in the Eastern High Arctic.** *Komatik series*, 2:1-364 (Calgary: The Arctic Institute of North America).

Stupart, R. F. [1887]: **The Eskimo of Stupart Bay.** *Proceedings of the Canadian Institute*, 3(4):93-114 (Toronto: Clark).

Taylor, William E. [1963]: **Archaeological collections from Joy Bay, Ungava Peninsula.** *The Arctic Circular*, 15(2):24-26 (Montréal).

Taylor, J. Garth [1975]: **Demography and adaptations of eighteenth-century Eskimo groups in Northern Labrador and Ungava.** pp:269-278 in "Prehistoric maritime adaptations of circumpolar zone", editor: William W. Fitzhugh, 405 p. (The Hague & Paris: World Anthropology, Mouton).

Death in traditional East Greenland: Age, causes, and rituals. A contribution from anthropology to archeology

Joëlle Robert-Lamblin

In the Arctic areas, and especially in East Greenland where the population came into contact with Westerners at a very late date[1], anthropological research and analysis, resulting from the reconstruction of ancient society by historical demography, can provide some answers to the questions asked by prehistorians and archaeologists, such as: What were the causes of death in nomadic hunting and gathering societies? At what age? What were the differences of the mortality rate between men and women?

Excavating burial sites can provide some explanations, but all deaths without ground burial escape our knowledge, although the dead, who did not leave visible traces, could have been numerous. At the end of the 19th century, for example, burial at sea was preferred because it gave the dead easier access to the best of the Worlds of the Dead. The body, tied in a leather shroud, was placed on the shore or slipped through the ice to disappear for ever into the sea. To this kind of burial organised by the family of the deceased may be added: Those lost at sea while hunting or travelling in umiaqs, persons who committed suicide by throwing themselves in the sea, individuals who had been murdered and whose body was ritually dismembered with the different parts being dispersed in different areas so they could not reappear to take revenge, as well as those who died from hunger and were abandoned without burial, or those the living had to eat in order to survive.

In this presentation I would like to survey our actual knowledge of mortality in Ammassalik during the period preceeding contact with the West, and during the early stages of Western presence in the area, spanning the period covering the end of the 19th and the beginning of the 20th centuries.

Data sources

Historical and demographic data are numerous for the population of Ammassalik. They start with the first nominative list established in 1884-1885 by Johannes Hansen (Hansêrak) who accompanied Holm, followed by that of 1892 established by Ryder during a short visit to the area, and by nominative censuses established almost yearly[2] by the first colonisers in charge of the local commercial organisation and the evangelization of the Ammassalimmiut. To these documents may be added vital registration data inscribed in parish registers since 1899, archive documents[3], observations by the first Danish visitors or by scientists having spent some time in the area (Holm, Hansêrak, Petersen, Thalbitzer, Rasmussen, Mikkelsen), and all the demographic and genealogical field research realized by the physician and anthropologist Robert Gessain in 1934-1935 and 1936, research completed by the ethnographical data collected by Paul-Emile Victor in 1934-1937.

Pursuing the research started by Robert Gessain, all the above information has been collated, cross checked and dated with maximum precision in order to reconstitute the genealogies of the whole Ammassalimmiut ethnic group. In addition, it was checked again at a later stage, whenever possible, between 1960 and 1990 with the eldest East Greenlanders (See Robert-Lamblin 1986:16-18). However, some unavoidable imprecisions, errors, or omissions still remain, given the difficulty of identifying certain individuals whose name changed from one census to another, and the impossibility of obtaining exact information on infant mortality, or on certain birth and death dates for the period preceeding 1915.

Age at death

Pre-contact Ammassalimmiut society is characterised by the low life expectancy of its members, inferior to 40 years for both sexes and lower for men than for women. Few individuals lived to or beyond 55 years: Only 4% in the census established at the discovery of this population in 1884[4].

In the extremely harsh environment of East Greenland, the main periods of risk for death were at birth and during the first days of life, and later, during the full activities of adulthood, that is to say, between 17-20 years and 45-50 years, the period when men spend most of their time hunting and women give birth to children.

Infant mortality

Prior to any kind of Western medical aid, one of the principal causes of death was infant mortality[5], and more particularly that of newborns. In traditional Ammassalimmiut society there were no midwives as such. Women gave birth alone or were helped by an old woman of the family.

The lack of hygiene for the mother as well as for the child during childbirth generated a high rate of mortality for both. Thus, on average, only three or four infants survived out of eight or nine deliveries per woman.

The presence of Greenlandic midwives trained in West Greenland or in Denmark (one in 1906, two in 1910, and three in 1923) lowered perinatal mortality at the beginning of the 20th century[6]. Figure 1 shows the evolution of infant mortality over three decades 1897-1926; for the previous period, we do not have sufficiently complete and precise information. Infant deaths occurred essentially during the first week of life, and more specifically at birth or during the hours immediately following (Fig. 1).

Newborn infanticide was carried out only in very particular cases: Either the child was malformed, handicapped, weak at birth, or was the result of a forbidden union, such as incest or illegitimacy. In other cases the child's close family or whole family group might have undergone a serious crisis such as famine, want, demise of the father or death of the mother at birth, and all new mouths to feed would represent an unbearable burden. The infant, particularly in the case of a girl, would be abandoned in the cold, thrown into the sea or buried alive (with his or her deceased mother).

Years	Infant mortality rate for 1000 births	% of deaths at birth or during the first days of life
1897-1901	284	55
1902-1906	225	64
1907-1911	143	35
1912-1916	128	47
1917-1921	123	24
1922-1926	146	60

Fig. 1 - Infant mortality among the Ammassalimmiut population during the years 1897-1926. Number of births for the period: 809; total number of deaths: 466; number of infant deaths (0-1 year): 137.

Child mortality

Beyond the first months of life, children had a good chance of survival into adulthood. Deaths occurring during childhood were essentially accidental: Falls, drowning while playing, dog bites. But children were always under the menace of tragic events touching their family group; when their fathers died or there was a famine in the area, they were the first to die of hunger or made to commit suicide with their mother. Several accounts collected in East Greenland mention these mothers, who, having lost their economic support, threw themselves into the icy ocean with their young children.

Adult mortality

Adults were exposed to multiple risks - men, in particular, during their hunting activities, women during childbirth. The dangers of the environment were not the only causes of death for adult men; homicides were also a frequent cause of death before colonization.

Elderly mortality

When we add to the above, various diseases and the famines which heavily affected the group at the end of the 19th century causing the death of whole families, it appears that dying of old age (over 55 years) was a very rare phenomenon in this population.

In Ammassalik, the suicide of the elderly, often mentioned among traditional Eskimo populations, resulted either from a personal decision, the person having decided to cut short his or her physical or moral sufferings, or from a real social pressure, for example, if the community was threatened by scarcity of food. Whatever the motive, personal or collective, the close kin of the person frequently helped him or her to carry out this act to its very end: to throw oneself from a cliff or disappear in a kayak (Holm 1911:147).

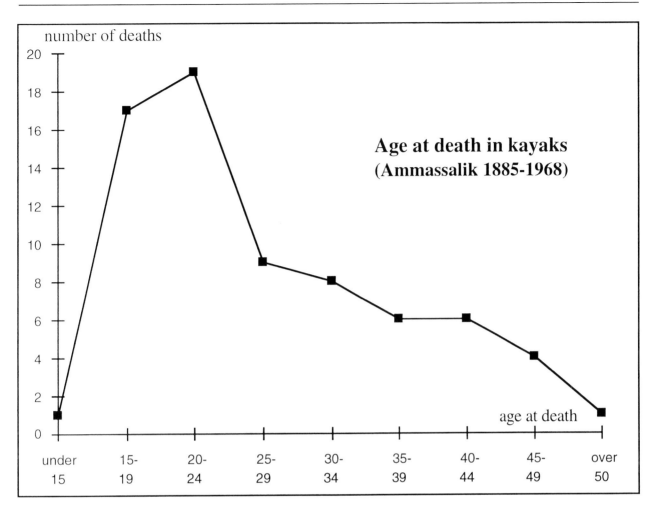

Fig. 2: Age at death of hunters who died in kayaks, in Ammassalik, for the period 1885-1968. (N=71 cases: 70 men and 1 women. We can note that among these deaths, 7 were accounted for as murders and 1 as suicide, and that the last known case dates back to 1968).

Causes of death according to sex

From the analysis of the causes of death, it appears that the types of mortality vary for each sex. This difference is first of all linked to environment and to the division of activities between men and women, but also to the social organisation of the group.

Male mortality

The adult male population is particularly exposed to the dangers of the polar environment: Icebergs overturning, storms, avalanches, ice breaking under the weight of the sled, or the hunter on foot. It was hunting - upon which in the past the whole group depended for its survival - which forced the men to go out in search of game, whatever the weather or the season.

In traditional East Greenlandic society, kayak accidents were the most frequent causes of death among men. Bad weather could catch up with the hunter, he could lose his balance when throwing the harpoon, or he could be carried away by the harpoon's line, or even

attacked by a walrus and have his kayak overturned. However, not all deaths occurring in kayaks were hunting accidents; there were also murders, perpetrated while the victim was in the kayak. In at least seven of the cases (Fig. 2), the two causes of death, kayak and homicide, overlap[7]. Another case is a kayak suicide (in 1913).

Fig. 2 shows the high frequency of deaths in kayaks among hunters aged 15 to 24 years: 51% of all deaths in a kayak concern these age groups. We should note here that there is a woman among the hunters who died in a kayak. She was born in 1918 and died in 1950, while hunting: She is an example of the rare cases of gender role inversion. On this subject Holm mentions two women hunters possessing a kayak, whom he met south of Ammassalik in 1884 (Holm 1911:187).

Returning to cases of homicide, their number appears to be very high considering the small size of the population (Fig. 3) and the tragedy represented by the death of any hunter, brutally depriving his family of its economic support[8]. These murderous acts originated in

Year of the census	Ammassalimmiut population Total (M number, W number)	Number of persons aged 15-54 years	Sex ratio at 15-54 years
1884	413 (M 193; W 220)	M 109; W 121	90
1892	293 (M 131; W 162)	M 72; W 91	79
1901	429 (M 204; W 225)	M 103; W 140	74
1911	547 (M 252; W 295)	M 123; W 152	81
1921	655 (M 313; W 342)	M 156; W 174	90

Fig. 3: Sex ratio in the age group between 15 and 54 years, for the Ammassalik population, according to various censuses. M = male; W = women.

rivalries between hunters or shamans, jealousy over women, and even the obligation for a man to revenge a member of his family who had been murdered (Rasmussen in Ostermann 1938:85-89). The vendetta type of family revenge, a murder for a murder, was the cause of a high number of deaths in the 19th century. Sometimes a man murdered another man simply because he suspected him of having bad intentions towards him. He thus anticipated a supposed malevolent action, at the same time exposing himself to the risks of retaliation from the deceased's family. Most often, the murderer, helped by one or two accomplices, killed his victim by throwing a harpoon in his back while he was hunting in his kayak. Sometimes, the killing took place on land, with a knife. The famous execution of Ilisimartek, who had murdered four men between 1886 and 1890, happened in 1892, using one of the very first guns introduced in the area. According to the information collected, there were 14 murders perpetrated on men between 1886 and 1896. Four of the victims were shamans (Uvia, Apalito, Kajamat, Simujok) who had themselves taken part in other murders, or were suspected of having stolen the soul of a person, causing his or her death.

A ritual was used to neutralize the power of a powerful enemy: his body was rapidly cut up at the joints and the head, eyes, and limbs were dispersed in different locations. The person would then be unable to reassemble himself as a whole being to come back and take revenge on the living (Victor & Robert-Lamblin 1993:28 + 287-288).

Female mortality

An important cause of death among women was childbirth and the period immediately following. We have already mentioned the very precarious conditions of childbirth in this traditional society, and the absence of specialised midwives, as well as the application of certain customs to facilitate delivery[9].

A certain number of mothers died of post natal haemorrhage or puerperal fever. For the 1897-1926 period (Fig. 1), I found 25 cases of women having died in childbirth or of its consequences; all of which, crossed with the 809 births registered during that period, gives us the very high figure of 3.1% of women dying while giving birth[10]. For seven of these, it was their first child. At death, the age of these women is distributed among the following age groups: 15-19 years: 2 women; 20-24 years: 5♀; 25-29 years: 6♀; 30-34 years: 6♀; 35-39 years: 4♀; 40-44 years: 2♀. The fate of children born thus was mostly that of their mother. Either they were born dead or died at birth, or they were buried alive with the mother, or were thrown into the sea, since in most cases there was no milk to feed them (the only available milk for infants, before Danish colonization, was women's milk). If, however, another woman could breast feed the infant he survived. In the period under consideration, seven children adopted by a new mother were able to survive in this way.

For this particular period it is interesting to compare deaths in kayaks for men (28 cases between 1897-1926) and deaths in childbirth for women (25 cases)[11]. We thus confiorm Bertelsen's data concerning the district of Uummannak in West Greenland for the period 1898-1908. He recorded 23 cases of male kayak deaths for 21 cases of death in childbirth (Bertelsen 1910:488 + 495).

If the suicide of elder individuals in traditional society concerned men and women equally, one cause of death could be considered as particularly feminine: Suicide while still young. Several traditional narrations tell of the tragic fate of wives whose husband had died. These women, deprived of their purveyor of game were fated to die if they did not rapidly find a new spouse. The custom of bigamy enabled the absortion of some of the surplus of young women lacking economic support. However, a certain number of young widows would kill themselves and their children, by throwing themselves into the sea, thus ending the pain of hunger and cold.

In this environment, where family migrations took place by boat during the short Arctic summer, an umiaq would sometimes overturn or sink, full of women and children, while adolescent boys and men accompanying the group in kayaks would survive. One of these accidents, for which we have very precise information, happened to Natanieli's umiaq in July 1914. According to the field notes of Paul-Emile Victor, twelve passengers on board the boat drowned (5 adult women, one mentally retarded youth of 17 years old, a 14 year old young girl and five children ranging from a few months to eight years). The only two survivors were the helmsman, the owner of the boat, and an 11-month-old baby.

Homicides of women were comparatively lower than those of men. There were, however, a few cases of women dying after being beaten by their husband.

Other causes of death

In addition to the other important causes of death for both men and women during the pre-contact period, we find famines and certain diseases.

When the Ammassalimmiut ethnic group was discovered in 1884, they had just undergone a terrible period of famine. According to information recorded by Holm, Mikkelsen (1934:46) estimated that between 1881 and 1883, some 70 individuals had died of hunger, which represents a loss equivalent to 15% of the total population.

An extremely cold winter during which the very thick pack ice covered with snow prevented the hunting of seals at the breathing hole, was succeeded by another equally cold winter.

Moreover, the intermediate season of summer had not been sufficiently mild, and thus the population was unable to make provision for the next winter. Dramatic tales of famine have long haunted the oral tradition of this society. In the second half of the 19th century, there were several periods of "great hunger" and of deadly cold (for the lamps were fueled with seal blubber), during which there was no more food left, no rind of blubber, root, or bone to gnaw. Humans started eating their dogs, their indispensible companions, then they chewed on leather straps, their leather clothes and blankets, the leather of their tents and boats. As the final resort, they would, with great apprehension, eat their dead in order to survive. The first victims of famine were the elderly and the young children.

In the publications of Holm (1911), Hansêrak (1933), Mikkelsen (1934), Rasmussen (1938), Rosing (1963) and Victor (1993) we find numerous elements which allow us to evaluate the effects of the famine on the population of Ammassalik between 1881 and 1883. At Qernertivartivit out of a total population of 19, including five hunters, two inhabitants went to find another location where there might be some food left; those who remained died of hunger and cold, except for two women who survived by eating their dead kin (of the 15 who died of hunger, 13 were eaten according to Holm, 1911:131-132). Ironically, Kunitse who had abandoned his family to find refuge elsewhere, and the two women (his wife and his mother-in-law) who had eaten their kin in order to survive, also died of hunger a few years later, in 1892-1893, while spending the winter at Qingeq (according to

Fig. 4: A kayak hunter looking for prey. Ammassalik 1972. (Photo: Joëlle Robert-Lamblin).

our documents there were then six dead at this location). When spring returned, only one of the 15 inhabitants was found alive: Ajatoq, in the house of Nunakitsit, in the area of Kulusuk (Holm 1911:132). There were also many deaths by famine during the winter of 1882-1883, at Inissalik, close to Isertoq, and at least six of the dead were eaten by the last survivors (Holm 1911:133).

Famine was present in several regions of East Greenland, during the period 1870-1895, as well as in the north of Ammassalik, at Kialineq, and further south at Anoritoq (Rasmussen in Ostermann 1938:56-58). Garde indicates that during the winter following the departure of Holm, in 1886-1887, there was again a famine and cases of anthropophagy at Ammassalik (Garde 1888:95). He adds that the reason given by the East Greenlanders to explain this calamity was that it was a punishment to the population, guilty of having stolen Holm's belongings. Regarding these catastrophies affecting this small population, such as continuous bad weather, disappearance of game, or unsuccessful hunting, it is interesting to note that they were generally attributed to a human fault. It may have been theft as in this case, but it could also be the transgression of a taboo, or the bad behaviour of men or women which were the causes of these punishments inflicted by the Great Forces of the Universe (particularly The Man of The Moon and the Woman of the Sea, mistress of sea animals). The essential function of the shaman was to attempt to re-establish order by identifying the cause of the trouble.

After the beginning of colonization, with the introduction of firearms, there were no longer famines in Ammassalik. But periods of want, when the Ammassalimmiut had to eat their dogs, are mentioned by Hedegaard (1894-1919), in 1906 and in 1908-1909.

Regarding fatal diseases in traditional society, the first physicians who spent the winter in Ammassalik, Knud Poulsen in 1898-1899 and Robert Gessain in 1934-1935, insist on the absence of infectious diseases in epidemic form among the inhabitants of Ammassalik before the first contact with Westerners (Gessain 1975:146). Deaths through disease, more frequent among women than men, were mostly due to respiratory illnesses (lung diseases and phthisis according to Poulsen 1904:148-149). Other causes of deaths were food poisoning by putrefied meat, abcesses and tumors (of the throat or abdomen), frostbite and gangrene (particularly in the legs among women), and very few cardiac diseases.

Particular cases of sudden insanity, of which there are several examples in oral literature (Victor & Robert-Lamblin 1993:74-78, 277-281), resulted in the killing of the insane by his close kin. The justification for this type of homicide was that the delirious person was endangering the whole group. The loss of sanity revealed that the person had made, in great secrecy, a tupilaq intended to kill someone by magic, but not having attained its intended victim, the evil spell had turned against its crea-tor. The killing of the insane individual corresponded to a necessity to protect, at any price, the inhabitants of the common house from malevolent spirits which had taken over one of their kin through his own fault. In our archives, three men (aged 20, 35 and 45) and two women (aged 31 and 42) died in that manner, between 1885 and 1911.

The first exchanges with Westerners provoked terrible epidemics among the Ammassalimmiut population. They had lived in great isolation and lacked immunity towards infectious and contagious diseases such as: The common cold, influenza, whooping cough, measels, poliomyelitis, small pox, and the like. Discounting the fatal diseases contracted in the south of the country by some visitors from Eastern Greenland who had come to trade in the 19th century (especially in 1872 and 1892), the first epidemic in the Ammassalik area was that of the winter 1892-1893, which followed the visit of Ryder. Disease and famine caused many deaths during that winter, and the succeeding epidemics also took a terrible toll[12].

Forms of burial

In conclusion, I shall briefly mention the customs and beliefs surrounding death, of which more ample description is given elsewhere. I shall only make remarks of the rituals and the numerous mourning taboos affecting the family of the deceased, more specically his wife and mother, and the person who touched the body to dress him and take him out of the house[13].

After a death, in non-Christian East Greenlandic society it was as important to protect the living from the great menace hanging over them at that time as to help the soul of the deceased reach the Country of the Dead with ease. All had to be accomplished very fast, but with infinite precautions, while strictly respecting the established rules and taboos, in order not to endanger the survival of the inhabitants of the place or to contaminate the sea game which would disappear as a result.

The deceased, dressed in his or her best clothes - kayak anorak for the man, amaut for the woman, the hood over the head and the clothes well tightened around the neck, the wrists and the ankles - was either wrapped in a large seal skin which was then sewn up, or in the leather cover of a kayak which was used as a shroud. The body was then tied at the ankles and, in great haste, dragged out of the house feet first, (or passed through a window for more speed) by the person who had dressed it, who had to be a close kin of the deceased.

The resting place was a grave consisting of a mound of flat stones covering the body or an opening in a rock, closed by stones. However, at the end of the last century, the most frequent form of burial was in the ocean. It was said that of the two Worlds which could be reached by the dead souls, the 'Under Sea World' was a better place. The 'Dead of the Sky' had only crows and berries to eat, while the dead at the bottom of the sea had plenty of sea mammals' meat and blubber. According to tradition, women who died in childbirth, hunters dead in kayaks and those who killed themselves by drowning were fated to rejoin the Under Sea World of the Dead. This explains why those suffering from physical or mental pain would put an end to their life and to that of their young children with a certain amount of serenity: They had the prospect of finding a better life in the nether world. Also, some persons anticipated their natural death for fear of not having a burial if there was no one who could undertake this task for them (either no more family members living, or kin already too weakened by disease or hunger).

The deceased took with him his personal possessions: For a man, for example, his drum, his hunting gear, sometimes his kayak; for a woman, her lamp, her sewing kit, her personal knife, some parts of her attire; for a child, his toys.

The house, its contents and inhabitants had then to be purified, before the start of the difficult mourning period for close kin.

Glossary

phthisis = lung tubercolosis

Joëlle Robert-Lamblin, Research Director, Anthropologie Biologique, Musée de l'Homme, Paris, France

Notes

(1): 1884: Discovery of the Ammassalimmiut ethnic group by the Dane Gustav Holm; 1894: Beginning of the Danish colonization.

(2): The years 1895-1899, 1901-1907, 1911, 1921, 1930.

(3): Particularly those of the administrator Hedegaard for the years 1895-1929. (Archives of the Arktisk Institut).

(4) Ages were estimated by J. Hansen (Hansêrak) from historical landmarks (Holm 1911:188) and corrected in our data according to information obtained later.

(5): Infant mortality represents more than 30% of the total deaths recorded in 1897-1916 (Robert-Lamblin 1986:39).

(6): A Danish nurse was then present in the area from 1932, and, in 1944, a permanent Danish doctor was appointed.

(7): These deaths occurred in 1890, 1895, 1896, 1906, 1926, 1933 and 1935.

(8): In 1884, a hunter had to feed an average of 4 to 5 persons.

(9): In particularly difficult cases, the woman who helped the mother in childbirth, rubbed her hands in seal oil to facilitate the birth.

(10): As a comparison, Bertelsen gives the figure of 2.2% of women having died in childbirth in West Greenland in the period 1851-1900 (Bertelsen 1910:477).

(11): 1897-1906: 9 men died in kayaks; 7 women died in childbirth; 1907-1916: 7 men died in kayaks; 8 women died in childbirth; 1917-1926: 12 men died in kayaks; 10 women died in childbirth.

(12): 1897 and 1898: epidemic amongst infants and common cold (mortality rate 51 per 1000 in 1897; 47 per 1000 in 1898). 1900: common cold (mortality rate 42 per 1000). 1910: whooping cough and influenza (mortality rate 63 per 1000). 1914 and 1915: influenza (mortality rate 77 per 1000 in 1914, 40 per 1000 in 1915). 1925: Spanish influenza and poliomyelitis (mortality rate 55 per 1000).

(13): See Holm 1911:74-80; Petersen 1966-1967; Rasmussen in Ostermann 1938:183-188; Victor & Robert-Lamblin 1993:17-20, 311-315 + 325-345.

References

Bertelsen, Alfred [1910]: **Om Dødeligheden i Grønland og om nogle af Dødsaarsagerne sammesteds.** *Bibliotek for laeger*, 102:459-504 (Copenhagen: Ugeskrift for Læger).

Garde, V. [1888]: **Nogle Bemaerkninger om Øst-Grønlands Beboere.** *Geografisk Tidsskrift*, 9:93-96 (Copenhagen: Kongelige Danske Geografiske Selskab).

Gessain, Robert [1975]: **Essai sur l'ethnonosologie des Ammassalimiut au XIXè siècle.** *Objets et Mondes*, 15(2):129-148 (Paris: Musée de l'Homme).

Hansen, J. (Hansêrak) [1911]: **List of the Inhabitants of the East Coast of Greenland made in the Autumn of 1884.** *Meddelelser om Grønland*, 39 (1):183-202 (Copenhagen: C. A. Reitzels Forlag) - Gustav Holm: Notes on the List.

Hansêrak, 1933 - see Thalbitser 1933.

Hedegaard, A. T. [1894-1919]: **Angmagssalik.** Manuscript, 90 p. (Copenhagen: Archive of the Arctic Institut).

Holm, Gustav [1911]: **Etnological sketch of the Angmagssalik Eskimo.** *Meddelelser om Grønland*, 39(1):1-147 (Copenhagen: C. A. Reitzels Forlag).

Mikkelsen, Einar [1934]: **De Østgrønlandske Eskimoers Historie.** 202 p. (Copenhagen: Gyldendalske Boghandel Nordisk Forlag).

Petersen J. (Ujuât) [1957]: **Ujuâts Dagbøger fra Østgrønland 1894-1935.** *Det Grønlandske Selskabs Skrifter*, 19:1-209 (Copenhagen: Det Grønlandske Selskab).

Petersen, Robert [1967]: **Burial-forms and death cult among the Eskimos.** *Folk*, 8-9:259-280 (Copenhagen: Dansk Etnografisk Forening).

Poulsen, K. [1904]: **Contributions to the Anthropology and Nosology of the East-Greenlanders.** *Meddelelser om Grønland*, 28(4):133-150 (Copenhagen: C. A. Reitzels Forlag).

Robert-Lamblin, Joëlle [1984]: **L'expression de la violence dans la société ammassalimiut (côte orientale du Groenland).** *Etudes Rurales*, juil.-déc.(95-96):115-129 (Paris: Laboratoire d'Anthropologie Sociale).

Robert-Lamblin, Joëlle [1986]: **Ammassalik, East Greenland - end or persistance of an isolate? Anthropological and demographical study on change.** *Med-delelser om Grønland, Man and Society*, 10:1-168 (Copenhagen: The Commission for Scientific Research in Greenland).

Rosing, Jens [1963]: **Sagn og Saga fra Angmagssalik.** 308 p. (Copenhagen: Rhodos).

Ryder, Carl [1895]: **Beretning om den Østgrønlandske Expedition 1891-1892.** *Meddelelser om Grønland*, 17(7): 1-147 (Copenhagen: C. A. Reitzels Forlag).

Thalbitzer, William (editor) [1914 & 1923]: **The Ammassalik Eskimo: contributions to the Ethnology of the East Greenland Natives.** *Meddelelser om Grønland*, 39(1-7):1-755 & 40(1-3):1-564 (Copenhagen: C. A. Reitzels Forlag).

Thalbitzer, William [1933]: **Den Grønlandske Kateket Hansêraks Dagbog om den Danske Konebaadsekspedition til Ammassalik i Østgrønland 1884-1885.** *Det Grønlandske Selskabs Skrifter*, 8:1-248 (Copenhagen: Det Grønlandske Selskab).

Victor, Paul-Emile & Joëlle Robert-Lamblin [1993]: **La Civilisation du Phoque. 2. Légendes, rites et croyances des Eskimo d'Ammassalik.** 424 p. (Biarritz: R. Chabaud, SAI).

Fig. 5: Kayak men, Ammassalik 1972. (Photo: Joëlle Robert-Lamblin).

Igloolik Island Before and After Jørgen Meldgaard

Graham Rowley and Susan Rowley

Igloolik Island Before Jørgen Meldgaard
by Graham Rowley

Igloolik Island lies in the eastern approaches to Fury and Hecla Strait, which separates Baffin Island from the mainland of Canada. It was here that Parry's second expedition, seeking a Northwest Passage by following the continental coast, was forced to spend the winter of 1822-1823 when stopped by ice blocking the strait (Parry 1824). The strong currents through the strait usually prevent patches of water from freezing completely even in mid-winter and also bring nutrients to the surface, resulting in rich marine resources, which were supporting, as they had for centuries, a human population. Parry found the people living in summer in tents and in winter in snow houses, though a few were in turf, stone, and whale bone *qarmat*.

Over the next hundred years the area was little visited by outsiders but in 1923 Rasmussen's Fifth Thule Expedition brought Therkel Mathiassen to carry out the first professional archaeological excavations in the Eastern Canadian Arctic. His work in Repulse Bay and Pond Inlet led to his definition of the Thule Culture. He visited Igloolik Island in the winter and noted old stone houses there which were similar to the Thule Culture houses he had excavated, and which he correlated with the Tuniit, who according to Inuit tradition had been displaced by their forefathers (Mathiassen 1927).

Diamond Jenness of the National Museum of Canada, after examining the museum's northern collections in the light of Mathiassen's work, believed that the Eastern Arctic had seen an earlier culture which had left artifacts very different from those of the Thule Culture.

He called this the Dorset Culture because many of these different artifacts had been found near Cape Dorset (Jenness 1925). Jenness' theory was not fully accepted as Mathiassen considered the Dorset material could be explained as local variations of the Thule Culture[1] (Mathiassen 1927: 164).

On my way to the Eastern Arctic in 1936 I asked Jenness what an archaeologist might usefully do there. He replied: "*Find a Dorset site which has no Thule material*". That summer I excavated on Southampton Island without finding such a site. In the winter, like Mathiassen, I sledged to Igloolik where there was now a Roman Catholic missionary, Father Bazin. He gave me a collection Inuit had made while digging turf for *qarmat* on Abverdjar (Avvajja), an adjacent island. The artifacts were all very different from what I had excavated the previous summer.

In Ottawa, Jenness confirmed by belief that they were all Dorset. In 1939, I returned to Igloolik to excavate at Abverdjar, where I located and excavated the site from which the collection Father Bazin had given me had been made (G. Rowley 1940). I also began to excavate at Arnaquaaksaat (NiHf-4) on Igloolik Island where I found both Thule houses and Dorset material, and where I thought I might learn something about the relationship between the two. I was at Arnaquaaksaat when the mission supply ship, the *M. V. Therese*, arrived in September, bringing the first trading post to Igloolik and taking me south to the war that had started two weeks earlier (G. Rowley 1996)[2].

In the archaeological reports of the Fifth Thule Expedition Mathiassen had frequently discussed the significance in the Eastern Canadian Arctic of the height of

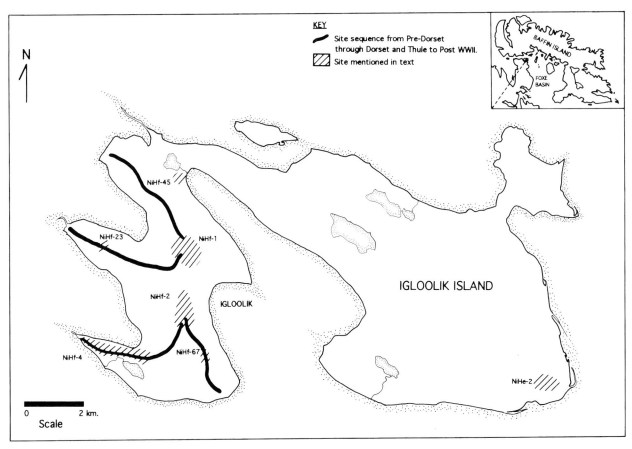

Fig. 1: Igloolik Island - Marked on the map are the sites mentioned by name in the text and the four known Pre-Dorset to Dorset site sequences on the island.

archaeological sites above sea level. Northern people have always depended mainly upon marine resources and have therefore usually lived close to the sea. During the Pleistocene Period the land was depressed by the weight of the ice covering it. When relieved of the pressure of the ice the land began to rise, here at the rate of about 1 m a century. The highest point of Igloolik Island is only 54 m above sea level and the island must first have begun to emerge from the sea between 5.000 and 6.000 years ago.

Archaeological sites excavated in the Igloolik area had all been at altitudes of not much more than 10 m above sea level and therefore could not have been more than 1.000 years old. In 1946 Father Guy Mary-Rousseliere noted raised beaches at Alarnerk (Alaniq) on the mainland close to Igloolik Island, with traces of old camp sites well away from the sea. Mary-Rousseliere also learnt from Monica Ataguttaaluk that the houses occupied by Tuniit were those where items belonging to the Dorset Culture were found (Mary-Rousseliere 1954, 1987).

When Jørgen Meldgaard visited the Foxe Basin area in 1954, he invited Mary-Rousseliere to join his party. Meldgaard had already excavated at the stratified Sermermiut site in Greenland, corroborating earlier excavations at Saqqaq of a culture earlier than the Dorset. At Igloolik he examined the higher land, discovering tent rings and other signs of habitation at the highest points of the island, thereby extending its prehistory back to 3810 +/- 302 B.P. (Maxwell 1985:78). At Kaleruserk (NiHf-1; Qalirusiq) and Lyon Hill (NiHf-2; Qalirusiq) he excavated artifacts different in many ways from those of the Dorset, but similar to his earlier Saqqaq finds. In the Eastern Arctic this is now referred to as the Pre-Dorset Culture.

Meldgaard continued his Igloolik research returning to Igloolik in 1957 and 1965 (Meldgaard 1960a, 1960b, 1962).

My daughter Susan was the next archaeologist to work in the Igloolik area and she will continue this account.

Igloolik Island - After Jorgen Meldgaard
by Susan Rowley

Igloolik Island is a small limestone island measuring 16 km by 8 km. As neither Meldgaard nor my father could have imagined there is now a thriving and growing community of over 1.000 inhabitants on the island. Roads, houses, community buildings and airstrips all require gravel for construction material and the cultural heritage of the community is constantly threatened by these demands. Our work has focused on offering Inuit youth an archaeological perspective on their heritage and in trying to stay one step ahead of the bulldozers. Fieldwork in 1987, 1988, and 1989 as well as discussions with Carolyn MacDonald, a teacher in the community, led to the establishment of the Igloolik Archaeology Field School. This school gives local high school students an opportunity to experience archaeological field techniques first hand while learning about their past. In 1996 a separate field school was offered as a university course for local teachers.

Meldgaard's pioneering research in Northern Foxe Basin provided the framework on which later PalaeoInuit research throughout the Canadian Arctic was based. In two short field seasons he located the first Pre-Dorset sites in the Canadian Arctic and also identified and excavated a sequence of sites from Early Dorset through to Terminal Dorset. His research led others to identify the Foxe Basin area as part of the 'core area' for PalaeoInuit cultural development. Our research has built upon Meldgaard's work.

We have added 110 sites to the five previously recorded and still have not completed the survey of the island. The sites span all time periods and include 36 Pre-Dorset sites, 26 Dorset sites, 54 NeoInuit sites (including three Thule sites with sod and whale bone *qarmat*), seven Post World War II sites and one European site. Owing to the rapid rate of isostatic rebound sites are rarely superimposed and there are only 8 sites with components of more than one archaeological culture. Meldgaard identified two site sequences following descending beach ridges on peninsulas from Pre-Dorset to Dorset. During 1989 we surveyed the remaining two peninsulas on the western half of the island and located two complete sequences of sites from Pre-Dorset through Late Dorset to Thule and up to the post-World War II period (Fig. 1).

Northern Foxe Basin has large herds of walrus and a high density of bearded seals. Both of these animals are large meat packages and are available throughout most of the year. The human population was therefore not as susceptible to unpredictable climatic events that can wipe out land mammals as were populations in some other regions. As a result of these resources, Igloolik Island was occupied continuously from the Early Pre-Dorset up to the present. While the occupation was continuous the population size was not at all constant. Our site survey

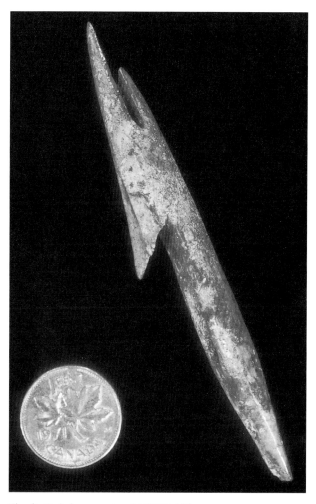

Fig. 2: Male harpoon head NiHf-2:310.

research indicates low population density in the late Pre-Dorset period and in the Middle Dorset period with higher densities during the Early Pre-Dorset, Early Dorset, and Late/Terminal Dorset periods. Not only are there more sites during the periods of greater population but the number of dwellings within sites also increases.

We have excavated one or more dwellings at four Pre-Dorset sites, three Early Dorset sites, two Late Dorset sites, one mixed Late Dorset and Neo-Inuit site and one Neo-Inuit site. As previously mentioned our research agenda is determined by the community's development plans. What follows is a short descriptive account of the Palaeo-Inuit research we have conducted as it corroborates or adds to Meldgaard's interpretations of Igloolik Island's archaeological record.

Pre-Dorset

Currently, three separate terms are commonly used for the earliest occupants of the eastern Arctic: Independence I, Early Pre-Dorset, and Early Saqqaq although Helmer (1994) has recently argued that they should all be referred to as the Initial Horizon of the Pre-Dorset period.

Fig. 3: Pre-Dorset tent ring with internal box hearth (NiHf-67 Feature 4).

When Meldgaard first excavated the Pre-Dorset sites on Igloolik Island he labeled them Saqqaq because of the similarities he saw with materials excavated from both the Sermermiut and Saqqaq sites in Greenland (1960a). Following the work of Collins (1954) this earliest material became identified as Pre-Dorset in the Eastern Canadian Arctic. The Igloolik material does indeed share many similarities with Saqqaq material as noted by Meldgaard. Two especially striking similarities have since been unearthed.

In 1988 at NiHf-2 we found two male harpoon heads (Fig. 2). These harpoon heads are common finds from Saqqaq sites and have been reported from two Independence I sites in the Canadian Arctic but are previously unknown from Pre-Dorset sites.

In 1957 Meldgaard excavated an antler artifact he and his Inuit assistants identified as a bow brace from Kaleruserk (NiHf-1; for an illustration of this object see Maxwell 1985:83). Later excavations at Qeqertasussuk in Greenland produced an identical object which proved to be a double ended scraper with both scrapers still in place (Grønnow 1994:211). These two artifacts are unique.

These finds support Meldgaard's belief that we are dealing with regional variations of an archaeological culture rather than with separate archaeological cultures.

The term Independence I is used in the Eastern Canadian Arctic to refer to a few sites that exhibit differences from Pre-Dorset sites. These differences include: Presence of male harpoon heads, linear settlement patterns as opposed to clustered settlement patterns, the construction of dwellings with axial features and box hearths, lithics with serrated edges, expanded end scrapers, and unpolished burins (McGhee 1979).

On Igloolik Island we have excavated male harpoon heads, found dwellings with axial features and box hearths, and recovered lithic materials commonly referred to as Independence I in Pre-Dorset contexts. For example, the male harpoon heads from NiHf-2 were recovered from the same dwelling as three female harpoon heads all of different Pre-Dorset types.

We have also surveyed Early PalaeoInuit sites with clustered settlement patterns as well as sites at similar elevations with linear settlement patterns. This research leads me to suggest that Independence 1 does not represent a separate and/or earlier migration of peoples into

Fig. 4: Late Dorset semi-subterranean dwelling (NiHf-4 Feature 4). Note axial feature of limestone and quartzite slabs with fire pit and pot stand. In the forground the moss mattress is visible while in the background the gravel under-mattress has been exposed.

the eastern Arctic. Rather, I would concur with Helmer (1994: 24) that the similarities override the differences and that the differences are due to seasonal variation, regional variation, and individual/group preferences rather than to separate and distinct occupations by different cultures.

Our research has revealed tremendous architectural variation throughout all time periods. This variation is manifested through differences in the form of dwellings, hearths, caches and other features. There is also variation in settlement patterns both in the location of sites and in the layout of dwellings within sites. This variation can be attributed to seasonal variation, inter-annual climatic variation, and individual preference.

During the Pre-Dorset period dwellings are oval in form and are either delineated by small rocks or substantial limestone slabs. They may or may not have guy rope rocks and they vary in size from 2.5 m by 2 m to 7.5 m by 5 m. Most of the dwellings cluster into two sizes:

1) a smaller group with measurements in the range of 3 m by 3 m and

2) a larger group with measurements in the range of 4 m by 5 m.

These dwellings may or may not have axial features. Some of the dwellings without axial features have internal box hearths (see Fig. 3). Still others have associated external box hearths or large external boulder hearths that are oval in shape. This variability is both inter and intra-site.

Some of the sites are located on top of beach ridges, others are excavated into the seaward slopes of beach ridges, and still others are constructed in the swales between the ridges.

At some sites the dwellings are clustered while in others they are laid out in a linear fashion along the beach ridge.

Most lithics produced during this period were made from chert, however, silicified slate, quartz and quartz crystals were also used. All these materials are present at the earliest sites on the island. However, through time we see changes in the cherts exploited suggesting changes in interaction spheres.

While we have had great success in locating the sources of many lithic quarries we have been able to identify the sources of only three of the almost twenty varieties of cherts we find.

Dorset

Meldgaard identified many dramatic changes in material culture between the 22 m and 23 m elevations. These included changes in technology, in architecture and in use of raw materials as well as the sudden disappearance of dogs and certain artifact types and the equally sudden appearance of other artifacts (1962:95). These changes led Meldgaard to identify the 22 m elevation as marking the transition between the Pre-Dorset and Dorset Cultures. In addition, they led him to argue that the Dorset Culture had been strongly influenced through either diffusion or migration by Indian cultures to the south - the infamous 'smells of the forest' (1960a:75; 1960b:593; 1962:95). Some of the changes Meldgaard noted have proven to be artifacts of limited excavation. For example, when Meldgaard wrote his papers triangular end blades were unknown from Pre-Dorset sites as were long straight microblades and sled shoes. All of which have since been identified.

In the Early Dorset period rectangular dwellings with external E-shaped hearths first occur. However, oval dwellings with axial features were still constructed (contra Meldgaard 1962:93). The earliest known long house on Igloolik Island (at NiHf-23) dates to this time period. Earlier long houses, dating to the Pre-Dorset period, have been reported nearby, on the west coast of Melville Peninsula at Cape McLoughlin (S. Rowley 1992).

At the beginning of the Early Dorset period there was a dramatic change in raw materials with the sudden appearance of slate. Meldgaard regarded the sudden appearance of slate as one strong indicator of the southern origins of the Dorset Culture. Contra Meldgaard, I would like to suggest another reason for the sudden appearance of slate in northern Foxe Basin. The slate found on Early Dorset sites is a very distinctive green slate we refer to as the Inuksugalik slate. Hubert Amarualik, Mark Ijjangiaq, Francois Quassa, Aipilik Innuksuk, and other Igloolik elders led us to the Inuksugalik and Uluksangnat slate sources. These quarries are located 30 km north-north-west of Igloolik Island and are both at elevations at or less than 22 m above sea level. Therefore, the Inuksugalik slate first became available during the Early Dorset period. The massive quantities of slate we find on Early Dorset sites on Igloolik Island and in northern Foxe Basin appear to be the result of peoples' experimentation with this new material. Following the Early Dorset period, the use of slate decreases dramatically, however, its use continues throughout the Dorset period. As the use of slate decreases the use of chert and quartz crystal increases.

Some features of the Pre-Dorset/Early Dorset transition noted by Meldgaard still remain. These include: the disappearance of dogs, bows and arrows and drilled holes; the sudden appearance of snow knife blades, composite boxes, and tip-fluting; and the radical changes in harpoon head, lamp and needle forms.

Fig. 5: "Caught in the Act" or "Surprized by Love". The first evidence of Dorset-Thule social interaction?

Our research generally supports Meldgaard's Igloolik harpoon head typology (nd) with some minor varitations and one addition. At the Qalirusiujak site (NiHf-45) we unearthed a new type of harpoon head. The Qalirusiujak type is only known from one specimen - NiHf-45:1299. It is a large antler harpoon head. The blade slit is cut away on one side and carefully carved out for a stemmed end blade. The remaining side of the blade slit has a slight notch for lashing. The socket is closed and the basal spurs are symmetric. The unique feature of this harpoon head is that the double line holes are placed one on top of the other rather than side by side. A harpoon head similar to this was reported by Jenness (1929) who regarded it as typical of Beothuk manufacture.

During the Late Dorset period the architectural variability to which we have become accustomed continues. Dwellings vary from possible snow houses, to simple rock outlines, to rectangular semi-subterranean dwellings without axial features, to semi-subterranean dwellings with axial features, pot stands, fire pits and well defined sleeping platforms with gravel and moss mattresses (Fig. 4), to jumbled rock masses with difficult to define borders and paved entrances. No Terminal Dorset houses with cold trap entrances have yet been identified on the island.

During the Late Dorset period there is increased experimentation with different raw materials, some exotic and some local. There is also a resurgence in the use of quartz. Meteoric iron and copper suddenly appear in small quantities during this period. Finds from two dwellings at Arnaquaaksaat (NiHf-4) include an iron knife blade in an antler handle, an iron end blade, a copper hook and a copper needle. This evidence and the evidence from other Late Dorset sites with metal finds indicates an increase in long distance trading relationships throughout the eastern Arctic during this time period.

The Dorset-Thule transition at Igloolik remains as much an archaeological mystery as ever despite the clear oral historical evidence of contact between the two peoples. At NiHf-4 Dorset material has been discovered at elevations as low as 7 m above sea level and Early Thule material has also been unearthed. Despite five seasons of excavation at this site we still have no clear evidence of contact unless the Dorset carving (Fig. 5) unearthed this summer could be considered as providing us with a first glimpse of Dorset-Thule social interaction!

Conclusion

The basic picture of Inuit prehistory as developed by Meldgaard for the Igloolik area still remains valid. Archaeological research on Igloolik Island continues to surprise and reward us with occasional new artifact types, and with both new discoveries and new sites every season.

Graham Rowley, Otawa, Canada and
Susan Rowley, Pitsbourgh, Pennsylvania, USA

Acknowledgements

As always, my first debt of gratitude is to the community of Igloolik for allowing us to excavate their heritage. I would particularly like to acknowledge the elders who have graciously shared their knowledge with us and the youth and teachers who have participated in the Igloolik Archaeology Field School. Logistical support for our research has been provided by the Nunavut Research Institute and I would like to thank all the staff of the Igloolik Research Centre for their efforts on our behalf through the years. Thanks also to the Baffin Divisional Board of Education, the Inuit Heritage Trust, the Prince of Wales Northern Heritage Centre, and the Canadian Conservation Institute. Carolyn MacDonald is the backbone of the field school and deserves special recognition. Finally, I would like to thank my family and Carolyn's family for all the different ways they have supported us.

Abbreviations

NiHf & NiHe are Borden site designations.

Notes

1: In 1933 Junius Bird on board the *Morrissey* spent part of an afternoon excavating at the large Thule site at Igloolik Point (NiHe-2) when their ship was unable to pass through Fury and Hecla Strait (Bartlett 1934).

2: During the next several years Inuit continued making archaeological collections which they gave to the Father Dutilly, a Roman Catholic priest who travelled on the *M. V. Therese*. These collections were made from the west coast of Hudson Bay and Foxe Basin. While most have poor provenience some of the collections are identified to the site where they were made.

References

Bartlett, Robert A. [1934]: **Sails over Ice**. 301 p. (New York: Charles Scribner's Sons).

Collins, Henry B. [1954]: **Archaeological Research in the North American Arctic**. *Arctic*, 7(3-4):296-306 (Calgary: The Arctic Institute of North America).

Grønnow, Bjarne [1994]: **Qeqertasussuk - the archaeology of a frozen Saqqaq site.** pp:197-238 in "Threads of Arctic Prehistory: Papers in honour of William E. Taylor, Jr.", editors: David Morrison & Jean-Luc Pilon, *Archaeological Survey of Canada, Mercury Series Paper*, 149:1-422 (Ottawa: Canadian Museum of Civilization).

Helmer, James [1994]: **Resurrecting the spirit(s) of Taylor's "Carlsberg Culture": Cultural traditions and cultural horizons in eastern Arctic Prehistory.** pp:15-34 in "Threads of Arctic Prehistory: Papers in honour of William E. Taylor, Jr.", editors: David Morrison & Jean-Luc Pilon, *Archaeological Survey of Canada, Mercury Series Paper*, 149:1-422 (Ottawa: Canadian Museum of Civilization).

Jenness, Diamond [1925]: **A new Eskimo culture in Hudson Bay.** *The Geographical Review*, 15(3):428-437 (*).

Jenness, Diamond [1929]: **Notes on the Beothuk of Newfoundland.** *National Musuem of Canada Bulletin*, 56:36-39, Annual Report for 1927 (Ottawa: National Museum of Canada).

Mary-Rousseliere, Guy [1954]: **The archaeological site of Pingerkalik.** *Eskimo*, 33(September):11-15 (Churchill: Diocese of Churchill-Hudson Bay).

Mary-Rousseliere, Guy [1987]: **How Old Monica Ataguttaaluk introduced me to Arctic Archaeology.** *Inuktitut*, 66:6-24 (Ottawa: Indian and Northrn Affairs Canada).

Mathiassen, Therkel [1927]: **Archaeology of the Central Eskimos.** *Report of the Fifth Thule Expedition 1921-1924*, 4(1):1-327 (Copenhagen: Gyldendanske Boghandel).

Maxwell, Moreau S. [1985]: **Prehistory of the Eastern Arctic.** 327 p. (New York: Academic Press).

McGhee, Robert [1979]: **The Palaeoeskimo occupations at Port Refuge, High Arctic Canada.** *Mercury Series. Archaeological Survey Paper*, 92:1-159 (Ottawa: National Museum of Man).

Meldgaard, Jørgen [1960a]: **Origin and Evolution of Eskimo Cultures in the eastern Arctic.** *Canadian Geographical Journal*, 60(2):64-75 (Ottawa: Royal Canadian Geographic Society).

Meldgaard, Jørgen [1960b]: **Prehistoric culture sequences in the eastern Arctic as elucidated by stratified sites at Iglulik.** pp:588-595 in "Men and cultures. Selected papers of the Fifth International Congress of Anthropological and Ethnological Sciences, 1956", editor: A. F. C. Wallace, 810 p. (Philadelphia: University of Pennsylvania Press).

Meldgaard, Jørgen [1962]: **On the Formative Period of the Dorset Culture.** pp:92-95 in "Prehistoric Cultural Relations between the Arctic and Temperate Zones of North America", editor: John M. Campbell, *Arctic Institute of North America, Technical Paper*, ll:1-181 (Montreal: Arctic Institute of North America).

Meldgaard, Jørgen [no date]: **Dorset Culture Harpoon Head Chronology.** Unpublished manuscript.

Parry, William E. [1824]: **Journal of a second voyage for the discovery of a North-west Passage from the Atlantic ot hte Pacific; performed in the years 1821-1822-1823, in His Majesty's Ships Fury and Hecla, under the orders of Captain William Edward Parry, R. N., F.R.S., and commander of the expedition.** 571 p. (London: John Murray).

Rowley, Graham W. [1940]: **The Dorset culture of the Eastern Arctic.** *American Anthropologist*, new series, 42:490-499 (Menasha, Wis.: American Anthropologist Society).

Rowley, Graham W. [1996]: **Cold Comfort: My love affair with the Arctic.** 255 p. (Montreal-Kingston: McGill-Queens's University Press).

Rowley, Susan [1992]: **Survey of three short range radar sites: Simpson Lake, Cape McLoughlin and Lailor River, N.W.T.** * p. Unpublished report on file with the Archaeological Survey of Canada (Ottawa).

Greenland and the National Museum of Denmark
The National Museum of Denmark and Greenland
Fragments of a piece of Museum History

Helge Schultz-Lorentsen

In the course of the last 50 years the society of Greenland has underwent a very rapid development.

From an isolated hunting and fishing population under Danish colonial administration, a modern society has been established. Its main bases are the industrial fishing, the prospect of finding and exploring mineral resources, plus the expectations of growing tourism. Denmark still provides substantial financial assistance but since the establisment of Home Rule in 1979 the Greenlanders themselves are fully responsible for the expenditure of these subsidies. Home Rule, based on community with Denmark and The Faroe Islands, has during the years taken over more and more administrative duties. Thus, the cultural sector was assumed in 1981.

In the rapid advancement of modern times the Greenlanders were not in time aware of the importance of preserving the remains of the original way of life and the former means of subsistence - the hunting culture.

So one has to be grateful that the National Museum of Denmark for more than hundred years has managed or supported systematic investigations and expeditions in order to gather knowledge about Greenlandic cultural history.

As time has passed, the National Museum of Denmark has received substantial culture-historical material, which, together with purchases and donations from Greenlanders and Danish administrators, forms an important basis for our knowledge about the Greenlanders' past, way of life, and culture.

This material, considered to consist of about 15.000 ethnographic and about 100.000 archaeologic items, has been stored in the National Museum of Denmark, which -until the assumption through Home Rule in 1981 - according to law took care of culture-historical research, collection and storage of relics of the past and the promoting of these.

In Greenland there had several times during the years been plans for establishing a museum. Nevertheless, half a century had to pass from the first idea, until the first Greenland Museum was opened in 1966. The Greenland Museum department did not until this incident establish itself officially.

Many years were then spent on eager and difficult preliminary work, in which the National Museum of Denmark - and not least the Department of Ethnography with curator Jørgen Meldgaard as the driving force - played an important role. Initially in the ante-natal period, later as midwife, and later again as advisor. After Home Rule had taken over the responsibility for the museum department and culture-historical research in Greenland the National Museum of Denmark took on the role as co-operative partner in a teamwork, which has echoed widely in the international museum society.

This development, which should be called an example of museum history, in fact began 50 years earlier. At a time when the National Museum of Denmark was rather regarded as an opponent, stealing Greenlandic relics.

The idea for a Greenland Museum was first expressed in Greenland in 1913, when the Council for

Fig. 1: The first Greenland Museum was established and housed in the "Ny Herrnhut" building.

South Greenland discussed a proposal from the Danish Administration and the National Museum of Denmark to prohibit foreign travellers and public employees in Greenland collecting and exporting objects from graves. It was found that this had happened on such a large scale that many cultural relics now rested in European and American museums, some collections being larger than that of the National Museum of Denmark.

Then the Danish Administration and the National Museum of Denmark together suggested that all finds of old Eskimo and Norse objects in the future should be handed over to the National Museum of Denmark.

'The Council for South Greenland' agreed that something had to be done to preserve the old cultural artefacts but found it unfair that the Greenlandic grave finds were exported and sent to the National Museum of Denmark.

"*The Greenlanders have no other history than that found in the graves, and it is of importance to acquire knowledge about the habits of the ancestors; that the population can get the opportunity to see the weapons and tools that were used*", one of the council members declared.

Wonder was also expressed over the interest, which suddenly grew in the National Museum of Denmark, which had remained passive and had not earlier considered the problem to be serious. The Council then suggested the establishment of a Greenland Museum, having first right to all finds of old Greenlandic and Norse items.

The following year the Council for South Greenland had to consider an estimate over the expenses concerning the foundation of a museum in the old mission building in 'Ny Herrnhut'. The Council decided to recommend that all necessary expenses for the museum were taken from the means of the Common Treasury.

In fact, 50 years had to pass before the first Greenland Museum could be inaugurated in 'Ny Herrnhut'.

The Council for South Greenland's reading of the proposal, put forward by the Danish Administration and the National Museum of Denmark in 1913, was followed up some years later with the issue of "General Circular of 19th April 1916 from the Ministry of the Interior Concerning Precautions for Saving Cultural Artefacts in Greenland." The circular prohibits excavation in Eskimo and Norse graves without special permission and instructs the authorities to take care that possible exports from Greenland go through the National Museum of Denmark in Copenhagen which must inspect the material having the right to take what is needed for the completion of the said collections. The circular ends:

"*The National Museum of Denmark assumes - should a folklore collection be established in Greenland - in the said inspections also to pick out such items as could be of value to such a collection, all in close arrangement with the Administration.*" A rule which should be regarded as quite fair. At that time the National Museum of Denmark was also that of Greenland.

Nothing else is heard about the Greenlandic museum-plans for the next many years. But as a positive result of the debates in the Council and the circular of 1916 a number of valuable relics was collected, both from West and East Greenland. The storage of these numerous relics naturally represented a problem, and since no one was directly responsible for solving this problem, the relics had a changeable existence over the years.

First they were stored in the attic in the Herrnhut building. Later a room in the attic in the Archives Building (a former hospital from 1856) was furnished and the relics moved to here in 1927. From then on they were designation as a Greenlandic folklore collection. But the building fell more and more into decay and was demolished in 1949. The collection was then stored in a warehouse attic.

The new Central Administration in Godthåb was in 1950 assigned two civil servants who in the following years played a vital role in the renewal of the museum idea: N. O. Christensen, head clerk of the administration and later governor, and C. F. Simony, chief constable and later High Court judge. The latter goty a residence in Ny Herrnhut.

Late in 1954 N. O. Christensen received a letter from one of the leading cultural figures of Greenland, priest and author Otto Rosing. Enclosed is a kind of memorandum which he calls "Reflections on a Greenlandic museum".

Otto Rosing mentions remembering that in 1914 there was a room in the attic in the Herrnhut Building where old things were stored, and he continues: *"Around 1915 my father sent different things from Angmagssalik, for example a model of an ice-harpoon - itsuarniut."*

Otto Rosing's "Reflections" which, in fact, are a cry for help, continue: *"I have often wondered about the great 'ignorance' regarding the way of life and the tools of our fathers and the energy and capability of the ancestors. The younger generation has no possibility to understand the ancestors' ingenuity and skilful crafts, because we have nothing to show of their tools and works; that is palpable proof of a special culture, a highly developed culture at that. - We Greenlanders, living today, are totally stripped of everything - lock, stock, and barrel - of old finds and similarly of national value. Everything has landed in Copenhagen."*

Otto Rosing continues: *"The National Museum of Denmark in Copenhagen is said to possess the world's largest Eskimo collection. Perhaps is it good that everything of national value from Greenland has landed there and has been in good hands for several years. We can not preserve old things ourselves, so we must be grateful, that the National Museum of Denmark has taken care of them and stored them properly. I expect that the National Museum of Denmark will hand over many, many things to our museums up here, if we ask them politely."*

N. O. Christensen forwarded 1954 Otto Rosing's "Reflections" to Helge Larsen (Chief curator 1963-1975 at the Department of Ethnography) and took the opportunity to tell, that *"everything, that exists of museum stuff in this town, is now stored in the attic in Ny Herrnhut. It has previously been stored in a warehouse attic, and unfortunately has been damaged, especially as some of the boxes have been robbed. The collection from the East Coast mentioned by Otto Rosing is among them."*

Helge Larsen answers N. O. Christensen, writing for example: *"Regarding the forwarded notes concerning*

Fig. 2: An example of the exhibition in the first Greenland Museum founded in the "Ny Herrnhut" building.

Fig. 3: The new National Museum of Greenland in a new built building in Nuuk.

one or more Greenlandic museums I can inform you that I have discussed the matter with Dr. Kaj Birket-Smith (Chief curator 1940-1963 at the Department of Ethnography), *and I can say on his behalf that there might well be a possibility that a few duplicates from the Department of Ethnography could be handed over to a future museum in Greenland but that we, on the other hand, do not possess as much duplicate material as might be imagined. We must also insist that Greenlandic museums must be regarded as provincial museums in relation to the National Museum of Denmark so that pieces of scientific value always must be sent to and remain in the National Museum of Denmark."*

Helge Larsen adds that he thinks, it is very important that new museums starts their own collections, *"because there is still ethnographic material in Greenland, and it has to be collected before it is too late."*

In Greenland the struggle to create an interest in and an understanding for the collection of more items has continued. That same year (1955) the Council granted 10.000 kr. for the restoration of the stable at Ny Herrnhut, whereto the collection was then moved, and another 5.000 kr. were granted for purchases in the years to come.

In 1956 four outstanding citizens of Nuuk/Godthåb wrote a paragraph in the Greenlandic newspaper Atuagagliutit/Grønlandsposten, saying that it was now time that a museum was established: *"All peoples developing and renewing their culture have an obligation to preserve the relics of their ancestors' culture. We should do the same,"* they called.

The paragraph demonstrated that the world's largest Eskimo culture-historical collection was in the National Museum of Denmark, while there was none in Greenland. But a hope was expressed that many of the duplicates in the storerooms of the National Museum of Denmark would return to Greenland, once a museum was established.

The paragraph was met with sympathy. A museum society was set up and the collection of tools, articles for everyday use, clothes, and skin boats was intensified. The relics were stored up in the small and modest, now restored, stable at Ny Herrnhut.

Jørgen Meldgaard, a recent M.A. in prehistoric archaeology, had in 1953 been employed as scientific member of the Department of Ethnography at the National Museum of Denmark.

The year before he, together with other students, participated in a reconnaissance expedition in the Godthåb Fjord.

During a visit to Godthåb Meldgaard established contact with N. O. Christensen and Simony who told about the museum plans and showed the collected items. This personal contact to the National Museum of Denmark later turned out to be of vital importance to the Greenlandic museum plans.

In 1961 something happened which undoubtedly added to a wider interest in the past:

N. O. Christensen turned up at the National Museum of Denmark, putting a skull on Meldgaard's desk, saying: *"Here is Erik the Red's head."*

The background for this somewhat surprising statement was that excavation for the foundation of a building had to be made in the sheep-breeding settlement of Kàgssiarssuk, which is situated in the place where Erik the Red in 985 A.D. settled down and named Brattahlid. A supposed former burial ground, filled with several bones and skulls, was found. The rumour spread across the fiord to the airfield Narsarsuaq, where N. O. Christensen was waiting for a plane to Denmark. He, at once, inspected the excavation and stopped it, but brought with him a skull to be shown at the National Museum of Denmark.

The next year a large-scale archaeologic excavation, led by Meldgaard and with the participation of Danish as well as foreign experts, was carried out. A number of Greenlandic teachers and students also took part as volunteers. The excavation of Thjodhilde's Church was widely mentioned in the newspapers and undoubtedly added to an increased interest in the past in Greenland.

1961 was also the year in which Jørgen Meldgaard wrote an extensive and highly detailed proposal for the Greenland Museum.

The proposal was forwarded to the Council by the National Museum of Denmark with an additional note from director P. V. Glob, who wrote:

"Of course the National Museum of Denmark is prepared to support the museum plans in any way, as well as it is willing to supplement the collections of the Green-land Museum, when it is finally established and approved."

Meldgaard's proposal opened with a review of which possibilities for grants exist according to the 'Statute for the Culture-Historical Local Museums', and which demands are made on quality and activities. It is noted that for a provincial museum there are further demands to a high standard of museum-technical quality and a professionally educated staff.

"In Greenland there seems to be a need - and the possibilities - for such a kind of museum," Jørgen Meldgaard wrote in the beginning of his proposal. Then Meldgaard reviewed the tasks and the exhibitions which should get priority.

Meldgaard realized that the proposal implied extensive collections but he thought that the Eskimo-Greenlandic collections already existed in the 'temporary museum', and that further methodical collection could expand these considerably. But he also predicted that, if necessary, the National Museum of Denmark might be willing to take out items from its Greenlandic collections and deposit them in a future Greenland Museum.

Meldgaard continued: *"For the Eskimo and general ethnographic exhibition the National Museum of Denmark will also be able to contribute and much will be acquired through exchange with foreign museums if Greenlandic ethnographic objects, such as kayaks and hunting devices, are offered."*

Fig. 4: An example of exhibition in the present National Museum of Greenland.

The need for space was thought to be fulfilled within the existing Herrnhut building, with temporary storage in the attic and a separate museum building. Two possibilities were suggested:

(1) A colonial building of considerable size, which would be moved to the area, or (2) a new building, for which Meldgaard made the preliminary drawings. His idea was a number of joined dome-shaped buildings, the basic idea being that they conjure up the notion of a group of igloos. The idea was that the aforementioned four collections make the permanent exhibitions and be placed in a dome each.

The Council responded that the establishment of a museum was certainly of interest, but since the proposal had been received so late, it had been impossible to discuss it in the session. The Council also wanted more information, especially absolute the cost of establishing and running such a museum.

The proposal was on the Council's agenda again in 1962, and this time a thorough budget, made by the National Museum of Denmark and the Ministry for Greenland, was enclosed. It estimates the building expenses to be about one million kroner and the running expenses about 100.000 kroner.

This time the Council resolved to declare that it had a positive attitude towards the proposal but, for the moment was unable to provide the necessary means to realize of the project. So, no fundamental consent to the suggested plans for a provincial museum and great disappointment both in Denmark and in Greenland.

In 1963 a somewhat reduced proposal was drawn up by N. O. Christensen, chairman of the Council. Now the wish for a separate exhibition building was withdrawn and efforts were concentrated upon the furnishing of a museum in Ny Herrnhut.

In his introductory speech the chairman said that if secure storage conditions for the now large and quite unique collection were not provided, the only proper thing to do would be to store all the collected objects in the National Museum of Denmark.

The Council then gave its fundamental consent to the establishment of a Greenland Museum as an independent institution, and furthermore promised, in advance, to contribute funding according to the statute for culture-historical museums. At the same time the Council appointed two members for the future governing body. So far so good. But more obstacles had to be moved before a museum could be opened.

A governing body had been established with N. O. Christensen as chairman and Jørgen Meldgaard and C. F. Simony as representatives from the National Museum of Denmark. In these years there was much correspondence between the chairman and the National Museum of Denmark about all the difficulties, large as well as small.

The collection had to be sorted out and registrated by a museum professional and the museum building had to be fireproof, so that the museum supervision could approve the museum as entitled to grants. Perhaps the worst thing was that the building was still used as official residence and neither the Council nor the Administration could promise when it would be free.

The Greenlandic museum affair was mentioned in Danish newspapers and headlines such as: *"Should the Greenland Museum be stored in the National Museum of Denmark?"* and *"The matter has reached a deadlock"* could be read. Under the headline: *"Difficulties for a Greenlandic museum"* the newspaper Information in 1964 brought a statement by chief curator Helge Larsen who wrote:

"The Council must decide whether the museum project should be carried out. From this side all that can be done has been done. Today, probably nobody knows when the museum in Godthåb will be a fact."

In early 1966 the Herrnhut building was at last handed over to the governing body, and that same year, on August 23, the Greenland Museum could be opened. On this occasion Jørgen Meldgaard made a speech, bringing greetings and congratulations to the Greenland Museum and the Council from the director, ending with these words:

"The National Museum of Denmark hopes to be able to contribute to the collections of the Greenland Museum later on. As a gift on the opening day I can deliver two costumes from the Netsilik Eskimos in Canada. Collected in 1923 by Knud Rasmussen."

A Greenland Museum was now a reality. That, which had been worked upon since the Council for South Greenland in 1913 brought up the idea for the first time, had now turned into reality.

From April 1, the following year the Greenland Museum was approved as a culture-historical local museum entitled to grants, but not until April 1972 did the museum supervisors approve the museum as a provincial museum, which meant better possibilities for grants.

The museum made its first archaeologic excavation in 1968. A Norse ruin at Qooqqut in the Godthåb Fjord. Of course it was done in close consultation with the National Museum of Denmark which, among other things, demanded that an experienced and professional person participated.

Incidentally, the correspondence between the Greenland Museum and the National Museum of Denmark was almost exclusively carried out between the chairman and Jørgen Meldgaard, who wrote on behalf of the National Museum of Denmark, and who on this as on many other occasions, gave advice and guidance to the new museum.

Meldgaard is also the one who in 1968 brought up a new idea for the strengthening of both the cooperation between the Greenland Museum and The National Museum of Denmark, and the strengthening of the possibilities for the National Museum of Denmark to expand its research in cooperation with the Greenland Museum.

A: The Greenland hunting Culture
B: History of Mankind, lecture hall & film
C: Prehistory Eskimo Cultures,
   incl. Canada & Alaska
D: Greenland Danish mixed Culture
E: Entrance hall

grundplan:

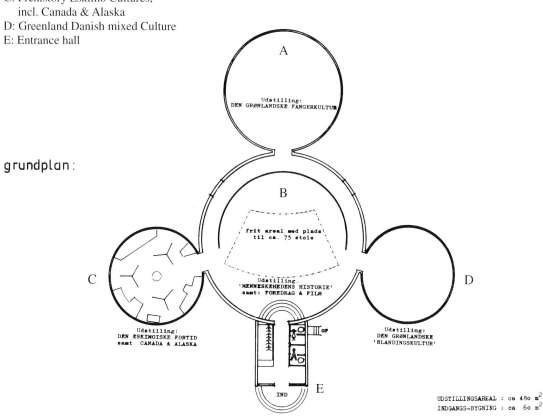

UDSTILLINGSAREAL : ca 480 m^2
INDGANGS-BYGNING : ca 60 m^2

Udstilling = Exhibition

længdesnit:

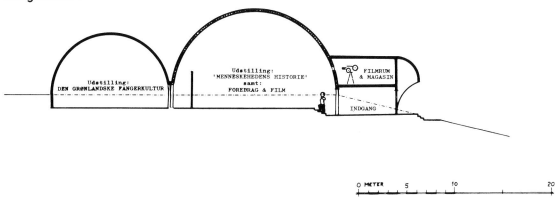

DET GRØNLANDSKE LANDSMUSEUM

skitseforslag til udstillingsbygning
for de eskimoisk-grønlandske samlinger

NATIONALMUSEET
Grønlandskontoret
Juni 1961
J.Meldgård

The idea was to establish a research station for Greenlandic ethnography and archaeology in Greenland, with a professional manager stationed in two-year terms. The research was to focus on the disappearing Greenlandic hunter culture and on the encounter with and integration into Danish culture.

The research station was also meant to provide consultative support - during a period of transition - for the Greenland Museum on the condition that the station was placed in Godthåb where there was a possibility of taking over the building then housing 'Marine-biological Station'.

The idea received a positive response from the board of the Greenland Museum, but it was never brought to life. There were several reasons, among them financial issues, but the main reason was probably that 'Marine-biological Station' remained in the building and still uses it.

Another project, having Meldgaard as its originator and prime mover, was the 'Inuit-Norse Project', an archaeologic excavation project in the Ameralik Fjord, carried out in 1976. The idea was that the Greenland Museum and Danish museum people together would try to throw light on the first encounter in Greenland between Eskimos and Europeans. The first encounter between two cultures. How did they live together? What did they learn from each other?

In the project local hunters and fishermen, eskimologists, archaeologists, zoologists, teachers, and students, Greenlanders as well as Danes, were to participate and 30 people were involved. The Inuit-Norse Examination involved two months of field-work and had great significance both for the reputation of the Greenland Museum outwardly, and for the future Danish-Greenlandic cooperation by means of the many good relations established between the participants.

The thought of transferring parts of the Greenlandic collections from the National Museum of Denmark to the Greenland Museum had, as has been mentioned, been proposed several times.

First time in 1961, in connection with the proposal put forward by the National Museum of Denmark for a Greenlandic museum, when director P. V. Glob, as aforementioned, promised to supplement the collections of a future Greenland Museum. The idea was repeated at the opening of the Greenland Museum in 1966.

10 years later - in 1976 - the question concerning "*the transfer of Greenlandic culture-historical valuables*" was raised in the Greenland Council. That same year, the Danish Minister for Cultural Affairs, during his visit to Greenland, expressed his wish to support the idea of transferring museum items to Greenland.

The Department of Ethnography at the National Museum of Denmark expressed the basic attitude that Greenlandic culture-historical valuables should be regarded as the Greenlandic people's property through the establishment of Home Rule and it was found just that considerable parts of the collections were transferred to Greenland. But it must be a condition that the Greenland Museum had reached such a level that the transferred items were not at risk of being damaged. Another necessary condition was that both parts had knowledge about the extent and contents of the collections in the National Museum of Denmark in order to make a objective estimation of what could possibly be transferred.

The physical space for the Greenland Museum in Ny Herrnhut became too limited over the years. So it was a considerable improvement of the situation when the Greenland Museum in 1980 could move into new and larger buildings, equipped with up-to-date exhibition rooms, depots, archives, administration and conservation department, and more. The board was now professionally educated and the economic conditions were better.

In 1982 Greenland celebrated the 1000-year anniversary of Erik the Red's settlements in the fjords of South Greenland. The National Museum of Denmark wished to take this opportunity to mark the fact that the responsibility for the museum system in Greenland had been taken over by the Home Rule from 1981. At the same time it wished to congratulate on the new settings in which the Greenland Museum could now work. And, last but, not least, it wanted to prove the good will to transfer Greenlandic cultural values to their place of origin.

Receiving great attention, not only from Greenland and Denmark but also from abroad, Queen Margrethe II, Lise Østergaard, the then Minister of Cultural Affairs, and Olaf Olsen, director of the National Museum of Denmark, carried out the official transfer of 204 aquarelles, 161 being painted by Greenland's national artist, the seal hunter Aron of Kangeq (1822-1869), and the rest by his contemporary, Jens Kreutzmann of Kangaamiut (1828-1899).

The first transfer had been made. And it would be the prelude to more and larger transfer projects. After a year of preparations and negotiations an agreement of cooperation between the National Museum of Denmark and the Greenland Museum was signed on October 31, 1983, and came into force on January 1, 1984.

The main point in the agreement was the establishing of a museum committee with six members, three appointed by the Greenlandic Administration Member for Culture and Education, and three appointed by the Danish Minister of Cultural Affairs. Furthermore, a secretariat to the committee had to be established. For practical reasons the committee would be placed in the Department of Ethnography at the National Museum of Denmark.

The main task of the Secretariat was to handle the tasks decided on by the Cooperation Committee according to its authority. It concerned first and foremost providing a basis for the transferring of culture-historical material in the form of knowledge as well as archaeo-

Fig. 6: The first museum committee was established i 1994. Here the committee is assembled Outside the National Museum of Greenland in Nuuk.
From left: Robert Petersen, Torben Lundbæk, Knud Krogh, Marianne Petersen, Claus Andreasen, Jørgen Meldgaard, Helge Schultz-Lorentzen.

logic, ethnographic, and ethnologic items from the National Museum of Denmark to the Greenland Museum. Another important task was to give the necessary help for the procurement of [preservation? safe?] archives, including both buildings and earthly relics, so that the Greenland Museum would become able to manage the regulations in the Greenlandic preservation act independently.

The first transferring project was carried out in 1985 and involved 748 ethnographic and 4.228 archaeologic items. The following transfers have been carried out according to a geographically defined plan, so that material from the Polar-Eskimo area was transferred in 1990. Then came ethnographic and archaeologic material from West Greenland. Now the transferral of Norse material and archaeologic material from North East Greenland is in execution. Until today, more than 2.000 ethnographic and 2.400 archaeologic items have been transferred.

At the same time, an important effort has been made to put all information about earthly relics into a database. Thus more than 6.000 localities are registered, including at least 25.000 relics.

The cooperation committee has two sessions a year and the resolutions are all agreed upon in broad unity. The formalized Danish-Greenlandic museum cooperation has now been working since 1984 and has functioned to the satisfaction of both parties. A cooperation which has reverberated around the museum world. Both in UNESCO and in ICOM (International Council of Museums) the Danish-Greenlandic cooperation has attracted a lot of attention.

In 1990 the Greenland Museum was renamed 'The Greenland National Museum and Archives'.

Helge Schultz-Lorenzen, head of the Greenland Secretariat.

References

Berglund, Joel [1994]: **Recovering the Past: The Greenland National Museum and Archives.** *Museum International*, 182, 46(2):26-29 (Paris: Unesco Quarterly Review).

Haagen, Birte [1995]: **Repatriation of Cultural Objects in Greenland.** *Yumtzilob*, Tijdschrift over de Americas, 7(3):225-243 (Haagen).

Schultz-Lorentsen, Helge [1987]: **Tilbage til Grønland -Det dansk-grønlandske museumsarbejde.** *National-museets Arbejdsmark*, 1987:177-192 (Copenhagen: National Museum of Denmark).

Schultz-Lorentsen, Helge [1988]: **Return of Cultural Proberty by Denmark to Greenland - From Dream to Reality.** *Museum International*, 160, 46(2):200-205 (Paris: Unesco Quarterly Review).

Schultz-Lorentsen, Helge [1988]: **Det dansk-grøn-landske museumsarbejde.** *Tidsskriftet Grønland*, 36(2-3):65-80 (Copenhagen: Det Grønlandske Selskab).

Schultz-Lorentsen, Helge [1990]: **Nye overførelser fra Nationalmuseet til Grønland.** *Tidsskriftet Grønland*, 38(4):113-120 (Copenhagen: Det Grønlandske Selskab).

Fig. 7: An example of the exhibition in the first Greenland Museum.

The Variety of Artistic Expression in Dorset Culture

Patricia D. Sutherland

In his book entitled "Eskimo Sculpture" Jørgen Meldgaard (1960a:11) wrote that "*a striking feature of Eskimo culture when studied as a whole is the quite amazing variety of artistic expression.*"

The truth of this statement is apparent to anyone who encounters the carvings, music and narrative art of contemporary Inuit. It is equally apparent in the variety of specimens residing in ethnographic collections made over the past century, ranging from Alaskan masks to Central Inuit clothing, and to the finely decorated tools and 'tupilak' carvings of Greenland. When one includes, as does Meldgaard, the ancient products of the Eskimo cultural tradition - the elaborately ornamented weapons of the Old Bering Sea Culture, the fantastic burial art of Ipiutak, and the unique carvings of the Dorset Culture - the variety of Eskimo artistic expression becomes even more remarkable.

While the degree of variability in the entire Eskimo cultural tradition is well appreciated, most scholars who have approached the subject have tended to treat the individual cultural expression of Eskimo art as a phenomenon that can be classified and typified in order to better express the differences between different cultural traditions. Thus "Dorset art", or "Ipiutak art" or "Alaskan Eskimo masks" are defined in a way which allows them to be compared with other such classes. Such definition risks implying a degree of uniformity which does not actually exist in the artistic tradition. The present paper approaches the artistic production of the Dorset Culture people through the perspective of the question: Is "Dorset art" as unitary a phenomenon as most scholars have generally assumed it to be?

Meldgaard's (1960a:24-26) brief description of Dorset art noted the vast spatial and temporal range of Dorset Culture, and suggested that there was a significant change in the amount of art produced in the late phase of the culture's existence. However, the style and function of the art was presented as a uniform manifestation which could be simply contrasted with the art of the contemporaneous Okvik and Ipiutak Cultures. The same approach was taken by Taylor (1967) and Swinton (1967) in their classic joint papers which form the basis of most archaeological opinion relating to the art of the Dorset Culture.

Taylor (1967:38), citing several examples of very similar specimens recovered from locations hundreds of kilometers apart, specifically noted the "geographic continuity or cultural consistency over the vast area" of Dorset occupation. Both Taylor and Swinton recognized the Dorset art recovered from subarctic Newfoundland as a distinctive regional variant, but the art of the vast Arctic region was presented as something which did not vary significantly either temporally or geographically.

The approach taken by these authors was, of course, conditioned by the material which was available at the time of their studies. Aside from a few scattered specimens from elsewhere, Meldgaard's collection of Dorset carvings was heavily centrered in the excavations which he and others had carried out in the region of Igloolik. Taylor's and Swinton's discussion was focussed on only 125 specimens, and again most of these came from the adjacent regions of Hudson Strait, Foxe Basin and northern Baffin Island. The accelerated archaeological activity of the past decades has multiplied the corpus of known Dorset specimens, and many of the newer collections derive from the Central Arctic, High Arctic, Labrador,

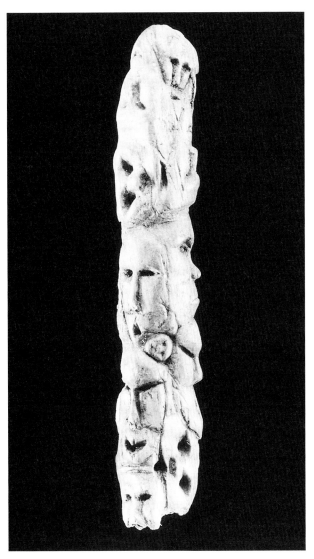

Fig. 1: Four forms of ivory "shaman's tube". From left to right: QiLd-2:12 (Early Dorset); KkHh-3:914 (Middle Dorset); NiHf-4:115 (Late Dorset); SiHw-1:453 (Late Dorset). Height of SiHw-1:453: 45 mm. (Photo Credit: Canadian Museum of Civilization).

Fig. 2: Antler baton carved with representations of human or human-like faces (SiHw-1:788). Length 103 mm. (Photo Credit: Canadian Museum of Civilization).

and Greenland where Dorset culture was poorly known a few decades ago.

The first attempt to explicitly study variability in Dorset art was carried out by Lyons (1982), whose innovative analysis compared the distribution of stylistic elements in five major collections comprising 585 specimens. On the basis of this work, Lyons was able to define stylistic differences between three Middle Dorset collections from the Igloolik region, northern Baffin Island and Newfoundland; collections from the Late Dorset period were distinctive from the earlier ones, but did not show the same pattern of regional differences. Lyons' interest was not in defining or explaining the nature of variability in Dorset art, but in using degrees of stylistic difference to test hypotheses relating to the culture history of the Dorset people. Her findings provided confirmation for the general impression of artistic differences which archaeologists had formed, as collections representing different regional and temporal variants of Dorset Culture had accumulated.

Fig. 3: Wooden specimens from Button Point, Bylot Island. Clockwise from upper left: PfFm-1:1780/1973 ("miniature kayak"); PfFm-1:1767 (abstract bear); PfFm-1: 1772-1777 (mask); PfFm-1:1750 (drum). Height of PfFm-1:1772: 175 mm. (Photo Credit: Canadian Museum of Civilization).

The definition and measurement of artistic variability is a difficult task, as the phenomenon is too complex to easily reduce to an objective and systematic analysis. Lyons should be commended for an admirable attempt at undertaking such a systematic inquiry, but she did not extend it to a more comprehensive treatment of the subject. No other attempts have been made to carry out such a treatment of Palaeo-Eskimo art, and the current paper does not pretend to do so. The following notes are based primarily on an examination of the approximately 800 carvings and decorated objects in the Palaeo-Eskimo collections of the Canadian Museum of Civilization, and are presented as a preliminary suggestion of the extent and nature of variability which exists in this material.

It is apparent that variation in Palaeo-Eskimo art occurs along several axes, which act in concert to define the form of individual specimens, and the nature of individual assemblages. The most apparent of these axes may be summarized as follows:

Temporal Variation

Information on the relative temporal positions of Dorset assemblages began to develop with Meldgaard's (1960b) excavations of the long occupational sequence in the vicinity of Igloolik. Stylistic comparison with assemblages from this sequence has remained a mainstay of Dorset temporal ascription, in conjunction with an accumulating series of radiocarbon dates. Meldgaard (1960a:24) was the first to recognize that the amount of artistic activity was not constant throughout the Dorset sequence, but that it increased significantly in the late period dating to the centuries around and after 1000 A.D.

For some time, this was the most recognized aspect of temporal variation in Dorset art. Taylor (1967:40) stated merely that *"Temporal variation is another sizable question"* which he did not attempt to answer; no reference was made to temporal position in the captions to the illustrations which accompany the Taylor and Swinton papers.

Fig. 4: Ivory carvings of animals from Brooman Point, Bathurst Island. Clockwise from upper left: QiLd-1:2291 (falcon); QiLd-1:819 (swimming bear); QiLd-1:2304 (muskox); QiLd-1:2299 (standing bear). Length of QiLd-1:2299: 41 mm. (Photo Credit: Canadian Museum of Civilization).

The first attempt to depict the processes of temporal variation which operated in Dorset art were made in a brief photograph caption published by Meldgaard (1960b: 70), in which he illustrated a series of 'floating bear' representations developing from a relatively naturalistic to increasingly abstract forms over a period of five centuries.

Swinton (1967:47) questioned the dating of this series, but appears to have concurred with the suggestion that a process of abstraction was operating over time in the activities of Dorset artists. Current knowledge continues to support the view that the flat and spatulate forms of abstract bear figures in Late Dorset assemblages developed from the skeletonized floating-bear images which first appear in Middle Dorset assemblages. However, parallel processes of stylistic change have not been defined in any other series of forms. The very abstract bear images occur in the same Late Dorset assemblages as the most naturalistic and realistic portrayals of bears known from any Dorset period.

The processes of temporal variation appear to be considerably more complex than the actions of a simple rule of increasing abstraction.

For example, while 'floating bears' become more abstract through time, the ivory containers termed 'shaman's tubes' become increasingly complex and representational (Fig. 1). The earliest known forms of these artifacts are simple hollow bell-shaped objects with small projections extending from the sides. Middle Dorset assemblages contain forms in which the upper corners have been transformed into a pair of bear heads facing one another across the top of the object; the bear heads are later transformed into walrus heads, with the tusks interlocking across the top of the container. In Late Dorset assemblages, the tubes with walrus heads also have sculpted or cut-out human faces added to the flat sides of the containers, and in some instances these are supplemented by other animal representations.

Other aspects of Dorset art appear to be subject to another process of temporal change, involving neither increasing complexity nor abstraction, but a simple increase in the varieties of representation over time. This is most apparent in representations of the human face, which in Pre-Dorset and Early Dorset assemblages generally approach the simple and elegant form represented in the miniature mask from the Tyara site.

Late Dorset assemblages also contain miniature masks, but the faces are not as simple or uniform, and human faces are also used as elements in objects as diverse as the shaman's containers noted above, and antler batons which are covered with a diversity of human and human-like representations (Fig. 2). The increase in artistic activity which is apparent in Late Dorset assemblages is associated with a general increase in variability, which applies to other objects as well as representations of the human face.

Another source of temporal variation appears in the existence of certain forms which occur in apparently uniform styles for a limited segment of the Dorset sequence. Bone disks which are perforated in the centre and marked with a pattern of radiating lines, usually numbering eight or sixteen, are found only in Early and Middle Dorset assemblages. Several other forms, including the antler batons mentioned above, are known only from the final few centuries of the Dorset sequence. The occurrence of such forms appears to be independent of any temporal process of development, providing an additional level of complexity to our attempts to understand the nature of variability through time. Such understanding must await more precise control on the temporal positions of most Dorset Culture assemblages.

Regional Variation

Bronshtein and Plumet (1995:42) have recently minimized the extent of regional variability in Dorset art, perceiving it as a phenomenon which evolved through uniform and contemporaneous changes over the entire area of Dorset occupation. However, as was noted earlier, scholars have long recognized the distinctive character of Newfoundland Dorset art, and Lyons' (1982) analysis documented the existence of two other regional traditions which existed during at least a portion of the Dorset temporal spectrum. The nature of such variation appears to be more complex than may be implied by simply ascribing it to regional cultural traditions which have diverged from one another as a result of isolation from one another.

This problem might be profitably approached through the suggestion that some of the variation which has been defined may be assemblage-specific rather than regional. The Button Point assemblage, for example, which Lyons used to define a distinct regional tradition, appears to represent a uniquely heavy emphasis on ritual activity and the artifacts associated with that activity: masks, drums, and a variety of small wooden figures (Figure 3). Although this assemblage shares certain elements with material recovered from other sites in adjacent regions of northern Baffin Island, it stands apart from these assemblages in the ritual-centred character of the majority of its artifacts.

Another such example is suggested by the Late Dorset assemblage from Brooman Point in the central High Arctic. While sharing many elements with the widespread Late Dorset tradition, this collection is unique in the large number of naturalistic animal representations, many of which are not perforated for attachment as amulets (Figure 4). This characteristic is not shared with roughly contemporaneous assemblages from Little Cornwallis Island, located only a few kilometers away. One suspects that more complete preservation of subarctic Dorset assemblages might indicate that the art of the Port aux Choix collection shares only general characteristics with other Newfoundland Dorset assemblages from sites in less environmentally rich locations.

The degree of difference between the artistic materials recovered from individual sites suggests that an analysis in terms of site assemblages rather than regional cultural traditions is more likely to provide a clear picture of Dorset cultural variability. Regional Dorset populations might usefully be considered as a mosaic of communities, each with its own unique cultural tradition, and continuing that tradition through time as they interact at various levels with other communities. The assemblage of carvings and decorated artifacts from any site would be conditioned by how this local tradition interpreted the broad cultural conventions of the evolving Dorset cultural tradition, as well as by the nature of activities which were carried out at this particular site. The latter factor would include the kind and level of ritual activities which were associated with particular classes of artifacts, as in the example of Button Point. It would also include subsistence activities, which appear to influence the choice of animal subjects represented at some sites; for example, carvings portraying walrus are most common in collections from the Igloolik region, where other archaeological evidence suggests a strong emphasis on walrus hunting.

In sum, regional differences have long been known to exist in Dorset art, but the nature of regional variation appears to be considerably more complex than can be simply ascribed to regional cultural traditions, and related to a number of interacting variables which are only poorly understood. Analysis in terms of the nature and amount of intra-regional variation between individual assemblages may be useful in elucidating the processes which produced variability between the art assemblages created by contemporaneous Dorset groups in various regions of the Arctic.

Intra-assemblage Variation

Perhaps the most striking aspect of variability in Dorset artistic production is that which occurs within single assemblages, including assemblages which appear to relate to a single relatively short-term occupation by a small community. This type of variability must be a reflection of many factors, including the number of people involved in artistic production and the variety of other activities in which they were involved. Swinton's

(1967:39) argument that Dorset artistic production was carried out by a relatively small number of skilled shaman-artists seems to be questioned by the amount of variability in the form and style of specimens in the numerous assemblages which are now available for study.

It is now apparent, for example, that decoration or the application of symbolic markings such as stylized skeletons or faces, is not limited to the ritual objects which Swinton (1967:37) considered to be the equipment of shamans. Such markings are found not only on weapons such as harpoon heads, where they may have been associated with hunting magic, but on utilitarian artifacts such as knife handles. The differing manner in which such markings are made on individual specimens, as well as the differing amounts of care taken in their application, suggest that such "artistic" activity was generally distributed throughout the community, and was not the preserve of the community shaman. Such an interpretation is supported by the wide range of artistic ability and craftsmanship which is apparent in the production of representational carvings. The concept that Dorset artists were uniformly skillful appears to have been influenced by our tendency to select only the best pieces for illustration in publications dealing with the subject; examination of entire assemblages reveals a much wider range of competence than is apparent from the perusal of publications on Dorset art.

Even in the case of specimens from a single assemblage representing the same class of standardized object (such as shamans' containers, spatulate objects, or antler batons), rarely is the degree of similarity sufficiently great to suggest that the specimens were produced by the same individual. Instead, one is impressed by the amount of individual variation which is expressed while producing an object which obviously adheres to a complex cultural prescription. This intimation that individual expression was an important characteristic of Dorset art is supported by the large number of specimens which are unique in concept and realization. Representations of a nesting eider duck with eggs carved on her breast, a diving falcon with outstretched talons, or a human head with inset ivory teeth (Figure 5) are each unique but not unusual in the corpus of Dorset art, suggesting that artistic activities were not as constrained by cultural mandates as has been commonly assumed.

Conclusions

This paper argues that an examination of the archaeological assemblages which have accumulated over the past decades indicates that the phenomenon known as "Dorset art" encompasses a much greater range of variability than has been generally assumed. An admittedly subjective review of this material suggests that the nature of variability, through time and through the contemporaneous social units of the Dorset world, was extremely complex.

Fig. 5: Human figure, wood with inset ivory teeth, northern Ellesmere Island (SlHq-1:29). Length 99 mm.
(Photo Credit: Canadian Museum of Civilization).

Earlier scholars are probably correct in recognizing that this art was closely related to shamanic religious practices. However, interpretations of Dorset art as the product of a uniform, conservative and constrained shamanic tradition has not facilitated a recognition of the variability apparent in the art, nor discussions of the meaning of such variability.

The carvings and decorated objects left by the Dorset people provide a unique opportunity to glimpse the artistic tradition of a small-scale society over a period of three thousand years. We should not be surprised to find that this art appears to have been subject to complex processes of innovation and change, similar to those which have influenced the development of artistic traditions in larger and more completely documented societies.

Patricia D. Sutherland, Canadian Museum of Civilization, Ottawa, Canada.

References

Bronshtein, Mikhail & Patrick Plumet [1995]: **Ékven: l'art préhistorique beeringien et l'approche russe de l'origine de la tradition culturelle esquimaude.** *Études Inuit/Inuit Studies*, 19(2):5-59 (Québec: Départment d'anthropologie, Université Laval).

Lyons, Diane [1982]: **Regionalism of Dorset Art Style: a Comparative Analysis of Stylistic Variability in Five Dorset Art Samples.** Master of Arts Thesis, Department of Archaeology, 192 p. (Calgary: University of Calgary).

Meldgaard, Jørgen [1960a]: **Eskimo Sculpture.** 48 p. (London: Methuen).

Meldgaard, Jørgen [1960b]: **Origin and Evolution of Eskimo Cultures in the Eastern Arctic.** *Canadian Geographical Journal*, 60(2):64-75 (Ottawa).

Swinton, George [1967]: **Prehistoric Dorset Art: The Magico-Religious Basis.** *The Beaver*, 298:32-47 (Winnipeg: The Hudson's Bay Company).

Taylor, William E. Jr. [1967]: **Prehistoric Dorset Art: The Silent Echoes of Culture.** *The Beaver*, 298:32-47 (Winnipeg: The Hudson's Bay Company).

Eskimo Art appreciated by an Artist

Eigil Knuth (1903-1997), Eskimo archeologist and sculptor, had Eskimo art as one of his favourite fields of study. Like George Swinton, art historian and visual artist, he endeavoured to highlight individual artists, and he emphasized the originality and creativity of Eskimo artists.

In his book, **Eskimo Sculpture**, Jørgen Meldgaard illustrated the specific qualities of some of the prehistoric carvings by reproducing an artistic experience by Eigil Knuth (Meldgaard 1959:15-16):

"Eskimo sculptures are small. They are meant to be handled and turned over; rarely do they have a base, and usually there is no front, no viewing angle ... Perhaps we ought to behold a work of art with the eyes of an artist unveiling the artifact. In 1939 Eigil Knuth excavated the carving seen above. It was found at Sophus Müllers Næs near the North East corner of Greenland in a ruin dating from the 14th-15th century.

These are extracts from his report: "I was kneeling in the ruins in front of the sleeping platform where various finds indicated that the women's place must have been, and I was chopping off another cake of blubber and mould. Then out rolled a small ivory figure of a woman c. 1 1/2 inches long, perfect and beautiful ...

I never dreamt that a desolate snow-covered coast in this faraway corner of the world was to be the setting for an intense artistic revelation. But that is how it was. She was daringly simple; in accordance with ancient Eskimo tradition her arms were only indicated as excrescences from the shoulders, the whole figure thereby becoming cross-shaped, frontal and symmetrical like the figures of Christ in early Romanesque crucifixes. And, even so, the tiniest detail stood out in beautiful relief: the breasts, the stomach, the waist, the knees, the calves, and the muscles of her back. The fact that all the forms were so com-

pressed and rigid was the very reason that the figure came to life with such concentrated force. The facial expression was immensely eloquent, and produced on a completely flat surface by means of dots and lines, which could hardly be felt, and became visible only after I had rubbed them with spit for some time; the likeness was so convincing that I knew exactly what the woman had looked like, knew all the flaws and charms of her body, and - thanks to the wonderful skill of the portrayal - even her personality ...

And this little woman, so full of life, whose stomach I was now gently rubbing, she was condemned to be imprisoned in some museum for relics of the past, would be given a number, and placed in a row with scores of trivial objects, killed like a butterfly on a pin. Or was she to be hidden away in drawer number something or other, far down in the basement, with other odds and ends of bone only to see daylight once in a decade when some bespectacled archeologist peered into the drawer ...

It so happened that I arrived from the South on a sled, living as primitive and natural a life as the Eskimo hunter who long since had come from the North and carved her out of a walrus tusk; and that was why I felt so sure that my impression of her was correct. If only a work of art could be seen more often under such conditions; for that is how it really should be seen: as an object dug out of the ground with the curiosity of a hunter, in the solitude of hundreds of miles of empty space. Then there is no temptation to play any tricks with it or make exaggerated statements."

The little woman was "imprisoned" in the National Museum of Denmark. Two decades later the bespectacled archeologist Jørgen Meldgaard peered into the drawer - and she was placed on a pedestal in the exhibition.

Who Makes Inuit Art?
Confessions of a Para-Anthropologist

George Swinton

In the current times of political and ethnical correctness, I do not hesitate to state from the outset that, when I speak and write about Inuit art matters, I decidedly do not do so within a white man's burden complex. My observations and personal opinions are based on, and touched by my interactions with Inuit artists and several figures in the socio-political world with whom I have become friends for over thirty years. In many ways, being a visual artist myself, I had professional and intellectual peer relationships with them, not merely exchanging thoughts and feelings but almost enculturising and enriching, rather than indigenising each other. It is partially in that sense that I dared to call myself a para-anthropologist who has greatly benefitted from these interrelationships.

The title of my essay could easily have read: "Who makes Inuit Art art?" But this might have led *a priori* to the idea that I did not believe that Inuit art and art are compatible. This would have been quite contrary to my intention of showing the nature of art making by Inuit as observed, appreciated, and collected by an artist who attempts to describe it as if he were an anthropologist. Which, alas, or God forbid, I am not, but many of my friends are. Thus it was with great delight that I accepted the invitation - the challenge? - to participate in honouring Meldgaard being part of Arctic research for 50 years. We have been friends for over 35 years and I have grown as fond of him as I have of his ideas and his writings.

We both have written about the prehistoric and contemporary arts by the peoples of the Arctic with equal enthusiasm but in inverse proportions. Much of what I have come to know about their arts - and also have become known for - is due to his sensitive and gentle revelations.

Likewise, when in 1970-1971 I put together my second book on sculpture made by contemporary Inuit (Swinton 1972), my major objective was to make available to the general public - as Jørgen did some ten years earlier (Meldgaard 1959-1960) - a compendium of what I, as a Western culture artist, thought was some of the best sculpture, regardless of size and differing aesthetic attitudes, produced in the previous twenty years. I also attempted to highlight individual artists, not merely because I thought that they were very good, but because their work stood out. Their work showed a spirit of individuality and inventiveness which - in Western art parlance - are called originality and creativity. To my non-anthropological Western artist eyes, they appeared to represent significant, new directions in the art by the constantly acculturating Inuit.

That specific feature, however, was precisely one of the major reasons why some of the purist anthropologists and/or traditionalists - most of whom, by the way, I knew and respected as scholars and writers in their respective fields - objected to it, as they also did to all other art expressions produced since the new wave of Eskimo art was "discovered" by James A. ("Jim") Houston in 1948-1949.

Their main thrust was that the acculturating Inuit could no longer be called "true Eskimo," nor could their art be "truly indigenous," both having come into existence only due to inauspicious acculturation, merely economic motivation, promotional schemes by the Canadian government, and Houston's clever entrepeneurship. In fact, as late as 1995, Houston's "Confessions of an Igloo Dweller" may have added further fuel to their purist fire.

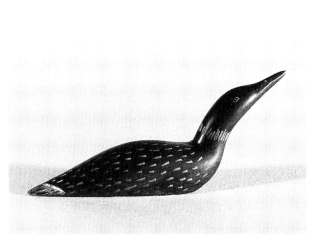

Fig. 1: Johnassie Kudlurok, Sanikiluaq 1993, "Loon" length 9.5 cm, a typical but quite exquisite Inuit souvenir carving. (Photo credit: George Swinton).

starting this essay by saying that its title might have been: "Who makes Inuit Art art?"

My reasoning is quite simple. As early as 1957, when I first went north to prepare a confidential report for the Hudson's Bay Company on the artistic and economic viability of "Eskimo Art," I started to have concerns about the denotative usage of this term. In an article subsequently published in *The Beaver*, I cautiously ventured to say *"no longer can we talk of Eskimo art when we see Eskimo sculpture, for some have become* [purely] *handicraft - skilful and 'charming' as it may be -* [but] *some of the inferior pieces are just Eskimo souvenirs. If* w e *do not make these classifications time will do it anyhow"* (Swinton 1958). I now equally agree and disagree with this statement, as categorically as I declared it in 1958. For I have become aware that the term "art" had then a totally different meaning for me from what it has today.

Then, my ideas were based on my observations in Povungnituk and Port Harrison (now Inukjuak), that not only did not all Inuit carve, but that there also existed several ranges between good and bad, simple and complex, expressionistic and naturalistic, and the like, that is

There were, however, others - notably Jørgen Meldgaard, Charles Martijn and Dorothy Jean Ray - who all, albeit for different reasons and from different points of view, did not join into purist and traditional tirades. They obviously were aware of the work ethics and art making motivations of the various peoples across the Arctic Ocean from Siberia to East Greenland, whether acculturating or not, going back to the past century. In fact, we know that what we may call "recorded Eskimo souvenir art productions" goes as far back as the first quarter of the 19th century, that means to the time when the initial large scale intrusions into the Arctic regions by whalers, traders, and explorers had already been well underway (Martijn 1964, Swinton 1965, 1992). So, when in the middle of the 20th century - to be exact in 1948-1949 - the new phase of what was then called Eskimo Art had its conspicuous beginning, it really was not a totally new venture, although it certainly was new in the context of commercial success, but not of economic motivation. For I cannot imagine why 19th century bartering should not be described as having economic motivation, nor why commercial success in art making is such a disgrace as it seems to be to cultural purists.

Here, of course, I have to confess that, as a practicing artist I, too, think with pleasure that art making can be commercially successful (compare Rembrandt as entrepreneur - Alpers 1988). On the other hand, I also know that commercial success can lead to malpractices but this is not inherent in commercial success itself. Furthermore, I know how easy it is to become obsessed in this regard in relation to all art. That is one of the reasons behind my

Fig. 2: Warehouse of the North West Company Inc. in Rexdale, Ontario, one of the two large wholesale companies of Inuit art. (Photo credit: North West Company Inc.).

Fig. 3: Arviat (Eskimo Point) in 1955. (Photo credit: Indian and Northern Affairs, Geert van den Steenhoven).

largely between artists and non-artist, very minor or souvenir makers. In other words, art making was to me not an ethnic chacteristic, nor was all Eskimo art "art" (in my sense of that word).

In my elitist, Western culture oriented linguistic perception of art history, the term "art" automatically implied an unequivocal sense of high or superior quality, all other simply was not "art." Therefore, when I talked or wrote about Eskimo art and, therefore, Eskimo sculpture, I unconsciously and spontaneously excluded all the indifferent work which I never considered to be "art." Which, of course, was the reason why I differentiated between them. But, intellectually, I no longer do. On the other hand, I found among the "minor art" carvings some excellent work which I illustrated in both my books.

Again, my reasoning is quite simple. It is primarily based on an exact translation or, better, transliteration, of that meaningful Inuktitut term *sananguaq*, as explained in detail in chapter 8, "Aesthetics - Inuit versus Kablunait", in both of my books on sculpture made by Inuit (Swinton 1972:129-134, 1992:129-134). I referred to the fact that, basically, there is no Inuktitut term for art and that the root *sana-* implies making, achieving, and carving, and the suffix *-nguaq* the idea of likeness and diminuative. *Sanaguaq*, therefore, means a little likeness which is achieved or carved - a sculpture! In other words, linguistically, it leads to an understanding of the basis of the contemporary Inuit sculpture where the aesthetic makeup entails the emphasis on making (or achieving) a likeness which is its own reality and not on the Western concept of beauty. In Inuit ethos and oral traditions, it seems to me, Inuit do not like to make personal quality distinctions or

value judgments and, in that sense, it should not come as a surprise that subject matter is the focal point of most Inuit art discussions, that is, what, and not merely how appealing, a work of art is.

In Inuit art of the past forty plus years, the emphasis was on truth and not on beauty, in contrast to Western art history practices which, almost exclusively, emphasise the major achievments only. At the same time, I wish to point out, as I did in my report to the Hudson's Bay Company, that *"Eskimo art is not an ethnic art form but art by a few remarkable individuals [artists!] who happen to be* inuit." That fact is the major reason why my books were safely titled "Sculpture <u>of</u> ..." and not "Eskimo (or Inuit) Sculpture." Today, however, I would be inclined to title it "Sculpture <u>by</u> ..."

The term *sananguaq* implies not only the concept of making, carving, and accomplishing, it also brings to the fore the differences which exist between art as process and art as product. In that sense, our value systems are totally different from theirs. Though different like apples and oranges, one is not superior to the other. To impute that their differing value judgments and hence thinking processes are inferior to ours - because it is they who are acculturating to us and not we to them - shows our often patronising attitude to them and to their culture. My thoughts, and the linguistic complexities involved in this regard, were just recently - and most timely for me - confirmed by an important interview published in the *Inuit Art Quarterly* (Mitchell 1996). There, Bill Nasogaluak (now from Yellowknife and Tuktoyaktuk in the Northwest Territories) very directly and decidedly dealt with the differing value systems and, thereby, invited further

Fig. 4: Pootoogook Jaw, Cape Dorset 1995, "Mother and Son Band", hight: 38.7 cm.
(Photo credit: Marion Scott Gallery, Brian Kardosh).

Fig. 5: Bill Nasogaluak, Tuktoyaktuk/Yellowknife 1995, "Sedna's Song", length: 52.1 cm.
(Photo credit: Inuit Art Quarterly, Richard Garner).

Fig. 6:   Oviloo Tunnillie, Cape Dorset 1995. "Torso", hight: 22.9 cm. (Photo credit: Marion Scott Gallery, Brian Kardosh).

Fig. 7: Judas Ullulaq, Gjoa Haven 1995, "Musk Ox", hight: 40.6 cm. (Photo credit: Marion Scott Gallery, Brian Kardosh).

Fig. 8: Fishing Derby in Repulse Bay, 1995, times have changed, fishing has now also become a competitive sport. (Photo credit: George Swinton).

first in 1964 and last in 1995 - it was and still is my favourite place in the Arctic.

On my last visit I spoke with many of the "old-timers" whom I had met when I was there first; their questions and their stories had hardly changed. Most had difficulties now in their hunting ventures, due to their age. But their communal life and social interaction had not changed a great deal, despite television, A.T.V.s, and a hotel with private bathrooms. The carvers still argued where the best stone could be found and everyone fondly remembered those who no longer were with us when I showed slides or photos of times past. But many of the younger people also were no longer there; they had gone - or wanted to go - south to Rankin Inlet, or west to Yellowknife, or even further south in all directions from Vancouver to Ottawa. While there were a few carvers who carved with interest (and one with passion) most considered it routine activity, "labour," mostly to "make an extra buck." The main issue here is that making "art" (in both its Inuit and Western sense) should almost never be a routine but, when it does become routine, it almost always shows. I must now explain how I use the terms almost, routine, and even art and artist.

The English word "artist" is a very vague term, especially in North America. Anybody who paints, sculpts, etches, etc. can call himself, or is commonly labelled an artist. Also, we used to have the bad habit of avoiding the use of this term when speaking even about the best of craftspeople, but did not hesitate to call some crooks cheque-artists and spoke about the art of forgery as well. In this regard the word art obviously does refer to art as process and, as suggested by Ingo Hessel, parallels the *sananguaq* art attitude of the Inuit makers of art. However, when Bill Nasogaluak calls himself an artist, he means precisely that, even in the Western elitist sense and in contrast to souvenir makers. While **we** have the tendency to misuse this term, **he** does not, as are others whom I know, or had known. In his interview he said

"... it's my life, my career. It's what drives me. It's something that I'm never going to give up. Whether I continue to make a living from it is irrelevant, I'm going to be doing art regardless."

When he makes carvings (he also paints) they are, in one way, *sananguaq* in the Inuktitut sense of that term, but not souvenir art, and he does so without the need for the Canadian Government label, the "igloo tag" - screaming "eskimo art esqimau" - which is supposed to be attached to all carvings made by Inuit. That label, intended to guarantee to the buying public the authenticity of the carvings as having been made by Inuit, also casually hinted that they are, in fact, art in the Western sense of the term. It is, partially at least, this label to which the purists really objected, while they had previously rejected the entire production as being not made by real Inuit, thinking of them as not being at all like the former, the not acculturated Inuit of previous times.

reflections on Inuit making art. Here are a few of the points he made which are highly relevant to my argument:

"I think of myself as an artist. I know that a lot of people from the South look at me as an Inuit artist, but I have never given it much thought because, to me, I am simply an artist. My subject matter happens to be very much drawn from my culture because I'm portraying what I know best ..." "... when you want to talk about the technical side of art ... there are restrictions in our language, but the storyline is better discussed in our language ..." "... I find Inuit are better at producing than appraising their own work ... when it comes to our own work, we tend to be reserved ..."

Those points - and several others he made in reply to the Editor's questions - clearly indicate, at least to me, his being so truly a "modern," a contemporary Inuk, utterly typical of forward thinking Inuit ideas and changed lifestyles.

The photos of Arviat (Eskimo Point 1955) and Repulse Bay (1990s) illustrate the ostensible, exterior changes. I had visited Repulse Bay on several occasions,

Fig. 9: Nick Sikkuark carving in 1991. This Inuit artist from Pelly Bay is one of the best carvers. He also teaches and writes. (Photo credit: Indian and Northern Affairs, Larry Ostrue).

"Can they really be called Eskimo?" they asked, and then denied that the Inuit of today are. Of course, they are not the Eskimo of old, but they are Eskimo none the less and their culture continues to change as mine has changed, now almost unrecognizable from when I was born during the first world war. "Almost" implies here hardly recognizable; obviously, *"no rule is so general, which admits not some exception."*

The same axiom applies to the word "routine" as it relates to Inuit art and, indeed, to most of the non-performing arts. Its etymology is similar to "rut" (a track worn by a wheel or habitual passage), both modified from the Middle French *routine* - route or the travelled way. The trouble with routine work in art is that it does become like being stuck in a rut. This is, quite naturally the nature of souvenir or tourist art all over the world. There are, of course, the proverbial exceptions and one is able to find small treasures (art) among such work - a true bonanza for the sensitive and judicious collector - but to the largest extent, while basic in subject matter, the work is marked by stereotyped repetition. Yet this does not disturb me, for I can, and do visualize the so many Inuit - call them artists or carvers - whom I have observed carv-

ing, out of unmitigated necessity, on the open tundra, in front of their tents or snow houses, in dinky, dusty spaces, and in co-op or government workshops making *sananguaq* art which we, however, are designating, with the Igloo tag, as Eskimo "art" in our Western sense. When first "discovered," it was called and promoted as a new cottage industry but soon thereafter as "art." But purists denounced it almost at once as souvenir industry, which a significant part of "Eskimo art" eventually became. Yet what is much more significant is that so much good and even excellent work (art) was, and still is being produced by so many people, quite staggering in numbers, in comparison to the actual Inuit population.

It needs to be added, that the Igloo tag - as the official symbol for Inuit art attached to every carving - has deceived many Inuit making souvenirs, whether small or large, into believing that they are making art in the Western (product oriented) and not in the Inuktitut (process oriented) sense of the word. For a long time, this imposed emphasis on product ("art") created for the artists, as opposed to the souvenir makers, an undue handicap vis-à-vis the *fine* art market and, especially so, in the eyes of international art critics and museum directors.

The Inuit souvenir market, as well as the benevolently intended but somewhat misleading label, discredited the credibility of Inuit art in general and, partially still does. While I am aware of the great variations which I, at least, perceive to exist, it is impossible to make dividing lines. There simply cannot be found sound or convincing, objective value judgments in art and, therefore, all I attempted to accomplish in this enquiry was to take as objective as possible a look at the nature and variety of making carvings by Inuit, which we now have become accustomed to call Inuit art. The accompanying photos and their captions will illustrate, I hope, most of what I have tried to portray better than I am able to describe with words.

References

Alpers, Swetlana [1988]: **Rembrandt's Enterprise**. 160 p. (Chicago: University of Chicago Press).

Houston, James A. [1951]: **Eskimo Sulptors**. *The Beaver*, Outfit 282, (June):34-39 (Winnipeg: Hudson's Bay Company).

Houston, James A. [1995]: **Confessions of an Igloo Dweller**. 322 p. (Toronto: McClelland & Stewart).

Martijn, Charles A. [1964]: **Canadian Eskimo Carving in Historical Perspective**. *Anthropos*, 59:546-549 (St. Augustin, Germany).

Meldgaard, Jørgen [1959]: **Eskimo Sculptur**. 48 p. (Copenhagen: J. H. Schultz Forlag).

Meldgaard, Jørgen [1960]: **Eskimo Sculpture**. 48 p. (London: Methuen).

Mitchell, Marybelle [1996]: **Bill Nasogaluak: Getting Past the Oral Tradition**. Interview. *Inuit Art Quarterly*, 11(3):28-35 (Ottawa).

Ray, Dorothy Jean [1961]: **Artists of the Tundra and the Sea**. 170 p. (Seattle: University of Washington Press).

Swinton, George [1958]: **Eskimo Carving Today**. *The Beaver*, Outfit 268, (Spring):40-47 (Winnipeg: Hudson's Bay Company).

Swinton, George [1965]: **Eskimo Sculpture/Sulpture Esquimaude**. 224 p. (Toronto: McClelland & Stewart).

Swinton, George [1972]: **Sculpture of the Eskimo**. 255 p. (Toronto: McClelland & Stewart).

Swinton, George [1992]: **Sculpture of the Inuit**. Revised and updated of 1972 book, 288 p. (Toronto: McClelland & Stewart).

George Swinton, C.M., B.A., LL.D., R.C.A., Winnipeg, Canada

Arctic Witnesses

Edmund Carpenter

Canada was fortunate in those who documented its northern frontier during the first half of this century. I shall speak of five: Knud Rasmussen (1879-1933), Peter Freuchen (1886-1957), Robert Flaherty (1884-1951), Richard Harrington (1911-), Bent Sivertz (1905-). I call them 'witnesses' in the sense that each bore honest witness to the events they observed. Unfortunately, later critics, without evidence, tried to discredit their work.

Knud Rasmussen

Raymond Firth, an English anthropologist, asked me which arctic ethnologist I admired most. I said, 'Rasmussen'. This astonished him. He said he found Rasmussen's writings 'unusable'. Unusable for what, he didn't say, but I suspect he saw ethnology as a science, and took exception to Rasmussen's humanism.

More recently, a critic of Rasmussen's Netsilik work wrote: '... *leaves much to be desired ... superficial ... should be used with utmost care ... haste ... failed to notice ... standards of scientific care and rigour not always maintained ... quality of data of a questionable nature ... considerable flaws*'.

Errors charged were slender. Rasmussen reported 259 people in 10 camps; his notes listed 260. He allegedly misidentified the sex of four infants and overestimated the incidence of infanticide.

During the seven months Rasmussen spent with the Netsilik, they moved around, reconstituting groups. There were births, deaths. Adoption & name-changing remained common. Under the circumstances, his census was a miracle in accuracy.

As for infanticide, the lower estimate came from Franz Van de Velde, an Oblate missionary. The good father spent 26 years (1938-1964) among the Netsilik. He knew them

Knud Rasmussen
1923

well. But was he unbiased about infanticide?

Rasmussen's most persistent critic was Lauge Koch, the geologist on several Thule Expeditions. Koch was a hater. Above all, he hated Rasmussen. He saw him as a showman explorer. When Rasmussen died at 54 years, Koch volunteered a highly critical obituary. He said Rasmussen could drive dogs and tell stories, little else. His main charge: romantic exaggeration.

To test this, I took a single song, specifically Aua's account of how, one particularly dark night, Uvavnuk was struck by a fire ball rushing through space. One side of this meteor was bear-like; the other side humanoid, but with bear incisors. The instant it entered her, 'all within her grew light', and she became a mighty shaman.

Regaining consciousness, she rushed back to the igloo, singing that nothing 'was hidden from her now'. There she revealed every offense committed by those present and thereby purified them all.

Suddenly, not knowing why, she sang:

imarjuble imna The great sea
aularjarmanga Has sent me adrift
ingerajarmanga It moves me as the
    weed
aqajaginarmanga in a great river.

narsugsup imna Earth and the great
    weather
aularjarmanga Move me,
ingerajarmanga Have carried me
    away
aulagarinarmanga And move my in
    ward parts with joy.

What saves this song from the conventional cry of those reborn is its form. One understands even now, decades later, why '*unattended lamps grew dim ... men and women sat in silence, hushed and overwhelmed*'.

Its two stanzas are paired. The first refers to Darkness beneath the waters. The second refers to Light beyond the Sky Dome. Their sequence records Uvavnuk's transmutation from the Depths of Darkness to Transcendent Radiance. Our closest parallel (not very close) might be "**Amazing Grace**".

Uvavnuk: once a river weed buffeted by currents Below is suddenly possesed by a storm spirit from Above and transformed into an *angakok* or shaman.

In a Cosmos conceived as three-tiered, with Earth as its center, *angakok*s could visit both Upper & Lower Worlds, then return to Earth with visions & messages. They acquired this gift after sickness, suffering or sin, through the intervention

Research members of the Fifth Thule Expedition. From left in front: Captain Peder Petersen, Knud Rasmussen, Peter Freuchen, Henrik Olsen. From left in the back: Kaj Birket-Smith, Therkel Matiassen, Helge Bangsted. (1921).
Photo p: 303+304 Courtesy: Departement of Ethnography, National museum of Denmark.

of some outside force. Here a meteor linked the terrestrial & divine.

Rasmussen offers four translations of Uvavnuk's song; Freuchen another. No version seems to have satisfied them. It's easy to see why. That song is as condensed as a scientific formula. No translation could ever be totally translucent. Something had to give.

In the first stanza, Rasmussen joined the third & fourth verses. This helped meaning, but sacrificed form. He varied his translations of identical verses in the two stanzas, again on behalf of meaning and again at the expense of form.

Etymologically, the stem *aqaja (qtuq)*, 'collects, has collected seaweed', sounds as if it might contain the notion of 'being removed from one's place without or against one's will'. In that sense, *aulargarinarmanga*, 'shakes me', might mean 'set me in motion without my own will'.

The play on words here requires that each stanza take some of its meaning from the other.

Aulagarinarmanga should probably have the same form as *aqajaginarmanga*, that is *aulgari(n)armanga*. In his Greenlandic version, Rasmussen records this final verse as *arlagarinermanga*, which he translates, 'And made me tremble with joy'. That translation better suits *arlagarinermanga* than *aulagari(n) armanga*, 'shakes me'.

Aulagarmanga, 'moves me', also means 'to be in a natural state'. To be moved by nature is to be in nature, to belong. Uvavnuk feels like a weed moved helplessly by the currents of life. Then, suddenly, she is possessed, transformed, endowed. Her response is joyful, her delight physical. She is granted the supreme gift: to see the epyream, the transcendent.

The 'joy' of which she speaks cannot be found in any literal reading

of the text. It appears primarily in the performance. Aua, Rasmussen's source, said Uvavnuk, 'intoxicated with joy', repeated her song incessantly and all listeners felt the same delight.

Perhaps Rasmussen, limited by his Greenlandic dialect, inquired of Aua the sense of *aulagarinarmanga* in this context. In any event, his translation extended beyond the text: it incorporated & preserved the essence of the whole event. His method came from literature. That he achieved results more accurate than those of his critics is worth reflection.

Peter Freuchen

In the winter of 1951-1952, with the help of my Eskimo host, Ohnainewk, I translated aloud in a crowded, Aivilik sod-hut, Peter Freuchen's novel "Eskimo". All present had heard of Freuchen. Several remembered him. His novel incorporated Aivilik &

Greenlandic experiences. My listeners confirmed events, added, corrected: not Iva, Mala's young wife, mistaken for a seal and killed by a whaler, but another, killed by a Mountie, the father of Pommeeolik, one of my listeners.

Mala, they said, was shot, not drowned. Enemies came upon him as he untangled dog traces, wounded him, released his dogs, broke his back by dropping his sled on him, then abandoned him to a wolf.

At least, that's how the man they knew died. I imagine there were other Malas, that Freuchen's Mala was a composite. Still, this audience found that figure so convincing, they claimed him.

In that novel, Freuchen shifted dates & details, but held the course. Conversations captured "**Eskimo**" cadences. Knud Rasmussen thanked him for a copy of "**Eskimo**". '*I found myself reading in Danish, but unconsciously thinking in Eskimo, which made me listen with astonishment and took me back to that environment.*'

Not everyone applauded. The Fifth Thule Expedition included two newcomers, the 'young scientists', Dr. Kaj Birket-Smith & Dr. Therkel Mathiassen. Birket-Smith dismissed Freuchen as a clown, a teller of tall tales, an embarrassment to the scientific community. The gap between them was probably there from the beginning.

Freuchen: Viking giant from a fishing village, arctic resident for fourteen years, married to an Eskimo orphan, Navarana.

Birket-Smith: plump aristocrat, self-styled scientist, new to the Arctic.

Freuchen didn't help. His field reports resemble scrapbooks. Scattered among facts & statistics are jokes, advice, squashed insects, clippings from his home newspaper. One clipping is a carnival ad for '*ASTA & ROSA: total weight 735 pounds, the world's stoutest, most beautiful giant ladies.*'

May 16, 1923

Dear Curator Thomsen:

Today, while wrapping boxes with collected objects, I find it natural to think of you. My misgivings are manifold. Birket-Smith and Mathiassen taught me to spray the objects with carbolic acid, then wrap them right away. I am not, thank God, a very learned person, though I have heard about killing bacteria. But, after two years in the same box, without drying, doesn't the skin crumble and the hair fall out? My old mother uses lavendar leaves with great success, but of course, I dare not disregard the instructions of the scholars.

Now they have left and the dust has settled. So, to kill time, I decided to make systemmatic collections among the locals so that people at home can get an idea of the way of life here. I find it a novel idea no one has come up with before. My method is to buy used things not made for presentation to museums. I ask you simply to store [the collection] away if it does not fit into the systems evolved here [by Birket-Smith].

I will not withhold from you that the conflict with Lauge Koch, whose cause remains completely unknown to Knud, pains him more than he is prepared to admit. He has done nothing but help Koch, so Koch's attitude towards him is quite odd not least considering all the help he keeps accepting from Knud. As you know, Mathiassen is Koch's friend and while indisputably a gentleman, it has often been obvious that the many courteous words spoken by both parties only disguised underlying disagreement.'

Nine months later, Freuchen advised Curator Thomsen that an umiak, commissioned by Birket-Smith, lacked oars & gear, which Awa, the maker, refused to produce without further payment.

'*Incidentally, this umiak is somewhat of a fake ... an obvious imitation of a European boat. The flaring stem is definitely not Eskimo. But since the*

museum adheres to the principle of placing umiaks in its African section, the new umiak will not detract from the overall impression of our collection.

The aforesaid Awa has also fashioned a kayak. Not having made kayaks for some years, he has come up with a specimen which nobody can squeeze into. Years ago I knew one Miss Alma Pedersen who toured the fairgrounds circuit as the lady lacking the lower part of her body. Perhaps she could be persuaded to perform in the kayak.

Awa seems to have been influenced by the kayaks he has seen with us ... I submit [this one] to the experts with the petition that they treat it with the same scepticism as Awa seems to have.

I regret that the scholars Kaj Birket-Smith and Therkel Mathiassen left us ignoramuses in the dark as to the various objects they acquired.

Signed: Lorenz Peter Elfrid Freuchen
Second in command,
Fifth Thule Expedition.
Decorated:
Silver Medal of Merit.
Hans Egede Medal.
M.A.
Fellow:
The American Geographical Society.
Member of:
Danish Temperance Society.
Society of Ornithology.
Geographical Society.
Danish Overseas League.
Greenland Society.
Society for Greenlandic Literature.
Maritime Association of Nykobing F.
Denied admission to Royal Society of Northern Antiquaries.
Height: 192 cm. Weight: 112 kilos.'

With hindsight, Freuchen's field reports are brilliant. But they weren't received as such. Koch, Birket-Smith & Mathiassen arrived back first and poisoned the land.

The contract called for equality, all members. Freuchen alone was denied a clothing allowance. Navarana, his wife, died of flu six months after the expedition began. Her contract went unpaid.

'By determining her pay to be zero, the Committee resorts to a legal technicality I have no reason to expect ... If the Committee insists that my late wife is to be the only unpaid party on the expedition, I request a statement specifying the areas in which she failed to live up to expectations while being on the expedition, since in my opinion non-payment is tantamount to discrediting her work.'

Freuchen's contract called for salaried employment after he returned, to write up his reports:

'The deal has always been that I was to get DK kroner 500 a month on a par with the university people ... The Board preferred to have acknowledged scientists apply for me as guarantors.'

Koch, as one of the appointed guarantors, withheld payment.

Freuchen's only Fifth Thule publication is on zoology. He's listed as second author, though he wrote most of it. It remains a classic.

On ethnology, nothing. Yet no one in the world, save Rasmussen, was better qualified to write about Eskimo life. That opportunity went to Birket-Smith & Mathiassen. Their contributions proved adequate, no more. Mathiassen made much of little. Birket-Smith erred in ways that Freuchen's intimate knowledge (and lack of pretensions) surely would have avoided. Birket-Smith & Mathiassen rose high in academia.

Knud Rasmussen had promised Freuchen the Thule trading post. The Board said, 'No.' Widowed, unemployed, with two motherless children, he wrote "**Eskimo**", a masterpiece. It tells of his love for Navarana. That love became legend in Greenland. Many now bear her name.

A second marriage failed. A successful third marriage, to a fashion editor, brought him to New York. He supported himself by writing. Some of this is very good, though nothing compares to "**Eskimo**". He became a celebrity character, playing red-neck at dinners. He won the *$64,000*

Question, a TV competition later exposed as rigged.

In 1950, Jørgen Meldgaard, a Danish archeologist, stopped over in New York enroute home from Alaska. He'd never met Freuchen. They arranged to meet at the Explorer's Club. After dinner, Freuchen, who never drank, beckoned Meldgaard to follow. No explanation. They took a cab far uptown to Harlem, climbed unlit stairs and entered a sparsely furnished room. An old, bed-ridden man greeted Freuchen. Clearly, few visitors came. Just as clearly, though unstated, Freuchen helped financially. Their host: Matthew Henson, Peary's invisible Black companion on that failed effort to reach the North Pole.

I once met Freuchen: raconteur, bard really, himself already a legend, yet what I remember most was his honesty. He told the truth.

One critic challenged his account of how, trapped in a make-shift shelter beneath his sled, Freuchen fashioned a turd into a tool, froze it, then chiseled his way out. The critic couldn't find this detail in any official report. No, replied Freuchen, he employed a euphemism to spare official sensitivity, but preserved that detail in fieldnotes.

That detail was worth preserving. It extended our record of a practice, common among Eskimos and those who learned from them, of using frozen perishables, including fish & hides, to replace missing parts of sleds & umiaks, and even to fashion temporary tools.

In 1981, long after Freuchen's death, Denmark's leading newspaper ran an article entitled, "**A Mythomaniac of Formidable Dimensions**". It quoted from a letter Freuchen wrote to his sister from arctic Canada in 1923. He spoke of mapping some 'measly little island', while snow fell and hungry dogs waited. 'But then', he wrote, 'one always has one's imagination to lean on.'

One always has, but Freuchen never availed himself of it. Meldgaard replied:

'For three years, Freuchen was the cartographer of the [Fifth Thule] expedition; he was a zoologist and ethnographer, indispensable aide of Knud Rasmussen, the expedition leader. Together with the Eskimos, Freuchen taught the scientists the art of surviving in the Arctic. And he taught everybody the art of co-existing with other people, of telling his fellow human beings the truth, the whole truth ... As a cartographer, he committed to paper the truth, the whole truth insofar as it could be observed in those harsh circumstances. No questionable coastline or island was entered on his maps. His truth was simple and unequivocal.'

Robert Flaherty

When Robert Flaherty's Arctic contributions first appeared, they received high praise from Arctic residents. With the film **Nanook of the North**, 1922, came international recognition.

Sixty years later, several critics placed the most unfavorable construction upon that film. None had ever been North or met an Eskimo or held a camera, yet each found Flaherty wanting in all particulars. Several charged him with racism, colonialism, dishonesty, falsification, insensitivity, much more.

They complained that Flaherty depicted Eskimos in a manner bearing little resemblance to reality. A book by Joanne Birnie-Danzkar, 1979, led the attack. Its frontespiece is identified as showing a church congregation at Lake Harbour, 1910-1911, printed from a Flaherty 'original glass plate'. That photograph, she says, reveals 'political connotations', perhaps reflecting 'serious disputes' between Flaherty and Bishop Fleming, missionary at Lake Harbour. It's described as 'close to an overt political statement' and cited as one of several photographs which 'shatter any myth of [Flaherty's] naivety'.

In fact, that photograph was taken by a Hudson's Bay Company clerk, A. A. Chesterfield, at Great

Whale River, circa 1902. The Flaherty *'original glass negative'* is actually a lantern slide, probably made for mission fund-raising. Chesterfield willed part of his estate to mission work. Clearly the motive behind this photograph was the exact opposite of what Birnie-Danzkar inferred.

In this same book, Birnie-Danzkar accuses Flaherty of costuming Nanook in bearskin pants for theatrical effect. Bearskin pants, she says, were unknown in this area. *'Flaherty would never have met Inuit wearing bearskin pants.'* Yet, when Flaherty first met Comock (identified by her as the model for Nanook), Comock wore bearskin pants.

Bearskin pants were then common in this area, a necessity created by a shortage of seal & caribou. Books, photographs, specimens, document their presence. The movie itself includes a second hunter wearing such pants. Yet Birnie-Danzkar assures us *'none wore such pants ... Flaherty dressed Allakariallak in bearskin pants, called him Nanook (the bear) and attempted to shoot bear hunting sequences in order to conform to preconceived and popularly held notions of the Inuit.'*

Those preconceived, popularly-held notions of the Eskimo happen to be true. Yet Flaherty's critics write on & on, error after error, each error used as weapon. Nothing is gained by trying to excuse those errors. They define the criticism.

She dismisses Flaherty's attempt to film a bear hunt as theatrical. Yet bear were taken in this area, in great number, sometimes by ancient means. She further charges Flaherty with renaming Nanook for theatrical effect. Yet the government census records this nickname long before Flaherty met him.

She calls Flaherty's portraits 'sentimental'. Many are. They were made to sell. He needed money. She says those portraits isolate subjects from daily life. Many do. Yet he also shot crowded scenes. These remain largely unpublished.

Robert Flaherty
Credit: Flaherty Study Center, Claremont.

Critics accused him of exaggerating the danger of dogs. Yet dogs were dangerous. Like the wolves with whom they sometimes bred, they instantly attacked any creature lying horizontally, including any child or adult who fell nearby. The dogs in Nanook were chained, for good reason.

Iris Barry dismissed "**Nanook**" as an enchanting romance: *'It convinced us it was fact though it wasn't at all (*"Nanook" *was actually taken in the latitude of Edinburgh, and acted by extremely sophisticated Eskimos)'*.

Temperature, not latitude, defines the Arctic: that region north of the tree-line with a July mean temperature below $50°F$ ($\div 45\frac{1}{2}$ C). The Belcher Islands, home to many of the Eskimos in "**Nanook**", fall within that definition. Its residents, far from being modern sophisticates, were exactly as portrayed: isolated traditionalists. The Belchers lay outside the area of commercial whaling. No trading post existed there. The channel separating the Belchers from the mainland, doesn't freeze solid every season. Cut off from the mainland by harsh seas and band rivalries, these isolated islanders were ideal candidates to represent traditional Eskimo life.

However, Barry is right in one sense: Flaherty *was* a Romantic, at least in the true sense of that word. Isaiah Berlin reminds us that:

'Until the Romantics came along, there was only one answer to any question. Truth was one, error was many. You might not know it, you may be too benighted to find it, but there must be one answer. The Romantics said the same question can have more than one answer. [They believed] *the answer wasn't something built into the universe.'*

"**Nanook of the North**" came out of that movement, proudly so. Prior to its release, most people believed we had nothing to learn from these hunters, save how to starve on a few fish or build snow-blocks into a shelter. Flaherty changed that view. He revealed a culture different from our own, but equally human, equally honorable.

He staged every scene. He had no choice. Filming a seal hunt in winter required rigging a line under the ice. Filming the interior of an igloo required cutting the igloo in half. Yet the film is wholly accurate.

Flaherty knew Eskimo life intimately. With great ingenuity, he made the necessary staging adjustment, then let his Eskimo friends act out their lives. They did so with all the self-confidence of people getting on with daily tasks. The result is surely the best film ever made of Eskimos.

I first saw that film in 1950, shortly after returning from the North. Had Flaherty been present, I would have bowed deeply. Never mind that scenes were staged: they rang true. Never mind that some Eskimos hammed it up: the way they filled themselves with pride was pure Eskimo.

Now I'm asked to believe that what I admired was false, not just "**Nanook of the North**", but all of Flaherty's work: full of racism, colonialism, ignorance, arrogance. These imagined distortions distract from real distortions - politically moti-vated, government financed, academ-ically embraced, beloved by the media.

'*The first step in liquidating a people*', writes the Czech historian Milan Hubl, '*is to erase its memory. Destroy its books, its culture, its his-tory. Then have somebody write new books, manufacture a new culture, invent a new history. Before long the nation will begin to forget what it is and what it was. The world around will forget even faster.*'

When they invented the Inuit, academics dismissed Flaherty's Eskimo friends as make-believe. Yet they were real enough. It simply required a Flaherty or Rasmussen, a Freuchen or Harrington, to recognize & greet them. '*Few people*', wrote Goethe, '*have the imagination for reality*'.

Richard Harrington

Westerners have been re-inventing Eskimos for centuries. Among the few to accept them as they found them was Richard Harrington. The result was a rare, rare record of hon-esty & compassion. His photographs speak for themselves. He himself says little. In an age of celebrity pho-tographers, he simply works. It's dis-turbing that photographs of this sen-sitivity remain largely unknown, unhonored.

As a commercial photographer, Harrington photographed penguins for Hallmark, news items for "**Parade Magazine**". He also pho-tographed the unsaleable. For whom? For the record? What record?

He went North many times. On his first six trips, 1948-1953, he trav-eled by sled. It was a time of famine. Of those charged with witnessing this ordeal, he alone brought back a truth-ful account. His photographs reveal silent dignity in the presence of per-sonal & cultural death.

No summer journalist, no sun-shine photographer, he made do, without complaint, whatever the hardship. His dogs starved, his hosts starved, he starved, spit blood,

endured frostbite. Of these ordeals, he says little, perhaps because he sur-vived, others did not. Several pho-tographs, within days of having been taken, became obituaries.

Yet scholars ignore his work and critics misrepresent it. With one exception: to their ever-lasting credit, the Canadian Museum of Photogra-phy chose his work - and his alone - for their inaugural exhibition, **The Incredible Journey**, 1987. It was the right choice.

It was also an isolated honor. Maria Tippett's **Between Two Worlds: A Photographer among the Inuit**, 1994, a book of unrelieved banality, begins by belittling Fla-herty, taking her lead, error for error, from Birnie-Danzker. She then moves on to Harrington:

'*late-romantic ... visual devices and iconographic clichés: action poses echoing Franz Boas's faked photographs; low-angled shots of sil-houetted figures popularized by Fla-herty ...*'

To this she adds the charge that Harrington obscured '*horrific condi-tions ... did nothing to explain*'. That explanation, she says, fell to Farley Mowat in **People of the Deer**, 1951.

Some model! Of the limitless errors in Mowat's best-seller, my favorite is his charge that traders encouraged the slaughter of caribou solely for their tongues which were bundled & shipped South. A 'Deer's Tongue' is the popular name for an arctic plant (*Liatris* sp.) used to flavor tobacco.

In 1996, a British Museum con-ference, **Imagining the Arctic**, rejected my essay on Harrington ('*contradicts the Conference's mea-sured insistence on a balanced approach*') and all but one of his pho-tographs ('*might offend modern Inuit*'). The title of that conference brings to mind Disney's '*imagineer-ing*'. So does its opening statement: '*We know that photographs are nei-ther truthful nor neutral "analo-gons" of reality*'.

I know no such thing.

'*No one will ever realize*', Har-rington wrote, '*what goes into the pictures I bring back.*' Fortunately, his diaries record just that, especially his 1950 diary, penciled among the starving Padleimiut:

February 8, 1950:
'*Came upon the tiniest igloo yet. Out-side: a single, mangy, starving dog lay motionles, sole survivor of a full team; a primus stove, half-drifted under; a broken komatik. Inside, a small woman [Tetuk], in clumsy clothes, large hood, with baby. She sat in darkness, without fuel. She speaks to me. I believe she said they are starving.*

Never before did the word cave-dwellers come to my mind, until I crawled into this small ante-room, bones strewn around, all sucked clean of marrow. [The anteroom] opened into a tiny lair, round, where I could not even stand upright. She hunched up there, no place for Kumok [my companion]. He knelt in the anteroom. We brought in some biscuits, thermos bottles. She chewed bits of hardtack, then gave it to the baby, nice & soggy. Baby gurgled.

They were out of nearly every-thing: matches, tea, kerosene. The first igloo I've seen without light or heat. We left tea, matches, kerosene, biscuits. And went on.

Later we met [her] husband [Annowtalik], a young man with a rifle and an empty game bag. He started with 6 dogs, now has one.'

Eight days later, at another camp, Harrington re-met Tetuk, her hus-band & infant.

February 16, 1950:
'*They all nearly starved, did not eat for several days, survived off a skinned fox carcass, eaten raw, plus caribou skin which Tetuk sheared of hair, chewed, then cooked over twigs until their matches gave out. But they did not kill their dogs.*

She & her husband went through an ordeal. Days without food or warmth, in the tiniest igloo, wearing grimy, greasy caribou clothes with-

out hair. Last dog died. Then he shot a caribou. They probably gorged, then walked 40-50 miles to this shack. He is young [20], but haggard, hardly moves. Now both have distended stomachs, are in pain, and he passes a great deal of gas. Baby still alive & well.'

February 27, 1950:

'Photographic interpretation of Eskimos is difficult, since they do not share our gestures. I could arrange, let's say, a picture of a man looking fondly at his wife - but he never does, rarely even looks at her directly. Their forms and ways of expression are very different [from ours]. They are not exhibitionists, nor show graceful moves or forms.

In an igloo, each one has his place: moving anything around at once makes a picture an unreality. A woman's place in [an] igloo is always the same corner. She would not sew in any other.'

The British Museum symposium, **Imagining the Arctic**, found the foregoing comments on Harrington unacceptable. Why?

One reason concerned money, specifically $10,000,000 claimed as compensation for the re-location in 1953 of Eskimos from Inukjuak to Grise Fiord & Resolute Bay. Harrington's photographs challenged the claim that relocatees had been exiled from a bountiful to a cruel land.

I cannot exaggerate the misery then prevailing at Inukjuak, known as the *'Hungry Coast'*. I believed then, and believe now, that relocation was a necessary, humane, practical solution to what often seemed a hopeless situation. I remember saying to Bent Sivertz, then Chief of the Arctic Service, *'If I were God, I wouldn't know what to do.'* Fortunately, he did. Relocation proved a great success. All evidence supports that conclusion.

Those seeking compensation described their former life at Inukjuak as an Eden of game, health, happiness, and their later life at Grise Fiord & Resolute Bay as a time of hunger,

Richard Harrington.
Photo: William Belsey.

cold, misery. The fascinating thing about this view is that it sustains itself without evidence.

Those seeking compensation called relocation a political act designed to establish sovereignty. Nonesense. If human flagpoles had been needed, surely uniformed officials would have been selected, not a handful of starving Eskimos, then publicly regarded as curiosities of uncertain affiliation. Academics created the sovereignty motive.

That claim was mere footnote in a national movement. After long delay, Canadians, like Americans, moved against racism, chauvinism, imperialism. This was most welcome. Yet, here & there, reform got out of hand. Most misdeeds were real enough. But this was not. It never happened. That mattered not at all. The mood was set, the public waiting.

Bent Sivertz

By now the reader must realize that a common theme runs through these profiles. Each tells of honesty collid-

ing with academia. With Bent Sivertz, that encounter approaches injustice.

Sivertz descended from Icelandic stock. He served as a seaman before the mast, then steam; put himself though university; captained *HMS KINGS* in wartime; founded & commanded the Royal Canadian Navigation School; then rose in government to Commissioner, Northwest Territories.

During the Second War, Canadian Eskimos still dressed in furs and traveled by sled. The web of custom & kinship knit together every person from birth to death. Yet, unobserved, changes occurred. TB spread. Caribou declined. Starvation followed. It was difficult to know what was happening.

In 1950, as Chief of the Arctic Division, Sivertz faced these problems. He assembled a team of *'arctic hands'* native & Western. How he found them, I don't know. Perhaps they found him. All were much like Sivertz himself: quiet, organized, intelligent, with absolute integrity. All were passionately committed to the welfare & rights of northern Canadians.

I was never part of that team, but I remain its life-long admirer. Gordon Robertson was then Deputy Minister of Northern Affairs. Henry Larsen commanded 'G' Division, RCMP. Graham Rowley served as scientific adviser to the Defence Research Board. It's hard to imagine arctic administration in better hands.

The initial problem was lack of information. In the past, Eskimos had been encouraged to remain self-uffient and shun Western outposts. The Second War reduced even this limited contact.

Once the crisis became clear, the government acted decisively. The ill were hospitalized. Families moved to government settlements. The Eskimos were saved. An exaggeration? No. The crisis was real, the outcome uncertain.

In 1953, the government relocated Eskimo volunteers from Quebec to the High Arctic. A great body of letters, photographs, medical records, observer's reports, testifies to the success of this move. It was uniformly applauded.

Then, suddenly, forty years later, criticism arose, without benefit of evidence. Anthropologists, gender activists, journalists and government-funded lawyers denounced this relocation as a violation of human rights.

Gerard Kenney's **Arctic Smoke & Mirrors**, 1994, documents all this. The only possible addition I can make to his accurate, eloquent book is to comment on the role of those anthropologists who denounced this relocation.

Anthropology is sometimes called a 'social science'. This legitimately applies only where it borrows from science, say carbon dating or genetics. Basically, anthropology is humanistic or political or both. Right now, politics dominate. So we ask: what political factors gave rise to this belated criticism?

In America at least, political correctness has overwhelmed academia. Practioners profess to speak from moral ground. Moral *superioritis* derives from the sinner redeemed syndrome. A Golden Glow cleanses past sins. No academic discipline got scrubbed cleaner than anthropology.

Revisionists, with an eye for funding & media attention, turned the Grise Fiord & Resolute Bay relocations into a small industry: over a dozen reports, at least three books, TV. It would be interesting to know how much public money, to date, has gone into this effort.

Those promoting this claim insisted that relocation was politically motivated, involuntary, a cruel hardship and a ghastly violation of rights. They searched, but found no such evidence. So they collected oral testimony. Even that was often contradicted by letters written by the same individuals, or their parents, extolling their new homes and urging relatives to join them.

A Royal Commission on Aboriginal Peoples was called. Thirty-three

Inuit were flown to Ottawa. Witnesses were neither sworn nor cross-examined. Immunity from libel was granted: no burden of proof required. Witnesses vilified those who had, in fact, saved their lives. They freely libeled & slandered Constable Ross Gibson, RCMP, accusing him, without evidence, of theft, lies, sexual misconduct. Gibson and his wife watched on TV.

Even before the hearings, Co-chair René Dussault called the relocation 'a human catastrophe'. After hearing only Inuit testimony, Commissioner Bertha Wilson, former Supreme Court Justice, spoke on television: '... *outraged ... injustice ... grieved ... pain and suffering ... no possible justification ... cruel and inhumane government policy ... raise the public awareness of this tragic episode ... bring pressure to bear on the federal government to make reparation ...*'.

These words ended TV coverage. The government's case went untelevised. Only one Commissioner resigned.

A bizarre tale. Due process, justice, evidence, common sense, turned upside down. One academic offered a F-paper. A lawyer spoke of *Nazi experiment*. Witnesses wept, accused, libeled. None of this made sense until one realized: this was a TV psychodrama masquerading as government in action. Real Commissioners, real Inuit, added a touch of verisimilitude.

Viewers could be forgiven if they mistook this for reality. In a modern sense, it was. But it had nothing to do with pre-TV reality. For that, three anchors were needed: sworn testimony, cross-examination, and an unbiased commission.

Nanook of the North was scripted, staged, acted. Yet it accurately portrayed Eskimo life. Can this be said of Inuit performances at the Royal Commission? Did they accurately portray Inuit? If so, then 'Eskimo' & 'Inuit' refer to different people.

In those hearings, Inuit lied. All people lie, of course, but Eskimos

lied so rarely, this astonished Whites. They had never before met people so truthful. Again & again one heard: 'Eskimos don't lie.' Yet these Inuit lied.

Inuit behavior differed from Eskimo behavior in another way. Ross Gibson's widow, who knew Eskimos well, wrote to Sivertz that sobbing Inuit, fleeing the room, were new to her. She thought they'd been coached. As they had. But perhaps they required less coaching than she thought. They were, after all, raised on TV.

Today the igloos & dogs are gone. The outer trappings of Eskimo culture dropped away long ago. What is left lies within. For Inuit activists, traditional attitudes of mind, shape of heart, if they survive at all, remain divorced from life, like a watch ticking in the pocket of a dead man. Inuit take their identity, their art, their entertainment, even their name, from the West.

The word 'Eskimo' was applied by the Montagnais to their northern neighbors, since at least the 16th century. Its meaning is now lost, but there's no reason to believe it was ever perjorative.

'Inuit' is an awkward term. Eskimo grammar traditionally shunned naked nouns and did so for reasons basic to Eskimo culture. 'Inuit' converts a suffix, meaning 'people', into a noun. It appeared in print as early as 1860, but gained acceptance only after official promotion, beginning in the late 50s. Many Eskimos outside of Canada decline to use it. Moreover, the title 'people' begs the question: who isn't?

Activists insist on the exclusive use of 'Inuit'. They condemn 'Eskimo' as racist and seek to censor all records where it appears. My hope is they will return to that proud name and accept those true records, not to imitate some lost ideal, but to realize that who they were, makes them what they are. When I'm in search of *me*, I don't want someone else's history. Rejecting your history means rejecting yourself.

Joint Bibliography

This is a list of all the references used by all the authors in this book. It has been collected in order to give the user easier access to the literature on the Arctic. Unfortunately, it has no been possible to get complete information. Lacking information is marked by a *. Abriviations: p. = pages; pp: = from page to page.

Aigner, J. [1981]: **Archaeological Remains in Pleistocene China.** *Forschungen zur Allgemeinen und Vergleichenden Archäologie*, 1:197-219, editor: H. Müller-Beck, 351 p. (München: Beck).

Alexandersen, Verner, Pia Bennike, Jens Peder Hart Hansen & Niels Lynnerup [1992]: **Biological Anthropology: prospects for a bio-cultural discipline.** *Arkæologiske Udgravninger i Danmark*, 1992:60-67 (Copenhagen: Det arkæologiske Nævn).

Alpers, Swetlana [1988]: **Rembrandt's Enterprise**. 160 p. (Chicago: University of Chicago Press).

AMAP [1997]: **Arctic Pollution Issues: A State of the Arctic Environment Report.** 188 p. (Oslo: Arctic Monitoring and Assessment Programme).

Amdrup, G. [1909]: **The former Eskimo Settlements on the East coast of Greenland between Scoresby Sund and the Angmagsalik District**. *Meddelelser om Grønland*, 28(4):285-328 (Copenhagen: Retizels Forlag).

Andersen, Sten [1981]: **Positivism kontra hermeneutik.** 119 p. (Göteborg: Förlaget Korpen).

Anderson, Douglas D. [1984]: **Prehistory of North Alaska**. pp:80-93 in "Handbook of North American Indians", Arctic, 5:1-829, editor: David Damas (Washington DC: Smithsonian Institution).

Anderson, Douglas D. [1988]: **Onion Portage: The Archaeology of a Stratified Site from the Kobuk River, Nort-** hwest Alaska. *Anthropological Papers of the University of Alaska*, 22(1-2):1-163 (Fairbanks, Alaska: University of Alaska Press).

Andreasen, Claus & H. Lange [1994]: **The Archaeology of Holm Land, Amdrup Land, and Henrik Krøyer Holme.** pp:163-165 in "Berichte zur Polarforshung. Reports on Polar Research 142/ 94. The 1993 North East Water Expedition Scientific cruise report of RV "Polarstern" Arctic Cruises ARK IX/2 and 3, USCG "Polar Sea" cruise NEWP and the NEWland expedition", editor: Hans-Jürgen Hirche & Gerhardt Kattner, 190 p. (Bremerhaven: Alfred-Wegener Institut für Polar- und Meeresforschung).

Andreasen, Claus & Henrik Elling [1991]: **De arkæologiske undersøgelser.** pp:54-65 in "Naturbevaring i Grønland", editor: Claus Andreasen, 132 p. (Nuuk: Attuakkiorfik).

Andreasen, Claus & Henrik Elling [1995]: **Biologisk-Arkæologisk kortlægning af Grønlands østkyst mellem 75°N og 79° 30'N. Del 7: Arkæologisk kortlægning mellem Dove Bugt (76° 30'N) og Lambert Land (79° 30'N) sommeren 1990.** *Teknisk Rapport*, 25:1-60 (Nuuk: Grønlands Hjemmestyre, Miljø og Naturforvaltning).

Andreasen, Claus [1986]: **Greenland's Museum Laws: An introduction to Greenland's Museums under Home Rule.** *Arctic Anthropology*, 23(1-2):239-246 (Madison: University of Wisconsin Press).

Andreasen, Claus [1996]: **A Survey of Paleo-Eskimo Sites in Northern East** Greenland. pp:177-189 in "The Paleo-Eskimo Cultures of Greenland - New Perspectives in Greenlandic Archaeology", editor: Bjarne Grønnow, 334 p., Publication 1 (Copenhagen: Danish Polar Center).

Andreasen, Claus [1997]: **Independence II in North East Greenland: Some new aspects.** *Ethnographical Series*, 18:23-32 (Copenhagen: The National Museum of Denmark).

Andreasen, Claus [1997]: **The Archaeology of NEWland - An Archaeological Perspective.** *Journal of Marine Systems*, 1997(10):41-46 (Amsterdam: Elsevier Science).

Anonymous [1861]: **Kalâdlit Okalluktualiait** II. Noungme.

Anonymous [1994]: **Fornyelse / Nutarterineq.** *Atuagagdliutit/Grønlandsposten*, 134(71):5 (Nuuk).

Anonymous [1995]: **Aqqaluk Lynge vil med i landsstyret / Aqqaluk Lynge naalakkersuinermi suleqataarusuppoq.** *Atuagagdliutit/Grønlandsposten*, 135(19): 10-11 (Nuuk).

Appelt, Martin & J. Pind [1996]: **Nunnguaq - a Saqqaq Site from the Godthåbsfiord.** pp:129-142 in "The Paleo-Eskimo Cultures of Greenland - New Perspectives in Greenlandic Archaeology", editor: Bjarne Grønnow, 334 p. (Copenhagen: Danish Polar Center).

Appelt, Martin [1995]: **Nunnguaq - en Saqqaq-plads fra Godthåbsfjorden. En gammel udgravning i nyt perspektiv.** 85

p. Unpublished master thesis from Department of Ethnology and Archaeology. University of Copenhagen.

Appelt, Martin [1997]: **Construction of an archeological "culture". Alikness and differences i early Greenland Paleo-Eskimo Cultures.** *Ethnographical Series*, 18:33-40 (Copenhagen: The National Museum of Denmark).

Archambault, M. F. [1981]: **Essai de caractérisation de la stéatite des sites dorsétiens et des carrières de l'Ungava, Arctique québécois.** *Géographie physique et Quaternaire*, 35(1):19-28 (Montréal: *).

Arneborg, Jette & Joel Berglund [1993]: **Gården under sandet / naasorissaasup illua sioqqanik matusimasoq.** *Forskning i Grønland / tusaat*, 4:7-19 (Copenhagen: Danish Polar Center).

Arneborg, Jette [1991]: **Kulturmødet mellem nordboer og eskimoer.** Unpublished PhD dissertation (Copenhagen: University of Copenhagen).

Arneborg, Jette [1993]: **Contacts between Eskimos and Norsemen in Greenland.** pp:23-37 in "Tolvte tværfaglige Vikingesymposium", editor: E. Roesdahl & P. Meulengracht Sørensen, * p. (Århus: Aarhus Universitet).

Arneborg, Jette [1996]: **Exchanges between Norsemen and Eskimos in Greenland?** pp:11-21 in "Cultural and Social Research in Greenland 95/96. Essays in Honour of Robert Petersen", editor: Birgitte Jacobsen, 332 p. (Nuuk: Ilisimatusarfik/Atuakkiorfik).

Arneborg, Jette [1997]: **Cultural Borders - Reflections on Norse-Eskimo Interaction.** *Ethnographical Series*, 18:41-46 (Copenhagen: The National Museum of Denmark).

Arnold, C. [1992]: **Repatriation of Skeletons to the Northwest territories: Past and Present.** *Information North*, 18(3):1-4 (Calgary: Arctic Institute of North America).

Auger, Réginald [1985]: **The Inuit in the Strait of Belle Isle.** *Archaeology in Newfoundland and Labrador, Annual Report*, 5:272-298, editor: J. Sproull-Thomson, 249 p. (St.John's, Newfoundland: Historic Resources).

Augustsson, J. E., A-M. Blennow, J. von Bonsdorff, I. Estham, L. Karlsson, M. Nockert, A. Piltz, J. Svanberg, G. Tegnér, P. Tångeberg & M. Ullén [1996]: **Den Gotiska Konsten**. 543 p. (Lund: Signum).

Bahnson, Anne & Birthe Haagen [1994]: **Vestgrønlandske dragter.** 28 p. (Copenhagen: National Museum of Denmark).

Bahnson, Anne [1996]: **Skinclothing in Greenland.** pp:60-88 in "Braving the cold, continuity an change in Arctic clothing", editors: C. Buis & J. Oosten, 213 p. (Leiden: Centre of Non-Western Studies).

Bahnson, Anne [1997]: **Ancient Skin Clothing passing through Copenhagen.** *Ethnographical Series*, 18:47-56 (Copenhagen: The National Museum of Denmark).

Balchen B., C. Ford & O. La Forge O. [1945]: **War below zero. The battle for Greenland.** 125 p. (London: George Allen & Unwin Ltd).

Bandi, Hans-Georg [1997]: **Arctic Prelude 1948 - A Summer Full of Experience in North-East Greenland.** *Ethnographical Series*, 18:57-69 (Copenhagen: The National Museum of Denmark).

Bandi, Hans-Georg & Jørgen Meldgaard [1952]: **Archaeological Investigations on Clavering Ø, Northeast Greenland.** *Meddelelser om Grønland*, 126(4):1-84 (Copenhagen: C. A. Reitzels Forlag).

Bandi, Hans-Georg [1969]: **Eskimo Prehistory.** 226 p. (College: University of Alaska Press).

Barr, William [1993]: **The Career and Disappearance of Hans K. E. Krueger, Arctic Geologist, 1886-1930**. *Polar Record*, 29(171):277-304 (Cambridge: Scott Polar Institute).

Barré, G. [1970]: **Reconnaissance archéologique dans la région de la Baie de Wakeham (Nouveau-Québec).** 107 p. (Montréal: La Société d'Archéologie Préhistorique du Québec).

Bartlett, Robert A. [1934]: **Sails over Ice**. 301 p. (New York: Charles Scribner's Sons).

Bay, Christian [1992]: **A phytogeographical study of the vascular plants of** northern Greenland - north of 74° northern latitude. *Meddelelser om Grønland, Bioscience*, 36:1-101 (Copenhagen: The Commission for Scientific Research in Greenland).

Benmouyal, Joseph [1972]: **Etude Archeologique de sites Eskimo aux Iles Belcher, T.N.O.** Dissertation submitted to the Graduate Faculty of the Department of Anthropology, University of Montreal, in partial fulfillment of the requirements for the degree of Master of Arts. Manuscript.

Berglund, Joel [1994]: **Recovering the Past: The Greenland Nationasl Museum and Archives.** *Museum International*, 182, 46(2):26-29 (Paris: Unesco Quarterly Review).

Berglund, Joel [1997]: **Two Dogs and a Dragon.** *Ethnographical Series*, 18:65-69 (Copenhagen: National Museum of Denmark).

Bertelsen, Alfred [1910]: **Om Dødeligheden i Grønland og om nogle af Dødsårsagerne sammesteds.** *Bibliotek for læger*, 102:459-504 (Copenhagen: Ugeskrift for Læger).

Bird, Junius [1945]: **Archaeology of the Hopedale Area, Labrador.** *Anthropological Papers of the American Museum of Natural History*, 39(2):121-186 (New York: American Museum of Natural History).

Birket-Smith, Kaj [1924]: **Ethnography of the Egedesminde District.** *Meddelelser om Grønland*, 66:1-484 (Copenhagen: C. A. Reitzels Forlag).

Birket-Smith, Kaj & Frederica de Laguna [1938]: **The Eyak Indians of the Copper River Delta, Alaska.** 592 p. *Det Kgl. Danske Videnskabernes Selskab.* (Copenhagen: Levin & Munksgaard).

Birket-Smith, Kaj [1948]: **Kulturens Veje.** 728 p. (Copenhagen: Jespersen og Pios Forlag).

Birket-Smith, Kaj [1953]: **The Chugach Eskimo.** *Nationalmuseets Skrifter, Etnografisk Række*, 6:1-262 (Copenhagen: National Museum of Denmark).

Birks, J. D. S. & N. Penford [1990]: **Observations on the ecology of Arctic Foxes Alopex lagopus in Eqalummiut Nunaat, West Greenland.** *Meddelelser* om Grønland, Bioscience, 32:1-26 (Copenhagen: The Commission for Scientific Research in Greenland).

Blumer, R. [1996]: **Première Expédition Archéologique Internationale en Thoukotka, Sibérie nord-orientale. Rapport de la contribution suisse aux travaux de l'été 1995.** Jahresbericht 1995:110-154 (Bern & Vaduz: Schweizerische-Liechtensteinische Stiftung für archäologische Forschungen im Ausland).

Bogoras, Waldemar [1929]: **Elements of the culture of the circumpolar zone.** American Anthropologist, 31(4):579-601 (Menasha, Wis.: American Anthropologist Society).

Braestrup, F. W. [1941]: **A study on the Arctic Fox in Greenland.** Meddelelser om Grønland, 131(4):1-101 (Copenhagen: C. A. Reitzels Forlag).

Bray, T. L. & T. W. Killion (editors) [1994]: **Reckoning with the Dead.** The Larsen Bay Repatriation and the Smithsonian Institution. 194 p. (Washington DC: Smithsonian Institution Press).

Breinholt-Larsen, Finn [1992]: **The quiet life of a revolution: Greenlandic Home Rule 1979-1992.** Études/Inuit/Studies, 16(1-2):199-226 (Quebec).

Brice-Bennett, Carol [1977]: **Land Use in the Nain and Hopedale Regions.** pp:97-203 in "Our Footprints are Everywhere", editor: Carol Brice-Bennett, 381 p. (Nain: Labrador Inuit Association).

Bronshtein, Mikhail & Patrick Plumet [1995]: **Ékven: l'art préhistorique beeringien et l'approche russe de l'origine de la tradition culturelle esquimaude.** Études/Inuit/Inuit Studies, 19(2):5-59 (Québec: Département d'anthropologie, Université Laval).

Bruemmer, Fred [1972]: **Les faces du diable.** Perspectives, 20 mai 1972:10-11 (Montréal: *).

Bruun de Neergaard, Helga [1962]: **Avigtat. Grønlandske skindmønstre.** 28 p (Copenhagen: Høst & Søns Forlag).

Bryan, Alan [1957]: **Results and interpretations of recent archeological research in Western Washington with circum-boreal implications.** Davidson Journal of Anthropology, 3(1):1-16 (*: *).

Bryson, Reid A. & W. M. Wendland [1967]: **Tentative Climatic Patterns for Some Late Glacial and Post-Glacial Episodes in Central North America.** pp:271-298 in "Life, Land and Water", editor: W. J. Meyer-Oakes, 416 p. (Winnipeg: University of Manitoba Press).

Buckland, Peter C., et al. [1996]: **Bioarchaeological and Climatological Evidence for the Fate of Norse Farmers in Medieval Greenland.** Antiquity, 70:88-96 (*: *).

Bugge, Aage & Augustinus Lynge [1951]: **Atuainiutitât** II. 254 p.(Nûk: Grønlandsdepartementip naqitertitai).

Carpenter, Edmund [1997]: **19th century Aivilik Drawings.** Ethnographical Series, 18:70-92 (Copenhagen: The National Museum of Denmark).

Carpenter, Edmund [1997]: **Arctic Witnesses.** Ethnographical Series, 18: 303-310 (Copenhagen: The National Museum of Denmark).

Chard, Chester [1958]: **The Western roots of Eskimo Culture.** pp: 2:20-27 in "Actas del XXXIII Congresso Internacional de Americanistas", San Jose, Costa Rica, 20-27 July, 1958. * p. (Costa Rica: *) (reprinted in Shimkin, "Western Siberian Archaeology").

Chernetsov, Valeri N. [1935]: **An Early Maritime Culture on the Yamal Peninsula.** Sovetskaya Etnografiya, 4-5:109-133 (*: *) (in Russian); English translation by Ludmila Bonnichson on file at Arctic Studies Center.

Chernetsov, Valeri N. [1970]: **On the Question of the Ancient Substratum in the Cultures of the Circumpolar Region.** pp:260-267 in "Selected Papers of the VIIth International Congress of Anthropological and Ethnological Sciences, 1964", editor: *, *, * p. (Moscow: Nauka).

Chernetsov, Valeri N. [1974]: **The Early History of the Lower Ob Region.** Translations from Russian Sources, 9:1-74, editor: Henry N. Michael, original in: V. N. Chernetsov & W. Mozhinskaya: "The Prehistory of Western Siberia", 377 p. (Montreal/London: Arctic Institute of North America/McGill-Queen's University Press).

Clark, P. U., & William W. Fitzhugh [1991]: **Postglacial relative sea level history of the Labrador coast and interpretation of the archaeological record.** pp:189-213 in "Paleoshorelines and prehistory: an investigation of method", editor: L. L. Johnson, 243 p. (Boca Raton, Fl: CRC Press).

Collins, Henry B. [1937]: **Archaeology of St. Lawrence Island, Alaska.** Smithsonian Miscellaneous Collections, 96(1): 1-431 (Washington DC: Smithsonian Institute Press).

Collins, Henry B. [1937]: **Culture migrations and contacts in the Bering Sea region.** American Anthropologist, 39(3): 375-384 (Menasha, Wis.: American Anthropologists Society).

Collins, Henry B. [1951]: **The origin and antiquity of the Eskimo.** Smithsonian Institution Annual Report for 1950:423-467 (Washington DC: Smithsonian Institution).

Collins, Henry B. [1954]: **Archaeological Research in the North American Arctic.** Arctic, 7(3-4):296-306 (Calgary: The Arctic Institute of North America).

Collins, Henry B. [1956]: **Archaeological Investigations on Southampton and Coats Islands, N.W.T.** Annual Report of the National Museum of Canada for 1954-1955. National Museum of Canada Bulletin, 142:*-* (Ottawa: *).

Cox, Steven L. [1978]: **Paleo-Eskimo Occupations of the North Labrador Coast.** Arctic Anthropology, 15(2): 96-118 (Madison: University of Wisconsin Press).

Crantz, David [1767]: **The history of Greenland: containing a description of the country, and its inhabitants; and particularly, a relation of the mission carried on for above these thirty years by the Unitas Fratrum, at New Herrnhut and Lichtenfels, in that country.** 2 vols. * p. & * p. (London: Printed for the Brethren's Society for the Furtherance of the Gospel among the Heathen, & sold by J. Dodsley).

D'Arrigo, Rosanne & Gordon Jacoby [1993]: **Secular Trends in High Northern Latitude Temperature Reconstructions Based on Tree Rings.** Climatic Change, 25:163-177 (Boston: Reidel Publishing Co.).

Dalager, Lars [1915]: **Grønlandske Relationer ... sammenskrevet ved Friderichshaabs Colonie i Grønland Anno 1752.** editor: Louis Bobé, *Det grønlandske Selskabs Skrifter*, 2:1-94 (Copenhagen: The Greenland Society).

Dam-Mikkelsen, Bente & Torben Lundbæk (editors) [1980]: **Etnografiske genstande i Det kongelige danske Kunstkammer 1650-1800. Ethnographic Objects in The Royal Danish Kunstkammer 1650-1800.** *Nationalmuseets skrifter, Ethnographical Series*, 17:1-260 (Copenhagen: National Museum of Denmark).

Dansgaard, W. & S. J. Johnsen [1971]: **Climatic Record Revealed by the Camp Century Ice Core.** pp:37-56 in "The Late Cenozoic Glacial Ages", editor: K. K. Turekian, 606 p. (New Haven: Yale University Press).

Dawkins, Boyd [1874]: **Cave hunting. Research on the Evidence of Caves Respecting the Inhabitants of Europe.** * p. (London: MacMillan and Company).

de Laguna, Frederica [1932-1933]: **A comparison of Eskimo and Paleolithic art.** *American Journal of Archaeology*, 36(4):477-511; 37(1):77-107 (*: *).

de Laguna, Frederica [1956]: **Chugach Prehistory. The Archaeology of Prince William Sound, Alaska.** * p. (Seattle: University of Washington Press).

de Laguna, Frederica [1977]: **Voyage to Greenland: A Personal Initiation into Anthropology.** 285 p. (New York: W. W. Norton), reprinted 1995 with new perface and illustrations (Prospect Heights, Illinois: Waveland Press).

de Laguna, Frederica [1997]: **The Fate of Krueger's Expedition.** *Ethnographical Series*, 18:93-98 (Copenhagen: The National Museum of Denmark).

Degerbøl, Magnus [1936]: **Animal Remains from the West Settlement in Greenland.** *Meddelelser om Grønland*, 88(3): 1-55 (Copenhagen: C. A. Reitzels Forlag).

Degerbøl, Magnus [1936]: **The Former Eskimo Habitation in the Kangerdlugssuak District, East Greenland.** *Meddelelser om Grønland*, 104(10):1-48 (Copenhagen: C. A. Reitzels Forlag).

Dektor, David [1996]: **Nenets in Yamal: opportunities in cultural continuity and preservation of tradition.** 29 page manuscript in Russian at Arctic Studies Center, Smithsonian Institute.

Desroiers, P. [1986]: **Pre-Dorset Surface Structures from Diana 1, Ungava Bay.** pp:3-25 in "Paleo-Eskimo Cultures in Newfounland, Labrador and Ungava", editor: *.*, *Reports in Archaeology*, 1:*-* (St.John's: Memorial University of Newfoundland).

Diklev, Torben & Bo Madsen [1992]: **Arkæologisk berejsning i Thule, 1991.** Unpublished report on file at Avernersuup Katersugaasivia, 42 p. (Qaanaaq: Thule Museum).

Dneprovsky, K. A. [1996]: **Archaeological Expedition in Chukotka of the State Museum of Oriental Art (Moscow).** 3 p. in "International Conference on Barents Spitsbergen Arctic 1996, Abstracts", * p. (Barentsburg).

Dodds, John W. [1973]: **The Several Lives Of Paul Fejos.** * p. (New York: The Wenner-Gren Foundation).

Downer, Alan S. [1993]: Comments to "The Return of the Ahayu:da. Lessons for Repatriation from Zuni Pueblo and the Smithsonian Institution" by William L. Merrill, EDmund J. Ladd, & T. J. Ferguson. *Current Anthropology*, 34:556-557 (Chicago: University of Chicago Press).

Dumond, Don E. [1987]: **The Eskimos and Aleuts.** (Revised Edition). 180 p. (London: Thames and Hudson).

Ebbesen, K. [1985]: **Fortidsminderegistrering i Danmark.** 150 p. (Copenhagen: Fredningsstyrelsen).

Egede, Hans [1741]: **Det gamle Grønlands Nye Perlustration.** 131 p. (Copenhagen: Johan Christoph Groth).

Egede, Hans [1925]: **Det gamle Grønlands Nye Perlustration eller Naturel-Historie 1741.** *Meddelelser om Grønland*, 54:1-442 (Copenhagen: C. A Reitzels Forlag).

Egede, Paul [1988]: **Efterretninger om Grønland 1721-1788.** *Det grønlandske Selskabs Skrifter*, 29:1-204 (Copenhagen: Det Grønlandskle Selskab).

Elling, Henrik [1992]: **De palæoeskimoiske kulturer i Nordgrønland og Nordøstgrønland i relation til de vestgrønlandske.** pp:30-69 in "*", editor: *.*, 270 p. (Nuuk: Grønlandsk kultur- og samfundsforskning & Ilisamatusarfik).

Elling, Henrik [1996]: **The Independence I and Old Nuuliit Cultures in Relation to the Saqqaq Culture.** pp:191-198 in "The Paleo-Eskimo Cultures of Greenland - New Perspectives in Greenlandic Archaeology", editor: Bjarne Grønnow, 334 p. (Copenhagen: Danish Polar Center).

Englund, Peter [1995]: **Förflutenhetens landskap. Historiska essäer.** 281 p. (Stockholm: Atlantis).

Evladov, Vladimir P. [1992]: **Across the Yamal tundra to the Byel'yi Island. An expedition to northern Yamal in 1928-1929.** [in Russian] Editor: Alexander Pika, * p. (Tyumen: Institute of the Problems of the Peoples of the North).

Fabricius, Otto [1962]: **A Precise Description of the Hunting of Terristrial Animals, of Fowling and Fishing by the Greenlanders.** *Meddelelser om Grønland*, 140(2):67-96 (Copenhagen: C. A. Reitzels Forlag).

Feodorova, Natalia V., A. P. Zykov, S. F. Koksharov, & L. M. Terekhova [1994]: **Ugrian Heritage: West Siberian antiquities from the collection of the Urals University.** * p. (Ekaterinburg: "Tyumentransgas" and Urals State University, History and Archaeology Institute, Russian Academy of Sciences) [Rusian / English].

Feodorova, Natalia V. [1996]: **Tiutey Sale, a site in northern Yamal: on the issue of the circumpolar maritime adaptation.** 45 p. Manuscript in Russian on file at the Arctic Studies Center (Washington DC: National Museum of the USA).

Fischer-Møller, K. [1937]: **Skeletal Remains of the Central Eskimos.** *Report of the Fifth Thule Expedition 1921-1924*, 3:1-104 (Copenhagen: Gyldendal).

Fitzhugh, William W. [1972]: **Environment Archeology and Cultural Systems in Hamilton Intel, Labrador: A Survey of the Central Labrador Coast from 3000 B.C. to the Present.** *Smithsonian*

Contributions to Anthropology, 16:1-299 (Washington DC: National Museum of the USA).

Fitzhugh, William W. [1974]: **Ground Slates in the Scandinavian Younger Stone Age with reference to circumpolar Maritime adaptations.** *Proceedings of the Prehistoric Society*, 40:45-58 (*: *).

Fitzhugh, William W. [1975]: **A Comparative Approach to Northern Maritime Adaptations.** pp:1-18, 339-386 in "Prehistoric Maritime Adaptations of the Circumpolar Zone", editor: William W. Fitzhugh, * p. (The Hague: Mouton).

Fitzhugh, William W. [1980]: **Preliminary Report on the Torngat Archaeological Project.** *Arctic*, 33(3):585-606 (Calgary: The Arctic Institute of North America).

Fitzhugh, William W. [1994]: **"Living Yamal": Preliminary field report for 1994.** 40 p. (Washington: National Museum of Natural History, Smithsonian Institution, Arctic Studies Center).

Fitzhugh, William W. [1994]: **Staffe Island 1 and the Northern Labrador Dorset-Thule Succession.** pp:239-268 in "Threads of Arctic Prehistory", editors: David Morrison & Jean-Luc Pilon, 422 p. (Quebec: Canadian Museum of Civilization).

Fitzhugh, William W. [1995]: **Archeological excavations in Yamal, 1994-1995: the "Living Yamal" Project.** 65 p. (Washington: National Museum of Natural History, Smithsonian Institution, Arctic Studies Center).

Fitzhugh, William W. [1997]: **Searching for the Grail[1997]: Virtual Archeology in Yamal and Circumpolar Theoty.** *Ethnographical Series*, 18:99-118 (Copenhagen: The National Museum of Denmark).

Ford, James A. [1959]: **Eskimo Prehistory in the Vicinity of Point Barrow, Alaska.** *Anthropological Papers*, 47(1):1-272 (New York: American Museum of Natural History).

Fortescue, Michael [1986]: **What Dialect Distribution can tell us of Dialect Formation in Greenland.** *Arctic Anthropology*, 23(1-2):413-422 (Madison: University of Wisconsin Press).

Fredskild, Bent [1973]: **Studies in the vegetational History of Greenland. Paleobotanical investigations of some Holocene lake and bog deposits.** *Meddelelser om Grønland*, 198(4):1-245 (Copenhagen: C. A. Reitzels Forlag).

Frisbie, Charlotte J. [1993]: Comments to "The Return of the Ahayu:da. Lessons for Repatriation from Zuni Pueblo and the Smithsonian Institution" by William L. Merrill, Edmund J. Ladd, & T. J. Ferguson. *Current Anthropology*, 34:558 (Chicago: University of Chicago Press).

Frohlich, Bruno & P. O. Pedersen [1992]: **Secular Changes Within Arctic and Sub-Arctic Populations: A Study of 632 Human Mandibles From The Aleutian Islands, Alaska and Greenland.** *Arctic Medical Research*, 51:173-188 (Oulu: Nordic Council for Arctic Medical Research).

Gad, Finn [1974]: **Fire detailkomplekser i Grønlands historie.** 283 p. (Copenhagen: Nyt Nordisk Forlag, Arnold Busch).

Garde, V. [1888]: **Nogle Bemaerkninger om Øst-Grønlands Beboere.** *Geografisk Tidsskrift*, 9:93-96 (Copenhagen: Kongelige Danske Geografiske Selskab).

Gendron, Daniel, Daniel Arsenault & Louis Gagnon [1996]: **A propos du sauvetage des pétroglyphes dorsétiens de Qajartalik dans le Nunavik: réplique de l'Institut culturel Avataq à la lettre de M. Patrick Plumet.** *Études/Inuit/Studies*, 20(2):117-122 (Québec: Département d'anthropologie, Université Laval).

Georgi, J. [1935]: **Mid-Ice: The Story of the Wegener Expedition to Greenland.** (New York: Dutton & Co).

Gerlach & Mason [1992]: **Calibrated Radiocarbon Dates and Cultural Interaction in the Western Arctic.** *Arctic Anthropology*, 29(1):54-81 (Madison: University of Wisconsin Press).

Gerlach, Craig S. & Owen K. Mason [1992]: **Calibrated radiocarbon dates and cultural interaction in the Western Arctic.** *Arctic Anthropology*, 29(1):54-81 (Madison: University of Wisconsin Press).

Gessain, Robert [1975]: **Essai sur l'ethnonosologie des Ammassalimiut au XIXè siècle.** *Objets et Mondes*, 15(2):129-148 (Paris: Musée de l'Homme).

GHM [1838-1845]: **Grønlands Historiske Mindesmærker I-III.** I:797 p., II: 791 p., III: 950 p. (Copenhagen: Det kongelige Nordiske Oldskrift-Selskab).

Giddings, James L. [1964]: **The archaeology of Cape Denbigh.** 331 p. (Providense, Rhode Island: Brown University Press).

Giddings, James Louis [1951]: **The Denbigh Flint Complex.** *American Antiquity*, 16(3):193-203 (Menasha, Wisconsin: Society for American Archeology).

Giddings, James Louis [1967]: **Ancient Men of the Arctic.** 409 p. (Lonson: Secker & Warburg).

Gilberg, Rolf [1994]: **Mennesket Minik (1888-1918). En grønlænders liv mellem 2 verdener.** 680 p. (Espergærde: ILBE).

Gilberg, Aage, Lisbet Gilberg, Rolf Gilberg & Mogens Holm [1978]: **Polar Eskimo Genealogy. Appendix: Polarskimo Genetical and Anthropological Markers.** *Meddelelser om Grønland*, 203(4):1-197 (Copenhagen: C. A. Reitzels Forlag).

Gjessing, Gutorm [1935]: **Fra Steinalder til jornalder i Finmark.** * p. (*: *).

Gjessing, Gutorm [1944]: **The Circumpolar Stone Age.** *Acta Arctica*, 9(2):1-70 (Copenhagen: Ejnar Munksgaard).

Gjessing, Gutorm [1948]: **Some problems in Northeastern Archeology.** *American Antiquity*, 13:298-302 (*: *).

Gjessing, Gutorm [1953]: **The Circumpolar Stone Age.** *Antiquity*, 107:131-136 (*: *).

Glahn, Henric Christopher [1771]: **Anmærkninger til de tre første Bøger af Hr. David Crantzes Historie om Grønland.** 388 p. (Copenhagen: Gerhard Giese Salicath).

Golovnev, Andrei V. [1992]: **An ethnographic reconstruction of the economy of the indigenous maritime culture of northwestern Siberia.** *Arctic Anthropology*, 29(1):96-103 (Madison: University of Wisconsin Press).

Golovnev, Andrei V. [1995]: **A Shaman's sledge at the Drovanoy-3 site.** pp:*-* in

"Peoples of Siberia - Rebirth and Development". Integration of Archaeological and Ethnographic research. Materials of the Third all-russian Scientific Seminar dedicated to the 110th anniversary of S. I. Rudenko's birth, editor: *, * p. (Omsk: *) [in Russian. English translation by Mila Bonnichson for "Living Yamal" program on file at Arctic Studies Center, Washington DC: National Museum of the USA].

Gordon, M. S. [1977]: **Animal Physiology: Principles and Adaptations.** 699 p. (New York: MacMillan Publishing Co., Inc.).

Gotfredsen, Anne Birgitte [1992]: **Nyt fra Saqqaq kulturen.** *Tusaat/Forskning i Grønland,* 1:39-45 (Copenhagen: Danish Polar Centre).

Gotfredsen, Anne Birgitte [1996]: **The Fauna of the Saqqaq Site Nipisat I, Sisimiut District, West Greenland: Preliminary results.** pp:97-110 in "The Paleo-Eskimo Cultures of Greenland - New Perspectives in Greenlandic Archaeology", editor: Bjarne Grønnow, 334 p. (Copenhagen: Danish Polar Centre).

Gotfredsen, Anne Birgitte [in press]: **Sea Bird Exploitation on Coastal Inuit sites, West and Southeast Greenland.** *International Journal of Osteoarchaeology.*

Greenberg, J. H., C. G. Turner II & Steven L. Zegura [1986]: **The Settlement of the Americas: A Comparison of the Linguistic, Dental and Genetic Evidence.** *Current Anthropology,* 27(5): 477-497 (Chicago: University of Chicago Press).

Griffin, James B. [1953]: **A preliminary statement on the pottery from Cape Denbigh, Alaska.** pp: 40-42 in: "Asia and North America: trans-pacific contacts", editor: Marion W. Smith, *Memoirs of the Society for American Archaeology,* 9:1-* (Salt Lake City: *).

Griffin, James B. [1960]: **Some Prehistoric Connections between Siberia and America.** *Science,* 131(3403):801-812 (*: *).

Grummesgaard-Nielsen, Stig [1995]: **Arkæologiske undersøgelser i forbindelse med anlæggelsen af en lufthavn ved Sisimiut.** Unpublished report at the National Museum of Greenland. 23 p. (Nuuk).

Gryazhnov, M. P. [1952]: **Some results of three years of archaeological work on the upper Ob.** [in Russian] *Brief reports of the Institute of Material Culture Studies,* 48:93-102 (*: *).

Grønlands Landsmuseum [1983]: **Fredning i Grønland.** Fortidsminder og bygninger. Materiale fra et seminar om den nye fredningslov afholdt i Nuuk, november 1982 (Nuuk: Grønlands Landsmuseum).

Grønlandssekretariatet (editor) [1985]: **Gustav Holm Samlingen. Genstande indsamlet på konebådsekspeditionen til Ammassalik 1883-85 / The Gustav Holm Collection. Objects collected by the Umiak-Expedition to Ammassalik 1883-1885.** 249 p. (Nuuk: Grønlands Landsmuseum, National Museum of Denmark & Grønlands Hjemmestyre, Pilersuiffik).

Grønnow, Bjarne (editor) [1996]: **The Paleo-Eskimo Cultures of Greenland - New Perspectives in the Early Prehistory of Greenland.** 334 p. (Copenhagen: Danish Polar Center).

Grønnow, Bjarne & Morten Meldgaard (editors) [1991]: **Qeqertasussuk. De første mennesker i Vestgrønland.** *Tidsskriftet Grønland,* 39(4-7):97-224 (Copenhagen: The Greenland Society).

Grønnow, Bjarne & Morten Meldgaard [1991]: **De første vestgrønlændere. Resultaterne af 8 års undersøgelser på Qeqertasussuk-bopladsen i Disko Bugt.** *Tidsskriftet Grønland,* 39(4-7):103-144 (Copenhagen: The Greenland Society).

Grønnow, Bjarne, Morten Meldgaard & Jørn Berglund Nielsen [1983]: **Aasivissuit - The Great Summer camp. Archaeological, ethnographical and zooarchaeological studies of a caribou-hunting site in West Greenland.** *Meddelelser om Grønland, Man & Society,* 5:1-96 (Copenhagen: The Commission for Scientific Research in Greenland).

Grønnow, Bjarne [1988]: **Nye perspektiver i Saqqaq-forskningen: en orientering om de tværfaglige undersøgelser på bopladsen Qeqertasussuk, Christianshåbs Kommune.** pp:21-38 in "Palæoeskimoisk forskning i Grønland", editor: Tinna Møbjerg, Bjarne Grønnow & Helge Schultz-Lorentzen, 102 p. (Århus: University of Aarhus Press).

Grønnow, Bjarne [1990]: **Prehistory in Permafrost. Investigations at the Saqqaq Site, Qeqertasussuk, Disco Bay, West Greenland.** *Journal of Danish Archaeology,* 7:24-39 (Odense: Odense University Press).

Grønnow, Bjarne [1994]: **Qeqertasussuk - the Archaeology of a Frozen Saqqaq Site in Disko Bugt, West Greenland.** pp:197-238 in "Treads of Arctic Prehistory: Papers in honour of William E. Taylor, Jr.", editors: David Morrison & Jean-Luc Pilon, *Mercury Series paper* 149:1-422 (Ottawa: Archaeological survey of Canada, Museum of Civilization).

Grønnow, Bjarne [1996]: **Driftwood and Saqqaq Culture Woodworking in West Greenland.** pp:73-89 in "Cultural and social research in Greenland 95/96. Essays in Honour of Robert Petersen", editor: Birgitte Jacobsen, 332 p. (Nuuk: Ilisimatusarfik/Atuakkiorfik).

Grønnow, Bjarne [1996]: **The Saqqaq Tool Kit - Technological and Chronological Evidence from Qeqertasussuk, Disko Bugt.** pp.17-37 in "The Paleo-Eskimo Cultures of Greenland. New Perspectives in Greenlandic Archaeology", editor: Bjarne Grønnow, 334 p. (Copenhagen: Danish Polar Center).

Grønnow, Bjarne [1997]: **The Saqqaq Harpoon: An Analysis of Early Palreo-Eskimo Harpoon Heads from Qeqertasussuk, West Greenland.** *Ethnographical Series,* 18:119-130 (Copenhagen: The National Museum of Denmark).

Gulløv, Hans Christian & Hans Kapel [1979]: **Haabetz Colonie 1721-1728. A Historical-archaeological Investigation of the Danish-Norwegian Colonization of Greenland.** *Publications of the National Museum, Ethnographical Series,* 16:1-245 (Copenhagen: National Museum of Denmark).

Gulløv, Hans Christian & Hans Kapel [1988]: **De palæoeskimoiske kulturer i Nuuk Kommune.** pp:39-58 in "Palæoeskimoisk forskning i Grønland", editors: Tinna Møbjerg, Bjarne Grønnow & Helge Schultz-Lorentzen, 102 p. (Århus: University of Aarhus Press).

Gulløv, Hans Christian [1983]: **Nuup kommuneani qangarnitsanik eqqaassutit - inuit-kulturip nunaqarfii / Fortidsminder i Nuuk Kommune - Inuit-**

kulturens bopladser. 245 p. (Nuuk: Kalaallit Nunaata katersugaasivia; Copenhagen: National Museum of Denmark).

Gulløv, Hans Christian [1985]: **Whales, Whalers, and Eskimos: The Impact of European Whaling on the Demography and Economy of Eskimo Society in West Greenland.** pp:71-96 in "Cultures in Contact. The European Impact on native Cultural Institutions in Eastern North America 1000-1800 A.D.", editor: William W. Fitzhugh, Anthropological Society of Washington Series, 320 p. (Washington, DC: Smithsonian Institution Press).

Gulløv, Hans Christian [1986]: **Introduction.** *Arctic Anthropology*, 23(1-2):1-18 (Madison: University of Wisconsin Press).

Gulløv, Hans Christian [1993]: **In Search of the Dorset Culture in the Thule Culture.** pp:201-214 in "The Paleo-Eskimo Cultures of Greenland: New Perspectives in Greenlandic Archaeology", editor: Bjarke Grønnow, *Proceedings from a Symposium, May 1992*, 334 p. (Copenhagen: Institute of Prehistorical Archaeology, University of Copenhagen.

Gulløv, Hans Christian [1995]: **"Olden times" in Southeast Greenland: New archaeological investigations and the oral tradition.** *Inuit Studies*, 19(1):3-36 (Quebec: Départment d'anthropologie, Université Laval).

Gulløv, Hans Christian [1996]: **Reading the Thule Culture - History between Archaeology and Ethnography.** *Cultural and Social research in Greenland*, 95/96: 90-106 (Nuuk: Ilisimatusarfik/ Atuakkiorfik).

Gulløv, Hans Christian [1996]: **Ved porten til Den nye Verden. Nationalmuseet og de russiske udgravninger ved Bering Strædet. Summary: At the gateway to the New World. The National Museum of Denmark and the Russian excavations on the Bering Strait coast.** *Nationalmuseets Arbejdsmark*, 1996:163-175 (Copenhagen: National Museum of Denmark).

Gulløv, Hans Christian [1997]: **The soul of the prey.** *Ethnographical Series*, 18: 131-140 (Copenhagen: The National Museum of Denmark).

Gulløv, Hans Christian [in print]: **From Middle Ages to Colonial Times. Archa-eological and Etnohistorical studies of the Thule Culture in Southwest Greenland, 1300-1800 A.D.** In *Meddelelser om Grønland* (Copenhagen: Ther Commission for Scientific Research in Greenland).

Gulløv, Hans Christian [in print]: **Ice summers and long-distance journeys - an Inuit perspective on the Little Ice Age.** "Proceedings from a Seminar on Climate and Man in the Arctic, March 1996" (Copenhagen: Danish Polar Center).

Gynther, Bent & Jørgen Meldgaard [1983]: **5 kapitler af Grønlands forhistorie.** 113 p. (Nuuk: Pilersuiffik) (Greenlandic edition 1983).

Gynther, Bent & Jørgen Meldgaard [1984]: **5 kapitler af Grønlands forhistorie / Kalaallit Nunaanni itsarsuup nalaa immikkoortut tallimat. Lærervejledning / Ilinniartitsisunut ilitsersusiaq.** 84/99 p. (Nuuk: Pilersuiffik).

Hakluyt, Richard [1903]: **The principal navigations, voyages and discoveries of the English nation.** 2:324-344 (Glascow: James MacLehose and Sons).

Hansen, J. (Hansêrak) [1911]: **List of the Inhabitants of the East Coast of Greenland made in the Autumn of 1884.** *Meddelelser om Grønland*, 39 (1):183-202 (Copenhagen: C. A. Reitzels Forlag).

Hansen, Jens Peder Hart & Hans Christian Gulløv (editors) [1989]: **The mummies from Qilakitsoq - Eskimos in the 15th century.** *Meddelelser om Grønland, Man & Society*, 12:1-199 (Copenhagen: The Commission for Scientific Research in Greenland).

Hansen, Jens Peder Hart, Jørgen Meldgaard & Jørgen Nordqvist (editors) [1985]: **Qilakitsoq. De grønlandske mumier fra 1400-tallet.** 216 p. (Nuuk: Grønlands Landsmuseum & Copenhagen: Christian Ejlers' Forlag) (English edition, London: British Museum Press 1991).

Hansen, Jens Peder Hart [1997]: **Chugach Remains Repatriated From Denmark.** *Newsletter*, Spring 1997:5-10 (Anchorage, Alaska: Keepers of the Treasures).

Hansen, Jens Peder Hart [1997]: **Repatriation of Eskimo human remains from Denmark.** *Ethnographical Series*, 18:141-148 (Copenhagen: The National Museum of Denmark).

Hansen, Keld (editor) [1971]: **Grønlandske fangere fortæller.** 207 p. (Holsteinsborg: Nordiske Landes Forlag).

Hansen, Keld [1997]: **Jigs from Greenland.** *Ethnographical Series*, 18:149-156 (Copenhagen: The National Museum of Denmark).

Hansen, Lars Ivar [1990]: **Samisk fangstsamfunn og norsk høvdingeøkonomi.** 275 p. (Oslo: *).

Harp Jr., Elmer [1997]: **Pioneer Settlements of the Belcher Islanmd, N.W.T.** *Ethnographical Series*, 18:157-168 (Copenhagen: The National Museum of Denmark).

Harper, Albert B. [1980]: **Origins and Divergence of Aleuts, Eskimos, and American Indians.** *Annals of Human Biology*, 7(6):547-554 (*: *).

Harper Kenn [1986]: **Give Me My Father's Body.** 275 p. (Frobisher Bay: Blacklead Books).

Hastrup, Kirsten [1983]: **Kulturelle kategorier som naturlige ressourcer. Exempler ra Islands historie.** "Samhälle och Ekosystem". *Forskningsrådsnämnden, rapport*, 83(7):40-54 (Stockholm: *).

Hastrup, Kirsten [1985]: **Culture and History in Medieval Iceland** . 285 p. [Oxford: Claredon Press).

Hastrup, Kirsten [1990]: **Nature and Policy in Iceland 1400-1800.** 367 p. (Oxford: Claredon Press).

Hastrup, Kirsten [1993]: **Native Anthropology: A Contradiction in Terms?** *Folk*, 35:147-161 (Copenhagen: Danish Ethnographical Society).

Hatt, Gudmund [1914]: **Arktiske Skinddragter i Eurasien og Amerika.** 255 p. (Copenhagen: J. H. Schultz Forlagsboghandel).

Hatt, Gudmund [1949]: **Asiatic Influence in American Folklore.** *Historisk-Filologiske Meddelelser*, 31(6):1-122 (Copenhagen: Kgl. danske videnskabernes Selskabs).

Hatting, Tove [1993]: **Oksefund fra Bukkerup og Turup.** *Fynske Minder*, 1993: 93-98 (*: *).

Haven, J. [1773]: **A brief account of the dwelling places of the Eskimos to the north of Naghvakh to Hudson Strait, their situation and subsistence.** Manuscrit inédit, * p. (London: Archives of the Moravian Church).

Haven, J. [1773]: **Extract of the voyage of the sloop George to reconnoitre the northern part of Labrador in the month of August and September 1773.** Manuscrit inédit, * p. (London: Archives of the Moravian Church).

Hedegaard, A. T. [1894-1919]: **Angmagssalik**. Manuscript, 90 p. (Copenhagen: Archive of the Arctic Institut).

Heinemeier, Jan, S. H. Nielsen & N. Rud [1993]: **Danish AMS datings, Århus 1992**. Arkæologisk udgravninger i Danmark 1992:291-304 (Copenhagen: Det Arkæologiske Nævn).

Helmer, James W. [1991]: **The Palaeo-Eskimo Prehistory of the North Devon Lowlands.** *Arctic*, 44(4):301-317 (Calgary: The Arctic Institute of North America).

Helmer, James [1994]: **Resurrecting the spirit(s) of Taylor's "Carlsberg Culture": Cultural traditions and cultural horizons in eastern Arctic Prehistory.** pp:15-34 in "Threads of Arctic Prehistory: Papers in honour of William E. Taylor, Jr.", editors: David Morrison & Jean-Luc Pilon, *Archaeological Survey of Canada, Mercury Series Paper*, 149:1-422 (Ottawa: Canadian Museum of Civilization).

Hjarnø, Jan [1974]: **Eskimo Graves from Upernavik District.** *Meddelelser om Grønland*, 202(1):7-35 (Copenhagen: C. A. Retizels Forlag).

Hjort, Christian [1997]: **Glaciation, climate history, changing marine levels and the evolution of the North-east Water Polynya - an overview.** *Journal of Marine Systems*, 1997(10):*-* (Amsterdam: Elsevier Science).

Hodder, Ian [1995]: **Reading the Past.** 221 p. (Cambridge: Cambridge University Press).

Hofstra, Tette & Kees Samplonius [1995]: **Viking expansion Northwards: Mediaval sources.** *Arctic*, 48(3):235-247 (Calgary: Arctic Institute of North America).

Holm, Gustav [1911]: **Etnological sketch of the Angmagssalik Eskimo.** *Meddelelser om Grønland*, 39(1):1-147 (Copenhagen: C. A. Reitzels Forlag).

Holtved, Erik [1944]: **Archaeological Investigations in the Thule District, I-II.** *Meddelelser om Grønland*, 141(1):1-308 & 141(2):1-184 (Copenhagen: C. A. Reitzels Forlag).

Holtved, Erik [1954]: **Archaeological Investigations in the Thule District, III: Nûgdlît and Comer's Midden.** *Meddelelser om Grønland*, 146(3):1-135 (Copenhagen: C. A. Reitzels Forlag).

Houston, James A. [1951]: **Eskimo Sulptors**. *The Beaver*, Outfit 282, (June):34-39 (Winnipeg: Hudson's Bay Company).

Houston, James A. [1995]: **Confessions of an Igloo Dweller.** 322 p. (Toronto: McClelland & Stewart).

Hrdlicka, Ales [1930]: **Anthropological Survey In Alaska**. *Forty-Sixth Annual Report of The Bureau of American Ethnology*. * p. (Washington, D.C.: Smithsonian Institute Press).

Hrdlicka, Ales [1933]: **The Eskimo of Kuskokwim.** *American Journal of Physical Anthropology*, 18(1):93-145 (New York: American Association of Physical Anthropologists).

Haagen, Birte [1995]: **Repatriation of Cultural Objects in Greenland.** *Yumtzilob*, Tijdschrift over de Americas, 7(3): 225-243 (Haagen).

Haakanson, Sven [1994]: **Yamal Field report**. pp:*-* in: "Living Yamal: preliminary field report for 1994", * p. (Washington: Arctic Studies Center, National Museum of Natural History).

Irving, W. [1962]: **A provisional comparison of some Alaskan and Asian stone industries.** pp:55-68 in "Prehistoric Cultural relation between the Arctic and Temperate Zones of North America", editor: J. M. Campbell, *Technical Papers*, 11:1-181 (Calgary: Arctic Institute of North America).

Jacoby, Gordon & Rosanne D'Arrigo [1989]: **Reconstructed Northern Hemisphere Annual Temperature Since 1671 Based on High-Latitude Tree-Ring Data from North America.** *Climatic Change*, 14:39-59 (Boston: Reidel Publishing Co.).

Jennes, Diamond [1941]: **An Archaeological Collection from the Belcher Islands.** *Annals of the Carnegie Museum*, 28:189-206 (Pittsburgh).

Jenness, Diamond [1925]: **A new Eskimo culture in Hudson Bay.** *The Geographical Review*, 15(3):428-437 (New York: *).

Jenness, Diamond [1928]: **Archaeological Investigations in Bering Strait, 1926.** *Annual Report of the National Museum of Canada for the Fiscal Year 1926, Bulletin*, 50:71-80 (Ottawa: National Museum of Canada).

Jenness, Diamond [1929]: **Notes on the Beothuk of Newfoundland.** *National Museum of Canada Bulletin*, 56:36-39, Annual Report for 1927 (Ottawa: National Museum of Canada).

Jochelson, Waldemar [1925]: **Archeaological Investigations In The Aleutian Islands.** Publication 367. * p. (Washington, D.C.: Carnegie Institution).

Johansen, Peter [1996]: **The Transformative Dragon. The Construction of Social Identity and the Use of Metaphors during the Nordic Iron Age.** *Current Swedish Archaeology*, 4:83-102 (Stockholm: *).

Johnson, John F. C. [1997]: **Ancient Chugach Native Remains are Back Home Again.** *Newsletter*, Spring 1997:3-4 (Anchorage, Alaska: Keepers of the Treasures).

Jones, Gwyn [1964]: **The Norse Atlantic Saga.** 246 p. (New York: Oxford University press).

Jones, Gwyn [1986]: **The Norse Atlantic Saga. Being the Norse Voyages of Discovery and Settlement to Iceland, Greenland, and North America.** 337 p. (New York: Oxford University Press).

Jordan, Richard H. & Susan Kaplan [1980]: **An Archaeological View of the Inuit/European Contact Period in Central Labrador.** *Etudes/Inuit/Studies*, 4(1-2):35-46 (Québec: Départment d'anthropologie, Université Laval).

Jordan, Richard H. [1974]: **Preliminary Report on Archaeological Investigations of the Labrador Eskimo in Hamilton Inlet in 1973.** *Man in the Northeast*, 8:77-89 (*: *).

Jordan, Richard H. [1977]: **Inuit Occupation of the Central Labrador Coast** since 1600 A.D. pp:43-48 in "Our Footprints are Everywhere", editor: Carol Brice-Bennett, 381 p. (Nain: Labrador Inuit Association).

Jordan, Richard H. [1978]: Archaeological Investigations of the Hamilton Inlet Labrador Eskimo: Social and Economic Responses to European Contact. *Arctic Anthropology*, 15(2):175-185 (Madison: University of Wisconsin Press).

Jordan, Richard H. [1979]: Inugsuk Revisited: An Alternative View of Neo-Eskimo Chronology and Culture Change in Greenland. pp: 149-170 in "Thule Eskimo Culture: An Anthropological Retrospective", editor: A. P. McCartney, *Mercury Series*, 88:1-569, Archaeological Survey of Canada (Ottawa: National Museum of Man).

Josefsen, N., M. Lynge, S. Egede, A. Egede & E. Motzfeldt [1964]: Rævejagt. pp:30-34 in "Lærebog i fangst for Syd- og Nordgrønland", editor: H. C. Christiansen, 132 p. (Copenhagen: Den Kongelige Grønlandske Handel).

Kalaallit Nunaanni Naatsorsueqqissaartarfik / Grønlands Statestik [1996]: Grønland 1996 Kalaallit Nunaat. Statistisk Årbog. Ukiumoortumik paasissutissat (Nuuk).

Kapel, Hans [1997]: The person who open an old grave makes a storm. Presavation in Greenland seen in a historian perspective. *Ethnographical Series*, 18:169-180 (Copenhagen: The National Museum of Denmark).

Kaplan, Susan A. [1980]: Neo-Eskimo Occupations of the Northern Labrador Coast. *Arctic*, 33(3):646-658 (Calgary: Arctic Instutute of North America).

Kaplan, Susan A. [1983]: Economic and Social Change in Labrador Neo-Eskimo Culture. Ph.D. dissertation, Department of Anthropology, Bryn Mawr College.

Kaplan, Susan A. [1985]: European Goods and Socio-Economic Change in Early Labrador Inuit Society. pp: 45-69 in "Cultures in Contact: The European Impact on Native Cultural Institutions in Eastern North America, A.D. 1000-1800", editor: W. Fitzhugh, 320 p. (Washington DC: Smithsonian Institution Press).

Kaplan, Susan A. [1997]: Analysis of an aspect of Labrador Neo-Eskimo Culture History. *Ethnographical Series*, 18: 181-186 (Copenhagen: The National Museum of Denmark).

Karlsson, L., M. Lindgren, M. Nockert, A. Piltz, J. Svanberg, P. Tåangeberg & M. Ullén [1995]: Den Romanska Konsten. 399 p. (Lund: Signum).

KHLNM [1982]: Kulturhistorisk Leksikon for Nordisk Middelalder. 5:*-* & 7:*-* (Copenhagen: Rosenkilde & Bagger).

Khlobystin, Leonid [1982]: Taimyr Archaeology and the Problems of the Origins of Archaeological Cultures of the Eurasian Far North. PhD dissertation submitted to the Institute of Archeology.

Kisbye Møller, J. [1985]: Jens Bielkes grønlandsberetning 1605. *Tidsskriftet Grønland*, 33(5-6-7):117-192 (Copenhagen: The Greenland Society).

Kleivan, Inge [1991]: Greenland's national symbols. pp:4-16 in "Greenland: Nationalism and Cultural Identity in Comparative perspectiv", editors: Susanne Dybbroe & Poul Brøbech Møller, *North Atlantic Studies*, 1(2):3-71 (Århus).

Kleivan, Inge [1991]: Historie og historier i Grønland. pp:234-258 in "Klaus Khan Baba: En etnografisk kalejdoskopi tilegnet Klaus Ferdinand den 19. april 1991", editors: Susanne Dybbroe et al., 398 p. (Århus: Aarhus University).

Kleivan, Inge [1992]: The Arctic Peoples' Conference in Copenhagen, November 22-25, 1973. *Études/Inuit/Studies*, 16(1-2):227-236 (Québec).

Kleivan, Inge [1997]: Poetry, Politics, and Archaeology in Greenland. *Ethnographical Series*, 18:187-194 (Copenhagen: The National Museum of Denmark).

Kleppe, Else Johansen [1977]: Archaeological material and ethnic identification: A study of Lappish material from Varanger, Norway. *Norwegian Archaeological Review*, 10(1-2):32-59 (Oslo: *).

Knuth, Eigil [1947]: Contributions to the Archaeology of North East Greenland. Manuscript at Peary Land Fondation (Copenhagen: Danish Polar Center).

Knuth, Eigil [1948]: Haandbog Dansk Pearyland Ekspedition 1948-49-50. 217 p. (Copenhagen: Dyra Bogtryk).

Knuth, Eigil [1952]: An Outline of the Archaeology of Peary Land. *Arctic*, 5(1):17-33 (Calgary: The Arctic Institute of North America).

Knuth, Eigil [1954]: The Paleo-Eskimo Cultures of Northeast Greenland elucidated by three new Sites. *American Antiquity*, 19(4):367-381 (Menasha, Wisconsin: Society for American Archeology).

Knuth, Eigil [1958]: Archaeology of the farthest North. pp:561-573 in "Proceedings of the 32nd Internatinal Congress of Americanists, 1956", editor: * *, * p. (Copenhagen: Munksgaard).

Knuth, Eigil [1967]: Archaeology of the Musk-Ox Way. Contributions de Centre d'Etudes Arctiques Finno-Scandinaves 5:1-70 (Paris: Ecole Pratique Des Hautes Etudes, Sorbonne, Centre d'Etudes Arctiques et Finno-Scandinaves).

Knuth, Eigil [1968]: The Indenpendence II Bone Artifacts and the Dorset-evidence in North Greenland. *Folk*, 10:61-80 (Copenhagen: Danish Ethnographical Society).

Knuth, Eigil [1978]: The "Old Nûgdlit Culture" Site at Nûgdlit Peninsula, Thule District, and the "Mesoeskimo" Site Below it. *Folk*, 19-20:15-48 (Copenhagen: Danish Ethnographic Society).

Knuth, Eigil [1978]: The Independence II Bone Artifacts and the Dorset-evidence in North Greenland. - *Folk*, 19-20:61-88 (Copenhagen: Danish Ethnographic Society).

Knuth, Eigil [1981]: Greenland News from between 81° and 83° North. *Folk*, 23:91-111 (Copenhagen: Danish Ethnographical Society).

Knuth, Eigil [1983]: The Northernmost Ruins on the Globe. *Folk*, 25:5-21 (Copenhagen: Danish Ethnographical Society).

Knuth, Eigil [1984]: Reports from the Musk-ox Way. (compilation of Knuth's published articles and expanded with ^{14}C-dates). Private edition, 173 p. (Copenhagen).

Korneliussen, Ole [1992]: **Uumasoqat**. 86 p. (Nuuk: Atuakkiorfik).

Korneliussen, Ole [1993]: **Glamhuller**. 68 p. (Nuuk: Atuakkiorfik). (Greenlandic editions: Putoq 1973 and Putoq nutaaq 1991).

Kosinskaya, L. & Natalia Feodorova [1994]: **An archeological inventory of the Yamal-Nenets Autonomous Area**. [in Russian] 114 p. (Ekaterinburg: Russian Academy of Sciences).

Kramer, Finn Erik & Hannah Jones [1992]: **Nipisat I - Nunaqarfik Saqqaq-kulturip kingusissuaneersoq / Nipisat I - en boplads fra den yngre Saqqaq kultur**. *Tusaat/Forskning i Grønland*, 1/92: 28-38 (Copenhagen: Danish Polar Centre).

Kramer, Finn Erik [1994]: **På sporet af Forhistorien**. *Tidsskriftet Grønland*, 42(7):217-226 (Copenhagen: The Greenland Society).

Kramer, Finn Erik [1996]: **Akia and Nipisat I: two Saqqaq sites in Sisimiut District, West Greenland**. pp:65-96 in "The Paleo-Eskimo Cultures of Greenland - New Perspectives in Greenlandic Archaeology", editor: Bjarne Grønnow, 334 p. (Copenhagen: Danish Polar Centre).

Kramer, Finn Erik [1996]: **The Paleo-Eskimo Cultures in Sisimiut District, West Greenland. Aspects of Chronology**. pp:39-64 in "The Paleo-Eskimo Cultures of Greenland - New Perspectives in Greenlandic Archaeology", editor: Bjarne Grønnow., 334 p. (Copenhagen: Danish Polar Centre).

Krenke, Nikolai [1992]: **Archaeological evidence of cultural interaction in the Ob Delta region in the 19th century**. *Kontaktstencil*, 36:131-140 (Turku: *).

Kroeber, A. L. [1939]: **Cultural and Natural Areas of Native North America**. * p. (Berkeley: University of California Press).

Krogh, Knud J. [1982]: **Erik den Rødes Grønland**. 266 p. (Copenhagen: National Museum of Denmark) (Original 1967).

Krueger, H. [1929]: **Recent Geological Research in the Arctic**, *American Journal of Science*, Series 5, 17:50-62 (New Haven, Connecticut).

Krupnik, Igor [1993]: **Arctic Adaptations: Native Whalers and Reindeer Herders of Northern Eurasia**. * p. (Hanover: Dartmouth College, University Press of New England) [1977 PhD thesis, published in Russian in 1989].

Krupnik, Igor [1996]: **Northern Peoples, Southern Records: the Yamal Nenets in Russian population counts, 1695-1988**. pp:67-91 in "Northern peoples, southern states: maintaining ethnicities in the circumpolar world", editor: Robert P. Wheelersburg, * p. (Umea: Cerum).

Kaalund, Bodil [1997]: **Aron fra Kangeq 1822-1869**. 126 p. (Copenhagen: Brøndum).

Labrèche, Y. [1988]: **Histoire de l'utilisation des ressources naturelles par les Inuit dans les estuaires de Kangiqsujuaq: perspective ethnoarchéologique**. pp: 512-516 in "Les recherches des étudiants dans le Nord canadien", editors: W. P. Adams & P. G. Johnson, 596 p. (Ottawa: Association Universitaire Canadienne d'Études Nordiques).

Labrèche, Y. [1991]: **Provisions, traditions et peuplement de la côte sud du détroit d'Hudson**. *Études Inuit Studies*, 15(2):85-105 (Québec: Départment d'anthropologie, Université Laval).

Labrèche, Y. [1992]: **Suite des fouilles sur l'île Ukiivik et entrevues à Kangiqsujuaq (1989)**. pp:227-228 in "Recherches archéologiques au Québec 1990", editors: A.-M. Balac et al., 241 p. (Québec: Association des archéologues du Québec).

Landes, Ruth [1938]: **Ojibwa Woman**. * p. (New York: Columbia University Press).

Langgård, Per [1990]: **Grønlandsk litteratur i 70-erne og 80-erne**. *Nordica - tidsskrift for nordisk tekshistorie og æstetik*, 7:15-37 (Odense: Odense Universitetsforlag).

Larsen, Helge & Froelich Rainey [1948]: **Ipiutak and the Arctic Whale Hunting Culture**. *Anthropological papers of the American Museum of Natural History*, 42:1-276 (New York: American Museum of Natural History).

Larsen, Helge & Jørgen Meldgaard [1958]: **Paleo-Eskimo Cultures in Disko Bugt, West Greenland**. *Meddelelser om Grønland*, 161(2):1-75 (Copenhagen: C. A. Reitzels Forlag).

Larsen, Helge [1934]: **Dødemandsbugten, An Eskimo Settlement on Clavering Island**. *Meddelelser om Grønland*, 102(1):1-185 (Copenhagen: C. A. Reitzels Forlag).

Larsen, Helge [1953]: **Archaeological Investigations in Alaska since 1939**. *Polar Record*, 6(45):593-607 (*: *).

Larsen, Helge [1968]: **Trail Creek. Final Report on the Excavation of two Caves on Seward Peninsula, Alaska**. *Acta Arctica*, 15:1-79 (Copenhagen: Munksgaard).

Lashook, L. P. [1968]: **The "Sirtya" - early inhabitants of the Subarctic**. pp:*-* in "Problems in the Anthropology and Historical Ethnography of Asia", * p. (Moscow: Nauka) [in Russian].

Laughlin, Marsh & J. W. Leach [1952]: **Supplementary Note On The Aleutian Core And Blade Industry**. *American Antiquity*, 18(1):69-70 (Washington DC: Society for American Archeology).

Laughlin, Sara B. [1990]: **Diagram of Angle Burin excavated from Anangula Blade Site 1974**. * p. (*: *).

Laughlin, Willam S. & A. B. Harper [1988]: **Peopling of the Continents: Australia and America**. pp.14-40 in "Biological Aspects Of Human Migration", editors: C. G. N. Mascie-Taylor & G. W. Lasker, * p. (New York: Cambridge University Press).

Laughlin, William S. [1951]: **Notes On An Aleutian Core And Blade Industry**. *American Antiquity*, 17(1):52-55 (Washington DC: Society for American Archeology).

Laughlin, William S. [1956]: **Anthropological Researches in Greenland**. *Fulbright Monitor*, 4(7):13-16 (*: *).

Laughlin, William S. [1956]: **Isolate Variation in Greenlandic Eskimo Crania**. *Acta Genetica et Statistica Media*, 6:3-12 (*: *).

Laughlin, William S. [1963]: **Eskmos and Aleuts: Their Origins and Evolution**. *Science*, 142:633-645 (*: *).

Laughlin, William S. [1997]: **Danish Arctic scholarship with a Foreign accent**. *Ethnographical Series*, 18:195-204 (Copenhagen: The National Museum of Denmark).

Lauritzen; Philip [1987]: **Myten om Minik.** 138 p. (Copenhagen: Gyldendal).

Le Blanc, R. J. [1994]: **The Crane Site and the Lagoon Complex in the Western Canadian Arctic.** pp:87-102 in "Threads of Arctic Prehistory: Papers in honour of William E. Taylor, Jr.", editors: David Morrison & Jean-Luc Pilon, *Mercury Series Paper*, 149:1-422 (Hull, Québec: Canadian Museum of Civilization).

Leakey, M. D. [1971]: **Olduvai Gorge.** 3:1-39 in "Excavations in Beds I and II, 1960-1963". 306 p. (Cambridge: Cambridge University Press).

Lee, Richard B. [1968]: **What Hunters Do for a Living, or, How to Make Out on Scarce Resources.** pp:30-48 in "Man the Hunter", editor: Richard B. Lee & Irven DeVore, 415 p. (Chicago: Aldine Publishing Company).

Lee, T. E. [1968]: **Archaeological discoveries, Payne Bay region, Ungava, 1966.** 2e édition, 1970, Travaux divers 20. 169 p. (Québec: Centre d'études nordiques, Université Laval).

Leskov, A. M. & Hansjürgen Müller-Beck [1993]: **Arktische Waljäger vor 3000 Jahren.** 208 p. (Mainz: Hase & Koehler).

Lévi-Strauss, Claude [1987]: **Det vilda tänkandet.** 289 p. (Malmö: Moderna Klassiker). Orginal title: **Lan pensée sauvage,** Paris 1962.

Liisberg, H. C. Bering [1897]: **Kunstkammeret. Dets stiftelse og ældste historie.** 192 p. (Copenhagen: Det Nordiske Forlag).

Lindgren, M., L. Lyberg, B. Sandström & A. G. Wahlberg [1993]: **Svensk Konsthistoria.** 542 p. (Lund: Signum).

Locher, G. W. [1932]: **The Serpent in the Kwakiutl Religion.** * p. (Leiden: Rijksuniversität Leiden).

Lyberth, Christian [1991]: **Indledning. Tema: Qeqertasussuk. De første mennesker i Vestgrønland.** *Tidsskriftet Grønland*, 39(4-5-6-7):98-99 (Copenhagen: The Greenland Society).

Lynge, Aqqaluk [1993]: **Inuit. Inuit Issittormiut kattuffiata oqaluttuassartaa / Histoire de la Conférence Circumpolaire Inuit / The Story of the Inuit Circumpolar Conference.** 123 p. (Nuuk: Atuakkiorfik).

Lynge, Arqaluk [1982]: **Til hæder og ære. Grønlands-digte / Tupigusullutik angalapput.** 84 p. Grafiske arbejder af Aka Høegh (Copenhagen: Brøndum).

Lynge, Bendt [1951]: **Aqigssiap oqalugtuai.** pp:91-97 in "Atuainiutitât II", editors: Bugge & Lynge, 254 p. (Nûk: Grønlandsdepartementip naqitertitai).

Lynge, Hans [1955]: **Inegpait.** *Meddelelser om Grønland*, 90(2):1-187 (Copenhagen: C. A. Reitzels Forlag).

Lynge, Hans [1981]: **Grønlands indre liv. Erindringer fra barndomsårene.** 106 p. (Nuuk: Det grønlandske Forlag).

Lynge, Kristoffer [1978]: **Kalâtdlit oqalugtuait oqalualâvilo** I-III. 360 p. (Nûk: Det grønlandske Forlag).

Lyons, Diane [1982]: **Regionalism of Dorset Art Style: a Comparative Analysis of Stylistic Variability in Five Dorset Art Samples.** Master of Arts Thesis, Department of Archaeology, 192 p. (Calgary: University of Calgary).

Majumder, P. P., William S. Laughlin, & R. E. Ferrell [1988]: **Genetic Variation in the Aleuts of the Pribilof Islands and the Eskimos of Kodiak Island.** *American Journal of Physical Anthropology*, 76:481-488 (New York: American Association of Physical Anthropologists).

Malmberg, Bertil [1965]: **Sproget og mennesket.** 197 p. (Copenhagen: J. H. Schultz Forlag).

Martijn, Charles A. [1964]: **Canadian Eskimo Carving in Historical Perspective.** *Anthropos*, 59:546-549 (St. Augustin, Germany).

Martinier, P.M. De La [1912]: **Puteshestviye v severnye strany** [A trip to the North]. *Zapiski Moskovskogo Arkheologicheskogo Instituta*, 15: (Moscow) [in Russian], Translated from the French, "Voyages des pays septentrionaux", Paris 1671].

Mary-Rousseliere, Guy [1954]: **The archaeological site of Pingerkalik.** *Eskimo*, 33(September):11-15 (Churchill: Diocese of Churchill-Hudson Bay).

Mary-Rousseliere, Guy [1987]: **How Old Monica Ataguttaaluk introduced me to Arctic Archaeology.** *Inuktitut*, 66:6-24 (Ottawa: Indian and Northrn Affairs Canada).

Mary-Rousselière, Guy [1976]: **The Paleo-Eskimo in Northern Baffinland.** pp:40-57 in "Eastern Arctic Prehistory: Paleoeskimo Problems", editor: Moreau S. Maxwell, *Memoirs of the Society for American Archaeology*, 31:1-* (Salt Lake City: Society for American Archaeology).

Mathiassen, Therkel [1925]: **Preliminary report of the Fifth Thule Expedition: Archaeology.** pp:206-215 in "Proceedings of the 21st International Congress of Americanists, 1924" (Goteborg: *).

Mathiassen, Therkel [1927]: **Archaeology of the Central Eskimos, the Thule Culture and its position with the Eskimo Culture.** *Report of the fifth Thule Expedition, 1921-1924*, 4(1):1-327 & 4(2):1-208 (Copenhagen: Gyldendal).

Mathiassen, Therkel [1930]: **Inugsuk - a mediaeval Eskimo settlement in Upernavik District, West Greenland.** *Meddelelser om Grønland*, 77(4):147-340 (Copenhagen: C. A. Reitzels Forlag).

Mathiassen, Therkel [1931]: **Ancient Eskimo Settlements in the Kangâmiut Area.** *Meddelelser om Grønland*, 91(1): 1-150 (Copenhagen: C. A. Reitzels Forlag).

Mathiassen, Therkel [1934]: **Contributions to the Archaeology of Disko Bay.** *Meddelelser om Grønland*, 93(2):1-192 (Copenhagen: C. A. Reitzels Forlag).

Mathiassen, Therkel [1936]: **kalâtdlit oqalugtuagssartáinik ilisimassavut.** atuagâraq 9, 32 p. (Nûk: kalâtdline qáumarsautigssîniaqatigît naqitertitât).

Mathiassen, Therkel [1958]: **The Sermermiut Excavations 1995.** *Meddelelser om Grønland*, 161(3):1-52 (Copenhagen: C. A. Reitzels Forlag).

Mathiasson, Therkel [1927]: **Archaeology of the Central Eskimos.** *Report of the Fifth Thule Expedition 1921-1924*, 4(1):1-328 & 4(2):1-208 (Copenhagen: Gyldendal).

Maxwell, Moreau S. [1973]: **Archaeology of the Lake Harbour District, Baffin Island.** *Archaeological Survey of Canada, Mercury Series*, Paper 6. * p. (Ottawa: *).

Maxwell, Moreau S. [1976]: **Eastern Arctic Prehistory. Paleo-Eskimo problems**. *Memoirs of the society for American Archaeology*, 31:*-* (*: *).

Maxwell, Moreau S. [1985]: **Eastern Arctic Prehistory.** 327 p. (London: Academic Press Inc Ltd).

Maxwell, Moreau S. [1985]: **Prehistory of Eastern Arctic.** 327 p. New World Archeological Record (New York: Academic Press Inc).

Maxwell, Moreau S. [1997]: **The Canadian Arctic in transition: Pre-Dorset to Dorset.** *Ethnographical Series*, 18:205-208 (Copenhagen: The National Museum of Denmark).

McCullough, Karen M. [1989]: **The Ruin Islanders - Early Thule Culture Pioneers in the Eastern High Arctic.** *Mercury Series*, 141:1-347, Archaeological Survey of Canada (Ottawa: Canadian Museum of Civilization).

McGhee, R. [1987]: **Peopling the Arctic.** pp:*-* in "Historical Atlas of Canada, Vol. I: From the Beginning to 1800, Plate 11", editors: R. C. Harris & G. J. Matthews, 69 plates (Toronto: University of Toronto Press).

McGhee, Robert [1972]: **Climate Change and the Development of Canadian Arctic Cultural Traditions.** pp: 39-60 in "Climatic Changes in Arctic Areas During the Past Ten Thousand Years", Acta Universitatis Ouluensis, Serie A, Geologica 1, editors: Y. Vasari et al., * p. (Oulu: *).

McGhee, Robert [1973]: **Paleoeskimo Occupations of Central and High Arctic Canada.** pp:15-39 in "Eastern Arctic Prehistory: Paleoeskimo Problems", editor: Moreau S. Maxwell, *Memoirs of the Society for American Archaeology*, 31:1-* (Washington DC).

McGhee, Robert [1979]: **The Paleo-Eskimo Occupations of Port Refuge, High Arctic Canada.** *Mercury Series, Archaeological Survey Paper*, 92:1-176 (Ottawa: National Museum of Man).

McGhee, Robert [1983]: **Possible Pre-Dorset culture connections to Scandinavia.** Presented at the Annual Meeting of the Canadian Archaeological Association. * p. (Halifax, Nova Scotia).

McGhee, Robert [1984]: **Contact Between Native North Americans and the Mediaeval Norse: a Review of the Evidence.** *American Antiquity*, 49(1):4-26 (Salt Lake City: *).

McGhee, Robert [1984]: **The Thule Village at Brooman Point, High Arctic Canada.** *Mercury Series Paper* 125:1-158 (Ottawa: Archaeological Survey of Canada, Canadian Museum of Civilization).

McGhee, Robert [1987]: **The Relationship between the Mediaeval Norse and Eskimos.** pp:51-60 in "Between Greenland and America. Cross-Cultural Contacts and the Environment in the Baffin Bay Area", editor: *, *, * p. (Groningen: Arctic Centre. University of Groningen).

McGhee, Robert [1996]: **Ancient People of the Arctic.** 244 p. (Vancouver: University of British Columbia Press 6 Hull: the Canadian Museum of Civilization).

McGhee, Robert [1997]: **Meeting Between Dorset Culture Palaeo-Eskimos and Thule Culture Inuit: Evidence from Brooman Point.** *Ethnographical Series*, 18:209-213 (Copenhagen: The National Museum of Denmark).

McGovern, Thomas H. [1979]: **The Paleoeconomy of Norse Greenland: Adaptation and extinction in a tightly bounded ecosystem.** 395 p. Ph.D. Dissertation (Ann Arbor, Michigan: University Microfilms, Columbia University).

McGovern, Thomas H. [1985]: **Contributions to the Paleo-Economy of Norse Greenland.** *Acta Archaeologica*, 54:73-122 (Copenhagen: Munksgaard).

Meese, D. A. [1994]: **The Accumulation Record from the GISP2 Core as an Indicator of Climate Change Throughout the Holocene.** *Science*, 266:1680-1682 (*: *).

Meldgaard, Jørgen, Peder Mortensen & Henrik Thrane [1964]: **Excavations at Tepe Guran, Lureistan. Preliminary Report of the Danish Archaeological Expedition to Iran 1963.** *Acta Archaeologica*, 34:97-133 (Copenhagen: Munksgaard).

Meldgaard, Jørgen [1952]: **A Palaeo-Eskimo Culture in West Greenland.** *American Antiquity*, 17(3):222-230 (Menasha: Society for American Archeology).

Meldgaard, Jørgen [1955]: **Dorset Kulturen. Den Dansk-Amerikanske Ekspedition til Arktisk Canada 1954.** *Kuml*, 1955:158-177 (Århus: Jysk Arkæologisk Selskab).

Meldgaard, Jørgen [1959]: **Eskimo Skulptur.** 48 p. (Copenhagen: J. H. Schultz Forlag).

Meldgaard, Jørgen [1960]: **Eskimo Sculpture.** 48 p. (London: Methuen).

Meldgaard, Jørgen [1960]: **Origin and evolution of Eskimo cultures in the Eastern Arctic.** *Canadian Geographical Journal*, 60(2):64-75 (Ottawa: Royal Canadian Geographic Society).

Meldgaard, Jørgen [1960]: **Prehistoric Culture Sequences in the Eastern Arctic as elucidated by Stratified Sites at Iglulik.** pp:588-595 in "Men and Cultures. Selected Papers of the Fifth International Congress of Anthropological and Ethnological Sciences, 1956", editor: Anthony F. C. Wallace, 810 p. (Philadelphia: University of Pennsylvania Press).

Meldgaard, Jørgen [1961]: **Sarqaq-folket ved Itivnera. Nationalmuseets undersøgelser i sommeren 1960.** *Tidsskriftet Grønland*, 9(9):15-23 (Copenhagen: The Greenland Society).

Meldgaard, Jørgen [1962]: **On the Formative Period of the Dorset Culture.** pp:92-95 in "Prehistoric Cultural Relations between the Arctic and Temperate Zones of North America", editor: John M. Campbell, *Arctic Institute of North America, Technical Paper*, ll:1-181 (Montreal: Arctic Institute of North America).

Meldgaard, Jørgen [1977]: **Inuit-Nordbo projektet. Arkæologiske undersøgelser i Vesterbygden i Grønland.** *Nationalmuseets Arbejdsmark*, 77:159-169 (Copenhagen: National Museum of Denmark).

Meldgaard, Jørgen [1977]: **Prehistoric Cultures in Greenland. Discontinuities in a Marginal Area.** pp:19-52 in "Continuity and Discontinuity in the Inuit Cultures of Greenland", Proceedings from Danish-Netherland Symposium 1976, editors: Hans P. Kylstra & Lies H. Liefferink, 125 p. (Groningen: Arctic Center, University of Groningen).

Meldgaard, Jørgen [1980]: **Den forhisto-riske bebyggelse.** pp:56-59 in "Holsteinsborg. Sisimiut kommune. Natur- og kulturforhold", 88 p. (Copenhagen: Ministeriet for Grønland/Geografisk Institut).

Meldgaard, Jørgen [1982]: **Aron - en af de mærkværdigste Billedsamlinger i Verden.** * p (Copenhagen: National Museum of Denmark).

Meldgaard, Jørgen [1982]: **Tjorhildes Kirke - den første fundberetning.** Tema: Nordboerne I. *Tidsskriftet Grønland*, 30(5-6-7):151-162 (Copenhagen: The Greenland Society).

Meldgaard, Jørgen [1983]: **Qajaa, en køkkenmødding i dybfrost. Feltrapport fra arbejdsmarken i Grønland.** *Nationalmuseets Arbejdsmark*, 1983:83-96 (Copenhagen: The National Museum of Denmark).

Meldgaard, Jørgen [1986]: **Dorset-Kulturen - udviklingstendenser og afbrydelser.** - pp:15-31 in "Vort sprog - vor kultur", Foredrag fra symposium afholdt i Nuuk i oktober 1981 arrangeret af Ilisimatusarfik og Kalaallit Nunaata Katersugaasivia, 220 p. (Nuuk: Pilersuiffik).

Meldgaard, Jørgen [1991]: **Bopladsen Qajaa i Jakobshavn Isfjord. En rapport om udgravninger i 1871 og 1982.** *Tidsskriftet Grønland*, 39(4-7):191-205 (Copenhagen: The Greenland Society).

Meldgaard, Jørgen [1995]: **Eskimoer og Nordboer i Det yderste Nord.** *Nationalmuseets Arbejdsmark*, 95:199-214 (Copenhagen: National Museum of Denmark).

Meldgaard, Jørgen [no date]: **Dorset Culture Harpoon Head Chronology.** Unpublished manuscript.

Meldgaard, Morten (editor) [1991]: **Qeqertasussuk. De første mennesker i Vestgrønland.** *Tidsskriftet Grønland*, 39(4-5-6-7):97-224 (Copenhagen: The Greenland Society).

Meldgaard, Morten [1986]: **The Greenland caribou - zoogeography, taxonomy, and population dynamics.** *Meddelelser om Grønland, Bioscience*, 20:3-88 (Copenhagen: The Commission for Scientific Research of Greenland).

Meldgaard, Morten [1988]: **The Great Auk, Pinguinus impennis (L.) in Greenland.** *Historical Biology*, 1:145-178 (London: Harwood Academy).

Meldgaard, Morten [1997]: **Sisikasiit - the place with the fox holes.** *Ethnographical Series*, 18:215-220 (Copenhagen: The National Museum of Denmark).

Merrill, William L, Edmund J. Ladd, & T. J. Ferguson [1993]: **The Return of the** Ahayu:da. *Current Anthropology*, 34: 523-567 (Chicago: University of Chicago Press).

Merriwether, D. A., F. Rothhammer, and R. E. Ferrell [1995]: **Distribution of the Four Founding Lineage Haplotypes in Native Americans Suggests a Single Wave of Migration for the New World.** *American Journal of Physical Anthropology*, 98:411-430 (New York: American Association of Physical Anthropologists).

Mikkelsen, Einar [1934]: **De Østgrønlandske Eskimoers Historie.** 202 p. (Copenhagen: Gyldendalske Boghandel Nordisk Forlag).

Mitchell, Marybelle [1996]: **Bill Nasogaluak: Getting Past the Oral Tradition.** Interview. *Inuit Art Quarterly*, 11(3):28-35 (Ottawa).

Moberg, Carl-Axel [1960]: **On some Circumpolar and Arctic Problems.** *Acta Arctica*, 12:67-74 (Copenhagen: Ejnar Munksgaard).

Moberg, Carl-Axel [1975]: **Circumpolar adaptation zones east-west and cross-economy contacts north-south: an outsider's query, especially on Ust'-Plouy.** pp:101-110 in "Prehistoric Maritime Adaptations of the Circumpolar Zone", editor: William W. Fitzhugh, 405 p. (The Hague: Mouton).

Morrison, D. [1991]: **The Diamond Jenness Collections from Bering Strait. Archaeological Survey of Canada.** *Mercury Series Paper* 144:1-171 (Hull: Canadian Museum of Civilisation).

Mozhinskaya, Wanda [1970]: **The Iron Age in north-western Siberia and its relation to the development of circumpolar region cultures.** pp:*-* in "Proceedings of the VII International Congress of Anthroplogical and Ethnological Sciences, Moscow, 1964", editor; *, *, * p. (Moscow: Nauka).

Mozhinskaya, Wanda [1974]: **Archaeological antiquities of the northern part of Western Siberia.** *Translations from Russian Sources*, 9:251-325, editor: Henry N. Michael, originally in: V. N. Chernetsov & W. Mozhinskaya: "The Prehistory of Western Siberia", * p. (Montreal / London: Arctic Institute of North America & McGill-Queen's University Press).

Murashko, Olga & Nikolai Krenke [1996]: **Burials of indigenous people in the Lower Ob region: dating, burial ceremonies, and technical interpretations.** *Arctic Anthropology*, 33(1):37-66 (Madison: University of Wisconsin Press).

Müller-Beck, Hansjürgen [1977]: **Excavations at Umingmak on Banks Island, N.W.T. 1970 and 1973.** Preliminary report. Urgeschitliche Materialhefte no. 1, * p. (*: Universität Tübingen).

Müller, R. [1906]: **Vildtet og Jagten i Sydgrønland.** 519 p. (Copenhagen: H. Hagerups Boghandel).

Müller-Beck, Hansjürgen [1997]: **A Heavy Duty Chopping Tool from a Birnirk House in Ekven.** *Ethnographical Series*, 18:221-226 (Copenhagen: The National Museum of Denmark).

Møbjerg, Tinna (editor) [1988]: **Palæoeskimoisk forskning i Grønland.** Indlæg fra et symposie på Moesgaard 1987. 102 p. (Århus: University of Aarhus Press).

Møbjerg, Tinna & Joëlle Robert-Lamblin [1990]: **The settlement Ikaasap Ittiva, East Greenland. An ethno-archaeological investigation.** *Acta Archaeologica*, 60:229-262 (Copenhagen: Munksgaard).

Møbjerg, Tinna & Stig Grummesgaard-Nielsen [1996]: **Excavations at Asummiut, West Greenland.** pp:55-59 in "Archaeological Field Work in the Northwest Territories, in 1994 and Greenland in 1993 and 1994", editor: Valovie Kenny, Margeret Bertulli, & Joel Berglund, *Archaeology Reports*, 17:1-76 (Prince of Wales: Northern Heritage Centre).

Møbjerg, Tinna [1981]: **Den palæoeskimoiske ressource-udnyttelse, som den kommer til udtryk gennem bopladspalcering og knoglefund.** pp: *-* in "Vort sprog - vor kultur". Foredrag fra symposium afholdt i Nuuk oktober 1981 arrangeret af Ilisimatusarfik og Kalaallit Nunaata Katersugaasivia. 220 p. (Nuuk: Pilersuiffik).

Møbjerg, Tinna [1986]: **A Contribution to Paleo-Eskimo Archaeology in Greenland.** *Arctic Anthropology*, 23(1-2):19-56 (Madison: University of Wisconsin Press).

Møbjerg, Tinna [1995b]: **Nipisat I. A Saqqaq site in Sisimiut District, West Greenland.** pp:88-94 in "Archaeological Field Work in the Northwest Territories, in 1994 and Greenland in 1993 and 1994", editor: Margeret Bertulli, Joel Berglund & Hans Lange, *Archaeology Reports*, 16:1-109 (Prince of Wales: Northern Heritage Centre).

Møbjerg, Tinna [1995]: **Sidste nyt fra Nipisat I - en Saqqaq boplads i Sisimiut Kommune, Vestgrønland.** *Tidsskriftet Grønland*, 43(2):45-54 (Copenhagen: The Greenland Society).

Møbjerg, Tinna [1997]: **New Aspects of the Saqqaq Culture in West Greenland.** *Ethnographical Series*, 18:227-236 (Copenhagen: National Museum of Denmark).

Møbjerg, Tinna, Bjarne Grønnow & Helge Schultz-Lorentzen [1988]: **Palæoeskimoisk forskning i Grønland. Indlæg fra et symposium på Moesgård 1987.** 102 p. (Århus: Aarhus Universitetsforlag).

Møgeltoft, Kista [1994]: **Udbrændte Politikere "Til politikernes hæder og ære" / "Tupigisaallutik angalapput".** *Atuagagdliutit / Grønlandsposten*, 134 (74):16 (Nuuk).

Møhl, Jeppe [1982]: **Ressourceudnyttelse fra norrøne og eskimoiske affaldslag belyst gennem knoglemateri-alet.** *Tidsskriftet Grønland*, 30(8-9):286-295 (Copenhagen: The Greenland Society).

Møhl, Jeppe [1986]: **Dog Remains from a Paleo-Eskimo Settlement in West Greenland.** *Arctic Anthropology*, 23 (1-2):81-89 (Madison: University of Wisconsin Press).

Møhl, Jeppe [1997]: **Greenland A Quaternary zoologcal View.** *Ethnographical Series*, 18:237-242 (Copenhagen: National Museum of Denmark).

Møhl, Ulrik [1972]: **Animal Bones from Itivnera, West Greenland. A Reindeer**

Hunting Site of the Sarqaq Culture. *Meddelelser om Grønland*, 191(6):1-23 (Copenhagen: C. A. Reitzels Forlag).

Nagle, Christopher [1982]: **1981 field investigations at Fleur de Lys soapstone quarry, Baie Verte, Newfoundland.** pp: 102-129 in "Archaeology in Newfoundland and Labrador 1981", editors: Jane Sproull Thomson & Callum Thomson, Annual Report 2, 237 p. (St. John's: Historic Resources Division, Government of Newfoundland and Labrador).

Nagy, M. [1994]: **A Critical Review of the Pre-Dorset/ Dorset Transition.** pp: 1-14 in "Threads of Arctic Prehistory: Papers in honour of William E. Taylor, Jr.", editors: David Morrison & Jean-Luc Pilon, *Mercury Series Paper*, 149:1-422 (Hull, Québec: Canadian Museum of Civilization).

Nationalmuseets Spørgeliste nr. 5. Fiskeri. (Copenhagen 1960: The National Museum of Denmark).

Native American Graves Protection and Repatriation Act (P.L. 101-601; 104 State 3048; 25 U.S.C. 3001-3013) November 16, 1992.

Nelson, E. W. [1889]: **The Eskimo about Bering Strait.** *Eighteenth annual report of the Bureau of American Ethnology, 1896-97*, 997 p. (Washington DC: Smithsonian Institute).

Nielsen, I. (redaktør) [1987]: **Bevar din arv.** Udgivet af Skov- og Naturstyrelsen i anledning af 100-året for 1937-lovens vedtagelse. 367 p. (Copenhagen: Skov- og Naturstyrelsen).

Nielsen, Martin [1955]: **Sîmuk qaers-ormio.** *Avangnâmioq*, 42:200-206 (Qeqertarssuaq: Avangnäta naqiterivia).

Nørlund, Poul [1924]: **Burried Norsemen at Herjolfsnes.** *Meddelelser om Grønland*, 67(1):1-270 (Copenhagen: C. A. Reitzels Forlag).

Osczevski, Randall J. [1944]: **"The Disappearance of Hans Krueger"**, *Polar Record*, 30(173):157-58 (Cambridge, England: Scott Polar Institute).

Osherenko, Gail [1995]: **Property rights and transformation in Russia: institutional change in the Far North.** *Europe-Asia Studies*, 47(7):1077-1108 (*: *).

Ostermann, H. [1921]: **Landjagten.** pp:110-113 in "Grønland i tohundredeaaret for Hans Egedes landing", editors: G. C. Amdrup, L. Bobé, A. S. Jensen & H. P. Steenby, *Meddelelser om Grønland*, 60:1-567 (Copenhagen: C. A. Reitzels Forlag).

Park, Robert W. [1993]: **The Dorset-Thule Succession in Arctic North America: Assessing Claims for Culture Contact.** *American Antiquity*, 58(2):203-234 (Salt Lake City: American Society for Archeology).

Parry, William E. [1824]: **Journal of a second voyage for the discovery of a North-west Passage from the Atlantic ot hte Pacific; performed in the years 1821-1822-1823, in His Majesty's Ships Fury and Hecla, under the orders of Captain William Edward Parry, R. N., F.R.S., and commander of the expedition.** 571 p. (London: John Murray).

Payne, F. F. [1889]: **Eskimo of Hudson's Strait.** *Proceedings of Canadian Institute*, ser. 3, 6:213-230 (Toronto: Clark).

Pedersen, Leif Toudal, Preben Gudmandsen & Henning Skriver [1993]: **North-East Water. A remote sensing study.** 64 p. (Lyngby: Remote Sensing Unit, Electromagnetics Institute, Technical University of Denmark).

Penrose, L. S. [1954]: **Distance Size and Shape.** *Annals of Eugenics*, 18:337-343.

Petersen, H. C. [1978]: **Rapport fra rejse til fåreholdersteder i Sydgrønland 5.-26. juni 1978.** 41 p. (Manuscript in Danish Polar Center, Copenhagen).

Petersen, H. C. [1986]: **Indtryk fra forskellige grønlandske indsamlingsstudier omkring ressourceudnyttelse og kulturkontakter.** pp:63-76 in "Vort sprog - vor kultur", editors: Robert Petersen & Rischel, 220 p. (Nuuk: Ilisimatusarfik & Kalaalit Nunaata Katersugaasivia).

Petersen J. (Ujuât) [1957]: **Ujuâts Dagbøger fra Østgrønland 1894-1935.** *The Greenland Societys Skrifter*, 19:1-209 (Copenhagen: The Greenland Society).

Petersen, Robert [1964]: **The Greenland Tupilak.** *Folk*, 6(2):73-102 (Copenhagen: Danish Ethnographical Society).

Petersen, Robert [1967]: **Burial-forms and death cult among the Eskimos.**

Folk, 8-9:259-280 (Copenhagen: Danish Ethnographical Society).

Petersen, Robert [1988]: **Palæoeskimoiske fund i Maniitsoq Kommune.** pp:59-68 in "Palæoeskimoisk forskning i Grønland", editors: Tinna Møbjerg et al., 102 p. (Århus: Aarhus Universiutets Forlag).

Petersen, Robert [1990]: **On the Material Element in the Supernatural Aspect of the Former Greenlandic Religion.** *Temenos*, 26:95-103 (Helsinki: Finnish Society for the Study of Comparative Religion).

Petersen, Robert [1997]: **On `Smell of forest' in Greenlandic Myths and Legends.** *Ethnographical Series*, 18:243-248 (Copenhagen: The National Museum of Denmark).

Pika, Alexander & D. Bogoyavlensky [1995]: **Yamal Peninsula: oil and gas development and problems of demography and health among indigenous populations.** *Arctic Anthropology*, 32(2):61-74 (Madison: University of Wisconsin Press).

Pintal, J-Y. [1994]: **A Groswater Site at Blanc-Sablon, Quebec.** pp:145-164 in "Threads of Arctic Prehistory: Papers in honour of William E. Taylor, Jr.", editors: David Morrison & Jean-Luc Pilon, *Mercury Series Paper*, 149: 1-422 (Hull, Québec: Canadian Museum of Civilization).

Pitul'ko, Vladimir [1991]: **Archeological data on the Maritime Cultures of the West Arctic.** *Fennoscandia Archaeologica*, 8:23-34 (*: *).

Pitul'ko, Vladimir [1993]: **An early Holocene site in the Siberian High Arctic.** *Arctic Anthropology*, 30(1):13-21 (Madison: University of Wisconsin Press).

Plumet, Patrick & P. Gangloff [1990]: **Contribution à l'archéologie et l'ethnohistoire de l'Ungava oriental: côte est, Killiniq, îles Button, Labrador septentrional.** *Paléo-Québec*, 19:1-286 (Québec: Presses de l'Université du Québec).

Plumet, Patrick [1979]: **Thuléens et Dorsétiens dans l'Ungava (Nouveau-Québec).** pp:110-121 in "Thule Eskimo culture: an anthropological retrospective", editor: A. P. McCartney, *Mercury Serie* 88, 586 p. (Ottawa: Musée National de l'Homme, Commission archéologique du Canada).

Plumet, Patrick [1985]: **Archéologie de l'Ungava : le site de la Pointe aux Bélougas (Qilalugarsiuvik) et les maisons longues dorsétiennes.** Préface de José Garanger, annexes de M.-F. Archambault & de M. Julien, *Paléo-Québec*, 18:1-471 (Montréal: Laboratoire d'archéologie, Université du Québec à Montréal).

Plumet, Patrick [1994]: **Le Paléoesquimau dans la baie du Diana (Arctique Quebecois).** pp:103-144 in "Threads of Arctic Prehistory: Papers in honour of William Taylor, Jr.", editor: David Morrison & Jean-Luc Pilon, Archaeological Survey of Canada. *Mercury Series Paper*, 149:1-422 (Hull, Quebec: Canadian Museum of Civilisation).

Plumet, Patrick [1996]: **A propos du sauvetage des pétroglyphes dorsétiens de Qajartalik dans le Nunavik (Arctique quiébécois). Questions et réflexions sur la politique de l'archéologie dans le Nunavik.** *Études/Inuit/Studies*, 20(2):112-116 (Québec: Départment d'anthropologie, Université Laval).

Plumet, Patrick [1997]: **L'importance Archéologique de la Région de Kangirsujuaq au Nunavik (Arctique Québécois). Un centre chamanique dorsétien?** *Ethnographical Series*, 18:249-260 (Copenhagen: The National Museum of Denmark).

Porsild, M. P. [1921]: **Dyrelivet.** pp:101-104 in "Grønland i tohundredeaaret for Hans Egedes landing", editors: G. C. Amdrup, L. Bobé, A. S. Jensen & Hans Peter Steenby, *Meddelelser om Grønland*, 60:1-567 (Copenhagen: C. A. Reitzels Forlag).

Pospisil, L. & William S. Laughlin [1963]: **Kinship Terminology And Kindred Among The Nunamiut Eskimo.** *Ethnology*, 11(2):180-189 (Pittsburgh: Department of Anthropology, University of Pittsburgh Press).

Poulsen, Jens (editor) [1970]: **agdlagarsiat.** 156 p. (Godthåb: Kalâtdlit-nunane naqiterisitsissarfik / Det Grønlandske Forlag).

Poulsen, K. [1904]: **Contributions to the Anthropology and Nosology of the East-Greenlanders.** *Meddelelser om Grønland*, 28(4):133-150 (Copenhagen: C. A. Reitzels Forlag).

Prokofyeva, E. D. [1964]: **The Nentsy.** pp:547-570 in "The Peoples of Siberia", editors: M. G. Levin & L. P. Potapov, 948 p. (Chicago: Chicago University Press).

Quimby, George I., Jr. [1940]: **The Manitunik Eskimo Culture of East Hudson Bay.** *American Antiquity*, 6: 148-165 (Washington DC: Society for American Archeology).

Rainey, Froelich G. [1947]: **The Whale Hunters of Tigara.** *Anthropological Papers*, 4(2):231-283 (New York: American Museum of Natural History).

Rainey, Froelich [1992]: **Reflections of a Digger.** * p. University Museum Publications, (Philladelphia: University of Pennsylvania).

Ramlau-Hansen, Laila [1994]: **Takorloortarpaa atuakkiortunngornissi / Drømmen om at skrive.** *Atuagagdliutit/ Grønlandsposten*, 134(15):10 (Nuuk).

Rasmussen, Holger [1979]: **Dansk museums historie. De kulturhistoriske museer.** 226 p. (Copenhagen: Dansk kulturhistorisk museumsforening).

Rasmussen, Knud [1924]: **Myter og sagn fra Grønland II: Vestgrønland.** 356 p. (Copenhagen: Gyldendalske Boghandel Nordisk Forlag).

Rasmussen, Knud [1929]: **Intellectual Culture of the Igloolik Eskimos.** *Report of the Fifth Thule Expedition 1921-1924*, 7(1):1-304 (Copenhagen: Gyldendal).

Rasmussen, Knud [1931]: **The Netsilik Eskimos: Social Life and Spiritual Culture.** *Report of the Fifth Thule Expedition 1921-1924*, 8(1-2):1-542 (Copenhagen: Gyldendal).

Rasmussen, Knud [1938]: **Knud Rasmussen's Posthumous Notes on the Life and Doings of the East Greenlanders in Olden Times.** Editor H. Ostermann, *Meddelelser om Grønland*, 109(1): 1-215 (Copenhagen: C. A. Reitzels Forlag).

Ray, Dorothy Jean [1961]: **Artists of the Tundra and the Sea.** 170 p. (Seattle: University of Washington Press).

Renfrew, Colin & Paul Bahn [1991]: **Archaeology. Theories, Methods, and Practice.** 543 p. (London: Thames and Hudson Ltd).

Renfrew, Colin [1984]: **Approaches to Social Archaeology**. 430 p. (Edinburgh: Edinburgh University Press).

Renouf, M. A. P. [1994]: **Two Transitional Sites at Port au Choix, Northwestern Newfoundland.** pp:165-196 in "Threads of Arctic Prehistory: Papers in honour of William E. Taylor, Jr.", editors: David Morrison & Jean-Luc Pilon, *Mercury Series Paper*, 149:1-422 (Hull, Québec: Canadian Museum of Civilization).

Riches, David [1982]: **Northern Nomadic Hunters-Gatherers: A Humanistic Approach.** 242 p. (New York: Academic Press).

Richling, Barnett [1993]: **Labrador's "Communal House Phase" Reconsidered.** *Arctic Anthropology*, 30(1): 67-78 (Madison: University of Wisconsin Press).

Rink, Henrik J. [1866]: **Eskimoiske Eventyr og Sagn**, I-II . 376 p. & 259 p. (Copenhagen: C. A. Reitzels Forlag).

Rink, Henrik J. [1871]: **Eskimoiske Eventyr og Sagn.** Supplement. 279 p. (Copenhagen: *).

Rink, Henrik J. [1871]: **Om Eskimoernes Herkomst.** *Aarbog for Nordisk Oldkundskab og Historie*, *(*):269-302 (Copenhagen: *).

Robert-Lamblin, Joelle [1979]: **Endogamy and Exogamy in two Arctic coummunityies: Aleut and East Geenlandic Eskimo.** pp:293-307 in "The First American: Origins, Affinities and Adaptations", editors: William S. Laughlin & A. B. Harper, * p. (New York: Gustav Fisher).

Robert-Lamblin, Joelle [1982]: **An Historical and Contemporary Demography of Akutan, An Aleution Village.** *Etudes/ Inuit/Studies*, 6(1):99-126 (Québec: Départment d'anthropologie, Université Laval).

Robert-Lamblin, Joëlle [1984]: **L'expression de la violence dans la société ammassalimiut (côte orientale du Groenland).** *Etudes Rurales*, juil.-déc.(95-96): 115-129 (Paris: Laboratoire d'Anthropologie Sociale).

Robert-Lamblin, Joëlle [1986]: **Ammassalik, East Greenland - end or persistance of an isolate? Anthropological and demographical study on change.** *Meddelelser om Grønland, Man and Society*, 10:1-168 (Copenhagen: The Commission for Scientific Research in Greenland).

Robert-Lamblin, Joëlle [1997]: **Death in traditional East Greenland: Age, causes and rituals. A contribution from anthropology to archaeology.** *Ethnographical Series*, 18:261-268 (Copenhagen: National Museum of Denmark).

Rosendahl, Phillip [1942]: **Jakob Danielsen en grønlandsk maler.** 80 p. (Copenhagen: Gyldendal).

Rosendahl, Phillip [1961]: **Grønlandsk jagt- og fangststatistik.** *Geografisk Tidsskrift*, 60:16-38 (Copenhagen: Det Kongelige Danske Geografiske Selskab).

Rosing, Jens [1963]: **Sagn og Saga fra Angmagssalik.** 308 p. (Copenhagen: Rhodos).

Rosing, Jens [1986]: **Havets enhjørning.** 83 p. (Århus: Wormianum).

Ross, W. Gillies [1984]: **An Arctic Whaling Diary: The Journal of Captain George Comer in Hudson Bay, 1903-1905.** * p. (*: *).

Roussell, Aage [1936]: **Sandnes and the Neighbouring Farms.** *Meddelelser om Grønland*, 88(2):1-219 (Copenhagen: C. A. Reitzels Forlag).

Rowley, Graham W. & Susan Rowley [1997]: **Igloolik Island Before and After Jørgen Meldgaard.** *Ethnographical Series*, 18:269-276 (Copenhagen: The National Museum of Denmark).

Rowley, Graham W. [1940]: **The Dorset Culture of the Eastern Arctic.** *American Anthropologist*, new series, 42:490-499 (Menasha: American Anthropologist Society).

Rowley, Graham W. [1996]: **Cold Comfort: My love affair with the Arctic.** 255 p. (Montreal-Kingston: McGill-Queens's University Press).

Rowley, Susan [1992]: **Survey of three short range radar sites: Simpson Lake, Cape McLoughlin and Lailor River, N.W.T.** * p. Unpublished report on file with the Archaeological Survey of Canada (Ottawa).

Ryder, C. [1895]: **Om den tidligere Eskimoiske bebyggelse af Scoresby Sund.** *Meddelelser om Grønland*, 17(6):281-374 (Copenhagen: C. A. Reitzels Forlag).

Ryder, Carl [1895]: **Beretning om den Østgrønlandske Expedition 1891-1892.** *Meddelelser om Grønland*, 17(7): 1-147 (Copenhagen: C. A. Reitzels Forlag).

Sahlins, Marshall [1972]: **Stone Age Economics.** 348 p. (London: *).

Saladin d'Anglure, Bernard [1962]: **Découverte de pétroglyphes à Qajartalik sur l'île de Qîlertaaluk.** *North*, 9(6):34-39 (Ottawa).

Saladin d'Anglure, Bernard [1963]: **Discovery of petroglyphs near Wakeham Bay.** *The Arctic Circular*, 15(1):7-14 (Montréal).

Saladin d'Anglure, Bernard [1965]: **Rapport succinct sur le travail effectué au cours de l'été pour le Musée national du Canada.** 15 p. Rapport déposé à la Commission archéologique du Canada (Ottawa).

Saladin d'Anglure, Bernard [1967]: **L'organisation sociale traditionnelle des Esquimaux de Kangirsujuaaq (Nouveau Québec).** *Travaux divers*, 17:1-204 (Québec: Centre d'Études Nordiques, Université Laval).

Salvesen, Astrid (translator) [1969]: **Norges Historie. Historien om de gamle norske kongene. Danernes færd til Jerusalem.** 136 p. (Oslo: *).

Sandell, H. & B. [1991]: **De palæoeskimoiske kulturer i Scoresby Sund.** *Tuusat/Forskning i Grønland*, 2/91:25-35 (Copenhagen: Dansk Polar Center).

Sandgreen, Otto [1987]: **Øje for øje, tand for tand.** 457 p. (Bagsværd: Otto Sandgreens Forlag).

Sapir, Edward [1916]: **Time Perpective In Aboriginal American Culture: A Study in Method.** Memoir 90, Anthropological Series 13:*-*, Department of Mines, Geological Survey (Ottawa: Government Print Bureau).

Schledermann, Peter [1972]: **The Thule Tradition in Northern Labrador.** M.A. Thesis, 147 p. (St.John's: Memorial University of Newfoundland).

Schledermann, Peter [1976a]: **Thule Culture Communal Houses in Labrador.** *Arctic*, 29(1):27-37 (Calgary: Arctic Institute of North America).

Schledermann, Peter [1976b]: **The Effect of Climatic/Ecological Changes on the Style of Thule Culture Winter Dwellings.** *Arctic and Alpine Research*, 8(1):37-47 (*, Colorado: Institute of Arctic & Alpine Research).

Schledermann, Peter [1990]: **Crossroads to Greenland: 3000 Years of Prehistory in the Eastern High Arctic.** *Komatic Series*, 2:1-364 (Calgary: The Arctic Institute of North America of The University of Calgary).

Schledermann, Peter [1993]: **Norsemen in the High Arctic?** pp:54-66 in "Viking Voyages to North America", editor: B. Laursen, * p. (Roskilde: The Viking Ship Museum).

Schledermann, Peter [1996]: **Voices in Stone. A Personal Journey into the Arctic Past.** *Komatic Series*, 5:1-221 (Calgary: The Arctic Institute of North America of the University of Calgary).

Schultz-Lorentzen, Helge [1997]: **Greenland and The National Museum of Denmark - The National Museum of Denmark and Greenland - Fragments of a piece of museum history.** *Ethnographical Series*, 18:277-286 (Copenhagen: National Museum of Denmark).

Schultz-Lorentsen, Helge [1987]: **Tilbage til Grønland - Det dansk-grønlandske museumsarbejde.** *Nationalmuseets Arbejdsmark*, 1987:177-192 (Copenhagen: National Museum of Denmark).

Schultz-Lorentsen, Helge [1988]: **Det dansk-grønlandske museumsarbejde.** *Tidsskriftet Grønland*, 36(2-3):65-80 (Copenhagen: The Greenland Society).

Schultz-Lorentsen, Helge [1988]: **Return of Cultural Proberty by Denmark to Greenland - From Dream to Reality.** *Museum International*, 160, 46(2):200-205 (Paris: Unesco Quarterly Review).

Schultz-Lorentsen, Helge [1990]: **Nye overførelser fra Nationalmuseet til Grønland.** *Tidsskriftet Grønland*, 38(4):113-120 (Copenhagen: The Greenland Society).

Schultz-Lorentzen, Helge [1987]: **Tilbage til Grønland - det dansk-grønlandske museumssamarbejde.** *Nationalmuseets Arbejdsmark*, 1987:177-192 (Copenhagen: National Museum of Denmark).

Schuster, Carl [1951]: **A survival of the Eurasiatic animal style in modern Alaskan Eskimo art.** pp:35-45 in "Selected Papers of the 29th Congress of Americanists. New York, 1949", editor: Sol Tax, (Chicago: University of Chicago Press).

Shimkin, D. B. [1960]: **Western Siberian archaeology (an interpretive summary).** pp:*-* in "Men and Cultures: selected papers of the 5th International Congress of Anthropology", * p. (Philadelphia.: *).

Simchenko, Yuri B. [1976]: **Culture of the reindeer hunters of Northern Eurasia: an ethnographic reconstruction.** [in Russian] * p. (Moscow: Nauka).

Simonsen, Povl [1972]: **The cultural concept in the Arctic Stone Age.** pp: 163-169 in "Circumpolar Problems", editor: G. Berg, * p. (New York: Pergamon Press).

Smidt, Poul [1972]: **Grønlandsk bitterhed i politisk digtning.** *Politiken*, 22 October (Copenhagen).

Solberg, Ole [1907]: **Beiträge zur Vorgeschichte der Osteskimo. Steinerne Schneidegeräte und Waffenschärfen aus Grönland.** *Videnskabsselskabets Skrifter*, II, *Historisk-Filologisk Klasse*, 2:1-92 (Oslo: *).

Solberg, Ole [1909]: **Eisenzeitfunde aus Ostfinmarken.** * p. (Christiania: *).

Sollas W. J. [1924]: **Ancient hunters and their modern representatives.** 3rd edition, * p. (New York: MacMillan Company).

Spaulding, Albert C. [1946]: **Northeastern archaeology and general trends in the northern forest zone.** pp:3:143-167 in "Man in Northeastern North America", editor: Frederick Johnson, Papers of the Robert S. Peabody Foundation, * p. (*: *).

Spencer, Robert F. [1959]: **The North Alaskan Eskimo: A Study in Ecology and Society.** *Bureau of American Ethno-logy Bulletin*, 171:1-490 (Washington DC: U.S. Government Printing Office).

Stanford, D. J. [1976]: **The Walpaka Site, Alaska. Its place in the Birnirk and Thule Cultures.** *Smithsonian Contributions to Anthropology*, 20:96-114 (Washington DC: The National Museum of America).

Stoklund, Marie [1982]: **Nordboruner.** *Tidsskriftet Grønland*, 30(5-7):197-206 (Copenhagen: The Greenland Society).

Stoklund, Marie [1993]: **Greenland Runes: Isolation or Cultural Contact?** pp:528-544 in "The Viking Age in Caithness, Orkney and the North Atlantic. Select papers from the proceedings of the eleventh Viking Congress, Thurso & Kirkwall, 22 August - 1 September 1989", editors: C. Batey, J. Jesch & C. D. Morris, * p. (*).

Storm, Gustav [1888]: **Islandske Annaler indtil 1578.** 667 p. (Christiania: *).

Strong, William D. [1930]: **A stone culture from northern Labrador and its relation to Eskimo-like cultures of the Northeast.** *American Anthropologist*, 32: 126-144 (*: *).

Stuiver, M. & G. W. Pearson [1993]: **High-precision bidecadal calibration of radiocarbon time scale, A.D. 1950-500 B.C. and 2500-6000 B.C.** *Radiocarbon*, 35(1):1-24 (Tucson: The University of Arizona Press).

Stupart, R. F. [1887]: **The Eskimo of Stupart Bay.** *Proceedings of the Canadian Institute*, 3(4):93-114 (Toronto: Clark).

Sutherland, Patricia [1996]: **Continuity and Change in the Paleo-Eskimo Prehistory of Northern Ellesmere Island.** pp:271-294 in "The Paleo-Eskimo Cultures of Greenland - New Perspectives in Greenlandic Archaeology", editor: Bjarne Grønnow, 334 p. (Copenhagen: Danish Polar Center).

Sutherland, Patricia [1996]: **Lost Visions. Forgotten Dreams.** Exhibition katalogue, 24 p. (Hull: Canadian Museum of Civilization).

Sutherland, Patricia [1997]: **The Variety of Artstic Expression in Dorset Culture.** *Ethnographical Series*, 18:287-293 (Copenhagen: National Museum of Denmark).

Swinton, George [1958]: **Eskimo Carving Today**. *The Beaver*, Outfit 268, (Spring):40-47 (Winnipeg: Hudson's Bay Company).

Swinton, George [1965]: **Eskimo Sculpture/Sulpture Esquimaude**. 224 p. (Toronto: McClelland & Stewart).

Swinton, George [1967]: **Prehistoric Dorset Art: The Magico-Religious Basis**. *The Beaver*, 298:32-47 (Winnipeg: The Hudson's Bay Company).

Swinton, George [1972]: **Sculpture of the Eskimo**. 255 p. (Toronto: McClelland & Stewart).

Swinton, George [1992]: **Sculpture of the Inuit**. Revised and updated of 1972 book, 288 p. (Toronto: McClelland & Stewart).

Swinton, George [1997]: **Who makes Inuit art? - Confessions by a para-anthropologist**. *Ethnographical Series*, 18:295-302 (Copenhagen: National Museum of Denmark).

Tauber, Henrik [1989]: **Age and diet of the mummified Eskimos from Qilakitsoq**. "The mummies from Qilakitsoq - Eskimos in the 15th century", editors: J. P. Hart Hansen & H. C. Gulløv, *Meddelelser om Grønland, Man & Society*, 12: 137-138 (Copenhagen: The Commission for Scientific Research in Greenland).

Taylor, J. Garth & Helga Taylor [1977]: **Inuit Lane Use and Occupancy in the Okak Region, 1776-1830.** pp:59-81 in "Our Footprints are Everywhere", editor: Carol-Brice Bennett, 331 p. (Nain: Labrador Inuit Association).

Taylor, J. Garth [1974]: **Labrador Eskimo Settlements of the Early Contact Period**. *Publications in Ethnology*, 9:1-102 (Ottawa: National Museum of Man).

Taylor, J. Garth [1975]: **Demography and adaptations of eighteenth-century Eskimo groups in Northern Labrador and Ungava.** pp:269-278 in "Prehistoric maritime adaptations of circumpolar zone", editor: William W. Fitzhugh, 405 p. (The Hague & Paris: World Anthropology, Mouton).

Taylor, J. Garth [1984]: **Historical Ethnography of the Labrador Coast.** *Handbook of North American Indians,*

Arctic, 5:508-521, editor: David Damas, 829 p. (Washington DC: Smithsonian Institution Press).

Taylor, J. Garth [1985]: **The Arctic Whale Cult in Labrador.** *Etudes/Inuit/Studies*, 9(2):121-132 (Québec: Départment d'anthropologie, Université Laval).

Taylor, J. Garth [1988]: **Labrador Inuit Whale Use During the Early Contact Period.** *Arctic Anthropology*, 25(1):120-130 (Madison: University of Wisconsin Press).

Taylor, J. Garth [1990]: **The Labrador Inuit Kashim (Ceremonial House) Complex**. *Arctic Anthropology*, 27(2):51-67) (Madison: University of Wisconsin Press).

Taylor, William E. jr. [1967]: **Summary of Archaeological Field work on Banks and Victoria Islands, Arctic Canada, 1965.** *Arctic Anthropology*, 4(1):221-243 (Madison: University of Wisconsin Press).

Taylor, William E. Jr. [1967]: **Prehistoric Dorset Art: The Silent Echoes of Culture.** *The Beaver*, 298:32-47 (Winnipeg: The Hudson's Bay Company).

Taylor, William E., Jr. [1968]: **The Arnapik and Tyara Sites; an Archaeological Study of Dorset Culture Origins.** *Memoir*, 22:*-* (Washington DC: Society for American Archaeology).

Taylor, William E. [1963]: **Archaeological collections from Joy Bay, Ungava Peninsula.** *The Arctic Circular*, 15(2): 24-26 (Montréal).

Taylor, William E. [1968]: **The Arnapik and Tyara Sites. An Archaeological Study of Dorset Culture Origins.** Memoirs of the Society for American Archaeology. *American Antiquity*, 33(4)2:1-129 (Salt Lake City).

Teillet, John V. [1988]: **A Reconstruction of Summer Sea Ice Conditions in the Labrador Sea Using Hudson's Bay Company Ships' Log-Books, 1751 to 1870.** M.A. Thesis, 161 p. (*: University of Manitoba).

Thalbitzer, William (editor) [1914 & 1923]: **The Ammassalik Eskimo: contributions to the Ethnology of the East Greenland Natives.** *Meddelelser om Grønland*, 39(1-7):1-755 & 40(1-3):1-564 (Copenhagen: C. A. Reitzels Forlag).

Thalbitzer, William [1933]: **Den Grønlandske Kateket Hansêraks Dagbog om den Danske Konebaadsekspedition til Ammassalik i Østgrønland 1884-1885.** *The Greenland Societys Skrifter*, 8:1-248 (Copenhagen: The Greenland Society).

Thomsen, Thomas [1917]: **Implements and Artefacts of the North East Greenlanders - finds from graves and settlements. Danmarks-ekspeditionen til Grønlands Nordøstkyst, 1906-1907**. *Meddelelser om Grønland*, 44(5):357-496 (Copenhagen: C. A. Reitzels Forlag).

Thostrup, Christian Bendix [1911]: **Ethnographic Description of the Eskimo Settlements and Stone Remains in North East Greenland**. *Meddelelser om Grønland*, 44(4):277-355 (Copenhagen: C. A. Reitzels Forlag).

Tindale, N. B. [1941]: **The Hand Axe Used in the Western Desert of Australia**. *Mankind*, 3(2):37-41 (London: *). Kraus reprint 1971 (Nekdeln, Liechtenstein).

Traverner, J. E. [1964]: **The Arctic Wintering of H.M.S. Hecla and Fury in Prince Regent Inlet, 1824-1825, by William Mogg**. *Polar Record*, 12(76):11-28. (Cambridge: Scott Polar Institute).

Tuck, James A. [1976]: **Newfoundland and Labrador Prehistory.** 127 p. (Ottawa: National Museum of Man).

Ubelaker, D. H. & L. G. Grant [1989]: **Human Skeletal Remains: Preservation or Reburial?** *Yearbook of Physical Anthropology*, 32:249-287 (New York: Wiley Uss).

Van Linshotten, * [1915]: **Dutch expeditions to the Arctic coast of Russia in 1594-1595.** *Zapiski po giografi*, 39(3-4):*-* (St. Petersburg: *) [in Russian].

Vartanyan, Sergei L., V. E. Garutt & Andrei V. Sher [1993]: **Holocene dwarf mammoths from Wrangel Island in the Siberian Arctic.** *Nature*, 362:337-340.

Vasil'ev, Valerii [1970]: **Siirtia - legenda ili real'nost'** [Siirtia: Legend or reality]. *Sovietskaya ethnographiya*, 1:151-157 (*: *) [in Russian. English translation on file at Washington DC: Arctic Studies Center, National Museum of the USA].

Vasil'ev, Valerii [1977]: **Nenets historical legends as a source for studies of the** ethnogenesis and ethnic history of the northern Samoyedic peoples. pp:113-126 in "Ethnic History and Folklore", editor: R. Lipets, * p. (Moscow: Nauka) [in Russian, translated into English by Ludmila Bonnichson for "Living Yamal" program, manuscript on file at Washington DC: Arctic Studies Center, National Museum of the USA].

Vebæk, Christian Leif [1992]: **Vatnahverfi. An Inland District of the Eastern Settlement in Greenland.** *Meddelelser om Grønland, Man & Society*; 17:1-132 (Copenhagen: The Commision for Scientific Research in Greenland).

Vibe, Christian [1967]: **Arctic animals in relation to climatic fluctuations.** *Meddelelser om Grønland*, 170(5): 1-227 (Copenhagen: C. A. Reitzels Forlag).

Vibe, Christian [1981]: **Pattedyr.** pp:364-459 in "Grønlands Fauna. Fisk, Fugle, Pattedyr", editor: Finn Salomonsen, 463 p. (Copenhagen: Nordisk Forlag).

Victor, Paul-Emile & Joelle Robert-Lamblin [1989]: **La Civilization du Phoque.** * p. (Paris: Armand Colin and Raymond Chabaud).

Victor, Paul-Emile & Joëlle Robert-Lamblin [1993]: **La Civilisation du Phoque. 2. Légendes, rites et croyances des Eskimo d'Ammassalik.** 424 p. (Biarritz: R. Chabaud, SAI).

Weiss, G. [1949]: **Das Arktische Jahr.** 168 p. (Braunschweig: Georg Westermann Verlag).

Wenzel, George [1995]: **Ningiqtuq: Resource Sharing and Generalized Reciprocity in Clyde River, Nunavat.** *Arctic Anthropology*, 32(2):43-60 (Madison: University of Wisconsin Press).

Weslawski, J. M. & J. Viktor [1994]: **Marine shallow coastal ecology - with special reference to the plankton development.** pp:145-150 in "Berichte zur Polarforshung. Reports on Polar Research 142/94. The 1993 North East Water Expedition Scientific cruise report of RV "Polarstern" Arctic Cruises ARK IX/2 and 3, USCG "Polar Sea" cruise NEWP and the NEWland expedition", editors: Hans-Jürgen Hirche & Gerhardt Kattner, 190 p. (Bremerhaven: Alfred-Wegener Institut für Polar- und Meeresforschung).

Wilson, C. [1983]: **Some Aspects of the Calibration of Early Canadian Temperature Records in the Hudson's Bay Company Archives.** pp:144-202 in "Climate Change in Canada 3", editor: C. R. Harrington, * p. (Ottawa: National Museum of Natural Sciences).

Wilson, David M. [1995]: **Vikingatidens Konst.** 238 p. (Lund: Signum).

Woollett, Jim [1996]: **Zooarchaeology and the Paleoeconomy of Uivak, Northern Labrador.** Paper presented at the Canadian Archaeological Association, Halifax, Nova Scotia.

Zachrisson, Inger [1993]: **Mötet mellan skandinaver och samer.** pp:7-22 in "Tolvte tværfaglige Vikingesymposium", editor: E. Roesdahl & P. Meulengracht Sørensen, * p. (Århus: Aarhus Universitet).

Zaslow, M. [1988]: **The northward expansion of Canada 1914-1967.** * p. (Toronto: McClelland & Stewart).

Zimmerman, Larry J. [1989]: **Human bones as symbols of power: Aboriginal American belief systems towards bones and "grave-robbing" archaeologists.** pp:211-216 in "Conflict in the archaeology of living traditions", editor: R. Layton, * p. (London: Unwin Hyman).

Zimmerman, Larry J. [1993]: Comments to "The Return of the Ahayu:da. Lessons for Repatriation from Zuni Pueblo and the Smithsonian Institution" by William L. Merrill, Edmund J. Ladd, & T. J. Ferguson. *Current Anthropology*, 34:562 (Chicago: University of Chicago Press).

Zordrager, C. G. [1723]: **Alte und neue Grónlándische Fischerei.** * p. (Leipzig).

Index of Place Names

West Greenland women and children outside Upernavik church.
Photo: Th. Krabbe, 2 July 1909. Courtesy: Dapartment of Ethnography, National Museum of Denmark.

Index of Personal Names

West Greenlanders at Ilulissat (Jakobshavn).
Photo: Th. Krabbe, 5 August 1906. Courtesy: Department of Ethnography, National Museum of Denmark.

East Greenlanders at Ammassalik. The man to the left is the shaman Ajukutok.
Photo: Th. Krabbe, 13 September 1908. Courtesy: Department of Ethnography, National Museum of Denmark.

West Greenlanders at Ny Herrnhut, c. 2 km south of Nuuk.
Photo: Th. Krabbe, 13 August 1906. Courtesy: Department of Ethnography, National Museum of Denmark.

Index of Subjects

Inughuit (Polar-Eskimo) women covering a wooden kayak frame with sealskin on the Fifth Thule Expedition.
Photo: Knud Rasmussen, Danish Island 1922. Courtesy: Department of Ethnography, National Museum of Denmark.

Ship: